Above right: Martha Hinrichs and Karen Parker, Test Kitchens Staff

Above: Linda Welch, Assistant Foods Editor; Beverly Morrow, Photo Stylist

Right: Diane Hogan, Laura Nestelroad, and Peggy Smith, Test Kitchens Staff

Meet the *Southern Living* Foods Staff

Year after year *Southern Living* continues to provide the South with irresistible recipes and a rich source of entertaining ideas. These recipes are tested, tasted, and reviewed by our staff of home economists in our test kitchens prior to publication.

Our team of food professionals work diligently to make *Southern Living* very special. A generous measure of "personal touch" goes into features planned by our Foods Editors who are responsible for selecting recipes, creating the magazine's food articles, and planning exciting food photographs.

Our test kitchen staff stock the kitchen and test the recipes. They confirm measurement of ingredients, numbers of servings, oven temperatures—all the specific information that makes *Southern Living* recipes completely reliable.

In addition, members of our foods staff are often involved in judging cook-offs throughout the country, planning and preparing special luncheons for visitors to *Southern Living,* and answering subscriber correspondence. Here the staff is introduced (left to right in each photograph).

Above: Susan Payne, Assistant Foods Editor; Margaret Chason, Associate Foods Editor
Below: Lynn Lloyd, Test Kitchens Director; Jean Wickstrom Liles, Foods Editor

Southern Living®
1981 ANNUAL RECIPES

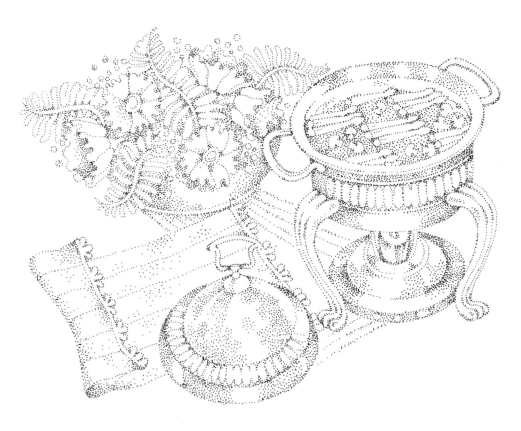

Oxmoor House, Inc., Birmingham

Cover: *You can make something in your
kitchen to please everyone on your
Christmas list. Clockwise from top:
Delicious Fruit Marmalade (page 285), Hot
Wine Mix (page 287), Christmas Brunch
Jam (page 286), Holiday Wreath (page
284), Gingerbread Muffins (page 285),
Delicious Fruit Marmalade (page 285),
Cherry Nut Nuggets (page 286), and
Three-C Bread (page 284).*

Page i: *Some of the best ways we know to
put sweet potatoes on the menu include
Louisiana Yam Pie (page 223), French-Fried
Sweet Potatoes (page 223), Sweet Potato-
Stuffed Orange Cups (page 223), Sweet
Potato Loaf Cake (page 224), and Sweet
Potato Muffins (page 224).*

Page iv: *Just about anything that grows in
the garden can be pickled. Besides
cucumbers, try corn, okra, or squash—and
don't forget the watermelon rind. Recipes
begin on page 173.*

Table of Contents

Southern Sun Tea (page 168)

Pork Chop Meal for Two (page 229)

Orange Breakfast Ring (page 229)

Our Year at Southern Living

Southern hospitality has always been a powerful tradition in an area where people enjoy cooking and entertaining in their homes. And for 15 years *Southern Living* has played an important part in furthering that tradition as Southern cooks—and a few Northern ones—have turned to our recipes to please family and friends. Year after year they find our food pages to be a primary source of irresistible recipes and entertaining ideas.

Now, for a third time, we offer a whole year of *Southern Living* recipes in a single volume. Our *1979 Annual Recipes* proved a best seller; then our *1980 Annual Recipes* surpassed it in sales and popularity. We're sure our readers will make *1981 Annual Recipes* our most successful collection yet.

1981 Annual Recipes brings together all of the recipes published in *Southern Living* during 1981. Organized month-by-month, the recipes not only spotlight seasonal foods, but also offer wonderful entertaining ideas for each season—springtime brunch menus, a cool salad bar party in hot July, appetizers for football festivities, an elegant holiday dinner party, plus many more festive ideas. In addition, each month you will discover new recipes for the microwave, recipes for those rush-rush days when you need something quick and easy, recipes for just the two of you. We

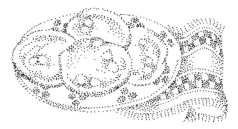

believe you will find this complete cookbook a valuable addition to your culinary library.

The food ideas come from the South's best cooks who each month favor us with thousands of their family's favorite recipes. Before these are published, they are tested, tasted, and evaluated by our staff of experienced home economists. Several factors are considered in evaluation: taste, appearance, ease of preparation, and cost of dish.

Although taste is of primary importance, the appearance of a dish adds much to its overall appeal. In view of the active pace of most people's lives and the increased cost of living, ease and cost are important factors considered in reviewing our recipes.

To keep the testing realistic, our home economists test each recipe in kitchens much like yours. Grocery shopping is done each week, and with seasonal fruits and vegetables testing is done while the produce is at its best in terms of flavor and price.

Yet *1981 Annual Recipes* is more than a collection of the year's recipes. It includes every food feature, 32 full-color photo pages illustrating many of the recipes and menus, and extensive cooking and kitchen guides. You will find tips for planning menus and buying food as well as helpful ideas for preparation and

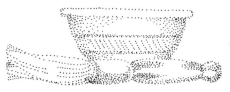

serving. To assist you in finding specific recipes, three detailed indices are included at the end of the book.

Enjoy your *1981 Annual Recipes*. After a busy but rewarding year, our foods staff presents to you the best of eating from 1981. A number of editors, photographers, and artists have contributed their talents to this book. All these ingredients make not only for pleasurable eating and reading throughout the year but also have culminated in our *1981 Annual Recipes*—a cookbook certain to be one of your favorites.

Jean Wickstrom Liles

January

If your New Year's resolutions include tightening your budget and your waistline, look for our delicious and affordable roasted chicken entrées in this chapter. Their ease in preparation doubles your benefits.

Whether or not you are a fan of black-eyed peas, don't challenge the Southern custom of eating them on New Year's Day! We guarantee your whole family will enjoy our readers' upbeat ideas for preparing them in such recipes as Black-Eyed Pea Dip and Mexi-Pea Salad.

And if you think January is not the time for fresh vegetables, turn to our stories about side dishes and salads. The possibilities are endless with crunchy fresh broccoli, cauliflower, and salad greens.

Presenting The Season's Fresh Vegetables

A vegetable side dish can be showy, yet simple. We prove that point with broccoli, brussels sprouts, and cauliflower—each prepared in ways that enhance their appeal while preserving their natural flavor.

Because broccoli turns a lovely, vibrant green when steamed, we recommend this gentle method of cooking. For the finishing touch, drizzle it with our subtle horseradish sauce or add pimiento, onion, and grated lemon rind for Carnival Broccoli.

The key to brussels sprouts is to cook them only until done. Overcooking results in flavor change and loss of color.

For an attractive cauliflower dish, we suggest mixing it with one or more colorful ingredients. Lemon twists and parsley add flavor and color to Cauliflower With Herb Butter, while green beans, celery, and pimiento dress up Sweet-and-Sour Cauliflower Salad.

BROCCOLI WITH HORSERADISH SAUCE

1 (1½-pound) bunch fresh broccoli
¾ cup commercial sour cream
½ teaspoon prepared horseradish
1½ teaspoons prepared mustard
Dash of salt
Paprika (optional)

Trim off large leaves of broccoli. Remove tough ends of stalks, and wash broccoli thoroughly. Make lengthwise slits in thick stalks. Arrange broccoli in steaming rack with stalks to center of rack. Place over boiling water; cover and steam 10 to 15 minutes or to desired degree of doneness. Place in serving dish.

Combine remaining ingredients except paprika in a small saucepan; heat thoroughly, stirring constantly. Spoon some sauce over broccoli; sprinkle with paprika, if desired. Serve the remaining sauce. Yield: 4 to 6 servings.
Mrs. Farmer L. Burns,
New Orleans, Louisiana.

Tip: Plastic bags that have been used to wrap dry foods, vegetables, and fruit can often be washed and reused.

CARNIVAL BROCCOLI

2 pounds fresh broccoli
½ cup sliced green onion
2 tablespoons butter or margarine
2 tablespoons chopped pimiento
1 teaspoon grated lemon rind
2 tablespoons lemon juice
1 teaspoon salt
⅛ teaspoon pepper

Trim off large leaves of broccoli. Remove tough ends, and wash broccoli thoroughly. Make lengthwise slits in thick stalks. Arrange broccoli in steaming rack with stalks to center of rack. Place over boiling water; cover and steam 10 to 15 minutes. Place in serving dish.

Sauté onion in butter until tender. Remove from heat, and stir in remaining ingredients. Pour mixture over broccoli. Yield: 6 servings. *Lucille Hall,*
Bakersfield, Missouri.

BRUSSELS SPROUTS WITH CASHEWS

2 pounds fresh brussels sprouts
3 cups water
2 chicken-flavored bouillon cubes
1½ cups sliced carrots
⅓ cup butter or margarine
¾ cup dry-roasted cashew halves
¼ teaspoon dried whole thyme, crushed
¼ teaspoon salt
⅛ teaspoon pepper

Wash brussels sprouts thoroughly. Combine water and bouillon cubes in a medium saucepan; bring to a boil. Add brussels sprouts and carrots; return to a boil. Reduce heat; cover and simmer 15 minutes or until vegetables are tender. Drain well, and place in serving bowl.

Melt butter in a small skillet; add cashews and seasonings. Cook on low heat for 3 to 4 minutes. Pour over vegetables. Yield: 6 to 8 servings.

CAULIFLOWER WITH HERB BUTTER

1 large head cauliflower
Juice of 1 lemon
¼ cup plus 1 tablespoon butter or margarine
1 tablespoon chopped fresh parsley
¼ teaspoon salt
¼ teaspoon dried whole basil
1 small clove garlic, crushed
Lemon twists
Parsley sprigs

Remove large outer leaves of cauliflower. Break cauliflower into flowerets; wash thoroughly. Arrange flowerets in steaming rack. Place over boiling water; cover and steam about 10 minutes or to desired degree of doneness. Arrange flowerets in serving dish, and sprinkle evenly with lemon juice.

Melt butter in a small saucepan; stir in chopped parsley, salt, basil, and garlic. Pour herb butter evenly over flowerets. Garnish with lemon twists and parsley sprigs. Yield: 6 servings.
Mrs. James L. Twilley,
Macon, Georgia.

SWEET-AND-SOUR CAULIFLOWER SALAD

1 (10-ounce) package frozen green beans
¼ cup sugar
¼ cup vinegar
¼ cup water
8 slices bacon
¾ pound cauliflower
½ cup diced celery
4 green onions, chopped
1 tablespoon chopped pimiento
1 tablespoon brown sugar
2 tablespoons vinegar
½ teaspoon salt

Cook green beans according to package directions; drain well. Add ¼ cup sugar, ¼ cup vinegar, and water; mix well. Cover and chill about 3 hours.

Cook bacon until crisp; drain well, reserving 2 tablespoons drippings. Crumble bacon, and set aside.

Break cauliflower into flowerets; wash thoroughly, and arrange in steaming rack. Place over boiling water; cover, and steam about 10 minutes or to desired degree of doneness.

Drain beans; add cauliflower, celery, onion, pimiento, and bacon. Toss lightly.

Combine reserved bacon drippings, brown sugar, 2 tablespoons vinegar, and salt in a small saucepan. Cook over low heat until thoroughly heated; pour over vegetable mixture, tossing gently. Serve immediately. Yield: 4 to 6 servings.
Mrs. Charles Simms,
Palestine, Illinois.

Ease Out Of The Season With Chicken

When the groaning board of the holidays is retired for another year, simple foods that are easy on both the cook and the waistline have special appeal. Chicken fills the bill—it's light, delicate, simple to prepare, and has minimum calories and fat. As a bonus, chicken is among the most economical meats you can buy.

The recipes we've tested take advantage of that economy—in all of them, you either bake or simmer the whole chicken. And while they save you money and ease up on calories, their complementary seasonings, sauces, and stuffings won't cheat you on flavor.

ROAST CHICKEN AND VEGETABLES

1 (5½-pound) baking hen
4 slices bacon, halved
6 large stalks celery
Salt
3 cups dry white wine or water
12 small red-skinned potatoes
16 baby carrots
2 tomatoes, cut into 8 wedges
½ cup whipping cream
¼ cup butter or margarine
½ cup water
¼ cup cornstarch

Remove giblets from cavity of chicken, and reserve for another recipe. Rinse chicken with cold water, and pat dry.

Fold bacon to form 1-inch pieces. Lift skin at neck of chicken, and insert bacon pieces. Fold skin over back, and secure with a wooden pick.

Cut 1 stalk of celery into 3-inch pieces; place in cavity of chicken. Lightly sprinkle cavity and skin of chicken with salt; truss chicken. Cut 2 stalks of celery into 6-inch pieces; place side by side in a large shallow roasting pan.

Place chicken, breast side up, on top of celery; add wine. Bake chicken at 375° for 2 hours and 15 minutes (25 minutes per pound) or until drumsticks are easy to move up and down; baste chicken frequently with pan juices.

Cut remaining 3 stalks of celery into 3-inch pieces. Wash potatoes; peel a strip around center of each, if desired. An hour before chicken is done, add celery, potatoes, and carrots to roasting pan; add tomato wedges during final 15 minutes of baking time.

Arrange chicken and vegetables on a platter; discard the celery used as a baking rack.

Pour pan juices into a large saucepan; add whipping cream and butter. Cook over low heat until butter melts, stirring occasionally. Combine water and cornstarch; stir well. Add to gravy; cook, stirring constantly, until sauce is thickened. Yield: 8 servings.

Note: If water is substituted for wine, 2 chicken-flavored bouillon cubes may be added. *Mrs. R. E. Coffman, Natchez, Mississippi.*

CHICKEN IN A POT

1 (3- to 3½-pound) broiler-fryer
1 small cooking apple, cored and quartered
2 tablespoons lemon juice
2 teaspoons onion salt
½ teaspoon dried whole rosemary
⅛ teaspoon instant minced garlic

Remove giblets from cavity of chicken, and reserve for another recipe. Rinse chicken with cold water, and pat dry.

Lift wingtips up and over back so they are under the bird; place apple in cavity. Truss chicken, and brush with lemon juice.

Place chicken, breast side up, in an ovenproof Dutch oven; sprinkle with remaining ingredients. Cover and bake at 375° for 1½ hours or until drumsticks are easy to move up and down. Yield: 4 to 6 servings. *Rita Scarberry, Ripley, West Virginia.*

LAZY DAY CHINESE CHICKEN

1 (3-pound) broiler-fryer
1 tablespoon vegetable oil
¼ cup dry sherry
¾ cup soy sauce
¼ cup water
¼ cup chopped green onion
3 cloves garlic, minced
1 tablespoon sugar
1 teaspoon minced fresh ginger
Hot cooked rice (optional)

Remove giblets from cavity of chicken, and reserve for another recipe. Rinse chicken with cold water, and pat dry. Lift wingtips up and over back so they are tucked under the bird.

Heat oil in a Dutch oven over high heat. Add chicken, and brown on all sides. Remove from heat, and turn chicken so breast side is up; pour sherry over chicken.

Combine next 6 ingredients, and pour into Dutch oven; return to heat. Reduce heat; cover and simmer 25 minutes. Turn chicken; simmer, uncovered, 10 minutes or until drumsticks are easy to move up and down. Serve chicken on a bed of rice with pan juices, if desired. Yield: 4 to 6 servings.
Steven John Choy, Silver Spring, Maryland.

CHICKEN-MUSHROOM DINNER

1 (3- to 3½-pound) broiler-fryer
1 teaspoon salt
¼ cup butter or margarine
½ pound fresh mushrooms, sliced
¼ teaspoon salt
¼ teaspoon white pepper
4 slices bacon, cooked and crumbled
2 tablespoons minced fresh parsley
3 tablespoons all-purpose flour, divided
1 teaspoon caraway seeds
1 teaspoon dried whole oregano
1 teaspoon paprika
2 medium potatoes, peeled and cut into ½-inch slices
½ cup Chablis or other dry white wine
1 cup chicken broth, divided

Remove giblets from cavity of chicken, and reserve for another recipe. Rinse chicken with cold water, and pat dry. Fold neck skin of chicken over back, and secure with a wooden pick. Lift wingtips up and over back so they are tucked under bird. Rub 1 teaspoon salt over skin of bird; set aside.

Melt butter; add mushrooms, ¼ teaspoon salt, and pepper. Sauté 5 minutes, stirring occasionally. Remove from heat; stir in bacon, parsley, and 2 tablespoons flour.

Stuff mushroom mixture into cavity of chicken. Close cavity, and secure with wooden picks; truss chicken. Place in a large ovenproof skillet, breast side up; sprinkle with caraway seeds, oregano, and paprika. Arrange potato slices around chicken; add wine and ½ cup chicken broth. Bake, uncovered, at 350° for 1½ hours or until drumsticks are easy to move up and down; baste occasionally with pan juices.

Combine 1 tablespoon flour and ½ cup chicken broth, stirring well; pour into skillet. Bake an additional 5 minutes. Yield: 4 to 6 servings.
Barbara M. Zollikofer, Towson, Maryland.

RICE-STUFFED CHICKEN

1 (3½-pound) broiler-fryer
Salt
½ cup chopped celery
¼ cup chopped onion
¼ cup sliced almonds
¼ cup butter or margarine
3 cups cooked regular rice or wild rice
2 tablespoons vegetable oil
1 cup chicken broth
2 tablespoons tomato paste
½ cup water

Remove giblets from chicken, and reserve for another recipe. Rinse chicken with cold water, and pat dry. Fold neck skin of chicken over back, and secure with a wooden pick. Lift wingtips up and over back so they are tucked under the bird. Salt cavity, and set aside.

Sauté vegetables and almonds in butter until vegetables are tender but not brown. Combine vegetable mixture and rice, stirring well; stuff into cavity of chicken. Close cavity, and secure with wooden picks; truss chicken.

Heat oil in a Dutch oven; add chicken, and brown on all sides. Turn chicken so breast side is up; remove from heat. Combine remaining ingredients, stirring well; pour mixture over chicken. Cover and cook over low heat 1½ hours. Yield: 4 to 6 servings.

Betty Hornsby,
Columbia, South Carolina.

Microwave Cookery

Quick And Light Microwave Menu

Dinner for four can be ready in a jiffy with this light and easy microwave menu. What's more, it's a nutritious and flavorful combination: haddock prepared in the Italian manner, Wilted Spinach Salad, a quick corn dish, and hot strawberry sauce to spoon over ice cream.

In each of the recipes, a time range for microwaving is given; this allows for the difference in wattage of microwave ovens. To prevent overcooking, always check for doneness at the lower end of the time range. Here are some pointers to ensure your success with these dishes.

—The eggs used in the spinach salad are similar to a hard-cooked product and can be prepared in the microwave oven. Just be sure to pierce the yolks before microwaving to prevent excessive steam build-up; otherwise, the yolks may burst.

—When preparing Haddock Italiano, arrange the fillets so that the thicker portions are to the outside of the baking dish. This promotes even cooking, as microwaves first enter food at the outside edges. Let the fish stand 2 to 3 minutes after microwaving; if it doesn't flake easily when tested with a fork, continue microwaving briefly.

—Microwave the corn dish while the fish is standing; that way, everything will be ready to serve at the same time. Stir the corn once during microwaving to mix heated and unheated portions.

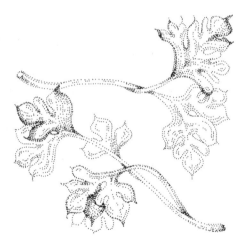

HADDOCK ITALIANO

2 tablespoons olive oil
1 tablespoon lemon juice
1 medium tomato, chopped
1½ cups sliced fresh mushrooms
¼ cup chopped onion
¼ cup chopped green pepper
2 tablespoons chopped fresh parsley
1 clove garlic, minced
½ teaspoon dried whole oregano
¼ teaspoon salt
1 (16-ounce) package frozen haddock fillets, thawed
Salt and pepper to taste

Combine first 10 ingredients in a 12- x 8- x 2-inch baking dish; stir well, being sure vegetables are evenly distributed in dish. Cover with heavy-duty plastic wrap; microwave at HIGH for 4 to 6 minutes or until onion is tender, stirring once. Push vegetable mixture to side of dish.

Sprinkle fillets with salt and pepper; arrange in baking dish with thickest portions to outside of dish (thinner portions may overlap, if necessary). Spoon vegetable mixture over fillets.

Cover and microwave at HIGH for 2 to 4 minutes, giving dish one half-turn during cooking. Let stand 2 to 3 minutes. If fish does not flake easily with a fork after standing, continue microwaving briefly. Yield: 4 servings.

QUICK CORN FIX-UP

2 tablespoons butter or margarine
¼ cup chopped green pepper
2 (12-ounce) cans vacuum-packed corn, drained
3 tablespoons chopped pimiento
⅛ teaspoon celery salt

Combine butter and green pepper in a 1½-quart casserole; cover with heavy-duty plastic wrap. Microwave at HIGH for 2 minutes or until green pepper is crisp-tender. Stir in corn, pimiento, and celery salt. Cover and microwave at HIGH for 3 to 4 minutes or until casserole is thoroughly heated, stirring once. Yield: 4 servings.

WILTED SPINACH SALAD

2 eggs
4 slices bacon
⅓ cup sliced green onion
¼ cup red wine vinegar
1 tablespoon sugar
1 tablespoon water
¼ teaspoon salt
About 5 cups fresh spinach, torn

Gently break each egg into a separate 6-ounce custard cup or microwave-safe coffee cup; pierce yolks with a wooden pick. Cover each cup with heavy-duty plastic wrap. Arrange cups about 2 inches apart in center of microwave oven.

Microwave at MEDIUM for 2 to 3 minutes or until eggs are almost set. Test eggs with a wooden pick (yolks should be just firm and whites should be almost set). Let eggs stand, covered, for 1 to 2 minutes to complete cooking. If eggs are not desired degree of doneness after standing, cover and continue microwaving briefly. Let eggs cool; chop finely, and set aside.

Place bacon on a microwave roasting rack in a 12- x 8- x 2-inch baking dish; cover with paper towel. Microwave at

HIGH for 4 to 5 minutes or until crisp. Remove bacon and rack, reserving drippings in dish. Crumble bacon, and set aside.

Add onion to bacon drippings, and cover with waxed paper. Microwave at HIGH for 3 minutes. Add vinegar, sugar, water, and salt. Microwave at HIGH for 2 minutes or until boiling.

Place spinach in a large bowl. Pour hot dressing over spinach. Add crumbled bacon and chopped egg; toss lightly, and serve immediately. Yield: 4 servings.

HOT STRAWBERRY SUNDAES

Vanilla ice cream
¾ cup strawberry preserves
2 tablespoons chopped pecans
2 tablespoons kirsch or cherry-flavored brandy

Scoop vanilla ice cream into 4 individual serving dishes; refreeze.

Combine strawberry preserves, pecans, and kirsch in a small bowl. Microwave at MEDIUM for 2 to 3 minutes or until preserves are thoroughly heated and partially melted. Spoon over ice cream, and serve sundaes immediately. Yield: 4 servings.

Crabs, shrimp, oysters, and fish make prize-winning Seafood Gumbo a meal in itself.

Simmer A Savory Gumbo

Many cooks insist that gumbo must simmer for hours in order to develop the proper flavor, texture, and aroma. Anita Williams' Seafood Gumbo, which won the 1980 Gulf Coast Gumbo Cookoff in Pensacola, Florida, and Chicken-Ham-Seafood Gumbo are full-flavored recipes that follow that theory. But we also found Easy Fish Gumbo to be savory, while being cooked in a fraction of the time.

Fresh crabs are among the delicacies in two of our gumbos. To clean fresh crabs, begin by pouring scalding water over crabs to kill them; remove large claws, and wash thoroughly. Turn each crab upside down, and lift the long, tapered point (the apron). Pull off shell, and remove the soft, spongy mass. Remove and discard legs. Wash crab thoroughly, and break body in half lengthwise; add to gumbo along with the crab claws.

SEAFOOD GUMBO

4 quarts water
1 (3½-ounce) package shrimp and crab boil
1 tablespoon salt
5 pounds fresh shrimp
2 tablespoons butter or margarine
1 tablespoon vegetable oil
3 large onions, chopped
2 (16-ounce) packages frozen cut okra
⅓ cup all-purpose flour
2 (28-ounce) cans whole tomatoes, undrained and finely chopped
2 fresh tomatoes, peeled and chopped
2 tablespoons tomato paste
3 fresh blue crabs, cleaned and broken in half
1 pint oysters, undrained
1 pound fish fillets, cut into 1-inch cubes
Dash of hot sauce
Hot cooked rice

Bring water, shrimp boil, and salt to a boil; add shrimp and return to a boil. Lower heat, and simmer 3 to 5 minutes. Drain well, reserving liquid; rinse shrimp with cold water, and chill. Peel and devein shrimp; chill until needed.

Heat butter and oil in a 10-quart pot; add onion, and sauté until tender. Add okra, and cook, stirring constantly, about 10 minutes.

Brown flour in an iron skillet over low heat until dark brown, stirring constantly. Stir flour into onion mixture; add tomatoes, and simmer 10 minutes. Stir tomato paste and reserved liquid into gumbo; simmer, uncovered, 2 to 3 hours, stirring occasionally (add additional water if necessary). Add crabs during last 20 minutes of cooking. Add shrimp, oysters, fish, and hot sauce during last 10 minutes of cooking. Serve gumbo over rice. Yield: about 6½ quarts.

Anita Williams,
Decatur, Georgia.

Tip: If soup or stew is too heavily salted, drop in a peeled, raw potato and cook for a few minutes. Remove the potato and taste the difference!

EASY FISH GUMBO

2 beef-flavored bouillon cubes
2 cups boiling water
½ cup chopped celery
½ cup chopped green pepper
½ cup chopped onion
1 clove garlic, minced
¼ cup vegetable oil
1 (28-ounce) can whole tomatoes, undrained
1 (10-ounce) package frozen cut okra, thawed
¼ teaspoon ground thyme
1 bay leaf
2 teaspoons salt
¼ teaspoon pepper
¼ teaspoon hot pepper sauce
1 pound fish fillets, cut into 1-inch cubes
Hot cooked rice

Dissolve bouillon cubes in boiling water; set aside.

Sauté celery, green pepper, onion, and garlic in hot oil in a Dutch oven until tender. Add bouillon, tomatoes, okra, and seasonings; mix well. Bring to a boil. Reduce heat; cover and simmer 30 minutes, stirring occasionally. Add fish; cover and simmer an additional 15 minutes or until fish flakes easily; remove bay leaf. Serve over rice. Yield: about 9 cups.

Mrs. Parke LaGourgue Cory,
Neosho, Missouri.

CHICKEN-HAM-SEAFOOD GUMBO

1 (2½-pound) broiler-fryer
1 quart water
¼ cup plus 2 tablespoons vegetable oil
¼ cup plus 2 tablespoons all-purpose flour
1 (16-ounce) package frozen cut okra
2½ cups chopped celery
½ cup chopped green pepper
2 medium onions, chopped
4 cloves garlic, minced
¼ pound ham, chopped
1 (12-ounce) can fresh oysters, undrained
6 fresh blue crabs, cleaned and broken in half
1 (8-ounce) can tomato sauce
1 tablespoon chopped fresh parsley
2 bay leaves, crumbled
2 tablespoons browning and seasoning sauce
2 teaspoons Creole seasoning
1 teaspoon dried whole thyme
¼ teaspoon garlic powder
1½ tablespoons Worcestershire sauce
¼ teaspoon liquid smoke
Juice of ½ lemon
Hot cooked rice
Gumbo filé (optional)

Place chicken in a Dutch oven; add water. Bring to a boil; cover, reduce heat, and simmer 1½ hours or until done. Remove chicken from broth, reserving broth. Cool chicken; remove meat from bones. Cut meat into bite-size pieces, and set aside.

Combine oil and flour in a heavy 5-quart Dutch oven over medium heat; cook, stirring constantly, until roux is the color of a copper penny.

Reduce heat to low; add okra, celery, green pepper, onion, and garlic. Cook, stirring occasionally, for 30 minutes. Add broth, chicken, and next 13 ingredients; stir well. Simmer, uncovered, for 3 hours, stirring occasionally. Serve over rice. If desired, thicken with gumbo filé; do not cook after adding filé. Yield: about 3½ quarts.

Joanne Champagne,
Covington, Louisiana.

Carrots At Their Best

Looking for a vegetable that can perk up a meal with color and flavor? Well, look no longer; here are some fresh carrot ideas that will stimulate appetites and brighten tables.

Eaten raw or cooked until tender, but not mushy, carrots are an appealing source of vitamin A. Try them scalloped and topped with breadcrumbs or marinated in a tangy dressing. For a healthy snack, select a sweet carrot muffin or a frosted cookie.

SCALLOPED CARROTS

2 pounds carrots, thinly sliced
¼ cup butter or margarine
¼ cup minced onion
¼ cup all-purpose flour
¼ teaspoon dry mustard
2 cups milk
1 teaspoon salt
¼ teaspoon celery salt
2 cups (8 ounces) shredded Cheddar cheese
2 tablespoons butter or margarine, melted
1 cup soft breadcrumbs

Cook carrots in a small amount of boiling salted water 12 to 15 minutes or until tender; drain and set aside.

Melt ¼ cup butter in a heavy saucepan over low heat; add onion, and cook until tender. Add flour and mustard, stirring until smooth. Cook 1 minute, stirring constantly. Gradually add milk; cook over medium heat, stirring constantly, until thickened and bubbly. Add salt, celery salt, and cheese, stirring until cheese melts.

Combine carrots and sauce in a lightly greased 2-quart casserole. Combine 2 tablespoons butter and breadcrumbs; sprinkle over casserole. Bake at 350° for 25 minutes or until sauce is bubbly. Yield: 8 servings.

Diane Stephens,
Memphis, Tennessee.

CARROT-PINEAPPLE MUFFINS

1 (8¼-ounce) can crushed pineapple, undrained
Milk
2 cups all-purpose flour
⅓ cup firmly packed brown sugar
1 tablespoon baking powder
½ teaspoon salt
2 tablespoons sugar
½ teaspoon ground cinnamon
¾ cup grated carrots
⅓ cup vegetable oil
1 egg, beaten
½ teaspoon vanilla extract

Drain pineapple, reserving juice. Add enough milk to pineapple juice to make ¾ cup liquid. Set aside.

Combine next 7 ingredients in a large bowl, stirring until carrots are well coated; make a well in center of mixture. Combine pineapple, milk mixture, oil, egg, and vanilla; add to dry ingredients, stirring just until moistened. Spoon into greased muffin pans, filling two-thirds full. Bake at 375° for 20 to 25 minutes or until done. Yield: about 1 dozen.

Doris Amonette,
Tulsa, Oklahoma.

CRISPY MARINATED CARROTS

1 pound carrots, thinly sliced
⅓ cup chopped onion
⅓ cup chopped green pepper
⅓ cup vinegar
3 tablespoons vegetable oil
⅓ cup sugar
¼ teaspoon prepared mustard
1 teaspoon Worcestershire sauce

Cook carrots in a small amount of boiling water about 5 minutes or until crisp-tender; drain. Combine carrots, onion, and green pepper; set aside.

Combine vinegar, oil, sugar, mustard, and Worcestershire sauce in a jar. Cover tightly, and shake vigorously. Pour over vegetables; toss lightly with a fork. Refrigerate overnight. Yield: 6 servings. *Margaret O. Kaminsky, Manassas, Virginia.*

FROSTED CARROT COOKIES

2 cups all-purpose flour
2 teaspoons baking powder
½ teaspoon salt
1 cup shortening
¾ cup sugar
1 cup mashed cooked carrots
2 eggs
¾ cup flaked coconut
Orange Frosting

Combine flour, baking powder, and salt; stir well. Set aside.

Cream shortening; gradually add sugar, beating until light and fluffy. Add carrots and eggs, beating well. Add dry ingredients, mixing well; stir in coconut.

Drop dough by heaping teaspoonfuls onto lightly greased cookie sheets, 2 inches apart. Bake at 400° for 8 to 10 minutes or until golden brown. Cool on cookie sheets 1 to 2 minutes; remove to racks, and cool completely. Frost with Orange Frosting. Yield: 4½ dozen.

Orange Frosting:

3 tablespoons butter or margarine, softened
1½ cups sifted powdered sugar
2 teaspoons grated orange rind
1 tablespoon orange juice

Combine all ingredients; beat until light and fluffy. Yield: about 1 cup.
Mrs. Ron Bain, Nashville, Tennessee.

Tip: Remove the tops of carrots before refrigerating. Tops drain the carrots of moisture, making them limp and dry.

Bring Luck With Black-Eyed Peas

If you follow the tradition of eating black-eyed peas on New Year's Day, then the following recipes will give you several choices of how to prepare your lucky dish.

Hopping John is always a favorite, and there are some unexpected dishes as well, like Mexi-Pea Salad, a spicy taco salad highlighted by the addition of good-luck peas. Or you might like to stir up some Black-Eyed Pea Dip, the perfect appetizer to serve for a New Year's celebration.

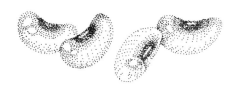

MEXI-PEA SALAD

¾ cup dried black-eyed peas
2½ cups water
1 pound ground beef
1 cup chopped onion, divided
½ cup chopped green pepper
1 tablespoon chili powder
½ teaspoon salt
⅛ teaspoon pepper
1 head lettuce, torn
2 tomatoes, peeled and coarsely chopped
2 avocados, peeled and chopped
1 cup (4 ounces) shredded Cheddar cheese
1 (8-ounce) can whole kernel corn, drained
1 (7-ounce) package tortilla chips, crushed
½ cup commercial Thousand Island dressing
½ cup commercial creamy Italian dressing

Sort and wash peas; place in a heavy saucepan. Cover with water, and bring to a boil; cook 2 minutes. Remove from heat. Cover and let soak 1 hour; drain.

Combine peas and 2½ cups water; bring to a boil. Reduce heat. Cover and simmer about 1¼ hours or until tender; drain. Cool and set aside.

Cook ground beef, ½ cup onion, and green pepper until tender; drain well. Stir in chili powder, salt, and pepper; let cool.

Combine peas, meat mixture, remaining onion, lettuce, tomatoes, avocados, cheese, corn, and chips in a large salad bowl; combine salad dressings, and pour over top. Toss gently before serving. Yield: 16 to 18 servings.
Julie Trammell, Snyder, Texas.

BLACK-EYED PEA SPAGHETTI

1 cup elbow spaghetti
5 cups frozen black-eyed peas
1 cup chopped onion
3 cloves garlic, minced
2 tablespoons bacon drippings
1 pound ground beef
2 (16-ounce) cans stewed tomatoes, undrained and chopped
1½ teaspoons chili seasoning
1 teaspoon seasoning salt
2 teaspoons garlic salt
½ teaspoon ground oregano
½ teaspoon dried whole basil
1½ teaspoons sugar
1 teaspoon salt
¼ teaspoon pepper
1 to 2 tablespoons Worcestershire sauce

Cook spaghetti according to package directions; drain and set aside.

Cook peas according to package directions; drain and set aside.

Sauté onion and garlic in bacon drippings in a large skillet until onion is tender. Add beef and cook, stirring constantly, until browned; drain off drippings. Add next 10 ingredients, mixing well; simmer 25 minutes, stirring occasionally. Stir in spaghetti and peas; simmer an additional 5 minutes. Yield: 8 to 10 servings. *Pat Gilbreath, Mabank, Texas.*

HOPPING JOHN WITH HAM

2 cups dried black-eyed peas
½ pound ham
2 quarts water
1 cup uncooked regular rice
1 cup chopped onion
1 cup chopped celery
2 teaspoons butter or margarine
½ to 1 teaspoon Italian seasoning
1 teaspoon sugar
1½ to 2 teaspoons salt
¼ teaspoon pepper

Sort and wash peas; place in a heavy saucepan. Cover with water, and bring to a boil; cook 2 minutes. Remove from heat. Cover and let soak 1 hour; drain.

Combine ham and 2 quarts water in a large Dutch oven. Bring to a boil. Reduce heat; cover and simmer 15 minutes. Add peas; bring to a boil. Reduce heat; cover and simmer 45 minutes. Add remaining ingredients; bring to a boil. Reduce heat; cover and simmer an additional 30 minutes or until black-eyed peas are done.

Remove ham; cut into small pieces. Stir ham into pea mixture. Yield: 10 to 12 servings. *Rubie M. Walker, Lynchburg, Virginia.*

SPICY HOT BLACK-EYED PEAS

3 slices bacon
1 (17-ounce) can black-eyed peas
1 (16-ounce) can whole tomatoes,
    undrained and chopped
1 cup chopped onion
1 large green pepper, chopped
1 clove garlic, minced
1 teaspoon ground cumin
1 teaspoon dry mustard
½ teaspoon curry powder
½ teaspoon chili powder
1 teaspoon salt
½ teaspoon pepper
Chopped fresh parsley

Cook bacon slices in a large skillet until crisp. Remove bacon; crumble and set aside.

Stir next 11 ingredients into bacon drippings in skillet; bring to a boil. Reduce heat, and simmer 20 minutes, stirring occasionally. Pour mixture into serving dish; sprinkle bacon and parsley over top. Yield: 6 servings.

Betty J. Moore,
Belton, Texas.

BLACK-EYED PEA DIP

1¾ cups dried black-eyed peas
5 cups water
5 jalapeño peppers, seeded and chopped
⅓ cup chopped onion
1 clove garlic
1 cup butter or margarine
2 cups (8 ounces) shredded sharp process
    American cheese
1 (4-ounce) can chopped green chiles
1 tablespoon jalapeño pepper liquid

Sort and wash peas; place in a heavy saucepan. Cover with water, and bring to a boil; cook 2 minutes. Remove from heat. Cover and let soak 1 hour; drain.

Combine peas and 5 cups water; bring to a boil. Reduce heat, cover, and simmer about 1 hour and 15 minutes or until tender; drain.

Combine peas, jalapeño peppers, onion, and garlic in container of electric blender; blend until smooth. Set aside.

Combine butter and cheese in top of a double boiler; bring water to a boil. Reduce heat to low; cook, stirring occasionally, until melted. Add chiles, pepper liquid, and pea mixture; stir well. Serve with corn chips. Yield: 6 cups.

Susan Blair,
Little Rock, Arkansas.

Tip: Freeze very soft cheese 15 minutes to make shredding easier.

Homemade Bread Made Easy

With the help of standard convenience products, homemade bread is easier to prepare than you've ever imagined. Our recipes for quick breads and rolls have been designed to help keep the busy cook on schedule.

Jam Teasers are easily assembled with refrigerated crescent rolls, orange marmalade, sour cream, coconut, and walnuts. A pound cake mix is the shortcut to Apricot-Nut Loaf. And biscuit mix is combined with Cheddar cheese, onion, and chopped parsley for savory Onion-Cheese Bread.

APRICOT-NUT LOAF

¾ cup chopped dried apricots
½ cup chopped walnuts
¼ cup all-purpose flour
¼ cup milk
¼ cup orange juice
3 eggs
1 (17-ounce) package pound cake mix
1 teaspoon grated orange rind
Orange Butter

Combine apricots, walnuts, and flour in a bowl, stirring well; set aside.

Combine milk, orange juice, and eggs; add pound cake mix and orange rind, stirring just until moistened. Fold in apricot mixture. Pour batter into greased and floured 9- x 5- x 3-inch loafpan. Bake at 325° for 1 hour and 15 minutes or until wooden pick inserted in center comes out clean. Cool in pan 10 minutes; remove from pan, and serve warm with Orange Butter. Yield: 1 loaf.

Orange Butter:

½ cup whipped butter or margarine
¼ teaspoon grated orange rind

Combine butter and orange rind; stir until mixed. Yield: ½ cup.

Doris Amonette,
Tulsa, Oklahoma.

JAM TEASERS

1 (8-ounce) can refrigerated crescent
    dinner rolls
About 3 tablespoons commercial sour
    cream
About 6 tablespoons orange marmalade
¼ cup chopped walnuts
¼ cup flaked coconut
2 tablespoons orange marmalade, melted
Additional chopped walnuts (optional)

Separate crescent dinner rolls into triangles. Spread each triangle with about 1 teaspoon sour cream and about 2 teaspoons marmalade. Sprinkle each evenly with walnuts and coconut; roll up, beginning at large end. Place seam side down, 1 inch apart on a greased baking sheet; curve into a crescent. Bake at 375° for 20 minutes or until golden brown. Remove from oven, and brush with melted marmalade; sprinkle with additional walnuts, if desired. Yield: 6 to 8 servings.

Mrs. W. J. Scherffius,
Mountain Home, Arkansas.

PUMPKIN BREAD

2 cups buttermilk pancake mix
¾ cup firmly packed brown sugar
1 teaspoon ground cinnamon
½ teaspoon ground nutmeg
½ teaspoon ground cloves
¼ teaspoon ground ginger
1 cup cooked, mashed pumpkin
⅓ cup vegetable oil
¼ cup milk
2 eggs, slightly beaten
½ cup chopped walnuts

Combine first 10 ingredients in a large mixing bowl. Beat 3 minutes at medium speed of an electric mixer. Stir in walnuts. Spoon batter into a greased 9- x 5- x 3-inch loafpan. Bake at 350° for 45 to 55 minutes or until a wooden pick inserted in center comes out clean. Cool in pan 10 minutes; remove from pan, and cool completely. Yield: 1 loaf.

Mrs. Steve Garvin,
Wilkesboro, North Carolina.

ONION-CHEESE BREAD

1 tablespoon butter or margarine
½ cup chopped onion
1½ cups biscuit mix
2 tablespoons chopped parsley
1 egg, beaten
1 cup (4 ounces) shredded sharp Cheddar
    cheese, divided
½ cup milk
1 tablespoon butter or margarine, melted

Melt 1 tablespoon butter in a small skillet; add onion, and cook until transparent. Combine onion, biscuit mix, parsley, egg, ½ cup cheese, and milk, stirring just until moistened. Spoon into a lightly greased 8-inch square baking pan; sprinkle with remaining cheese. Drizzle with 1 tablespoon melted butter. Bake at 400° for 25 to 30 minutes or until golden brown. Yield: 6 to 8 servings. *Mrs. J. O. Branson, Thomasville, North Carolina.*

Salads To Fool The Season

If you think that it has to be summer to enjoy a really good salad, it's time to fool the season using these recipes. Each shows how one or two special ingredients can turn basic salad greens into a fresh winter delight.

Canned asparagus spears top off a lettuce, spinach, and broccoli combination in Garden Salad Toss.

For a zesty chef's salad, toss avocado, tender strips of chicken, bacon, and blue cheese with romaine and Boston lettuce. A vinaigrette dressing blends the flavors.

Crispy bacon and hot bacon drippings are the secret to Hill Country Salad, a wilted lettuce salad.

VINAIGRETTE CHEF'S SALAD

2 whole chicken breasts, cooked, skinned, and boned
1 tablespoon lemon juice
1 medium avocado, peeled, seeded, and coarsely chopped
3 cups torn Boston lettuce
3 cups torn romaine lettuce
1 cup chopped celery
6 slices bacon, cooked, drained, and crumbled
2 medium tomatoes, cut into eight wedges
3 hard-cooked eggs, sliced
1 (4-ounce) package blue cheese, crumbled
½ cup commercial vinaigrette salad dressing

Chill chicken; cut into thin strips. Sprinkle lemon juice over avocado, and toss gently.

Combine chicken, avocado, and remaining ingredients in a large bowl; toss carefully. Yield: 6 to 8 servings.
Ella Brown, Proctor, Arkansas.

GARDEN SALAD TOSS

2 cups torn iceberg lettuce
3 cups torn spinach
1 cup broccoli flowerets
¼ teaspoon garlic powder
¼ teaspoon salt
⅛ teaspoon pepper
¼ cup commercial oil-and-vinegar salad dressing
1 (14½-ounce) can asparagus spears, drained
Mayonnaise (optional)
Paprika (optional)

Combine lettuce, spinach, and broccoli in a large bowl; toss gently. Sprinkle with garlic powder, salt, and pepper. Add dressing, and toss. Divide greens equally on 6 salad plates. Arrange asparagus spears on top of greens; garnish with mayonnaise and paprika, if desired. Yield: 6 servings.
Marilyn Baquet, Baton Rouge, Louisiana.

HILL COUNTRY SALAD

5 slices bacon
5 to 7 cups torn leaf lettuce
3 green onions, chopped
2 tablespoons cider vinegar
1 teaspoon sugar
¼ teaspoon salt

Cook bacon until crisp; drain, reserving ¼ cup drippings. Crumble bacon, and set aside.

Place lettuce in a large bowl; sprinkle with onion, vinegar, sugar, and salt. Drizzle reserved hot bacon drippings over greens, tossing gently. Sprinkle with bacon, and serve immediately. Yield: 6 servings. *Edna Chadsey, Corpus Christi, Texas.*

COMBO SALAD BOWL

1 cup fresh green bean pieces
1 medium head lettuce, torn
3 tomatoes, peeled and chopped
2 tablespoons chopped parsley
1 or 2 hard-cooked eggs, chopped
¼ cup whipping cream
2 tablespoons olive oil
1 tablespoon prepared mustard
1 tablespoon vinegar
1 tablespoon tarragon vinegar
½ to 1 cup croutons

Cook beans, uncovered, in boiling water for 20 minutes or just until tender; drain and cool.

Combine green beans, lettuce, tomatoes, parsley, and eggs in a large salad bowl; set aside.

Combine whipping cream, olive oil, mustard, and vinegar in a saucepan; stir well. Place over medium heat and cook, stirring constantly, until thickened. Pour warm dressing over vegetable mixture; toss gently. Top with croutons, and serve immediately. Yield: 8 servings.
Mrs. George Sellers, Albany, Georgia.

Curry Blends In Nicely With Shrimp, Lamb

Curry, a blend of as many as 16 different spices, is one of the world's oldest seasonings. Essential to the blend are ginger, turmeric, red pepper, and coriander, while a wide range of other spices may be added to give each curry its distinctive flavor.

Whether you select a mild or a hot curry powder is a matter of individual taste, but you will want to use your choice in the following recipes. Our selections range from a shrimp curry and a lamb curry served with traditional condiments to a tangy curry dip delicious served with fresh vegetables.

CURRY DIP

1 cup mayonnaise
1 tablespoon finely grated onion
1 teaspoon garlic salt
1 teaspoon curry powder
1 teaspoon prepared horseradish
1 teaspoon tarragon vinegar

Combine all ingredients, mixing well. Chill at least 3 hours; serve with fresh vegetables. Yield: about 1 cup.
Patricia Pashby, Memphis, Tennessee.

LAMB CURRY WITH RICE

¾ pound boneless lamb, cut into 1½-inch
    cubes
3 tablespoons vegetable oil
1 medium onion, minced
1 cooking apple, peeled and chopped
¼ cup melted butter or margarine
3 tablespoons all-purpose flour
1 cup milk
1 tablespoon curry powder
1 tablespoon lemon juice
1½ teaspoons salt
¼ teaspoon ground ginger
Dash of pepper
Hot cooked rice

Cook lamb in oil until brown; drain and set aside.

Sauté onion and apple in butter until tender. Add flour and cook 1 minute, stirring constantly. Gradually add milk; cook over medium heat, stirring constantly, until thickened and bubbly. Stir in next 5 ingredients. Add lamb to sauce mixture; serve over rice.

Serve with several of the following condiments: currants, raisins, peanuts, onion, green pepper, or orange sections. Yield: 4 servings.
Regina Campbell,
Universal City, Texas.

SOUR CREAM AND SHRIMP CURRY

⅓ cup chopped onion
¼ cup chopped green pepper
1 clove garlic, minced
2 tablespoons melted butter or margarine
1 (8-ounce) carton commercial sour cream
1¼ pounds medium shrimp, peeled, deveined, and cooked
1 teaspoon curry powder
¼ teaspoon salt
Pepper to taste
Hot cooked rice

Sauté onion, green pepper, and garlic in butter until tender. Add remaining ingredients except rice; cook over low heat until thoroughly heated, stirring often. Serve over rice. Yield: about 4 servings.
Mrs. R. M. Lancaster,
Brentwood, Tennessee.

Tip: Treat yourself and your family to a dinner cooked right at the table. Tempura, fondues, and stir-fry dishes prepared in woks or electric skillets save time and energy.

Pork By Popular Demand

Pork is such a simple food that it inspires people who love to cook to new heights of creativity. Our readers have come up with several new ways to serve this favorite—and each is so good you'll be proud to serve it to company.

All dressed up, Stuffed Pork Shoulder makes a pretty entrée for a fancy dinner or a family get-together. This recipe provides extra stuffing as a side dish—a Southern tradition.

Pork chops offer even more possibilities: Barbecue them in a sweet sauce, stuff them with a sage-flavored mixture, or bake them with apples.

The Chinese Spareribs work well in the oven, bringing a smoky-sweet flavor indoors for the winter.

BAKED PORK CHOPS AND APPLES

2 tablespoons butter or margarine
½ cup chopped onion
6 (1-inch-thick) pork chops
1 teaspoon salt
⅛ teaspoon pepper
4 cooking apples, peeled, cored, and sliced
1 cup water
3 tablespoons brown sugar
½ teaspoon dry mustard
¼ teaspoon ground cloves

Melt butter in large skillet; add onion and sauté until tender. Remove onion, and set aside. Brown pork chops on both sides in butter; sprinkle with salt and pepper.

Arrange chops in a 13- x 9- x 2-inch baking dish. Cover with apple slices; sprinkle with onion. Combine remaining ingredients, and pour over chops. Cover and bake at 375° for about 1 hour. Yield: 6 servings.
Mrs. Roy Sweeney,
Louisville, Tennessee.

BARBECUED PORK CHOPS

4 (½-inch-thick) pork chops
½ cup chopped onion
¼ cup firmly packed brown sugar
¼ cup catsup
¼ cup vinegar
¼ cup water
1 tablespoon Worcestershire sauce
1 teaspoon salt
1 teaspoon paprika
¼ teaspoon pepper

Place pork chops in a 9-inch square baking dish. Combine remaining ingredients; mix well, and pour over chops. Bake at 300° for 1 hour. Yield: 4 servings.
Billie Taylor,
Afton, Virginia.

EASY STUFFED PORK CHOPS

1 cup soft breadcrumbs
½ cup peeled, diced cooking apple
2 teaspoons minced onion
2 teaspoons minced fresh parsley
½ teaspoon salt
⅛ teaspoon pepper
¼ teaspoon rubbed sage
¼ cup plus 2 tablespoons milk
4 (1½-inch-thick) pork chops, cut with pockets

Combine first 8 ingredients; stir well. Stuff mixture into pockets of pork chops; place the chops in a shallow baking pan. Cover and bake at 350° for 30 minutes. Uncover and bake an additional 30 minutes or until done, basting often with pan drippings. Yield: 4 servings.
Mrs. C. R. Field,
Bryson City, North Carolina.

CHINESE SPARERIBS

5 pounds spareribs
¼ cup chopped onion
2 cloves garlic, minced
1 (10-ounce) jar plum jelly
⅓ cup soy sauce
¼ cup dark corn syrup
2 teaspoons ground ginger

Cut ribs into serving-size pieces; place in a 13- x 9- x 2-inch baking dish. Combine remaining ingredients in a saucepan, and bring to a boil. Remove from heat, and pour over ribs. Cover and refrigerate 2 hours.

Bake ribs, covered, at 350° about 2 hours, turning halfway through baking. Yield: about 6 servings.

Mrs. Tommy W. Ellison,
Matthews, North Carolina.

STUFFED PORK SHOULDER

4 cups soft breadcrumbs
¼ cup chopped celery
¼ cup finely chopped green pepper
¼ cup minced onion
1 (7-ounce) can whole kernel corn, drained
5 tablespoons melted butter or margarine
2 eggs, beaten
1 teaspoon salt
1 (4- to 5-pound) boned Boston pork shoulder

Combine first 8 ingredients; mix well.

Untie roast, and spoon breadcrumb mixture into the opening formed by boning. Spoon remaining stuffing into a greased shallow casserole. Set aside.

Tie roast securely with string, and place on a rack in a roasting pan. Bake 40 minutes per pound at 325° or until desired degree of doneness. Bake extra dressing at 325° for 15 to 20 minutes. Remove string, and slice to serve. Yield: about 8 servings.

Mary Ellen Shull,
Melbourne, Florida.

A pork shoulder is as simple to stuff as a turkey. The butcher does most of the work first by boning the meat.

HAM-AND-MUSHROOM QUICHE

Pastry for two 9-inch quiche dishes or pieplates
1 bunch green onions, chopped
2 tablespoons melted butter or margarine
2 cups (8 ounces) shredded Swiss cheese
6 slices bacon, cooked and crumbled
1 (8-ounce) can sliced mushrooms, drained
2 cups coarsely shredded ham
8 eggs, beaten
1½ cups evaporated milk
1 clove garlic, crushed
½ teaspoon salt
½ teaspoon dry mustard
Dash of ground nutmeg
Dash of white pepper

Line two 9-inch quiche dishes or pieplates with pastry; trim excess pastry from edges. Fold edges under and flute. Prick bottom and sides of pastry with a fork. Bake at 425° for 6 to 8 minutes. Let cool on wire rack.

Sauté onion in butter until tender. Combine onion, cheese, bacon, mushrooms, and ham; toss gently. Spoon half of mixture into each pastry shell.

Combine remaining ingredients; beat well. Pour half of egg mixture into each pastry shell. Bake at 350° for 30 to 40 minutes or until set. Yield: two 9-inch quiches.

Note: Unbaked quiche may be covered with aluminum foil and frozen. To serve, thaw overnight in refrigerator; bake at 350° for 40 to 50 minutes.

Dale W. Barr,
Birmingham, Alabama.

PORK SPAGHETTI BAKE

1 pound ground pork
½ pound bulk pork sausage
1 large onion, minced
1 large green pepper, minced
2 cloves garlic, minced
1 tablespoon vegetable oil
1 (6-ounce) can tomato paste
1 cup ripe olives, sliced
1 (17-ounce) can cream-style corn
1 (4-ounce) can sliced mushrooms, drained
1 cup (4 ounces) shredded Cheddar cheese
6 ounces spaghetti, broken into 2-inch pieces
1 tablespoon sugar
1 tablespoon Worcestershire sauce
1½ teaspoons salt
½ teaspoon pepper
¼ cup grated Parmesan cheese

Cook ground pork, sausage, onion, green pepper, and garlic in oil in a

Dutch oven until meat is browned; drain off drippings. Add remaining ingredients except Parmesan cheese; stir well. Spoon into a greased 12- x 8- x 2-inch baking dish; sprinkle Parmesan cheese over top. Cover and refrigerate 8 to 10 hours or overnight.

Let come to room temperature; bake at 375° for 30 to 35 minutes or until lightly browned. Yield: 8 to 10 servings.

Mrs. W. J. Lichtenegger,
Poplar Bluff, Missouri.

Make Pralines Like The Experts

Probably no one knows more about making pralines than the folks at Evans Creole Candy Co. in New Orleans. The factory has eight praline variations, ranging from the original pecan to the strawberry-coconut variation.

But Evans offers more than just a variety of candy to sample. You can watch the actual candymaking process through glass in the company's modern facility at 848 Decatur Street, in the French Market area. In addition to sampling the candy, you can purchase boxes to be mailed anywhere in the United States.

So you can enjoy the flavor of New Orleans at home, Evans shares the recipe for its most popular praline—Original Pecan Pralines.

ORIGINAL PECAN PRALINES

2 cups firmly packed brown sugar
¼ cup water
2½ cups mixed pecan pieces and halves
1 tablespoon butter

Combine sugar and water in a 2-quart saucepan; heat to boiling, stirring constantly. Stir in pecans; cook until mixture reaches the soft ball stage (235°). Remove from heat; stir in butter.

Immediately drop by tablespoonfuls onto waxed paper; let stand until firm. Yield: about 1½ dozen.

Tip: To freshen air throughout the house, boil 1 tablespoon of whole cloves in a pan of water for a few minutes.

Revive Winter Meals With Fresh Oranges

An orange is so good all by itself, eaten as nature made it, that it's easy to forget how many other good things it can be. Starting with the basic fruit, section it, slice it, or squeeze it to enjoy that delightful flavor from entrée to dessert.

Lemon and lime aren't the only kinds of citrus that turn a meringue pie into sheer heaven. Try our Orange Meringue Pie and watch for the smiles. Or fill hollowed orange shells with a rich, creamy orange mixture—no baking—for a special Orange Cream dessert.

Beneath the gorgeous meringue topping Orange Meringue Pie has a citrusy filling made with fresh orange juice and rind.

ORANGE CREAM

6 large oranges
3½ to 4 cups miniature marshmallows, divided
1 teaspoon grated orange rind
1 egg, beaten
1 cup whipping cream, whipped

Slice tops from oranges, scalloping or notching edges, if desired. Gently remove fruit, leaving shells intact. Remove membrane from fruit; cut fruit and drain off juice, reserving ⅓ cup. Set fruit aside.

Melt 3 cups marshmallows in top of double boiler; stir in reserved orange juice and orange rind. Gradually add egg, and cook 5 minutes, stirring constantly. Chill thoroughly.

Stir until well blended; fold in whipped cream, oranges, and remaining marshmallows. Spoon mixture into orange shells; chill. Yield: 6 servings.
Mrs. John R. Allen,
Dallas, Texas.

SPICY ORANGE SLICES

8 to 10 oranges
4 cups sugar
1 cup vinegar
½ cup water
10 whole cloves
2 (2-inch) sticks cinnamon

Cut oranges into ½-inch slices; remove seeds, and discard end pieces. Place oranges in a Dutch oven, and cover with water. Bring to a boil; reduce heat, cover, and simmer 1 hour. Drain.

Combine remaining ingredients in a Dutch oven. Bring to a boil; cook 5 minutes over medium heat, stirring constantly. Add oranges; cover, and simmer 1 hour. Remove from heat, and pack orange slices into hot sterilized jars; fill with syrup, leaving ½-inch headspace. Seal with ⅛-inch layer of paraffin. Yield: 4 pints.
Mrs. Ron Bain,
Nashville, Tennessee.

PERSIAN CHICKEN SALAD

3 cups cubed cooked chicken
2 small oranges, peeled and sectioned
8 canned apricot halves, quartered
¼ cup sliced green onion
¼ cup lemon or lime juice
¼ cup vegetable oil
½ teaspoon salt
¼ teaspoon pepper
8 large romaine leaves

Combine first 4 ingredients. Combine lemon juice, vegetable oil, salt, and pepper; mix well. Pour over chicken mixture; toss gently. Serve on romaine leaves. Yield: 6 to 8 servings.
Lilly S. Bradley,
Salem, Virginia.

ORANGE MERINGUE PIE

1½ cups sugar
¼ cup plus 2 tablespoons cornstarch
¼ teaspoon salt
1½ teaspoons grated orange rind
3 cups orange juice
¼ cup plus 2 tablespoons lemon juice
4 eggs, separated
3 tablespoons butter or margarine
1 baked 9-inch pastry shell
¼ teaspoon cream of tartar
½ cup sugar
Fresh orange slices (optional)

Combine 1½ cups sugar, cornstarch, salt, and orange rind in a heavy saucepan. Gradually add orange juice, lemon juice, and egg yolks. Bring mixture to a boil, stirring constantly; stir in butter. Cook over medium heat 10 to 12 minutes or until smooth and thickened. Pour filling into pastry shell.

Beat egg whites (at room temperature) and cream of tartar until foamy. Gradually add ½ cup sugar, 1 tablespoon at a time, beating until stiff peaks form. Spread meringue over filling, sealing to edge of pastry. Bake at 350° for 10 to 12 minutes or until golden brown. Chill overnight. Garnish with orange slices, if desired. Yield: one 9-inch pie.
Mrs. E. A. Kraus,
Louisville, Kentucky.

February

Our title "Chocolate! Indulge Yourself" seems an appropriate one for our salute to the favorite sweet because that is what we did while testing the recipes! We ate chocolate cheesecakes every afternoon for a week before finding just the right blend.

On Valentine's Day, why not send a baked greeting instead of a card? We offer several cookie choices as well as an icing to decorate them. The whole test kitchens staff lent a hand at decorating ours and thoroughly enjoyed it. You try it, too!

And don't miss Spaghetti Pie. One of our editors tried it at the home of a friend and found it so delicious that she charmed him out of the recipe, bringing it back to share with you.

Mix Up A Quick Bread

Pop open a steaming hot muffin, and smother it with butter. Slice a fresh loaf of oatmeal bread filled with raisins. Bite into a delicate coffee cake, and discover swirls of cranberry. These breads boast the old-fashioned flavor of home baking with quick methods well suited for today's busy cooks. The surprise ingredients make these breads taste like they took all day to bake. You'll know better. Using baking powder and soda for leavening cuts preparation time.

BANANA WHEAT BREAD

2 cups whole wheat flour
¼ cup wheat germ
1 teaspoon salt
1 teaspoon soda
1½ cups mashed ripe banana
¼ cup vegetable oil
½ cup honey
2 eggs
1 teaspoon vanilla extract
½ cup chopped pecans

Combine dry ingredients in a large bowl; stir well. Combine banana, oil, honey, eggs, and vanilla; mix well. Make a well in center of dry ingredients; add banana mixture, and stir just until moistened. Stir in pecans. Spoon into a well-greased and floured 9- x 5- x 3-inch loafpan. Bake at 350° for 1 hour or until bread tests done. Yield: 1 loaf.
*Terri Burke,
Elkins, West Virginia.*

OATMEAL RAISIN BREAD

2¼ cups all-purpose flour
¾ cup quick-cooking oats, uncooked
¼ cup whole bran cereal
¾ cup firmly packed brown sugar
1 tablespoon plus 1 teaspoon baking powder
1 teaspoon salt
1½ teaspoons ground cinnamon
½ teaspoon ground cloves
2 eggs, beaten
1½ cups milk
½ cup vegetable oil
1 cup raisins
⅓ cup quick-cooking oats, uncooked
¼ cup firmly packed brown sugar
1 tablespoon butter, melted

Combine first 8 ingredients in a large bowl. Combine eggs, milk, and oil.

Make a well in center of dry ingredients; add liquid ingredients, and stir just until moistened. Stir in raisins.

Pour into a lightly greased and floured 9- x 5- x 3-inch loafpan. Combine remaining ingredients; sprinkle over batter, and press gently. Bake at 325° for 70 minutes or until a wooden pick inserted in center comes out clean. Cool in pan 10 minutes; remove to cooling rack. Cool completely. Yield: 1 loaf.
*Margaret W. Cotton,
Franklin, Virginia.*

CRANBERRY COFFEE CAKE

½ cup butter or margarine, softened
1 cup sugar
2 eggs
2 cups all-purpose flour
1 teaspoon baking powder
1 teaspoon soda
½ teaspoon salt
1 (8-ounce) carton commercial sour cream
1 teaspoon almond extract
1 (16-ounce) can whole-berry cranberry sauce
½ cup chopped pecans
Glaze (recipe follows)

Cream butter; gradually add sugar, beating until light and fluffy. Add eggs, one at a time, beating well after each addition. Combine dry ingredients; add to creamed mixture alternately with sour cream, beating well after each addition. Add almond extract; mix well.

Spoon one-third of mixture into a greased and floured 10-inch tube pan or Bundt pan. Spread one-third cranberry sauce over batter. Repeat layers twice more, ending with cranberry sauce. Sprinkle pecans over top.

Bake at 350° for 1 hour or until cake tests done. Let cool 5 minutes before removing from pan. Drizzle glaze over top. Yield: one 10-inch coffee cake.

Glaze:

¾ cup powdered sugar
½ teaspoon almond extract
1 tablespoon warm water

Combine all ingredients; stir well. Yield: glaze for one 10-inch cake.

LIGHTLY LEMON COFFEE CAKE

¾ cup evaporated milk
2 tablespoons vinegar
1 teaspoon soda
½ cup butter or margarine, softened
1 cup sugar
2 eggs
1 teaspoon grated lemon rind
1¾ cups sifted cake flour
2 teaspoons baking powder
½ teaspoon salt
½ cup firmly packed brown sugar
1 tablespoon ground cinnamon
1 cup sifted powdered sugar
2 tablespoons lemon juice

Combine evaporated milk and vinegar in a small bowl; stir in soda. Set aside.

Cream butter; gradually add sugar, beating until light and fluffy. Add eggs and lemon rind; beat well. Combine flour, baking powder, and salt; add to creamed mixture alternately with milk mixture, beating well.

Spread half of batter in a greased and floured 10-inch tube pan. Combine brown sugar and cinnamon; sprinkle half of mixture over batter. Spoon remaining batter into pan; sprinkle with remaining cinnamon-sugar. Bake at 350° about 45 to 50 minutes or until a wooden pick inserted in center comes out clean. Cool in pan 5 minutes; remove from pan.

Combine powdered sugar and lemon juice; spoon over cake. Yield: one 10-inch coffee cake.

PINEAPPLE MUFFINS

2 cups all-purpose flour
2 teaspoons baking powder
½ teaspoon soda
½ teaspoon salt
½ cup firmly packed brown sugar
1 egg, well beaten
1 (8-ounce) carton commercial sour cream
1 (8-ounce) can crushed pineapple, undrained
⅓ cup melted shortening
½ cup chopped pecans

Combine first 5 ingredients in a large bowl; stir well. Combine egg, sour cream, pineapple, and shortening. Make a well in center of dry ingredients; add pineapple mixture, and stir just until moistened. Stir in pecans. Spoon into greased muffin pans, filling two-thirds full. Bake at 400° for 20 to 25 minutes or until brown. Yield: 1½ dozen.
*Mrs. Paul C. Wood,
New Orleans, Louisiana.*

Chocolate! Indulge Yourself

Temptation should not always be resisted. We can think of no better reasons to yield than these luscious chocolate desserts. Rich, dark, and sweet, they are simply impossible to resist.

Perhaps the richest of all are the Pots de Crème, a delectable offering made with sweet baking chocolate and whipping cream. Chocolate Cheesecake, laced with rum, is a super-rich combination of cream cheese, sour cream, and semisweet chocolate morsels.

Chocolate-Orange Mousse is flavored with a subtle hint of orange, then topped with mounds of whipped cream. And Chocolate-Peanut Clusters are a glorious mixture of chocolate, peanut butter, and Spanish peanuts.

Substitutions

For each of these recipes we specify the type of chocolate we used for testing. If you need to make substitutions, use the following as a guide:

—Substitute 3 tablespoons unsweetened cocoa powder plus 1 tablespoon shortening for each 1-ounce square unsweetened chocolate.

—Use 2 ounces unsweetened chocolate, 7 tablespoons sugar, and 2 tablespoons shortening for each cup (6 ounces) semisweet chocolate morsels.

—When melted, semisweet chocolate morsels and semisweet squares can be used interchangeably.

Garnishes

The crowning touches to these chocolate delicacies are the garnishes. Two special ones are chocolate leaves and curls, and they are easier to prepare than you might think.

For **chocolate leaves,** select such nonpoisonous leaves as mint or rose leaves. Wash leaves and pat dry with paper towels. Melt 1 or 2 (1-ounce) squares semisweet chocolate over hot water in a double boiler; let cool slightly.

Using a small spatula, spread a ⅛-inch layer of chocolate on the back of each leaf, spreading to edges. Place leaves on a waxed paper-lined cookie sheet, chocolate side up; freeze until chocolate is firm, about 10 minutes.

Grasp leaf at stem end, and carefully peel leaf away from chocolate. Chill chocolate leaves until ready to use. (Handle carefully since leaves are thin and will melt quickly from the heat of your hand.)

For **chocolate curls,** melt 4 (1-ounce) squares semisweet chocolate over hot water in a double boiler. (This amount is needed for length and width of chocolate strip. Excess may be reused.) Pour chocolate out in a stream onto a waxed paper-lined cookie sheet. Spread chocolate with a spatula into a 3-inch-wide strip. (Vary the length of curls by altering the width of strip.) Smooth top of strip with spatula.

Chill until chocolate partially cools and feels slightly tacky but is not firm. (If chocolate is too hard, curls will break; if too soft, chocolate will not curl.)

Gently pull a vegetable peeler across length of chocolate until curls form, letting chocolate curl up on top of peeler. (If chocolate becomes too firm, remelt and repeat process.) Transfer curls to a tray by inserting a wooden pick in end of curl. (Curls will melt from heat of hand.) Chill curls until ready to use.

POTS DE CREME

2 (4-ounce) packages sweet baking
   chocolate
2 tablespoons sugar
1 cup whipping cream
4 egg yolks
1 teaspoon vanilla extract
Whipped cream
Chocolate curls

Melt chocolate over hot water in top of double boiler. Stir in sugar. Gradually add whipping cream, stirring until smooth. Remove from heat.

Beat yolks well with a wire whisk. Gradually stir about one-fourth of chocolate mixture into yolks; quickly add to remaining chocolate mixture, stirring constantly. Stir in vanilla.

Spoon into small cordial glasses. Refrigerate. Garnish with whipped cream and chocolate curls. Yield: 6 servings.

Mrs. Joe DeJournette,
Thurmond, North Carolina.

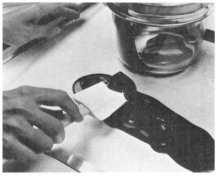

Chocolate curls—*Spread melted chocolate into a 3-inch-wide strip on waxed paper; chill until chocolate feels slightly tacky. Pull a vegetable peeler across length of chocolate, letting chocolate curl up on top of peeler.*

Chocolate leaves—*Spread a ⅛-inch layer of melted chocolate on back of each leaf; freeze until firm. When firm, grasp leaf at stem end and carefully peel leaf away from chocolate.*

CHOCOLATE CHEESECAKE

1⅓ cups chocolate wafer crumbs
2 tablespoons sugar
¼ teaspoon ground cinnamon
¼ cup butter, softened
1½ cups semisweet chocolate morsels
2 eggs
½ cup sugar
2 teaspoons rum
1 (8-ounce) carton commercial sour cream
2 (8-ounce) packages cream cheese, cubed and softened
2 tablespoons butter, melted
Whipped cream
Chocolate leaves

Combine wafer crumbs, 2 tablespoons sugar, cinnamon, and ¼ cup butter; mix well. Firmly press into bottom of a 10-inch springform pan; set aside.

Melt chocolate morsels over hot water in top of a double boiler. Set aside.

Combine eggs, ½ cup sugar, rum, and sour cream in container of an electric blender; process 15 seconds. Continue blending, and gradually add chocolate and cream cheese. Add melted butter; blend well. Pour cheese mixture into chocolate crust. Bake at 325° for 45 minutes or until cheesecake is set in center. Cool at room temperature for at least 1 hour. Chill at least 6 hours. Remove sides of springform pan. Before serving, garnish with whipped cream and chocolate leaves. Yield: 10 to 12 servings.

CHOCOLATE MINT SOUFFLE

Vegetable oil
1 (6-ounce) package semisweet chocolate morsels
1 envelope unflavored gelatin
1 cup sugar, divided
6 eggs, separated
½ cup milk
¼ cup water
1 teaspoon peppermint extract
1 cup whipping cream, whipped

Cut a piece of aluminum foil long enough to fit around a 1-quart soufflé dish, allowing a 1-inch overlap. Fold aluminum foil lengthwise into thirds. Lightly oil one side of foil. Wrap around dish, oiled side touching dish, allowing foil to extend 2 inches above rim to form a collar. Secure with cellophane tape.

Place chocolate morsels in container of electric blender; blend at high speed 15 seconds or until finely chopped. (Do not overprocess.) Set aside.

Combine gelatin and ½ cup sugar in top of double boiler. Combine egg yolks, milk, and water; beat well. Pour egg yolk mixture into gelatin; stir to dissolve gelatin. Bring water to a boil in bottom of double boiler. Reduce heat to low; cook, stirring constantly, until mixture thickens and coats a metal spoon. Pour into a large mixing bowl. Cool to room temperature (15 to 20 minutes); stir in peppermint.

Beat egg whites (at room temperature) until foamy. Gradually add remaining sugar, 1 tablespoon at a time, beating until stiff peaks form.

Reserve 1 tablespoon chocolate; fold remaining chocolate and whipped cream into custard. Fold egg whites into custard. Pour into soufflé dish; sprinkle with reserved chocolate. Chill until firm (4 to 5 hours). Remove collar to serve. Yield: 6 to 8 servings.

Margaret Cotton,
Franklin, Virginia.

CHOCOLATE-ORANGE MOUSSE

6 (1-ounce) squares semisweet chocolate
1 teaspoon grated orange rind
¼ cup firmly packed brown sugar
2 egg yolks
2 eggs
1 tablespoon orange juice
1 cup whipping cream, whipped
Additional whipped cream
Mandarin oranges

Melt chocolate over hot water in top of double boiler. Cool.

Combine orange rind, sugar, egg yolks, and eggs in container of electric blender; blend until light and foamy. Add chocolate and orange juice; blend well. Fold in whipped cream. Pour into small individual serving dishes; chill until set. Garnish each with additional whipped cream and mandarin orange slices. Yield: 4 to 5 servings.

Nancy Mettrick,
Miami, Florida.

CHOCOLATE-PEANUT CLUSTERS

2 tablespoons peanut butter
1 (6-ounce) package butterscotch morsels
1 (6-ounce) package semisweet chocolate morsels
2 cups salted Spanish peanuts

Combine peanut butter, butterscotch morsels, and chocolate morsels in a heavy saucepan; place over low heat and cook, stirring constantly, until melted. Stir in peanuts. Drop by rounded teaspoonfuls onto waxed paper; chill until firm. Store in a covered container in refrigerator. Yield: about 4 dozen.

Mrs. Gary Witschy,
Marietta, Georgia.

Slice Into Tostada Pizza

If you like both pizza and Mexican food, you'll love Tostada Pizza. It starts with an easy biscuit mix crust, then adds toppings of refried beans, ground beef, chiles, lettuce, tomatoes, onion, and cheese.

TOSTADA PIZZA

2 tablespoons yellow cornmeal
2 cups biscuit mix
½ cup cold water
1 pound ground beef
¾ cup water
3 tablespoons chopped, seeded canned green chiles
1 (1.25-ounce) package taco seasoning mix
1 (16-ounce) can refried beans
2 cups (8 ounces) shredded sharp process American cheese, divided
3 cups shredded iceberg lettuce
1 large tomato, chopped
½ cup chopped onion
Taco sauce

Sprinkle a well-greased 12-inch pizza pan with cornmeal.

Combine biscuit mix and ½ cup water in a medium bowl; stir vigorously with a fork until a soft dough is formed. Turn out on a floured surface; knead lightly about 5 times. Roll dough into a 14-inch circle. Fit dough into pizza pan; crimp edges. Bake at 425° for 10 to 12 minutes or until browned.

Cook ground beef in a medium skillet until browned; drain. Add ¾ cup water, chiles, and taco mix, stirring well. Bring to a boil; reduce heat and simmer, uncovered, 10 minutes or until thickened.

Spread beans evenly over pizza crust, leaving a ½-inch border around edges. Spoon meat mixture over beans. Bake at 425° for 8 to 10 minutes. Sprinkle top with 1 cup cheese; bake an additional 2 minutes or until cheese melts. Top with lettuce, tomato, onion, and remaining cheese. Cut into wedges; serve with taco sauce. Yield: one 12-inch pizza.

Betty Wise,
Duncanville, Texas.

A Tender Approach To Round Steak

Tenderizing techniques can turn less expensive round steak into a delicacy suitable for company.

For Cheese-Stuffed Steaks and Swiss Steak Surprise, the meat is pounded with a meat mallet before cooking to break down some of the tough meat fibers. Slicing the meat diagonally across the grain, a technique used for Barbecued Beef and Pepper Steak and Rice, also makes for more tender steak.

Other recipes rely on the moist-heat method of cooking in a covered skillet to tenderize the steak. Whichever method you choose, you'll find that round steak can rival many of the more expensive cuts of beef.

CHEESE-STUFFED STEAKS

1 (32-ounce) jar spaghetti sauce
1 teaspoon dried whole basil
⅛ teaspoon garlic powder
2 (1-pound) top round steaks, ½ inch thick
½ teaspoon pepper
1 cup (4 ounces) shredded mozzarella cheese
2 eggs
1 tablespoon milk
½ cup herb-seasoned stuffing mix
¾ cup grated Parmesan cheese, divided
⅓ cup all-purpose flour
2 tablespoons vegetable oil
Hot cooked noodles

Combine spaghetti sauce, basil, and garlic powder in a saucepan; bring to a boil over medium heat. Reduce heat, and simmer 15 to 20 minutes. Set aside.

Trim excess fat from steaks. Sprinkle steaks with pepper; pound to ⅛-inch thickness. Cut each steak into 4 pieces. Place about ¼ cup mozzarella in center of 4 steak pieces. Top with remaining steak pieces; secure with wooden picks.

Combine eggs and milk; beat well. Combine stuffing mix and ½ cup Parmesan cheese.

Dredge steaks in flour, and dip in egg mixture; dredge in stuffing mixture. Brown steaks in hot oil. Remove to lightly greased shallow 2-quart casserole; top with sauce, and sprinkle with remaining ¼ cup Parmesan cheese. Cover and bake at 350° for 1 hour. To serve, cut each steak in half; serve over noodles. Yield: 8 servings.

Susan Settlemyre,
Raleigh, North Carolina.

PEPPER STEAK AND RICE

1 pound boneless round steak
2 tablespoons butter or margarine
1 medium-size green pepper, cut into strips
1 large onion, cut into rings
½ cup chopped celery
1 (4-ounce) can sliced mushrooms, undrained
¼ cup soy sauce
Pepper to taste
3 tablespoons water
1 teaspoon cornstarch
1 tablespoon water
Hot cooked rice

Trim excess fat from steak. Partially freeze steak, and slice across the grain into 2- x ¼-inch strips.

Melt butter in a large skillet. Sauté green pepper, onion, and celery in butter. Remove vegetables, reserving drippings in skillet.

Brown steak in reserved drippings. Add sautéed vegetables, mushrooms, soy sauce, pepper, and 3 tablespoons water; cover and simmer 30 minutes or until meat is tender. Remove meat and vegetables and reserve the drippings in skillet.

Combine cornstarch and 1 tablespoon water, stirring until cornstarch is dissolved. Add cornstarch mixture to liquid in skillet; cook, stirring constantly, until smooth and thickened. Return meat and vegetables to skillet. Serve over rice. Yield: 4 servings.

Jean S. Williams,
Jefferson, Georgia.

FRENCH QUARTER STEAK

1 pound boneless round steak
¼ cup all-purpose flour
1 teaspoon salt
2 teaspoons paprika
½ teaspoon pepper
¾ cup chopped onion
⅓ cup chopped green pepper
2 tablespoons vegetable oil
½ cup uncooked regular rice
1 (28-ounce) can tomatoes, undrained
1 cup water

Trim excess fat from steak; cut steak into serving-size pieces.

Combine flour, salt, paprika, and pepper. Dredge steak in flour mixture; reserve excess flour mixture.

Sauté onion and green pepper in hot oil in large skillet; remove vegetables, and set aside. Brown steak on both sides in remaining oil. Add sautéed vegetables, rice, tomatoes, and water; sprinkle with reserved flour mixture. Cover and simmer 1 hour, stirring occasionally. Yield: 4 to 6 servings.

Mrs. Parke LaGourgue Cory,
Neosho, Missouri.

SWISS STEAK SURPRISE

2 pounds boneless round steak
¼ cup all-purpose flour
¼ teaspoon salt
¼ teaspoon celery salt
¼ teaspoon pepper
3 tablespoons vegetable oil
1 medium onion, minced
1 (4-ounce) can mushroom pieces, undrained
⅔ cup water
½ cup commercial sour cream

Trim excess fat from steak. Pound steak to ¼-inch thickness; cut into serving-size pieces.

Combine flour, salt, celery salt, and pepper. Dredge steak in flour mixture; reserve excess flour mixture. Brown steak in hot oil in large skillet. Add onion and mushrooms; sprinkle with reserved flour mixture; add water, and bring to a boil. Reduce heat and simmer, covered, about 50 to 60 minutes, stirring occasionally. Stir in sour cream. Yield: 6 to 8 servings.

Mrs. William S. Bell,
Chattanooga, Tennessee.

Tip: To peel small white onions easily, pour boiling water over onions in a bowl and let stand 1 minute; drain and cover with cold water. Peel when cool.

Tenderize round steak by pounding it with a meat mallet prior to cooking.

SKILLET STEAK 'N POTATOES

1½ pounds boneless round steak, ½ inch thick
¼ cup all-purpose flour
2 teaspoons salt
¼ teaspoon pepper
2 tablespoons vegetable oil
1 (10½-ounce) can beef broth, undiluted
1 cup water
4 medium potatoes, thinly sliced
2 medium onions, thinly sliced
Chopped fresh parsley (optional)

Trim excess fat from steak; cut into serving-size pieces.

Combine flour, salt, and pepper. Dredge steak in flour mixture. Brown steak in hot oil. Add broth and water; cover and simmer 30 minutes. Turn meat, and top with potatoes and onion. Cover and simmer 20 minutes or until potatoes are done. Sprinkle with parsley, if desired. Yield: 6 servings.
Mrs. F. W. Armstrong,
Dallas, Texas.

BARBECUED BEEF

2 pounds boneless top round steak
2 tablespoons vegetable oil
2 medium onions, chopped
1 medium-size green pepper, chopped
2 tablespoons vinegar
2 tablespoons dry mustard
1½ teaspoons salt
1⅓ cups catsup
⅓ cup water
Hot cooked rice or hamburger buns

Trim excess fat from steak. Partially freeze steak, and slice across the grain into 2- x ¼-inch strips.

Brown steak in hot oil. Add onion and green pepper; cook until tender. Add next 5 ingredients; cover and simmer 1 hour or until meat is tender, stirring occasionally. Serve barbecued beef over hot rice or hamburger buns. Yield: 6 to 8 servings.
Ann B. Martin,
Greenwood, South Carolina.

SAVORY STUFFED ROUND STEAK

2 pounds boneless round steak, ½ inch thick
2 tablespoons butter or margarine
½ cup chopped celery
¼ cup chopped onion
2 cups (½-inch) bread cubes
½ teaspoon salt
½ teaspoon rubbed sage
⅛ teaspoon pepper
1 tablespoon water
All-purpose flour
3 tablespoons vegetable oil
1 (10¾-ounce) can cream of mushroom soup, undiluted
2 teaspoons Worcestershire sauce
1 clove garlic, minced
½ cup water
Hot cooked rice (optional)

Trim excess fat from steak; pound steak to ¼-inch thickness. Cut steak into 4 equal pieces.

Melt butter in a large skillet; sauté celery and onion in butter until tender. Remove from heat. Stir in bread cubes, salt, sage, pepper, and 1 tablespoon water. Place one-fourth of mixture on each piece of steak, spreading to within ½ inch of edge. Roll up each piece, jellyroll fashion; secure with wooden picks, and cut in half crosswise. Dredge each steak roll in flour, and brown in hot oil in large skillet.

Combine soup, Worcestershire sauce, garlic, and ½ cup water; stir well, and pour over steak rolls. Cover and simmer 1 hour, stirring occasionally. Serve with rice, if desired. Yield: 8 servings.
Mrs. John R. Taylor, Jr.,
Jonesboro, Tennessee.

Tip: When freezing meat patties, steaks, or chops, separate with two thicknesses of wrapping material between them so that the pieces can be separated without thawing more than needed.

Microwave Cookery

Tips For Microwave Shortcuts

Visitors to our *Southern Living* test kitchens almost always comment on the presence of a microwave oven in each kitchen. In addition to using these to develop our microwave recipes, our home economists have found microwave ovens valuable for shortcuts in conventional recipe preparation. Here are some of their time-saving tips.

Softening

—Soften hard ice cream by microwaving at MEDIUM LOW. One pint will take 15 to 30 seconds; one quart, 30 to 45 seconds; and one-half gallon, 45 seconds to 1 minute.

—One stick of butter or margarine (½ cup) will soften in 1 minute when microwaved at LOW.

—Soften one 8-ounce package of cream cheese by microwaving at MEDIUM LOW for 2 to 2½ minutes. One 3-ounce package of cream cheese will soften in 1½ to 2 minutes.

Reheating

—Refrigerate coffee in a glass container. Reheat one cup by microwaving at HIGH for 2 to 2½ minutes.

—Store leftover pancakes or waffles in the refrigerator. To reheat, place 4 on a glass pizza plate or microwave-safe platter; microwave at MEDIUM HIGH for 1½ to 1¾ minutes.

—Reheat a slice of two-crust pie, and top with ice cream for a special treat. A slice that has been refrigerated will heat in 30 to 45 seconds at HIGH. Slices stored at room temperature will heat in 20 to 30 seconds each.

—Reheat one serving of soup in the serving bowl. Microwave a 1½-cup serving at HIGH for 2 to 2½ minutes.

Melting

—One stick of butter (½ cup) will melt in 1 minute at HIGH.

—Unwrap caramels from a 14-ounce package, and place in a deep 1-quart bowl. Microwave at HIGH about 2½ minutes, stirring 3 times.

—Place a 1-ounce square of unsweetened chocolate in a custard cup; microwave at HIGH for 1½ to 2 minutes.

—Place 6 ounces of semisweet chocolate morsels in a small bowl; microwave at HIGH for 1½ minutes, stirring once.

A 14-ounce package of caramels will melt at HIGH in about 2½ minutes.

Warm liqueurs at HIGH for about 15 seconds before igniting.

Combine the next 8 ingredients in a medium saucepan, mixing well. Simmer sauce 10 minutes.

Arrange half of eggplant slices in a lightly greased 13- x 9- x 2-inch baking dish. Top with half of mozzarella cheese. Spoon half of tomato mixture over cheese. Repeat layers. Top with Parmesan cheese. Bake at 350° for 30 to 40 minutes or until sauce is bubbly. Yield: 6 to 8 servings.

Lynn Katzenmeyer,
Bowie, Maryland.

Thawing

—Remove frozen orange juice concentrate from container, and place in a microwave-safe serving pitcher. Microwave at HIGH for 30 to 45 seconds; add water.

—Microwave a 4½-ounce carton of frozen whipped topping at MEDIUM LOW for 1 minute.

—Microwave 1 pound of frozen bacon at MEDIUM LOW for 4 to 6 minutes.

—Thaw a 1-pound package of frozen frankfurters in microwave oven at MEDIUM LOW for 5 to 6 minutes, turning package over once.

—Microwave a whole turkey (up to 10 pounds) at MEDIUM LOW for 10 minutes per pound.

Warming

—Most baby foods can be warmed in the original glass container. (Most meats should not be microwaved. Carefully check labels before microwaving any baby foods.) To warm, remove metal lid and microwave at HIGH for 25 to 30 seconds.

—Warm liqueurs for flaming at HIGH; allow about 15 seconds for 2 tablespoons to ¼ cup.

—Ice cream sauces can be warmed in the original container. Remove lid, and microwave at HIGH about 45 seconds for an 11-ounce jar.

—Warm a 12-ounce container of maple syrup (with cap removed) at HIGH about 25 seconds.

Serve Eggplant, Italian Style

If you like Italian food, you'll want to try this recipe for Eggplant Parmigiana. Dried oregano, basil, and thyme are used to flavor a savory tomato sauce that is layered with fried eggplant and mozzarella cheese.

EGGPLANT PARMIGIANA

1 egg, slightly beaten
1 cup milk
1 tablespoon vegetable oil
1 cup all-purpose flour
2 medium eggplant, peeled and cut into ½-inch slices
Hot vegetable oil
1 (29-ounce) can tomato sauce
1 (12-ounce) can tomato paste
1 (16-ounce) can tomatoes, drained
¼ cup Burgundy
1 teaspoon dried whole oregano
½ teaspoon dried whole basil
¼ teaspoon dried whole thyme
¼ teaspoon garlic salt
10 ounces sliced mozzarella cheese
½ cup grated Parmesan cheese

Combine egg, milk, and 1 tablespoon vegetable oil; gradually add to flour, beating until smooth. Dip eggplant in flour mixture; fry in hot oil until golden brown. Drain well on paper towels, and set aside.

Potatoes Fill This Soup

This time of year, a steaming bowl of homemade soup is always welcome. In just the time it takes to simmer potatoes, you can have a satisfying meal-in-a-bowl. Whipping cream and milk make this soup so rich and thick that the chunks of potato, celery, and onion actually float.

CREAMY POTATO SOUP

4 cups peeled, cubed potatoes
1 cup (¾-inch slices) celery
1 cup coarsely chopped onion
2 cups water
2 teaspoons salt
1 cup milk
1 cup whipping cream
3 tablespoons butter or margarine, melted
1 tablespoon dried parsley flakes
½ teaspoon caraway seeds
⅛ teaspoon pepper

Combine potatoes, celery, onion, water, and salt in a large Dutch oven. Simmer, covered, about 20 minutes or until potatoes are tender.

Mash mixture once or twice with a potato masher, leaving some vegetable pieces whole. Stir in remaining ingredients; return to heat and cook, stirring constantly, until soup is thoroughly heated. Yield: about 7 cups.

Margie G. McGee,
Richmond, Virginia.

Tip: Keep celery fresh and crisp by wrapping in paper towels; place in plastic bag in refrigerator. The towels absorb excess moisture.

Send Valentines From Your Kitchen

Instead of making Valentines from red construction paper and white lace doilies, send your special greetings with Valentine cookies you bake yourself.

Valentine Butter Cookies are basic sugar cookies that are rolled, cut into heart shapes, and sprinkled with red decorator sugar before baking. Cinnamon and nutmeg flavor Sugar 'n Spice Cookies, which can be decorated with Royal Icing after baking. Our recipe for the icing is suitable for decorating cookies and can be used on any rolled and cut sugar cookie. If you prefer, cans of commercial red decorative icing may be substituted.

For a delicate, buttery sugar cookie, try Easy Roll-Out Shortbread, cut with cookie cutters, or Melt-Away Butter Cookies, pressed into hearts with a cookie gun or cookie press. Light and luscious as their name implies, they simply melt in your mouth.

Send Valentine greetings with special homemade cookies.

CHERRY-ALMOND DROPS

2¼ cups all-purpose flour
¾ teaspoon salt
½ teaspoon soda
1 cup butter or margarine, softened
1 cup firmly packed brown sugar
1 teaspoon almond extract
½ teaspoon vanilla extract
2 eggs
2 cups blanched almonds, chopped
½ cup maraschino cherries, chopped

Combine flour, salt, and soda; set aside. Combine butter and sugar in a large mixing bowl; cream until light and fluffy. Stir in flavorings. Add eggs, one at a time, beating well after each addition. Add dry ingredients, mixing well. Stir in almonds and cherries.

Drop batter by heaping teaspoonfuls onto lightly greased cookie sheets. Bake at 350° for 10 to 12 minutes or until lightly browned. Cool on wire racks. Yield: about 7½ dozen.

Stephanie E. Creim,
Bellevue, Washington.

MELT-AWAY BUTTER COOKIES

1¼ cups butter, softened
¾ cup powdered sugar
2½ cups all-purpose flour
½ teaspoon vanilla extract
½ teaspoon lemon extract

Cream butter; gradually add sugar, beating until light and fluffy. Add flour, and mix well. Stir in flavorings.

Use a cookie gun or cookie press to shape dough into hearts, following manufacturer's instructions. Place cookies on ungreased cookie sheets, and bake at 325° for 15 minutes. Store in airtight containers, placing waxed paper between layers of cookies. Yield: about 7 dozen.

Florence L. Costello,
Chattanooga, Tennessee.

Tip: Measure the dry ingredients before liquids when cooking; you won't have to wash measuring spoons or cups in between measuring.

VALENTINE BUTTER COOKIES

½ cup butter, softened
½ cup shortening
1 cup sugar
3 eggs
3½ cups all-purpose flour
2 teaspoons cream of tartar
1 teaspoon soda
1½ teaspoons vanilla extract
Red decorator sugar crystals

Cream butter and shortening; gradually add sugar, beating until light and fluffy. Add eggs, one at a time, beating well after each addition.

Combine flour, cream of tartar, and soda; add to creamed mixture, beating well. Stir in vanilla. Chill dough 2 hours.

Work with half of dough at a time; store remainder in refrigerator. Roll dough out on a lightly floured board to ¼-inch thickness; cut out with heart-shaped cookie cutter. Place on ungreased cookie sheets. Sprinkle cookies with decorator sugar crystals. Bake at 425° for 6 to 8 minutes or until lightly browned.

Store in airtight containers, placing waxed paper between layers of cookies. Yield: about 5½ dozen.

Nina L. Andrews, Tappahannock, Virginia.

SUGAR 'N SPICE COOKIES

⅔ cup shortening
¾ cup sugar
1 egg
1 tablespoon plus 1 teaspoon milk
2 cups all-purpose flour
1½ teaspoons baking powder
2 teaspoons ground cinnamon
¾ teaspoon ground nutmeg
¼ teaspoon salt
1 teaspoon vanilla extract

Cream shortening; gradually add sugar, beating until light and fluffy. Add egg and milk; beat well.

Combine flour, baking powder, cinnamon, nutmeg, and salt; add to creamed mixture, beating well. Stir in vanilla. Chill dough for 1 hour.

Roll dough out on a lightly floured board to ¼-inch thickness; cut out with heart-shaped cookie cutter. Place on lightly greased cookie sheets. Bake at 375° for 6 to 8 minutes or until lightly browned. Store in airtight containers, placing waxed paper between layers. Yield: about 5 dozen.

Note: Cookies may be frosted with Royal Icing, if desired.

Carol Anne Smith, Aiken, South Carolina.

RED-SUGAR COOKIES

½ cup butter or margarine, softened
½ cup sugar
½ cup powdered sugar
1 egg
½ cup vegetable oil
2¼ cups all-purpose flour
½ teaspoon cream of tartar
½ teaspoon soda
½ teaspoon vanilla extract
Red decorator sugar crystals

Cream butter; gradually add sugar, beating until light and fluffy. Add egg, beating well. Beat in oil.

Combine flour, cream of tartar, and soda; add to creamed mixture, beating well. Stir in vanilla. Chill dough 2 hours.

Shape dough into 1-inch balls; dip into decorator sugar crystals. Place 2 inches apart on ungreased cookie sheets, and flatten with a fork. Bake at 350° for 8 to 10 minutes. Store in airtight containers; place waxed paper between layers of cookies. Yield: about 5½ dozen.

Note: Substitute ½ cup sugar plus ¾ teaspoon ground cinnamon for sugar crystals, if desired.

Kathryn Ryan, Noblesville, Indiana.

EASY ROLL-OUT SHORTBREAD

1 cup butter, softened
¾ cup firmly packed brown sugar
3 cups all-purpose flour
Pinch of salt

Cream butter; gradually add sugar, beating until light and fluffy.

Combine flour and salt; add to creamed mixture, beating well.

Roll dough out on a lightly floured board to ¼-inch thickness; cut out with 3-inch cookie cutter. Place on ungreased cookie sheets. Bake at 300° for 30 to 35 minutes or until lightly browned. Store in airtight containers with waxed paper between layers of cookies. Yield: about 2 dozen.

Rosemary Clapham, Austin, Texas.

ROYAL ICING

3 large egg whites
½ teaspoon cream of tartar
1 (16-ounce) package powdered sugar, sifted
Red paste food coloring

Combine egg whites and cream of tartar in a large mixing bowl. Beat at medium speed of electric mixer until frothy. Add half of powdered sugar, mixing well. Add remaining sugar, and beat 5 to 7 minutes at high speed or until mixture is stiff and holds a peak.

Color desired amount of icing with red paste food coloring, leaving remaining icing white. Prepare decorating bags with metal tips. Decorate cookies as desired with red and white icing. Yield: about 2 cups icing.

Note: Icing dries very quickly; keep covered at all times with a damp cloth.

Depend On Salmon For Flavor

Few foods can equal the convenience and versatility of canned salmon. It can be served straight from the can or combined with other foods in a variety of appealing salads, entrées, or appetizers. As an added bonus, canned salmon is relatively low in calories and an excellent source of protein.

When the occasion calls for an appetizer or snack, dip into a mixture of salmon and cream cheese, rolled up log-style and coated in pecans. For an easy main dish, select Salmon Casserole or Baked Salmon Croquettes; both are delicious ways to serve this special fish.

SALMON DILL MOUSSE

1 (15½-ounce) can red salmon
2 envelopes unflavored gelatin
¼ cup lemon juice
½ cup peeled, seeded, and chopped cucumber
½ cup chopped onion
½ cup chopped celery
½ teaspoon dried whole dillweed
½ teaspoon salt
1 cup mayonnaise
1 cup whipping cream
Lettuce leaves
Cucumber slices (optional)
Lemon slices (optional)

Drain salmon, reserving liquid; add enough water to salmon liquid to measure 1 cup. Combine salmon liquid and gelatin in a small saucepan; cook over medium heat until gelatin is dissolved, stirring constantly. Remove from heat, and set aside.

Remove skin and bones from salmon; flake salmon with a fork.

Place half of liquid, half of salmon, and half of next 8 ingredients in container of electric blender; process until smooth. Pour mixture into a lightly oiled 6½-cup mold. Repeat blending procedure with remaining half of ingredients; add to mold. Chill until firm. Unmold on lettuce leaves. Garnish with cucumber and lemon, if desired. Serve with assorted crackers. Yield: one (6-cup) mousse.

Note: Recipe may be prepared in a food processor. Position knife blade in processor bowl; add ingredients. Process until smooth, and proceed as directed.

Sandra Russell, Maitland, Florida.

BAKED SALMON CROQUETTES

1 (15½-ounce) can pink salmon
Milk
¼ cup butter or margarine
2 tablespoons finely chopped onion
⅓ cup all-purpose flour
½ teaspoon salt
¼ teaspoon pepper
1 tablespoon lemon juice
1 cup crushed corn flakes, divided

Drain salmon, reserving liquid; add enough milk to salmon liquid to measure 1 cup; set aside.

Melt butter in a heavy saucepan over low heat; add onion and cook until tender. Add flour, stirring until smooth. Cook 1 minute, stirring constantly. Gradually add milk mixture; cook over medium heat, stirring constantly, until thickened and bubbly. Stir in salt and pepper; set aside.

Remove skin and bones from salmon; flake salmon with a fork. Add lemon juice, ½ cup corn flakes, and white sauce, stirring well. Refrigerate mixture until chilled; shape into croquettes. Roll in remaining corn flakes. Place on a lightly greased baking sheet; bake at 400° for 30 minutes. Yield: 8 servings.
Gayle Wallace,
Memphis, Tennessee.

SALMON LOG

1 (15½-ounce) can red salmon
1 (8-ounce) package cream cheese, softened
1 tablespoon lemon juice
2 teaspoons grated onion
¼ teaspoon salt
¼ teaspoon liquid smoke
¾ cup chopped pecans
3 tablespoons minced fresh parsley

Drain salmon, and remove skin and bones. Flake salmon with a fork; add cream cheese, lemon juice, onion, salt, and liquid smoke; stir well. Chill mixture several hours or overnight.

Shape salmon mixture into a log. Combine pecans and parsley; stir well. Roll salmon log in pecan mixture, and chill several hours. Yield: one 10-inch log.
Mrs. Herman Moore,
Dunwoody, Georgia.

Tip: Stains or discolorations inside aluminum utensils can be removed by boiling a solution of 2 to 3 tablespoons cream of tartar, lemon juice, or vinegar to each quart of water in the utensil for 5 to 10 minutes.

SALMON CASSEROLE

½ cup diced carrots
¼ cup coarsely chopped onion
1 (15½-ounce) can pink salmon
1 cup cooked elbow macaroni
1 (10½-ounce) can cream of celery soup, undiluted
½ teaspoon salt
¼ teaspoon pepper
2 tablespoons butter or margarine, melted
½ cup fine dry breadcrumbs
1 cup (4 ounces) shredded medium Cheddar cheese

Cook carrots and onion in boiling salted water until tender; drain.

Drain salmon, and remove skin and bones. Flake salmon into small chunks; add carrots, onion, and macaroni, mixing well. Stir in soup, salt, and pepper. Spoon into a greased 1½-quart casserole. Combine butter and breadcrumbs; sprinkle over casserole. Bake at 375° for 20 minutes. Top with cheese the last 5 minutes of baking. Yield: 4 to 6 servings. *Mrs. Earl L. Faulkenberry, Lancaster, South Carolina.*

She Makes The Most Of Her Food Processor

Since she started using a food processor, Susan Abrams of Rockville, Maryland, has found it very convenient to rely on only one small appliance.

"I rarely use any other appliance now," she said. "I use the processor for all my slicing, chopping, and shredding, and I even mix cakes in the processor using the plastic blade."

Susan also takes advantage of the processor to make baby food. "I steam vegetables for a few minutes and then run them through the processor using the chopping blade," she explained. "Most fruits don't need to be steamed. Even sturdier fruits like apples can be processed raw. They take about 30 or 40 seconds in the processor."

She then freezes individual servings of baby food in plastic bags. When ready to serve, she places them in boiling water until they are warm.

One of Susan's favorite vegetable dishes is ratatouille. She uses the slicing, knife, and shredding blades for this quick food processor version.

RATATOUILLE NICOISE

¾ bunch fresh parsley
2 cloves garlic, peeled
1 large onion
3 zucchini
1 medium eggplant
2 medium-size green peppers, seeded and quartered
2 ounces Parmesan cheese
⅓ cup olive oil
3 tablespoons all-purpose flour
5 medium tomatoes, peeled and sliced
1 tablespoon capers
Salt and pepper

Wash parsley, and dry thoroughly (wet parsley will not process well). Cut leaves from stems. Position knife blade in processor bowl; then add parsley leaves. Process until the parsley is evenly chopped, pulsing 4 to 5 times. Remove parsley, and set aside.

Position knife blade in processor bowl. Drop garlic cloves through food chute with processor running; process 3 to 5 seconds or until garlic is minced. Remove garlic, and set aside.

Cut onion into quarters. Position slicer blade in processor bowl. Add onion; slice, applying firm pressure with food pusher. Set aside.

Position zucchini in food chute; slice, applying firm pressure with food pusher. Set aside. Pare eggplant, and cut into wedges. Position eggplant in food chute; slice, applying moderate pressure with food pusher. Set aside.

Position green pepper in the food chute; slice, applying moderate pressure with food pusher. Set aside.

Position shredding blade in processor bowl. Cut Parmesan cheese (at room temperature) to fit food chute; shred, applying firm pressure with food pusher. Set aside.

Heat oil in a large skillet. Add garlic and onion; sauté until onion is transparent. Dredge zucchini and eggplant in flour; add to onion mixture. Stir in green pepper. Cover and cook vegetable mixture over low heat for 15 minutes, stirring occasionally.

Add tomatoes and capers; simmer, uncovered, for 10 minutes or until mixture is thick. Season to taste with salt and pepper. Sprinkle with parsley and Parmesan cheese just before serving. Yield: 8 to 10 servings. *Susan Abrams, Rockville, Maryland.*

Time-Saving Salad Suggestions

If you've wished for a salad that could be prepared ahead of time, the selections below could be just what you've been looking for. Congealed, marinated, or simply chilled, each one of these salads combines crispy ingredients for the freshest of flavors.

GARDEN MARINADE

1 (6-ounce) jar marinated artichoke hearts, drained
2 carrots, thinly sliced diagonally
1 green pepper, cut into strips
1 cup sliced cauliflower flowerets
1½ cups sliced fresh mushrooms
2 cups chopped celery
1 (8-ounce) can water chestnuts, drained and sliced
3 green onions, chopped
¼ cup vegetable oil
½ cup sugar
½ cup vinegar
1 tablespoon water
⅛ teaspoon salt

Combine first 8 ingredients in a large shallow dish; set aside.

Combine remaining ingredients, mixing well. Pour marinade over vegetables, and toss lightly. Cover and chill 8 to 10 hours or overnight. Drain before serving. Yield: 8 servings.

Nancy H. Aden,
Midlothian, Virginia.

CREAMY BROCCOLI AND CAULIFLOWER SALAD

1 cup mayonnaise
1 (8-ounce) carton commercial sour cream
½ teaspoon dried parsley flakes
½ teaspoon dried dillweed
½ teaspoon onion salt
½ teaspoon Beau Monde seasoning
1 bunch broccoli
1 head cauliflower
2 hard-cooked eggs, coarsely chopped
10 ripe olives
2 pimientos, chopped
1 small onion, chopped

Combine first 6 ingredients; mix well, and set aside.

Trim off large leaves of broccoli. Remove tough ends of lower stalks, and wash broccoli thoroughly. Remove flowerets, and cut stems into 1-inch pieces; set all aside.

Remove outer leaves of cauliflower. Break cauliflower into flowerets, and wash thoroughly.

Combine broccoli (flowerets and stem pieces), cauliflower, eggs, olives, pimiento, and onion in a large bowl. Spoon dressing mixture over top; toss gently to coat. Refrigerate 8 to 10 hours or overnight. Yield: 8 to 10 servings.

Betty Wise,
Duncanville, Texas.

CAULIFLOWER-LEMON SALAD

1 cup diced cauliflower
1 (3-ounce) package lemon-flavored gelatin
2 cups boiling water
1 tablespoon cider vinegar
½ teaspoon salt
1 teaspoon chopped red sweet pepper or pimiento
1 teaspoon chopped green pepper
¼ cup diced celery
Lettuce leaves (optional)
Mayonnaise (optional)

Cook cauliflower, covered, in a small amount of boiling salted water 1 to 2 minutes; drain and cool.

Dissolve gelatin in boiling water; stir in vinegar and salt. Chill until consistency of unbeaten egg white. Stir in cauliflower, red and green pepper, and celery. Pour into lightly oiled individual molds; chill until set. Unmold each salad on lettuce leaves and garnish with mayonnaise, if desired. Yield: 4 to 6 servings.

Mrs. Gene Coleman,
Whispering Pines, North Carolina.

SHOEPEG CORN SALAD

1 (12-ounce) can vacuum-packed shoepeg whole kernel corn, drained
¼ cup chopped green pepper
2 tablespoons diced pimiento
½ cup chopped celery
1 cup peeled and thinly sliced cucumber
½ cup thinly sliced red onion
⅓ cup vegetable oil
3 tablespoons sugar
1½ teaspoons salt
3 tablespoons red wine vinegar

Combine first 6 ingredients; set aside.

Combine remaining ingredients; stir well, and pour over vegetables. Toss gently; cover and chill 8 to 10 hours. Drain. Yield: 4 to 6 servings.

Mrs. Charles R. Simms,
Palestine, Illinois.

LAYERED CREAMY POTATO SALAD

8 medium potatoes
1 cup minced fresh parsley
1 large onion, minced
1 cup mayonnaise, divided
1 (8-ounce) carton commercial sour cream
1½ teaspoons celery seeds
1 teaspoon salt
2 teaspoons prepared horseradish

Cook potatoes in boiling salted water about 30 minutes or until tender; drain and cool slightly. Peel and thinly slice potatoes; set aside. Combine parsley and onion; mix well, and set aside.

Combine mayonnaise, sour cream, celery seeds, salt, and horseradish; stir well.

Place one-third of the potatoes in a 13- x 9- x 2-inch baking dish; top with one-third of mayonnaise mixture then one-third of onion-parsley mixture. Repeat layers twice. Chill 8 hours. Yield: 8 to 10 servings.

Joan B. Piercy,
Memphis, Tennessee.

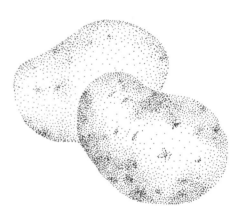

ZESTY RICE SALAD

2 cups cooked rice, chilled
¼ cup plus 1 tablespoon finely chopped onion
¼ cup plus 1 tablespoon finely chopped sweet pickle
½ teaspoon salt
Dash of pepper
½ cup mayonnaise
½ teaspoon prepared mustard
2 teaspoons diced pimiento
2 hard-cooked eggs, chopped
Lettuce leaves (optional)

Combine all ingredients except lettuce leaves. Mix salad well, and refrigerate until thoroughly chilled. Serve on lettuce leaves, if desired. Yield: 4 to 6 servings.

Ruby Bonelli,
Pearland, Texas.

Put The Spotlight On Vegetables

At this time of year, fresh vegetables taste especially good. Prepared with imagination and flair, wintertime vegetables—acorn squash, turban squash, broccoli, and eggplant—can be the main attraction on any menu.

These selections include an eggplant casserole layered with a well-seasoned mushroom-tomato sauce, a fruit-stuffed acorn squash, and a puffy broccoli soufflé.

BAKED ACORN SQUASH

3 medium acorn squash
Salt
2 tablespoons butter or margarine
1 (8¼-ounce) can crushed pineapple, drained
1¼ cups peeled, chopped cooking apple
2 tablespoons brown sugar
1 tablespoon butter or margarine

Cut squash in half, and remove seeds. Place cut side down in a shallow baking dish. Add ½ inch boiling water. Bake at 350° for 40 minutes. Turn cut side up, and sprinkle with salt; set aside.

Melt 2 tablespoons butter; add pineapple, apple, and sugar, mixing well. Spoon mixture into squash shells. Dot each with ½ teaspoon butter. Return to oven, and bake 30 minutes. Yield: 6 servings.
Patricia Chapman,
Huntsville, Alabama.

LEBANESE EGGPLANT

1 medium eggplant, peeled and diced
½ cup chopped onion
1 clove garlic, pressed
½ cup sliced fresh mushrooms
¼ cup olive oil
1 tablespoon all-purpose flour
1 (16-ounce) can tomatoes, undrained
½ teaspoon salt
½ teaspoon brown sugar
¼ teaspoon dried whole basil
⅛ teaspoon pepper
2 tablespoons grated Parmesan cheese
¼ cup slivered almonds, toasted (optional)

Cook eggplant in boiling salted water 8 to 10 minutes or just until eggplant is tender; drain well.

Sauté onion, garlic, and mushrooms in olive oil until tender. Add flour, stirring until smooth. Add tomatoes, salt, sugar, basil, and pepper; bring to a boil. Remove from heat.

Layer half of eggplant and half of tomato mixture in a lightly greased 1-quart casserole; repeat layers. Top with Parmesan cheese and sprinkle with almonds, if desired. Bake at 375° for 25 minutes. Yield: 6 servings.
Paula Patterson,
Houston, Texas.

GLAZED TURBAN SQUASH

1 (3½-pound) turban squash
Salt
1 cup peach jam
2 tablespoons orange juice

Remove small upper portion of squash, cutting down to seeds. Remove seeds to form a cavity; discard upper portion of squash and seeds. Sprinkle cavity with salt. Place squash, cut side down, in a 9-inch square baking pan. Fill pan with 1 inch water. Bake at 375° for 1 hour or until tender. Remove squash from pan; peel, and cut into 1-inch cubes. Set aside.

Combine jam and orange juice in a saucepan; cook, stirring frequently, over medium heat until thoroughly heated.

Place squash in a 9-inch square baking dish; pour jam mixture evenly over squash. Bake at 300° for 15 minutes. Yield: 8 to 10 servings.
Mrs. Ted Zahrfeld,
Highland, Michigan.

BROCCOLI SOUFFLE

3¼ cups chopped broccoli
½ cup mayonnaise
¼ cup all-purpose flour
1½ cups milk
¾ cup grated Parmesan cheese
1 teaspoon salt
4 eggs, separated

Lightly butter a 2-quart soufflé dish. Cut a piece of aluminum foil long enough to fit around dish, allowing a 1-inch overlap. Fold foil lengthwise into thirds, and lightly butter one side. Wrap foil, buttered side touching dish, so it extends 3 inches above rim to form a collar. Secure with string.

Cook broccoli in a small amount of boiling salted water about 7 to 8 minutes or until crisp-tender; drain well.

Combine mayonnaise and flour in a heavy saucepan, stirring until smooth.

Cook over low heat 1 minute, stirring constantly. Gradually add milk; cook over medium heat, stirring constantly, until thickened and bubbly. Add cheese and salt; stir until cheese melts.

Beat egg yolks. Gradually stir about one-fourth of hot white sauce into yolks; add to remaining hot mixture, stirring constantly. Add broccoli; stir well.

Beat egg whites (at room temperature) until stiff but not dry; gently fold into broccoli mixture. Spoon into prepared soufflé dish. Bake at 300° for 1 hour and 15 minutes or until puffed and golden. Remove collar, and serve immediately. Yield: 5 to 6 servings.
Catherine Bearden,
Bostwick, Georgia.

Hot Sandwiches For Chilly Days

Lighten up lunch or liven up supper with one of these hot and saucy sandwiches. Add a serving of coleslaw, potato salad, or a choice of relishes, and enjoy an easy but nourishing meal.

Our hearty Open-Face Chili Burgers are festively topped with lettuce, olives, onion rings, and chiles. The ground beef is simmered with onion in a taco-flavored tomato sauce. And if you'd like an idea for leftover sliced chicken, try our Saucy Chick-Wiches.

OPEN-FACE CHILI BURGERS

1½ pounds ground beef
½ cup chopped onion
1 (8-ounce) can tomato sauce
1 (1¼-ounce) package taco seasoning mix
6 hamburger buns
12 slices tomato
1 cup (4 ounces) shredded Cheddar cheese
¾ cup shredded lettuce
¼ cup chopped stuffed olives
1 small onion, cut into rings and separated
1½ tablespoons chopped red and green chiles

Brown meat and onion in a large skillet; drain. Stir in tomato sauce and taco seasoning; simmer 5 minutes.

Split and toast hamburger buns; spread with meat mixture. Place tomato

slice on each sandwich, and sprinkle with cheese; bake at 400° for 4 minutes or until cheese melts. Top with lettuce, olives, onion, and chiles. Yield: 12 servings.
Dorothy Cox,
Snyder, Texas.

BARBECUED BEEF SANDWICHES

1½ pounds ground beef
¾ cup finely chopped celery
¾ cup finely chopped onion
½ cup finely chopped green pepper
1 (8-ounce) can tomato sauce
¼ cup catsup
2 tablespoons brown sugar
2 tablespoons barbecue sauce
2 tablespoons vinegar
1 tablespoon prepared mustard
1 tablespoon Worcestershire sauce
1½ teaspoons salt
¼ teaspoon pepper
8 to 10 hamburger buns

Brown meat in a large skillet; drain. Add celery, onion, and green pepper; cook 5 minutes or until onion is tender. Add next 9 ingredients; cover and simmer 1 hour. Serve on hamburger buns. Yield: 8 to 10 servings. *Sherry Smith,*
Afton, Tennessee.

SAUCY CHICK-WICHES

4 slices cooked chicken
4 slices bread, toasted and buttered
8 slices tomato
4 slices process American cheese
1 (10½-ounce) can chicken gravy

Arrange chicken on toast; top with tomato slices. Broil 4 inches from heat for 3 minutes or until hot. Top with cheese, and broil until melted. Heat gravy, and spoon over sandwiches. Yield: 4 servings. *Melody Fowler,*
Devine, Texas.

Tangy Ideas For Celery

Here are two good reasons why celery is a staple in Southern kitchens: a tangy appetizer spread to enjoy with crackers and a sweet-and-sour vegetable salad tossed with an oil-and-vinegar dressing.

SWEET-AND-SOUR VEGETABLE SALAD

1 (17-ounce) can English peas, drained
1 (17-ounce) can French-style green beans, drained
1 medium-size green pepper, coarsely chopped
1 small onion, chopped
4 stalks celery, sliced
1 (2-ounce) jar diced pimiento, drained
½ cup cider vinegar
¼ cup vegetable oil
¾ cup sugar
1½ teaspoons water
¼ teaspoon salt

Combine first 6 ingredients; toss gently. Combine remaining ingredients, mixing well. Pour dressing over vegetables; toss. Cover and refrigerate overnight. Yield: 8 to 10 servings.
Joyce Eastham,
Proctorville, Ohio.

ANTIPASTO SPREAD

2 (4-ounce) cans mushroom stems and pieces, drained and finely chopped
1 (14-ounce) can artichoke hearts, drained and finely chopped
1 (10-ounce) jar pimiento-stuffed olives, drained and finely chopped
1 (6-ounce) can ripe olives, drained and finely chopped
¼ cup chopped green pepper
½ cup chopped celery
¾ cup vinegar
¾ cup olive oil
¼ cup instant minced onion
2½ teaspoons Italian seasoning
1 teaspoon onion salt
1 teaspoon salt
1 teaspoon seasoned salt
1 teaspoon garlic salt
1 teaspoon sugar
1 teaspoon cracked black pepper

Combine first 6 ingredients, mixing well; set aside. Combine remaining ingredients in a saucepan; bring to a boil. Pour dressing over vegetables; place in a large jar with a tight-fitting lid. Shake jar to stir ingredients; refrigerate overnight. Serve spread with assorted crackers. Yield: about 7 cups.
Mrs. George Sellers,
Albany, Georgia.

Tip: Depending on condition when purchased, fresh mushrooms can be refrigerated for 7 to 10 days.

Frozen Vegetables Save Time

Although there's nothing quite like the flavor of garden-fresh vegetables, commercially frozen foods offer a good alternative when favorites are out of season. Often the prices are lower than their fresh or canned counterparts, and you'll rely on their speed and convenience in cooking.

Some recipes, such as Squash Pats, exclusively use frozen vegetables. Others like Zucchini-and-Corn Medley combine the frozen product with fresh food available year-round.

SQUASH PATS

1 (10-ounce) package frozen yellow squash
1 egg, beaten
¼ cup all-purpose flour
¼ cup cornmeal
2 teaspoons baking powder
½ teaspoon salt
1 medium onion, finely chopped
Vegetable oil

Cook squash according to package directions; drain well. Mash squash. Combine squash and egg; stir well.

Combine flour, cornmeal, baking powder, and salt; stir well. Add squash mixture and onion; stir until blended.

Drop squash mixture by heaping tablespoonfuls into hot oil. Cook until golden brown; turn and flatten to about ½-inch thickness. Cook until golden brown, and drain well on paper towels. Yield: 15 squash patties. *Jean McCoy,*
Pineville, North Carolina.

ZUCCHINI-AND-CORN MEDLEY

1 tablespoon bacon drippings
⅓ cup chopped onion
½ cup chopped green pepper
1 clove garlic, minced
1 (16-ounce) package frozen whole kernel corn, thawed
4 cups thinly sliced zucchini
1 teaspoon salt
¼ teaspoon pepper

Heat bacon drippings in a large skillet. Add remaining ingredients; cover and cook over medium heat 5 to 10 minutes or until zucchini is crisp-tender. Stir occasionally. Yield: 8 to 10 servings. *Pauline Miller,*
Elk City, Oklahoma.

OKRA-TOMATO BAKE

½ pound bacon
1 medium onion, finely chopped
1 (10-ounce) package frozen cut okra, thawed
1 small green pepper, finely chopped
2 tablespoons instant rice
1 (16-ounce) can whole tomatoes, undrained
1 tablespoon sugar
Dash of garlic salt
¼ teaspoon salt
⅛ teaspoon pepper
1 tablespoon grated Parmesan cheese
¼ cup fine dry breadcrumbs
1 tablespoon butter or margarine, melted

Cook bacon in a large skillet until crisp; drain on paper towels, reserving bacon drippings in skillet. Crumble bacon, and set aside.

Cook onion and okra in reserved bacon drippings until lightly browned. Drain on paper towels; place in a lightly greased 1½-quart casserole. Add green pepper, rice, and crumbled bacon; mix well.

Combine tomatoes, sugar, garlic salt, salt, and pepper in container of electric blender; blend on low speed 1 to 2 minutes. Pour over mixture in casserole; top with Parmesan cheese. Combine breadcrumbs and butter; mix well. Sprinkle on top of casserole. Bake at 350° about 45 minutes. Yield: 6 servings. *Mrs. H. Mark Webber, New Port Richey, Florida.*

FRENCH QUARTER GREEN BEANS

3 (9-ounce) packages frozen French-style green beans
3 tablespoons butter or margarine
1 (10¾-ounce) can cream of mushroom soup, undiluted
1 (3-ounce) package cream cheese, softened
1 teaspoon dried onion flakes
1 (8-ounce) can water chestnuts, drained and sliced
¼ teaspoon garlic salt
¼ teaspoon pepper
1½ cups (6 ounces) shredded Cheddar cheese
1 (2½-ounce) package slivered almonds
Paprika

Cook green beans according to package directions; drain. Melt butter in a Dutch oven; add soup and cream cheese. Cook over low heat, stirring constantly, until cream cheese is melted

and mixture is smooth. Remove from heat; stir in green beans, onion flakes, water chestnuts, garlic salt, pepper, and shredded Cheddar cheese.

Spoon mixture into a lightly greased 1¾-quart casserole. Top with almonds; sprinkle with paprika. Bake, uncovered, at 375° for 45 minutes. Yield: 8 servings. *Martha L. Taylor, Greenville, South Carolina.*

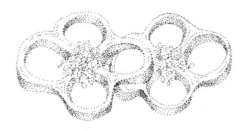

Stir-Fry A Crowd Pleaser

Even people who think they don't like Chinese food like Sweet-and-Sour Pork. None of the ingredients is mysterious or "foreign," but the stir-fry method of cooking is decidedly Oriental. Each chunk of pork and piece of pepper is bathed in a smooth, sweet sauce, which should suit even the most confirmed American in the family.

SWEET-AND-SOUR PORK

2 tablespoons peanut oil
1¼ pounds boneless pork shoulder, cut into 1-inch cubes (about 2½ cups)
1 teaspoon garlic salt
⅛ teaspoon pepper
1¾ cups water
2 medium-size green peppers, cut into 1-inch pieces
½ cup raisins
⅓ cup sugar
⅓ cup vinegar
2 tablespoons cornstarch
¼ cup soy sauce
3 cups hot cooked rice

Pour oil around top of preheated wok, coating sides; allow to heat at medium high (325°) for 2 minutes. Add pork, and stir-fry about 5 to 6 minutes. Add garlic salt, pepper, and water. Reduce heat to low (225°); cover and simmer about 25 minutes or until pork is very tender.

Add green pepper; cook, uncovered, about 4 minutes. Stir in raisins, sugar,

and vinegar. Dissolve cornstarch in soy sauce, and add to pork mixture. Cook, stirring constantly, until thickened and bubbly. Serve over hot cooked rice. Yield: 4 to 5 servings. *Lois Rodriquez, Henryetta, Oklahoma.*

Make Your Own Beef Jerky

Early explorers packed their saddlebags with sun-dried beef jerky for their meat supply on long journeys. Today's backpackers, campers, and skiers can enjoy a modern version of beef jerky. Produced by a method similar to the old-fashioned sun-drying method, this jerky is oven dried for 10 hours.

Simply cut lean meat into long, thin strips about 1 inch wide. Sliced with the grain, it will be more tender. The result is a chewy, seasoned snack you can enjoy on your next outdoor excursion.

BEEF JERKY

1 (1- to 2-pound) flank steak
½ cup soy sauce
Garlic salt to taste
Lemon pepper to taste

Cut steak with the grain in long strips no more than ¼ inch thick. Combine meat and soy sauce; toss to coat evenly. Drain and discard soy sauce.

Sprinkle both sides of strips lightly with seasonings. Place strips in a single layer on an ungreased cookie sheet. Bake at 150° for 10 hours. (Do not allow temperature to go above 150°.) Yield: ¼ to ½ pound jerky.

Note: Partially freeze meat for easier slicing. Store jerky in airtight container. *Anne Ringer, Warner Robins, Georgia.*

Right: Roast Chicken and Vegetables (page 3) offers wonderful flavor while economizing on calories and the food budget.

Page 28: Brighten winter meals with a simple presentation of fresh vegetables: Brussels Sprouts With Cashews, Cauliflower With Herb Butter, and Broccoli With Horseradish Sauce (recipes on page 2).

Hot's The Word For These Sandwiches

A sandwich can be more than cold cuts between two slices of bread. It can be a bacon cheeseburger so robust you have to eat it with a fork, a ham and Swiss cheese sandwich baked in a loaf and served with a sauce, or an open-face crabmeat sandwich broiled until golden.

OPEN-FACE CRAB TOMATO SANDWICHES

1 egg, slightly beaten
1 (3-ounce) package cream cheese, softened
1 teaspoon lemon juice
2 tablespoons chopped fresh parsley
2 tablespoons grated Parmesan cheese
3 tablespoons mayonnaise
½ cup crabmeat
6 slices bread, crusts removed
2 large tomatoes

Combine first 6 ingredients; mix well. Stir in crabmeat; set aside. Toast one side of bread; turn. Slice each tomato into 3 slices; place on untoasted side of bread.

Spread crab mixture evenly over tomato slices. Broil sandwiches about 6 inches from heat until golden brown. Yield: 6 servings. *Betty Hornsby, Columbia, South Carolina.*

CHEESY BACON BURGERS

6 slices bacon
2 pounds ground beef
1 small onion, chopped
1 cup catsup
1 (2½-ounce) jar sliced mushrooms, drained
Salt and pepper to taste
2 cups (8 ounces) shredded medium Cheddar cheese
8 hamburger buns

Fry bacon in a large skillet until crisp. Drain bacon; crumble, and set aside. Drain off all bacon drippings. Add ground beef to skillet and brown; drain. Stir in bacon, onion, catsup, mushrooms, salt, and pepper. Cover and simmer 10 to 15 minutes. Sprinkle cheese over top, and heat until cheese melts. To serve, spoon over split hamburger buns. Yield: 8 servings. *Joan T. Palmer, Fieldale, Virginia.*

BAKED HAM SANDWICHES

¼ cup butter or margarine, softened
1 tablespoon mayonnaise or salad dressing
2 tablespoons prepared mustard
2 tablespoons diced onion
1½ teaspoons poppy seeds
8 hamburger buns
8 slices cooked ham
8 slices Swiss cheese

Combine first 5 ingredients, mixing well. Spread mixture on both sides of hamburger buns. Place 1 ham slice and 1 cheese slice on bottom of each bun; cover with top of bun. Wrap each sandwich in aluminum foil. Bake at 450° for 15 minutes. Yield: 8 servings. *Pam Sigler, Lexington, Kentucky.*

HAM HIDEAWAYS

1 (16-ounce) can sauerkraut, drained
1 teaspoon lemon pepper marinade
1 teaspoon dried dillweed
1 (32-ounce) package frozen bread dough, thawed
¼ cup mayonnaise or salad dressing, divided
16 slices ham
8 slices Swiss cheese
Jezebel Sauce

Combine sauerkraut, lemon pepper, and dillweed; stir well, and set aside.

Flatten 1 loaf of bread dough on a lightly floured surface; roll into a 12- x 14-inch rectangle. Spread 2 tablespoons mayonnaise over dough. Place 8 ham slices on one side of dough; place half the sauerkraut mixture over ham. Top with 4 cheese slices; fold dough in half, making sure edges are even. Using a fork dipped in flour, press edges together to seal.

Repeat procedure using remaining loaf of bread dough, mayonnaise, ham, sauerkraut mixture, and cheese. Place sandwiches on a lightly greased jellyroll pan. Bake at 400° for 10 minutes; reduce heat to 350°, and bake about 15 minutes or until golden brown. Serve with Jezebel Sauce. Yield: 8 servings.

Jezebel Sauce:

1 cup pineapple preserves
1 cup apple jelly
1 tablespoon prepared horseradish
1 teaspoon Creole mustard

Combine all ingredients, mixing well. Yield: about 2 cups. *Emily Smith, Fayetteville, North Carolina.*

Make It Down Home With Hominy

If you'd like something different to add to your breakfast and brunch menus, turn to hominy for an economical alternative.

Hominy, sausage links, and vegetables are cooked together to serve six in Hominy-Sausage Skillet. Or for a more adventurous way to serve hominy, try Chile-Hominy Casserole. It includes lots of cheese, sour cream, and chopped green chiles.

HOMINY-SAUSAGE SKILLET

1 pound pork sausage links, cut crosswise into halves
¼ cup chopped onion
1 tablespoon all-purpose flour
½ teaspoon chili powder
1 (16-ounce) can stewed tomatoes, undrained
1 (16-ounce) can hominy, drained
1 (10-ounce) package frozen lima beans
¼ cup chopped green pepper
½ teaspoon Worcestershire sauce
½ teaspoon salt
¼ teaspoon pepper

Cook sausage in a large skillet until browned; drain off drippings. Add onion; cook until tender but not brown. Combine flour and chili powder; stir into sausage mixture. Add remaining ingredients. Cover and simmer 10 to 15 minutes or until beans are tender. Yield: 6 servings.

Mrs. William Strieber, San Antonio, Texas.

CHILE-HOMINY CASSEROLE

2 cups (8 ounces) shredded Cheddar or Longhorn cheese, divided
1 (29-ounce) can hominy, drained
1 (4-ounce) can chopped green chiles, drained
1 (8-ounce) carton commercial sour cream

Combine 1 cup cheese and remaining ingredients; stir well. Spoon into a lightly greased 2-quart casserole. Sprinkle top with remaining cheese. Bake, uncovered, at 350° for 20 to 30 minutes. Yield: 6 servings. *Sandy Preston, Biloxi, Mississippi.*

Freeze Dessert In A Muffin Cup

The flavor of coffee seems to be turning up in a number of interesting recipes. One in particular combines coffee, almonds, vanilla, and coconut to come up with a melt-in-your-mouth tortoni. As far as we're concerned, this dessert is just as tasty as it is easy to prepare. Since it is made ahead and frozen in paper-lined muffin cups, it's ready whenever you need it.

COFFEE-ALMOND TORTONI

1 cup whipping cream
½ cup sugar, divided
1 teaspoon vanilla extract
¼ teaspoon almond extract
2 egg whites
¼ cup finely chopped toasted almonds
¼ cup flaked coconut, toasted
1 teaspoon instant coffee powder

Combine whipping cream, ¼ cup sugar, vanilla, and almond extract in a medium mixing bowl; beat until soft peaks form.

Beat egg whites (at room temperature) until foamy. Gradually add remaining sugar, beating until soft peaks form. Fold in whipped cream mixture and half the almonds and coconut; spoon half of mixture into 8 paper-lined muffin cups.

Stir coffee powder into remaining portion of tortoni; spoon over whipped cream mixture. Sprinkle with remaining almonds and coconut; cover and freeze until firm. Yield: 8 servings.

Note: Cups may be removed from muffin tins and stored in freezer bags.
Sandy Wallace,
Mobile, Alabama.

A Special Chocolate Pie

Easier than it looks, this Chocolate-Amaretto Mousse Pie can be made in a matter of minutes. The filling is a creamy blend of whipped topping mix, chocolate pudding, and almond-flavored liqueur.

CHOCOLATE-AMARETTO MOUSSE PIE

2 (1.5-ounce) envelopes whipped topping mix
1½ cups milk
2 (4⅛-ounce) packages chocolate instant pudding and pie filling mix
¼ cup amaretto or other almond-flavored liqueur
1 baked 9-inch pastry shell, cooled
1 (8-ounce) container frozen whipped topping, thawed (optional)
Chocolate shavings (optional)

Prepare topping mix according to package directions. Add milk, pudding mix, and amaretto; beat 2 minutes at high speed of electric mixer. Spoon mixture into pastry shell. Top with whipped topping and chocolate shavings, if desired. Chill at least 4 hours. Yield: one 9-inch pie.
Barbara Bartolomeo,
Houston, Texas.

A Catch Of Fish Favorites

Whether you prefer flounder, haddock, trout, or halibut, there are probably as many fish recipes as there are fish in the sea. And our readers have shared some of their favorites.

Helen Boatman of Chapel Hill, North Carolina, bakes fresh flounder fillets in a white wine sauce. Mrs. Pierre J. Bouis of Kenner, Louisiana, suggests a wine sauce with fresh shrimp for trout.

Chinese-Style Fried Halibut, featuring a sweet-and-sour sauce, is a specialty from Cynthia Harper of Snow Hill, North Carolina.

FILLET OF FLOUNDER IN WINE SAUCE

3 tablespoons butter or margarine
3 tablespoons all-purpose flour
1 (10¾-ounce) can cream of mushroom soup, undiluted
¾ cup dry white wine
3 tablespoons grated Parmesan cheese
2 tablespoons chopped fresh parsley
½ teaspoon salt
⅛ teaspoon pepper
1 pound flounder fillets
Grated Parmesan cheese (optional)

Melt butter over low heat; add flour, stirring until smooth. Add soup and wine; cook, stirring constantly, until thickened. Stir in cheese, parsley, salt, and pepper.

Arrange fish in a lightly greased 13- x 9- x 2-inch baking dish. Pour sauce over fish. Sprinkle additional Parmesan cheese on top, if desired. Bake, uncovered, at 375° for 30 minutes. Yield: 4 servings.
Helen Boatman,
Chapel Hill, North Carolina.

BAKED HADDOCK

2 pounds fresh or frozen haddock fillets, thawed
1 large tomato, chopped
1 small green pepper, finely chopped
⅓ cup lemon juice
1 tablespoon vegetable oil
2 teaspoons instant minced onion
¾ to 1 teaspoon dried whole basil
2 teaspoons salt
¼ teaspoon pepper
4 drops hot sauce

Arrange fillets in a single layer in a lightly greased 13- x 9- x 2-inch baking dish. Combine remaining ingredients; mix well, and spoon over fish. Bake 5 to 8 minutes at 500° or until fish flakes easily with a fork. Yield: 6 servings.
Doris Garton,
Shenandoah, Virginia.

CHINESE-STYLE FRIED HALIBUT

½ cup vinegar
1 cup sugar
1⅓ cups water
3 chicken bouillon cubes
1 large green pepper, cut into strips
1 (15¼-ounce) can pineapple chunks, drained
1½ tablespoons cornstarch
1½ teaspoons soy sauce
1½ teaspoons water
2 pounds halibut steaks or fillets
½ cup all-purpose flour
1 teaspoon salt
Hot vegetable oil

Combine vinegar, sugar, 1⅓ cups water, bouillon cubes, green pepper, and pineapple in a medium saucepan; simmer 10 minutes. Combine cornstarch, soy sauce, and 1½ teaspoons water; stir well. Gradually add cornstarch mixture to pineapple mixture;

cook over low heat, stirring constantly, until thickened.

Rinse fish, and pat dry. Combine flour and salt; stir well. Dredge fish in flour mixture; fry in ⅛ inch hot oil (375°) until golden brown. Do not overcook; drain on paper towels. Serve pineapple sauce over fish. Yield: 6 to 8 servings. *Cynthia Harper, Snow Hill, North Carolina.*

TROUT IN WINE SAUCE

½ pound medium shrimp
1½ cups boiling salted water
4 trout fillets (about 1 pound)
1 cup all-purpose flour
½ teaspoon salt
¼ teaspoon pepper
¼ cup butter or margarine, melted
4 green onions, chopped
¼ cup all-purpose flour
1½ cups milk
½ teaspoon salt
Pinch of white pepper
½ cup dry vermouth

Add shrimp to boiling salted water; return to a boil. Lower heat, and simmer 3 to 5 minutes. Drain well; rinse with cold water. Let cool. Peel and devein shrimp, and set aside.

Rinse trout fillets, and pat dry. Combine 1 cup flour, ½ teaspoon salt, and ¼ teaspoon pepper; dredge fish in seasoned flour. Sauté fish in butter in a large skillet until lightly browned, turning once. Remove fish; drain on paper towels, and set aside. Reserve butter in skillet.

Stir onion into butter; coat completely. Add ¼ cup flour and cook 1 minute, stirring constantly. Gradually add milk; cook over medium heat, stirring constantly, until sauce is thickened and bubbly. Remove from heat and set aside.

Add shrimp, ½ teaspoon salt, white pepper, and vermouth to sauce; stir well.

Carefully place trout fillets in wine sauce; simmer until thoroughly heated. Yield: 4 servings. *Mrs. Pierre J. Bouis, Kenner, Louisiana.*

Tip: As a rule, thawed fish should not be kept longer than one day before cooking: The flavor is better if it is cooked immediately after thawing.

Cooking For Two Without Leftovers

When cooking for two people, adapting recipes can sometimes be difficult, especially if you don't want to eat leftovers for a week. These recipes make it easy, since they yield two servings.

There's a clam chowder that's a cinch to make and just the right amount for a wintertime lunch or a casual supper. For a special entrée, try Veal and Carrots in Wine Sauce; it's a main dish and a side dish in one. And what about bread for two? We recommend cornbread that bakes on top of the range in a small skillet—just enough for two.

VEAL AND CARROTS IN WINE SAUCE

½ to ¾ pound (¼-inch-thick) veal
2 tablespoons all-purpose flour
½ teaspoon salt
Dash of pepper
⅛ teaspoon dried whole marjoram
1 clove garlic
2 tablespoons vegetable oil
3 medium carrots, peeled and cut in half crosswise
½ cup white wine

Cut veal into 2-inch pieces. Combine flour, salt, pepper, and marjoram; dredge veal in flour mixture.

Sauté garlic in oil 1 minute; add meat, and cook until browned. Discard garlic. Add carrots and wine; cover and simmer 30 minutes. Yield: 2 servings. *Bobbi Harris, San Antonio, Texas.*

FRIED RICE FOR TWO

1 tablespoon butter or margarine
1 egg, well beaten
2 tablespoons vegetable oil
3 green onions, chopped
⅓ cup chopped green pepper
⅔ cup cooked rice
⅔ cup diced cooked ham
1 (8½-ounce) can English peas, drained
Freshly ground pepper (optional)
Soy sauce (optional)

Heat butter in a skillet or wok; add egg, and scramble until firm. Chop egg into small pieces; set aside.

Heat oil in skillet over medium heat. Add onion and green pepper; sauté until tender. Do not overcook. Stir in rice, ham, peas, and egg. Stir-fry 2 to 3 minutes. Sprinkle with pepper, if desired. Reduce heat; cover and simmer about 10 minutes. Serve with soy sauce, if desired. Yield: 2 servings. *H. Maxcy Smith, St. Petersburg, Florida.*

MACARONI SALAD FOR TWO

1 cup cooked elbow macaroni, cooled
1 hard-cooked egg, chopped
2 tablespoons chopped celery
2 tablespoons chopped onion
3 tablespoons mayonnaise or salad dressing
1 teaspoon sugar
1 teaspoon vinegar
¼ teaspoon salt
¼ teaspoon prepared mustard
Pepper to taste

Combine all ingredients, stirring lightly; cover and chill several hours before serving. Yield: 2 servings. *Stella Stitt, Houston, Texas.*

SKILLET CORNBREAD

Vegetable oil
¼ cup all-purpose flour
¼ cup cornmeal
1 teaspoon baking powder
¼ teaspoon salt
1 egg, beaten
¼ cup milk

Pour a small amount of oil in an 8-inch iron skillet; cover and heat over very low heat on top of range until very hot.

Combine flour, cornmeal, baking powder, and salt; stir in egg, milk, and 1 tablespoon vegetable oil. Pour batter into hot skillet; cover, and place over very low heat. Cook 5 minutes; turn and cook, covered, an additional 5 minutes or until golden brown. Yield: 2 servings. *Janet Baker, Metairie, Louisiana.*

CLAM CHOWDER

1 slice bacon
2 tablespoons diced onion
1 small potato, peeled and diced
½ cup water
½ teaspoon salt
Dash of pepper
1 (8-ounce) can minced clams, undrained
1 cup milk
1 tablespoon butter

Cook bacon until crisp; drain on paper towels, and reserve drippings. Sauté onion in reserved drippings until tender; set aside.

Combine potato, water, salt, and pepper in a saucepan; cook over medium heat just until potato is tender. Stir in clams, milk, butter, and onion; simmer 3 minutes or until heated through. Sprinkle bacon over each serving of chowder. Yield: 2 servings.

Shelly Albritton,
Shubuta, Mississippi.

Pineapple Makes This Cheesecake Special

Nothing could be more flavorful than a simple, velvety-smooth cheesecake, unless it's our Pineapple Cheesecake with a pineapple-sour cream topping. Try this one, and you may never serve the plain version again.

PINEAPPLE CHEESECAKE

2 cups graham cracker crumbs
1½ tablespoons sugar
3 tablespoons butter or margarine, melted
3 (8-ounce) packages cream cheese, softened
1 cup sugar
4 eggs
1 (8¼-ounce) can crushed pineapple
1 tablespoon lemon juice
1 teaspoon grated lemon rind
¼ cup sugar
1½ cups commercial sour cream
½ teaspoon vanilla extract

Combine graham cracker crumbs, 1½ tablespoons sugar, and butter; mix well. Press into bottom and halfway up sides of a 10-inch springform pan; set aside.

Beat cream cheese at medium speed of electric mixer until light and fluffy. Gradually add 1 cup sugar, beating well. Add eggs, one at a time, beating well after each addition.

Drain pineapple, reserving ¼ cup liquid. Stir pineapple, lemon juice, and lemon rind into cheese mixture; spoon into crust. Bake cheesecake at 325° for 1 hour and 15 minutes or until set. Cool thoroughly.

Combine reserved pineapple liquid and ¼ cup sugar; cook over medium heat until sugar dissolves and mixture begins to thicken. Cool thoroughly. Stir in sour cream and vanilla.

Spread sauce over top of cheesecake; chill well before serving. Yield: one 10-inch cheesecake. *Susan Settlemyre, Raleigh, North Carolina.*

Microwave Cookery

Why Not A Spaghetti Pie?

For a homemade spaghetti dinner that's quick to prepare, how about Spaghetti Pie? Cooked spaghetti is shaped to form a pie shell that holds a savory tomato-meat sauce. A topping of pepperoni and sliced olives makes this dish totally irresistible.

Using a microwave oven, you can make Spaghetti Pie in about 30 minutes.

SPAGHETTI PIE

½ (12-ounce) package vermicelli
2 tablespoons butter or margarine
⅓ cup grated Parmesan cheese
2 eggs, well beaten
1 pound ground beef
½ cup chopped onion
¼ cup chopped green pepper
1 (8-ounce) can stewed tomatoes, undrained
1 (6-ounce) can tomato paste
1 teaspoon sugar
¾ teaspoon dried whole oregano
½ teaspoon salt
½ teaspoon garlic salt
1 cup cream-style cottage cheese
½ cup (2 ounces) shredded mozzarella cheese
8 to 12 pepperoni slices
2 pimiento-stuffed olives, sliced
2 teaspoons chopped fresh parsley

Cook vermicelli according to package directions; drain. Stir butter and Parmesan cheese into hot vermicelli. Add eggs, stirring well. Spoon mixture into a 10-inch pieplate. Use a spoon to shape the spaghetti into a pie shell. Microwave at HIGH, uncovered, 3 minutes or until set. Set aside.

Crumble beef in a shallow 2-quart casserole; stir in onion and green pepper. Cover with heavy-duty plastic wrap, and microwave at HIGH 5 to 6 minutes, stirring at 2-minute intervals; drain well. Stir in tomatoes, tomato paste, and seasonings. Cover and microwave at HIGH 3½ to 4 minutes, stirring once; set aside.

Spread cottage cheese evenly over pie shell. Top with meat sauce. Cover with heavy-duty plastic wrap, and microwave at HIGH 6 to 6½ minutes; sprinkle with mozzarella cheese. Microwave, uncovered, at HIGH 30 seconds or until cheese begins to melt.

Garnish with pepperoni, olives, and parsley. Microwave, uncovered, at HIGH 1 minute. Let stand 10 minutes before serving. Yield: 4 to 6 servings.

Bill Phillips,
Albertville, Alabama.

Tip: Have your oven thermostat professionally checked at least once a year. Another way to occasionally check oven temperature is to prepare a cake mix according to package directions; the cake should cook the entire recommended time and test done (a wooden pick inserted in the center should come out clean).

Offer A Distinctive Avocado Dish

Avocados are one of the most welcome ingredients around. In this collection of recipes, they lend their nutty flavor to dishes ranging from a colorful salad to a yogurt-topped omelet.

For full flavor, avocados must be ripe. To speed ripening, place them in a brown paper bag. Storing in the refrigerator delays ripening. Once an avocado is cut, immediately rub the flesh with lime or lemon juice to help prevent discoloration.

AVOCADO-GARBANZO SALAD

½ cup commercial French salad dressing
1 (15-ounce) can garbanzos, drained
¼ head lettuce, chopped
1 ripe avocado, peeled, seeded, and
    quartered
1 medium tomato, cut into wedges
2 hard-cooked eggs, quartered
¼ cup pimiento-stuffed olives
½ cup (2 ounces) shredded Monterey Jack
    cheese

Pour French dressing over garbanzos. Marinate in refrigerator 3 to 4 hours.

Place lettuce on serving platter; arrange avocado, tomato, and eggs over lettuce. Spoon garbanzos over avocado; top with olives. Sprinkle with cheese. Yield: 4 servings. *Mrs. H. S. Wright, Leesville, South Carolina.*

YOGURT-AVOCADO OMELET

1 ripe avocado
Lemon juice
4 eggs
¼ cup water
½ teaspoon salt
2 tablespoons butter or margarine,
    divided
6 thin slices tomato
½ cup alfalfa sprouts, divided
¼ cup plain yogurt, divided
2 tablespoons chopped walnuts, divided

Peel avocado; remove seed. Reserve 2 slices avocado for garnish; chop remaining avocado. Sprinkle avocado with lemon juice; set aside.

Combine eggs, water, and salt; mix just until blended. Heat 1 tablespoon butter in a 10-inch omelet pan or heavy skillet over medium heat until slightly golden at the edges.

Pour in half of egg mixture. As mixture starts to cook, gently lift edges of omelet with a spatula, and tilt pan so uncooked portion flows underneath.

Place half of chopped avocado on half of omelet; top with 3 tomato slices and half of alfalfa sprouts. Carefully fold omelet in half, and place on a warm platter. Top with 1 avocado slice, 2 tablespoons yogurt, and 1 tablespoon walnuts. Repeat procedure with remaining ingredients. Yield: 2 servings.

Doris Amonette, Tulsa, Oklahoma.

Tip: Get in the habit of grocery shopping with a list. Watch newspapers for advertised "specials," then plan a week's menus around bargains in foods the family enjoys.

Avocado can add distinct flavor to many dishes, including Avocado-Garbanzo Salad.

CEVICHE IN AVOCADO SHELLS

1 pound trout, boned, skinned, and diced
1 cup lemon or lime juice
3 tablespoons olive oil
1 medium onion, chopped
1 (4-ounce) can green chiles, drained and
    chopped
1 medium tomato, peeled and chopped
Pinch of dried whole oregano
¼ teaspoon salt
⅛ teaspoon pepper
3 ripe avocados

Place fish in a glass or earthenware bowl (do not use metal); pour lemon juice over fish. Cover and refrigerate at least 1 hour. Drain fish. Add remaining ingredients except avocado; mix well.

Cut avocados in half lengthwise; remove seed. Scoop out some of avocado to form deeper shells; chop pulp, and add to fish mixture. Fill avocado shells with fish mixture. Yield: 6 servings.

Doris Garton, Shenandoah, Virginia.

CHILLED AVOCADO SOUP

1 large ripe avocado, peeled and cubed
1½ cups chicken broth
1 (8-ounce) bottle clam juice
1 (8-ounce) carton commercial sour cream
¼ cup grated onion
¼ teaspoon salt
2 drops of hot sauce
Dash of chili powder

Combine avocado, broth, and clam juice in container of food processor or electric blender; process until smooth. Add remaining ingredients; stir well. Chill thoroughly. Serve with tortilla chips. Yield: 5 cups.

Kathleen D. Stone,
Houston, Texas.

End Meals With A Light Dessert

If you consider your meal incomplete without dessert, these recipes should offer some ideas for light desserts to accompany any meal.

Frozen raspberries, whipped cream, and orange-flavored liqueur are the special ingredients for light and airy Raspberry Mousse. There is also a recipe that revives old-fashioned boiled custard. The soft, almost liquid texture and delicate flavor of Perfect Boiled Custard make it ideal for serving with fruit.

APPLESAUCE-GRAHAM CRACKER PUDDING

1½ cups graham cracker crumbs
¾ cup firmly packed brown sugar
½ cup chopped pecans or walnuts
¼ cup plus 2 tablespoons butter or margarine, melted
½ teaspoon ground cinnamon
2 cups applesauce
1½ tablespoons lemon juice

Combine first 5 ingredients; stir well. Press half of crumb mixture into a buttered 9-inch baking pan.

Spoon applesauce evenly over crust; sprinkle with lemon juice. Top with remaining crumb mixture.

Bake at 400° for 20 to 25 minutes. Yield: 6 to 8 servings.

Nancy S. Register,
Columbus, Georgia.

PERFECT BOILED CUSTARD

2 eggs
¼ cup sugar
1½ tablespoons all-purpose flour
⅛ teaspoon salt
2 cups milk, scalded
½ teaspoon vanilla extract

Beat eggs in top of a double boiler on medium speed of an electric mixer until frothy. Combine sugar, flour, and salt, stirring well; gradually add to eggs, beating until thick.

Gradually stir about one-fourth of hot milk into egg mixture; add remaining milk, stirring constantly.

Bring water in bottom of double boiler to a boil. Reduce heat to low; cook, stirring occasionally, 20 minutes or until custard thickens and coats a metal spoon. Stir in vanilla. Pour custard into serving bowl and chill. Yield: 4 servings. *Mrs. Sidney I. McGrath,*
Hopkinsville, Kentucky.

ORANGE CAKE SQUARES

½ cup shortening
1⅓ cups sugar
2 eggs
1 cup milk
1 teaspoon orange extract
1 teaspoon grated orange rind
2 cups all-purpose flour
1 tablespoon baking powder
¼ teaspoon salt
Orange Glaze

Cream shortening; gradually add sugar, mixing well. Add eggs, one at a time, beating well after each addition.

Combine milk, extract, and orange rind; set aside.

Combine flour, baking powder, and salt; add to creamed mixture alternately with milk mixture, beginning and ending with flour mixture. Beat 3 minutes

on medium speed of an electric mixer; pour into a greased and floured 13- x 9- x 2-inch baking pan. Bake at 350° for 30 minutes or until a wooden pick inserted in center comes out clean. Pour Orange Glaze over warm cake, spreading evenly. Cut cake into squares to serve. Yield: 15 to 18 servings.

Orange Glaze:

2 cups sifted powdered sugar
¼ cup fresh orange juice
2 teaspoons grated orange rind

Combine all ingredients; stir until smooth. Yield: about 1 cup.

Marcella R. White,
Pensacola, Florida.

RASPBERRY MOUSSE

2 (10-ounce) packages frozen raspberries, thawed
1 envelope unflavored gelatin
⅓ cup orange juice
¼ cup sugar
2 tablespoons Triple Sec or other orange-flavored liqueur
2 egg whites, stiffly beaten
1½ cups whipping cream, whipped
Additional whipped cream

Drain raspberries, reserving juice. Add enough water to juice to make 1 cup. Process raspberries in food mill or container of electric blender. Strain raspberries, and discard the seeds.

Soften gelatin in orange juice. Combine raspberry juice, pulp, gelatin mixture, and sugar in a saucepan; bring to a boil, stirring constantly. Remove from heat, and cool.

Stir liqueur into mixture; chill until consistency of unbeaten egg white.

Fold egg whites and whipped cream into raspberry mixture. Spoon into individual serving dishes; chill until firm. Garnish with additional whipped cream. Yield: 6 servings. *Helen J. Wright,*
Leesville, South Carolina.

Tip: To get maximum volume when beating cream, evaporated milk, or reconstituted dry milk, use a deep metal or glass bowl and have cream, bowl, and beaters very cold before starting.

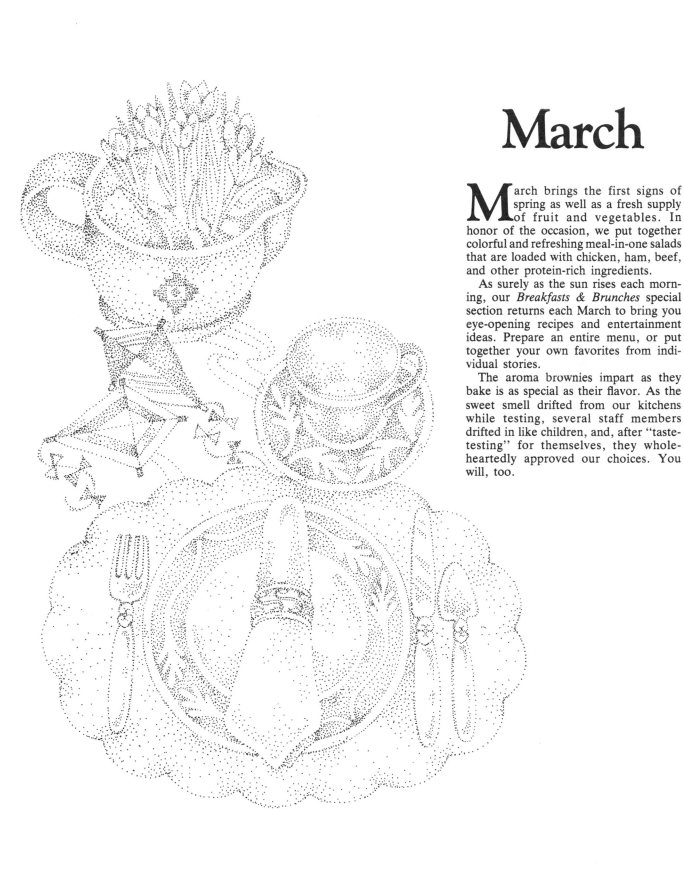

March

March brings the first signs of spring as well as a fresh supply of fruit and vegetables. In honor of the occasion, we put together colorful and refreshing meal-in-one salads that are loaded with chicken, ham, beef, and other protein-rich ingredients.

As surely as the sun rises each morning, our *Breakfasts & Brunches* special section returns each March to bring you eye-opening recipes and entertainment ideas. Prepare an entire menu, or put together your own favorites from individual stories.

The aroma brownies impart as they bake is as special as their flavor. As the sweet smell drifted from our kitchens while testing, several staff members drifted in like children, and, after "taste-testing" for themselves, they wholeheartedly approved our choices. You will, too.

Substantial Salads Bridge The Season

As spring arrives, so does a fresh supply of fruit and vegetables just right for colorful salads. To make a salad a satisfying meal in itself, toss in chunks of meat, seafood, or other protein-rich foods.

Simple preparation makes main dish salads a great spur-of-the-moment party menu idea. Recipes like Flavorful Tuna Salad and Full o' Beans Salad are based on ingredients you'll likely have on hand and can be mixed up in minutes. With salad entrées you'll find buffet settings a snap to assemble and serve. A bread and beverage round out the meal.

When time allows you to plan ahead, congealed or marinated salads eliminate last-minute preparation. As an added advantage, the flavors blend and may actually improve with overnight chilling. We found Super Shrimp Salad especially worth the wait.

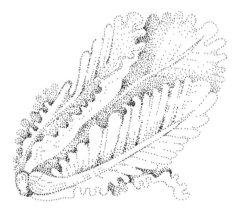

POTATO-CORNED BEEF SALAD

2 cups sliced cooked potatoes
1 (12-ounce) can corned beef, cubed
3 hard-cooked eggs, sliced
½ cup diced cooked carrots
¼ cup diced green pepper
2 tablespoons minced onion
2 tablespoons chopped pimiento
½ cup mayonnaise
2 tablespoons vinegar
1 tablespoon prepared mustard
¼ teaspoon pepper
Lettuce (optional)

Combine first 7 ingredients, mixing well. Combine the mayonnaise, vinegar, mustard, and pepper; add to potato mixture, and toss gently. Serve on lettuce, if desired. Yield: 4 servings.
Sherry Boger Phillips,
Knoxville, Tennessee.

MEXICAN SALAD

1 to 1½ pounds ground beef
1 (1.25-ounce) package taco seasoning
1 head iceberg lettuce, coarsely shredded
2 to 3 tomatoes, chopped
1 (15½-ounce) can kidney beans, drained
1 or 2 (8-ounce) packages tortilla chips
1 or 2 green onions, chopped
1 (8-ounce) jar taco sauce
2 cups (8 ounces) shredded Cheddar cheese
1 (16-ounce) jar low-calorie Thousand Island dressing

Brown meat, and drain well; stir in taco seasoning, and simmer 5 minutes. Combine meat mixture with remaining ingredients, and toss well. Serve immediately. Yield: 12 servings. *Debra Rich,*
Vancouver, Washington.

FRUITED HAM SALAD

1 (15¼-ounce) can pineapple chunks
1 banana, sliced
1 avocado, sliced
½ medium cantaloupe, cut into balls
1¼ pounds smoked ham, cut into thin strips
Lettuce leaves
Pineapple Salad Dressing

Drain pineapple, reserving juice. Pour pineapple juice over banana and avocado, tossing lightly to coat fruit. Drain fruit, reserving juice for use in dressing.

Combine fruit and ham; toss gently. Chill 3 to 4 hours. Spoon into a lettuce-lined bowl, and serve with Pineapple Salad Dressing. Yield: 6 servings.

Pineapple Salad Dressing:

½ cup sugar
1 tablespoon all-purpose flour
Reserved pineapple juice
1 egg, beaten
2 tablespoons vegetable oil
2 tablespoons lemon juice

Combine sugar and flour in a small saucepan. Add enough water to reserved pineapple juice to measure ¾ cup. Add pineapple juice and remaining ingredients to sugar mixture, mixing well. Cook over low heat until thickened, stirring constantly. Chill thoroughly. Yield: about 1½ cups.
Edna B. Chadsey,
Corpus Christi, Texas.

Tip: For a small amount of grated onion, place onion pieces in garlic press.

CONGEALED HAM SALAD

1 envelope unflavored gelatin
¼ cup cold water
1½ cups hot water
1 tablespoon vinegar
1 tablespoon lemon juice
½ teaspoon salt
1 cup finely chopped ham
1 cup finely shredded cabbage
1 cup finely chopped celery
6 sweet pickles, finely chopped
2 whole pimientos, finely chopped
Lettuce leaves

Soften gelatin in cold water; add hot water, and stir until gelatin dissolves. Stir in vinegar, lemon juice, and salt. Chill until consistency of unbeaten egg white.

Add next 5 ingredients to thickened gelatin, stirring well. Pour into an oiled 1-quart mold, and chill until firm. Unmold salad on lettuce-lined platter. Yield: 6 to 8 servings. *Helen Bates,*
Fort Worth, Texas.

HAM 'N EGG SALAD

10 hard-cooked eggs, chopped
2 cups chopped ham
¼ cup chopped sweet pickle
¼ cup sliced pimiento-stuffed olives
1 stalk celery, sliced
1 tablespoon minced onion
½ cup mayonnaise
2 tablespoons milk
2 teaspoons vinegar
¾ teaspoon salt
Lettuce leaves
Tomato wedges

Combine first 6 ingredients, tossing gently. Combine next 4 ingredients, and fold into ham mixture. Chill well. Serve on lettuce leaves, and garnish with tomato wedges. Yield: 4 to 6 servings.
Linda C. Swan,
Culloden, West Virginia.

CURRIED CHICKEN SALAD WITH ASPARAGUS

1 pound fresh asparagus spears
3 cups chopped cooked chicken
3 small stalks celery, finely chopped
1 small onion, grated
¾ to 1 cup mayonnaise
1 teaspoon lemon juice
½ teaspoon curry powder
¼ teaspoon salt
⅛ teaspoon white pepper

Snap off tough ends of asparagus, and remove scales from stalks with a knife or vegetable peeler. Cut asparagus into 1½-inch pieces.

Cook asparagus, covered, in a small amount of boiling salted water about 6 to 8 minutes or until crisp-tender; drain. Arrange asparagus in a serving dish; chill.

Combine chicken, celery, and onion; toss well. Combine remaining ingredients, and mix well; stir into chicken mixture. Chill 3 to 4 hours. To serve, spoon chicken salad over asparagus. Yield: 6 servings.

Note: One (14½-ounce) can cut asparagus, drained and chilled, may be substituted for fresh asparagus.

Gale Purser,
Jackson, Mississippi.

CHOP SUEY SALAD

1 cup sliced ripe olives
1 medium-size green pepper, sliced in 1-inch strips
4 cups mixed salad greens
1 cup canned bean sprouts, drained and rinsed
1 (8-ounce) can water chestnuts, drained and thinly sliced
1 cup sliced green onion
¾ cup chopped celery
1 cup thinly sliced cooked chicken
1 tablespoon mayonnaise or salad dressing
2 tablespoons lemon juice
1 tablespoon vegetable oil
⅓ cup soy sauce
4 slices bacon, cooked and crumbled

Combine first 8 ingredients. Combine remaining ingredients except bacon; mix thoroughly. Pour dressing over salad just before serving, tossing lightly. Sprinkle with bacon. Yield: 4 servings.

Jane Crum,
North Little Rock, Arkansas.

CHICKEN SALAD AMANDINE

½ cup slivered almonds
¼ cup butter or margarine
4 cups cubed cooked chicken breasts
1 (15¼-ounce) can crushed pineapple, well drained
1 cup chopped celery
½ cup mayonnaise
1 teaspoon salt
6 pineapple slices
Lettuce leaves
Almond Salad Dressing

Sauté almonds in butter until golden brown, stirring occasionally; drain well.

Combine half of almonds and next 5 ingredients, mixing well. Cover and chill several hours or overnight.

Place sliced pineapple on lettuce leaves; top with chicken salad. Spoon dressing over salad, and sprinkle with remaining almonds. Yield: 6 servings.

Almond Salad Dressing:

1 cup mayonnaise
¼ cup amaretto or other almond-flavored liqueur

Combine ingredients, and mix until smooth. Chill thoroughly. Yield: about 1¼ cups.

Emily W. Booth,
Sandston, Virginia.

SUPER SHRIMP SALAD

3 cups water
1 pound large shrimp
¼ pound lump crabmeat
¼ cup chopped celery
½ cup chopped green pepper
2½ tablespoons chopped sweet pickle
1 shallot, minced
1½ teaspoons minced fresh parsley
½ cup sliced ripe olives
½ cup sliced pimiento-stuffed olives
1 cup commercial Italian salad dressing
2 tablespoons olive oil or walnut oil
1½ teaspoons lemon juice
Leaf lettuce
½ medium head iceberg lettuce, coarsely shredded
2 medium tomatoes, cut in wedges

Bring water to a boil; add shrimp, and return to a boil. Lower heat, and simmer 3 to 5 minutes. Drain well; then rinse with cold water. Peel and devein shrimp.

Combine shrimp and next 11 ingredients in an airtight container; cover and refrigerate overnight.

Line a serving platter with leaf lettuce, and top with iceberg lettuce; spoon on shrimp mixture. Garnish with tomato wedges. Yield: 4 to 6 servings.

Alzina Toups,
Galliano, Louisiana.

Tip: Prices of fresh vegetables and fruit change with the seasons. Buy seasonal fresh foods when most plentiful and at peak quality in your area.

FLAVORFUL TUNA SALAD

¾ cup pitted ripe olives
2 (7-ounce) cans tuna, drained and flaked
½ cup chopped celery
1 cup mayonnaise
2 teaspoons lemon juice
½ teaspoon prepared mustard
½ teaspoon onion powder
½ teaspoon ground ginger
Lettuce leaves (optional)
Baked patty shells (optional)

Set aside 10 olives; chop remaining olives. Combine tuna, chopped olives, and celery.

Combine mayonnaise, lemon juice, mustard, onion powder, and ginger; mix well, and pour over tuna mixture. Stir gently, and chill until serving time.

If desired, serve in lettuce-lined patty shells or on lettuce leaves. Garnish with reserved olives. Yield: 10 servings.

Lilly B. Smith,
Richmond, Virginia.

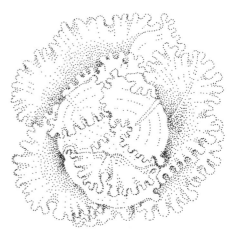

CHEESY LAYERED SALAD

1 head lettuce, shredded
Dash of salt
Dash of pepper
2 tablespoons sugar
2 hard-cooked eggs, sliced
1 (10-ounce) package frozen English peas
1 pound bacon, cooked and crumbled
2 cups (8 ounces) shredded Swiss cheese
1 cup mayonnaise or salad dressing

Layer half of lettuce in a 2½-quart bowl; sprinkle with salt, pepper, and 1 tablespoon sugar. Line sides of bowl with egg slices.

Spoon peas evenly over lettuce, and sprinkle with remaining sugar. Layer with remaining lettuce, bacon, and cheese. Spread mayonnaise evenly over top. Cover salad tightly, and chill 24 hours. Yield: 6 servings. *Patty Merritt,*
Jacksonville, North Carolina.

FULL O' BEANS SALAD

1 (15½-ounce) can kidney beans, drained
1 (15-ounce) can garbanzo beans, drained
½ cup diced Cheddar cheese
½ cup sliced celery
¼ cup chopped onion
½ cup commercial Italian salad dressing
¼ cup sweet pickle relish, drained
½ teaspoon prepared mustard
Lettuce leaves
6 slices bacon, cooked and crumbled

Combine first 5 ingredients, and set aside. Combine salad dressing, relish, and mustard; stir well, and pour over bean mixture. Mix well; then chill. Serve on lettuce leaves, and sprinkle with bacon. Yield: 6 servings.
James L. Strieber,
Odenton, Maryland.

Sauce Up Your Spaghetti

A plate of plain spaghetti doesn't have much to say, but pile on the sauce and the taste will speak for itself. A meatball sauce is certainly one of the most popular toppings, but spaghetti can be dressed in a variety of ways.

For a meatless version, serve Spaghetti With Zucchini Sauce. This savory blend of tomatoes, zucchini, and onions sautéed in olive oil is seasoned with bay leaf, basil, and oregano. It's great topped with Parmesan cheese.

Italian Spaghetti, packed with garlic, mushrooms, and onions, features Italian sausage for added flavor. And what about spaghetti as a side dish? We suggest Spaghetti Alla Carbonara—a rich blend of cream, bacon, garlic, parsley, and Parmesan cheese tossed with hot spaghetti.

SPAGHETTI ALLA CARBONARA

1 (1-pound) package spaghetti
3 eggs, beaten
1 cup grated Parmesan cheese, divided
½ cup whipping cream
8 slices bacon, cooked and crumbled
¼ cup chopped fresh parsley
¼ teaspoon dried whole basil
1 clove garlic, crushed
¼ cup butter or margarine

Cook spaghetti according to package directions; drain and keep warm.

Combine eggs and ½ cup cheese, stirring well.

Heat whipping cream in a heavy saucepan until scalded. Stir in bacon, parsley, basil, and garlic.

Combine spaghetti, egg mixture, whipping cream mixture, and butter; toss gently until butter is melted. Spoon spaghetti into serving bowl, and sprinkle remaining ½ cup cheese over top. Yield: 6 to 8 servings. *Tammy Smith,*
Talbott, Tennessee.

SPAGHETTI WITH MEATBALLS

2 tablespoons butter or margarine
½ cup chopped onion
1 (28-ounce) can tomatoes, undrained
1 (6-ounce) can tomato paste
1 tablespoon chopped parsley
Salt
Pepper
Dash of ground oregano
1 pound ground beef
2 tablespoons grated onion
2 tablespoons vegetable oil
Hot cooked spaghetti

Melt butter in a large skillet. Add chopped onion, and sauté until tender. Add tomatoes, tomato paste, parsley, ½ teaspoon salt, ¼ teaspoon pepper, and oregano. Cover and cook over low heat 30 minutes, stirring occasionally. Remove cover, and cook 30 minutes.

Combine ground beef, grated onion, 1 teaspoon salt, and ¼ teaspoon pepper; mix well. Shape into 1½-inch meatballs. Cook in oil over medium heat until no longer pink; drain. Add to sauce; cook over low heat 15 minutes. Serve over spaghetti. Yield: 4 servings.
Mary Dishon,
Stanford, Kentucky.

ITALIAN SPAGHETTI

1 pound Italian link sausage, cut into ½-inch pieces
2 tablespoons olive oil
1 large onion, chopped
½ pound fresh mushrooms, sliced
2 cloves garlic, minced
2 (15-ounce) cans tomato puree
1 teaspoon dried parsley flakes
1 teaspoon dried whole oregano
1 teaspoon dried whole basil
Hot cooked spaghetti

Cook sausage in oil in a Dutch oven until done. Add onion, mushrooms, and garlic; cook, stirring occasionally, until tender. Drain. Add tomato puree, parsley, oregano, and basil. Cover and cook sauce over low heat about 1 hour, stirring occasionally.

Serve sauce over spaghetti. Yield: 4 servings.
Carol Horn,
Huntsville, Alabama.

SPAGHETTI WITH ZUCCHINI SAUCE

1 medium onion, sliced
¼ cup olive oil
4 medium zucchini, sliced
3 medium tomatoes, quartered
¾ teaspoon salt
1 bay leaf
¼ teaspoon pepper
¼ teaspoon dried whole basil
¼ teaspoon dried whole oregano
Hot cooked spaghetti
Grated Parmesan cheese

Sauté onion in oil until tender. Add remaining ingredients except spaghetti and cheese; cook sauce over low heat 10 minutes, stirring occasionally. Remove bay leaf.

Serve over spaghetti; sprinkle with Parmesan cheese. Yield: 4 to 6 servings.
Mrs. O. V. Elkins,
Raleigh, North Carolina.

Tip: Properly canned foods have been sterilized and won't spoil as long as the container remains airtight. However, most canned foods have a "shelf life" of approximately one year—they then may begin to slowly lose flavor and nutrients. If you use large amounts of canned foods, date them at time of purchase and use the oldest first.

BREAKFASTS&BRUNCHES™

Greet The Morning, Southern Style

Morning is a time of fresh breezes, a day's new possibilities, smiles as bright as a sunrise. In the kitchen, where everyone's day begins, a good cook can capture that feeling. It's luxurious to dawdle over a delightfully endless brunch, but a snack on-the-run that's prepared with special care can say "good morning" in the same way.

Our readers have a host of fresh ideas to help you add that special Southern touch to the first meal of the day. In this year's *Breakfasts & Brunches* section, you'll discover new ways with old favorites and some surprises that may become new favorites. We've tested everything from breads using delicious natural grains to a soufflé that bakes in a tomato shell. Try just one recipe or a whole menu; our idea is to start every morning at the top.

One of the best morning gatherings we've heard of begins with the glint of sun on water at the North River Yacht Club in Tuscaloosa, Alabama. Dorothy and Amos Burns love to sail, but their guests are just as delighted with the delectable meal that comes first. Several times throughout spring and summer, friends gather on the tri-level terraces of the club's Captain's Cabin for a brunch that satisfies the heartiest sailors among them. "We all like getting together to enjoy such a pretty time of day," says Dorothy.

Keeping an eye on wind and weather, guests arrive to be greeted with an icy glass of Refreshing Orange Punch. When the sun's rays grow stronger, they retreat to rockers on the cabin's shady porch to enjoy Parmesan Sesame Sticks and good conversation.

Dorothy concentrated on color, flavor, and ease of preparation when choosing her menu. "When serving food outdoors like this, just about everything has to be done ahead of time," she remarks. Cheese Fondue, served with cherry tomatoes and chunks of ham and turkey, is stirred together at home and then heated in a chafing dish or fondue pot at lakeside. Accompanying dishes are equally convenient to prepare.

A successful brunch is the sum of its side dishes, and Dorothy's add up deliciously. While a Hash Brown Potato Casserole bakes, the salad and vegetable are removed from the refrigerator. The resulting colorful combination is bright with green broccoli spears and red tomato aspic. Dorothy uses a ring mold for the aspic and fills it with her Artichoke-Rice Salad.

Pecan-Topped Coffee Cake and steaming coffee, along with fresh fruit for dipping in sour cream and cinnamon, brown sugar, or coconut complete the menu. The cantaloupe, green grapes, strawberries, and pineapple are prepared well in advance of brunchtime. The coffee cake, made ahead and baked in the morning, is tasty and easy to serve.

Maybe you can use some of the Burns' ideas for a brunch, whether you are serving sailors or your own family.

Refreshing Orange Punch
Parmesan Sesame Sticks
Cheese Fondue
with
Ham, Turkey, and Cherry Tomatoes
Hash Brown Potato Casserole
Marinated Broccoli
Spicy Tomato Aspic
Artichoke-Rice Salad
Pecan-Topped Coffee Cake
Fresh Fruit
Coffee

REFRESHING ORANGE PUNCH

1 (6-ounce) package orange-flavored
  gelatin
1½ cups sugar
2 quarts boiling water
2 quarts orange juice
2 quarts pineapple juice
¼ cup plus 2 tablespoons lemon juice

Dissolve gelatin and sugar in boiling water; cool. Stir in remaining ingredients, and serve over ice. If desired, the punch can be made ahead and frozen; remove from freezer the night before serving. Yield: about 1½ gallons.

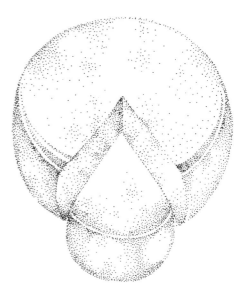

PARMESAN SESAME STICKS

12 slices bread, crusts removed
¼ cup butter or margarine, melted
¼ cup grated Parmesan cheese
2 tablespoons sesame seeds

Cut each slice of bread into 4 sticks, and place on ungreased cookie sheets. Brush with butter; then sprinkle evenly with cheese and sesame seeds. Bake at 350° for 10 to 15 minutes or until golden brown. Yield: 4 dozen.

Marinated Broccoli can be prepared well in advance and chilled until serving time.

MARINATED BROCCOLI

2 bunches fresh broccoli
1½ cups cider vinegar
¼ cup cold water
½ cup vegetable oil
2 tablespoons sugar
1 tablespoon dillseeds
1 teaspoon salt
1 teaspoon pepper
½ teaspoon minced garlic
Ripe olives
Pimiento strips

Trim off large leaves of broccoli and tough ends of lower stalks. Wash broccoli thoroughly, and cut into serving-size spears; arrange spears in a single layer in dish.

Combine next 8 ingredients in a jar; cover tightly, and shake vigorously. Pour over broccoli. Cover and chill at least 12 hours, stirring occasionally.

Before serving, remove broccoli from marinade; garnish with olives and pimiento. Yield: 12 servings.

CHEESE FONDUE

3 (10¾-ounce) cans Cheddar cheese soup, undiluted
3 cups (12 ounces) shredded Cheddar cheese or grated Parmesan cheese
6 green onions, finely chopped
¼ cup plus 2 tablespoons commercial cocktail sauce
⅛ teaspoon hot sauce
3 tablespoons cooked, crumbled bacon

Combine Cheddar cheese soup and shredded cheese in a saucepan or fondue pot. Place over medium heat; cook, stirring occasionally, until cheese melts and the mixture is smooth.

Add onion, cocktail sauce, and hot sauce; cook, stirring often, until thoroughly heated. Sprinkle with bacon. Place over fondue heating unit to keep hot. Serve with cherry tomatoes and chunks of ham and turkey. Yield: 12 servings.

HASH BROWN POTATO CASSEROLE

1 (32-ounce) package frozen hash brown potatoes, thawed
¾ cup butter or margarine, melted
½ cup chopped onion
1 (10¾-ounce) can cream of chicken soup, undiluted
1 (8-ounce) carton commercial sour cream
1 cup (4 ounces) shredded Cheddar cheese
2 cups corn flakes
Lemon twist (optional)
Parsley sprigs (optional)

Combine potatoes, ½ cup butter, onion, soup, sour cream, and cheese; stir well. Spoon into a greased 2½-quart casserole.

Crush cereal, and stir in remaining butter. Sprinkle over potato mixture. Bake at 350° for 50 minutes. Garnish with a lemon twist and parsley, if desired. Yield: 10 to 12 servings.

SPICY TOMATO ASPIC

3 packages unflavored gelatin
5½ cups tomato juice
⅓ cup lemon juice
1 tablespoon grated onion
1 clove garlic, minced
1 teaspoon dillweed or dillseeds
½ teaspoon dried whole basil
½ teaspoon dried whole oregano
1 small bay leaf, crushed
Leaf lettuce
Parsley
Lemon twists

Soften gelatin in ½ cup tomato juice; set aside.

Combine remaining tomato juice and next 7 ingredients in a large saucepan; bring to a boil. Reduce heat, and simmer 10 minutes. Strain tomato juice mixture; add gelatin, stirring until dissolved. Pour into a lightly oiled 5½-cup ring mold, and chill until set.

Unmold on a lettuce-lined serving plate, and garnish with parsley and lemon twists. Yield: 12 servings.

Note: Center of aspic may be filled with Artichoke-Rice Salad, if desired.

ARTICHOKE-RICE SALAD

1 (8-ounce) package chicken-flavored
  vermicelli-rice mix
1 (6¼-ounce) package fried rice mix with
  almonds
½ cup chopped green pepper
½ cup chopped green onion
½ cup chopped pimiento-stuffed olives
2 (6-ounce) jars marinated artichoke
  hearts, drained and sliced
½ cup mayonnaise
1 teaspoon curry powder

Prepare rice mixes according to package directions, omitting margarine. Cool.

Combine rice and remaining ingredients, tossing lightly; chill. Yield: 12 servings.

Note: The salad may be spooned into the center of Spicy Tomato Aspic, if desired.

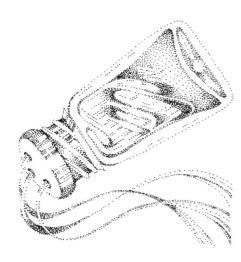

PECAN-TOPPED COFFEE CAKE

⅔ cup butter or margarine
1 cup sugar
½ cup firmly packed brown sugar
2 eggs
1 teaspoon vanilla extract
2 cups all-purpose flour
1 teaspoon baking powder
1 teaspoon soda
½ teaspoon salt
1 teaspoon ground cinnamon
1 cup buttermilk
1 cup coarsely chopped pecans
½ cup firmly packed brown sugar
½ teaspoon ground cinnamon

Cream butter; gradually add 1 cup sugar and ½ cup brown sugar, beating well. Add eggs, one at a time, beating well after each addition. Stir in vanilla.

Combine flour, baking powder, soda, salt, and 1 teaspoon cinnamon. Add to creamed mixture alternately with buttermilk, beginning and ending with flour mixture; mix well after each addition.

Pour batter into a greased and floured 13- x 9- x 2-inch baking pan. Combine pecans, ½ cup brown sugar, and ½ teaspoon cinnamon; stir well, and sprinkle over batter.

Cover and chill 8 to 10 hours or overnight. Uncover batter, and let come to room temperature. Bake at 350° for 35 minutes or until wooden pick inserted in center comes out clean. Yield: 12 to 15 servings.

Lively Ideas For Pancakes And Waffles

Pancakes, waffles, and French toast get a lively new taste and party-pretty good looks with our special sauces and fillings. And no one but you will know that some of the recipes have shortcuts like commercial pancake and biscuit mixes.

For starters, make pancakes from a commercial mix. Roll them around a sweet apricot filling (as you would crêpes), sprinkle with powdered sugar, top with whipped cream and pecans, and you've got Apricot Delight.

Chopped walnuts added to waffle batter make Crunchy Brunch Waffles. Instead of serving them with plain maple syrup, warm the syrup and add fresh strawberries and bananas. Spoon over the steaming-hot waffles, and top with a dollop of sour cream.

Our French toast is a breeze because you make it the night before. Soak slices of French bread overnight in a seasoned egg and milk mixture; the slices are ready to cook the next morning. Serve them with luscious Orange Butter while they're hot.

CRUNCHY BRUNCH WAFFLES

2 cups all-purpose flour
1½ teaspoons baking powder
1 teaspoon ground ginger
½ teaspoon soda
¼ teaspoon salt
2 eggs
1½ cups buttermilk
½ cup maple syrup
¼ cup plus 2 tablespoons shortening,
  melted
½ to ¾ cup finely chopped walnuts
Strawberry-Banana Sauce
½ to ¾ cup commercial sour cream

Combine first 5 ingredients; stir well. Beat eggs at medium speed of an electric mixer until thick and lemon colored. Add flour mixture, buttermilk, syrup, and shortening; beat until smooth.

Pour about 1¼ cups batter into a hot, lightly oiled waffle iron. Quickly sprinkle about 3 tablespoons walnuts over batter. Cook about 5 minutes or until done. Repeat process until all batter is used.

Spoon Strawberry-Banana Sauce over each waffle and top with a dollop of sour cream. Yield: 12 (4-inch) waffles.

Strawberry-Banana Sauce:

1½ cups maple syrup
1 pint strawberries, hulled and halved
1 cup sliced bananas

Combine all ingredients in a heavy saucepan. Cook over medium-high heat 10 minutes, stirring occasionally. Serve hot. Yield: about 3½ cups.

Deborah Jo Grams,
Lake Worth, Florida.

Tip: Remember that deep green, bright yellow, or orange fruit and vegetables are good sources of vitamin A. Good sources of vitamin C are citrus fruit, deep green vegetables, and potatoes.

FRENCH TOAST WITH ORANGE BUTTER

12 (1-inch-thick) slices French bread
6 eggs
4 cups milk
½ teaspoon salt
½ teaspoon ground nutmeg
½ teaspoon vanilla extract
2 tablespoons butter or margarine, divided
Orange Butter

Place bread in a 13- x 9- x 2-inch pan. Combine eggs, milk, salt, nutmeg, and vanilla; beat well. Pour mixture over bread; cover and refrigerate overnight.

Melt 1 tablespoon butter in an electric skillet at 300°; remove 6 slices of bread from dish, and cook in butter 10 to 12 minutes on each side or until cooked through. Repeat procedure with remaining butter and bread. Serve hot with Orange Butter. Yield: 6 servings.

Orange Butter:

1 cup butter, softened
½ cup orange juice
½ cup powdered sugar

Cream butter until light and fluffy. Add orange juice and powdered sugar; beat until thoroughly blended. Yield: about 2 cups.   *Ruth Carr, Lyndon, Kentucky.*

APRICOT DELIGHT

1 (17-ounce) can apricot halves
1½ tablespoons butter
2 tablespoons all-purpose flour
3 tablespoons sugar
1 tablespoon lemon juice
¼ cup coarsely chopped pecans
½ cup whipping cream
1 tablespoon powdered sugar
1 cup commercial pancake mix
¼ cup powdered sugar
Chopped pecans (optional)

Drain apricots, reserving 1 cup liquid. Cut apricots into fourths.

Melt butter in a heavy saucepan over low heat; add flour, stirring until smooth. Cook 1 minute, stirring constantly. Gradually add reserved apricot juice, 3 tablespoons sugar, and lemon

juice. Cook over medium heat, stirring constantly, until thickened and bubbly. Stir in apricots and ¼ cup pecans.

Beat whipping cream until foamy; gradually add 1 tablespoon powdered sugar, beating until soft peaks form. Chill well.

Prepare pancake batter according to package directions, using 1 cup mix. For each pancake, pour about ⅓ cup batter onto a hot, lightly greased griddle or skillet. When pancakes have a bubbly surface and slightly dry edges, turn to cook the other side.

Spoon ¼ cup apricot mixture down center of each pancake. Roll up, and place seam side down on a warm serving platter or individual plates. Pour remaining apricot sauce over pancakes. Sprinkle with ¼ cup powdered sugar. Top pancakes with a dollop of whipped cream; sprinkle with chopped pecans, if desired. Yield: 4 servings.
Nancy Cochrane, Nashville, Tennessee.

PANCAKES WITH FRUIT TOPPING

2 cups biscuit mix
1 egg
1⅓ cups milk
1 cup 100% natural cereal, crushed
Fruit Topping

Combine biscuit mix, egg, and milk; beat until smooth. Stir in cereal.

For each pancake, pour about ¼ cup batter onto a lightly greased hot griddle or skillet. When pancakes have a bubbly surface and slightly dry edges, turn to cook other side. Serve with Fruit Topping. Yield: 14 (4-inch) pancakes.

Fruit Topping:

1 (16-ounce) can sliced peaches
½ cup apricot preserves
⅓ cup maraschino cherries, cut in half
¼ cup butter
2 teaspoons lemon juice
½ teaspoon vanilla extract
3 medium bananas, cut into ¼-inch slices

Drain peaches, reserving ¼ cup syrup.

Combine peaches, reserved syrup, and remaining ingredients except the

bananas in a medium saucepan. Bring mixture to a boil, stirring occasionally; reduce heat, and add bananas. Simmer until bananas are heated through. Serve hot. Yield: 3¾ cups.   *Beth Oliver, Camilla, Georgia.*

Citrus Makes A Better Jam

Marmalade is great for more than just spreading on breakfast toast. It can also be used as fillings for baked goods and as toppings for meat and vegetables.

In making marmalade, the rind is tenderized in boiling water. The remaining ingredients are then added and the mixture cooked to the proper consistency. Commercial thickening agents are never added to marmalade, since citrus rind is unusually rich in pectin.

ORANGE MARMALADE

1 quart orange sections
1 quart thinly sliced orange rind
1 cup thinly sliced lemon
1½ quarts water
About 5¾ cups sugar

Combine orange sections, orange rind, lemon slices, and water in a large heavy Dutch oven. Bring to a boil; reduce heat, and simmer 5 minutes. Cover and let stand 12 to 18 hours in a cool place.

Uncover; bring to a boil, and boil rapidly about 40 minutes. Measure amount of fruit and liquid; add 1 cup sugar per 1 cup fruit and liquid. Stir well; bring to a boil. Boil rapidly 10 to 15 minutes or until mixture registers 220° on a candy thermometer; stir mixture frequently.

Quickly pour mixture into hot sterilized jars, leaving ¼-inch headspace; cover at once with metal lids, screwing bands tight. Process in boiling-water bath for 10 minutes. Yield: 6 half-pints.

MIXED CITRUS MARMALADE

4½ quarts water
1½ cups thinly sliced grapefruit rind
½ cup thinly sliced orange rind
1½ cups chopped grapefruit sections
¾ cup chopped orange sections
½ cup thinly sliced lemon
About 2¼ cups sugar

Combine 1½ quarts water and grapefruit and orange rind in a large Dutch oven; bring to a boil. Boil, uncovered, 5 minutes; drain. Repeat procedure.

Combine 1½ quarts water, rind, chopped fruit, and lemon slices; bring to a boil, and boil 5 minutes. Cover and let stand 12 to 18 hours in a cool place.

Uncover; bring mixture to a boil, and boil 35 to 40 minutes or until rind is tender. Measure amount of fruit and liquid; add 1 cup sugar per 1 cup fruit and liquid. Stir well; bring mixture to a boil, and boil until mixture registers 220° on a candy thermometer, stirring frequently.

Pour marmalade into hot sterilized jars, leaving ¼-inch headspace; cover at once with metal lids, and screw metal bands tight. Process in boiling-water bath for 10 minutes. Yield: about 3 half-pints.

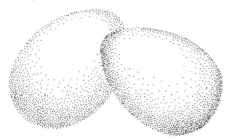

Stir The Eggs Into A Special Main Dish

For many Southerners, the morning can't begin without eggs. Happily that doesn't mean that eggs have to be served in the usual ways. These recipes prove that, and deliciously, with main dishes that are just right for a festive brunch or special breakfast.

Quiche is always a nice choice for a midmorning meal, and ours is rich with eggs and flavored with bacon, spinach, and lots of Swiss cheese. Royal Brunch Crêpes is an appealing alternative. Light and delicate from the eggs stirred into the batter, the crêpes are filled with a broccoli-tuna mixture and baked in a lightly seasoned cheese sauce.

Omelet lovers will delight in one that is wrapped around a creamy sausage-mushroom filling, while those who opt for ham and eggs can enjoy them with a cheesy sauce. For hefty appetites, we suggest the delicious Farmer's Breakfast.

OMELET WITH SAUSAGE FILLING

½ cup butter or margarine, divided
1 cup sliced fresh mushrooms
½ pound bulk pork sausage
2 tablespoons all-purpose flour
½ cup milk
¼ teaspoon salt
Pepper
1 (8-ounce) carton commercial sour cream
8 eggs
¼ cup cold water

Melt 2 tablespoons butter in a skillet. Add mushrooms; sauté until tender.

Crumble sausage in a skillet; cook until browned, stirring occasionally. Drain well, and set aside.

Melt 2 tablespoons butter in a heavy saucepan over low heat; add flour, stirring until smooth. Cook 1 minute, stirring constantly. Gradually add milk; cook over medium heat, stirring constantly, until thickened and bubbly. Stir in mushrooms, sausage, salt, dash of pepper, and sour cream.

Combine eggs, water, and dash of pepper; beat well.

For each omelet, melt 1 tablespoon butter in a 10-inch skillet until just hot enough to sizzle a drop of water; pour in one-fourth of egg mixture. As mixture starts to cook, gently lift edges of omelet and tilt pan to allow uncooked portion to flow underneath.

When mixture is set and no longer flows freely, spoon on one-fourth of mushroom sauce. Fold omelet in half, and place on a warm platter. Repeat procedure with remaining ingredients. Yield: 4 servings. *Charlotte Farmer, Richmond, Virginia.*

HAM AND EGGS ON TOAST WITH CHEESE SAUCE

6 thin slices cooked ham
3 English muffins, split and toasted
2 tablespoons vinegar
1 teaspoon salt
6 eggs
Cheese sauce (recipe follows)
1½ teaspoons paprika
Fresh parsley sprigs (optional)

Fold ham slices in half, and place on muffin halves.

Fill a skillet with 2 to 3 inches of water; add vinegar and salt. Bring water to a boil. Break eggs, one at a time, into a saucer; carefully slip each egg into skillet. Reduce heat; simmer eggs over low heat about 3 to 5 minutes or until desired degree of doneness.

Place each egg on a muffin half, and top with cheese sauce. Sprinkle with paprika; garnish with parsley, if desired. Yield: 3 servings.

Cheese Sauce:

1 tablespoon plus 1½ teaspoons butter or margarine
1 tablespoon plus 1½ teaspoons all-purpose flour
1 cup milk
¼ cup whipping cream
1 cup (4 ounces) shredded Cheddar cheese
¼ teaspoon ground nutmeg
⅛ teaspoon salt
⅛ teaspoon red pepper
⅛ teaspoon pepper

Melt butter in a heavy saucepan over low heat; add flour, stirring until smooth. Cook 1 minute, stirring constantly. Gradually add milk and whipping cream; cook over medium heat, stirring constantly, until thickened and bubbly. Stir in remaining ingredients. Cook just until cheese melts, stirring constantly. Yield: about 1⅔ cups.
Mrs. Edward H. Blythe, Sr., Franklin, Virginia.

Tip: Refrigerate cheese in its original wrap until opened. After opening, rewrap tightly in plastic wrap, plastic bags, or aluminum foil, or place in airtight containers.

ROYAL BRUNCH CREPES

4 eggs
¼ teaspoon salt
2 cups all-purpose flour
2¼ cups milk
¼ cup butter or margarine, melted
Broccoli Filling
Cheese sauce (recipe follows)
Fresh parsley sprigs (optional)

Combine eggs and salt, beating well. Add flour alternately with milk, beginning and ending with flour; mix well after each addition. Add ¼ cup melted butter; beat well. Refrigerate batter 1 hour (this allows flour particles to swell and soften so the crêpes are light in texture).

Brush the bottom of an 8-inch crêpe pan with melted butter; place the pan over medium heat until butter is just hot, not smoking.

Pour about 3 tablespoons batter into pan; quickly tilt pan in all directions so batter covers the pan in a thin film. Cook about 1 minute.

Lift edge of crêpe to test for doneness. Crêpe is ready for flipping when it can be shaken loose from pan. Flip crêpe, and cook about 30 seconds on other side (this side is rarely more than spotty brown).

Stack crêpes between layers of waxed paper to prevent sticking. Set aside 18 crêpes; freeze the remaining crêpes for other uses.

Spoon about 2 tablespoons Broccoli Filling onto center of each crêpe. Roll up crêpes and place, seam side down, in 2 lightly greased 9-inch baking dishes; spoon on cheese sauce. Bake at 350° for 15 to 20 minutes or until bubbly. Garnish with parsley, if desired. Serve immediately. Yield: 9 servings.

Broccoli Filling:

1 (10-ounce) package frozen chopped broccoli
2 tablespoons butter or margarine
1 medium onion, chopped
1 (7-ounce) can tuna, drained and flaked
1 (10¾-ounce) can cream of mushroom soup, undiluted
¼ teaspoon salt
¼ teaspoon pepper

Cook broccoli according to package directions; drain.

Melt butter in a large skillet; add onion, and sauté until tender. Stir in broccoli, tuna, soup, salt, and pepper; heat thoroughly. Yield: about 2⅓ cups.

Cheese Sauce:

2 tablespoons butter or margarine
2 tablespoons all-purpose flour
1 cup milk
1 cup (4 ounces) shredded Cheddar cheese
¼ teaspoon Dijon mustard
¼ teaspoon salt
1 (4-ounce) jar diced pimiento, drained

Melt butter in a heavy saucepan over low heat; add flour, stirring until smooth. Cook 1 minute, stirring constantly. Gradually add milk; cook over medium heat, stirring constantly, until thickened and bubbly. Add cheese, mustard, and salt, stirring until cheese melts. Stir in pimiento. Yield: about 1¼ cups.
Marylou Coffin,
Albuquerque, New Mexico.

SPINACH QUICHE

Pastry for 9-inch quiche dish
½ pound fresh spinach, torn
1 tablespoon butter or margarine
1 medium onion, chopped
6 slices bacon, cooked and crumbled
1 cup (4 ounces) shredded Swiss cheese
4 eggs
2 cups half-and-half or whipping cream
½ teaspoon salt
¼ teaspoon white pepper
Dash of ground nutmeg

Line a 9-inch quiche dish with pastry; trim away all but about ½ inch around edges. Fold under edges of pastry to form a standing rim; then flute. Bake at 400° for 3 minutes; remove from oven, and gently prick with a fork. Bake 5 additional minutes. Cool on rack.

Cook spinach 8 to 10 minutes or until tender in a small amount of salted water. Drain well, and squeeze spinach to remove excess liquid. Set aside.

Melt butter in a skillet; add onion, and sauté until barely tender. Set aside.

Sprinkle bacon and cheese in pastry shell; top with spinach. Beat eggs until foamy; add half-and-half, salt, pepper, nutmeg, and onion. Mix well, and pour into pastry shell.

Bake at 350° for 1 hour or until a knife inserted about an inch from center comes out clean. Let stand 10 minutes before serving. Yield: one 9-inch quiche.
Alice-Marie Darnell,
Marietta, Georgia.

FARMER'S BREAKFAST

6 slices bacon, cut into 2-inch pieces
1 small green pepper, cut into 1-inch strips
2 tablespoons finely chopped onion
3 large potatoes, cooked, peeled, and cubed
½ cup (2 ounces) shredded sharp Cheddar cheese
6 eggs
Salt and pepper

Fry bacon in a medium skillet over low heat until crisp; remove bacon, reserving 3 tablespoons drippings in skillet. Set bacon aside to drain.

Add green pepper, onion, and potatoes to skillet; cook over medium heat for about 5 minutes or until the potatoes are browned.

Sprinkle cheese over potatoes, and stir until cheese melts. Break eggs into skillet; cook over low heat, stirring gently, until done. Season to taste with salt and pepper. Sprinkle with bacon, and serve immediately. Yield: 6 servings.
Mrs. Greg Robertson,
Durham, North Carolina.

Right: *Whether or not you're served breakfast in bed, we think you'll agree that Apricot Delight (page 42) is an extra-special way to start the morning.*

Above left: *Fresh fruits dipped in sour cream and rolled in cinnamon, brown sugar, or coconut complete a festive brunch that also includes Cheese Fondue and Hash Brown Potato Casserole. Menu begins on page 39.*

Above right: *The filling for this Spinach Quiche (page 44) is rich with eggs and enhanced with bacon and Swiss cheese.*

Right: *Start your morning off with an eye-opening beverage. Clockwise: Champagne Blossom Punch, New Orleans Milk Punch, or Tropical Smoothie (recipes on page 50).*

What's Breakfast Without Grits?

To a Southerner, grits are as necessary for a good breakfast as bacon and eggs. Generations of Southerners have included steaming-hot grits, topped with butter, as a part of their daily diet.

Over the years, imaginative cooks have devised some pleasant variations of "plain" grits. Sarah Countryman of Monroeville, Alabama, created Nassau Grits, a colorful blend of bacon, green peppers, tomatoes, and grits; it's a good choice for a brunch menu.

Linda Sutton, of Winston-Salem, North Carolina, brightens the flavor of grits by adding a little orange rind and juice, plenty of eggs, and some brown sugar. Linda tells us this recipe for Orange Grits once won her first place in a grits-cooking contest.

GARLIC GRITS CASSEROLE

½ cup uncooked quick-cooking grits
1 (6-ounce) roll garlic cheese, cubed
¼ cup melted margarine
2 eggs, slightly beaten
1 cup milk

Cook grits according to package directions. Add cheese and margarine, stirring until cheese melts. Combine eggs and milk; stir into grits. Spoon into a lightly greased 1 quart casserole. Bake at 350° for 45 minutes or until golden brown and set. Yield: 4 servings.
Susan R. Smith,
Martinez, Georgia.

ORANGE GRITS

12 slices bacon
3 cups water
1 teaspoon salt
1 cup uncooked quick-cooking grits
¼ cup butter or margarine
1 teaspoon grated orange rind
1 cup orange juice
4 eggs, slightly beaten
2 tablespoons brown sugar

Cook bacon until crisp. Drain and crumble; set aside.

Bring water and salt to a boil; add grits. Cook over medium heat for 3 minutes, stirring constantly. Remove from heat; add butter, orange rind, orange juice, and eggs, mixing well.

Pour mixture into a greased 1½-quart baking dish. Sprinkle with brown sugar. Bake at 350° for 45 minutes or until knife inserted in center comes out clean. Top casserole with crumbled bacon. Yield: 6 to 8 servings.
Linda H. Sutton,
Winston-Salem, North Carolina.

NASSAU GRITS

8 slices bacon
1 medium onion, chopped
2 small green peppers, finely chopped
1 (16-ounce) can tomatoes, undrained and chopped
¼ teaspoon sugar
6 cups water
1 teaspoon salt
1½ cups uncooked regular grits

Cook bacon slices in skillet until crisp. Drain bacon; crumble and set aside. Pour off drippings, reserving 2 tablespoons in skillet.

Sauté onion and green pepper in drippings; stir in tomatoes and sugar. Bring to a boil; reduce heat and simmer 30 minutes, stirring occasionally.

Bring water and salt to a boil; add grits. Cook 10 to 20 minutes, stirring frequently, until grits are thickened. Remove from heat; stir in tomato mixture. Spoon into serving dish; sprinkle bacon on top. Yield: 8 servings.
Sarah Hestle Countryman,
Monroeville, Alabama.

GRUYERE CHEESE GRITS

1 quart milk
½ cup butter or margarine, divided
1½ cups (6 ounces) shredded Gruyère cheese
1 cup uncooked regular grits
1 teaspoon salt
⅛ teaspoon pepper
⅓ cup grated Parmesan cheese

Place milk in a large heavy saucepan; bring to a boil. Add ¼ cup butter and Gruyère cheese; stir until cheese melts. Slowly add grits; boil until thick, stirring constantly. Stir in salt and pepper.

Over very low heat, beat mixture with an electric mixer on low speed for 5 minutes. Remove from heat; pour mixture into a lightly greased 8-inch square pan. Melt remaining butter; add Parmesan cheese, mixing well. Spread over top of grits mixture. Bake at 400° for 30 minutes. Yield: 8 to 10 servings.
Mrs. William A. Caldwell,
Mesa, Arizona.

Fresh-As-The-Morning Side Dishes

When planning a brunch, choose fruit and vegetable side dishes that are equal to the occasion. We suggest Tomato Cheese Puffs, tomato shells baked with a cheesy soufflé-like filling. Fruit in White Wine and Brandied Peaches With Mincemeat offer the luxury of advance preparation. And don't overlook the hash browns. They're always welcome.

BRANDIED PEACHES WITH MINCEMEAT

1 (29-ounce) can peach halves
1 (3-inch) cinnamon stick
6 whole cloves
2 tablespoons brandy
¾ to 1 cup prepared mincemeat

Drain peaches, reserving syrup. Combine syrup, cinnamon stick, and cloves in a small saucepan; bring to a boil. Reduce heat, and simmer 5 minutes. Remove from heat, and stir in brandy. Pour brandy mixture over peaches, and chill well.

Arrange peach halves, cut side up, in a serving dish; spoon mincemeat into center of each. Yield: 6 to 8 servings.
Evelyn P. Martens,
Richmond, Virginia.

Morning menus boast color and flavor with Fruit in White Wine, Hash Brown Potatoes, and Tomato Cheese Puffs.

FRUIT IN WHITE WINE

Ascorbic-citric powder
3 pears, sliced
2 apples, sliced
2 bananas, sliced
1 (16-ounce) can sliced peaches, drained
1 pint strawberries, sliced
About 1 tablespoon sugar
¾ cup Sauterne or other white wine
2 tablespoons flaked coconut

Prepare an ascorbic-citric solution according to manufacturer's directions. Toss pears, apples, and bananas separately in prepared solution; drain fruit.

Layer fruit (in order listed) in a 2-quart serving bowl, sprinkling each layer lightly with sugar. Pour wine over fruit, and sprinkle with coconut. Refrigerate for at least 2 hours before serving. Yield: 10 to 12 servings.

Mrs. Travis M. Bedsole, Jr.,
Mobile, Alabama.

HASH BROWN POTATOES

¼ cup bacon drippings
2 tablespoons butter or margarine
4 cups diced cooked potatoes
⅔ cup minced onion
2 tablespoons minced fresh parsley
2 cloves garlic, minced
Salt and pepper to taste

Melt bacon drippings and butter in a 9-inch skillet. Add remaining ingredients, stirring gently until coated. Cook mixture, uncovered, turning occasionally until browned on all sides (about 20 minutes). Yield: 4 servings.

Ella Stivers,
Abilene, Texas.

TOMATO CHEESE PUFFS

6 large tomatoes
½ teaspoon salt
1 cup milk
1 cup soft breadcrumbs
1 cup (4 ounces) shredded Cheddar cheese
1 tablespoon butter or margarine
3 eggs, separated

Cut off top of each tomato; scoop out pulp, leaving shells intact. (Save pulp for use in other recipes.) Sprinkle cavity of each tomato with salt; invert on paper towels to drain.

Combine milk, breadcrumbs, cheese, and butter in a heavy saucepan; cook over medium heat, stirring constantly, until cheese melts and mixture is thoroughly heated.

Beat egg yolks until thick and lemon colored. Gradually stir about one-fourth of hot mixture into yolks; add to remaining hot mixture, stirring constantly.

Beat egg whites until stiff peaks form; fold into yolk mixture. Spoon into tomato shells, and place in a 12- x 8- x 2-inch baking dish. Bake at 350° for 35 to 40 minutes or until puffed and lightly browned. Serve puffs immediately. Yield: 6 servings.

Marie Webb,
Roanoke, Virginia.

Tip: Brush a small amount of oil on grater before shredding cheese for easier cleaning.

Take A Healthy Look At Breakfast

Breakfast is the most important meal of the day. It doesn't have to be elaborate, but if it's high in nutritional value, it will get your day off to a healthy start.

If the breakfast order at your house is for cereal and milk, serve a homemade granola cereal. Easy Granola combines oats, wheat germ, coconut, sunflower kernels, pecans, and sesame seeds, toasted to a golden brown and mixed with raisins and dates.

A steaming-hot bowl of Breakfast Oatmeal, Swiss Style, flavored with the old-fashioned sweetness of honey and fruit, is very satisfying and will stay with you all morning. It is topped with wheat germ and toasted almonds.

Slice into Pumpkin-Oatmeal Loaf and you'll find a nutritional blend of oats, dates, raisins, and pecans. And for breakfast on the run, there's Fruit and Nut Granola Bars. They also make a great after-school snack.

FRUIT AND NUT GRANOLA BARS

½ cup butter or margarine
½ cup light corn syrup
1 cup miniature marshmallows
2 cups 100% natural cereal
1 cup salted peanuts
½ cup dried apricots or dates, coarsely
    chopped
½ cup raisins
1 cup powdered sugar
1 tablespoon butter or margarine,
    softened
2 tablespoons orange juice
½ teaspoon vanilla extract

Combine ½ cup butter, corn syrup, and marshmallows in a large saucepan. Cook over medium heat until butter and marshmallows melt, stirring constantly. Cook 2 minutes longer, stirring constantly. Remove from heat; stir in cereal, peanuts, fruit, and raisins, mixing well. Pour into a well-greased 13- x 9- x 2-inch pan. Chill 1 hour.

Combine powdered sugar, 1 tablespoon butter, orange juice, and vanilla, mixing well. Spread over cereal mixture; chill. To serve, cut into bars; store in refrigerator. Yield: about 2½ dozen.
Susan Settlemyre,
Raleigh, North Carolina.

BREAKFAST OATMEAL, SWISS STYLE

3 cups water
½ (8-ounce) package mixed dried fruit,
    chopped
1 teaspoon salt
1⅓ cups quick-cooking oats, uncooked
2 tablespoons honey
2 tablespoons wheat germ
¼ cup slivered almonds, toasted

Bring water to a boil in a 2-quart saucepan. Stir in fruit and salt; return to a boil. Add oats and honey; cook, stirring frequently, 1 minute. Remove from heat. Cover, and let stand 3 minutes.

Stir oatmeal; spoon into serving bowls. Sprinkle each serving with 1½ teaspoons wheat germ and 1 tablespoon almonds. Serve with milk. Yield: 4 servings.
Mrs. Harvey Kidd,
Hernando, Mississippi.

EASY GRANOLA

7¾ cups regular oats, uncooked
1¼ cups flaked coconut
¾ cup firmly packed brown sugar
1 cup wheat germ
1 cup chopped pecans
½ cup salted sunflower kernels
½ cup sesame seeds
1½ teaspoons salt
¾ cup vegetable oil
⅓ cup water
1½ teaspoons vanilla extract
½ to 1 cup raisins
½ to 1 cup chopped dates

Combine first 8 ingredients in a large mixing bowl; set aside.

Combine oil, water, and vanilla; stir well, and pour over oat mixture. Toss gently to coat; place mixture in two 15- x 10- x 1-inch jellyroll pans. Bake at 250° for 35 to 40 minutes, stirring every 10 minutes; cool. Stir in raisins and dates. Store granola in airtight containers. Serve as a cereal with milk. Yield: about 14½ cups. *Mrs. A. C. Frese III,*
Birmingham, Alabama.

WHEAT BRAN BISCUITS

2 cups all-purpose flour
1 tablespoon baking powder
1 teaspoon salt
¼ cup unprocessed bran
¼ cup shortening
¾ to 1 cup milk

Combine flour, baking powder, salt, and bran; cut in shortening until mixture resembles coarse meal. Stir in enough milk to form a soft dough. Turn dough out on a lightly floured surface; knead 4 or 5 times.

Roll dough to ⅜-inch thickness; cut with a 2¾-inch biscuit cutter. Place biscuits on a lightly greased baking sheet; bake at 475° for 15 minutes or until lightly browned. Serve warm with butter and honey. Yield: 1 dozen.
Mrs. Thomas R. Smith,
Columbus, Mississippi.

PUMPKIN-OATMEAL LOAF

1 cup quick-cooking oats, uncooked
1 cup finely chopped dates
1 cup chopped raisins
1 cup chopped pecans
1½ cups hot milk
1 teaspoon vanilla extract
2 eggs, beaten
½ cup canned pumpkin
2 cups all-purpose flour
¾ cup sugar
1 tablespoon plus 1 teaspoon baking
    powder
1 teaspoon salt
1 teaspoon ground cinnamon
¼ teaspoon ground nutmeg

Combine oats, dates, raisins, pecans, and milk; mix well, and let stand 10 minutes. Stir in vanilla, eggs, and pumpkin.

Combine remaining ingredients; mix well, and gradually stir into oat mixture. Spoon into a greased and floured 9- x 5- x 3-inch loafpan; bake at 350° about 1 hour and 5 minutes or until a wooden pick inserted in center comes out clean. Cool on a wire rack. Yield: 1 loaf.
Mrs. J. W. Hopkins,
Abilene, Texas.

Tip: To prevent fruit or nuts from sinking to the bottom of bread or cake batter, shake them in a bag with a small amount of flour to dust lightly before adding to batter.

A Pleasant Surprise In A Glass

Whether you're preparing a simple family breakfast or entertaining with a gala brunch, the beverage doesn't have to be predictable. These recipes offer you some refreshing choices.

HOMEMADE TOMATO JUICE

12 medium tomatoes, cored and cut into quarters
½ cup water
⅓ cup coarsely chopped onion
2 stalks celery, coarsely chopped
1 teaspoon minced fresh parsley
1 bay leaf
1 teaspoon salt
¼ teaspoon paprika
¼ teaspoon sugar

Combine first 6 ingredients in a Dutch oven; bring to a boil. Reduce heat; cover and simmer 30 minutes.

Remove from heat, and put vegetable mixture through a food mill or sieve. Stir in salt, paprika, and sugar. Chill thoroughly. Serve over ice, if desired. Yield: about 2 quarts.

Peggy Fowler Revels,
Woodruff, South Carolina.

TROPICAL SMOOTHIE

1 quart orange juice
1 cup fresh strawberries
2 large bananas
6 ice cubes
Whole strawberries

Combine half of first 4 ingredients in container of electric blender; process until frothy. Pour into stemmed glasses, and garnish each with a whole strawberry. Repeat procedure with remaining ingredients. Yield: about 2 quarts.

Mrs. John Rucker,
Louisville, Kentucky.

CHAMPAGNE BLOSSOM PUNCH

⅓ cup frozen orange juice concentrate, thawed and undiluted
⅓ cup frozen lemonade concentrate, thawed and undiluted
1 (25.4-ounce) bottle Riesling, chilled
1 (25.4-ounce) bottle champagne, chilled
Lemon, lime, or orange slices (optional)

Combine first 3 ingredients, stirring well. Gradually add champagne (do not stir). Garnish each serving with a lemon slice, if desired. Yield: about 2 quarts.

Marge Killmon,
Annandale, Virginia.

CREAMY COFFEE PUNCH

2 quarts hot strong coffee
½ cup sugar
2 cups milk
1½ teaspoons vanilla extract
1 quart vanilla ice cream
Whipped cream (optional)

Combine coffee and sugar, stirring until sugar dissolves. Chill thoroughly. Combine coffee mixture, milk, and vanilla; mix well. Add ice cream by scoopfuls, stirring gently. Ladle into serving cups; if desired, top each with whipped cream. Yield: about 3½ quarts.

Kendall Happy,
Dallas, Texas.

NEW ORLEANS MILK PUNCH

1½ cups milk
1½ cups half-and-half
½ cup plus 2 tablespoons white crème de cacao
¼ cup plus 2 tablespoons bourbon
2 tablespoons powdered sugar
2 egg whites
Cracked ice (optional)
Ground cinnamon or nutmeg (optional)

Combine first 6 ingredients in container of electric blender; blend until frothy. If desired, serve over cracked ice and sprinkle with cinnamon. Yield: about 1¼ quarts. *William H. Tilly, Jr.,*
Birmingham, Alabama.

Doughnuts Without Holes

Homemade doughnuts—does the thought bring to mind a complicated process of rolling out the dough and cutting it in the traditional doughnut shape? That's not the case with Dutch Doughnuts. These small, round doughnuts are made by dropping spoonfuls of batter into hot oil and frying.

You won't even miss the doughnut hole when you bite into the raisins and candied orange peel scattered inside.

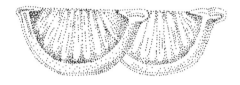

DUTCH DOUGHNUTS

1½ cups milk, scalded
1 envelope plus 1 teaspoon dry yeast
3 cups all-purpose flour
2 tablespoons sugar
1 teaspoon salt
2 tablespoons chopped raisins
2 tablespoons chopped candied orange peel
1½ teaspoons grated lemon rind
2 eggs, beaten
Vegetable oil
Powdered sugar

Cool milk to lukewarm (105° to 115°); add yeast, and let the mixture stand 5 minutes.

Combine flour, sugar, salt, raisins, orange peel, and lemon rind in a large bowl; stir. Add yeast mixture and eggs; stir until dough is smooth. Cover, and let rise in a warm place (85°), free from drafts, until doubled in bulk. Stir dough down.

Pour oil into a skillet to a depth of 1 inch; heat to 375°. Drop dough by tablespoonfuls into hot oil; cook 5 to 7 minutes, turning once, until brown. Drain on paper towels; sprinkle with powdered sugar. Yield: about 2½ dozen.

Pam Snellgrove,
LaGrange, Georgia.

Let Rice Surprise You

That box of rice hiding on the kitchen shelf can be the key to any meal of the day and every course of the meal. White rice is a highly compatible ingredient and can be just as exciting as the wild and brown varieties—yet far more economical.

The Southern rice belt of Arkansas, Texas, Louisiana, and Mississippi is a source of rice itself—and also of tasty rice recipes. From Louisiana comes a classic Creole Jambalaya. This spicy combination of rice, shrimp, sausage, tomatoes, and seasonings just needs a salad and bread to make a complete meal. For lunch, one Mississippi reader suggests a Rice Salad. It's more flavorful when the salad is made the day before serving and refrigerated overnight.

Rice can also be served before the meal as an appetizer. Rice Balls are coated with breadcrumbs, fried, and served hot with spicy Dijon mustard. They're also great as a side dish for brunch.

And for an old-fashioned Southern dessert, there's Creamy Rice Pudding. This version can be served warm or cold with your choice of fruit, toasted almonds, or coconut.

CREOLE JAMBALAYA

1 pound smoked sausage, sliced
1 cup chopped green pepper
1 cup chopped onion
1 clove garlic, crushed
1 tablespoon all-purpose flour
1 (28-ounce) can tomatoes, undrained
2½ cups water
2 tablespoons chopped fresh parsley
2 cups uncooked regular rice
2 tablespoons Worcestershire sauce
2 teaspoons salt
½ teaspoon dried whole thyme
¼ teaspoon red pepper
1½ pounds shrimp, peeled and deveined

Cook sausage until browned in a large Dutch oven. Drain off all but 2 tablespoons pan drippings. Add green pepper, onion, and garlic; cook until vegetables are tender. Add flour, and stir until well blended. Stir in tomatoes, water, and parsley; bring to a boil. Add remaining ingredients except shrimp; return to a boil. Reduce heat, and simmer, covered, 20 minutes. Add shrimp; cover and cook 10 minutes. Yield: 12 servings. *DeLea Lonadier, Montgomery, Louisiana.*

SPANISH RICE

2 cloves garlic, crushed
¼ cup chopped celery
¼ cup vegetable oil
1 (28-ounce) can tomatoes
1 (6-ounce) can tomato paste
1½ cups uncooked regular rice
2 teaspoons salt
1 bay leaf
Dash of red pepper
1½ pounds ground beef
¾ cup chopped green pepper
1 tablespoon chili powder
1 teaspoon sugar
1 (10½-ounce) can beef broth, undiluted

Cook garlic and celery in hot oil in a large skillet until tender.

Drain tomatoes, reserving juice. Add enough hot water to tomato juice to equal 2 cups. Combine tomatoes, tomato juice, tomato paste, rice, salt, bay leaf, and red pepper. Add to garlic and celery mixture; stir well. Bring to a boil. Reduce heat, and simmer, covered, 10 minutes. Remove bay leaf.

Cook ground beef and green pepper until beef is browned; drain. Stir in chili powder, sugar, and beef broth. Combine rice mixture and meat mixture; place in a 13- x 9- x 2-inch baking dish. Bake at 350° for 35 minutes. Yield: 8 to 10 servings. *Mrs. J. W. Riley, Jr., Kingsport, Tennessee.*

RICE SALAD

3 cups chicken broth
1¼ cups uncooked regular rice
1 cup vegetable oil
2 tablespoons vinegar
1 teaspoon salt
⅛ teaspoon pepper
⅛ teaspoon red pepper
1 cup chopped ripe olives
2 hard-cooked eggs, chopped
1½ cups chopped celery
¼ cup chopped dill pickle
1 small onion, minced
1 (2-ounce) jar diced pimiento, drained
1 medium-size green pepper, chopped
½ cup mayonnaise
2 tablespoons prepared mustard

Bring chicken broth to a boil; add rice. Reduce heat, and cook, covered, 25 minutes or until rice is tender and chicken broth is absorbed.

Combine vegetable oil, vinegar, salt, and pepper in a large bowl, mixing well. Stir in rice. Allow mixture to cool. Add remaining ingredients; mix well. Chill overnight. Yield: 10 servings. *June Campbell, Greenville, Mississippi.*

RICE BALLS

4 cups water
2 teaspoons salt
1 cup uncooked regular rice
1 egg, beaten
1 cup (4 ounces) shredded sharp Cheddar cheese
2 eggs
2 tablespoons water
1¼ cups fine dry breadcrumbs
Vegetable oil
Dijon mustard (optional)

Bring 4 cups water and salt to a boil in a Dutch oven; stir in rice. Reduce heat, and cook, covered, about 40 minutes or until water is absorbed. Cool slightly; stir in beaten egg and cheese, mixing well.

Combine 2 eggs and water; beat well. Set aside.

Shape rice mixture into balls 1¼ inches in diameter. Roll balls in breadcrumbs; dip in egg mixture; coat again with breadcrumbs. Deep fry in hot oil until golden brown. Serve with Dijon mustard, if desired. Yield: about 3 dozen. *Aileen Wright, Nashville, Tennessee.*

CREAMY RICE PUDDING

1 quart milk
1 cup uncooked regular rice
½ teaspoon salt
1½ teaspoons vanilla extract
4 egg yolks, beaten
½ cup sugar
½ cup half-and-half
1 teaspoon ground cinnamon

Combine first 4 ingredients in a medium saucepan. Cover and cook over very low heat about 30 minutes or until rice is tender and milk is absorbed. Stir mixture occasionally.

Combine remaining ingredients in a small bowl. Gradually stir about one-fourth of hot rice mixture into yolk mixture; add yolk mixture to remaining rice mixture. Cook over low heat, stirring constantly, until mixture comes to a boil; remove from heat. Serve warm or cold with fruit, toasted almonds, or coconut. Yield: 10 to 12 servings. *Mary Dishon, Stanford, Kentucky.*

Tip: If a recipe calls for yolks only, use leftover whites to make meringue shells or meringue topping.

Cornish Hens, Stuffed And Baked To Perfection

When the occasion calls for a sophisticated entrée, nothing fills the bill like a beautifully garnished platter of baked Cornish hens. Here are two delicious versions that both feature a rich, moist stuffing of rice and mushrooms. Elegant Cornish Hens are basted with a seasoned soy sauce mixture during baking, while Cornish Hens Flambé are flamed in brandy for their final touch.

A note on how to flambé the hens. To produce enough fumes to ignite, the brandy must be heated quickly. Warm the brandy, ignite it, and pour the flaming liquid evenly over the food.

An alternate method is to warm the spirit, pour it over the food, and then ignite. But in testing this method, we found that the alcohol dispersed and diluted when poured over the food, making it more difficult to ignite.

ELEGANT CORNISH HENS

1 (6-ounce) package long grain and wild rice mix
1 chicken bouillon cube
4 (1- to 1½-pound) Cornish hens
½ cup chopped onion
½ cup chopped celery
1 tablespoon butter or margarine, melted
¼ pound fresh mushrooms, sliced
1 teaspoon grated lemon rind
1 teaspoon poultry seasoning
¼ cup vegetable oil
¼ cup lemon juice
2 tablespoons soy sauce
1 teaspoon paprika
½ teaspoon garlic salt
Dash of white pepper
Lemon slices (optional)
Parsley (optional)

Cook rice according to package directions, adding bouillon cube with rice and seasoning envelope.

Remove giblets from hens; reserve for another use. Rinse hens with cold water, and pat dry.

Sauté onion and celery in butter; add mushrooms, and cook 1 to 2 minutes. Combine rice, vegetables, lemon rind, and poultry seasoning, stirring well.

Stuff hens lightly with the rice mixture. Close cavities, and secure with wooden picks; truss.

Combine next 6 ingredients, stirring well. Brush hens with soy sauce mixture, and place breast side up in 13- x 9- x 2-inch baking pan. Bake at 325° for 1¼ to 1½ hours, depending on size of hens; baste often with soy sauce mixture. Garnish with lemon slices and parsley, if desired. Yield: 4 servings.

Mrs. Leo Cole,
Lake Charles, Louisiana.

CORNISH HENS FLAMBE

1 large onion, minced
2 tablespoons butter or margarine, melted
2 cups mushrooms, sliced
½ cup diced cooked ham
1½ cups cooked wild rice
2 to 4 tablespoons brandy
¼ teaspoon dried whole marjoram
¼ teaspoon dried whole thyme
6 (1- to 1½-pound) Cornish hens
Salt
Coarsely ground black pepper
2 to 4 tablespoons dry sherry
¼ cup chicken broth
¼ cup brandy

Sauté onion in butter until tender. Add mushrooms and ham; cook 3 to 5 minutes or until mushrooms are tender. Combine mushroom mixture, rice, 2 to 4 tablespoons brandy, marjoram, and thyme.

Remove giblets from hens; reserve for another use. Rinse hens with cold water, and pat dry; sprinkle with salt and pepper. Stuff hens lightly with rice mixture. Close cavities, and secure with wooden picks; truss. Place hens breast side up in a 15- x 10- x 1-inch jellyroll pan. Bake hens at 350° for 1¼ to 1½ hours, depending on size of hens.

Place hens on serving platter. Combine sherry and chicken broth; brush over hens. Heat ¼ cup brandy in a small saucepan over medium heat. (Do not boil.) Ignite with a long match, and pour over hens. After flames die down, serve immediately. Yield: 6 servings.

Mrs. H. S. Wright,
Leesville, South Carolina.

Tip: Immediately before using fresh mushrooms, wipe them clean or quickly rinse them in a colander; never immerse mushrooms in water.

Spinach Goes Rich And Cheesy

Spinach remains one of the most popular vegetables around because it can be prepared in so many delicious ways. The bonus is that it is low in calories and high in vitamins and iron. Here fresh spinach is the basis for some rich and cheesy dishes—a puffy soufflé, casserole, and even a filling for crêpes.

When buying spinach, remember that 1 pound of fresh spinach yields about 1½ cups cooked. Select spinach that has large, crisp leaves that are dark green; avoid wilted or crushed greens. If time is a factor, substitute one 10-ounce package frozen spinach for 1 pound fresh.

SPINACH-RICOTTA CREPES

1⅓ cups all-purpose flour
¾ teaspoon salt
4 eggs, beaten
2 tablespoons vegetable oil
1⅓ cups milk
Spinach-Ricotta Filling
1 (15-ounce) can herb-flavored tomato sauce
1 cup (4 ounces) shredded mozzarella cheese

Combine flour, salt, and eggs; mix well. Blend in oil and milk, beating until smooth. Refrigerate at least 2 hours. (This allows flour particles to swell and soften so crêpes are light in texture.)

Brush the bottom of an 8-inch crêpe pan or heavy skillet with vegetable oil; place over medium heat until just hot, not smoking.

Pour 3 tablespoons batter in pan; quickly tilt pan in all directions so batter covers pan in a thin film. Cook crêpe about 1 minute.

Lift edge of crêpe to test for doneness. Crêpe is ready for flipping when it can be shaken loose from pan. Flip crêpe, and cook about 30 seconds on other side. (This side is rarely more than spotty brown and is the side on which the filling should be placed.)

Remove crêpe from pan, and repeat procedure until all batter is used.

Place ⅓ cup Spinach-Ricotta Filling off-center on each crêpe. Roll crêpe over filling. Place, seam side down, in a 13- x 9- x 2-inch baking dish. Cover with aluminum foil; bake at 375° for 30 minutes. Remove foil; pour tomato

Our Cheesy Spinach Soufflé comes out light and puffy.

sauce over crêpes; sprinkle with shredded cheese. Bake, uncovered, an additional 5 minutes. Yield: 1 dozen.

Note: Crêpes may be made in advance. Stack crêpes between layers of waxed paper, and cover tightly with plastic wrap or aluminum foil; store in refrigerator or freeze until needed.

Spinach-Ricotta Filling:

2 pounds fresh spinach
1 large onion, chopped
1 clove garlic, minced
1 tablespoon vegetable oil
1 (16-ounce) carton ricotta cheese
1 cup (4 ounces) shredded mozzarella
  cheese
½ cup grated Parmesan cheese
3 eggs, beaten
1 tablespoon lemon juice
½ teaspoon salt
½ teaspoon ground nutmeg
¼ teaspoon pepper

Remove stems from spinach; wash leaves thoroughly, and tear into large pieces. Cook spinach in a small amount of boiling water 5 to 10 minutes or until tender. Drain; place on paper towels, and squeeze until barely moist. Finely chop spinach; set aside.

Sauté onion and garlic in hot oil until tender but not brown. Combine onion mixture, spinach, and remaining ingredients; stir well. Yield: enough filling for 1 dozen crêpes. *Gloria Pedersen, Brandon, Mississippi.*

CHEESY SPINACH SOUFFLE

1 pound fresh spinach
¼ cup butter or margarine
1 tablespoon minced onion
¼ cup plus 1 tablespoon all-purpose flour
1 cup milk
1 cup (4 ounces) shredded Cheddar cheese
½ teaspoon salt
⅛ teaspoon pepper
3 eggs, separated
⅛ teaspoon cream of tartar
2 tablespoons grated Parmesan cheese

Remove stems from spinach; wash leaves thoroughly, and tear into large pieces. Cook spinach in a small amount of boiling water 5 to 10 minutes or until tender. Drain; place on paper towels, and squeeze until barely moist.

Lightly butter a 5-cup soufflé dish. Cut a piece of aluminum foil long enough to circle the dish, allowing a 1-inch overlap. Fold foil lengthwise into thirds, and lightly butter one side. Wrap foil around dish, buttered side against the dish, so it extends 3 inches above the rim. Secure foil with string.

Melt butter in a large saucepan; sauté onion in butter until tender. Add flour and cook 1 minute, stirring constantly. Gradually add milk; cook over medium heat, stirring constantly, until thickened and bubbly. Add Cheddar cheese, salt, and pepper; stir until cheese melts. Stir in the spinach.

Beat egg whites (at room temperature) and cream of tartar until stiff peaks form.

Beat yolks until thick and lemon colored; stir into spinach mixture. Fold in egg whites. Spoon into prepared soufflé dish; sprinkle with Parmesan. Bake at 350° for 45 minutes. Remove collar before serving. Yield: 4 to 6 servings.
Sandra Russell, Maitland, Florida.

SPINACH FRITTATA

1 pound fresh spinach
3 tablespoons butter or margarine
½ pound fresh mushrooms, sliced
¼ cup finely chopped onion
8 eggs
½ teaspoon seasoning salt
Dash of pepper
3 tablespoons butter or margarine
⅓ cup grated Parmesan cheese

Remove stems from spinach; wash leaves thoroughly, and tear into large pieces. Cook spinach in a small amount of boiling water 5 to 10 minutes or until tender. Drain; place on paper towels, and squeeze until dry. Finely chop spinach; set aside.

Melt 3 tablespoons butter in a skillet; sauté mushrooms and onion in butter until tender but not brown; drain on paper towels.

Beat eggs slightly; add seasonings, and beat until frothy. Stir spinach and mushroom mixture into eggs.

Melt 3 tablespoons butter in a large ovenproof skillet. Pour egg mixture into skillet; cook over medium-low heat 7 minutes or until eggs are set. Remove from heat; sprinkle with cheese.

Place oven rack about 6 inches from broiler element; broil frittata 2 to 3 minutes. Cut into wedges to serve. Yield: 4 to 6 servings.
Nancy Summers, Altamonte Springs, Florida.

CREAMED SPINACH

1 pound fresh spinach
¼ cup butter or margarine
1 medium onion, chopped
1 clove garlic, crushed
½ cup commercial sour cream
Dash of salt
¼ teaspoon pepper
Pinch of ground nutmeg
Paprika

Remove stems from spinach; wash leaves thoroughly, and tear into large pieces. Cook spinach in a small amount of boiling water 5 to 10 minutes or until tender. Drain; place on paper towels, and squeeze until barely moist.

Melt butter in a large skillet; sauté onion and garlic in butter until tender. Stir in next 4 ingredients. Add the spinach, and cook over low heat until thoroughly heated; sprinkle with paprika. Yield: 4 servings.   *Dorsella Utter,*
Columbia, Missouri.

Cooking Through Texas

Lillian Bertram Marshall recently completed a culinary tour of the South for a cookbook for *Southern Living.* Excerpted here are a few of the best tall stories and most coveted recipes from the Southwest that appear in her book *Cooking Across the South.*

A study of Southern foodways quite logically begins with soups, for in them is found the most infinite variety. And by way of looking at the South's soups in some sort of order, one could well go straight to Texas and commence with chili. Texas occupies a larger chunk of the South than any other state, so if a Texan's story ever seems larger than life, it is only because the rest of us do not understand the principle of sheer bigness. Among the legends, none is more colorful than the story of chili. Chili was part of the life support system in the vastness of Texas untouched by the sea; it could be made any time a beef or venison was slaughtered.

It must be remembered that during the nearly three hundred years of Spanish rule Texans consisted of Mexican, Irish, English, French, Italian, and African immigrants. It was not until the early 1800s that Southerners, most of North European extraction, poured in

from Georgia, Tennessee, Alabama, and the Carolinas. Latecomers to Texas, then, found Mexican chilies there ahead of them, plenty of beef on the hoof, and dried beans (to be eaten alone or with chili) in every trail kit.

While the Indians maintain that they have been making chili for as long as there have been winters and that Texas stole chili from them, historians are fairly certain that "the world's greatest restorative" was first cooked in Texas border towns in the early 1800s. The dish remained somewhat localized until 1893 when "San Antonio Chilly" created a sensation at the Chicago World's Fair.

Will Rogers' reverent term for this native American dish was "a bowl of blessedness." He did not live to see the cheerful madness called "The Annual World Championship Chili Cook-Off," first held in Terlingua, Texas, in 1967. The ingredients at this gathering seem to have gotten out of hand, but spirits soar as contestants gather from everywhere plus England to vie for the championship pot of chili. Nothing is sacred as cooks throw in armadillo meat, tequila, peppers from Sri Lanka—even a handful of "mother earth, to sift out the impurities," as a Shawnee from Oklahoma remarked during the cook-off a few years ago.

There are many ways to make chili, and each method has its wild-eyed adherents. Meat cubed or coarsely ground, with or without beans, and so on. And on. The original San Antonio Chilly laid on the peppers and left out the beans. What chili recipes do have in common is their satisfying, delicious, rib-sticking quality. That is what sustained the weary cowpoke when the weather turned sour and threatened to freeze him to his horse. And no matter what the recipe, or how it laid waste to his taste buds, nothing could have been further from his mind than to express dissatisfaction with the chuck wagon cook's kettle of chili. . . .

TEXAS CHAMPIONSHIP CHILI

2 large onions, chopped
3 cloves garlic, minced
1 jalapeño pepper, finely chopped
1 tablespoon peanut oil
3 pounds boneless chuck roast, finely diced
1 teaspoon cumin seeds
1½ tablespoons whole oregano leaves
1 (1½-ounce) can chili powder
1 (28-ounce) can whole tomatoes, undrained
3½ cups water
1½ teaspoons instant corn masa (optional)
Shredded Cheddar cheese (optional)

Sauté onion, garlic, and jalapeño pepper in oil until tender; set aside. Combine meat, cumin, and oregano in a Dutch oven; cook until the meat is browned. Add onion mixture, chili powder, tomatoes, and water; bring to a boil. Reduce heat and simmer 2 to 3 hours, stirring frequently.

For thicker chili, combine corn masa with small amount of cold water to make a paste; add to chili, stirring constantly. Top with shredded cheese, if desired. Yield: 5 to 7 servings.

We can only surmise how stale and unprofitable eating must have been before the discovery of fire. But once our common ancestor lit the fire under the first barbecue, we entered the era of eating for pleasure as well as for sustenance. The extremes of temperature in the South notwithstanding, it is a rare household these days that does not boast some sort of facility for outdoor meat cookery. And entertaining at barbecues is as firmly entrenched in the South as it is in California. . . .

You can draw more people to a political barbecue in Texas or Kentucky than you could to a public hanging. The late Vice President Alben W. Barkley of Kentucky probably delivered more orations with blistered lips than any other political figure in history, with the possible exception of the late President Lyndon B. Johnson. It is interesting to note, however, that they probably preferred different meats. In western Kentucky, mutton is king; in Texas, beef. Oddly enough, eastern Kentuckians consume practically no mutton or lamb. . . .

In Texas . . . I found . . . three imperatives of barbecuing: the dry mix, the mopping sauce, and the barbecue sauce. The mopping liquid, which usually does not even taste good, is used during cooking to flavor and moisten the meat. Barbecue sauce is served with the meat at the table. . . .

Purists claim that when we put spicy red sauce on meat during the cooking we are not truly barbecuing. Convenience must be served, however, even in Texas; thus many barbecue recipes exist that can be easily prepared in the home kitchen.

DENTON, TEXAS, BARBECUED BEEF BRISKET

⅓ cup molasses
⅓ cup prepared mustard
½ cup firmly packed brown sugar
3 tablespoons Worcestershire sauce
¼ teaspoon hot sauce
½ cup pineapple juice
¾ cup wine vinegar
1 teaspoon chili powder
1 tablespoon minced onion
1 (4- to 6-pound) beef brisket

Combine all ingredients except beef, mixing well. Place meat in heavy plastic bag and pour marinade over it. Squeeze air from bag, and fasten bag. Place bag in a 13- x 9- x 2-inch baking dish; marinate in refrigerator at least 4 to 6 hours, or overnight.

Drain meat and reserve marinade. Grill meat over medium heat until browned. Cover grill and cook 15 minutes. Turn meat and baste with reserved marinade. Grill 15 minutes longer.

Wrap meat in heavy foil, leaving room for marinade. Cut hole in top of foil and pour marinade through hole over the meat. Continue grilling for 1½ to 2 hours, or until meat is very tender. To serve, slice thin diagonal slices. Yield: 12 to 15 servings.

Unlike barbecue, which we fondly believe to have its roots in the South, the story of sausage-making in the South is a compilation of methods, brought from all over the world, to use up the last morsels of a precious meat. Give a side of pork, beef, or venison to a Mexican-American, a Texan of German background, an Appalachian or Ozark Mountain man, and an Italian-Floridian. The result will be four distinctly different sausages, each more delicious than the other.

In my childhood, hog-killing time was a period of generalized tension; all the

meat had to be treated quickly even in cold weather. But when it was time to make the sausage, there came the annual crisis in my parents' marriage. My father liked it hot; my mother enjoyed a more delicate approach to the spicing. Here is my father's recipe.

PORK SAUSAGE

1 pound salt
2 to 4 tablespoons rubbed sage
2 to 4 tablespoons black pepper
1½ tablespoons red pepper
  (3 tablespoons for hot sausage)
50 pounds pork, ¼ to ⅓ fat by weight

Combine seasonings and rub well into cut-up meat. Grind twice. Stuff into casings. Smoke 2 to 4 hours over green hickory and hang to store. If sausage is not smoked, it should be frozen after taking seasonings for 2 days.

Stuffing Sausage

For those who . . . want to try their hand at stuffing their own sausage, here are some simple instructions.

For those recipes that require stuffing sausage into casings, natural casings (the cleaned intestines of pigs or sheep) are preferable to artificial ones, as they are edible. They are available, clean and ready to use, packed in salt. Meat packing companies will sell them, and many butcher shops will be happy to order them. They are inexpensive; for a dollar or two, the home sausage maker can have a season's supply, and with little effort, can make professional-looking sausages.

To use the casings, take them out of the salt, estimating roughly 2 inches per 1 ounce of meat to be processed. The unused portion, closed and in a cool place, will keep indefinitely. Cut casings into manageable yard-long pieces and rinse away the salt by running tepid tap water through each length. Blot excess water; knot one end. Slip the open end over the sausage stuffing attachment, drawing the casing over the tube to within an inch of the knotted end. Fill the casing, using the free hand to equalize the meat as it goes in. Or, if no sausage stuffing attachment is available, use a funnel or cake decorator without a tube attached. In any case, the casings should not be too tightly stuffed, lest they burst under the pressure. Fill to within about 2 inches of the end, leaving enough casing to tie

off. Form individual sausages by twisting the finished casing at desired intervals. As an alternative, the sausage may be left in one long coil. Before freezing or serving, hang the stuffed sausage to dry for twenty-four hours outdoors in a breezy spot, or indoors with an electric fan blowing. . . .

In the South, even after other grain crops became established, the people kept eating cornbread because they liked it, not because they had to. They invented a wide variety of breads made from corn, beginning with the elementary ones picked up from the Indians. The Indians who greeted the first settlers on the Eastern Seaboard used corn in many ways; it was their staple food. But unlike the tribes of the Southwest, they had no ovens. Their bread was a cornmeal mush or "platter" bread made of parched corn and baked in cakes by the sun's heat.

The story of Indian fry bread may be of interest at this point, as there may be others who labor, as I did, under the misapprehension that fry bread was made from corn. The Indians who gave corn cultivation and cookery to the colonists were not, at that time, making fry bread at all. And when they did, they made it from wheat flour.

The story of Indian fry bread is an unhappy one, as I received it from Mrs. Raymond Red Corn, of Pawhuska, Oklahoma. Claiming little or no Indian blood, Waltena Red Corn is Osage mostly by marriage. The Red Corns own the Ha-Pah-Shu-Tse Restaurant and are students of Indian history.

The origin of Indian fry bread runs like this. The Eastern tribes were moved off their lands in the early 1800s and relocated in the West. Their corn fields were left behind. The rations, or "commodities," issued by the government included flour, not cornmeal. "This was when they came up with a 'fry bread.' It had to be made of flour," said Mrs. Red Corn.

"It is made by different tribes in different ways. Ours is rolled and cut in squares; others pinch off a piece and flatten it by patting and pulling before dropping it in hot fat. . . ."

INDIAN FRY BREAD

2 cups all-purpose flour
2 tablespoons baking powder
½ teaspoon salt
Vegetable oil for deep frying

Sift or stir dry ingredients in mixing bowl to blend thoroughly. Slowly add sufficient water to form a stiff dough. Cover bowl with towel; let stand 30 minutes. Pinch off balls of dough with floured hands, and work out into 5-inch circles. Drop into oil heated to 360°, and fry until golden brown. Yield: 7 or 8 fry breads.

SOUTHERN CORNBREAD

2 eggs
2 cups buttermilk
2 cups cornmeal
1 teaspoon salt
1 teaspoon soda
2 teaspoons baking powder
2 tablespoons bacon drippings, melted

If skillet or muffin irons are to be used, grease and place in oven when it is turned on; they should be smoking hot. If tin pan or muffin rings are used, grease them.

Beat eggs in a medium mixing bowl; add buttermilk. Combine dry ingredients; stir into egg mixture. Stir in drippings.

Pour into a hot, well-greased 9- or 10-inch skillet or 18 muffin cups or one 9-inch square baking pan. Bake at 475° about 25 minutes if using skillet or baking pan, and about 15 to 20 minutes for muffins. Serve hot with butter. Yield: one 9- or 10-inch loaf or about 1½ dozen muffins.

HOT WATER HOECAKE

2 cups cornmeal
3 cups boiling water
2 tablespoons shortening
1 teaspoon salt
1 egg, beaten
About ½ cup milk
Butter

Stir cornmeal slowly into boiling water in a medium saucepan. Add shortening, salt, egg, and enough milk to make a stiff batter. Form into small ½-inch-thick cakes; fry on a hot greased griddle. Turn when brown on bottom side and brown on the other side. Serve hot with butter. Yield: about 20 small hoecakes.

A Flavor Lift For Leftover Roast

Leftover roast beef can be as special as the first time around with these two recipes. Carry-Along Beef Pies call for chopped roast beef and vegetables to be baked in a flaky turnover pastry. And Roast Beef Salad can be spread between bread slices or stuffed into a tomato shell.

CARRY-ALONG BEEF PIES

½ teaspoon instant beef bouillon granules
2 tablespoons boiling water
1¾ cups chopped cooked roast beef
½ cup chopped cooked potatoes
½ cup chopped cooked carrots
1 medium onion, chopped
2 tablespoons sweet pickle relish
2 tablespoons catsup
⅛ teaspoon ground savory
¼ teaspoon salt
Dash of pepper
Flaky Pastry

Dissolve bouillon in boiling water. Combine next 9 ingredients; pour bouillon over top. Stir and set aside.

Divide pastry dough in half; roll one part out to ⅛-inch thickness on a lightly floured board. Cut into four 5½-inch squares; repeat with remaining dough. Place about ⅓ cup meat mixture in center of each square, and fold pastry in half diagonally to make a triangle. Moisten edges with water, and press with a fork to seal. Prick tops with fork.

Place beef pies on lightly greased baking sheets, and bake at 425° for 25 to 30 minutes or until lightly browned. Yield: 8 servings.

Flaky Pastry:

3 cups all-purpose flour
1½ teaspoons salt
1 cup plus 3 tablespoons shortening
9 to 10 tablespoons cold water

Combine flour and salt; cut in shortening with pastry blender until mixture resembles coarse meal. Sprinkle cold water evenly over surface; stir with a fork until all ingredients are moistened. Shape dough into a ball. Yield: enough for 8 beef pies.
Pam Snellgrove,
LaGrange, Georgia.

Tip: Use an extra set of dry measuring cups as scoops in canisters of flour, sugar, and grains to save time.

ROAST BEEF SALAD

4 cups ground cooked roast beef
½ cup chopped celery
½ cup chopped sweet pickle
1 tablespoon prepared mustard
1 cup mayonnaise
¼ teaspoon salt

Combine all ingredients, mixing well; chill 1 to 2 hours. Yield: 8 servings.
Gloria Pedersen,
Brandon, Mississippi.

Greet Guests With Tasty Appetizers

The easiest way to get a party off to a good start is to serve a variety of appealing appetizers. As guests start nibbling, the ice is magically broken; everyone relaxes and feels welcome.

Stuff mushroom caps with a rich cream cheese mixture, or stir up a tangy mustard sauce for tiny smoked sausages. And be sure to include plenty of Avocado Dip; it's always popular when served with fresh vegetables, chips, or crackers.

HAM AND PIMIENTO SPREAD

1½ cups finely chopped cooked ham
1 (4-ounce) jar chopped pimiento, drained
½ cup chopped parsley
½ cup mayonnaise

Combine all ingredients; stir well. Chill. Serve on party rye bread or crackers. Yield: about 3 cups.
Eleanor K. Brandt,
Arlington, Texas.

SMOKED SAUSAGES WITH MUSTARD SAUCE

1 cup half-and-half
½ cup sugar
3 tablespoons dry mustard
½ teaspoon salt
2 tablespoons all-purpose flour
2 egg yolks
¼ cup vinegar
Cocktail-size smoked link sausages

Pour ¾ cup half-and-half into a small saucepan; place over low heat, stirring occasionally until bubbly.

Combine next 5 ingredients with remaining half-and-half, mixing well; gradually add heated half-and-half, and mix well. Return mixture to saucepan; cook over low heat, stirring constantly, until smooth and thickened.

Remove sauce from heat, and gradually stir in vinegar. Serve with sausages. Yield: about 2 cups. *Susan Leftwich, DeSoto, Texas.*

ELEGANT CHEESE-STUFFED MUSHROOMS

1½ pounds small fresh mushrooms
1 (8-ounce) package cream cheese, softened
Dash of salt
Dash of Worcestershire sauce
Dash of ground nutmeg
Freshly ground black pepper to taste
1 cup grated Parmesan cheese

Rinse mushrooms, and pat dry; remove stems. (Mushroom stems may be used in other recipes.) Place caps on a greased baking sheet.

Combine remaining ingredients except 2 tablespoons Parmesan cheese; mix well. Spoon mixture into mushroom caps; sprinkle each with reserved cheese. Bake mushrooms at 350° for 20 minutes. Yield: 4 dozen.
Mrs. Quentin Bierman, Dunwoody, Georgia.

BOURBON CHEESE BALL

4 cups (1 pound) shredded sharp Cheddar cheese
¼ cup mayonnaise
2 to 4 tablespoons bourbon
1 teaspoon lemon juice
Dash of red pepper
½ cup ground pecans
Paprika
Parsley sprigs

Combine cheese and mayonnaise; blend until smooth. Add bourbon, lemon juice, and red pepper; beat well. Stir in pecans. Chill 1 hour.

Shape cheese mixture into a ball; roll in paprika. Garnish with parsley. Chill. Yield: 1 cheese ball. *Eva G. Key, Isle of Palms, South Carolina.*

AVOCADO DIP

1 ripe avocado, peeled and mashed
2 (3-ounce) packages cream cheese, softened
2 tablespoons milk
1 tablespoon lemon juice
1 tablespoon grated onion
¼ teaspoon salt

Combine first 3 ingredients; beat until smooth. Add remaining ingredients, and blend well. Serve with fresh vegetables or crackers. Yield: about 1½ cups.
Katie Bender, Rickman, Tennessee.

Versatile, Affordable Chicken Livers

One of the best ways to relieve your food budget is by serving chicken livers as an entrée. Distinctive in flavor, they combine well with ingredients like bacon, mushrooms, and onions.

Try Chicken Livers With Rice for a quick and easy family dish, or Sautéed Chicken Livers—an entrée special enough for any occasion. You can also enjoy livers in appetizer servings. For Chicken Liver and Bacon Roll-Ups the livers are dipped in Dijon mustard and then baked until crisp in a coating of cracker crumbs.

SAUTEED CHICKEN LIVERS

1 pound chicken livers, cut into bite-size pieces
3 tablespoons butter or margarine, melted
½ pound fresh mushrooms, sliced
½ cup sliced onion
1 teaspoon all-purpose flour
½ teaspoon salt
1 (14½-ounce) can tomatoes, undrained
½ cup dry white wine
2 teaspoons chopped fresh parsley
½ teaspoon Worcestershire sauce
Hot cooked rice or toast points

Sauté chicken livers in butter 5 minutes or until brown. Remove livers, and drain on paper towels, reserving drippings in skillet. Sauté mushrooms and onion in drippings until onion is golden. Stir in flour and salt. Add tomatoes, wine, parsley, and Worcestershire

sauce; bring to a boil. Reduce heat and cook 5 minutes, stirring often. Add chicken livers; simmer 5 additional minutes. Serve over rice or toast points. Yield: 4 servings. *Sarah J. Phelps, Baltimore, Maryland.*

CHICKEN LIVER AND BACON ROLL-UPS

1 pound chicken livers
3 tablespoons Dijon mustard
10 to 12 slices bacon, cut in half
½ cup cracker crumbs

Dip chicken livers lightly in mustard. Wrap a half slice of bacon around each, and secure with a wooden pick. Coat livers with crumbs. Place in an 8-inch square baking dish; bake at 425° for 25 minutes. Yield: 6 to 8 appetizer servings. *Mrs. H. J. Sherrer, Bay City, Texas.*

CHICKEN LIVERS STROGANOFF

¾ pound chicken livers
1 (4-ounce) can sliced mushrooms, drained
1 medium onion, chopped
¾ cup vermouth
½ teaspoon dried whole rosemary, crushed
¼ teaspoon dried whole thyme
1 teaspoon salt
¾ cup commercial sour cream
Hot cooked noodles

Combine first 7 ingredients in a medium saucepan; bring to a boil. Reduce heat and simmer, covered, 20 minutes. Stir in sour cream; cook over medium heat, stirring constantly, until mixture is thoroughly heated. Serve over hot cooked noodles. Yield: 4 servings.
Sam Jones, Tallahassee, Florida.

Tip: It's a good idea to learn as much as you can about the metric system of measuring since these measurements are now appearing on some canned foods. To give you an idea of some new measurements: 1 cup flour equals 140 grams; 1 cup butter equals 200 grams; and 1 cup sugar equals 190 grams.

CHICKEN LIVERS WITH RICE

1 (4-ounce) can sliced mushrooms
1 pound chicken livers
¼ cup chopped green pepper
1½ tablespoons butter or margarine,
    melted
2 tablespoons catsup
Hot cooked rice

Drain mushrooms, reserving liquid.
Add enough water to liquid to make ¾
cup; set aside.

Sauté chicken livers and green pepper
in butter until livers are browned. Stir
in mushrooms, reserved liquid, and catsup; bring to a boil. Reduce heat.
Cover and simmer 10 minutes, stirring
occasionally. Serve over rice. Yield: 4
servings.   *Esther Hench,*
              Fort Lauderdale, Florida.

Two Choices For Lamb

The mild, delicate flavor of lamb
lends itself to many seasonings, particularly ginger, parsley, and garlic. A delicious example is Lamb Hawaii—the
outside of the meat is rubbed with
lemon juice and rind, and a seasoned
filling is rolled up inside. For another
elegant presentation, try Crown Roast
of Lamb; it's easier to prepare and
serve than you might think.

When selecting lamb, look for meat
that is pinkish-red with a fine, velvety
texture. Since lamb is from young sheep
less than a year old, most cuts are
tender with only a thin layer of fat
around the outside of the cut.

Regal, impressive, and delicious best describe this Crown Roast of Lamb.

CROWN ROAST OF LAMB

1 (3½- to 4-pound) crown roast of lamb
Salt and pepper
1 (8-ounce) package herb-seasoned stuffing
    mix
1 pound ground lamb
2 tablespoons minced onion
Fresh parsley sprigs (optional)
Whole spiced peaches (optional)

Sprinkle roast with salt and pepper;
place on a rack in a shallow roasting
pan, bone end up.

Combine stuffing mix, ground lamb,
and onion, stirring well. Spoon stuffing
into center of roast. Place a folded strip
of aluminum foil over exposed ends of
ribs. Roast at 325° for 1 hour and 45
minutes to 2 hours (30 minutes per
pound) or until meat thermometer registers 175° to 180°. Garnish roast with
parsley and peaches, if desired. Yield: 8
servings.   *Florence L. Costello,*
              Chattanooga, Tennessee.

LAMB HAWAII

1 (5- to 6-pound) leg of lamb, boned
2 tablespoons lemon juice
1½ tablespoons grated lemon rind
1 (8-ounce) can crushed pineapple,
    undrained
2 tablespoons butter or margarine
2 tablespoons minced fresh parsley
1 tablespoon chopped onion
½ clove garlic, crushed
½ teaspoon salt
½ teaspoon ground ginger
⅛ teaspoon pepper
2 cups toasted breadcrumbs
Salt and pepper
Ground ginger
2 tablespoons melted butter or margarine

Remove the fell (tissuelike covering)
from lamb with a sharp knife. Rub cavity and outside of lamb with lemon juice
and rind; cover lamb, and chill 2 to 3
hours.

Drain crushed pineapple, reserving
juice; set aside.

Melt 2 tablespoons butter in a large
skillet; add next 6 ingredients. Cook
over low heat 3 to 4 minutes. Stir in
pineapple; cook 5 minutes. Add breadcrumbs, mixing well.

Stuff dressing into cavity (do not
pack). Tie lamb securely with string.
Season to taste with salt, pepper, and
ginger. Place lamb on a rack in roasting
pan; pour 2 tablespoons melted butter
over lamb. Insert meat thermometer,
making sure end of thermometer does
not touch fat.

Bake, uncovered, at 425° for about 10
minutes or until lightly browned. Cover
and lower heat to 350°; bake 30 to 35
minutes per pound or until meat thermometer registers 175° to 180°, basting
frequently with reserved pineapple
juice. Yield: 8 servings.
                 Mrs. Charles R. Simms,
                    Palestine, Illinois.

A Medley of Banana Favorites

Peel a banana, and you get a quick snack or light dessert. Add other ingredients, and enjoy Banana-Nut-Raisin Bread, an old-fashioned meringue-topped pudding, or a flaming sauce to spoon over ice cream.

In addition to their good taste, bananas are high in vitamin A and potassium, low in sodium, and—something that may surprise you—one medium banana contains only 85 calories.

ELEGANT BANANAS FOSTER

½ cup butter or margarine
1½ cups firmly packed brown sugar
4 medium bananas, sliced
1 to 2 tablespoons imitation banana
    extract
Dash of ground cinnamon
¼ cup rum
Vanilla ice cream

Melt butter in a large skillet; add sugar, and cook over medium heat until bubbly. Add bananas; heat 2 to 3 minutes, basting constantly with syrup. Stir in banana extract and cinnamon.

Place rum in a small, long-handled pan; heat just until warm. Ignite with a long match, and pour over bananas. Baste bananas with sauce until flames die down. Serve immediately over ice cream. Yield: 6 servings.

*Mrs. Charles Price,
Houston, Texas.*

BASIC BANANA PUDDING

⅓ cup all-purpose flour
⅔ cup sugar
2 cups milk
2 eggs, separated
½ teaspoon vanilla extract
Vanilla wafers
4 bananas, sliced
¼ teaspoon cream of tartar
¼ cup sugar

Combine flour and ⅔ cup sugar in a heavy saucepan, mixing well; gradually stir in milk and egg yolks. Cook over medium heat, stirring constantly, until thickened. Let mixture cool slightly, and stir in vanilla.

Arrange a layer of vanilla wafers in a lightly greased 8-inch square baking dish; top with half of bananas and half of pudding. Repeat layers.

Beat egg whites (at room temperature) until soft peaks form; add cream of tartar, beating slightly. Gradually add ¼ cup sugar, 1 tablespoon at a time, beating until stiff peaks form. Spread meringue over pudding, sealing to edge of dish. Bake at 350° for 10 to 12 minutes or until golden brown. Yield: 4 to 6 servings.
*Myra Schisler,
Jonesboro, Arkansas.*

BANANA-NUT-RAISIN BREAD

½ cup butter or margarine, softened
1 cup sugar
2 eggs
2 cups mashed ripe bananas
2 cups all-purpose flour
1 teaspoon baking powder
1 teaspoon soda
½ teaspoon salt
½ cup chopped pecans
½ cup raisins

Cream butter; gradually add sugar, beating well. Add eggs, one at a time, beating well after each addition. Add bananas, and mix until smooth.

Combine flour, baking powder, soda, and salt; add to creamed mixture, stirring just enough to moisten. Stir in chopped pecans and raisins.

Pour batter into a greased and floured 9- x 5- x 3-inch loafpan. Bake at 350° for 1 hour to 1 hour and 10 minutes. Cool in pan 10 minutes. Remove to wire rack to complete cooling. Yield: 1 loaf.
*Annmarie DeMattia,
Garland, Texas.*

STRAWBERRY-BANANA SMOOTHIE

3 ripe bananas, broken into 1-inch pieces
1 (10-ounce) package frozen strawberries
1 cup vanilla ice cream
½ cup light rum

Combine all ingredients in container of electric blender; finish filling with ice. Process until smooth. Yield: 5 cups.
*Kathy Wall,
Birmingham, Alabama.*

Tip: Ripe bananas can be refrigerated to keep them an additional 3 to 5 days. Or peel, mash, and freeze in airtight containers for use in baking.

Steam Artichokes For The First Course

For a distinctive appetizer, serve Steamed Artichokes with the classic accompaniment, clarified butter. The artichokes are nutritious, attractive, and easier to prepare than you'd imagine. And because they are available during the spring months only, they are a delicacy of sorts.

To give this stately vegetable a different flavor twist, add celery leaves, onion, or garlic to the steaming pot. Or substitute herb butter or hollandaise sauce for the clarified butter.

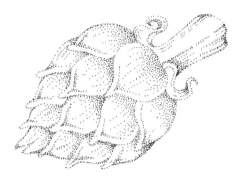

STEAMED ARTICHOKES

6 artichokes
Lemon wedge
Clarified butter (recipe follows)

Wash artichokes by plunging up and down in cold water. Cut off the stem end, and trim about ½ inch from top of each artichoke. Remove any loose bottom leaves. With scissors, trim away about ¼ of each outer leaf. Rub top and edges of leaves with a lemon wedge to prevent discoloration.

Place artichokes in a large Dutch oven with about an inch of water. Cover tightly, and heat to boiling; reduce heat, and simmer 35 to 45 minutes or until leaves pull out easily. Spread leaves apart; pull out the fuzzy thistle center (choke) with a spoon.

Arrange the artichokes on serving plates, and serve with clarified butter. Yield: 6 servings.

Clarified Butter:

1 cup butter

Melt butter over low heat in a 1-quart saucepan, without stirring. When completely melted, the butter will separate, with a milky layer atop a clear layer. Remove from heat; slowly pour the clear layer into a dish, reserving the milky layer in pan. Discard pan liquid. Yield: about ¾ cup.

Mix Up A Cheesecake In The Processor

Like many good cooks across the South, Sara Scott of Dothan, Alabama, relies more and more on her food processor. A busy mother of three, Sara has found that using the processor allows her to prepare many dishes that otherwise would be too time consuming.

One of her favorite recipes, Lemon Cheesecake With Orange-Pineapple Glaze, is a good example of how she saves time with the help of her food processor. For the crust, she processes vanilla wafers and lemon zest with the knife blade until they are finely ground. She then adds sugar and butter and lets the processor do the mixing. She also blends the filling in the processor.

Here Sara shares her cheesecake recipe along with her Creamy French Dressing, which is also prepared in the food processor.

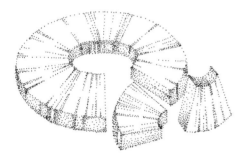

inches up sides of a buttered 9-inch springform pan; put in refrigerator to chill.

Position knife blade in dry bowl. Add 1⅓ cups sugar and remaining 1 teaspoon lemon zest; top with cover. Process 15 seconds or until zest is finely chopped. Remove cover, and add cream cheese and egg yolks. Top processor with cover, and blend 1 minute or until smooth. With processor running, pour vanilla through food chute; process 10 seconds or until well mixed.

Beat egg whites (at room temperature) until stiff peaks form. Fold egg whites into cream cheese mixture. Pour batter into prepared crust, and bake at 350° for 50 to 60 minutes or until the cheesecake is set. Cool; chill at least 3 hours. Spread Orange-Pineapple Glaze over cheesecake, and garnish with orange slices. Yield: 8 to 10 servings.

Orange-Pineapple Glaze:

3 tablespoons sugar
1 tablespoon cornstarch
1 (15¼-ounce) can crushed pineapple
About ¼ cup orange juice
2 tablespoons Grand Marnier or other orange-flavored liqueur

Combine sugar and cornstarch in a heavy saucepan; stir well.

Drain pineapple, reserving juice. Add enough orange juice to pineapple juice to equal 1 cup. Stir juice and liqueur into sugar mixture. Cook over medium heat until mixture is thickened and translucent. Cool glaze completely. Stir in pineapple. Yield: about 1½ cups.

LEMON CHEESECAKE WITH ORANGE-PINEAPPLE GLAZE

3 cups vanilla wafers
2 tablespoons sugar
2 teaspoons lemon zest, divided
¼ cup butter or margarine, melted
1⅓ cups sugar
3 (8-ounce) packages cream cheese, softened
4 eggs, separated
1 teaspoon vanilla extract
Orange-Pineapple Glaze
Orange slices

Position knife blade in processor bowl. Add vanilla wafers, 2 tablespoons sugar, and 1 teaspoon lemon zest; top with cover. Process 35 to 40 seconds or until finely ground.

With processor running, pour butter through food chute; process 15 to 20 seconds or until well mixed. Press crumb mixture into bottom and 1½

CREAMY FRENCH DRESSING

¼ cup vinegar
2 teaspoons lemon juice
3 cloves garlic
1 tablespoon plus 1 teaspoon Creole mustard
1 teaspoon salt
½ teaspoon pepper
⅛ teaspoon sugar
¾ cup vegetable oil
2 tablespoons olive oil
¼ cup plus 1 tablespoon whipping cream

Position knife blade in processor bowl; add vinegar, lemon juice, and garlic, and top with cover. Process 30 seconds or until garlic is finely chopped.

Add mustard, salt, pepper, and sugar; process until well mixed. With processor running, pour oil through food chute in a slow steady stream. Pour cream through food chute, and process until well mixed. Yield: 1⅓ cups.

Microwave Cookery

Baked Potatoes Ready In Minutes

Baked potatoes—whether stuffed or smothered with a rich sauce or loaded with butter and sour cream—are an accompaniment you can always count on to enhance a meal.

Thanks to the microwave oven, enjoying potatoes no longer means an hour from oven to table and wrapping them in foil to keep the skins from drying out. With microwaving, baked potatoes are ready in minutes, with the skin still soft and supple.

The basic procedure for microwaving potatoes is given here, along with some tips to ensure good results. You'll also find some of the best potato fix-ups you'll ever taste.

—Prick potatoes with a fork before microwaving to allow excess steam to escape; otherwise, they may burst.

—Potatoes continue to cook after the microwave cycle is complete, so let them stand 5 minutes before checking for doneness. Don't ever attempt to microwave potatoes until they are done, as they will be overcooked after standing.

—When cooking several potatoes, arrange them in a circle with at least 1 inch between each.

Prick potatoes before microwaving to prevent excess steam build-up.

—When microwaving more than two potatoes, ensure even cooking by turning them over and rearranging once during microwaving cycle.

—If you don't plan to serve the potatoes immediately after microwaving, wrap them in foil to keep them warm.

MICRO-BAKED POTATOES

Rinse potatoes, and pat dry; prick several times with a fork. Arrange potatoes on paper towels in microwave oven, leaving 1 inch between each. (If microwaving more than 2 potatoes, arrange them in a circle.)

Microwave at HIGH according to the following times, turning and rearranging potatoes once. Let potatoes stand 5 minutes before serving. (If potatoes are not done after standing, microwave briefly and let stand 2 minutes.)

Number of Potatoes	Minutes at HIGH
1	4 to 6
2	7 to 8
3	9 to 11
4	12 to 14
6	16 to 18

Note: These times are for cooking medium-size potatoes (6 to 7 ounces). If potatoes are larger, allow more time.

JALAPENO-HAM STUFFED POTATOES

4 medium baking potatoes
3 tablespoons butter or margarine
½ cup diced ham
½ cup (2 ounces) shredded Monterey Jack cheese with jalapeño peppers
1 (8-ounce) carton commercial sour cream
½ teaspoon celery salt
½ teaspoon pepper

Microwave the potatoes according to Micro-Baked Potatoes recipe; let cool to touch. Slice away skin from top of each potato; carefully scoop out pulp, leaving shells intact. Mash pulp.

Place butter in a 1-cup glass measure; microwave at HIGH for 30 to 45 seconds or until melted. Combine butter, potato pulp, ham, cheese, sour cream, celery salt, and pepper; mix well. Stuff shells with potato mixture.

Place stuffed potatoes on a microwave-safe serving platter. Microwave at HIGH for 5 to 7 minutes or until thoroughly heated, giving dish one half-turn. Yield: 4 servings.

CHEESY BACON-STUFFED POTATOES

4 medium baking potatoes
6 slices bacon
⅓ cup chopped green onion
⅓ cup shredded Cheddar cheese
1 (8-ounce) carton commercial sour cream
1 teaspoon salt
½ teaspoon pepper
Paprika

Microwave the potatoes according to Micro-Baked Potatoes recipe; let cool to touch. Slice away skin from top of each potato; carefully scoop out pulp, leaving shells intact. Mash pulp.

Place bacon on a bacon rack in a 12- x 8- x 2-inch microwave-safe baking dish; cover with waxed paper. Microwave at HIGH for 6 to 7 minutes or until bacon is crisp. Remove bacon and rack, reserving 3 tablespoons drippings in dish. Drain bacon; crumble and set aside.

Microwave onion in drippings at HIGH for 2 to 3 minutes or until tender. Combine onion, potato pulp, bacon, cheese, sour cream, salt, and pepper; mix well. Stuff shells with potato mixture, and sprinkle with paprika.

Place stuffed potatoes on a microwave-safe serving platter. Microwave at HIGH for 5 to 7 minutes or until thoroughly heated, giving dish one half-turn. Yield: 4 servings.

POTATOES WITH CHIVES

4 medium baking potatoes
¼ cup plus 2 teaspoons butter or margarine
1 tablespoon plus 1 teaspoon seasoned dry breadcrumbs
1 (3-ounce) package cream cheese with chives
⅓ cup half-and-half
¾ teaspoon salt
¼ teaspoon pepper

Microwave the potatoes according to Micro-Baked Potatoes recipe; let cool to touch. Slice away skin from top of each potato; carefully scoop out pulp, leaving shells intact. Mash pulp.

Place butter in a 1-cup glass measure; microwave at HIGH for 45 seconds to 1 minute or until melted. Transfer 2 teaspoons melted butter to a small mixing bowl; add breadcrumbs, and mix well.

Place cream cheese in a medium-size glass mixing bowl. Microwave at MEDIUM LOW for 1 to 2 minutes or until softened. Add potato pulp, half-and-half, remaining butter, salt, and pepper; mix well. Stuff shells with potato mixture, and sprinkle with breadcrumbs.

Place potatoes on a microwave-safe serving platter. Microwave at HIGH for 5 to 7 minutes or until thoroughly heated, giving dish one half-turn. Yield: 4 servings.

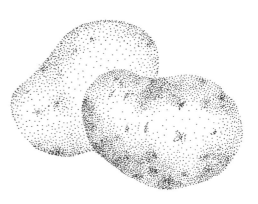

SHRIMP-SAUCED POTATOES

4 medium baking potatoes
2 (4¼-ounce) cans tiny shrimp, drained
2 tablespoons butter or margarine
2 teaspoons all-purpose flour
¼ teaspoon salt
½ cup whipping cream
½ cup commercial sour cream
1 tablespoon chili sauce
½ teaspoon dry mustard
2 teaspoons parsley flakes

Microwave the potatoes according to Micro-Baked Potatoes recipe. Wrap in foil to keep hot.

Prepare shrimp according to label directions; set aside.

Place butter in a 4-cup glass measure; microwave at HIGH for 30 to 40 seconds or until butter melts. Add flour and salt, stirring until smooth. Gradually add whipping cream, stirring well. Microwave at HIGH for 1 minute; stir well. Microwave at HIGH for 30 seconds to 1 minute, stirring at 30-second intervals, until thickened and bubbly.

Stir shrimp, sour cream, chili sauce, and seasonings into sauce. Microwave at MEDIUM HIGH for 1 minute or until thoroughly heated, stirring once.

Split potatoes lengthwise, and fluff pulp with a fork. Spoon on sauce. Yield: 4 servings.

Sweet Rolls Even A Novice Can Make

If freshly baked sweet rolls glazed with a caramel-pecan topping sound like a wonderful way to start the day, then you'll want to bake our delightful Pecan Rolls. You don't have to be an expert bread baker to make these rolls; just follow baking instructions carefully.

A tip to novice yeast dough bakers: Use a cooking thermometer to measure the temperature of the liquid (milk and melted butter in this recipe). If the liquid is too hot when added to the yeast, the yeast will be destroyed and the bread will not rise. If the liquid is too cool, the yeast will not activate and again the bread will not rise.

PECAN ROLLS

3¼ to 3½ cups all-purpose flour
¼ cup sugar
1 teaspoon salt
1 package dry yeast
¼ cup butter or margarine
1 cup milk
1 egg
¼ cup plus 2 tablespoons butter or
    margarine
½ cup plus 2 tablespoons firmly packed
    brown sugar
2 tablespoons milk
1 cup pecan halves
3 tablespoons butter or margarine, melted
¼ cup plus 1 tablespoon firmly packed
    brown sugar, divided
Ground cinnamon

Combine 1¼ cups flour, ¼ cup sugar, salt, and yeast in a large bowl; mix well.

Melt ¼ cup butter in a small saucepan; add 1 cup milk, and heat until very warm (120° to 130°). Add butter mixture and egg to yeast mixture; blend on low speed of electric mixer until moistened. Beat 3 minutes at high speed. Stir in 1½ cups flour until mixture leaves sides of bowl.

Turn dough out onto a floured surface; knead in ½ to ¾ cup flour. Continue kneading until dough is smooth and elastic (about 7 minutes).

Place dough in a greased bowl, turning to grease top. Cover with a damp cloth, and let rise in a warm place (85°), free from drafts, 1 hour or until dough is doubled in bulk.

Melt ¼ cup plus 2 tablespoons butter in a small saucepan; add ½ cup plus 2 tablespoons brown sugar, and bring to a boil, stirring constantly. Remove from heat; add 2 tablespoons milk, stirring until smooth.

Pour sugar mixture into a greased 13- x 9- x 2-inch baking pan; place pecans, right side down, evenly over sugar mixture. Set aside.

Punch dough down, and divide in half. Roll each half into a 16- x 7-inch rectangle, and brush with 3 tablespoons melted butter. Sprinkle 2½ tablespoons brown sugar and cinnamon on each rectangle.

Starting at the wide end, roll up each strip in jellyroll fashion; pinch edges together to seal. Cut each roll into 1-inch slices. Place slices over pecans in prepared pan. Cover and let rise in a warm place (85°), free from drafts, 1 hour or until doubled in bulk.

Bake at 400° for 15 minutes or until golden brown. Remove from oven; invert on platter. Yield: about 2½ dozen.
Mrs. Walter Wickstrom,
Pelham, Alabama.

Flavor Dessert With Coffee

Here's a dessert that not only looks different, but has an unusual and delightful taste. Strong cold coffee and ground almonds flavor a rich, buttery filling, which is then sandwiched between layers of ladyfingers. A whipped cream topping is spread over the dessert, and toasted almonds add the finishing touch to Mocha-Almond Dessert.

MOCHA-ALMOND DESSERT

1 cup unsalted butter, softened
½ cup sugar
5 egg yolks
¼ cup plus 3 tablespoons cold strong
    coffee
2 teaspoons vanilla extract
¼ cup plus 1 tablespoon toasted ground
    almonds
8 to 10 ladyfingers, split lengthwise
1 cup whipping cream, whipped
Sliced almonds, toasted

Cream butter; gradually add sugar, beating until light and fluffy and sugar is dissolved. Add egg yolks, one at a time, beating well after each addition.

Gradually add coffee to creamed mixture, beating well. Stir in vanilla and ground almonds.

Arrange ladyfingers around sides of a 1½-quart mold; spoon in half of creamed mixture. Top with a layer of ladyfingers, and add remaining creamed mixture. Top evenly with remaining ladyfingers. Cover; chill 24 hours.

Unmold dessert onto a serving plate. Spread whipped cream evenly over dessert. Garnish with sliced almonds. Yield: 8 servings.   *Florence Costello,*
Chattanooga, Tennessee.

Munch On Cheesy Tortillas

Diane Coats of Houston lives close enough to Mexico to know a good tortilla when she tastes one. That's why we were anxious to try her recipe for Cheesy Tortillas. If you've never made this Mexican bread from scratch, you'll be surprised at how tender and crisp it can be.

CHEESY TORTILLAS

2 cups all-purpose flour
1½ teaspoons baking powder
1 teaspoon salt
3 tablespoons shortening
¾ cup cold water
Vegetable oil
3 cups (12 ounces) shredded Longhorn
    cheese
Salt

Combine first 3 ingredients; cut in shortening until mixture resembles coarse meal. Add water; stir well. Turn dough out on a heavily floured surface; knead 10 to 12 times or until thoroughly mixed. Form dough into 12 equal-size balls; let dough rest 15 to 20 minutes.

Place stockinette cover on rolling pin; flour well. Roll each ball of dough into a 6- to 7-inch circle. Cook dough circles in an ungreased skillet over medium heat 1 minute; lift edge, and flip tortilla. Cook an additional 1 minute; do not brown. Place tortillas on a towel to cool; then stack between layers of waxed paper.

Heat 1 inch oil to 375° in a large skillet. Fry tortillas, one at a time, until brown on each side; drain well on paper towels.

Place tortillas on cookie sheets; sprinkle each tortilla with about ¼ cup cheese. Broil tortillas 3 to 4 inches from heat until cheese melts; sprinkle lightly with salt. Serve immediately. Yield: 1 dozen.

Note: Tortillas may be frozen after they are cooked in an ungreased skillet; thaw before frying. *Diane Coats, Houston, Texas.*

Discover The Flavor Of Poppy Seeds

Poppy seeds can be more than just a decorative topping for breads. Stir them into muffin or cake batter, mix them into a savory dressing for fruit salads, or use them to perk up refrigerated rolls. Their crunchy texture and that special nutty flavor are a pleasant surprise every time.

For a quick dinner roll you'll be proud to serve guests, we suggest Poppy Seed Onion Rolls. Start with refrigerated dinner rolls, and dip them into a mixture of butter, poppy seeds, and onion. This easy bread tastes delectably homemade.

Poppy Seed Muffins, made in minutes from commercial biscuit mix, are sweet and light. The nutlike taste of the poppy seeds are complemented by raisins. And we think any fresh fruit salad is better when drizzled with Poppy Seed Dressing.

POPPY SEED MUFFINS

1½ cups biscuit mix
½ cup sugar
1 tablespoon poppy seeds
¾ cup raisins, chopped
1 egg, beaten
¾ cup commercial sour cream
1 teaspoon vanilla extract

Combine biscuit mix, sugar, and poppy seeds; make a well in center of mixture. Add remaining ingredients, stirring just until moistened. Spoon into greased muffin pans, filling one-half full. Bake at 400° for 20 minutes or until muffins test done. Yield: 1 dozen. *Mrs. Gary Willcox, Austin, Texas.*

POPPY SEED ONION ROLLS

¼ cup butter or margarine, melted
1 tablespoon instant minced onion
1 tablespoon poppy seeds
1 (11-ounce) package refrigerated bakery-style dinner rolls

Combine butter, onion, and poppy seeds. Dip rolls in butter mixture, and place in a 9-inch round cakepan. Bake at 350° for 20 to 25 minutes or until golden brown. Yield: 8 rolls. *Shirley Hodge, Delray Beach, Florida.*

FRESH APPLE SLAW

1 (8-ounce) carton commercial sour cream
3 tablespoons lemon juice
1 tablespoon sugar
1 tablespoon poppy seeds
¾ teaspoon salt
⅛ teaspoon pepper
4 cups finely shredded cabbage
4½ cups thin apple wedges

Combine first 6 ingredients; mix well. Combine cabbage and apples; pour sour cream mixture over top. Stir well; chill at least 1 hour before serving. Yield: 8 servings. *Carla C. Hunter, Fort Valley, Georgia.*

POPPY SEED DRESSING

¾ cup sugar
1 cup vegetable oil
⅓ cup cider vinegar
1 tablespoon onion juice or ⅛ teaspoon grated onion
1 teaspoon salt
1 teaspoon dry mustard
1½ tablespoons poppy seeds

Combine all ingredients except poppy seeds in container of electric blender; process on high until well blended. Stir in poppy seeds. Chill thoroughly; stir well before serving. Yield: 1¾ cups. *Mrs. Sam Meyer, Atlanta, Georgia.*

POPPY SEED LOAF CAKE

½ cup butter or margarine
1 cup sugar
¼ cup poppy seeds
1 teaspoon vanilla extract
2 eggs
1½ cups all-purpose flour
1 teaspoon baking powder
½ teaspoon salt
½ cup half-and-half
Glaze (recipe follows)

Cream butter; gradually add sugar, beating until light and fluffy. Add poppy seeds, vanilla, and eggs; mix well. Combine dry ingredients; add to creamed mixture alternately with half-and-half, beginning and ending with flour mixture.

Pour batter into a greased and floured 8½- x 4½- x 3-inch loafpan. Bake at 350° for 50 minutes or until wooden pick inserted in center comes out clean. Cool in pan 10 minutes; remove from pan. Pour glaze over cake and cool completely. Yield: 1 loaf cake.

Glaze:

1 cup sifted powdered sugar
½ teaspoon vanilla extract
Juice of 1 lemon or lime

Combine all ingredients, mixing well. Yield: about ½ cup. *Lee Hunt, Fort Lauderdale, Florida.*

Tip: To test for doneness in baking a butter or margarine cake, insert a wooden pick or wire cake tester into the center of the cake in at least two places. The tester should come out clean if the cake is done. The cake should be beginning to shrink from the pan's sides. If the cake is pressed with a finger in the center, it should come back into shape at once. If cake tests done, remove from oven and invert cakepan 5 minutes (or time specified in the instructions); then loosen the cake from the sides and bottom of the pan. Invert it onto a plate or cake rack and turn it right side up on another cake rack so that air may circulate around it. This prevents sogginess.

Nutty Cocoa Brownies and Nutty Blonde Brownies are two good reasons for baking a batch of brownies.

These Brownies Come Out Moist And Chewy

Moist, chewy brownies are just about everyone's favorite. Some prefer them frosted, some like them chock-full of nuts, and others choose blonde brownies dotted with chocolate morsels.

CHOCOLATE-PECAN BROWNIES

½ cup butter or margarine
2 (1-ounce) squares unsweetened chocolate
1 cup sugar
½ cup all-purpose flour
1 teaspoon baking powder
2 eggs
1 teaspoon vanilla extract
1 cup chopped pecans

Combine butter and chocolate in top of double boiler; bring water to a boil. Reduce heat to low, and cook until the chocolate melts.

Combine sugar, flour, and baking powder in a mixing bowl; add chocolate mixture, mixing well. Add eggs; beat well. Stir in vanilla and pecans. Pour mixture into a greased 9-inch square baking pan. Bake at 350° for 25 to 30 minutes. Cool and cut into squares. Yield: 3 dozen (1½-inch) squares.

Mary Lou Lesniak,
Owatonna, Minnesota.

NUTTY BLONDE BROWNIES

⅓ cup butter or margarine, softened
1 cup firmly packed brown sugar
1 egg
1 teaspoon vanilla extract
1 cup all-purpose flour
¼ teaspoon soda
¼ teaspoon salt
½ to 1 cup semisweet chocolate morsels
½ cup chopped pecans

Cream butter; gradually add brown sugar, beating well. Add egg and vanilla; beat well.

Combine flour, soda, and salt; add to creamed mixture, and mix well. Stir in chocolate morsels and pecans. Spread mixture in a greased 12- x 7½- x 1½-inch baking pan. Bake at 350° for 20 to 25 minutes. Cool and cut into squares. Yield: about 3 dozen (1½-inch) squares.

Grace Bravos,
Reisterstown, Maryland.

NUTTY COCOA BROWNIES

2 cups sugar
2 cups self-rising flour
1 teaspoon soda
¼ cup plus 1 tablespoon cocoa
1 cup butter or margarine
1 cup water
½ cup buttermilk
2 eggs, beaten
1 teaspoon vanilla extract
Frosting (recipe follows)

Combine sugar, flour, soda, and cocoa; stir well, and set aside.

Combine butter and water in a small saucepan; cook over medium heat, stirring occasionally, until butter melts. Pour over dry ingredients. Beat on medium speed of electric mixer about 1 minute. Add buttermilk, eggs, and vanilla; beat just until blended.

Pour into a greased and floured 18- x 12- x 1-inch jellyroll pan. Bake at 400° for 15 to 20 minutes or until a wooden pick inserted in center comes out clean.

Immediately spread frosting over brownies. Cool and cut into squares. Yield: 4½ dozen (2-inch) squares.

Frosting:

1 (16-ounce) package powdered sugar, sifted
Dash of salt
¼ cup cocoa
½ cup butter or margarine
⅓ cup milk
1 teaspoon vanilla extract
1 cup chopped pecans

Combine sugar, salt, and cocoa; stir well, and set aside.

Combine butter and milk in a heavy saucepan. Cook over low heat, stirring occasionally, until butter melts. Pour into cocoa mixture; beat until smooth. Stir in vanilla and pecans. Yield: enough for 4½ dozen (2-inch) squares.

Mrs. Jack K. Wyatt,
Pembroke Pines, Florida.

Tip: Clean, dry coffee cans make ideal baking containers for gift breads and fruitcakes.

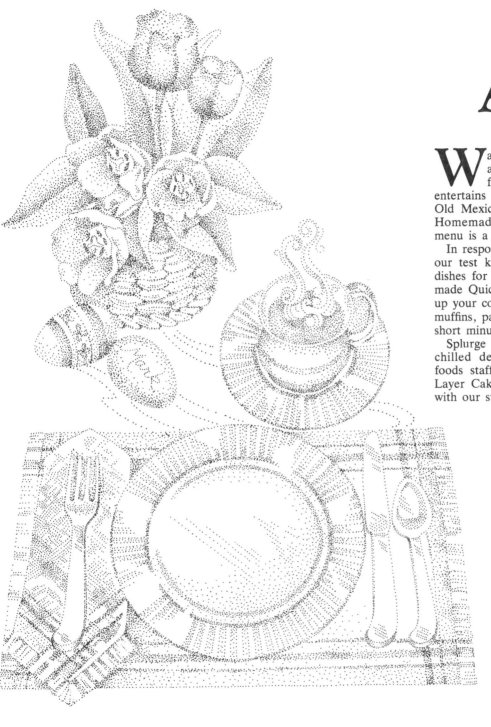

April

Warm April days inspire parties all around the South, and we found an Austin hostess who entertains with the flair and flavor of Old Mexico. From Hacienda Salad to Homemade Salsa Picante, her entire menu is a feast of flavors worth trying.

In response to many reader requests, our test kitchens developed new main dishes for your microwave. Our homemade Quick Bread Mix will also speed up your cooking, as you can now serve muffins, pancakes, and waffles in a few short minutes.

Splurge for dessert with one of our chilled desserts or layer cakes. The foods staff's favorite? Stately Coconut Layer Cake—and you won't go wrong with our step-by-step directions.

Mexico Comes Alive With A Party

The pungent aroma of chiles, onions, and tomatoes drifts across the lawn to welcome guests to Maline and Dudley McCalla's Mexican party. As they enter the airy stucco home, it's like stepping into Old Mexico.

Maline's knowledge of south-of-the-border cuisine is evident when the buffet foods are served. Chilaquiles Con Pollo, a spicy chicken-and-tortilla casserole, is the highlight of the menu. Accompanying the casserole are Mexican Marinated Mushrooms, Jalapeño Rice Casserole, and Maline's popular Hacienda Salad—topped with a choice of tangy salad dressings or Homemade Salsa Picante. This fiery sauce gets its warmth from fresh serrano chiles or jalapeño peppers.

No authentic Mexican menu would be complete without black beans. The traditional recipe is transformed into Frijoles Con Cerveza with the addition of beer. It's served with sour cream.

With all this highly seasoned food, a tall glass of refreshing Sangría, filled with floating fruit slices, is in order. And the menu ends on an equally cool note as guests reach for an ice cream cone filled with several dips of homemade Caramel-Vanilla Helado.

Mexico Inspires A Party

Maline McCalla of Austin, Texas, serves up a spicy and colorful party buffet. Most of Maline's recipes can be prepared ahead and microwaved just before serving. The menu includes a variety of Mexican flavors—from fiery Homemade Salsa Picante to cool creamy Caramel-Vanilla Helado.

Chilaquiles Con Pollo
Jalapeño Rice Casserole
Frijoles Con Cerveza
Mexican Marinated Mushrooms
Hacienda Salad
Homemade Salsa Picante
Tostados
Sangría
Caramel-Vanilla Helado

CHILAQUILES CON POLLO

1 (3- to 3½-pound) broiler-fryer
6 cups water
1 teaspoon salt
4 (8-ounce) packages frozen corn tortillas, thawed
Vegetable oil
2 (10¾-ounce) cans cream of mushroom soup, undiluted
2 (10¾-ounce) cans cream of chicken soup, undiluted
2 (10-ounce) cans tomatoes and green chiles
2 (16-ounce) cans stewed tomatoes
1 fresh serrano chile or jalapeño pepper, broiled, peeled, seeded, and chopped
4 medium onions, chopped
1 bunch green onions, chopped
1½ teaspoons garlic powder
1 teaspoon ground cumin
5 cups (20 ounces) shredded Cheddar cheese
3 cups (12 ounces) shredded Monterey Jack cheese

Place chicken in a Dutch oven; add water and salt. Bring to a boil; reduce heat and simmer, covered, 1½ hours or until tender. Remove chicken from broth; cool and cut into bite-size pieces. Strain broth, and set aside 1⅓ cups (reserve the remaining broth for use in another recipe).

Using tongs, carefully arrange 3 tortillas in ⅛-inch-deep hot oil in a large skillet; cook 3 to 5 seconds on each side. Drain tortillas on paper towels. Repeat cooking procedure with remaining tortillas; add oil to skillet if necessary. Tear each tortilla into 8 pieces; set aside. Reserve oil in skillet.

Combine reserved broth, soup, tomatoes and green chiles, stewed tomatoes, and serrano chile in a Dutch oven; simmer 30 minutes, stirring frequently.

Sauté onion, garlic powder, and cumin in reserved oil until onion is tender but not brown. Stir onion and chicken into soup mixture.

Spread one-fourth of tortillas in a 13- x 9- x 2-inch baking dish. Sprinkle half of Cheddar cheese over tortillas, and pour one-fourth of sauce over cheese. Spread one-fourth of tortillas over sauce. Pour one-fourth of sauce over tortillas; sprinkle top with half of Monterey cheese.

Repeat layering sequence in another 13- x 9- x 2-inch baking dish. Bake casseroles at 350° for 20 to 30 minutes or until bubbly. Yield: 24 servings.

Note: Casseroles may be frozen before baking; thaw completely, and bake as directed. To broil fresh chiles, refer to the procedure in Homemade Salsa Picante.

JALAPENO RICE CASSEROLE

3 cups uncooked regular rice
3 cups chicken broth
3 tablespoons butter or margarine
3 fresh jalapeño peppers, broiled, peeled, seeded, and chopped
3 (8-ounce) cartons commercial sour cream
4½ cups (18 ounces) shredded Monterey Jack cheese

Combine first 3 ingredients in a large saucepan; bring to a boil. Cover; reduce heat, and simmer 25 minutes. Stir jalapeño pepper into rice.

Spoon rice into a lightly buttered shallow 3-quart casserole; spread sour cream over rice. Sprinkle cheese evenly over sour cream. Bake at 350° for 25 to 30 minutes or until cheese is melted. Yield: 20 to 24 servings.

Note: To broil fresh jalapeño peppers, refer to procedure in Homemade Salsa Picante.

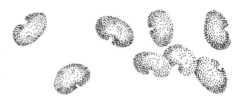

FRIJOLES CON CERVEZA
(Beans With Beer)

1 pound dried black beans
6 cups water
1 (12-ounce) can beer
1 teaspoon garlic powder
1 teaspoon salt
Chopped fresh cilantro or parsley
Commercial sour cream

Sort beans, and rinse thoroughly. Combine beans and water in a Dutch oven; let sit overnight. Bring bean mixture to a boil; reduce heat and simmer, uncovered, 2 hours. Add beer, garlic powder, and salt to bean mixture; stir well. Cook an additional 30 minutes. Sprinkle cilantro over beans; serve with sour cream. Yield: 12 to 16 servings.

MEXICAN MARINATED MUSHROOMS

2 pounds large fresh mushrooms, coarsely chopped
5 (7-ounce) cans green chile salsa
1 (5-ounce) jar pimiento-stuffed olives, drained
1 teaspoon salt
Chopped fresh cilantro or parsley

Combine first 4 ingredients; stir well. Cover and refrigerate overnight. Sprinkle cilantro over mixture before serving. Yield: 20 to 24 servings.

Note: This mixture may be stored in refrigerator several days. If desired, 4 cups Homemade Salsa Picante (see recipe) may be substituted for the green chile salsa.

HACIENDA SALAD

1 medium head iceberg lettuce, torn
1 bunch green onions, thinly sliced
2 medium tomatoes, cut into wedges
1 avocado, peeled, seeded, and chopped
1 (15-ounce) can ranch-style beans, drained
1 cup (4 ounces) shredded Cheddar cheese
1 (10½-ounce) package corn chips
3 sprigs fresh cilantro, chopped, or 1 teaspoon dried cilantro leaves
⅛ teaspoon garlic powder
Salt and pepper to taste
Homemade Salsa Picante (optional)

Combine all ingredients except Homemade Salsa Picante in a large salad bowl; toss gently. Serve with Homemade Salsa Picante or choice of salad dressings. Yield: 20 to 24 servings.

HOMEMADE SALSA PICANTE

3 fresh serrano chiles or jalapeño peppers
3 tomatillos or 1 medium-size green tomato, cored
1 bunch green onions, cut into 1-inch pieces
2 medium tomatoes, cored and cut into eighths
1 medium avocado, peeled and cut into 1-inch pieces
15 sprigs fresh cilantro or parsley
Juice of 4 limes (about ½ cup)
½ cup olive oil
1 teaspoon garlic powder
1 teaspoon ground cumin
1 teaspoon salt
Pinch of sugar

Place chiles or peppers on a baking sheet; broil 3 to 4 inches from heat, turning often with tongs, until blistered on all sides. Immediately place chiles in a plastic bag; fasten securely, and let steam 10 to 15 minutes. Remove peel of each chile.

Cut a small slit in side of each chile, and rinse under cold water to remove seeds. (Wear rubber or plastic gloves when rinsing and cutting chiles if you have sensitive skin.) Remove stems from chiles; quarter each chile, and set aside.

Remove husks from tomatillos. Place tomatillos in a small saucepan; add water to cover. Bring water to a boil; drain. Cut tomatillos into 6 wedges, and set aside.

Combine all ingredients in container of electric blender (or use food processor fitted with knife blade). Process 10 to 15 seconds or until chopped to desired texture. Chill before serving. Yield: about 4½ cups.

SANGRIA

1 gallon Burgundy
1 quart orange juice
1 quart lemon-lime carbonated beverage
2 cups cherry or peach brandy
⅓ cup lime or lemon juice
Lemon slices
Lime slices
Orange slices

Combine first 5 ingredients in a large punch bowl; stir gently. Garnish with fruit slices; serve over ice. Yield: about 1⅔ gallons.

CARAMEL-VANILLA HELADO
(Caramel-Vanilla Ice Cream)

2 (14-ounce) cans sweetened condensed milk
4 eggs
2 cups sugar
1 quart half-and-half
2 cups whipping cream
1 quart milk
Sugar ice cream cones

Pour sweetened condensed milk into two 8-inch pieplates. Cover with foil. Place each pieplate in a larger shallow pan filled with ¼ inch hot water. Bake at 425° for 1 hour and 20 minutes or until the condensed milk is thick and caramel colored (add hot water to casseroles as needed). Remove foil when done; let caramelized milk cool.

Beat eggs in a large bowl at medium speed of electric mixer until thick and lemon colored. Gradually add sugar, beating until mixture is light and fluffy. Add caramelized milk, half-and-half, and whipping cream, beating constantly until well mixed.

Pour caramelized milk mixture into container of a 1½-gallon hand-turned or electric ice cream freezer; add milk, stirring well. Freeze according to manufacturer's directions. Let ice cream ripen 1 hour before serving. Serve ice cream in ice cream cones. Yield: 1½ gallons.

Note: For a very firm ice cream, pack in freezer containers, and let harden in freezer before serving. Recipe may be halved and prepared in a 1-gallon ice cream freezer.

Pile Up A Taco

If you like tacos but find them just too messy to eat, here's a suggestion. Instead of stuffing all the ingredients into a taco shell, use corn chips as the base.

A savory meat mixture is spooned over the chips, followed by any combination of toppings. It's a great way to serve tacos to a crowd.

CORN CHIP TACOS

2½ pounds ground beef
1 large onion, chopped
2 teaspoons chili powder
2 teaspoons dried whole oregano
2 teaspoons ground cumin
2 teaspoons salt
¼ cup sugar (optional)
¼ teaspoon garlic powder
2 (8-ounce) cans tomato sauce
3 (6-ounce) cans tomato paste
4 cups water
1 (10-ounce) package corn chips
1 large onion, chopped
2 green peppers, chopped
1 avocado, peeled, seeded, and chopped
1 small head iceberg lettuce, shredded
3 tomatoes, chopped
1 cup sliced ripe or pimiento-stuffed olives
2 cups (8 ounces) shredded Cheddar cheese
Taco or picante sauce

Cook beef and 1 large onion in a Dutch oven until meat is browned. Drain. Add next 9 ingredients; simmer 1 hour over low heat, stirring mixture occasionally.

Arrange corn chips on serving plates. Spoon meat mixture over chips. Layer with desired amounts of onion, green pepper, avocado, lettuce, tomato, and olives. Top with cheese. Serve with taco or picante sauce. Yield: 10 to 12 servings.
Betty Melton,
Brookston, Texas.

Tempura Puts The Light Touch On Frying

There's no denying the popularity of fried foods in the South, and more and more Southerners are discovering that there's a way to enjoy them on the lighter side. It's the Japanese dish known as tempura.

For tempura, pieces of seafood and fresh vegetables are dipped into a thin batter and quickly fried in deep, hot oil. The crisp, delicate coating that results allows maximum food flavor and minimum fat retention.

The secret to the crispness of tempura is very hot cooking oil and icy-cold food and batter. Here are some other things that you'll need to know to master the technique.

The Basics

Among fresh vegetables suitable for tempura are broccoli, carrots, eggplant, green pepper, mushrooms, onions and green onions, pea pods, sweet potatoes, and squash (both yellow and zucchini). Do not use tomatoes, cucumbers, cabbage, or other vegetables with a high water content. Fish, scallops, and shrimp are all suitable.

Since tempura requires a very fast cooking process, there's no time to cut and wash food once cooking begins. Prepare all food well in advance, allowing time for thorough chilling.

Most vegetables can be cut as you choose, but fibrous ones, such as carrots and broccoli stems, should be cut on the diagonal to expose more surface area and ensure even cooking. Drying the vegetables is essential; otherwise, they will spatter when they hit the hot oil.

Seafood should also be well chilled. For shrimp, peel and devein, leaving the tail intact to ease handling.

Two batter recipes are included here; one is a basic tempura batter, while the other is a Southernized version made with cornmeal. Assemble all ingredients for the batter, and mix it while the oil is heating in the wok. Be sure to use ice-cold water in the batter. If preparing a lot of tempura, you may want to set the bowl of batter in a bowl of ice to keep it cold throughout the cooking process.

Peanut oil, vegetable oil, or a combination of oils can be used for tempura. Heat the oil to 375° before beginning cooking. Measure the temperature with a deepfat thermometer or use the following method: Toss a bread cube into the hot oil; if it sinks to the bottom and immediately comes to the surface and turns golden brown, the oil is ready.

Cooking and Serving

Dip a few pieces of vegetables or seafood into the batter, and drop them into the hot oil. Don't cook too many at one time, as this will lower the temperature of the oil, which slows cooking and makes the coating soggy. As the pieces of food hit the hot oil, the icy batter expands. This puffing and swelling generates steam that helps cook the food.

Since tempura should be served as it is cooked, fry an assortment of foods at one time—a few pieces of seafood along with a choice of vegetables. Cook each piece until golden brown; then briefly drain on the tempura rack or paper towels.

Serve tempura with a sauce for dipping. We offer two choices: Mustard-Sour Cream Sauce and Basic Tempura Sauce, which has a soy sauce base.

BASIC TEMPURA

1 cup ice water
1 egg
1 cup all-purpose flour
Fresh vegetables
Seafood
Peanut oil

Combine water and egg, mixing well. Add flour; stir until well blended, but do not beat. Batter should be lumpy.

Dip well-chilled vegetables and seafood into batter, a few pieces at a time. Drop into deep oil heated to 375°, and fry until golden brown. Drain on tempura rack or paper towels. Serve immediately. Yield: about 1⅔ cups batter.
Yukie McLean,
Birmingham, Alabama.

CORNMEAL TEMPURA

½ cup all-purpose flour
½ cup cornmeal
2 tablespoons cornstarch
1 teaspoon baking powder
½ teaspoon salt
2 egg whites, lightly beaten
1 cup ice water
Fresh vegetables
Seafood
Peanut oil

Combine dry ingredients; add egg whites and water. Stir until well blended, but do not beat. Batter should be lumpy.

Dip well-chilled vegetables and seafood into batter, a few pieces at a time. Drop into deep oil heated to 375°, and fry until golden. Drain on tempura rack or paper towels. Serve immediately. Yield: about 1⅔ cups batter.
Charles Walton,
Birmingham, Alabama.

BASIC TEMPURA SAUCE

½ cup soy sauce
½ cup sweet cooking rice wine
1¼ cups water
¼ teaspoon monosodium glutamate

Combine all ingredients, stirring well; bring to a boil. Serve hot. Yield: about 2¼ cups.
Yukie McLean,
Birmingham, Alabama.

MUSTARD-SOUR CREAM SAUCE

⅓ cup commercial sour cream
⅓ cup plain yogurt
3 tablespoons Dijon mustard
2 teaspoons prepared horseradish
1 teaspoon dry sherry
½ teaspoon hot sauce
¼ teaspoon Worcestershire sauce

Combine all ingredients, stirring well. Chill sauce until serving time. Yield: about 1 cup.
Charles Walton,
Birmingham, Alabama.

Serve Vegetables Fresh And Crisp

For side dishes as crisp and refreshing as the season, serve the vegetables uncooked. Besides delighting you with crunchy textures, fresh flavors, and vibrant colors often lost during cooking, fresh vegetables also offer more nutrients than their cooked counterparts.

Easy, quick preparation is another plus. In just the time it takes to cut or slice the vegetables into bite-size pieces, toss with other ingredients, and allow to marinate, you'll have delectable dishes like Cauliflower-Broccoli Medley, Pickled Spinach, and Tomato Bowl.

For Cauliflower-Broccoli Medley, bite-size pieces of uncooked vegetables chill in a mayonnaise-base dressing.

MARINATED MUSHROOMS

½ cup olive oil
3 tablespoons tarragon vinegar
2 teaspoons dried parsley flakes
½ teaspoon salt
⅛ teaspoon pepper
1 pound fresh mushrooms, sliced

Combine all ingredients except mushrooms in a large bowl; stir well. Add mushrooms, tossing gently to coat. Chill for about 4 to 6 hours before serving. Yield: 4 servings. *Gail Hail, Moody, Texas.*

PICKLED SPINACH

2 cups torn spinach
1 cup chopped tomato
¼ cup chopped green pepper
¼ cup vinegar
⅓ to ½ cup vegetable oil
2 slices bacon, cooked and crumbled
Lettuce leaves (optional)

Combine first 5 ingredients, tossing gently. Chill at least 15 minutes. Sprinkle bacon over top; serve on lettuce leaves, if desired. Yield: 4 servings. *Aimee A. Goodman, Knoxville, Tennessee.*

TOMATO BOWL

¼ cup chopped fresh parsley
¼ cup vegetable oil
2 tablespoons cider vinegar
2 teaspoons prepared mustard
1 teaspoon salt
1 teaspoon sugar
¼ teaspoon pepper
1 clove garlic, minced
6 firm, ripe small tomatoes, sliced

Combine the first 8 ingredients, mixing well.

Place tomato slices in serving bowl, and pour dressing over all. Cover and let stand at room temperature 20 minutes before serving. Yield: 8 to 10 servings. *Mrs. John R. Armstrong, Farwell, Texas.*

CAULIFLOWER-BROCCOLI MEDLEY

1 head cauliflower
1 bunch broccoli
2 small onions, sliced and separated into rings
½ cup mayonnaise
⅓ cup vegetable oil
⅓ cup vinegar
¼ cup sugar
½ teaspoon salt
¼ teaspoon pepper
2 slices bacon, cooked and crumbled

Wash cauliflower, and remove green leaves. Separate the cauliflower into flowerets, slicing the large ones into bite-size pieces.

Trim off large leaves of broccoli. Remove tough ends of lower stalks, and wash broccoli thoroughly. Cut into bite-size pieces.

Combine vegetables in a large bowl. Combine remaining ingredients except bacon; add to vegetables, tossing gently. Chill several hours or overnight. Garnish with bacon. Yield: 6 to 8 servings. *Gwyn Prows Groseclose, Longwood, Florida.*

CUCUMBER AND ONION IN SOUR CREAM

½ cup commercial sour cream
1 tablespoon sugar
1 tablespoon vinegar
½ teaspoon salt
2 medium cucumbers, thinly sliced
2 small onions, thinly sliced

Combine sour cream, sugar, vinegar, and salt; add cucumber and onion, tossing gently. Cover and chill 24 hours, stirring occasionally. Yield: 4 servings. *Louise Spraggins, Birmingham, Alabama.*

Tip: Use a stiff vegetable brush to scrub vegetables rather than peel them. Peeling is not necessary for many vegetables and causes a loss of vitamins found in and just under the skin.

Our Layer Cakes Are Classic

Moist and feathery light, layer cakes have been a favorite dessert for as long as Southerners have been baking. And with every bite of cake comes a creamy bit of frosting.

Consider three tender layers of cake spread with a lemon-orange filling, frosted with fluffy white icing, and covered with coconut (fresh, of course). Small wonder it's called Stately Coconut Layer Cake. Blue Ribbon Carrot Cake boasts an orange-cream cheese frosting that's also spread between the layers. The frosting for our caramel layer cake is extra creamy, thanks to a base of whipping cream.

For success with these and our other layer cakes, see the article that follows on page 71 for some tips and techniques. We have also included a chart outlining causes of cake failures.

BROWN SUGAR MERINGUE CAKE

½ cup butter or margarine, softened
¾ cup firmly packed brown sugar
⅓ cup honey
3 eggs
2 cups all-purpose flour
½ teaspoon salt
1 teaspoon baking powder
¾ teaspoon soda
1 teaspoon ground cinnamon
¼ teaspoon ground cloves
½ teaspoon ground allspice
1¼ cups buttermilk
½ cup ground walnuts
½ cup ground golden raisins
1 teaspoon grated lemon rind
1 tablespoon honey
Brown Sugar Meringue Frosting

Cream butter; gradually add brown sugar, beating until light and fluffy. Add ⅓ cup honey, beating until smooth. Add eggs, one at a time, beating well after each addition.

Combine flour, salt, baking powder, soda, and spices; add to creamed mixture alternately with buttermilk, beginning and ending with flour mixture. Mix well after each addition.

Pour batter into 2 greased and floured 9-inch round cakepans. Bake at 350° for 20 to 25 minutes or until a wooden pick inserted in center comes out clean. Cool in pans 10 minutes; remove layers from pans, and let cool completely.

Combine walnuts, raisins, lemon rind, and 1 tablespoon honey; mix well. Spread over one cake layer, and top with about 1 cup Brown Sugar Meringue Frosting. Place second cake layer on top. Spread the remaining frosting on top and sides of cake. Yield: one 2-layer cake.

Brown Sugar Meringue Frosting:

1 cup firmly packed brown sugar
3 egg whites
1 tablespoon light corn syrup
½ teaspoon cream of tartar
Dash of salt
¼ cup water
1 teaspoon vanilla extract

Combine all ingredients except vanilla in top of a double boiler; beat 1 minute at high speed of electric mixer. Place over boiling water, and beat for 7 to 8 minutes or until stiff peaks form. Remove from heat; add vanilla, and beat an additional 2 minutes. Yield: enough to frost one 2-layer cake.

Susan Settlemyre,
Raleigh, North Carolina.

BLUE RIBBON CARROT CAKE

2 cups all-purpose flour
2 teaspoons soda
½ teaspoon salt
2 teaspoons ground cinnamon
3 eggs, well beaten
¾ cup vegetable oil
¾ cup buttermilk
2 cups sugar
2 teaspoons vanilla extract
1 (8-ounce) can crushed pineapple, drained
2 cups grated carrots
1 (3½-ounce) can flaked coconut
1 cup chopped walnuts
Buttermilk Glaze
Orange-Cream Cheese Frosting

Combine flour, soda, salt, and cinnamon; set aside.

Combine eggs, oil, buttermilk, sugar, and vanilla; beat until smooth. Stir in flour mixture, pineapple, carrots, coconut, and chopped walnuts. Pour batter into 2 greased and floured 9-inch round cakepans.

Bake at 350° for 35 to 40 minutes or until a wooden pick inserted in center comes out clean. Immediately spread Buttermilk Glaze evenly over layers. Cool in pans 15 minutes; remove from pans, and let cool completely.

Spread Orange-Cream Cheese Frosting between layers and on top and sides of cake. Store cake in refrigerator. Yield: one 2-layer cake.

Buttermilk Glaze:

1 cup sugar
½ teaspoon soda
½ cup buttermilk
½ cup butter
1 tablespoon light corn syrup
1 teaspoon vanilla extract

Combine sugar, soda, buttermilk, butter, and corn syrup in a Dutch oven. Bring to a boil; cook 4 minutes, stirring often. Remove from heat, and stir in vanilla. Yield: about 1½ cups.

Orange-Cream Cheese Frosting:

½ cup butter, softened
1 (8-ounce) package cream cheese, softened
1 teaspoon vanilla extract
2 cups sifted powdered sugar
1 teaspoon grated orange rind
1 teaspoon orange juice

Combine butter and cream cheese, beating until light and fluffy. Add vanilla, powdered sugar, rind, and juice; beat until smooth. Yield: enough for one 2-layer cake.

Grace Bravos,
Reisterstown, Maryland.

STATELY COCONUT LAYER CAKE

1 cup shortening
2 cups sugar
4 eggs
3 cups sifted cake flour
2½ teaspoons baking powder
½ teaspoon salt
1 cup milk
1 teaspoon almond extract
1 teaspoon vanilla extract
Lemon-Orange Filling
Luscious White Frosting
1 small fresh coconut, grated

Cream shortening; gradually add sugar, beating until light and fluffy. Add eggs, one at a time, beating well after each addition.

Combine flour, baking powder, and salt; add to creamed mixture alternately with milk, beginning and ending with flour mixture. Mix well after each addition. Stir in flavorings.

Pour batter into 3 greased and floured 9-inch round cakepans. Bake at 375° for 20 to 25 minutes or until a wooden pick inserted in center comes out clean. Cool in pans 10 minutes; remove layers from pans, and let cool completely.

Spread Lemon-Orange Filling between layers; spread top and sides with Luscious White Frosting, and sprinkle with coconut. Yield: one 3-layer cake.

Lemon-Orange Filling:

½ cup sifted cake flour
1 cup sugar
¼ teaspoon salt
¼ cup water
2 tablespoons grated orange rind
1 tablespoon grated lemon rind
1¼ cups orange juice
¼ cup lemon juice
4 egg yolks, well beaten

Combine flour, sugar, salt, and water in a heavy saucepan; mix well. Stir in fruit rind and juice. Cook over medium heat, stirring constantly, until mixture thickens and boils.

Gradually stir about one-fourth of hot mixture into egg yolks; add to remaining hot mixture, stirring constantly. Return to a boil; cook 1 to 2 minutes, stirring constantly. Remove from heat, and let cool completely. (Mixture will be thick.) Yield: about 2½ cups.

Luscious White Frosting:

1½ cups sugar
½ teaspoon cream of tartar
⅛ teaspoon salt
½ cup hot water
4 egg whites
½ teaspoon almond extract
½ teaspoon coconut extract

Combine sugar, cream of tartar, salt, and water in a heavy saucepan. Cook over medium heat, stirring constantly, until clear. Cook without stirring until candy thermometer registers 240° (soft ball stage).

Beat egg whites until soft peaks form; continue to beat, slowly adding syrup mixture. Add flavorings; continue beating until stiff peaks form and frosting is thick enough to spread. Yield: enough for one 3-layer cake.

Mrs. Earl L. Faulkenberry,
Lancaster, South Carolina.

CREAMY CARAMEL LAYER CAKE

¾ cup butter, softened
2 cups sugar
3 cups sifted cake flour
2 teaspoons baking powder
1 cup milk
1 teaspoon vanilla extract
5 egg whites (at room temperature)
Creamy Caramel Frosting

Cream butter; gradually add sugar, beating until light and fluffy.

Combine flour and baking powder; add to creamed mixture alternately with milk, beginning and ending with flour

Accurate measuring is the beginning of a successful cake. When a recipe calls for all-purpose flour, no sifting is necessary. However, cake flour should always be sifted before measuring.

mixture. Stir in vanilla. Mix well after each addition. Beat egg whites until stiff peaks form; fold into creamed mixture.

Pour batter into 2 greased and floured 9-inch round cakepans. Bake at 350° for 25 to 30 minutes or until a wooden pick inserted in center comes out clean. Cool in pans 10 minutes; remove layers from pans, and let cool completely.

Spread Creamy Caramel Frosting between layers and on top and sides of cake. Yield: one 2-layer cake.

Creamy Caramel Frosting:

3 cups sugar
2 cups whipping cream
¼ cup butter
¼ cup light corn syrup
1 tablespoon vanilla extract

Combine all ingredients except vanilla in a buttered heavy saucepan; cook over medium heat, stirring often, until a candy thermometer reaches 240° (soft ball stage). Let cool slightly; add vanilla, and beat until spreading consistency. Yield: enough for one 2-layer cake. *Florence L. Costello,*
Chattanooga, Tennessee.

A Perfect Cake Is A Matter Of Technique

A perfect layer cake results not from luck but from accurate measuring and proper mixing and baking. To ensure your success use the tips and techniques that follow. You'll also find that the chart included here will be helpful in diagnosing and correcting cake failures.

—Position the oven rack in the center of the oven. Unless otherwise specified in the recipe, always preheat the oven when baking cakes.

—Be sure to use the correct pan size.

—Grease cakepans with shortening; do not use oil, butter, or margarine. Lightly dust pans with flour.

—Let eggs, butter, and milk reach room temperature before mixing.

—When a recipe calls for all-purpose flour, no sifting is necessary unless specified; simply spoon the flour into the measuring cup, leveling it with a straight edge. However, always sift cake flour before measuring.

—Cream shortening thoroughly. Gradually add sugar, and beat until

Add dry and liquid ingredients alternately, beginning and ending with dry. Beat well after each addition, but only until batter is smooth; overbeating results in cake with heavy texture.

CAKE FAILURE CHART

Problem	Possible Cause
Cake falls	Oven not hot enough Undermixing Insufficient baking Opening oven door during baking Too much leavening, liquid, or sugar
Peaks in center	Oven too hot at start of baking Too much flour Not enough liquid
Sticks to pan	Cake cooled in pan too long Pan not greased and floured
Cracks and falls apart	Removed from pan too soon Too much shortening, leavening, or sugar
Sticky crust	Insufficient baking Oven not hot enough Too much sugar
Heavy texture	Overmixing when flour and liquid added Oven temperature too low Too much shortening, sugar, or liquid
Coarse texture	Inadequate mixing or creaming Oven temperature too low Too much leavening
Dry texture	Overbaking Overbeaten egg whites Too much flour or leavening Not enough shortening or sugar

light and fluffy. (Beating will take about 7 minutes with a standard mixer, longer with a portable type.)

—Add only one egg at a time, and beat 1 minute after each addition.

—Add dry and liquid ingredients alternately to creamed mixture, beginning and ending with dry ingredients. Beat well after each addition, but only until the batter is smooth; do not overbeat. Using a rubber spatula, scrape sides and bottom of bowl often during beating.

—Stagger cakepans so they do not touch each other or the sides of the oven. If they must be placed on separate racks, stagger the pans so air can circulate around them.

—Keep the oven door closed until minimum baking time has elapsed.

—Test the cake for doneness before removing it from the oven (underbaking can cause a cake to fall). The cake is done when a wooden pick inserted in the center comes out clean or if the cake springs back when lightly touched.

—Let the layers cool completely before adding filling and frosting. Lightly brush the cake to remove loose crumbs.

—To keep the cake plate looking neat, place three or four strips of waxed paper over the edges. Position the cake on the plate, and fill and frost it; then carefully pull out the strips of waxed paper.

—When filling the cake, place the first two layers with the bottom side up;

place the last layer so the top side is up.

—Frost the sides of the cake first, then the top. Before you begin, you may want to spread a thin layer of frosting on the sides to set any remaining crumbs.

Before filling and frosting a layer cake, place three or four strips of waxed paper over the edges of the cake plate to keep it looking neat. Simply pull out the paper when the cake is frosted.

Custom-Made Burgers Suit Every Taste

Hamburgers get a lift with these recipes, which are custom-made to suit every taste. Enjoy them with or without the bun, piled with condiments, or covered with a special sauce.

Be sure to try our Pizza Burgers—the patties are flavored with Parmesan cheese, onion, and olives, while sliced tomatoes and melted mozzarella cheese provide the finishing touch.

TERIYAKI BURGERS

1 pound ground beef
1 cup soft breadcrumbs
2 tablespoons finely chopped onion
1 egg, slightly beaten
1 tablespoon plus 1 teaspoon sugar
2 tablespoons soy sauce
2 tablespoons water
1 small clove garlic, crushed
Dash of ground ginger
4 hamburger buns, split and toasted

Combine all ingredients except hamburger buns; mix well and shape into 4 patties. Broil 4 to 5 inches from heat for

5 minutes on each side or until desired degree of doneness.

Place patties on bottom of buns; cover with bun tops. Yield: 4 servings.
Cheryl Keener,
Lenoir, North Carolina.

PIZZA BURGERS

1 pound ground beef
¼ cup plus 2 tablespoons grated Parmesan cheese
¼ cup plus 2 tablespoons finely chopped onion
¼ cup catsup
10 ripe olives, chopped
1 teaspoon salt
1 teaspoon dried whole oregano
4 hamburger buns, split and toasted
4 tomato slices
3 slices mozzarella cheese, cut into ½-inch strips

Combine first 7 ingredients; mix well, and shape into 4 patties. Broil 5 inches from heat for 6 minutes on each side or until desired degree of doneness.

Place patties on bottom of buns; top each with slices of tomato and cheese. Broil until cheese melts. Cover with top half of buns. Yield: 4 servings.
Hedy Samuels,
Southern Pines, North Carolina.

GLORIFIED HAMBURGERS

1 pound ground beef
½ cup finely chopped celery
1 small onion, finely chopped
½ cup catsup
1 tablespoon Worcestershire sauce
½ teaspoon salt
¼ teaspoon pepper
1 cup (4 ounces) shredded Cheddar cheese
4 hamburger buns
Mayonnaise

Cook beef until lightly browned, stirring constantly; drain well. Add next 6 ingredients; simmer 10 minutes, stirring occasionally. Stir in cheese.

Spoon mixture onto bottom half of buns. Spread about 1 teaspoon mayonnaise on the cut side of each bun top; place on top of beef mixture. Wrap hamburgers in aluminum foil; bake at 300° for 20 minutes. Yield: 4 servings.
Mrs. Dean Piercy,
Memphis, Tennessee.

HAMBURGERS WITH TOMATO SAUCE

1 pound ground beef
½ cup soft breadcrumbs
¼ teaspoon salt
Dash of pepper
1 (8-ounce) can tomato sauce
2 tablespoons instant minced onion
2 tablespoons brown sugar
1 teaspoon Worcestershire sauce
1 teaspoon prepared mustard

Combine beef, breadcrumbs, salt, and pepper; mix well. Shape into 4 patties about ¾ inch thick. Cook in a medium skillet until brown on each side; drain.

Combine remaining ingredients, stirring well; pour over patties. Simmer 10 minutes. Yield: 4 servings.
Carol S. Noble,
Burgaw, North Carolina.

Choose An Aspic For Lunch

Next time you have friends over for lunch, round out the menu with one of these glistening molded salads. Sunshine Apple Aspic is on the crunchy side, filled with bits of apple, green pepper, and onion. If you favor tomato aspic, try our well-seasoned Herbed Tomato Aspic or Cheesy Vegetable Aspic, with a tomato soup and cream cheese base.

SUNSHINE APPLE ASPIC

3 envelopes unflavored gelatin
1 cup cold water
3 cups boiling water
¾ cup sugar
1½ teaspoons salt
⅓ cup cider vinegar
¼ cup lime juice
2 large sweet green apples, unpeeled and chopped
1 large green pepper, chopped
½ cup chopped green onion
Lettuce
Apple slices

Soften gelatin in cold water. Add boiling water, sugar, and salt; stir until gelatin is dissolved. Stir in vinegar and lime juice; chill until consistency of unbeaten egg white. Fold in apple, green pepper, and onion.

Spoon into a lightly oiled 9- x 5- x 3-inch loafpan; chill until firm. Unmold on lettuce, and garnish with apple slices. Yield: 8 to 10 servings.
Marie LaZelle,
Grove, Oklahoma.

CHEESY VEGETABLE ASPIC

1 (10¾-ounce) can tomato soup, undiluted
2 (3-ounce) packages cream cheese
1 envelope unflavored gelatin
¼ cup cold water
½ cup boiling water
⅓ cup finely chopped carrot
⅓ cup finely chopped onion
⅓ cup finely chopped green pepper
½ cup mayonnaise
¼ teaspoon salt

Place soup in a heavy saucepan; bring to a boil over medium heat, stirring constantly. Add cream cheese, and stir until completely melted.

Soften gelatin in cold water; stir in boiling water. Add to soup mixture; stir in vegetables, mayonnaise, and salt. Pour into a 10- x 6- x 2-inch dish; chill until firm. Yield: 8 servings.
Mrs. J. E. Printup,
Hendersonville, North Carolina.

HERBED TOMATO ASPIC

3 envelopes unflavored gelatin
¾ cup cold water
2½ cups tomato juice, divided
1 (6-ounce) can tomato paste
¼ cup vinegar
3 tablespoons lemon juice
1½ teaspoons dried whole basil
1 teaspoon salt
1 teaspoon sugar
⅛ teaspoon black pepper
⅛ teaspoon onion powder
½ teaspoon Worcestershire sauce

Soften gelatin in water. Bring 1 cup tomato juice to a boil; remove from heat and add gelatin, stirring until dissolved. Add tomato paste, and stir until blended. Add remaining tomato juice and remaining ingredients; stir well. Pour into a lightly oiled 6-cup mold; chill until firm. Yield: 6 to 8 servings.
Martha Edington,
Oak Ridge, Tennessee.

Microwave Cookery

Main Dishes Especially For The Microwave

In answer to numerous requests for more main dishes prepared in the microwave, here are four recipes that our test kitchens developed especially for the microwave oven.

Lots of cheese goes into Cheesy Pork Casserole, a hearty combination of egg noodles, vegetables, and ground pork. For a sandwich meal, we suggest crabmeat, tomato slices, and a creamy spread layered on toasted English muffins. Equally delicious are Creamed Ham and Chicken and the delicate Spinach-Mushroom Quiche.

DELUXE CRABMEAT SANDWICHES

⅓ cup finely chopped celery
¼ cup mayonnaise
1 teaspoon lemon juice
4 slices tomato
1 (6-ounce) package frozen crabmeat, thawed and drained
2 tablespoons finely chopped onion
2 English muffins, split and toasted
Salt and pepper to taste
½ cup (2 ounces) shredded Cheddar cheese

Combine chopped celery, mayonnaise, and lemon juice; mix well, and spread over tomato slices. Set aside.

Combine crabmeat and onion in a small bowl; mix well. Microwave at HIGH for 3 to 4 minutes or until thoroughly heated, stirring twice. Drain well. Spoon hot crab mixture onto English muffins, and place in an 8-inch square baking dish.

Top sandwiches with tomato slices, and sprinkle with salt and pepper. Top with cheese. Microwave at HIGH for 1 minute to 1 minute 15 seconds or until cheese begins to melt. Yield: 2 to 4 servings.

Tip: Use LOW setting on the microwave oven to soften cheese for cutting or spreading, leftover icings or frostings, honey and spreads, and butter or cream cheese.

CREAMED HAM AND CHICKEN

2 tablespoons butter or margarine
3 tablespoons all-purpose flour
⅛ teaspoon celery salt
¾ cup chicken broth
¾ cup half-and-half
1 cup cubed cooked ham
1 cup cubed cooked chicken
1 tablespoon chopped fresh parsley
Baked patty shells or hot cooked rice

Place butter in a 4-cup glass measure; microwave at HIGH for 30 to 40 seconds or until butter melts. Blend in flour and celery salt. Gradually add chicken broth and half-and-half, stirring well. Microwave at HIGH for 1½ minutes; stir well. Microwave at HIGH for 2½ to 3½ minutes, stirring at 1-minute intervals, until thickened and bubbly.

Add ham, chicken, and parsley to sauce; stir well. Microwave at MEDIUM HIGH for 1½ to 2 minutes or until thoroughly heated. Serve in patty shells or over rice. Yield: 4 servings.

CHEESY PORK CASSEROLE

1¼ pounds ground pork
1 cup chopped fresh mushrooms
½ cup chopped onion
4 ounces (3 cups uncooked) medium egg noodles, cooked and drained
2 cups (8 ounces) shredded process American cheese, divided
1 (17-ounce) can small English peas, drained
1 (10¾-ounce) can cream of mushroom soup, undiluted
¼ teaspoon salt
⅛ teaspoon pepper

Crumble pork into a 3-quart casserole; stir in mushrooms and onion. Cover with heavy-duty clear plastic wrap; microwave at HIGH for 5 to 7 minutes or until pork is done, stirring twice. Drain off excess drippings.

Add noodles, 1½ cups cheese, peas, soup, and seasonings; stir well. Cover and microwave at MEDIUM HIGH for 9 to 11 minutes or until thoroughly heated, stirring once. Sprinkle with remaining cheese. Cover and cook at MEDIUM for 1½ to 2½ minutes or until cheese melts. Yield: 6 to 8 servings.

SPINACH-MUSHROOM QUICHE

1 (10-ounce) package frozen chopped spinach
1 cup (4 ounces) shredded Monterey Jack cheese
Microwaved quiche pastry (recipe follows)
1 (4-ounce) can sliced mushrooms, well drained
3 eggs, beaten
1½ cups half-and-half
½ teaspoon salt
⅛ teaspoon ground nutmeg
⅛ teaspoon pepper
2 tablespoons grated Parmesan cheese
Ground nutmeg

Pierce spinach package with a fork; place package in a flat baking dish. Microwave at HIGH for 5 to 7 minutes or until done, giving dish one half-turn during cooking. Remove spinach from package, and drain well. Place spinach between paper towels, and squeeze until spinach is barely moist.

Sprinkle Monterey Jack cheese in microwaved pastry shell; top with spinach and mushrooms. Combine eggs, half-and-half, salt, ⅛ teaspoon nutmeg, and pepper; pour into quiche shell. Sprinkle with Parmesan cheese and additional ground nutmeg.

Microwave at MEDIUM HIGH for 7 to 12 minutes or until a knife inserted off-center comes out clean (center will be slightly soft). Let stand 10 minutes before serving. Yield: one 9½-inch quiche.

Microwaved Quiche Pastry:

1 cup all-purpose flour
½ teaspoon salt
⅓ cup plus 1 tablespoon shortening
2 to 3 tablespoons cold water
3 to 4 drops of yellow food coloring (optional)

Combine flour and salt; cut in shortening with pastry blender until mixture resembles coarse meal. Combine water and food coloring if extra color is desired (pastry will not brown in microwave oven). Sprinkle water evenly over flour mixture; stir with a fork until all of the ingredients are moistened. Shape into a ball.

Place dough on a lightly floured surface, and roll it into a circle 2 inches larger than inverted 9½-inch quiche dish. Fit pastry loosely into dish. Trim edges, and fold under to form a standing rim; then flute.

Place a piece of heavy-duty plastic wrap over pastry; cover with dried beans or peas. Microwave at HIGH for 5½ to 7 minutes or until pastry is opaque and bottom is dry. Yield: pastry for one 9½-inch quiche.

Give A New Look To Vegetables

If you've slipped into a routine of serving the same vegetable dishes meal after meal, you may want to look over these recipes. The dishes are not elaborate, just favorite vegetables prepared with a different twist.

You'll find broccoli and onions baked in a cream cheese sauce and topped with buttered breadcrumbs, as well as Stir-Fried Cabbage and Scalloped Potatoes With Pimiento.

LAREDO RANCH BEANS

1 pound dried pinto beans
8 cups water
½ pound salt pork, diced
1 clove garlic, minced
2 cups chopped onion
2 tablespoons Worcestershire sauce
1 teaspoon chili powder
1 teaspoon prepared mustard
2 cups peeled, diced tomatoes
¼ teaspoon salt
⅛ teaspoon pepper

Sort and wash beans; place in a large Dutch oven. Cover with water, and add pork. Bring to a boil; reduce heat, and simmer 1 hour. Add remaining ingredients; cover and cook over low heat 30 minutes. Uncover and continue to cook over low heat about 30 minutes. Yield: 8 to 10 servings.
Margaret Beasley,
Timpson, Texas.

BROCCOLI-ONION DELUXE

1 to 1½ pounds fresh broccoli, cut into
    1½-inch pieces
3 small onions, quartered
2 tablespoons butter or margarine
2 tablespoons all-purpose flour
1 cup milk
1 (3-ounce) package cream cheese, cut
    into cubes
¼ teaspoon salt
⅛ teaspoon white pepper
½ cup (2 ounces) shredded process sharp
    American cheese
2 tablespoons butter or margarine, melted
1 cup soft breadcrumbs

Cook broccoli and onion in a small amount of boiling water 3 to 4 minutes or until tender. Drain well.

Melt 2 tablespoons butter in a heavy saucepan over low heat; add flour, stirring until smooth. Cook 1 minute, stirring constantly. Gradually add milk;

cook over medium heat, stirring constantly, until thickened and bubbly. Remove from heat; add cream cheese, and stir until melted. Stir in salt and pepper. Pour over vegetables; stir gently. Spoon into a lightly greased 1½-quart casserole; top with cheese. Cover and bake at 350° for 25 minutes.

Combine remaining butter and breadcrumbs; toss gently. Uncover casserole, and sprinkle with buttered breadcrumbs; bake 5 additional minutes or until golden brown. Yield: 6 servings.
Mrs. Jack Corzine,
St. Louis, Missouri.

STIR-FRIED CABBAGE

1 tablespoon vegetable oil
1 onion, thinly sliced
4 cups coarsely shredded cabbage
1 cup thinly sliced celery
½ cup chicken broth
2 tablespoons soy sauce

Heat oil in a wok or large skillet. Add remaining ingredients; cook over high heat, stirring constantly, until cabbage is crisp-tender. Yield: 8 servings.
Mrs. Vaiden Hiner,
Abilene, Texas.

ORIENTAL CAULIFLOWER

1 medium head cauliflower
1 medium onion, chopped
½ cup diced celery
3 sprigs fresh parsley, chopped
1 tablespoon butter or margarine, melted
1 tablespoon cornstarch
1 beef or chicken-flavored bouillon cube
1 cup hot water
1 tablespoon soy sauce
Dash of pepper

Wash cauliflower, and break into flowerets. Cook, covered, in a small amount of boiling salted water about 8 to 10 minutes or until crisp-tender; drain.

Sauté onion, celery, and parsley in butter until tender. Remove from heat; add cornstarch, stirring until blended. Dissolve bouillon in 1 cup hot water; gradually add to vegetable mixture, stirring constantly. Add soy sauce and pepper; cook over medium heat, stirring constantly, until smooth and thickened. Pour over cauliflower in serving dish. Yield: 6 servings.
Mrs. Donald C. Vanhoy,
Salisbury, North Carolina.

BAKED VEGETABLE MEDLEY

1½ cups fresh corn (about 3 ears)
¾ cup peeled, chopped tomato
⅓ cup cornmeal
2 cups (8 ounces) shredded Cheddar
    cheese
1 medium onion, chopped
1 medium-size green pepper, chopped
2 eggs, beaten
¾ cup milk
½ teaspoon salt
Dash of pepper

Combine first 6 ingredients; let stand 30 minutes. Spoon into a lightly greased 12- x 8- x 2-inch baking dish. Combine remaining ingredients; pour over vegetables. Bake at 325° for 35 to 40 minutes or until set. Yield: 8 to 10 servings.
Mrs. J. B. Arthur,
San Antonio, Texas.

Take A Little Thyme

Thyme, known as "the poor man's herb" because it's so easy to grow, rates as a best seller in supermarkets. Southerners enjoy thyme's sweet but pungent taste and trust the herb to flavor even their most renowned dishes.

Like any herb, store thyme in an airtight container away from light and heat to preserve its potency; if space permits, your freezer provides ideal storage. The herb stays free flowing and will be ready to spice up your meals.

CREAMY BROCCOLI SOUP

1 (10¾-ounce) can cream of potato soup,
    undiluted
1 (10¾-ounce) can cream of celery soup,
    undiluted
1¼ cups milk
1 teaspoon Dijon mustard
½ teaspoon dried whole thyme
¼ teaspoon dry mustard
¼ teaspoon dried whole basil (optional)
1 (10-ounce) package frozen chopped
    broccoli

Heat soup in a 2-quart saucepan; gradually add milk, stirring until smooth. Add remaining ingredients; cook over low heat 40 minutes, stirring occasionally. Yield: about 5 cups.
Susun A. Houston,
Tucker, Georgia.

April 75

BEEF STEW WITH PARSLEY DUMPLINGS

⅓ cup all-purpose flour
2½ teaspoons salt
¼ teaspoon pepper
3 pounds lean beef for stewing, cut into 1-inch cubes
¼ cup butter or margarine
3 cups water
½ cup chopped celery tops
1½ teaspoons dried whole thyme
4 whole cloves
2 sprigs fresh parsley
1 bay leaf
1 pound boiling onions
1 pound carrots, cut in half crosswise
1½ pounds small new potatoes
2 medium turnips, peeled and quartered
2 stalks celery, cut into 1-inch pieces
¼ cup water
3 tablespoons all-purpose flour
½ cup milk
1 egg
2 tablespoons chopped fresh parsley
2 cups biscuit mix

Combine ⅓ cup flour, salt, and pepper; dredge meat in flour mixture, and brown in butter in an 8-quart Dutch oven. Stir in next 6 ingredients; bring to a boil. Reduce heat; cover and simmer 2 hours, stirring occasionally.

Add onion, carrots, and potatoes; cover and cook over medium heat 20 minutes. Stir in turnips and celery; cover and cook 20 to 25 minutes.

Combine ¼ cup water and 3 tablespoons flour, stirring until smooth. Stir into stew; cook until thickened.

Combine milk, egg, and 2 tablespoons parsley; stir well. Add milk mixture to biscuit mix, and stir just until all ingredients are moistened. Drop by tablespoonfuls onto stew. Cook, uncovered, over low heat 10 minutes. Cover and cook 10 additional minutes. Yield: 10 to 12 servings. *Lilly B. Smith, Richmond, Virginia.*

FANCY FOWL

4 whole chicken breasts, split, skinned, and boned
3 slices cooked ham, cut into thin strips
1 cup (4 ounces) shredded Swiss cheese
Salt
White pepper
Dried whole thyme
1 cup all-purpose flour
¼ cup butter or margarine
3 tablespoons chopped shallots
2 cups sliced fresh mushrooms
1 cup dry white wine
1 cup whipping cream
2 tablespoons tomato paste
Hot cooked rice

Place each chicken breast on a sheet of waxed paper; flatten to ¼-inch thickness, using a meat mallet or rolling pin.

Place 4 to 5 strips of ham horizontally across each chicken breast; sprinkle cheese evenly over chicken. Sprinkle with salt, pepper, and thyme. Fold long sides of chicken to center; fold in sides of chicken to center, and secure with wooden picks. Dredge chicken in flour.

Melt butter in large skillet; add chicken and sauté, turning gently, until tender. Transfer chicken to an ovenproof dish, reserving drippings in pan; keep chicken warm in oven.

Add shallots and mushrooms to reserved pan drippings; sauté until onion is browned. Combine wine, whipping cream, and tomato paste, stirring until smooth; add to mushroom mixture. Cook over low heat 10 to 15 minutes or until thickened, stirring constantly. Pour mixture over chicken, and serve with rice. Yield: 8 servings. *Ted J. Kleisner, Savannah, Georgia.*

His Recipes Are For Entertaining

After a busy day in the nation's capital, Rick Mann, a Washington, D.C., attorney, heads for his Bethesda, Maryland, home to pursue his favorite hobby—cooking. Rick learned to cook when he was a law student, beginning outside on the grill. He has since experimented with all types of foods, and lately he's taken to Chinese and Mexican cuisines.

One of Rick's favorite recipes for entertaining is Hot Chicken Supreme. "It's great because it can be made up to the point of adding the noodles, then frozen," he says. "The recipe can be multiplied to feed as many as you want. I've fed up to 30 with this recipe."

Rick suggests serving his Hot Chicken Supreme with a fresh green salad, hot brandied fruit, and French bread.

Another one of Rick's favorites is Breaded Baked Chicken, chicken breasts coated in breadcrumbs and Parmesan cheese. Preparation time is minimal. Following Rick's recipes, we've included specialties from other men who enjoy cooking.

HOT CHICKEN SUPREME

3 whole chicken breasts, cooked and diced
1½ cups chopped celery
1 cup (4 ounces) shredded sharp Cheddar cheese
1 cup mayonnaise
¼ cup milk
¼ cup slivered almonds, toasted
¼ cup chopped pimiento
2 tablespoons dry sherry
2 teaspoons chopped onion
½ teaspoon poultry seasoning
½ teaspoon grated lemon rind
1 (3-ounce) can Chinese noodles

Combine all ingredients except noodles; stir well. Spoon chicken mixture into a greased 1½-quart casserole, and top with noodles. Bake at 350° for 30 minutes. Yield: 6 to 8 servings.

BREADED BAKED CHICKEN

2 cups French breadcrumbs
½ cup grated Parmesan cheese
1 to 2 teaspoons garlic salt
½ to 1 teaspoon pepper
3 whole chicken breasts, halved and skinned
½ cup butter or margarine, melted

Combine breadcrumbs, cheese, garlic salt, and pepper. Dip chicken in butter; then dredge in breadcrumb mixture. Place in a lightly greased 13- x 9- x 2-inch baking pan; sprinkle with remaining crumb mixture.

Bake at 350° for 45 minutes or until done. Yield: 6 servings.

CHICKEN LIVERS WITH MARSALA WINE SAUCE

½ cup all-purpose flour
½ cup milk
1 egg, beaten
1 tablespoon butter, melted
¼ teaspoon salt
Dash of ground nutmeg
1 egg white
1 cup all-purpose flour
½ teaspoon salt
⅛ teaspoon pepper
1 pound chicken livers
3 tablespoons butter, melted
Vegetable oil
Marsala Wine Sauce

Combine first 6 ingredients; mix until smooth. Refrigerate 1 hour.

Beat egg white (at room temperature) until stiff peaks form; fold into batter.

Combine 1 cup flour, ½ teaspoon salt, and pepper; stir well. Dredge livers in flour mixture, and sauté in 3 tablespoons butter about 5 minutes or until browned (livers should still be pink inside). Drain well on paper towels.

Dip livers into batter, and fry in deep oil heated to 375°. Cook until golden, turning once. Drain on paper towels. Serve hot with Marsala Wine Sauce. Yield: 4 servings.

Marsala Wine Sauce:

½ cup plus 2 tablespoons milk
1½ tablespoons butter
1½ tablespoons all-purpose flour
⅛ teaspoon salt
2 tablespoons Marsala wine

Scald milk. Combine half the milk, butter, flour, and salt in container of electric blender; process at low speed until smooth. Add remaining milk, and process at high speed until frothy.

Pour sauce in a small saucepan, and add wine to sauce. Cook over low heat, stirring constantly, until thickened and thoroughly heated. Yield: about ⅔ cup.
Wayne Kroeger,
Fort Lauderdale, Florida.

HOT TEXAS CHILI

1½ pounds lean ground beef
½ pound bulk pork sausage
2 medium onions, chopped
1 (8-ounce) can tomato sauce
1 medium-size green pepper, chopped
1 jalapeño pepper, seeded and chopped
1 clove garlic, minced
2 tablespoons chili powder
½ teaspoon salt
¼ teaspoon dried whole oregano
1 cup beer
¼ cup instant corn masa, divided
¼ teaspoon red pepper
Chopped onion (optional)
Commercial sour cream (optional)

Combine ground beef, sausage, and 2 chopped onions in a large Dutch oven; cook over medium heat, stirring to crumble meat, until meat is browned and onion is tender. Add tomato sauce and 1 cup water; simmer 15 minutes. Add green pepper, jalapeño pepper, garlic, chili powder, salt, oregano, and beer; bring to a boil. Gradually stir a small amount of hot mixture into 2 tablespoons masa; add to remaining hot mixture, stirring constantly. Reduce heat; cover and simmer 30 minutes, stirring occasionally.

Gradually add ½ cup water to remaining masa, stirring until smooth.

Add to chili mixture, and stir well. Add an additional 1 cup water and red pepper; simmer 15 to 20 minutes. Serve with additional chopped onion and sour cream, if desired. Yield: 6 to 8 servings.
Jay Jerome,
Charlottesville, Virginia.

BLOODY MARY-TOMATO ASPIC

4 envelopes unflavored gelatin
3¾ cups tomato juice, divided
¼ cup water
1 teaspoon celery salt
1 tablespoon Worcestershire sauce
1½ teaspoons hot sauce
½ teaspoon aromatic bitters
Lettuce
Cottage cheese

Soften gelatin in ¾ cup tomato juice and ¼ cup water; let stand 5 minutes.

Combine 3 cups tomato juice, celery salt, Worcestershire, hot sauce, and bitters in a saucepan; bring to a boil. Remove from heat and add gelatin mixture, stirring until gelatin dissolves.

Pour into an oiled 4½-cup ring mold; chill until firm. Unmold on lettuce-lined serving plate, and fill center with cottage cheese. Yield: 8 to 10 servings.
Robert V. Allen,
Memphis, Tennessee.

HOMEMADE MUSTARD

½ cup sugar
¼ cup plus 1 tablespoon dry mustard
½ teaspoon salt
2 tablespoons all-purpose flour
1 cup milk
1 egg yolk
½ cup vinegar

Combine sugar, mustard, salt, and flour in a small saucepan; stir well. Combine remaining ingredients; beat well. Gradually add milk mixture to mustard mixture; cook over low heat, stirring constantly, until thickened and bubbly. Cool thoroughly, and store in refrigerator. Yield: 1¾ cups.
Dr. Henry Orr,
Opelika, Alabama.

Tip: Raw eggs separate more easily while still cold from the refrigerator, but let whites reach room temperature to get maximum volume when beating.

Bake This Special Easter Bread

Hot Cross Buns were traditionally baked for serving on Good Friday, but now they're enjoyed throughout Lent. These slightly sweet buns are filled with currants and marked with a cross made of powdered sugar frosting.

HOT CROSS BUNS

4 to 4½ cups all-purpose flour
2 packages dry yeast
¾ teaspoon ground cinnamon
¾ cup milk
⅓ cup sugar
½ cup vegetable oil
¾ teaspoon salt
3 eggs
⅔ cup currants
1 egg white, slightly beaten
1 cup powdered sugar
1 tablespoon milk
½ teaspoon vanilla extract

Combine 2 cups flour, yeast, and cinnamon; mix well.

Scald milk; stir in ⅓ cup sugar, oil, and salt. Let cool to lukewarm (105° to 115°). Gradually add milk mixture to flour mixture, beating at low speed of electric mixer. Add eggs; beat 3 minutes at high speed. Stir in currants and enough remaining flour to make a soft dough.

Place dough in a well-greased bowl, turning to grease top. Cover and let rise in a warm place (85°), free from drafts, about 1½ hours or until doubled in bulk. Punch down dough; cover and let rest 10 minutes.

Divide dough into 18 pieces; shape into balls, and place 2 inches apart on greased cookie sheets. Cover and let rise in a warm place (85°), free from drafts, about 1 hour or until doubled in bulk.

Using a sharp knife, cut a shallow cross on top of each bun; brush each with egg white. Bake at 375° for 12 to 15 minutes; cool on wire racks.

Combine powdered sugar, milk, and vanilla; mix well. Pipe into cross-shaped indentation on each bun. Yield: 1½ dozen.
Peggy Fenderson,
Stillwater, Oklahoma.

Bake Homemade Rolls For Dinner

Homemade yeast rolls are one of the nicest things that can happen to dinner. They add a flavor that can't be matched by commercial products, and the aroma that fills the house while they bake is an added bonus.

If lack of time keeps you from baking rolls, select the recipe for Refrigerator Dinner Rolls. The dough keeps in the refrigerator for several days, then takes only an hour to rise and another 12 minutes to bake.

REFRIGERATOR DINNER ROLLS

2 packages dry yeast
⅓ cup sugar
2 cups warm water (105° to 115°)
6½ to 7 cups all-purpose flour
2 teaspoons salt
1 egg
⅓ cup shortening, melted

Combine yeast and sugar in a large bowl; add warm water, stirring until yeast dissolves. Stir in 3½ cups flour and salt; beat with a wooden spoon about 2 minutes or until smooth. Add egg and shortening, mixing well. Add just enough remaining flour to make a soft dough.

Turn dough out onto a lightly floured surface, and knead about 2 minutes or until smooth. Place in a well-greased bowl, turning to grease top. Cover and refrigerate about 2 hours or until doubled in bulk. (Dough may be stored in refrigerator several days.)

Punch dough down. Shape into ¾-inch balls; place 3 balls in each cup of well-greased muffin pans. Cover and let rise in a warm place (85°), free from drafts, 1 hour or until doubled in bulk. Bake at 400° about 12 minutes or until golden brown. Yield: about 2 dozen.
Lois Rodriquez,
Henryetta, Oklahoma.

COTTAGE CHEESE ROLLS

2 packages dry yeast
½ cup warm water (105° to 115°)
2 cups cream-style cottage cheese
¼ cup sugar
1½ teaspoons salt
½ teaspoon soda
2 eggs
About 5 cups all-purpose flour

Dissolve yeast in warm water. Combine cottage cheese, sugar, salt, soda, eggs, yeast mixture, and 1 cup flour in a large mixing bowl; mix well.

Gradually add remaining flour, and mix well. Place dough in a well-greased bowl, turning to grease top. Cover and let rise in a warm place (85°), free from drafts, 45 minutes or until dough is doubled in bulk.

Turn dough out onto a lightly floured surface. Divide dough in half. Divide each half into 12 equal portions; roll into balls. Place in 2 well-greased 9-inch baking pans. Cover and let rise in warm place (85°), free from drafts, 45 minutes or until doubled in bulk. Bake at 350° about 20 minutes or until golden brown. Yield: 2 dozen. *Carolyn Ferguson,*
Piney Flats, Tennessee.

SUPER PARKERHOUSE ROLLS

2 packages dry yeast
½ cup warm water (105° to 115°)
1½ cups milk
½ cup sugar
2 teaspoons salt
¼ cup shortening
About 5½ cups all-purpose flour
1 egg, beaten
Butter or margarine, melted

Dissolve yeast in warm water, and set aside.

Scald milk in a small saucepan; add sugar, salt, and shortening, stirring until shortening melts. Cool to lukewarm. Add 2 cups flour; beat until smooth. Add yeast mixture and egg; beat well. Stir in remaining flour to make a soft dough.

Turn dough out onto a lightly floured surface, and knead until smooth and elastic (about 8 to 10 minutes). Place in a well-greased bowl, turning to grease top. Cover and let rise in a warm place (85°), free from drafts, 1½ hours or until doubled in bulk.

Punch dough down. Roll out to ¼-inch thickness on a lightly floured surface; cut into 3-inch circles, and brush with butter.

Make a crease across each circle, and fold one half over. Gently press edges to seal. Place on greased cookie sheets. Cover; let rise in a warm place (85°), free from drafts, 45 minutes or until doubled in bulk. Bake at 400° for 10 to 12 minutes or until golden brown. Yield: about 3 dozen rolls.
Billie Taylor,
Afton, Virginia.

EASY YEAST ROLLS

2 tablespoons warm water (105° to 115°)
1 package dry yeast
3 tablespoons sugar
2 cups buttermilk
1 teaspoon soda
5 cups all-purpose flour
1 tablespoon baking powder
1½ teaspoons salt
1 cup shortening

Combine water, yeast, and sugar; let stand 5 minutes.

Combine buttermilk and soda, mixing well. Combine flour, baking powder, and salt; mix well. Cut shortening into flour mixture with pastry blender until mixture resembles coarse meal.

Combine yeast mixture, buttermilk mixture, and flour mixture; stir well.

Turn dough out onto a heavily floured surface, and knead about 8 times. Shape into a ball; place in a greased bowl, turning to grease top. Cover and let rise in a warm place (85°), free from drafts, 1½ hours or until doubled in bulk.

Roll dough out to ½ inch thickness on a lightly floured surface. Cut into 2-inch circles. Place rolls, sides touching, in two lightly greased 13- x 9- x 2-inch baking pans. Cover and let rise in a warm place (85°), free from drafts, 45 minutes or until doubled in bulk.

Bake at 450° for 10 to 15 minutes or until golden brown. Yield: about 3 dozen rolls. *Judy Dorton,*
Monroe, North Carolina.

Right: *Rice finds a place in a variety of tasty dishes: Spanish Rice, Rice Balls, and Creole Jambalaya (recipes on page 51).*

Page 82: *Fresh strawberries and whipped cream are a natural combination in one of the South's favorite desserts, Strawberry Shortcake (page 96).*

Left: *Spread between the three moist layers of Stately Coconut Layer Cake (page 70) is a tangy lemon-orange filling, a delectable complement to the coconut-covered white frosting.*

Above: *This menu is as colorful as spring: Shrimp Salad, Broccoli Puff, Tomato Refresher, French Lemon Spirals, and Wine Spritzers (recipes on page 94).*

These Menus Speed Up Dinner

Searching for company-good meals that are quick to prepare, well balanced, and economical? Letters from *Southern Living* readers suggest that is one of their biggest challenges.

Whether you're a beginning or experienced cook, you can serve elegant meals to family and friends without spending hours in the kitchen. Careful organization and some fast but flavorful recipes are the trick.

We offer two menus from *Southern Living*'s *The Quick & Easy Cookbook* designed to help you get dinner on the table almost effortlessly.

Linguine in Clam Sauce
Italian Peas
Tomato, Onion, and Cucumber in Italian Dressing
Hot Garlic French Bread
Peach Melba

LINGUINE IN CLAM SAUCE

3 cloves garlic, minced
½ cup melted butter or margarine
4 (4-ounce) cans sliced mushrooms, drained
2 (6½-ounce) cans minced clams, drained
½ cup chopped parsley
½ teaspoon salt
1 teaspoon pepper
8 ounces linguine or spaghetti, cooked and drained
Grated Parmesan cheese

Sauté garlic in butter in large skillet over low heat for 1 minute. Add mushrooms and cook 5 minutes. Stir in clams, parsley, salt, and pepper. Heat thoroughly. Combine linguine and mushroom mixture, toss well, and heat until hot. Top with Parmesan cheese. Yield: 4 to 6 servings.

ITALIAN PEAS

2 (10-ounce) packages frozen English peas
4 slices bacon
¼ cup minced onion
1 tablespoon water
2 tablespoons butter or margarine
¼ cup shredded lettuce
½ teaspoon salt
1 teaspoon chopped pimiento

Cook peas according to package directions. Dice bacon and cook in medium skillet until crisp; remove bacon and reserve drippings. Cook onion in bacon drippings until soft; remove and drain. Drain skillet. Put water and butter in skillet; add peas and lettuce; cook until lettuce is wilted, about 10 minutes. Add bacon, onion, and salt. Add pimiento just before serving. Yield: 4 to 6 servings.

Note: Two (16-ounce) cans English peas can be substituted for frozen English peas.

TOMATO, ONION, AND CUCUMBER IN ITALIAN DRESSING

6 tomatoes, peeled and sliced
1 onion, sliced
2 cucumbers, sliced
¼ cup commercial Italian dressing

Combine all vegetables in salad bowl; add Italian dressing. Refrigerate until ready to serve. Yield: 4 to 6 servings.

HOT GARLIC FRENCH BREAD

1 (8-ounce) loaf French bread
½ cup butter or margarine, softened
1 teaspoon garlic salt

Slice French bread into ½-inch slices. Butter one side of each slice. Sprinkle with garlic salt. Wrap in aluminum foil; heat. Yield: 6 servings.

PEACH MELBA

1 (10-ounce) package frozen raspberries, thawed and drained
3 tablespoons sugar
1½ pints vanilla ice cream
1 (29-ounce) can peach halves, drained
Whipped cream (optional)

Puree raspberries and sugar in a blender. Spoon ice cream into dessert dishes; top each with a peach half, round side up; cover with raspberry puree. Serve with whipped cream, if desired. Yield: 4 to 6 servings.

Note: Melba sauce can be served with other canned or fresh fruits.

Broiled Pork Chops
With Crabapple Peaches
Asparagus With Hot Wine Mayonnaise
Buttered Summer Squash
California Green Salad
Seasoned Breadsticks
Blueberry Crumble

BROILED PORK CHOPS WITH CRABAPPLE PEACHES

1 (16-ounce) can cling peach halves
1 (16-ounce) jar spiced crabapples
6 (1¼- to 1½-inch-thick) loin pork chops
Salt and pepper
Parsley sprigs

Drain peaches and crabapples; reserve peach juice. Place pork chops on rack in broiler pan. Place pan 6 to 7 inches from heat. Broil 15 to 17 minutes on first side; season with salt and pepper. Turn chops and broil second side 15 minutes, basting with peach juice. During last 5 minutes of broiling, place a crabapple in each peach half and arrange on broiler rack with chops. Continue broiling until chops are browned and peaches and crabapples are heated through, brushing fruit and chops with peach juice. Place chops and fruit in serving dish. Garnish with parsley sprigs. Yield: 6 servings.

ASPARAGUS WITH HOT WINE MAYONNAISE

3 (10-ounce) packages frozen asparagus spears
Hot Wine Mayonnaise

Cook asparagus spears according to package directions. Drain thoroughly. Place warm asparagus in flat serving dish, and top with Hot Wine Mayonnaise. Yield: 6 servings.

Hot Wine Mayonnaise:

1 tablespoon instant minced onion
¼ cup Sauterne
2 tablespoons parsley flakes
1 tablespoon lemon juice
¾ cup mayonnaise

Combine onion and wine; let stand 10 minutes. Add remaining ingredients. Heat over hot, but not boiling, water. Yield: 1 cup sauce.

Tip: Always turn saucepan and skillet handles toward the back of the range to prevent accidents.

BUTTERED SUMMER SQUASH

1½ pounds yellow squash, washed and
    sliced
1 teaspoon salt
1 medium onion, chopped
3 tablespoons butter or margarine

Place squash in medium saucepan with tight lid. Cover with water; drain water off completely. Add salt and onion. Cover and cook over medium heat about 3 to 4 minutes. Do not lift cover. Reduce heat to lowest temperature; simmer 6 minutes. Remove cover; add butter. Replace cover; turn off heat. Keep covered until butter melts or ready to serve. Yield: 6 servings.

CALIFORNIA GREEN SALAD

1 large head iceberg lettuce
Garlic salt
Freshly ground pepper
Commercial Italian dressing
2 avocados, peeled and diced

Tear lettuce into bite-size pieces in salad bowl. Add garlic salt and pepper. Toss lightly with dressing to coat the leaves. Add avocado. Toss lightly and serve at once. Yield: 6 servings.

SEASONED BREADSTICKS

Bread slices
Butter or margarine, softened
Onion salt or garlic salt
Grated Parmesan cheese
Oregano

Toast bread under broiler on one side; butter other side and sprinkle with onion salt, Parmesan cheese, and oregano. Remove crusts and cut into ½-inch strips. Toast buttered side until lightly browned. Yield: 4 sticks per slice.

BLUEBERRY CRUMBLE

2 (16-ounce) packages frozen blueberries,
    thawed
⅓ cup sugar
1 tablespoon lemon juice
½ cup quick-cooking oats, uncooked
½ cup all-purpose flour
½ cup firmly packed brown sugar
1 teaspoon ground cinnamon
¼ cup butter or margarine

Combine blueberries, sugar, and lemon juice; place in buttered 8-inch square baking dish. Combine oats, flour, brown sugar, and cinnamon; cut in butter until mixture resembles coarse meal. Spread over fruit mixture. Bake at 350° for 30 to 35 minutes. Serve warm, plain or with cream. Serve leftovers cold topped with whipped cream or ice cream. Yield: 6 servings.

Note: Any fruit can be substituted for blueberries.

Spring Blooms With Chilled Desserts

Spring is a time of rainbow pastel colors and light and pretty desserts. And these chilled specialties seem made to order for the season.

Strawberry Delight is a luscious mixture of whipped cream, strawberries, egg whites, sugar, and lemon juice that's whipped and frozen in a crunchy sweet crust. The taste will remind you of strawberry ice cream.

For a switch from the usual cheesecake, try Orange Cheesecake—it is made in an electric blender. And when you're short on time, stir up some Glorified Vanilla Sherry Dessert; it has only four ingredients. Just mix, freeze, and enjoy.

MAPLE NUT DESSERT

1 envelope unflavored gelatin
½ cup cold water
3 eggs, separated
¾ cup maple-flavored syrup
¼ teaspoon salt
10 coconut macaroons, crumbled
¾ cup chopped pecans
1½ cups whipping cream, whipped
    and divided
10 ladyfingers, split lengthwise

Combine gelatin and cold water; let stand 5 minutes.

Beat egg yolks until thick and lemon colored. Combine egg yolks, syrup, and salt in a small saucepan; cook over medium heat 5 minutes or until thickened, stirring constantly.

Stir gelatin into egg mixture. Chill until partially set (about 20 minutes).

Combine chilled mixture, macaroons, and pecans, stirring well. Beat egg whites (at room temperature) until stiff peaks form. Fold egg whites and 2 cups whipped cream into chilled mixture. Line sides of a 10-cup bowl with ladyfingers. Pour in filling, and spread remaining 1 cup whipped cream evenly over the top. Chill several hours or overnight. Yield: 8 servings.

Mrs. Clyde W. Shahan,
Rome, Georgia.

ORANGE CHEESECAKE

15 graham cracker squares, crushed
2 tablespoons sugar
¼ teaspoon ground cinnamon
¼ cup butter, melted
2 eggs
½ cup sugar
1 (8-ounce) carton commercial sour cream
2 teaspoons vanilla extract
2 (8-ounce) packages cream cheese,
    softened and cut into 1-inch pieces
2 tablespoons butter, melted
1 (11-ounce) can mandarin oranges
¼ cup Cointreau or Triple Sec
½ cup orange juice
1½ tablespoons cornstarch

Combine first 4 ingredients; press into a buttered 9-inch round cakepan. Bake at 400° for 6 minutes. Cool.

Combine eggs, ½ cup sugar, sour cream, and vanilla in container of electric blender; blend for 15 seconds. Gradually add cream cheese, and continue blending. Add 2 tablespoons butter, blending until well mixed.

Pour cheese mixture into prepared crust. Bake at 325° for 35 minutes or until set in center. (Filling will be very soft but will firm up as cake cools.)

Drain mandarin oranges, reserving ½ cup liquid; set liquid aside. Combine mandarin oranges and Cointreau; let sit 30 minutes.

Drain mandarin oranges, reserving Cointreau. Combine reserved ½ cup mandarin orange liquid, reserved Cointreau, orange juice, and cornstarch; stir well. Cook over low heat 5 minutes or until thickened; cool slightly. Arrange oranges on top of cheesecake; top with glaze. Chill 6 hours or overnight before serving. Yield: 8 servings.

Tip: Make certain your refrigerator or freezer is cold enough. Refrigerator temperature should be maintained at 34°F to 40°F and freezer temperature at 0°F or lower. To allow the cold air to circulate freely, foods should not be overcrowded.

Freeze a sweet, delicate filling between a crunchy pecan topping and crust for Strawberry Delight. It's like strawberry ice cream . . . only better.

pan; stir well. Bake at 350° for 20 minutes, stirring occasionally; cool.

Combine strawberries, sugar, lemon juice, and egg whites in a large mixing bowl; beat at high speed of electric mixer 10 to 12 minutes or until stiff peaks form. Fold in whipped cream.

Press about two-thirds of crumb mixture into a 9-inch springform pan; spoon in strawberry mixture. Sprinkle remaining crumbs on top; freeze until firm. Garnish with fresh strawberries, if desired. Yield: 8 to 10 servings.

Janice Humphreys,
Roanoke, Virginia.

GLORIFIED VANILLA SHERRY DESSERT

1 quart vanilla ice cream, softened
8 almond macaroons, crumbled
¾ cup finely chopped pecans or walnuts
½ cup cream sherry

Combine all ingredients; stir well. Pour into an 8-inch square pan; freeze until partially set, stirring occasionally. Freeze until firm. Cut into squares to serve. Yield: 9 servings.

Mrs. Herbert W. Rutherford,
Baltimore, Maryland.

ORANGE PUDDING

6 eggs, separated
1 cup sugar
¼ cup cornstarch
¼ teaspoon salt
1 quart milk
1 teaspoon vanilla extract
8 oranges, peeled, chopped, and drained
¾ cup sugar

Beat egg yolks; set aside. Combine 1 cup sugar, cornstarch, and salt in a heavy saucepan; stir well. Add milk; cook to boiling point, stirring constantly (do not boil). Remove from heat.

Stir about one-fourth of hot mixture gradually into yolks; add to remaining hot mixture, stirring constantly. Cook over medium heat, stirring constantly, until smooth and thickened. Stir in vanilla. Pour into large mixing bowl and chill.

Stir orange pieces carefully into pudding. Beat egg whites (at room temperature) until foamy; gradually add ¾

cup sugar, 1 tablespoon at a time, beating until stiff peaks form. Fold egg whites into pudding, and serve immediately. Yield: 12 to 14 servings.

Elizabeth Kraus,
Louisville, Kentucky.

STRAWBERRY DELIGHT

1 cup all-purpose flour
½ cup chopped pecans
½ cup butter or margarine, melted
¼ cup firmly packed brown sugar
1 (10-ounce) package frozen strawberries, thawed
1 cup sugar
2 teaspoons fresh lemon juice
2 egg whites
1 cup whipping cream, whipped
Sliced fresh strawberries (optional)

Combine flour, pecans, butter, and brown sugar in an 8-inch square baking

Onions, Honey Glazed Or Crispy Fried

The onion, one of the most valued ingredients in Southern cooking, is the basis for some zesty side dishes, an excellent soup, and crispy fried onion rings.

Try them sautéed with sherry and topped with Parmesan cheese or baked with a honey sauce. And for an old favorite, serve onion soup topped with a thick, crusty layer of melted Swiss cheese.

When selecting onions, choose those that are bright, clean, firm, and well shaped with dry skins. Small onions are best for boiling whole, stewing, or creaming. Medium onions are usually just right for stuffing, while the larger ones make good slices for fried onion rings, salads, or sandwiches. Store onions in a cool, dark, dry place that is well ventilated to prevent sprouting or decay.

HONEY ONIONS

4 medium onions
2 tablespoons tomato juice
1½ tablespoons honey
1 tablespoon butter or margarine
½ teaspoon salt
⅛ teaspoon paprika

Peel onions, and cut in half crosswise. Place onion halves, cut side up, in a 12- x 8- x 2-inch baking dish.

Combine remaining ingredients; stir well. Pour over onions, and bake at 350° for 1 hour. Yield: 8 servings.

Rose Marie Rousse,
Murray, Kentucky.

GOURMET ONIONS

5 medium onions, sliced
½ teaspoon sugar
½ teaspoon salt
½ teaspoon pepper
⅓ cup butter or margarine
½ cup dry sherry
¼ cup grated Parmesan cheese

Combine onion, sugar, salt, and pepper; stir gently. Melt butter in a heavy skillet; add onion mixture and cook, stirring frequently, 5 to 8 minutes. Stir in sherry, and cook an additional 2 to 3 minutes. Spoon into serving dish; sprinkle with cheese. Yield: 6 servings.

Mrs. Charles W. Kelly,
Somerville, New Jersey.

CHEESE AND LIMAS
IN ONION SHELLS

6 medium onions
1 (10-ounce) package frozen baby lima beans
¼ cup catsup
¼ teaspoon rubbed sage
Dash of pepper
1 cup (4 ounces) shredded sharp process American cheese
¼ cup water
6 slices bacon, cooked and crumbled

Peel onions, and cut a slice from each top. Cook onions in boiling salted water about 15 minutes or until tender but not mushy. Cool; remove center of onions, leaving shells intact. Chop onion centers, and set aside.

Cook beans according to package directions; drain. Combine beans, catsup, sage, pepper, and half of cheese; stir well. Fill onion shells with bean mixture; place in a 10- x 6- x 2-inch baking dish.

Spoon chopped onion centers evenly around onion shells; pour water over chopped centers. Bake at 375° for 25 minutes. Sprinkle remaining cheese and bacon over onion shells, and bake 5 additional minutes. Yield: 6 servings.

Mrs. J. W. Hopkins,
Abilene, Texas.

FAVORITE FRIED ONION RINGS

1 extra-large Spanish onion or 3 large Bermuda onions
About 1 quart milk
1 cup all-purpose flour
1 teaspoon salt
2 eggs
1 tablespoon vegetable oil
Vegetable oil

Peel onion; cut into ¼-inch slices, and separate into rings. Place rings in a large bowl, and cover with milk; refrigerate 30 minutes. Drain on paper towels, reserving ⅔ cup milk.

Combine flour and salt; stir well. Add eggs, reserved milk, and 1 tablespoon oil; beat until smooth.

Dip rings into batter; fry in deep hot oil (375°) until golden on both sides (3 to 5 minutes). Drain well on paper towels. Yield: 4 to 6 servings.

Janis Moyer,
Farmersville, Texas.

SUPERB ONION SOUP

6 medium-size yellow onions, coarsely chopped
½ cup peanut oil
1 (25.4-ounce) bottle dry red wine
1 teaspoon dried whole thyme
1 large bay leaf
4 (10½-ounce) cans beef consommé
5 cups water
French bread, cut into ½-inch-thick slices
6 cups (24 ounces) shredded Swiss cheese

Sauté onion in oil in a large Dutch oven until tender. Add wine, thyme, and bay leaf; bring to a boil, and cook 5 minutes. Add consommé and water; reduce heat. Simmer, uncovered, for 20 minutes, stirring occasionally.

Ladle soup into individual baking dishes. Top each with a slice of bread, and sprinkle with cheese. Place under broiler 2 to 3 minutes or until cheese melts. Yield: 13 cups.

Mrs. Charles G. Hays,
Rockmart, Georgia.

Bake It In A Pepper

Among the many kinds of baked, stuffed vegetables, the green pepper is perhaps the all-time favorite. A firm, fresh green pepper makes a perfect container for your favorite stuffing of meats, rice, and vegetables. Some of our readers' favorites include Mexican-flavored Taco Peppers; a spicy beef, corn, and celery filling; and one with ham, corn, and tomatoes.

When choosing peppers for stuffing, select firm, shiny, and medium- to dark-green ones. The wide stocky peppers make especially good containers.

BEEFY STUFFED GREEN PEPPERS

6 large green peppers
1 pound ground beef
¾ cup chopped onion
¼ cup chopped green pepper
1 clove garlic, crushed
⅓ cup chopped celery
1 (17-ounce) can cream-style corn
1 teaspoon salt
⅛ teaspoon pepper
Dash of red pepper
½ cup Italian breadcrumbs
¼ cup (1 ounce) shredded Cheddar cheese

Cut off tops of green peppers; remove seeds. Cook peppers 5 minutes in boiling salted water to cover; drain and set aside.

Cook ground beef, onion, chopped green pepper, garlic, and celery until beef is browned and vegetables are tender, stirring often; drain off excess drippings.

Add corn, salt, and pepper; cook, stirring often, until thoroughly heated. Fill green peppers with meat mixture; place in an 8-inch square baking dish. Combine breadcrumbs and cheese; sprinkle over peppers. Bake at 350° about 15 minutes or until top is lightly browned. Yield: 6 servings.

Clydia Dicharry,
Greenwell Springs, Louisiana.

TACO PEPPERS

6 medium-size green peppers
1 (15-ounce) can tamales
1 (15-ounce) can chili with beans
1 cup (4 ounces) shredded sharp Cheddar cheese, divided
¼ cup chopped onion
¼ cup catsup
1½ cups tortilla chips, crushed

Cut green peppers in half lengthwise; remove seeds

Remove wrappers from tamales, and cut into ¼-inch slices. Combine tamales, chili, ½ cup cheese, onion, and catsup; stir well. Fill peppers with tamale mixture; place in an electric skillet, and pour ¼ inch hot water into skillet. Cover and simmer 25 minutes. Sprinkle remaining cheese over peppers; top with chips. Simmer, uncovered, 1 to 2 minutes or until cheese melts. Yield: 6 servings. *Mrs. William T. Hunter, Princeton, Kentucky.*

HAM-AND-CORN STUFFED PEPPERS

8 medium-size green peppers
3 quarts water
¼ teaspoon salt
2 cups diced cooked ham
½ cup chopped onion
2 cups soft breadcrumbs, divided
¾ cup peeled, chopped tomato
1 cup drained whole kernel corn
¼ cup butter or margarine

Cut green peppers in half lengthwise; remove seeds. Combine water and salt in a large Dutch oven; bring to a boil. Add peppers and boil 5 minutes; drain and set aside, reserving ¼ cup liquid.

Put ham and onion through food chopper or food processor. Remove to a mixing bowl; stir in 1 cup breadcrumbs, tomato, and corn. Fill peppers with meat mixture; sprinkle remaining 1 cup crumbs on top, and dot with butter. Place peppers in a 15- x 10- x 1-inch baking pan; pour reserved liquid around peppers. Bake at 350° for 45 minutes. Yield: 8 servings. *Mrs. Lewis R. Carroll, Easton, Maryland.*

Cabbage: The Winner By A Head

Our readers have shared with us some wonderful new ways to prepare fresh cabbage. There's a delicious version of cabbage rolls filled with ground beef and rice, two versions of cabbage baked with a cheesy sauce, and a convenient overnight coleslaw.

Besides its versatility, cabbage is packed with minerals and the vitamins

A and C. In fact, the United Fresh Fruit and Vegetable Association points out that cabbage is so high in vitamin C that, ounce for ounce, it ranks right along with orange juice.

In selecting a head of cabbage, choose one that is firm and heavy for its size. Cabbage leaves should be fresh, crisp, and free from bruises.

BEEF STUFFED CABBAGE ROLLS

1 pound ground beef
⅓ cup uncooked regular rice
1 egg, beaten
1½ teaspoons salt
⅛ teaspoon pepper
6 large cabbage leaves
1 medium onion, thinly sliced
2 tablespoons butter or margarine, melted
1 (10¾-ounce) can tomato soup, undiluted
1¼ cups water
½ cup chopped celery
1 teaspoon minced fresh parsley
3 tablespoons lemon juice
1 teaspoon sugar
1 teaspoon salt
⅛ teaspoon pepper

Combine ground beef, rice, egg, 1½ teaspoons salt, and ⅛ teaspoon pepper; stir well.

Cook cabbage leaves in boiling salted water 5 to 8 minutes or until just tender; drain. Place equal portions of meat mixture in center of each cabbage leaf; fold ends over, and fasten with wooden pick.

Sauté onion in butter in a large skillet until tender but not brown. Add tomato soup and remaining ingredients, stirring well; simmer 10 minutes.

Place cabbage rolls in the tomato mixture; cover and simmer 1½ to 2 hours. Yield: 6 servings. *Mrs. S. Korzun, Holiday, Florida.*

CHEESE SCALLOPED CABBAGE

1 medium cabbage, cored and cut into small wedges
½ cup butter or margarine
¼ cup all-purpose flour
2 cups milk
½ teaspoon salt
¼ teaspoon pepper
Dash of ground nutmeg
2 cups (8 ounces) shredded medium Cheddar cheese
1 cup soft breadcrumbs

Cook cabbage in a small amount of boiling water until tender; drain well.

Melt butter in a heavy saucepan over low heat; add flour and cook 1 minute, stirring constantly. Gradually add milk; cook over medium heat, stirring constantly, until thickened and bubbly. Stir in salt, pepper, and nutmeg. Remove from heat; add the shredded cheese, stirring until melted.

Place half the cabbage in a greased 2½-quart casserole; top with half the cheese sauce. Repeat layers; top with breadcrumbs. Bake at 350° for 30 to 35 minutes. Yield: 8 servings. *Jeanne Lee Smith, Louisville, Kentucky.*

SMOTHERED CABBAGE WEDGES

1 medium cabbage
½ cup finely chopped green pepper
¼ cup finely chopped onion
¼ cup butter or margarine, melted
¼ cup all-purpose flour
2 cups milk
½ teaspoon salt
⅛ teaspoon pepper
½ cup mayonnaise or salad dressing
¾ cup (3 ounces) shredded medium Cheddar cheese
3 tablespoons chili sauce

Cut cabbage into 8 wedges, removing core; cover and cook 10 minutes in a small amount of lightly salted boiling water. Drain well; place cabbage wedges in a 13- x 9- x 2-inch baking dish.

Sauté green pepper and onion in butter until tender. Add flour and cook 1 minute, stirring constantly. Gradually add milk; cook over medium heat, stirring constantly, until thickened and bubbly. Stir in salt and pepper. Pour sauce over cabbage. Bake at 375° for 20 minutes.

Combine mayonnaise, cheese, and chili sauce; mix well. Spoon sauce over cabbage wedges, and bake 5 additional minutes. Yield: 8 servings. *Opal M. Rogers, Tempe, Arizona.*

OVERNIGHT CABBAGE SLAW

1 medium cabbage, shredded
1 small onion, grated
1 medium-size green pepper, finely
   chopped
8 pimiento-stuffed olives, sliced
¾ cup sugar
¾ cup vinegar
½ cup vegetable oil
1 teaspoon celery seeds
1 teaspoon dry mustard
1 teaspoon salt
⅛ teaspoon pepper

Combine cabbage, onion, green pepper, and olives in a large bowl; sprinkle with sugar.

Combine remaining ingredients in a medium saucepan; boil 3 minutes. Pour over vegetables, stirring well. Chill overnight. Yield: 8 to 10 servings.

Faye Beard,
Lipscomb, Alabama.

Don't Let The Jicama Fool You

You could mistake it for a brown turnip unpeeled, a potato when diced, and a water chestnut when tasted, but these similarities make the jicama a most versatile vegetable.

New to many Southern supermarkets, the jicama fries up much like a potato, and our version of French-Fried Jicama sports a crunchy coating. Since it maintains its crispness when cooked, you'll enjoy the jicama as an economical substitute for water chestnuts. And don't miss the sweet taste of raw jicama, a favorite in many fruit and vegetable salads.

Our test kitchen recommends not peeling the jicama until just before using it. Wrapped in a plastic bag, it will keep in the refrigerator for up to two weeks.

FRENCH-FRIED JICAMA

1 large (about 2 pounds) jicama, peeled
¾ cup all-purpose flour
½ teaspoon salt
½ teaspoon paprika
Hot vegetable oil
Salt

Cut jicama into thin strips. Soak in cold water about 10 minutes. Combine flour, salt, and paprika in a shallow dish. Drain jicama, and pat dry; coat well with flour mixture. Fry in hot oil about 1 inch deep until lightly browned. Drain well on paper towels; sprinkle with salt. Yield: 4 to 5 servings.

PARSLEYED JICAMA

About 2½ cups water
1 large (about 2 pounds) jicama, peeled
   and cut into ½-inch cubes
1 teaspoon salt
4 tablespoons butter or margarine
Dash of sugar
Dash of pepper
¼ cup chopped fresh parsley

Bring water to a boil; add jicama, salt; 1 tablespoon butter, sugar, and pepper. Reduce heat, and simmer about 30 minutes. Drain. Melt remaining butter, and stir in parsley; pour over hot jicama, and toss gently. Yield: 4 to 5 servings.

Flame A Peach Sundae

Flaming desserts are dramatic and surprisingly easy. Canned peach pie filling is combined with sherry, orange marmalade, and brandy. Just heat the sweet sauce, ignite, and spoon over ice cream, all in a matter of minutes. The end result is a glowing success.

PEACH SUNDAES FLAMBE

1 (21-ounce) can peach pie filling
¼ cup cream sherry
½ cup orange marmalade
¼ cup brandy
2 pints vanilla ice cream
Chopped pecans (optional)

Combine pie filling, sherry, and marmalade in a medium saucepan; heat thoroughly, stirring gently. Transfer mixture to chafing dish or flambé pan to keep warm. Heat brandy in small saucepan over medium heat (do not boil). Ignite with a long match, and pour over peach mixture. After flames die down, serve immediately over individual servings of ice cream. Sprinkle with pecans, if desired. Yield: 6 servings.

James L. Strieber,
San Antonio, Texas.

Make The Main Dish Meatless

As meat prices continue to rise, more and more Southerners are looking for alternative entrées. Here we offer three meatless main dishes, all designed to trim the food budget and satisfy hearty appetites.

Sautéed Vegetables With Spaghetti is a colorful dish flavored with a medley of six garden-fresh vegetables. Cheese and Mushroom Crêpes are filled with a cream cheese-mushroom filling and topped with a Swiss cheese sauce. Cheese and hard-cooked eggs provide two sources of protein in Continental Cheese Bake, which is topped with rye bread before baking.

CHEESE AND MUSHROOM CREPES

2 cups all-purpose flour
½ teaspoon salt
4 eggs
1 cup milk
1 cup water
¼ cup butter or margarine, melted
Vegetable oil
Mushroom filling (recipe follows)
1¾ cups Rich Cheese Sauce
¼ cup (1 ounce) shredded Swiss cheese

Combine flour, salt, and eggs; mix well. Add milk, water, and butter; beat until smooth. Refrigerate batter at least 2 hours. (This allows flour particles to swell and soften so that the crêpes will be light in texture.)

Brush the bottom of a 6- or 7-inch crêpe pan or heavy skillet with vegetable oil; place the skillet over medium heat until the oil is hot, not smoking.

Pour 3 tablespoons batter into pan; quickly tilt pan in all directions so batter covers the pan in a thin film. Cook about 1 minute.

Lift edge of crêpe to test for doneness. Crêpe is ready for flipping when it can be shaken loose from pan. Flip the crêpe, and cook about 30 seconds on the other side. (This side is rarely more than spotty brown and is the side on which filling is placed.) When crêpes are done, place on a towel to cool. Stack between layers of waxed paper to prevent sticking.

Spread ¼ cup mushroom filling in center of each crêpe; roll up and place, seam side down, in a buttered 13- x 9- x 2-inch baking dish. Spread 1¾ cups of

Rich Cheese Sauce over crêpes, and sprinkle with cheese. Bake at 375° for 10 to 15 minutes. Yield: 7 servings.

Mushroom Filling:

3 tablespoons minced shallots
¼ cup butter or margarine
½ pound fresh mushrooms, sliced
1 (8-ounce) package cream cheese, softened
1 egg
1¾ cups Rich Cheese Sauce

Sauté shallots in butter for 2 minutes; add mushrooms, and sauté an additional 3 minutes.

Combine cream cheese and egg, beating until fluffy. Add mushroom mixture and 1¾ cups Rich Cheese Sauce; stir well. Yield: 3½ cups.

Rich Cheese Sauce:

¼ cup butter or margarine
¼ cup plus 1 tablespoon all-purpose flour
2¾ cups milk, scalded
¼ cup whipping cream
¾ cup (3 ounces) shredded Swiss cheese
⅛ teaspoon ground nutmeg
⅛ teaspoon pepper
Pinch of salt

Melt butter in a heavy saucepan over low heat; add flour, stirring with a whisk until smooth. Cook 1 minute, stirring constantly. Gradually add milk; cook over medium heat, stirring constantly, until thickened and bubbly. Stir in remaining ingredients; cook over low heat until cheese melts, stirring constantly. Yield: about 3½ cups.

Betty Arthur,
Evergreen, Colorado.

CONTINENTAL CHEESE BAKE

1 medium onion, sliced and separated into rings
1 tablespoon butter or margarine
8 hard-cooked eggs, sliced
2 cups (8 ounces) shredded Swiss cheese
1 (10¾-ounce) can cream of mushroom soup, undiluted
¾ cup milk
1 teaspoon prepared mustard
½ teaspoon salt
¼ teaspoon dried dillweed
¼ teaspoon pepper
6 slices rye bread, buttered and cut into triangles

Sauté onion in butter until tender; place in a lightly greased 12- x 8- x 2-inch baking dish. Top with egg slices, and sprinkle with cheese. Combine soup, milk, and seasonings; beat well,

and pour over cheese. Top with bread, buttered side up, overlapping each triangle.

Bake at 350° for 30 minutes or until bubbly. Place under broiler (6 inches from source of heat), and broil about 1 minute or until the bread is lightly browned. Yield: 6 to 8 servings.

June Johnson,
Mocksville, North Carolina.

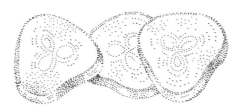

SAUTEED VEGETABLES WITH SPAGHETTI

1 (7-ounce) package spaghetti or vermicelli
1 small onion, chopped
3 tablespoons butter or margarine
2 medium zucchini, cut into 2- x ¼-inch spears
¾ cup peeled, chopped cucumber
½ cup grated carrot
½ cup chopped green pepper
2 medium tomatoes, coarsely chopped
3 tablespoons chopped fresh parsley
Dash of pepper
Grated Parmesan cheese

Cook spaghetti according to package directions; drain.

Sauté onion in butter in a large skillet for 2 minutes. Add zucchini, cucumber, carrot, and green pepper; sauté 5 minutes. Add remaining ingredients except Parmesan cheese; reduce heat to low, and cook 5 minutes.

Combine vegetables and spaghetti, tossing well. Sprinkle with Parmesan cheese before serving. Yield: 4 servings.

Mrs. John H. Kolek,
Lakeland, Florida.

Discover Some Saucy Secrets

Whether the dish is meat, seafood, eggs, or vegetables, one of the easiest ways to transform plain fare into something special is by adding a sauce.

Perhaps the most well known and certainly the most versatile of the sauces is white sauce. Not only can its consistency be varied from thin to thick just

by increasing the butter and flour, but a white sauce is also the basis of a number of other popular sauces, such as Mornay and mushroom.

The lemony flavor of hollandaise is especially good with vegetables, seafood, or chicken. A variation of this favorite is béarnaise sauce, and our recipe is quickly prepared in the blender.

Success with sauces depends on carefully—and exactly—following recipe instructions. For example, the basis of several of the sauces included here is a flour and butter mixture called a roux. The 1 minute of cooking and stirring specified for the roux in these recipes is essential, for this releases the starch (thickening agent) from the flour and prevents the sauce from lumping.

REMOULADE SAUCE

1 cup mayonnaise
1½ teaspoons lemon juice
3 tablespoons chopped chives
3 tablespoons chopped fresh parsley
2 teaspoons Dijon mustard

Combine all ingredients, stirring until smooth. Cover and chill at least 2 hours. Serve over meats or seafood. Yield: about 1 cup.

Patricia Pashby,
Memphis, Tennessee.

BASIC WHITE SAUCE

Thin White Sauce:

1 tablespoon butter or margarine
1 tablespoon all-purpose flour
1 cup milk
Salt and white pepper to taste

Medium White Sauce:

2 tablespoons butter or margarine
2 tablespoons all-purpose flour
1 cup milk
Salt and white pepper to taste

Thick White Sauce:

3 tablespoons butter or margarine
3 tablespoons all-purpose flour
1 cup milk
Salt and white pepper to taste

Melt butter in a heavy saucepan over low heat; add flour, stirring until smooth. Cook 1 minute, stirring constantly. Gradually add milk; cook over medium heat, stirring constantly, until mixture is thickened and bubbly. Stir in salt and pepper. Yield: 1 cup.

MORNAY SAUCE

2 tablespoons margarine
2 tablespoons all-purpose flour
¼ teaspoon salt
Dash of pepper
1 small bay leaf
1 teaspoon dried parsley flakes
1½ teaspoons instant minced onion
1 cup milk
¾ cup (4 ounces) cubed Gouda cheese

Melt margarine in a heavy saucepan over low heat; add next 6 ingredients, stirring until smooth. Cook 1 minute, stirring constantly. Gradually add milk; cook over medium heat, stirring constantly, until thickened and bubbly. Discard bay leaf; add cheese, stirring until melted.

Serve over poached eggs, chicken, or seafood. Yield: about 1¼ cups.

Pat Mann,
Bradenton, Florida.

BLENDER BEARNAISE SAUCE

3 egg yolks
2 tablespoons lemon juice
¼ teaspoon salt
Dash of red pepper
⅔ cup butter, melted
2 tablespoons white wine
1 tablespoon tarragon vinegar
2 teaspoons minced shallots
1 teaspoon dried whole tarragon
¼ teaspoon pepper

Combine egg yolks, lemon juice, salt, and red pepper in container of electric blender; set on high speed, and process 3 seconds.

Turn blender to low speed; add butter to yolk mixture in a slow, steady stream. Turn blender to high speed, and process until thick.

Combine wine, vinegar, shallots, tarragon, and pepper in a small saucepan; cook over high heat until almost all liquid evaporates. Add to mixture in blender, and process at high speed 4 seconds.

Serve over meat, seafood, or chicken. Yield: about ¾ cup.

HOLLANDAISE SAUCE

4 egg yolks
½ cup butter or margarine, softened
2 tablespoons lemon juice
¼ teaspoon salt

Combine egg yolks and one-third of butter in top of double boiler. Bring water to a boil (water in bottom of double boiler should not touch top pan). Reduce heat to low; cook, stirring constantly, until butter melts. Add second third of butter; stir constantly until butter begins to melt. Add the remaining butter, stirring constantly until melted.

Remove pan from water, and stir rapidly for 2 minutes. Stir in lemon juice, 1 teaspoonful at a time; add salt. Place over boiling water; cook, stirring constantly, 2 to 3 minutes or until smooth and thickened. Immediately remove from heat.

Serve over vegetables, seafood, or chicken. Yield: about 1 cup.

Betty Lancaster,
Alexandria, Virginia.

MUSHROOM SAUCE

2 tablespoons butter
¾ cup sliced fresh mushrooms
2 tablespoons all-purpose flour
1 cup half-and-half
½ cup (2 ounces) shredded process American cheese
¼ to ½ teaspoon salt
¼ teaspoon white pepper

Melt butter in a heavy saucepan over low heat; add mushrooms, and sauté until tender. Add flour, stirring until smooth. Cook 1 minute, stirring constantly. Gradually add half-and-half; cook over medium heat, stirring constantly, until thickened and bubbly. Add the cheese, and stir until melted. Season with salt and pepper.

Serve the sauce over meats or vegetables. Yield: about 1¾ cups.

Mary Dishon,
Stanford, Kentucky.

Mix Up Breakfast In Minutes

With our Quick Bread Mix, pancakes, waffles, and muffins are just minutes away. It's simply a matter of adding egg and liquid to the mix, giving it a quick stir, and baking.

Our test kitchens staff prepared each recipe using milk as the liquid, then water. While we found the milk versions to have a richer flavor, water was a highly acceptable substitute.

QUICK BREAD MIX

6 cups all-purpose flour
1 cup instant nonfat dry milk solids
¼ cup baking powder
2 teaspoons salt
½ cup sugar
¾ cup shortening

Combine first 5 ingredients, and sift 3 times. Cut in the shortening until thoroughly mixed. Place in an airtight container, and store in a cool, dry place; it will keep for 6 to 8 weeks. Yield: 8½ cups.

Muffins:

⅓ cup milk or water
1 egg, slightly beaten
1 cup Quick Bread Mix

Combine milk and egg, mixing well. Place Quick Bread Mix in a bowl, and make a well in center. Pour in liquid ingredients, and stir just until dry ingredients are moistened.

Fill greased muffin cups about two-thirds full. Bake at 400° for 20 minutes. Yield: 5 muffins.

Waffles:

¾ cup milk or water
1 egg, separated
1 cup Quick Bread Mix

Combine milk and beaten egg yolk, mixing well; add to the Quick Bread Mix, mixing well.

Beat egg white until soft peaks form; fold gently into batter. Bake in a preheated, lightly oiled waffle iron. Yield: two 8-inch waffles.

Pancakes:

1 cup Quick Bread Mix
⅔ cup milk or water
1 egg, slightly beaten

Combine all ingredients, stirring just until blended. For each pancake, pour about 2 tablespoons batter onto a hot, lightly greased griddle. When pancakes are bubbly on top and slightly dry at edges, turn to cook other side. Yield: about seven 5-inch pancakes.

Tip: When food boils over in the oven, sprinkle the burned surface with a little salt. This will stop smoke and odor from forming and make the spot easier to clean. Also, rubbing damp salt on dishes in which food has been baked will remove brown spots.

Casseroles Tailored For Two

If you're cooking for two and find it difficult to serve a casserole without having leftovers, here are some delightful solutions. Each of the recipes is a special version of an old favorite tailor-made to serve just two.

Always popular, ground beef is served up right in Cornbread Casserole, lasagna, or Hamburger Pie. In Elegant Crêpes Divan, crêpes are filled with a chicken and asparagus mixture.

ELEGANT CREPES DIVAN

⅓ cup plus 3 tablespoons all-purpose flour
½ teaspoon sugar
⅛ teaspoon salt
½ cup buttermilk
¼ cup milk
1 egg, slightly beaten
Vegetable oil
Chicken Divan Filling
Creamy Chicken Sauce
½ cup grated Parmesan cheese, divided
⅓ cup mayonnaise
½ cup whipping cream, whipped

Combine first 5 ingredients, beating until smooth. Add egg, and beat well; stir in ¾ teaspoon oil. Refrigerate batter for 1 hour. (This allows flour particles to swell and soften so the crêpes will be light in texture.)

Brush the bottom of a 6-inch crêpe pan with oil; place pan over medium heat until just hot, not smoking.

Pour 3 tablespoons batter into pan; quickly tilt pan in all directions so batter covers the pan in a thin film. Cook batter 1 minute.

Lift edge of crêpe to test for doneness. Crêpe is ready for flipping when it can be shaken loose from pan. Flip the crêpe, and cook about 30 seconds on other side. (This side is rarely more than spotty brown and is the side on which the filling is placed.)

Place crêpes on a towel to cool. Stack crêpes between layers of waxed paper to prevent sticking.

Spoon ¼ cup Chicken Divan Filling into center of each crêpe; roll up, and place seam side down in a lightly oiled 9-inch square baking dish.

Spread ¼ cup Creamy Chicken Sauce over crêpes; then sprinkle with ¼ cup Parmesan cheese. Cover and bake at 375° for 25 minutes.

Fold mayonnaise into whipped cream, and spread over crêpes; sprinkle with remaining cheese. Broil 5 inches from heating element about 3 minutes or until golden. Yield: 2 servings.

Chicken Divan Filling:

1 cup chopped cooked chicken
⅓ cup chopped cooked ham
¼ cup Creamy Chicken Sauce
½ (10-ounce) package frozen cut asparagus, thawed

Combine all ingredients; stir gently. Yield: about 1½ cups.

Creamy Chicken Sauce:

½ cup undiluted cream of chicken soup
Dash of ground nutmeg
1 teaspoon Worcestershire sauce

Combine all ingredients. Stir well. Yield: ½ cup.
Tommye Foster, Houston, Texas.

QUICK CHICKEN CASSEROLE

¼ cup minced celery
1 tablespoon minced green pepper
1 tablespoon grated onion
1½ tablespoons butter or margarine
½ cup undiluted cream of mushroom soup
⅓ cup commercial sour cream
2 tablespoons dry white wine
1 cup chopped cooked chicken
1 (8-ounce) can green beans, drained
½ cup soft breadcrumbs
1 tablespoon butter or margarine, melted

Sauté celery, green pepper, and onion in 1½ tablespoons butter for 5 minutes.

Combine soup, sour cream, and wine, stirring well. Stir together celery mixture, soup mixture, chicken, and beans; spoon into a lightly greased 1½-quart casserole. Combine breadcrumbs and butter; sprinkle over casserole. Bake at 350° for 20 minutes or until thoroughly heated. Yield: 2 servings.
Mrs. James Tuthill, Virginia Beach, Virginia.

LASAGNA FOR TWO

½ pound ground beef
1 clove garlic, minced
1 tablespoon vegetable oil
1 (8-ounce) can tomato sauce
½ teaspoon salt
⅛ teaspoon pepper
⅛ teaspoon dried whole oregano
5 lasagna noodles
¼ pound mozzarella cheese, sliced
½ cup ricotta cheese
¼ cup grated Parmesan cheese

Sauté beef and garlic in oil in a 10-inch skillet until meat is browned. Drain off drippings. Add tomato sauce, salt, pepper, and oregano; cover and simmer about 15 minutes, stirring occasionally.

Cook noodles according to package directions; drain. Layer half of noodles, mozzarella, ricotta, meat sauce, and Parmesan cheese in a lightly greased 1½-quart casserole. Repeat layers. Bake at 375° for 15 minutes. Yield: 2 servings.
Mary V. Berube, Mechanicsville, Maryland.

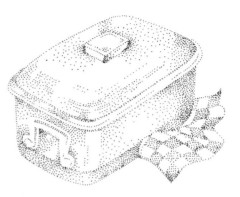

CORNBREAD CASSEROLE

½ pound ground beef
¼ cup chopped onion
½ cup chopped green pepper
1 (8¾-ounce) can whole kernel corn, drained
½ cup undiluted tomato soup
¼ cup sliced pimiento-stuffed olives
½ teaspoon salt
Dash of pepper
¼ cup all-purpose flour
¼ cup cornmeal
¾ teaspoon baking powder
¾ teaspoon sugar
Dash of salt
1 egg, slightly beaten
½ cup milk
1 tablespoon vegetable oil

Cook ground beef, onion, and green pepper until meat is browned and vegetables are tender, stirring to crumble meat. Discard pan drippings. Add corn, soup, olives, ½ teaspoon salt, and pepper; stir until combined. Spoon mixture into a lightly greased 1-quart casserole; then set aside.

Combine flour, cornmeal, baking powder, sugar, and a dash of salt. Add egg, milk, and oil; stir until dry ingredients are just moistened (mixture will be thin). Pour over casserole, and bake at 375° for 30 to 40 minutes or until golden brown. Yield: 2 servings.
Elizabeth Hale, Galax, Virginia.

HAMBURGER PIE

2 tablespoons chopped onion
1 tablespoon vegetable oil
½ pound ground beef
1 (8-ounce) can green beans, drained
½ cup undiluted tomato soup
¼ teaspoon salt
⅛ teaspoon pepper
1 cup seasoned mashed potatoes
Paprika

Sauté onion in oil until tender. Add ground beef; cook over medium heat until meat is browned. Drain well.

Combine beef mixture, beans, soup, salt, and pepper; stir well. Spoon meat mixture into a greased 1-quart casserole. Spread mashed potatoes evenly over top. Sprinkle with paprika. Bake at 350° about 30 minutes. Yield: 2 servings.   *Mrs. L. R. Koenig,*
Charleston, South Carolina.

SAUSAGE-NOODLE BAKE

1 cup sliced smoked sausage
2 tablespoons finely chopped onion
1 (8½-ounce) can English peas, drained
1 (10¾-ounce) can cream of chicken soup, undiluted
1 (5-ounce) package medium egg noodles, cooked
¼ teaspoon salt
½ cup milk
2 tablespoons butter or margarine, melted
1 cup herb-seasoned stuffing mix

Combine first 7 ingredients, stirring well. Spoon into a lightly greased 1½-quart casserole.

Combine butter and stuffing mix; sprinkle over casserole. Bake at 350° for about 30 minutes or until bubbly. Yield: 2 to 3 servings. *Gordon H. Grappone,*
Glen Allen, Virginia.

Cookies You Don't Bake

No-bake cookies are quick to make and delicious to eat, but best of all, children love to prepare them. These two recipes feature the flavors children love most—chocolate and peanuts.

The only cooking these recipes require is done on the top of the stove. Then the mixture is spooned onto waxed paper.

Older children can measure, mix, and cook these simple recipes, while younger children can help measure and mix. Also, it's a good idea to transfer the cooked mixture to a cool bowl before shaping or spooning cookies.

PEANUT-DATE BALLS

½ cup butter or margarine
¼ cup firmly packed dark brown sugar
1 egg, beaten
1 cup chopped dates
¼ cup salted peanuts, chopped
1 teaspoon vanilla extract
2 cups crisp rice cereal
Powdered sugar

Combine butter, brown sugar, egg, and dates in a heavy skillet; cook over low heat, stirring constantly, 5 minutes or until mixture is thickened. Add peanuts and vanilla; stir well.

Combine date mixture and crisp rice cereal; stir well. Allow mixture to cool to touch. Shape cookie mixture into 1-inch balls; place on waxed paper. Sprinkle cookies with powdered sugar. Yield: about 3 dozen.   *Marie Hayman,*
Lake Worth, Florida.

CHOCOLATE-NUT CHEWS

1½ cups sugar
½ cup cocoa
½ cup evaporated milk
⅓ cup butter or margarine
⅓ cup peanut butter
1½ cups quick-cooking oats, uncooked
½ cup chopped pecans or walnuts
1 teaspoon vanilla extract

Combine sugar, cocoa, milk, and butter in a heavy saucepan. Cook over medium heat, stirring constantly, until mixture reaches a slow boil (mixture will bubble around sides). Cook 2 additional minutes, stirring constantly.

Remove from heat; add peanut butter, and stir until smooth. Stir in oats, pecans, and vanilla. Drop mixture by tablespoonfuls onto waxed paper. Cool. Yield: about 4½ dozen.

Sharon Bramlett,
Clyde, North Carolina.

Tip: Use muffin pans to make extra-large ice cubes for punch.

Have The Clambake At Home

There's something for everybody at this backyard clambake. Besides the clams, there's lobster, chicken, and vegetables—all cooked on the grill in two airtight foil packages.

BACKYARD CLAMBAKE

24 steamer clams
2 (1-pound) live lobsters
1 small broiler-fryer, quartered
2 ears fresh corn, halved
2 large potatoes, cut into 8 wedges each
2 medium onions, quartered
1 teaspoon salt
¼ teaspoon pepper
½ cup water
1 cup melted butter

Scrub clams, and set aside.

Plunge lobsters headfirst into boiling salted water; remove with tongs. Place each lobster on its back; insert a sharp knife between body shell and tail segment, cutting down to sever spinal cord. Cut in half lengthwise. Remove the stomach (located just back of the head) and the intestinal vein (running from the stomach to the tip of the tail). Do not discard the green liver and coral roe; they are both delicious.

Cut two 36- x 18-inch pieces of heavy-duty aluminum foil; line each with cheesecloth. In center of each piece, place 2 chicken quarters; arrange 2 lobster halves and 12 clams around chicken. Then arrange 2 halves of corn, 8 potato wedges, and 4 onion quarters around the seafood in each package. Sprinkle each package with ½ teaspoon salt and ⅛ teaspoon pepper.

Pour ¼ cup water into each package. Gather up edges of cheesecloth, and tie with string. Bring foil up to cover the cheesecloth and form an airtight package.

Place packages on grill over medium-hot coals; cook for 45 to 50 minutes or until chicken is done. Remove from grill, open foil, and cut the cheesecloth package. Drizzle the seafood, chicken, and vegetables with 1 cup melted butter. Yield: 4 servings.   *Ruth Wilson,*
Siler City, North Carolina.

May

With the sunny days of May come a number of celebrations, such as bridal showers and graduation teas. Recipes for Pecan Cheese Wafers and Party Mints, among others, will make food the talk of the party.

Another reason to celebrate is the arrival of fresh strawberries, as light and refreshing as the season. How could you go wrong with the ruby red fruit piled into a cream puff or spread with whipped cream into a cake roll?

You may have been making meat loaf for years, but have you made it in the microwave? We will tell you how. And if you're wondering about cooking with wine or cooking with herbs, this chapter includes tips for that, too.

Take The Luncheon Outdoors

Along with warm days and bright-blue skies, May brings graduations and all the festivities that precede June weddings—even the weather is reason enough for celebration. So what better time to take a party outdoors.

We suggest a luncheon served on a sunny deck or terrace, and the menu we've put together is as colorful and lighthearted as spring itself.

A zesty shrimp salad sets the pace for this festive meal, while the piping-hot Broccoli Puff and icy-cold Tomato Refresher offer delightful contrast in both flavor and color. To enjoy with it all, there are lemony yeast rolls and refreshing Wine Spritzers.

Shrimp Salad
Broccoli Puff   Tomato Refresher
French Lemon Spirals
Wine Spritzers

SHRIMP SALAD

5 quarts water
1 cup celery leaves
2 tablespoons salt
½ cup pickling spice
Juice and rind of 2 lemons
2 small onions, chopped
5 pounds medium shrimp
4 small onions, sliced
14 bay leaves
2½ cups vegetable oil
1½ cups vinegar
1 teaspoon salt
1 tablespoon plus 2 teaspoons celery seeds
¼ cup plus 1 tablespoon capers, drained
Dash of hot sauce
Watercress or leaf lettuce

Combine first 6 ingredients, and bring to a boil; add shrimp, and cook 5 minutes. Drain well, and rinse shrimp in cold water; peel and devein.

Combine shrimp, sliced onion, and bay leaves in a large shallow dish. Combine next 6 ingredients, mixing well. Pour over shrimp; cover and chill 24 hours. Remove shrimp from marinade with a slotted spoon, and serve on a bed of watercress or lettuce. Yield: 8 to 10 servings.   *Mildred Sherrer,*
Bay City, Texas.

BROCCOLI PUFF

2 (10-ounce) packages chopped broccoli
3 eggs, separated
1 tablespoon all-purpose flour
Pinch of ground nutmeg
1 cup mayonnaise
1 tablespoon butter or margarine, softened
¼ teaspoon salt
¼ teaspoon pepper
¼ cup plus 1 tablespoon grated Parmesan cheese

Cook broccoli according to package directions; drain well. Beat egg yolks; add flour, mixing well. Stir in nutmeg, mayonnaise, butter, salt, pepper, and cheese. Add broccoli, mixing lightly.

Beat egg whites (at room temperature) until stiff but not dry; gently fold into broccoli mixture. Pour into a lightly buttered 9-inch square baking dish. Bake at 350° for 30 minutes. Cut into squares to serve. Yield: 9 servings.
Sandra Russell,
Maitland, Florida.

TOMATO REFRESHER

2 small green peppers, diced
⅔ cup diced celery
2 small onions, diced
1 tablespoon salt
¼ teaspoon pepper
¼ cup vinegar
¼ cup sugar
1 cup cold water
6 medium tomatoes, sliced

Combine first 8 ingredients, and pour over tomatoes. Cover and chill 3 to 4 hours. Yield: 8 servings.
Claire A. Bastable,
Chevy Chase, Maryland.

FRENCH LEMON SPIRALS

1 package dry yeast
2½ cups all-purpose flour, divided
½ cup milk
¼ cup plus 2 tablespoons butter or margarine
¼ cup sugar
2 eggs, beaten
1 tablespoon plus 1 teaspoon grated lemon rind, divided
¼ cup butter or margarine, softened
½ cup sugar

Combine yeast and 1 cup flour, mixing well. Combine milk, 6 tablespoons butter, and ¼ cup sugar; heat just until warm (115° to 120°), stirring to melt

butter. Add to yeast mixture, mixing well. Stir in eggs and 2 teaspoons lemon rind.

Beat mixture at low speed of electric mixer for 30 seconds, scraping bowl often; beat at high speed for 3 minutes. Stir in 1½ cups flour, and mix well. Cover and chill 2 to 3 hours.

Divide dough in half; place on a well-floured surface, and roll each half into a 12- x 7-inch rectangle. Spread each with 2 tablespoons butter, and sprinkle with ¼ cup sugar and 1 teaspoon lemon rind. Roll up jellyroll fashion, starting at long side. Cut each roll into 12 slices, and place on well-greased baking sheets. Cover and let rise in a warm place (85°), free from drafts, for 1 hour. Bake at 375° for 12 to 15 minutes. Yield: 2 dozen.   *Betty Rabe,*
Little Rock, Arkansas.

WINE SPRITZERS

1 (25.4-ounce) bottle white wine
1 (28-ounce) bottle club soda
Lemon slices
Lime slices

Combine wine and club soda; mix gently. Pour into ice-filled glasses, and garnish with lemon and lime slices. Yield: 8 to 10 servings.

Sweeten The Season With Strawberries

Whole and unadorned, the ruby-red strawberry sparks taste buds as is, the simplest way to eat the fruit. While we can't improve on the strawberry's perfection, we can give you more ways to enjoy it.

Plump, juicy strawberries just seem to call for whipped cream. The two are a natural for some of spring's sweetest desserts. Spread them between layers of shortcake, or stuff them into a delicate cream puff.

For Strawberry Mousse, the whipped cream is folded into the pureed berries, while for Strawberries Zabaglione, the whole berries are stuffed with a whipped cream and wine mixture.

But don't restrict strawberries to desserts. We've included recipes for a fresh fruit salad, chunky preserves, and an icy beverage.

When selecting strawberries, choose those that are bright red and well rounded, as they will not ripen after they are picked. Small to medium-size berries are often the tastiest, while large ones tend to have hollow centers.

STRAWBERRY CREAM PUFFS

1 cup water
½ cup butter
1 cup all-purpose flour
4 eggs
1 cup whipping cream
2 tablespoons powdered sugar
1 quart strawberries, sliced
Whole strawberries
Mint leaves

Combine water and butter in saucepan; bring to a boil. Add flour all at once, stirring vigorously over low heat for approximately 1 minute or until mixture leaves sides of pan and forms a smooth ball. Remove from heat, and allow to cool slightly.

Add eggs, one at a time, beating with a wooden spoon after each addition; beat until batter is smooth. Drop rounded ¼ cupfuls of batter 3 inches apart on an ungreased baking sheet.

Bake at 400° for 35 to 40 minutes or until golden brown and puffed. Cool away from drafts. Cut top off cream puffs; pull out and discard soft dough inside.

Beat whipping cream until foamy; gradually add powdered sugar, beating until soft peaks form. Fold about three-quarters of sliced strawberries into whipped cream; fill cream puffs with strawberry mixture. Arrange the remaining sliced strawberries on top; replace tops of cream puffs. Arrange on platter, and garnish with whole strawberries and mint leaves. Yield: 8 servings.

STRAWBERRY MOUSSE

1 quart strawberries
½ cup sugar
3 envelopes unflavored gelatin
½ cup cold water
1 cup boiling water
2 cups whipping cream
½ cup sifted powdered sugar
Whole and sliced strawberries

Puree 1 quart strawberries in container of an electric blender; add ½ cup sugar, and process until blended.

Soften gelatin in ½ cup cold water in a large bowl. Add boiling water, stirring until gelatin completely dissolves; cool.

Stir strawberry mixture into gelatin; chill until the consistency of unbeaten egg white.

Beat whipping cream until foamy; gradually add powdered sugar, beating until soft peaks form. Fold whipped cream into strawberry mixture. Spoon into lightly oiled 2-quart mold. Refrigerate until set.

Unmold on serving plate, and garnish with whole and sliced strawberries. Yield: 10 to 12 servings.
Mrs. Parke LaGourgue Cory,
Neosho, Missouri.

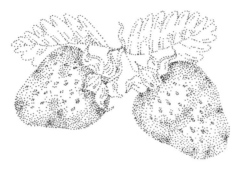

STRAWBERRIES 'N CREAM SPONGE CAKE ROLL

3 egg yolks
1 teaspoon vanilla extract
5 egg whites
½ teaspoon cream of tartar
¼ teaspoon salt
¾ cup sifted powdered sugar
½ cup all-purpose flour
Powdered sugar
2 cups sliced strawberries
2 tablespoons sugar
2 cups whipping cream
3 tablespoons sugar
Whole strawberries (optional)

Grease a 15- x 10- x 1-inch jellyroll pan with vegetable oil, and line with waxed paper. Grease waxed paper with vegetable oil; set aside.

Beat egg yolks until light and lemon colored; stir in vanilla, and set aside.

Beat egg whites until foamy; add cream of tartar and salt, beating until stiff but not dry. Fold in ¾ cup powdered sugar. Fold yolk mixture into whites. Gradually fold flour into egg mixture. Spread batter evenly in prepared pan. Bake at 350° for 10 to 12 minutes.

Sift powdered sugar in a 15- x 10-inch rectangle on a linen towel. When cake is done, immediately loosen from sides

of pan, and turn out on sugar. Peel off waxed paper. Starting at narrow end, roll up cake and towel together; cool on a wire rack, seam side down.

Combine 2 cups strawberries and 2 tablespoons sugar; set aside.

Beat whipping cream until foamy; gradually add 3 tablespoons sugar, beating until soft peaks form.

Unroll cake and remove towel. Spread cake with sliced strawberries and half the whipped cream; reroll. Place on serving plate, seam side down; spread remaining whipped cream on all sides. Garnish with whole strawberries, if desired. Chill until serving time. Yield: 8 to 10 servings. *Mrs. W. P. Chambers,*
Louisville, Kentucky.

STRAWBERRIES ZABAGLIONE

2 egg yolks
2 tablespoons sugar
2 tablespoons Marsala wine, sherry, or port
1 cup whipping cream
¼ cup sifted powdered sugar
30 large strawberries

Combine egg yolks, 2 tablespoons sugar, and wine in top of a double boiler; beat with an electric mixer at medium speed until well blended. Place over boiling water. Reduce heat to low; cook about 5 minutes or until soft peaks form, beating constantly at medium speed of an electric mixer. Remove mixture from heat.

Spoon the mixture into a medium bowl; place in a larger bowl of ice. Beat about 2 minutes or until cool; refrigerate 30 minutes.

Combine whipping cream and powdered sugar in a small bowl; refrigerate 30 minutes. Add whipping cream to cooked mixture; beat until stiff.

Make two perpendicular slices down pointed end of each strawberry, cutting to within ½ inch of stem end. Carefully spread out quarter sections of the strawberry to form a cup. Fill each strawberry with the cream mixture, using a pastry bag. Refrigerate until ready to serve. Yield: 10 to 15 servings.
Scarlet Keck,
Williamson, West Virginia.

Tip: Hull strawberries after washing so that they won't absorb too much water and become mushy.

CREPES WITH FRUIT FILLING

⅔ cup all-purpose flour
1 cup milk
2 tablespoons vegetable oil
3 eggs
1 tablespoon sugar
¼ teaspoon salt
¼ teaspoon ground mace
Vegetable oil
Fruit filling (recipe follows)
1 (8-ounce) carton commercial sour cream
Fresh mint (optional)

Combine flour and milk, beating until smooth. Add 2 tablespoons vegetable oil, eggs, 1 tablespoon sugar, salt, and mace; beat 3 minutes. Refrigerate batter 1 hour. (This allows flour particles to swell and soften so the crêpes are light in texture.)

Brush the bottom of a 7-inch crêpe pan with vegetable oil; place the pan over medium heat until it is just hot, not smoking.

Pour 2 to 2½ tablespoons batter into pan; quickly tilt pan in all directions so batter covers the pan in a thin film. Cook crêpe 1 minute.

Lift edge of crêpe to test for doneness. Crêpe is ready for flipping when it can be shaken loose from pan. Flip the crêpe, and cook about 30 seconds on other side. (This side is rarely more than spotty brown and is the side on which the filling is placed.)

When crêpes are done, place on a towel and allow to cool. Stack between layers of waxed paper to prevent crêpes from sticking.

Place about ½ cup fruit filling in center of each crêpe; roll up, and place seam side down on a serving platter. Spoon sour cream over crêpes. Garnish with fresh mint, if desired. Yield: 12 crêpes.

Fruit Filling:

1 quart strawberries, sliced
4 cups fresh or frozen sliced peaches, thawed
1 tablespoon lemon juice
½ cup sugar
½ teaspoon ground cinnamon

Combine strawberries, peaches, lemon juice, sugar, and cinnamon, mixing well. Yield: about 6 cups.

Mrs. J. Wells,
Fairfax, Virginia.

Tip: Submerge a lemon or orange in hot water for 15 minutes before squeezing to yield more juice.

STRAWBERRY SHORTCAKE

1 quart strawberries, sliced
¼ to ½ cup sugar
½ cup butter or margarine, softened and divided
2 cups all-purpose flour
¼ cup sugar
1 tablespoon plus 1 teaspoon baking powder
¼ teaspoon salt
Dash of ground nutmeg
½ cup milk
2 eggs, separated
¼ cup sugar
1 cup whipping cream
¼ cup sifted powdered sugar
Whole strawberries

Combine sliced strawberries and ¼ to ½ cup sugar; stir gently, and chill 1 to 2 hours.

Butter two 9-inch cakepans with ½ tablespoon butter each; set aside.

Combine flour, ¼ cup sugar, baking powder, salt, and nutmeg in a large mixing bowl; cut in remaining butter with pastry blender until mixture resembles coarse meal.

Combine milk and egg yolks; beat well. Add to flour mixture; stir with a fork until a soft dough forms. Pat dough out evenly into cakepans. (Dough will be sticky; moisten fingers with egg whites as necessary.)

Beat egg whites until stiff but not dry. Brush surface of dough with beaten egg whites; sprinkle evenly with ¼ cup sugar. Bake at 450° for 10 to 12 minutes or until layers are golden brown. Cool on wire racks. (Layers will be thin.)

Beat whipping cream until foamy; gradually add powdered sugar, beating until soft peaks form.

Place 1 cake layer on serving plate. Spoon on half of whipped cream, and arrange half of sliced strawberries on top. Repeat procedure with remaining cake, whipped cream, and strawberries, reserving small amount whipped cream. Garnish top of cake with remaining whipped cream and whole berries. Yield: 8 to 10 servings.

STRAWBERRY SLURP

2 cups strawberries
¼ to ¾ cup sifted powdered sugar
Ice cubes

Combine strawberries and sugar in container of a 5-cup electric blender. Add ice to within 1 inch of container top; blend well. Yield: about 5 cups.

Bob Stephens,
Luling, Louisiana.

SPRINGTIME FRUIT SALAD

1 fresh pineapple, peeled, cored, and cubed
1 quart strawberries
½ cup fresh or frozen blueberries, thawed
½ cup fresh or frozen raspberries, thawed
1 (11-ounce) can mandarin oranges, drained
2 cups orange juice
1 cup sugar
¼ cup cream sherry
½ teaspoon almond extract
½ teaspoon vanilla extract

Combine fruit in a large bowl. Combine remaining ingredients, stirring until sugar dissolves. Pour over fruit mixture, tossing lightly. Chill 2 to 3 hours. Yield: about 14 to 16 servings.

Dr. David A. Miller,
Corpus Christi, Texas.

STRAWBERRY PRESERVES

5 cups firm, ripe strawberries
3 cups sugar
1 tablespoon lemon juice

Combine strawberries and 1 cup sugar in a Dutch oven. Bring to a boil and cook 10 minutes, stirring frequently. Stir in remaining sugar; boil an additional 5 minutes, stirring frequently. Stir in lemon juice.

Pour strawberry mixture into a 13- x 9- x 2-inch pan; skim off foam with metal spoon. Let stand, uncovered, in a cool place 12 hours. Shake pan occasionally (do not stir) so that berries will absorb syrup and remain plump and whole.

Pour preserves into hot sterilized jars, leaving ½-inch headspace; cover at once with metal lids, and screw metal bands tight. Process in boiling-water bath 20 minutes. Yield: 3 cups.

Louise L. Bryant,
Norfolk, Virginia.

Flavorful, Yet Affordable Chicken

We receive letters daily from readers requesting recipes that cut the food bill without sacrificing flavor. Serving chicken is still one of the best ways we know to fight inflation.

Some of our recipes may be quickly assembled from ingredients you have on hand, such as tangy Barbecued Chicken Bake or Oven-Fried Parmesan Chicken. Add some special ingredients, and serve a special meal with Artichoke Chicken or Sherry Chicken With Rice.

SHERRY CHICKEN WITH RICE

3 whole chicken breasts, split
Salt and pepper to taste
Paprika
½ cup butter or margarine
1 (10¾-ounce) can cream of mushroom
  soup, undiluted
1 (3-ounce) can sliced mushrooms,
  undrained
½ cup chopped onion
½ cup slivered almonds
¼ cup cooking sherry
¼ teaspoon dried whole basil
¼ teaspoon dried whole rosemary
Hot cooked rice

Rinse chicken breasts with cold water and pat dry. Place chicken in a 13- x 9- x 2-inch baking dish. Sprinkle with salt, pepper, and paprika.

Melt butter in a medium saucepan; stir in remaining ingredients except rice, and pour over chicken. Bake at 350° for 1 hour or until done. Serve chicken and gravy over rice. Yield: 6 servings.
Cindy Fields,
Courtland, Virginia.

ARTICHOKE CHICKEN

3 whole chicken breasts, split and skinned
¼ cup vegetable oil
2 to 3 carrots, cut in 2-inch pieces
½ pound fresh mushrooms, sliced
1 (14-ounce) can artichokes, drained and
  halved
½ cup chopped green onion
½ cup sliced water chestnuts
⅛ teaspoon dried whole thyme
½ teaspoon salt
⅛ teaspoon pepper
1½ cups chicken broth
½ cup cooking sherry
2 tablespoons cornstarch

Brown chicken in hot oil in large skillet; add carrots. Cover and simmer 5 minutes. Add mushrooms, artichokes, onion, water chestnuts, thyme, salt, and pepper; cover and simmer 10 minutes.

Combine broth, sherry, and cornstarch in a small saucepan; stir well. Cook over medium heat, stirring constantly, until sauce is thickened.

Place chicken and vegetables in a greased 13- x 9- x 2-inch baking dish. Pour sauce over top; bake at 375° for 45 minutes or until done, basting occasionally with pan drippings. Yield: 6 servings. *Mrs. William E. Treadwell,*
Ellenwood, Georgia.

BARBECUED CHICKEN BAKE

1 (4-pound) broiler-fryer
1½ to 2 cups catsup
1 cup water
¼ cup vinegar
¼ cup firmly packed brown sugar
½ cup chopped onion
1 stalk celery, chopped
1 tablespoon prepared mustard
1 tablespoon Worcestershire sauce
Dash of hot sauce
2 tablespoons vegetable oil

Remove giblets from cavity of chicken, and reserve for another recipe. Rinse chicken with cold water, and pat dry. Fold neck skin of chicken over back, and secure with a wooden pick. Lift the wingtips up and over back so they are tucked under the chicken. Truss chicken, and set aside.

Combine remaining ingredients except vegetable oil in a large saucepan. Bring to a boil; reduce heat, and simmer 30 minutes.

Heat oil in a Dutch oven; add chicken, and brown on all sides. Place in a 13- x 9- x 2-inch baking pan. Pour sauce over chicken, and cover pan tightly with aluminum foil. Bake at 350° for 1½ hours or until done. Yield: 4 to 6 servings.
Peggy F. Revels,
Woodruff, South Carolina.

OVEN-FRIED PARMESAN CHICKEN

1 cup fine cracker crumbs
¼ cup plus 2 tablespoons grated
  Parmesan cheese
1 tablespoon dried parsley flakes
1 teaspoon salt
⅛ teaspoon pepper
Dash of garlic powder
1 (2½- to 3-pound) broiler-fryer, cut up
  and skinned
½ cup butter or margarine, melted

Combine first 6 ingredients, and stir mixture well.

Rinse chicken with cold water, and pat dry. Dip chicken in butter, and dredge in cracker crumb mixture. Place chicken in a 13- x 9- x 2-inch baking pan. Bake at 350° for 1 hour or until done. Yield: 4 to 6 servings.
Mrs. Charles Peterson,
Kennesaw, Georgia.

CHICKEN IN WHITE WINE

1 (3- to 3½-pound) broiler-fryer
½ cup Chablis or other dry white wine
1 (10¾-ounce) can cream of mushroom
  soup, undiluted
1 (4-ounce) can sliced mushrooms,
  drained
Pepper to taste
Hot cooked rice
1 (8-ounce) carton commercial sour cream

Remove giblets from cavity of chicken, and reserve for another recipe. Rinse chicken with cold water and pat dry. Lift wingtips up and over back so they are tucked under bird. Truss chicken, and place in a 13- x 9- x 2-inch baking pan.

Combine wine, soup, mushrooms, and pepper; stir well, and pour over chicken. Cover with aluminum foil, and bake at 350° for 1½ hours or until drumsticks are easy to move up and down. Place chicken on a bed of rice; keep warm.

Pour pan juices into a saucepan; stir in sour cream. Cook over low heat until thoroughly heated; do not boil. Serve gravy with chicken and hot rice. Yield: 4 to 6 servings. *Jean S. Williams,*
Jefferson, Georgia.

Tip: Chicken to be roasted will brown without fat, but the skin will be crisper if it is brushed with fat or oil before putting it in the oven.

Soup: Some Like It Hot, Some Cold

Nutritious and satisfying soups can be whatever you want them to be—first course or main dish, plain or fancy, hot or cold. They can be made with ingredients you already have on hand and need not simmer for hours to be good.

Served piping hot, Chicken Soup and Turkey-Corn Chowder combine poultry and vegetables to satisfy the heartiest appetites. Those who opt for a light soup can choose Cream of Cucumber Soup or Gazpacho. To really dress up a meal, ladle them into frosty bowls.

TURKEY-CORN CHOWDER

¼ cup butter or margarine
1 medium onion, chopped
2 cups water
2 chicken bouillon cubes
3 cups diced cooked turkey or chicken
1 cup sliced celery
5 medium potatoes, cubed
1 (17-ounce) can whole kernel corn, drained
1 (17-ounce) can cream-style corn
1 quart milk
Salt and pepper to taste
Chopped fresh parsley (optional)
Paprika (optional)

Melt butter in a Dutch oven; add onion, and sauté until tender. Stir in water, bouillon cubes, turkey, celery, and potatoes; cook 20 to 30 minutes or until potatoes are tender. Add corn and milk; season with salt and pepper. Simmer until thoroughly heated. Sprinkle with parsley and paprika, if desired. Yield: about 8 to 10 servings.
Thelma Olson,
Lexington, Oklahoma.

CHICKEN SOUP

1 (2½- to 3-pound) broiler-fryer
1 tablespoon salt
½ cup butter or margarine
About 1 quart boiling water
1 large potato, cubed
1 medium onion, coarsely chopped
2 (17-ounce) cans cream-style corn
1 (28-ounce) can tomatoes, undrained
½ teaspoon pepper

Combine chicken, salt, butter, and boiling water in a Dutch oven. Bring to a boil; reduce heat, and cook until

chicken is tender. Remove chicken from broth; let cool, and remove meat from bones.

Add potato and onion to broth. Bring to a boil; reduce heat, and cook until vegetables are tender. Add chicken and remaining ingredients. Simmer 30 to 45 minutes, stirring occasionally. Yield: about 8 servings.
Pauline Horn,
Carthage, Mississippi.

FISHERMAN'S STEW

2 tablespoons butter or margarine
1 cup diced white potatoes
1 cup thinly sliced celery
2 (10½-ounce) cans oyster stew, undiluted
2 (7-ounce) cans tuna, drained and flaked
1 (17-ounce) can English peas, drained
3 cups milk
2 tablespoons diced onion
1 teaspoon salt
2 tablespoons chopped fresh parsley
Pinch of red pepper
Additional chopped fresh parsley (optional)

Melt butter in a large Dutch oven; add potatoes and celery. Sauté until potatoes are lightly browned and celery is tender.

Stir in next 8 ingredients. Place stew over medium-low heat until thoroughly heated, stirring occasionally. If desired, garnish each serving with additional chopped fresh parsley. Yield: 8 to 10 servings.
Nancy Monroe,
Elizabethtown, North Carolina.

CREAM OF CUCUMBER SOUP

2 cups peeled and sliced cucumber
¼ cup chopped celery
1 cup chicken broth or chicken bouillon
1 cup milk or half-and-half
3 tablespoons butter or margarine, melted
2 tablespoons all-purpose flour

Combine all ingredients in container of electric blender, and process until smooth. Chill soup 3 to 4 hours. Yield: 4 to 6 servings.
Note: The soup may also be served hot; sprinkle with dillweed, if desired.
Nell Little,
Jonesboro, Tennessee.

GAZPACHO

2 cups finely chopped tomato
1 cup finely chopped celery
1 cup finely chopped green pepper
1 cup finely chopped cucumber
1 cup sliced green onion
1 (4-ounce) can chopped green chiles
2 (8-ounce) cans tomato sauce
½ to 1 cup water
¼ cup vinegar
¼ cup vegetable oil
1 tablespoon salt
2 teaspoons Worcestershire sauce
Dash of pepper

Combine first 6 ingredients in a large bowl. Combine remaining ingredients, stirring well; pour over vegetables, and toss lightly. Cover and chill 6 to 8 hours. Stir soup gently before serving. Yield: 6 to 8 servings.
Mrs. John Mosley,
Franklin, Arizona.

CREAMY POTATO SOUP

1 onion, chopped
2 tablespoons butter or margarine
6 cups milk
1 tablespoon salt
1½ cups instant mashed potato flakes

Sauté onion in butter until tender; stir in milk and salt. Heat just until mixture begins to boil. Remove from heat, and stir in potato flakes. Serve soup hot. Yield: 6 servings.
June Bostick,
Fruitland, Maryland.

Tip: Check foods closely as you are shopping to be sure they are not spoiled before you purchase them. Do not buy cans that are badly dented, leaking, or bulging at the ends. Do not select pre-sealed packages on which the seal has been broken.

Look What's Quick And Easy

More and more nowadays, the call is out for quick and easy recipes. The good news is that they don't have to sacrifice flavor for convenience.

Zucchini Omelet, filled with vegetables and cheese, is ready in minutes. For a quick entrée using leftover ham, we suggest Ham Patties. Ground cooked ham is mixed with a few simple ingredients, shaped into patties, and then browned in a skillet.

And homemade biscuits aren't time consuming at all when they're Easy Cheese Biscuits. Just mix four simple ingredients, and drop spoonfuls of batter onto a baking sheet. They're quick enough for an early-morning breakfast, and they're easy enough to prepare after a busy day.

HAM PATTIES

½ cup fine dry breadcrumbs
1¾ cups ground cooked ham
1 egg, beaten
¼ cup milk
3 tablespoons sweet pickle relish
1½ teaspoons dry mustard
3 tablespoons butter or margarine, melted

Remove 2 tablespoons breadcrumbs, and set aside. Combine remaining breadcrumbs, ham, egg, milk, pickle relish, and dry mustard; mix well, and shape into 4 patties.

Coat patties with reserved breadcrumbs; cook over medium heat in butter until brown on both sides, turning once. Yield: 4 servings. *Jodie McCoy, Tulsa, Oklahoma.*

ZUCCHINI OMELET

½ tablespoon butter or margarine
⅓ cup chopped zucchini
¼ cup chopped green onion
¼ cup chopped tomato
Dash of salt
Dash of pepper
4 eggs
2 tablespoons water
¼ teaspoon salt
¼ teaspoon dried whole basil
⅛ teaspoon celery salt
⅛ teaspoon pepper
2 tablespoons butter or margarine
¼ cup (1 ounce) shredded Swiss cheese

Melt ½ tablespoon butter in a small saucepan or skillet. Add zucchini, onion, and tomato; sauté 2 to 3 minutes or just until tender. Stir in dash of salt and pepper; set aside.

Combine eggs, water, remaining salt, basil, celery salt, and remaining pepper; mix well. Melt 2 tablespoons butter in a 10-inch skillet until just hot enough to sizzle a drop of water; pour in egg mixture. As mixture starts to cook, gently lift edges of omelet, and tilt the pan to allow the uncooked portion to flow underneath.

When mixture is set and no longer flows freely, sprinkle zucchini mixture on half of omelet and cheese on remaining half. Fold omelet in half, and place on a warm platter. Yield: 2 servings.
Cynthia Stewart Neely, Charlotte, North Carolina.

QUICK-AND-EASY FRUIT SALAD

1 (15¼-ounce) can pineapple chunks
1 (16-ounce) can chunky mixed fruit
1 (3¾-ounce) package vanilla instant pudding and pie filling mix
3 tablespoons orange-flavored instant breakfast drink
2 large bananas, sliced

Drain pineapple and mixed fruit, reserving pineapple juice. Combine juice, pudding mix, and instant breakfast drink; stir well.

Combine fruit and dressing; toss gently. Chill. Yield: 4 servings.
Mrs. John A. Wyatt, Palmyra, Tennessee.

EASY CHEESE BISCUITS

¼ cup butter or margarine, softened
2 cups self-rising flour
1 cup buttermilk
1½ cups (6 ounces) shredded Cheddar cheese

Cut butter into flour until mixture resembles coarse crumbs; add remaining ingredients, and stir well. Drop by tablespoonfuls, 2 inches apart, onto a large greased baking sheet. Bake at 425° for 12 to 15 minutes or until golden. Yield: about 1½ dozen.
Gloria Pedersen, Brandon, Mississippi.

Tip: Lower oven temperature 25° when using heat-proof glass dishes to ensure even baking.

Is It Pudding Or Cake?

These puddings both have a cakelike texture. Chocolate Cake Pudding is rich in flavor and just as delicious with or without that extra dollop of whipped cream.

LEMON PUDDING

1 cup sugar
3 tablespoons all-purpose flour
¼ teaspoon salt
2 eggs, separated
1 cup milk
1½ teaspoons lemon rind
3 tablespoons lemon juice
Whipped cream (optional)

Combine sugar, flour, and salt.

Beat egg yolks. Add milk, lemon rind, and lemon juice; beat well. Add to dry ingredients, and mix well. Beat egg whites until stiff; fold into lemon mixture. Pour into a greased 1-quart casserole. Place casserole in a pan of warm water. Bake at 350° for 35 minutes or until a knife inserted in center comes out clean.

Serve warm with whipped cream, if desired. Yield: 6 servings.
Gladys Weldon, Cullman, Alabama.

CHOCOLATE CAKE PUDDING

¾ cup sugar
1 cup all-purpose flour
2 tablespoons cocoa
2 teaspoons baking powder
¼ teaspoon salt
½ cup milk
3 tablespoons butter or margarine, melted
1 teaspoon vanilla extract
½ cup sugar
½ cup firmly packed brown sugar
¼ cup cocoa
1½ cups water
Whipped cream or ice cream (optional)

Sift ¾ cup sugar, flour, 2 tablespoons cocoa, baking powder, and salt into a 9-inch square pan. Stir in milk, butter, and vanilla; spread evenly in pan.

Combine next 3 ingredients and sprinkle over batter. Pour water over top. Bake pudding at 350° for 40 minutes. Serve with whipped cream or ice cream, if desired. Yield: 6 servings.
Mrs. Galen Jones, Ackerman, Mississippi.

Icy Beverages Give A Warm Welcome

These icy-cold beverages will offer a friendly welcome to guests at your next party, whether you're entertaining a large group or just a few friends. They all sparkle with fruit juices and carbonated beverages.

Spirited Fruit Punch combines limeade and pineapple juice with light rum, while citrus and Chablis flavor Wine Welcomer. For Summertime Bourbon Slush, chunks of a frozen mixture of bourbon, ginger ale, and pineapple juice are scooped into tall glasses, and lemon-lime carbonated beverage is poured over.

Southerners, of course, love their iced tea, and our Ginger Tea is especially light and refreshing with fruit juice and ginger ale added.

Ginger Tea is a refreshing blend of iced tea, fruit juices, and ginger ale.

APRICOT COOLER

½ cup lemonade-flavor drink mix
2 (12-ounce) cans apricot nectar, chilled
2 (12-ounce) bottles lemon-lime carbonated beverage, chilled

Combine drink mix and apricot nectar in a pitcher; stir well. Slowly pour in carbonated beverage, and serve over crushed ice in tall glasses. Yield: 6 cups.
*Heather Riggins,
Nashville, Tennessee.*

GINGER TEA

2 cups tea
Juice of 2 oranges
Juice of 1 lemon
¼ cup sugar
2 cups ginger ale
Orange slices (optional)
Lemon slices (optional)

Combine first 5 ingredients, mixing well. Serve over ice. Garnish glasses with orange and lemon slices, if desired. Yield: 4½ cups. *Maybelle Pinkston, Corryton, Tennessee.*

PINK LADY PUNCH

1 quart cranberry juice cocktail, chilled
1 quart pineapple juice, chilled
1 to 1½ cups sugar
2 quarts ginger ale, chilled

Combine all ingredients; stir well. Serve over ice. Yield: 1 gallon.
Mrs. E. Lamar McMath, Jacksonville, Florida.

WINE WELCOMER

2 cups orange juice
1 (6-ounce) can frozen lemonade concentrate, thawed and undiluted
1 cup Cointreau or other orange-flavored liqueur
1 (25.4-ounce) bottle Chablis or other dry white wine, chilled
1 (33.8-ounce) bottle club soda
Orange slices (optional)

Combine first 4 ingredients in a punch bowl; add club soda and ice, stirring gently. Garnish with orange slices, if desired. Yield: about 12 cups.
Lilly S. Bradley, Salem, Virginia.

SPIRITED FRUIT PUNCH

1 (8.5-ounce) can cream of coconut
1 (6-ounce) can frozen limeade concentrate, thawed and undiluted
1 (46-ounce) can pineapple juice
1½ cups light rum
1 (33.8-ounce) bottle ginger ale, chilled
Ice ring

Combine first 4 ingredients; chill. To serve, combine chilled mixture and ginger ale in a punch bowl with an ice ring. Yield: about 3¼ quarts.
Hildegard Wolverton, Auburn, Alabama.

Tip: Before trying a new recipe, read through it at least once before beginning; check carefully to see if all ingredients are on hand.

SUMMERTIME BOURBON SLUSH

2¼ cups pineapple juice
1½ cups ginger ale
¾ cup bourbon
Lemon-lime carbonated beverage

Combine juice, ginger ale, and bourbon; stir well, and freeze until firm.

Break frozen mixture into chunks. Scoop into tall glasses, filling one-third to one-half full. Add carbonated beverage; stir until slushy. Yield: 4½ cups.

Note: The pineapple mixture may be stored, covered, in the freezer for several months. *Jayne Perala, Salem, Virginia.*

Do Something Different With Vegetables

Good things happen when you take a familiar vegetable and prepare it a different way. For instance, have you ever tried frying zucchini? Our recipe is reminiscent of fried green tomatoes. Speaking of that Southern favorite, we've found there's a great way to fry ripened tomatoes too, in Fried Red Tomatoes.

And for cooks who rely on the potato as a staple in their menus, we've got a recipe for Savory Stuffed Potatoes. These baked potatoes are scooped out of the shell, mixed with sour cream, sprinkled with Parmesan, and baked again in the shell. It's a sure way to liven up a plain baked potato.

CAULIFLOWER WITH CHEESE SAUCE

½ teaspoon salt
1 head cauliflower, broken into flowerets
2 tablespoons butter or margarine
2 tablespoons all-purpose flour
½ teaspoon salt
Dash of pepper
Dash of paprika (optional)
1 cup milk
1 cup (4 ounces) shredded Cheddar cheese
Parsley sprigs (optional)

Bring 1 inch of water and ½ teaspoon salt to a boil in a saucepan; add cauliflower. Cover and cook 8 to 10 minutes or until crisp-tender. Drain and keep warm.

Melt butter in a saucepan over low heat. Add flour, ½ teaspoon salt, and pepper, stirring until smooth; if desired, add the paprika. Cook 1 minute, stirring constantly. Gradually add milk; cook over medium heat, stirring constantly, until thickened and bubbly. Add cheese, and stir until melted.

Arrange cauliflower on a platter, and spoon cheese sauce over top. Garnish with parsley sprigs, if desired. Yield: 6 to 8 servings. *Margaret Steele, Jackson, Kentucky.*

BROCCOLI-RICE CASSEROLE

1 (10-ounce) package frozen chopped broccoli
½ cup chopped onion
½ cup butter or margarine
1⅓ cups cooked rice
1 (8-ounce) jar process cheese spread
1 (10¾-ounce) can cream of mushroom soup, undiluted

Combine broccoli and onion; cook according to package directions. Drain and add remaining ingredients; stir well. Pour into a greased 2-quart shallow casserole. Bake at 350° about 30 minutes. Yield: 6 to 8 servings. *Myra Musick, Grapeland, Texas.*

SAVORY STUFFED POTATOES

5 or 6 medium baking potatoes
Vegetable oil
⅓ cup butter or margarine
½ cup milk
½ cup commercial sour cream
2 teaspoons salt
⅛ teaspoon pepper
2 tablespoons grated Parmesan cheese
Chopped chives

Wash potatoes and rub skins with oil. Bake at 400° for 1 hour or until done.

Allow potatoes to cool to touch. Slice skin away from top of each potato. Carefully scoop out pulp, leaving shells intact; spoon pulp into a mixing bowl. Add butter, milk, sour cream, salt, and pepper; beat with an electric mixer until fluffy. Stuff potato shells with potato mixture; sprinkle with cheese. Bake at 400° for 15 minutes. Remove from oven; top with chives. Yield: 5 or 6 servings. *Mrs. Doug Hail, Moody, Texas.*

MINTED CARROTS

⅓ cup sliced water chestnuts
2 tablespoons margarine, melted and divided
2 cups cooked sliced carrots, drained
⅓ cup sifted powdered sugar
1 teaspoon dried mint leaves or 1 tablespoon chopped fresh mint leaves
¼ teaspoon ground cinnamon

Sauté water chestnuts in 1 tablespoon margarine for 5 minutes; combine with carrots, and place in a 1-quart casserole. Add remaining 1 tablespoon margarine.

Combine remaining ingredients; sprinkle over carrot mixture. Cover and bake at 350° for 20 minutes, stirring frequently. Yield: 4 servings. *Eunice Palmer, Morris Chapel, Tennessee.*

CABBAGE CHOP SUEY

2 tablespoons shortening
3 cups shredded cabbage
1 cup thinly sliced celery
1 cup thinly sliced green pepper
1 medium onion, thinly sliced
1½ teaspoons salt
¼ teaspoon pepper
Chow mein noodles (optional)

Heat shortening in a large skillet over medium heat. Add vegetables, tossing lightly. Cover and cook over low heat for 5 minutes. Add salt and pepper; cook, uncovered, for 1 minute, stirring gently. Sprinkle with chow mein noodles, if desired. Yield: 5 to 6 servings. *Marilyn Hershberger, Due West, South Carolina.*

PEAS, COUNTRY STYLE

8 slices bacon
½ cup chopped onion
½ cup chopped green pepper
2 (16-ounce) cans English peas, drained
¼ cup chopped parsley
1 teaspoon sugar
¼ teaspoon pepper

Fry bacon until crisp; crumble and set aside. Reserve 2 tablespoons bacon drippings. Sauté onion and green pepper in drippings until tender. Add remaining ingredients except bacon. Cover and cook over low heat 5 minutes, stirring occasionally. Garnish with bacon. Yield: about 6 servings. *Mrs. Max E. Ayer, Elizabethton, Tennessee.*

SUMMER SQUASH CASSEROLE

4 medium-size yellow squash, cut into
    ¼-inch slices
⅓ cup chopped onion
⅓ cup butter or margarine, melted
2 hard-cooked eggs, chopped
½ cup cubed Cheddar cheese
1 cup corn chips, crushed

Cook squash in a small amount of boiling salted water until tender; drain. Sauté onion in butter; add squash, stirring to mix. Spoon mixture into a lightly greased 1-quart casserole. Top with eggs, cheese, and corn chips. Bake casserole at 350° about 15 minutes or until cheese melts. Yield: 4 servings.
Mrs. J. C. Ellis,
Comanche, Texas.

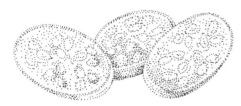

FRIED RED TOMATOES

1 tablespoon Dijon mustard
1½ teaspoons Worcestershire sauce
1 teaspoon sugar
½ teaspoon salt
¼ teaspoon paprika
Dash of red pepper
2 medium tomatoes, chilled and cut into
    ½-inch slices
Cornmeal
Hot bacon drippings

Combine first 6 ingredients; stir to mix well. Spread mixture onto both sides of tomato slices, and coat with cornmeal. Sauté in about ¼ inch hot bacon drippings until lightly browned and crisp. Drain and serve hot. Yield: 4 servings.
Mrs. William B. Marks,
Harrisonburg, Virginia.

ZUCCHINI FRY

1 pound zucchini, cut into ½-inch
    slices
Salt and pepper to taste
2 eggs, well beaten
About 1 cup cornmeal
Hot vegetable oil

Sprinkle zucchini with salt and pepper. Dip into egg, and dredge in cornmeal. Fry zucchini in hot vegetable oil over medium heat until golden brown, turning once. Serve hot. Yield: 4 to 6 servings.
Carolyn Beyer,
Fredericksburg, Texas.

Use Herbs To Enhance Flavor

Cooking with herbs is an art that's easy to master, and the rewards are delicious. Much of the fun of cooking with herbs is experimenting for new flavor combinations, but remember that herbs should enhance the flavor of food, not disguise it. Here are a few helpful hints for the use of dried and fresh herbs as well as some recipes for both.

—To substitute dried herbs for fresh, use one-third the amount specified, since the flavor of dried herbs is stronger.

—Store dried herbs in airtight containers in a cool, dry place to preserve freshness. Herbs lose flavor with age, so it's a good idea to label containers with storage date. To determine freshness, crush a small amount in a mortar and pestle; a fresh aroma should be apparent.

—Help to release the flavor of dried herbs by crushing them gently before using them.

—Add ground and delicately flavored herbs late in the cooking period to prevent the flavor from being steamed out. However, firm herbs such as bay leaves require long, slow cooking to bring out their flavor.

—When using fresh herbs, remember to snip them with scissors into the desired size rather than chopping or crushing them. If your plants are yielding faster than your cooking demands, remember that most fresh herbs, such as chives, may be frozen for later use.

MINTED CHICKEN

1 (2½- to 3-pound) broiler-fryer
Butter or margarine
Salt and pepper
1 cup fresh mint leaves
1 tablespoon chopped fresh mint
Commercial mint sauce (optional)

Rinse chicken with cold water, and pat dry. Rub outside of chicken lightly with butter. Sprinkle chicken inside and outside with salt and pepper. Place 1 cup fresh mint in cavity of chicken.

Place chicken, breast side up, on a rack in a shallow roasting pan. Bake at 375°, basting occasionally, for 1 hour and 15 minutes or until done. Sprinkle remaining mint over chicken during last 10 minutes of baking. Serve with mint sauce, if desired. Yield: 4 to 6 servings.
Dale H. Hollabaugh,
Constantine, Kentucky.

HERBED NEW POTATOES

1½ pounds new potatoes
¼ cup melted butter or margarine
3 tablespoons chopped fresh parsley
1 tablespoon chopped fresh chives
1 tablespoon lemon juice
1½ teaspoons chopped fresh dillweed
Salt and pepper to taste

Pare a 1-inch strip around center of each potato. Cover potatoes, and cook in boiling salted water 25 minutes or until tender. Drain potatoes, and set aside.

Combine remaining ingredients, stirring well. Pour over potatoes, coating thoroughly. Yield: 6 servings.
Carol T. Keith,
Fincastle, Virginia.

HERBED TOMATOES

1 (28-ounce) can whole tomatoes, drained
1¼ cups chicken- and herb-flavored
    stuffing mix, divided
1 small onion, finely chopped
1½ teaspoons sugar
1 teaspoon salt
¼ teaspoon dried whole oregano
¼ teaspoon dried rosemary
1 tablespoon butter or margarine

Cut tomatoes in quarters, reserving juice that accumulates. Combine tomatoes, reserved juice, 1 cup stuffing mix, onion, sugar, salt, oregano, and rosemary; mix well. Pour into a greased 1-quart casserole. Sprinkle with ¼ cup stuffing mix, and dot with butter. Bake at 375° for 45 minutes. Yield: 3 to 4 servings.
Mrs. J. W. Craft,
Harlan, Kentucky.

Tip: Use a timer when cooking. Set the timer so it will ring at various intervals, and check the progress of the dish. However, try to avoid opening the oven door unless necessary.

His Recipes Have That Special Added Touch

When he's in the kitchen, Dr. Lamar Miller of Dothan, Alabama, adds a dab of one ingredient and a sprinkle of the next until his recipe is just right.

"I've been cooking all my life," he says. "My mother went back to work during the war, so I guess I've known how to put breakfast on the table from the time I was 10 years old."

Although Miller's wife still does the bulk of the cooking for them and their five children, he likes to take over the kitchen sometimes—especially at breakfast. "I get tired of the same old regular scrambled eggs," he explained. "So one morning I was experimenting and came up with my Special Scrambled Eggs." According to Miller, it's the mayonnaise that makes the eggs special, and our test kitchen agrees that they are unusually light, creamy, and tasty.

Another one of Dr. Miller's favorite recipes is Broiled Tomatoes With Mushroom Sauce. He says he first ate them at a St. Louis restaurant, and "they were so good that when I got home, I experimented around until I found a recipe that tasted just like them." Miller points out that the recipe is best when you start with a "good, ripe, firm tomato." And the touch of wine really sets off the mushroom sauce.

Following Dr. Miller's specialties are recipes from other men cooks.

BROILED TOMATOES WITH MUSHROOM SAUCE

¾ teaspoon beef-flavored bouillon granules
¼ cup hot water
⅔ cup sliced fresh mushrooms
2 tablespoons butter or margarine, melted
2 tablespoons white wine
1½ teaspoons instant blending flour
2 large tomatoes
¼ cup fine dry breadcrumbs
1 teaspoon dried whole oregano
1 tablespoon grated Parmesan cheese
2 tablespoons lemon juice
2 teaspoons vegetable oil
Dash of salt

Dissolve beef bouillon in water, and set aside.

Sauté mushrooms in butter in a heavy skillet until tender. Stir in wine. Add flour, stirring until smooth. Cook 1 minute, stirring constantly. Gradually add bouillon; cook over medium heat, stirring constantly, until slightly thick and bubbly. Keep warm while broiling tomatoes.

Remove stems from tomatoes; cut in half crosswise. Combine remaining ingredients; lightly press mixture over top of tomato halves. Broil 6 inches from heat about 7 minutes or just until topping is lightly browned. Spoon mushroom sauce over hot tomatoes. Yield: 4 servings.

SPECIAL SCRAMBLED EGGS

3 eggs
1 tablespoon buttermilk
1½ tablespoons mayonnaise
Salt and pepper to taste
1 tablespoon butter or margarine
1 slice bacon, cooked and crumbled

Combine eggs, buttermilk, mayonnaise, salt, and pepper; beat with fork until well blended.

Melt butter in a small skillet; add egg mixture. Cook over low heat until eggs are partially set, lifting edges gently to allow uncooked portions to flow underneath. Cook until eggs are set but still moist. Sprinkle with bacon, and serve immediately. Yield: 1 to 2 servings.

PEANUT BUTTER ICE CREAM

4 eggs
2 cups sugar
¾ cup crunchy peanut butter
6 cups milk
1 quart half-and-half
1 tablespoon vanilla extract
1 teaspoon salt

Beat eggs with electric mixer at medium speed until frothy. Gradually add sugar, beating until thick. Add peanut butter, beating until blended. Add remaining ingredients; mix well.

Pour mixture into freezer can of a 1-gallon hand-turned or electric freezer. Freeze according to manufacturer's instructions. Let ripen at least 1½ hours. Yield: about 1 gallon.

SPINACH AND ARTICHOKE CASSEROLE

2 (10-ounce) packages frozen chopped spinach
½ cup butter or margarine
2 (3-ounce) packages cream cheese
1 (8½-ounce) jar artichoke hearts, drained and chopped
¼ teaspoon pepper
1 tablespoon lemon juice
1 tablespoon Parmesan cheese
1 tablespoon seasoned breadcrumbs

Cook spinach according to package directions; drain well. Set aside.

Combine butter and cream cheese in a saucepan; cook over low heat, stirring constantly, until butter is melted and cream cheese is softened.

Combine spinach, artichoke hearts, cream cheese mixture, pepper, and lemon juice; stir well. Spoon into a lightly greased 1½-quart casserole dish; sprinkle with cheese and breadcrumbs. Bake at 325° for 30 minutes or until bubbly. Yield: 8 servings. *Tony Jones, Atlanta, Georgia.*

CHEESY VEGETABLE CASSEROLE

2 (10-ounce) packages frozen mixed vegetables
1 cup chopped celery
⅓ cup chopped onion
1 cup mayonnaise
½ cup (2 ounces) shredded sharp Cheddar cheese
¼ teaspoon salt
⅛ teaspoon pepper
2 cups bite-size Cheddar cheese crackers, crushed
¼ cup butter or margarine, melted
½ cup (2 ounces) shredded sharp Cheddar cheese

Cook frozen mixed vegetables according to package directions; drain well.

Combine cooked vegetables, celery, onion, mayonnaise, ½ cup cheese, salt, and pepper; spoon into a greased 2-quart casserole. Combine remaining ingredients; sprinkle over top. Bake at 300° for 30 to 40 minutes. Yield: about 8 servings. *James O. Michelinie, Louisville, Kentucky.*

Tip: If a recipe calls for egg whites at room temperature, separate the whites from the yolks an hour ahead of preparation time.

CHICKEN LIVERS IN WINE SAUCE

1 (6-ounce) package long grain and wild rice
2 tablespoons minced onion
1 clove garlic, minced
3 tablespoons butter or margarine
2 tablespoons all-purpose flour
1 cup beef broth, undiluted
¼ cup all-purpose flour
½ teaspoon salt
¼ teaspoon pepper
1 pound chicken livers
2 tablespoons butter or margarine, melted
3 tablespoons sweet Madeira wine

Cook rice according to directions on the package.

Sauté onion and garlic in 3 tablespoons butter until tender. Add 2 tablespoons flour, stirring until smooth. Cook 1 minute, stirring constantly. Gradually add broth; cook over medium heat, stirring constantly, until thickened and bubbly; set aside.

Combine ¼ cup flour, salt, and pepper; stir well. Dredge livers in flour mixture. Sauté livers in 2 tablespoons butter, stirring often, about 15 minutes or until done. Stir sauce and wine into livers; cook just until heated through. Serve over rice. Yield: 4 servings.

T. O. Davis,
Waynesboro, Mississippi.

SWEET-AND-SOUR PORK

½ cup dry sherry
½ cup soy sauce
1 pound boneless pork, cut into 1-inch cubes
½ cup cornstarch
½ cup all-purpose flour
Vegetable oil
1 medium-size green pepper, cut into 1-inch pieces
1 large onion, cut into 1-inch pieces
1 carrot, thinly sliced
1 (8-ounce) can pineapple chunks, drained
1 tablespoon soy sauce
¾ cup sugar
3 tablespoons cornstarch
¼ cup soy sauce
½ cup red wine vinegar
⅔ cup water
Hot cooked rice

Combine sherry, ½ cup soy sauce, and pork; mix well, and let stand at room temperature for 1 hour. Drain, reserving the marinade for use in other recipes.

Combine ½ cup cornstarch and flour. Dredge pork in flour mixture, coating

well; deep fry in hot oil (375°) for 5 to 6 minutes or until golden brown. Drain and set aside. Keep warm.

Heat 2 tablespoons oil in a large skillet; add green pepper, onion, carrot, and pineapple. Cook 1 minute, stirring occasionally. Then add 1 tablespoon soy sauce; cook an additional minute. Remove vegetables, and keep warm.

Combine sugar and 3 tablespoons cornstarch; stir until blended. Gradually add ¼ cup soy sauce, vinegar, and water; cook, stirring constantly, until thickened and bubbly. Stir in pork and vegetables. Serve over rice. Yield: about 4 servings.

Fred Ralls,
Dallas, Texas.

THOUSAND ISLAND DRESSING

1 cup mayonnaise
½ cup chili sauce
3 tablespoons coarsely chopped pimiento-stuffed olives
¼ teaspoon onion powder
1 tablespoon chopped fresh parsley
1 tablespoon chopped pimiento
½ teaspoon lemon juice
1 tablespoon honey
12 capers

Combine mayonnaise and chili sauce, stirring well. Stir in remaining ingredients. Chill before serving. Store in refrigerator. Yield: about 2 cups.

William A. Thornburg,
Long Beach, Mississippi.

Let The Sweetness Be Honey

Back-to-nature food buffs prize honey because it's one of the few sweeteners that can be used in the unrefined state, but there's also a lot to be said for its wonderful flavor. With these recipes, you can enjoy honey's natural goodness—and sweetness—in Dutch Apple Pie, Tomato-Honey French Dressing, and a whole-grain yeast bread.

When buying honey, remember that lighter colored honeys have a mild flavor, while the darker colored ones (orange, tupelo, and buckwheat) are stronger flavored. Here are a few other pointers.

—Lightly grease measuring cups and spoons before using them to measure honey; this will make the sticky honey easier to remove.

—To keep honey easy to pour, store it at room temperature.

—Reliquify the honey if sugar crystals form in the jar, by letting the jar stand in warm water for a few minutes.

HONEY-GLAZED HAM SLICE

½ cup firmly packed brown sugar
½ cup honey
½ teaspoon dried mustard
6 whole cloves
1 (1-pound) fully cooked ham slice (about 1 inch thick)
2 slices canned pineapple
4 maraschino cherries, halved

Combine brown sugar, honey, mustard, and cloves in a small saucepan; mix well. Bring to a boil; boil 2 to 3 minutes, stirring occasionally.

Bake ham slice at 325° for 10 minutes. Arrange pineapple slices and cherries on top of ham; spoon on glaze. Bake an additional 15 minutes, basting twice with drippings. Yield: 4 servings.

Mrs. Guy C. Palmer,
Wagoner, Oklahoma.

HINT O' HONEY LOAVES

2¼ cups milk, scalded
¼ cup butter or margarine
⅓ cup honey
2½ teaspoons salt
2 packages dry yeast
½ cup warm water (105° to 115°)
2 cups regular oats, uncooked
6 to 7 cups all-purpose flour
2 tablespoons butter or margarine, melted

Combine milk, ¼ cup butter, honey, and salt; stir until butter melts. Let cool to 105° to 115°.

Combine yeast and warm water in a large bowl; let stand 5 minutes. Add milk mixture, oats, and 2 cups flour; mix well. Stir in enough remaining flour (about 4 to 5 cups) to make a soft dough.

Turn dough out onto a lightly floured surface, and knead until smooth and elastic (about 8 to 10 minutes).

Place dough in a greased bowl, turning to grease top. Cover and let rise in a warm place (85°), free from drafts, 1 hour or until doubled in bulk.

Punch dough down; cover and let rest 10 minutes. Divide dough in half, and shape each portion into a loaf. Place in greased 9- x 5- x 3-inch loafpans, and brush with melted butter.

Cover and let rise 40 minutes or until doubled in bulk. Bake at 350° for 40 minutes or until loaves sound hollow when tapped. Remove from pans, and cool on wire racks. Yield: 2 loaves.
Sue-Sue Hartstern,
Louisville, Kentucky.

HONEY TEA

2 tablespoons black tea leaves
1 tablespoon whole cloves
4 cups boiling water
½ cup orange juice
¼ cup plus 2 tablespoons honey
¼ cup lime juice

Combine tea and cloves in a tea ball; place in teapot. Add boiling water; cover and let steep 5 minutes. Remove teaball, and stir in orange juice, honey, and lime juice. Yield: 5 cups.
Glenda Wasson,
Sikeston, Missouri.

TOMATO-HONEY FRENCH DRESSING

1 cup vegetable oil
½ cup catsup
½ cup honey
⅓ cup cider vinegar
½ teaspoon onion salt
½ teaspoon paprika
¼ teaspoon garlic powder
¼ teaspoon celery salt

Combine all ingredients in container of electric blender; process on low speed 1 minute or until smooth. Chill thoroughly. Stir well before serving. Yield: 2 cups. *Dorothy Apgar,*
Flagler Beach, Florida.

DUTCH APPLE PIE

Pastry for double-crust 9-inch pie (recipe follows)
6 cups peeled, thinly sliced cooking apples
¾ cup honey
¼ cup all-purpose flour
½ teaspoon ground cinnamon
½ teaspoon ground nutmeg
Dash of salt
2 tablespoons butter or margarine
½ cup whipping cream

Line a 9-inch pieplate with half of pastry; set aside.

Combine apples and honey, tossing gently. Combine flour, spices, and salt, stirring well; spoon over apple mixture, tossing gently.

Spoon filling evenly into pastry shell, and dot with butter. Cover with top crust, and slit in several places to allow steam to escape; seal and flute edges. Cover edges of pie with aluminum foil, and bake at 425° for 40 minutes.

Remove the aluminum foil from edge of pie. Pour whipping cream in slits of top crust. Bake pie 5 additional minutes. Yield: one 9-inch pie.

Double-Crust Pastry:

2 cups all-purpose flour
½ teaspoon salt
⅔ cup shortening
4 to 6 tablespoons cold water

Combine flour and salt; cut in shortening with pastry blender until mixture resembles coarse meal. Sprinkle cold water evenly over surface; stir with a fork until all dry ingredients are moistened. Shape dough into a ball; chill. Divide in half, and roll each portion to ⅛-inch thickness on a lightly floured surface. Yield: pastry for one double crust 9-inch pie. *Grace Edwards,*
Greenville, South Carolina.

These Fritters Come Out Crisp

For happy faces, serve a batch of hot and crispy fritters. Our ham fritters are substantial enough for a main dish. Or if you prefer your fritters sweet, try our delicious version of apple fritters dusted with powdered sugar.

For perfect fritters, crisp outside and moist inside, be sure the oil is hot enough to fry them quickly. Slide spoonfuls of batter into the heated oil at the side of the pan. If the batter sticks to the spoon, simply dip the bowl of the spoon into the hot oil before picking up each spoonful of batter.

HAM FRITTERS WITH CREAMY SAUCE

1 cup all-purpose flour
1 teaspoon salt
1 teaspoon baking powder
2 eggs, beaten
¼ cup milk
1 tablespoon melted shortening
1 cup chopped cooked ham
Hot vegetable oil
Creamy Sauce

Combine flour, salt, and baking powder; stir in eggs and milk. Add shortening, and mix well. Stir in ham. Drop batter by tablespoonfuls into deep oil heated to 375°. Fry until golden. Drain on paper towels. Serve hot with Creamy Sauce. Yield: about 2 dozen.

Creamy Sauce:

¼ cup shortening
¼ cup all-purpose flour
2 cups milk
1 teaspoon salt
1 cup (4 ounces) shredded Cheddar cheese

Melt shortening in heavy saucepan over low heat; add flour, and stir until smooth. Cook 1 minute, stirring constantly. Gradually add milk; cook over medium heat, stirring constantly, until thickened and bubbly. Stir in salt and cheese; cook, stirring constantly, until cheese is melted. Yield: about 2 cups.
Mrs. Kenneth Corley,
Plantersville, Mississippi.

APPLE FRITTERS

1 egg, beaten
1 cup milk
1 cup unpeeled, cored, finely chopped apple
¼ cup sugar
¼ teaspoon salt
1 teaspoon grated orange rind
3 tablespoons orange juice
½ teaspoon vanilla extract
2 cups all-purpose flour
1 tablespoon baking powder
Hot vegetable oil
Sifted powdered sugar

Combine first 8 ingredients; mix well. Stir flour and baking powder together; add to apple mixture, and stir well. Drop mixture by teaspoonfuls into deep oil heated to 375°. Fry fritters until golden (about 3 minutes). Drain on paper towels. Dust with powdered sugar. Serve hot. Yield: about 5 dozen. *Mrs. Howard W. Phillips,*
Springfield, Missouri.

Sesame Seeds Liven Things Up

The South has its own special name for sesame seeds. In areas of the coastal South they have been called "bene" or "benne" seeds ever since they were introduced to the region from Africa.

Here they add a nutlike taste and a spritely crunch to dishes as diverse as fried catfish and fried green onions.

■ This recipe won second prize in a national catfish cooking contest.

CATFISH SESAME

1 egg, beaten
2 tablespoons milk
½ cup cracker crumbs
3 tablespoons sesame seeds
2 pounds fresh or frozen catfish fillets
Salt
White pepper
¼ cup all-purpose flour
Vegetable oil
Lemon Parsley Sauce

Combine egg and milk; mix well, and set aside.

Combine cracker crumbs and sesame seeds; stir well, and set mixture aside.

Sprinkle fillets with salt and pepper; dredge in flour. Dip each fillet into egg mixture, and roll in crumb mixture.

Fry in 1-inch-deep hot oil (360°) for 4 to 5 minutes on each side; drain on paper towels. Serve with Lemon Parsley Sauce. Yield: 4 servings.

Lemon Parsley Sauce:

⅓ cup finely chopped onion
¼ cup finely chopped parsley
¼ cup lemon juice

Combine all ingredients in a saucepan, mixing well; bring to a boil. Yield: about ⅓ cup. *Bill Oransky, Richboro, Pennsylvania.*

HAWAIIAN SESAME CHICKEN

1 (2½- to 3-pound) broiler-fryer, cut up
1 tablespoon sesame seeds
2 tablespoons vegetable oil
¼ cup sugar
2 tablespoons cornstarch
⅛ teaspoon ground ginger
1 (15¼-ounce) can crushed pineapple, undrained
1 cup water
⅓ cup soy sauce
1 clove garlic, crushed

Brown chicken and sesame seeds in oil in a large skillet.

Combine sugar, cornstarch, and ginger in a medium saucepan; mix well. Add next 4 ingredients; cook over medium heat, stirring constantly, until thickened and bubbly.

Pour sauce over chicken; cover and simmer 45 minutes or until tender. Yield: 6 servings. *Cindy Murphy, Cleveland, Tennessee.*

FRIED GREEN ONIONS

¾ cup all-purpose flour
1 teaspoon baking powder
½ teaspoon salt
⅔ cup water
2 tablespoons sesame seeds
20 green onions, cut into 5-inch lengths
Vegetable oil

Combine flour, baking powder, and salt; stir well. Gradually add water to flour mixture, stirring until smooth. Stir in sesame seeds.

Dip onions in batter, and fry in deep oil heated to 375°. Fry until golden, turning once. Drain well on paper towels. Serve warm. Yield: 10 servings. *Ellen Hanna, England, Arkansas.*

SESAME WHEAT CRISPS

¾ cup unbleached all-purpose flour
½ cup wheat germ
¼ cup toasted sesame seeds
1 teaspoon baking powder
1 teaspoon sugar
½ teaspoon salt
⅓ cup butter or margarine
3 to 4 tablespoons cold water
Sesame seeds

Combine first 6 ingredients; stir well. Cut in butter with pastry blender until mixture resembles coarse meal. Sprinkle water evenly over surface; stir with a fork until all dry ingredients are moistened. Shape into a ball.

Roll dough to ⅛-inch thickness on a lightly floured surface. Cut dough into 3- x 1½-inch rectangles, and place on ungreased cookie sheets. Sprinkle lightly with additional sesame seeds. Bake at 375° for 12 to 14 minutes or until golden brown. Yield: about 2½ dozen. *James L. Strieber, San Antonio, Texas.*

Breads That Say Good Morning

You'll want to linger over that first cup of coffee when there's a freshly baked cinnamon roll or coffee cake to go with it. Raisin Cinnamon Rolls and Orange Marmalade Swirl Coffee Cake entice you with a heavenly aroma and taste that only come with home-baked bread. And be sure to try our Orange Muffins. Filled with dates and pecans, they have a sweet orange glaze drizzled over them.

EVER-READY BRAN MUFFINS

1 (15-ounce) package wheat bran flakes cereal with raisins
5 cups all-purpose flour
3 cups sugar
1 tablespoon plus 2 teaspoons soda
2 teaspoons salt
4 eggs, beaten
1 quart buttermilk
1 cup vegetable oil

Combine first 5 ingredients in a very large bowl; make a well in center of mixture. Add eggs, buttermilk, and oil; stir just enough to moisten dry ingredients. Cover and store in refrigerator until ready to bake. (Batter can be kept in refrigerator up to 6 weeks.)

To bake, spoon batter into greased muffin pans, filling two-thirds full. Bake at 400° for 12 to 15 minutes. Yield: about 5½ dozen. *Margaret M. Lewis, Bowling Green, Virginia.*

WHEAT GERM-PRUNE MUFFINS

1 egg
¾ cup milk
¼ cup vegetable oil
1 cup all-purpose flour
¾ cup regular wheat germ
¼ cup sugar
2 teaspoons baking powder
½ teaspoon salt
1 cup chopped prunes

Combine egg, milk, and oil in a medium bowl; beat with electric mixer on medium speed until well blended.

Combine dry ingredients; add to liquid mixture, and stir until moistened. Stir in prunes. Spoon into greased muffin pans, filling two-thirds full. Bake at 400° for 18 to 20 minutes or until done. Yield: about 9 muffins.

Charlene Stroud, Laurens, South Carolina.

ORANGE MUFFINS

½ cup chopped dates
½ cup chopped pecans
2 tablespoons all-purpose flour
1 cup shortening
1 cup sugar
2 eggs, beaten
2 cups all-purpose flour
1 teaspoon soda
¼ teaspoon salt
⅔ cup buttermilk
Orange glaze (recipe follows)

Combine dates, pecans, and 2 tablespoons flour; stir well and set aside.

Cream shortening; gradually add sugar, beating until light and fluffy. Add eggs, one at a time, beating well after each addition. Combine 2 cups flour, soda, and salt. Alternately add dry ingredients and buttermilk to creamed mixture, beginning and ending with dry ingredients. Stir in reserved date-and-pecan mixture (batter will be very thick).

Fill greased muffin pans one-half full. Bake at 375° for 15 to 20 minutes or until muffins test done.

Place cake racks on waxed paper. Remove muffins from pan; place on racks, and spoon orange glaze over hot muffins. Yield: about 2 dozen.

Orange Glaze:

½ cup sugar
Grated rind of ½ orange
About ⅓ cup orange juice

Combine all ingredients in a saucepan; cook over low heat, stirring until sugar dissolves. Yield: about ½ cup.

Gazelle Baxter,
Leoma, Tennessee.

RAISIN CINNAMON ROLLS

3½ cups all-purpose flour
1 package dry yeast
1¼ cups milk
¼ cup sugar
¼ cup shortening
1 teaspoon salt
1 egg, beaten
½ cup sugar
¼ cup butter or margarine, melted
2 teaspoons ground cinnamon
½ cup raisins
Glaze (recipe follows)

Combine 2 cups flour and yeast in a large bowl; stir well and set aside. Combine milk, ¼ cup sugar, shortening, and salt in a saucepan; cook over medium

heat until mixture reaches 120° to 130°. Add milk mixture to yeast mixture, mixing well. Add egg, and mix at low speed of electric mixer for 30 seconds; beat at high speed for 3 minutes, scraping sides of bowl.

Stir in remaining 1½ cups flour, and mix with a spoon. Place dough in a greased bowl, turning to grease top. Cover; let rise in a warm place (85°), free from drafts, until doubled in bulk (about 1½ to 2 hours).

Divide dough in half. Turn each half out on a lightly floured surface; roll each into a 16- x 8-inch rectangle. Combine ½ cup sugar, butter, and cinnamon; spread half of mixture over each rectangle, and top each with ¼ cup raisins. Roll jellyroll fashion, beginning with the long side. Moisten edge of long side and seal. Cut rolls into 1-inch slices, and place slices cut side down in 2 greased 9-inch square baking pans.

Cover; let rise in a warm place, free from drafts, until doubled in bulk (about 1 hour). Bake at 375° for 20 to 25 minutes. While rolls are warm, drizzle with glaze. Yield: 3 dozen.

Glaze:

1 cup sifted powdered sugar
1 to 2 tablespoons milk
½ teaspoon vanilla extract

Combine all ingredients, and beat until smooth. Yield: about ½ cup.

Debra Hawkins,
Oswego, South Carolina.

ORANGE MARMALADE SWIRL COFFEE CAKE

1 package dry yeast
¼ cup warm water (105° to 115°)
1 cup milk
1 teaspoon salt
¼ cup sugar
½ cup shortening or margarine
3¼ cups all-purpose flour
2 eggs, beaten
½ teaspoon vanilla extract
1 cup orange marmalade, divided

Dissolve yeast in water. Scald milk; add salt, sugar, and shortening, and cool to lukewarm (105° to 115°). Add 1 cup flour to milk mixture, and beat well. Add yeast mixture, eggs, and vanilla; beat well. Add remaining 2¼ cups flour to make a thick batter; beat until smooth. Cover, and let rise in a warm place (85°), free from drafts, until doubled in bulk (about 1 hour).

Stir batter and pour into two greased 9-inch round cakepans; let rise until doubled in bulk, about 1 hour. Make a swirl design on top of batter with a floured spoon; fill grooves using ½ cup marmalade for each coffee cake. Bake at 375° for 30 to 35 minutes. Yield: two 9-inch coffee cakes.

Mrs. L. M. Barker,
Elfrida, Arizona.

BUBBLE BREAD

1 cup milk, scalded
½ cup shortening
½ cup sugar
1 teaspoon salt
1 package dry yeast
2 eggs, beaten
About 3½ cups all-purpose flour
1 cup sugar
2 teaspoons ground cinnamon
1 cup raisins
1 cup finely chopped pecans or walnuts
½ cup margarine, melted

Combine milk, shortening, ½ cup sugar, and salt; cool to lukewarm (105° to 115°). Add yeast and stir to dissolve. Stir in eggs. Gradually add flour to make a soft dough; mix well. Knead for 10 minutes on a lightly floured surface. Place in a greased mixing bowl, turning to grease top. Let rise in a warm place (85°), free from drafts, until doubled in bulk (about 1½ hours).

Combine 1 cup sugar, cinnamon, raisins, and pecans; set aside.

Punch dough down, and roll with hands into 1½-inch balls; dip each in melted margarine, and roll in sugar mixture. Place balls in staggered rows and layers in a well-greased, one-piece, 10-inch tube pan. Sprinkle remaining sugar mixture between each ball while arranging. Pour remaining margarine over top. Let rise in a warm place until doubled, about 1 hour. Bake at 350° for 45 to 50 minutes. Invert on a serving platter. Yield: one 10-inch coffee cake.

Mrs. W. P. Chambers,
Louisville, Kentucky.

Tip: Sifting flour, with the exception of cake flour, is no longer necessary. Simply stir the flour, gently spoon it into a dry measure, and level the top. Powdered sugar, however, should usually be sifted to remove the lumps.

Vegetables Enjoy A Simple Preparation

Imagination and ease of preparation combine to make these impressive vegetable side dishes. For the most part, cooking time is kept to a minimum.

Fresh zucchini is baked in a bubbly casserole that's sparked with Parmesan cheese and mushrooms. A simple combination of carrots, celery, and onion is cooked in white wine.

MARINATED ASPARAGUS

1 (15-ounce) can asparagus spears, drained
¼ cup vegetable oil
1 tablespoon parsley flakes
3 tablespoons vinegar
2 tablespoons chopped pimiento
¾ teaspoon salt
¼ teaspoon pepper

Place asparagus in a small shallow dish. Combine remaining ingredients in a jar, and shake vigorously; pour over asparagus. Cover and chill at least 4 hours. Yield: about 4 servings.

Mrs. John A. Wyatt,
Palmyra, Tennessee.

SPECIAL CARROTS

1 pound carrots, thinly sliced
½ cup chopped celery
¼ cup chopped onion
¼ cup dry white wine
2 tablespoons sugar
2 tablespoons margarine
⅛ teaspoon dried dillweed

Combine all ingredients in a large saucepan. Cover and cook over medium heat 15 to 20 minutes or until tender. Yield: 6 servings.

Mrs. Philip H. Pedlow,
Richmond, Virginia.

MUSHROOMS AU GRATIN

3 tablespoons butter or margarine
1 pound fresh mushrooms, halved
⅓ cup chopped onion
Salt and pepper
1 (8-ounce) carton commercial sour cream
1 tablespoon all-purpose flour
Grated Parmesan cheese
Dry breadcrumbs

Melt butter in a large skillet; add mushrooms, onion, salt, and pepper. Cover and simmer over medium-low heat 7 to 10 minutes or until tender; drain.

Spoon mushrooms into a lightly greased shallow 1½-quart baking dish. Combine sour cream and flour; mix well, and spread over mushrooms. Sprinkle with cheese and breadcrumbs. Broil 3 to 5 minutes or until lightly browned. Yield: 4 servings.

Eunice H. Tinsley,
Huntington, West Virginia.

SKILLET TOMATOES

4 large firm tomatoes, halved
1 tablespoon butter or margarine, melted
1 teaspoon sugar
1 teaspoon salt
1 tablespoon chopped fresh parsley
1 clove garlic, crushed
1 tablespoon vinegar
2 tablespoons olive oil

Cook tomatoes in butter in a skillet, cut side down, about 5 minutes; turn. Combine remaining ingredients, stirring well; pour over tomatoes, and simmer an additional 5 minutes. Yield: 8 servings.

Lynn Rollins,
Chapel Hill, North Carolina.

ZUCCHINI PARMESAN

2½ pounds zucchini, thinly sliced
⅔ cup chopped onion
1 cup sliced fresh mushrooms
3 tablespoons vegetable oil
2 (6-ounce) cans tomato paste
1 teaspoon salt
½ teaspoon garlic salt
⅛ teaspoon pepper
⅔ cup grated Parmesan cheese, divided

Sauté zucchini, onion, and mushrooms in hot oil 5 to 6 minutes, stirring occasionally. Remove from heat; stir in tomato paste, salt, pepper, and ⅓ cup Parmesan cheese. Spoon into a 2-quart casserole dish; sprinkle with remaining cheese. Cover and bake at 350° for 30 minutes or until bubbly. Yield: 8 servings.

Mrs. R. P. Vinroot,
Matthews, North Carolina.

Wine Makes The Difference

There's nothing like the subtle flavor of wine for transforming even the most everyday dish into something quite special. Take Carrots in White Wine, for example; a little Chablis and seasonings make these cooked carrots like none you've ever tasted. That's just one example of how our readers cook with wine—there's more.

Generally speaking, white wine is used for poultry and seafood dishes. We illustrate that point deliciously with fillets of sole and two variations on chicken.

Red wine is usually reserved for dishes made with red meats and game. In our Beef Burgundy With Pearl Onions, the Burgundy goes into the sauce for simmering cubes of round steak.

If you'd like to do some experimenting on your own, just substitute wine for some of the liquid in your favorite recipes, using the general rule above. Since the alcohol in wine evaporates during cooking and only the flavor is left behind, you need not hesitate to use wine in dishes for family meals.

BEEF BURGUNDY WITH PEARL ONIONS

1 (1½-pound) top round steak (½ inch thick)
2 tablespoons butter or margarine
½ cup Burgundy or other dry red wine
1 cup tomato puree
½ cup hot water
2 tablespoons tomato paste
2 cloves garlic, minced
2 whole cloves
1 (2-inch) stick cinnamon
1 bay leaf
Salt and pepper to taste
1 (16-ounce) jar onions, drained
Hot cooked rice

Cut steak into 2-inch squares; brown in butter in a heavy Dutch oven. Add wine, and simmer 3 to 5 minutes.

Combine tomato puree, hot water, and tomato paste; mix well, and pour over steak. Stir in seasonings; cover and simmer over low heat 1½ hours. Add onions; cover and simmer an additional 30 minutes. Discard cinnamon stick and bay leaf. Serve beef and sauce over rice. Yield: 6 servings.

Mrs. Loren D. Martin,
Knoxville, Tennessee.

SOLE FILLETS IN WINE SAUCE

1½ cups water
½ pound shrimp
¼ cup plus 1 tablespoon butter or
    margarine
¼ pound fresh mushrooms, sliced
½ cup chopped green onions or scallions
3 tablespoons all-purpose flour
1 cup half-and-half
½ cup Chablis or other dry white wine
3 tablespoons capers
Dash of salt
Dash of pepper
Dash of paprika
½ teaspoon curry powder
4 large sole fillets

Bring water to a boil; add shrimp, and return to a boil. Lower heat, and simmer 3 to 5 minutes. Drain well, and rinse shrimp with cold water. Chill; then peel and devein.

Melt 2 tablespoons butter in a heavy skillet; add mushrooms and onion, and sauté until tender.

Melt remaining butter in a heavy saucepan over low heat; add flour, stirring until smooth. Cook 1 minute, stirring constantly. Gradually add half-and-half and wine; cook sauce over medium heat, stirring constantly, until thickened and bubbly. Stir in sautéed mushrooms and onion, capers, and the seasonings.

Cut four 12-inch square pieces of aluminum foil; place a sole fillet in center of each. Top each fillet with one-fourth of shrimp and sauce. Fold aluminum foil securely to seal. Place foil packages on a baking sheet, and bake at 425° for 40 minutes. Yield: 4 servings.
Mrs. Rodger Giles,
Augusta, Georgia.

CHICKEN AND MUSHROOMS IN WINE SAUCE

1 (2½- to 3-pound) broiler-fryer, cut up
Salt and pepper
¾ cup Chablis or other dry white wine
2 tablespoons vegetable oil
1 medium onion, finely chopped
1 clove garlic, minced
1 teaspoon all-purpose flour
⅛ teaspoon paprika
½ teaspoon dried whole basil
2 bay leaves
3 sprigs fresh parsley
1 small stalk celery, cut in half
2½ to 3 cups sliced fresh mushrooms
¼ cup half-and-half
1 egg yolk, beaten

Sprinkle chicken pieces with salt and pepper; place in a 13- x 9-x 2-inch

baking dish. Add wine; cover and refrigerate 2 to 3 hours. Remove chicken, reserving wine; pat chicken dry with paper towels. Brown chicken in hot oil in a large skillet over medium heat. Remove chicken pieces from the skillet, and set aside; reserve pan drippings.

Sauté onion and garlic in pan drippings about 2 minutes. Reduce heat to low; add flour, stirring well. Stir in reserved wine; cook until bubbly, stirring constantly.

Return chicken to skillet; stir in ½ teaspoon salt, ⅛ teaspoon pepper, paprika, basil, bay leaves, parsley, and celery. Cover and simmer over medium heat 30 to 35 minutes or until chicken is tender. Transfer chicken to serving platter, and keep warm. Discard bay leaves, parsley, and celery.

Add mushrooms to pan drippings; cook 3 to 4 minutes, stirring constantly. Combine half-and-half and egg yolk, beating well. Gradually add to mushrooms; cook, stirring constantly, until thickened and bubbly. Pour over chicken. Yield: 6 servings.
Lilly S. Bradley,
Salem, Virginia.

BAKED CHICKEN IN WINE

4 pounds chicken legs and thighs, skinned
1 teaspoon salt
½ to 1 teaspoon pepper
1 teaspoon paprika
½ cup all-purpose flour
Vegetable oil
2 medium onions, chopped
2 medium-size green peppers, chopped
½ cup sliced fresh mushrooms
2 (16-ounce) cans tomatoes, undrained
    and coarsely chopped
1 teaspoon ground thyme
2 teaspoons curry powder
½ cup Chablis or other dry white wine
Hot cooked rice or noodles

Sprinkle chicken with salt, pepper, and paprika; dredge in flour, and brown on all sides in hot oil. Drain chicken,

and place in a 13- x 9- x 2-inch baking dish; reserve pan drippings.

Add onion, green pepper, and mushrooms to pan drippings; sauté until tender. Stir in tomatoes, thyme, and curry powder; pour over chicken. Cover and bake at 350° for 30 minutes. Add wine, and bake an additional 20 minutes. Serve over rice or noodles. Yield: 10 to 12 servings. *Mrs. Leo Scherle,*
Louisville, Kentucky.

CARROTS IN WHITE WINE

¾ pound baby carrots
½ cup Chablis or other dry white wine
3 tablespoons butter or margarine
½ teaspoon salt
Dash of pepper
1½ teaspoons dried parsley flakes
1½ teaspoons dried mint flakes
1½ teaspoons dried whole thyme

Cook carrots in a small amount of boiling water 5 minutes; drain off liquid. Add wine to carrots, and bring to a boil. Boil about 10 minutes or until wine is almost absorbed. Add remaining ingredients, stirring until the butter is melted. Yield: about 4 servings.
Mrs. C. D. Marshall,
Culpeper, Virginia.

FRESH MUSHROOM SOUP

1 pound fresh mushrooms
¼ cup plus 2 tablespoons butter or
    margarine
2 cups minced onion
½ teaspoon sugar
¼ cup all-purpose flour
1 cup water
1¾ cups chicken broth
1 cup dry vermouth
½ teaspoon salt
¼ teaspoon pepper

Slice one-third of mushrooms, and finely chop the remainder. Melt butter; add onion and sugar, sautéing until onion is tender. Add mushrooms; cook 5 minutes, stirring often. Stir in flour; cook 2 minutes, stirring constantly.

Stir in water; then add all of the remaining ingredients.

Bring soup to a boil, and reduce heat; simmer, uncovered, 10 minutes. Yield: 8 cups. *Mrs. Steve Garvin,*
Wilkesboro, North Carolina.

Time For Cooking Out

The tantalizing aroma of meat sizzling over glowing coals is a sure sign that Southerners have once again taken to the outdoors for a favorite warm-weather pastime: cooking out. When you bring out your grill, take along some of these terrific new ways for enjoying that juicy steak, ham slice, chicken, roast, or those pork chops and hamburgers.

Marinating opens up a whole new dimension of flavors for grilled meats, besides making them juicier and more tender. For Barbecued Ham Slices, the marinade has an orange marmalade base; used also for basting, it glazes the ham with tangy sweetness.

Flank Steak Teriyaki gets its distinctive taste from an oil and vinegar marinade flavored with honey, soy sauce, garlic, and ginger. For pork chops, the combination is wine, oregano, garlic, and basil.

And look at the ingredients for Flavorful Grilled Hamburgers. Besides catsup, onion, and Worcestershire sauce in these juicy burgers, you'll also taste a hint of molasses, nutmeg, and cinnamon. Delicious!

SECRET SIRLOIN STEAK

¼ cup Worcestershire sauce
2 tablespoons instant minced onion
2 tablespoons lemon or lime juice
2 tablespoons olive oil
¾ teaspoon salt
½ teaspoon instant minced garlic
1 (3-pound) sirloin steak
2 tablespoons butter or margarine, melted
1 tablespoon chopped fresh parsley
1 teaspoon Worcestershire sauce

Combine first 6 ingredients, mixing well; pour into a large shallow dish, and add steak. Marinate in refrigerator 4 hours or overnight, turning occasionally.

Remove steak from marinade; place on grill 5 inches from hot coals; grill about 8 to 12 minutes on each side or to desired degree of doneness. Place the steak on a heated platter.

Combine butter, parsley, and 1 teaspoon Worcestershire sauce, and pour over steak. Yield: 6 to 8 servings.
Mrs. Jack Corzine,
St. Louis, Missouri.

FLANK STEAK TERIYAKI

1 (1¾- to 2-pound) flank steak
¾ cup vegetable oil
¼ cup soy sauce
¼ cup honey
2 tablespoons chopped onion
2 tablespoons cider vinegar
1 clove garlic, minced
1½ teaspoons ground ginger

Place steak in a shallow baking dish. Combine remaining ingredients, mixing well. Pour over steak; cover and marinate in the refrigerator 4 hours, turning steak occasionally.

Remove steak from marinade, reserving marinade for basting. Grill 5 inches from hot coals about 4 minutes on each side (for rare), turning frequently and basting with marinade.

To serve, slice across grain into thin slices. Yield: 4 to 6 servings.
Mrs. W. A. Reid, Jr.,
Tuscumbia, Alabama.

GRILLED PEPPER ROAST

1 (2½- to 3-pound) shoulder roast (about 2 inches thick)
2 teaspoons unseasoned meat tenderizer
1 cup red wine vinegar
½ cup vegetable oil or olive oil
2 tablespoons instant minced onion
3 tablespoons lemon juice
2 teaspoons dried whole thyme
1 teaspoon dried whole marjoram
1 bay leaf, crumbled
2 tablespoons whole peppercorns, coarsely crushed

Moisten roast with water; sprinkle both sides with meat tenderizer. Pierce surface of roast several times with a fork.

Combine next 7 ingredients, mixing well; pour into a large shallow dish, and add roast. Marinate in refrigerator for 2 to 3 hours, turning roast occasionally.

Remove roast from marinade, reserving marinade for basting. Pound 1 tablespoon pepper into each side of roast, and place 6 inches from hot coals; grill to desired degree of doneness (30 minutes for rare), turning frequently and basting with marinade. Yield: 6 to 8 servings.

Note: If desired, roast may be marinated overnight in refrigerator.
Joanne Wagoner,
Louisville, Kentucky.

FLAVORFUL GRILLED HAMBURGERS

¼ cup plus 2 tablespoons catsup
2 tablespoons molasses
1½ tablespoons Worcestershire sauce
1 small onion, cut into 8 wedges
1 clove garlic
2 bay leaves
1 teaspoon salt
½ teaspoon pepper
¼ teaspoon ground nutmeg
¼ teaspoon ground cinnamon
3 pounds ground chuck

Combine first 10 ingredients in container of electric blender, and process until smooth. Add to ground chuck, mixing well. Shape into 6 patties about ¾ inch thick.

Grill patties 3 to 5 inches from slow coals for 4 to 7 minutes on each side or until desired degree of doneness. Yield: 6 servings. *Will D. Sampson,*
Dallas, Texas.

BARBECUED HAM SLICES

½ cup orange marmalade
¼ cup prepared mustard
1 teaspoon Worcestershire sauce
¼ cup plus 2 tablespoons water
6 (6- to 8-ounce) slices fully cooked ham (about 1 inch thick)

Combine first 4 ingredients, and mix well; pour into a large baking dish. Add ham slices, turning to coat; marinate in refrigerator about 1 hour.

Remove ham from marinade, reserving marinade for basting. Place ham 4 to 5 inches from slow to medium coals; grill 30 to 45 minutes, turning frequently and basting with marinade. Yield: 6 servings. *Charlotte A. Pierce,*
Greensburg, Kentucky.

MARINATED GRILLED PORK CHOPS

¼ cup red wine vinegar
2 tablespoons Chablis or other dry white wine
1 tablespoon vegetable oil
1 teaspoon Worcestershire sauce
½ teaspoon dried whole oregano
½ teaspoon garlic salt
¼ teaspoon dried whole basil
4 (½-inch-thick) pork chops

Combine first 7 ingredients, mixing well; pour into a shallow baking dish, and add pork chops. Marinate in the refrigerator for about 2 hours, turning chops every 30 minutes.

Remove chops from marinade, reserving marinade for basting. Place chops 4 to 5 inches from slow to medium coals; grill 30 to 45 minutes or until done; turning frequently and basting with marinade. Yield: 4 servings.

Susan H. Martel,
San Antonio, Texas.

SCALLOP-BACON KABOBS

¼ cup vegetable oil
¼ cup lemon juice
¼ cup Chablis or other dry white wine
¼ cup soy sauce
2 tablespoons chopped fresh parsley
½ teaspoon salt
½ teaspoon pepper
¼ teaspoon garlic powder
1 pound fresh scallops or frozen scallops, thawed
1 small pineapple, cut into 1-inch pieces
18 to 24 fresh mushroom caps
3 large green peppers, cut into 1-inch squares
18 to 24 cherry tomatoes
12 slices bacon, cut in half

Combine first 8 ingredients in a large bowl, mixing well. Add scallops, pineapple, and vegetables; toss to coat, and marinate in refrigerator 1 to 1½ hours.

Cook the bacon until transparent (not crisp); drain. Alternate bacon, scallops, pineapple, and vegetables on skewers.

Place kabobs 4 to 5 inches from hot coals; grill 10 to 12 minutes or until bacon is crisp, turning kabobs frequently and basting them with marinade. Yield: 6 servings.

Mildred Sherrer,
Bay City, Texas.

GRILLED YOGURT-LEMON CHICKEN

1 (8-ounce) carton plain yogurt
¼ cup red wine vinegar
1 tablespoon lemon juice
1 clove garlic, minced
1 teaspoon ground coriander
1 teaspoon dry mustard
½ teaspoon ground ginger
½ teaspoon pepper
⅛ teaspoon ground cloves
5 drops hot sauce
1 (3-pound) broiler-fryer, cut up

Combine first 10 ingredients, mixing well; pour into a large shallow baking dish. Add chicken, turning to coat; cover and marinate in refrigerator 1½ hours.

Remove chicken from marinade, reserving marinade for basting. Grill about 6 inches from medium-hot coals 1 hour or until done, turning frequently and basting with marinade. Yield: about 4 to 6 servings.

Joan McCormick,
Tabb, Virginia.

Pork: A Year-Round Favorite

Pork is a year-round favorite—whether it be in the form of chops, roasts, ribs, or ground meat. Everyone has favorite ways to prepare this versatile meat, and this group of recipes includes some of the most popular: ribs baked in a tangy barbecue sauce, sweet-and-sour pork, a boneless roast filled with a savory breadcrumb stuffing.

A word about preparation: To preserve its delicate flavor and juiciness, cook pork until well done but avoid overcooking. For best results, use a meat thermometer to ensure that the larger cuts of meat are thoroughly cooked. The meat is done when the thermometer registers 170°.

BARBECUED PORK SHOULDER

1 (3½- to 4-pound) pork shoulder roast
1 cup catsup
½ cup firmly packed brown sugar
2 teaspoons salt
1 teaspoon pepper
1 to 2 tablespoons chili powder
¼ cup plus 2 tablespoons vinegar
2 tablespoons lemon juice
¼ cup Worcestershire sauce
2 teaspoons prepared mustard
Hamburger buns (optional)

Cover roast with lightly salted water in a large Dutch oven. Cover and cook over medium heat 2 to 2½ hours or until tender. Drain, and slice thinly; place in a shallow 2-quart baking dish.

Combine next 9 ingredients, stirring well. Spoon sauce over sliced roast, turning slices to coat. Bake at 300° for 45 minutes. Serve on buns, if desired. Yield: 6 servings.

Brentz Moore,
Kenton, Tennessee.

STUFFED PORK ROAST

1 (4- to 5-pound) boneless pork shoulder roast or pork loin roast
Salt, pepper, and poultry seasoning to taste
4 cups soft breadcrumbs
1 cup chopped celery
¾ cup chopped onion
1 teaspoon ground sage
1 teaspoon salt
¼ teaspoon pepper
½ cup butter or margarine, melted

Cut a wide, deep pocket in roast. Season roast on all sides with salt, pepper, and poultry seasoning. Combine remaining ingredients, and stuff into pocket. Secure roast with metal skewers. Bake at 325° about 35 to 40 minutes per pound or until thermometer registers 170°. Yield: 8 to 10 servings.

Mrs. Leslie McIver,
Holly Springs, North Carolina.

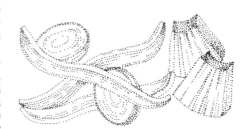

SWEET-AND-SOUR PORK

1 (20-ounce) can pineapple chunks
1½ pounds boneless pork shoulder, cut into 2-inch strips
3 tablespoons vegetable oil
½ cup water
¼ cup firmly packed light brown sugar
2 tablespoons cornstarch
½ teaspoon salt
¼ cup cider vinegar
2 tablespoons soy sauce
1 small green pepper, cut into strips
1 small onion, thinly sliced
Hot cooked rice

Drain pineapple, reserving juice; set both aside.

Brown pork in oil in a large skillet; stir in water. Cover and simmer 1 hour or until tender. Combine sugar, cornstarch, and salt in a medium bowl; stir in reserved pineapple juice, vinegar, and soy sauce. Add to pork and cook, stirring constantly, until smooth and thickened. Add pineapple, green pepper, and onion; toss lightly, and cook 2 to 3 minutes. Serve over rice. Yield: 4 to 6 servings.

Dorothy L. Anderson,
Manor, Texas.

BARBECUED SPARERIBS

3 pounds spareribs
½ cup chopped onion
1 clove garlic, minced
¼ cup butter or margarine, melted
2 (8-ounce) cans tomato sauce
⅓ cup water
¼ cup Worcestershire sauce
2 tablespoons lemon juice
2 tablespoons vinegar
2 teaspoons chili powder
2 teaspoons salt
4 drops of hot sauce

Place spareribs in shallow baking pan. Bake, uncovered, at 325° for 1½ hours. Drain off pan drippings.

Sauté onion and garlic in butter in a medium saucepan. Add remaining ingredients; bring to a boil. Pour over ribs, and bake 45 to 60 minutes or until tender, basting occasionally. Yield: 6 servings.
*Karol Stephenson,
Washington, Georgia.*

PORK CHOPS JARDINIERE

4 (½-inch-thick) pork chops
1 tablespoon vegetable oil
2 chicken bouillon cubes
1½ cups boiling water
1 to 1¼ teaspoons salt
½ teaspoon sugar
½ teaspoon pepper
2 medium stalks celery, chopped
1 medium carrot, chopped
1 tablespoon all-purpose flour
Mashed potatoes (optional)

Brown pork chops on both sides in hot oil in a large skillet; drain off pan drippings.

Dissolve chicken bouillon cubes in boiling water. Stir in next 6 ingredients; pour over pork chops. Bring to a boil; cover and simmer 1 hour or until tender. Serve over mashed potatoes, if desired. Yield: 4 servings.
*Alda Reynolds,
Lincolnton, North Carolina.*

SAUSAGE CASSEROLE

1 large onion, finely chopped
1 pound bulk pork sausage
1 (4-ounce) package (2 envelopes) chicken noodle soup mix
½ cup uncooked regular rice
4½ cups water
1 (4-ounce) package slivered almonds (optional)

Brown onion and sausage in a large skillet, stirring to crumble sausage; drain. Add soup mix, rice, water, and almonds, if desired; mix well, and simmer 7 minutes. Spoon into a greased 2½-quart casserole; bake at 400° for 30 minutes. Yield: 5 to 6 servings.
*Joan Prescott,
Savannah, Georgia.*

HAM BALLS WITH SPICED
CHERRY SAUCE

2 cups ground cooked ham
⅓ cup dry breadcrumbs
¼ cup milk
1 egg, beaten
⅛ teaspoon pepper
¼ cup vegetable oil
¼ cup hot water
1 cup cherry preserves
2½ tablespoons lemon juice
¾ teaspoon ground cinnamon
¼ teaspoon ground cloves

Combine first 5 ingredients, mixing well. Shape into 1½-inch balls. Heat vegetable oil in a skillet over medium heat; add ham balls, and cook until browned on all sides.

Pour off drippings, and add ¼ cup hot water to skillet. Cover and simmer 15 to 20 minutes.

Combine cherry preserves, lemon juice, cinnamon, and cloves in a small saucepan. Place over low heat, and cook until mixture comes to a low boil, stirring occasionally.

Place ham balls in a chafing dish or on a warm platter, and cover with sauce. Yield: 4 to 6 servings.
*Mrs. A. Stancill,
Bel Air, Maryland.*

Soup And Salad,
Texas Style

With a warm Texas spring promising a hot summer, it's time to think about lighter menus—soup-and-salad meals, to be specific. The recipes included here are distinctively Southwestern, all originating in Texas kitchens.

Spring Gazpacho and Monterey Jack Cheese Soup are superb examples of how two Texans prepare soup. One is cold and crispy with vegetables, while the other is spicy with green chiles and served piping hot. For appetites that demand more than just soup, we suggest adding a salad, and offer two choices.

MONTEREY JACK CHEESE SOUP

1½ tablespoons butter or margarine
1½ tablespoons all-purpose flour
3 cups milk, divided
½ cup finely chopped onion
½ cup peeled, diced tomato
2 canned green chiles, seeded and chopped
1 small clove garlic, minced
1 cup chicken broth
1½ cups (6 ounces) shredded Monterey Jack cheese
½ teaspoon salt
Dash of pepper

Melt butter in a heavy saucepan over low heat; add flour, stirring until smooth. Cook 1 minute, stirring constantly. Gradually add 1½ cups milk; cook over medium heat, stirring constantly, until thickened and bubbly. Set aside.

Combine onion, tomato, chiles, garlic, and chicken broth; cook over medium heat about 3 minutes or until vegetables are tender. Remove from heat, and gradually stir in white sauce; return to low heat. Add 1½ cups milk and remaining ingredients; cook, stirring constantly, until cheese is melted. Serve immediately. Yield: about 6 cups.
*Carol Barclay,
Portland, Texas.*

SPRING GAZPACHO

4 large tomatoes, peeled and chopped
1 medium-size green pepper, chopped
1 large cucumber, peeled and chopped
1 small onion, chopped
3 small green onions, thinly sliced
2 cloves garlic, crushed
1 cup cocktail vegetable juice or tomato juice
2 cups water
3 tablespoons vinegar
¼ cup olive oil
1½ teaspoons salt
Freshly ground pepper to taste

Combine all ingredients in a large bowl, stirring well. Chill several hours before serving. Yield: about 7½ cups.
*Mrs. Don H. Eldridge,
Houston, Texas.*

MEXICAN SALAD

½ cup mayonnaise
¼ cup chopped green onion
2 tablespoons chili sauce
2 teaspoons cider vinegar
1 teaspoon onion salt
½ teaspoon chili powder
4 drops of hot sauce
1 (12-ounce) can whole kernel corn, drained
1 (8½-ounce) can red kidney beans, drained
1 (6-ounce) can pitted ripe olives, drained and halved
4 cups shredded lettuce

Combine first 7 ingredients, stirring well; chill thoroughly. Combine remaining ingredients, tossing gently. Serve with dressing. Yield: 6 to 8 servings.
Dee Little,
Kilgore, Texas.

SOUTHWEST SALAD

½ cup vegetable oil
¼ cup tarragon vinegar
1 clove garlic, minced
1 teaspoon sugar
½ teaspoon salt
½ teaspoon onion powder
½ teaspoon dry mustard
½ teaspoon paprika
¼ teaspoon celery salt
3 drops of hot sauce
6 cups torn mixed salad greens
1 cup drained garbanzo beans
1 dozen cherry tomatoes, halved
⅓ cup pitted ripe olives, sliced
1 large green onion, chopped
1 avocado, peeled and coarsely chopped

Combine first 10 ingredients in a jar; cover tightly, and shake vigorously. Chill several hours. Combine remaining ingredients in a large salad bowl. Shake dressing well, and pour over salad; toss gently. Yield: 6 to 8 servings.
Mrs. Richard F. Ledyard,
Beaumont, Texas.

Make These Cinnamon Rolls Flat

Cinnamon Crisps are often referred to in bakeries as elephant ears because of their large, flat shape. They're crisp, yet chewy—perfect for breakfast on the run and great for snacks.

They're made with a yeast dough and flattened to ⅛-inch thickness. Brushing them with melted butter and sprinkling on cinnamon, sugar, and nuts before baking makes them nice and crisp.

CINNAMON CRISPS

1¼ cups milk, scalded
¼ cup sugar
¼ cup shortening
1 teaspoon salt
About 3½ cups all-purpose flour
1 package dry yeast
1 egg
¼ cup butter or margarine, melted
½ cup sugar
½ cup firmly packed brown sugar
½ teaspoon ground cinnamon
1 cup sugar
1 teaspoon ground cinnamon
½ cup finely chopped pecans
¼ cup butter or margarine, melted

Combine milk, ¼ cup sugar, shortening, and salt; stir until shortening melts. Cool to 105° to 115°.

Combine 2 cups flour and yeast. Add milk mixture and egg to dry ingredients, mixing at low speed of electric mixer. Beat 30 seconds on low speed. Scrape bowl, and beat 3 minutes at high speed. Stir in enough remaining flour to make a soft dough (1 to 1½ cups).

Place dough in a greased bowl, turning to grease top. Cover and let rise in a warm place (85°), free from drafts, 1½ to 2 hours or until doubled in bulk.

Combine ¼ cup butter, ½ cup sugar, brown sugar, and ½ teaspoon ground cinnamon; divide in half. Set aside.

Punch dough down, and divide in half. Turn dough onto a heavily floured surface (dough will be very soft). Roll out each dough ball to a 12-inch square. Spread half the sugar mixture on each square. Roll up each square in jellyroll fashion; seal edges. Cut each roll into 1-inch slices. Place slices on a greased cookie sheet 4 to 5 inches apart. Flatten each roll to 3 inches in diameter. Cover and let rise in a warm place (85°), free from drafts, 30 minutes.

Combine 1 cup sugar, 1 teaspoon cinnamon, and pecans. Set aside.

Cover rolls with waxed paper; roll out to ⅛-inch thickness with a rolling pin.

Brush with ¼ cup butter. Sprinkle each roll with about 1 tablespoon sugar mixture; cover with waxed paper. Gently roll again with rolling pin. Bake at 400° for 10 to 12 minutes or until golden brown. Immediately remove to cooling rack. Yield: 2 dozen. *Mrs. Terry Tolle,*
Waynesville, North Carolina.

Serve These Sandwiches Hot

If you're tired of your usual repertoire of cold sandwiches, try these new sandwich ideas—they're both served toasty hot from the oven.

Hot dog buns are filled with a spicy mixture of frankfurters, Cheddar cheese, hard-cooked egg, and pickles, then baked until hot.

And our Crispy Chicken Sandwich is filled with a creamy chicken filling, given a crunchy coating, then baked until golden.

HOT DOG JUBILEE

6 frankfurters, finely chopped
½ cup (2 ounces) shredded Cheddar cheese
2 hard-cooked eggs, chopped
2 tablespoons chopped sweet pickle
3 tablespoons catsup
1 teaspoon prepared mustard
2 tablespoons vegetable oil
¼ teaspoon salt
6 hot dog buns, split

Combine frankfurters, cheese, eggs, and pickle, stirring well. Combine catsup, mustard, oil, and salt; mix well and pour dressing over frankfurter mixture. Toss lightly to mix.

Spoon mixture into hot dog buns; wrap each in aluminum foil, and bake at 350° for 25 minutes or until heated through. Yield: 6 sandwiches.
Mrs. Bruce Fowler,
Woodruff, South Carolina.

Tip: For a delicious way to use leftover hot dog buns, cut horizontally into thin slices, butter, sprinkle with Parmesan cheese or garlic powder, and toast until golden brown.

CRISPY CHICKEN SANDWICH

1½ cups chopped cooked chicken
1 (10¾-ounce) can cream of mushroom
  soup, undiluted
1 (10¾-ounce) can cream of chicken soup,
  undiluted
2 tablespoons chopped pimiento
2 tablespoons chopped onion
1 (8-ounce) can water chestnuts, drained
  and thinly sliced
20 slices of bread, crusts removed
4 eggs, slightly beaten
2 tablespoons milk
1 (6-ounce) bag potato chips, crushed

Combine chicken, soup, pimiento, onion, and water chestnuts, mixing well. Spread evenly on 10 slices of bread; top with remaining slices. Wrap sandwiches individually in freezer wrap and freeze.

When ready to use sandwiches, combine eggs and milk; mix well. Dip each frozen sandwich into egg mixture, and coat on all sides with crushed potato chips. Place on a lightly greased baking sheet, and bake at 300° for 1 hour. Yield: 10 sandwiches. *Jane Crum, Morrilton, Arkansas.*

Salads In Savory Combinations

When you want to lend variety to the meal, the salad is the place to start.

Springtime Spinach Salad combines crisp lettuce and dark green spinach with ripe olives and fresh mushrooms. A tangy dressing made with garlic and chives is the finishing touch.

Fresh fruit and yogurt make a popular salad, and our Yogurt Fruit Salad makes this choice even better with the addition of honey, chopped pecans, and a touch of lemon juice.

And for a salad to serve as the main dish, we suggest Crab-Avocado Salad or Salmon-and-Macaroni Salad.

YOGURT FRUIT SALAD

2 tablespoons honey
1 tablespoon lemon juice
3 oranges, peeled and sectioned
1 medium apple, unpeeled and diced
2 bananas, sliced
1 cup chopped pecans
1 (8-ounce) carton plain yogurt

Combine honey and lemon juice in a large bowl; stir well. Add fruit and pecans, tossing gently to coat. Chill thoroughly. Fold in yogurt just before serving; toss gently. Yield: 6 servings.
Mrs. David Culp, Abilene, Texas.

SALMON-AND-MACARONI SALAD

1 (8-ounce) package elbow macaroni
1 (15½-ounce) can red salmon, drained
  and flaked
1 medium onion, finely chopped
1 cucumber, sliced
¼ cup chopped fresh parsley
¼ cup plus 2 tablespoons vegetable oil
2 tablespoons vinegar
2 teaspoons salt
½ teaspoon dry mustard
¼ teaspoon pepper
Salad greens

Cook macaroni according to package directions; drain. Rinse with cold water, and drain.

Combine macaroni with next 4 ingredients. Combine remaining ingredients except salad greens, and stir well. Pour dressing over salmon mixture, stirring lightly; cover and chill.

To serve, spoon mixture into a bowl lined with salad greens. Yield: 6 to 8 servings. *Edna Chadsey, Corpus Christi, Texas.*

OLIVE CLUBHOUSE SALAD

1 cup uncooked elbow macaroni
1 cup ripe olives, sliced
½ cup chopped celery
⅓ cup chopped green onion
3 tablespoons diced pimiento
2 tablespoons chopped dill pickle
2 tablespoons chopped sweet pickle
1 tablespoon chopped fresh parsley
½ cup mayonnaise
1 tablespoon vinegar
¼ teaspoon salt
Dash of pepper
Lettuce leaves

Cook macaroni according to package directions; drain. Rinse with cold water, and drain.

Combine macaroni with next 7 ingredients; set aside. Combine mayonnaise, vinegar, salt, and pepper; stir well. Add to macaroni mixture, stirring lightly. Chill 2 to 3 hours.

Spoon salad into a bowl lined with lettuce leaves. Yield: 6 servings.
Mrs. J. W. Hopkins, Abilene, Texas.

CRAB-AVOCADO SALAD

1½ cups flaked fresh crabmeat
1 (10-ounce) package frozen English peas,
  thawed
1 (8-ounce) carton commercial sour cream
4 green onions, finely chopped
6 slices bacon, cooked and crumbled
½ teaspoon salt
¼ teaspoon pepper
2 avocados, sliced

Combine all ingredients except avocado; gently toss. Chill thoroughly. Serve salad on avocado slices. Yield: 8 servings. *Marge Killmon, Annandale, Virginia.*

SPRINGTIME SPINACH SALAD

½ cup vegetable oil
¼ cup wine vinegar
1½ teaspoons lemon juice
¼ teaspoon salt
Dash of hot sauce
1 clove garlic, minced
1 tablespoon chopped chives or green
  onion tops
6 cups torn lettuce
2 cups torn spinach
6 large fresh mushrooms, sliced
½ cup sliced ripe olives

Combine first 7 ingredients in a jar; cover tightly, and shake well. Chill several hours.

Combine remaining ingredients in a salad bowl; add dressing, and toss gently. Yield: about 8 servings.
Mrs. John R. Taylor, Jr., Jonesboro, Tennessee.

Right: *Two of the best things that can happen to a summer day are Honeydew Fruit Boats (page 147) and Minted Melon Cocktail (page 146).*

Page 118: *Try shrimp and vegetable tempura served over rice and accompanied by Basic Tempura Sauce and Mustard-Sour Cream Sauce (recipes on page 68).*

Above: *Along with the harvest of fresh corn comes some of summer's finest dishes.*
Clockwise: Corn Relish (page 129), Creole Corn (page 128), and Foil-Baked Corn on the
Cob (page 128).

Left: *Kabobs of Skewered Steak With Vegetables (page 124) make firing up the grill well*
worth the effort.

Everything's Coming Up Parties

Teas, showers, and receptions seem to become the rule in spring rather than the exception. For these, a rather distinctive type of party food is called for—a light, refreshing punch, pretty finger sandwiches, dainty mints, and tiny cakes. Our readers have some delectable and appropriate suggestions.

Try using a food processor to prepare the cucumber sandwiches. Using both white and wheat bread and cutting the sandwiches into decorative shapes make them especially attractive.

When preparing sandwiches in advance, keep them from drying out by placing them in a shallow container lined with a damp towel and waxed paper. Separate the layers with waxed paper, and cover with another layer of waxed paper and a damp towel; store in the refrigerator.

DAINTY CUCUMBER SANDWICHES

1 small onion, peeled and cut into chunks
1 cucumber, peeled and cut into chunks
1 (8-ounce) package cream cheese, softened
¼ teaspoon salt
Dash of garlic powder
Dash of red pepper
3 drops green food coloring (optional)
1 (16-ounce) loaf thin-sliced white bread
1 (16-ounce) loaf thin-sliced wheat bread

Position knife blade in food processor bowl; add onion and cucumber. Process 3 to 5 seconds. Stop processor, and scrape sides of bowl with a rubber spatula. Process 3 to 5 additional seconds or until vegetables are finely chopped. Remove vegetables, and drain well.

Position plastic blade in bowl. Cut cream cheese into about 1-inch pieces; place in processor bowl. Process 8 to 10 seconds or until smooth.

With processor running, add vegetables and seasonings through food chute; process 20 to 25 seconds or until well combined. Add food coloring, if desired; process about 5 seconds. Scrape sides of bowl; process 5 seconds or until mixture is well combined.

Remove crust from bread, and cut into assorted shapes. Spread filling on half the pieces; top with remaining pieces. Yield: about 8 dozen.

Carolyn Langley,
Lake Charles, Louisiana.

PECAN-CHEESE WAFERS

2 cups (8 ounces) shredded sharp Cheddar cheese
1 cup butter or margarine, softened
2 cups all-purpose flour
½ teaspoon salt
Dash of pepper
2 cups crisp rice cereal
Pecan halves

Combine cheese and butter; mix well. Combine flour, salt, and pepper; add to creamed mixture, mixing well. Stir in cereal. Chill 2 hours.

Shape dough into 1-inch balls; place on ungreased cookie sheets, and flatten to ⅓-inch thickness. Top each with a pecan half. Bake at 350° for 8 minutes. Yield: about 6½ dozen.

Mrs. Ray Sizemore,
Keysville, Virginia.

CHOCOLATE-PEPPERMINT SQUARES

½ cup butter, softened
1 cup sugar
2 eggs
½ cup all-purpose flour
Pinch of salt
2 (1-ounce) squares unsweetened chocolate, melted
½ cup chopped pecans or walnuts
Peppermint Filling
Chocolate Glaze

Cream butter; gradually add sugar, beating until mixture is light and fluffy. Add eggs, one at a time, beating well after each addition.

Combine flour and salt; add to the creamed mixture, and beat well. Add chocolate, beating until thoroughly blended; stir in pecans.

Pour batter into a greased 9-inch square pan. Bake at 350° for 20 minutes. Cool cake thoroughly (layer will fall while cooling).

Spread Peppermint Filling over cake layer, and chill thoroughly (filling will be very thin).

Spread or drizzle Chocolate Glaze over filling; chill thoroughly. Cut into 1-inch squares. Store in refrigerator. Yield: about 5 dozen.

Peppermint Filling:

1 cup sifted powdered sugar
2 tablespoons butter, softened
1 tablespoon milk
½ to ¾ teaspoon peppermint extract

Combine all ingredients, beating until smooth. Yield: about ½ cup.

Chocolate Glaze:

2 (1-ounce) squares semisweet chocolate, melted
1 tablespoon butter, melted

Combine ingredients; stir well. Yield: about ¼ cup. *Vivian Conner,*
Dale, Indiana.

PARTY MINTS

½ cup unsalted butter, softened
1 (1-pound) package powdered sugar, sifted
3 tablespoons warm water
2 to 3 drops oil of peppermint
Paste food coloring

Cream butter; gradually add sugar, beating well. Stir in water and oil of peppermint. Using a very small amount of paste food coloring, tint the mint mixture as desired.

Drop coupler into decorating bag, and push it as far down into bag as possible. Insert a No. 195 star metal tip over tip of coupler, and screw coupler ring over metal tip.

Spoon mint mixture into decorating bag; fold corners of bag over, creasing it until all air is pressed out. (A decorating bag for each color of mint is helpful but not necessary.)

To make mints, hold tube perpendicular to surface and squeeze out a star onto waxed paper; stop pressure, and lift off tube. Let mints dry at room temperature 36 to 48 hours.

Note: If a firmer, drier mint is desired, transfer mints to paper toweling after 36 hours; then let dry an additional 12 hours. Yield: about 10 dozen.

Carolyn Epting,
Leesville, South Carolina.

SPECIAL PARTY PUNCH

7 cups pineapple juice, chilled
1½ pints vanilla ice cream
1 pint orange sherbet
3 cups ginger ale, chilled

Pour pineapple juice into punch bowl; add the ice cream and sherbet by small scoopfuls. Add ginger ale, and stir slightly. Serve punch immediately. Yield: about 3½ quarts.

Darlene Dakin,
Drakesboro, Kentucky.

Enjoy The Richness Of Buttermilk

As far as Southern cooks are concerned, buttermilk is a staple. Here it adds rich flavor to a variety of baked products—from griddle cakes to rolls.

BUTTERMILK GRIDDLE CAKES

2 cups all-purpose flour
3 tablespoons sugar
2 teaspoons baking powder
1 teaspoon salt
½ teaspoon soda
1 egg
1½ cups buttermilk
3 tablespoons shortening, melted
Maple syrup (recipe follows)

Combine dry ingredients. Combine egg and buttermilk; slowly stir into dry ingredients. Add shortening, mixing lightly.

Drop mixture by heaping tablespoonfuls onto a hot, lightly greased griddle. Turn pancakes when the tops are bubbly and edges are brown. Serve hot with maple syrup. Yield: 4 to 6 servings.

Maple Syrup:

2 cups water
4 cups sugar
2 teaspoons imitation maple flavoring

Heat water to boiling in a medium saucepan; add sugar and reduce heat. Stir until sugar is dissolved (do not let mixture boil). Remove from heat, and add maple flavoring. Serve warm. Store in refrigerator. Yield: 4 cups.
Ansel L. Todd,
Royston, Georgia.

BUTTERMILK REFRIGERATOR ROLLS

1 package dry yeast
½ cup warm water (105° to 115°)
½ cup shortening, melted
4½ cups all-purpose flour
¼ cup sugar
1 tablespoon plus 1 teaspoon baking powder
1 teaspoon salt
½ teaspoon soda
2 cups buttermilk

Dissolve yeast in warm water in a large mixing bowl; let stand 5 minutes. Stir in melted shortening.

Combine dry ingredients in a small bowl. Add dry ingredients and buttermilk to yeast mixture; mix well. Turn dough out on a well-floured surface; knead gently until dough can be handled. Shape dough into a ball; place in a greased bowl, turning once to grease top. Cover the dough, and refrigerate until needed (dough will keep 1 week).

Shape dough into rolls, as desired; place on lightly greased baking sheets. Bake at 400° for 8 to 10 minutes or until lightly browned. Yield: about 2 dozen.
Mrs. Larry Doskocil,
Lott, Texas.

BUTTERMILK-LEMON PIE

3 eggs
1½ cups sugar
½ cup buttermilk
3 tablespoons butter or margarine, melted
1 tablespoon all-purpose flour
2 tablespoons lemon juice
1 teaspoon lemon extract
1 unbaked 9-inch pastry shell

Beat eggs; add next 6 ingredients, and mix well. Pour into pastry shell.

Bake at 425° for 10 minutes; place foil over edges of crust, and bake 5 to 10 minutes longer or until set. Let cool on a wire rack. Yield: one 9-inch pie.
Mrs. Raymond Simpson,
Cleveland, Tennessee.

WILLIAMSBURG ORANGE CAKE

2½ cups all-purpose flour
1½ cups sugar
1½ teaspoons soda
¼ teaspoon salt
1½ cups buttermilk
½ cup butter or margarine, softened
¼ cup shortening
3 eggs
1½ teaspoons vanilla extract
1 tablespoon grated orange rind
1 cup golden raisins, chopped
½ cup finely chopped pecans
Williamsburg Butter Frosting

Combine first 10 ingredients in a large mixing bowl; beat with an electric mixer for 30 seconds on low speed. Beat 3 minutes on high speed. Stir in chopped raisins and pecans.

Pour batter into a greased and floured 13- x 9- x 2-inch baking pan. Bake at 350° for 45 to 55 minutes; cool.

Frost with Williamsburg Butter Frosting. Yield: one 13- x 9- x 2-inch cake.

Williamsburg Butter Frosting:

⅓ cup butter or margarine, softened
3 cups sifted powdered sugar
1 tablespoon grated orange rind
3 to 4 tablespoons orange juice or orange-flavored liqueur

Cream butter and sugar until fluffy. Add orange rind and juice; beat until smooth. Yield: frosting for one 13- x 9- x 2-inch cake.
Margie L. Warthan,
Avery, Texas.

Microwave Cookery

Microwave The Meat Loaf

Thanks to the microwave oven, meat loaf that used to take 1 to 1½ hours to bake now becomes a quickly prepared entrée—ready in just 7 to 18 minutes.

The actual time required for microwaving meat loaf varies with the amount of moisture in the meat, as well as the wattage of the microwave oven. Meat with a high moisture content will require more microwaving time than meat with a low moisture content. Also, a microwave oven with a lower wattage requires more time to complete cooking than one of higher wattage. Our recipes give a time range to allow for these factors.

To prevent overcooking, always check for doneness at the lower end of the range. Meat loaf is done when it is fairly firm to the touch. Since it will continue to cook after the microwaving cycle is complete, let it stand for 5 minutes before serving. Here are some other pointers.

Shaping the Loaf

Meat loaves can be shaped in a variety of ways for microwaving. A ring-shaped loaf cooks the quickest because the microwaves can enter from the inside of the ring, as well as from the outside. Round loaves are a good choice for microwave cooking because there are no corners that may overcook.

The traditional loaf shapes work well in most ovens. However, overcooking on the corners can occur in some ovens. Reducing the power from HIGH to MEDIUM usually eliminates the problem. Keep in mind that a meat loaf microwaved at MEDIUM will require about twice as much time to cook as one microwaved at HIGH.

Since the shape of the loaf affects cooking time, refer to the chart to help you determine how much time to allow for various shapes (times are based on loaves made with 1½ pounds of meat).

Shape	Minutes at HIGH
Ring	7 to 12
Round	14 to 18
Loaf	14 to 18
Individual	9 to 13

Individual Pineapple Loaves cook in just 9 to 13 minutes. Then they're topped with crushed pineapple and microwaved to heat the topping.

Use a custard cup to keep a ring-shaped loaf in shape during cooking.

Converting Conventional Recipes

Almost any meat loaf recipe can be converted to microwave cooking. Just compare it to a similar microwave recipe for amount of meat and other ingredients, cooking time, and power setting.

Because there is less evaporation in microwave cooking, the liquid called for in conventional recipes should be reduced. During our testing, we achieved best results by decreasing the liquid and adding an extra egg so the total liquid is about half (the extra egg should be counted as a liquid ingredient). For example, if a conventional recipe calls for 1 cup milk and one egg, decrease the milk to ¼ cup and use two eggs. The extra egg plus the ¼ cup milk equals about ½ cup or half the liquid called for in the conventional recipe.

SWEDISH MEAT LOAF

¾ pound ground beef
¾ pound ground pork
1 cup soft breadcrumbs
¼ cup finely chopped onion
2 eggs, beaten
1¾ cups half-and-half, divided
½ teaspoon salt
¼ teaspoon pepper
¼ teaspoon ground allspice
3 tablespoons butter or margarine
3 tablespoons all-purpose flour
½ teaspoon salt
¼ teaspoon pepper

Combine meat, breadcrumbs, onion, eggs, ¼ cup half-and-half, ½ teaspoon salt, ¼ teaspoon pepper, and allspice; mix well. Shape into a 6-inch round loaf in a 12- x 8- x 2-inch baking dish. Cover with waxed paper. Microwave at HIGH for 14 to 18 minutes or until firm to the touch, giving dish a half-turn after 7 minutes. Drain off excess drippings. Cover meat loaf with aluminum foil to keep warm.

Place butter in a 4-cup glass measure; microwave at HIGH for 45 seconds to 1 minute or until melted. Blend in flour, ½ teaspoon salt, and ¼ teaspoon pepper; gradually add remaining half-and-half. Microwave at HIGH for 1½ minutes; stir well. Microwave at HIGH for 2½ to 3½ minutes or until sauce is thickened and bubbly, stirring at 1-minute intervals.

Transfer meat loaf to serving platter. Serve with sauce. Yield: 6 servings.

CHEESY PIZZA MEAT LOAF

1 pound ground beef
½ pound hot bulk pork sausage
1½ cups soft breadcrumbs
2 eggs, beaten
1 (8-ounce) can tomato sauce
3 tablespoons finely chopped onion
3 tablespoons finely chopped green pepper
½ teaspoon garlic salt
½ teaspoon dried whole oregano
1 (2½-ounce) jar sliced mushrooms, drained
¾ cup (3 ounces) shredded mozzarella cheese

Combine meat, breadcrumbs, eggs, ⅓ cup tomato sauce, onion, green pepper, garlic salt, and oregano; mix well. Press mixture into a 9-inch pieplate; cover with waxed paper. Microwave at HIGH for 14 to 18 minutes or until firm to touch, giving dish a half-turn after 7 minutes. Using a baster, drain off excess drippings.

Spread remaining tomato sauce evenly over meat loaf, and arrange mushrooms over sauce. Microwave at HIGH for 2 minutes. Sprinkle with cheese, and microwave at MEDIUM HIGH for 2 to 3 minutes or until most of cheese is melted. Let stand 5 minutes before serving. Cut into wedges to serve. Yield: 6 servings.

INDIVIDUAL PINEAPPLE LOAVES

1 (8¼-ounce) can crushed pineapple
1½ pounds ground beef
1⅓ cups cracker crumbs
½ cup finely chopped green pepper
2 eggs, beaten
¾ teaspoon salt
¼ to ½ teaspoon curry powder
¼ teaspoon pepper

Drain pineapple, reserving 2 tablespoons juice. Set pineapple aside.

Combine reserved juice and remaining ingredients except pineapple; mix well. Pack meat mixture into six 6-ounce custard cups. Arrange cups in a ring in microwave oven. Microwave at HIGH for 9 to 13 minutes or until firm to the touch, rearranging cups after 5 minutes.

Invert loaves on a microwave-safe serving platter or glass pizza plate, and spoon pineapple evenly over each. Microwave at MEDIUM HIGH for 1½ to 2 minutes. Let stand 5 minutes before serving. Yield: 6 servings.

ORIENTAL MEAT LOAF

1½ pounds ground beef
½ cup fine dry breadcrumbs
2 eggs, beaten
½ cup finely chopped onion
½ cup finely chopped green pepper
⅓ cup finely chopped water chestnuts
3 tablespoons catsup
2 tablespoons soy sauce
½ teaspoon salt
¼ teaspoon pepper
2 tablespoons catsup
1 tablespoon soy sauce
1 tablespoon brown sugar
½ teaspoon dry mustard

Combine first 10 ingredients, and mix well. Shape into a 10- x 5-inch slightly rounded loaf in a 12- x 8- x 2-inch baking dish. Cover with waxed paper. Microwave at HIGH for 14 to 18 minutes or until firm to touch, giving dish a half-turn after 7 minutes. Drain off excess drippings.

Combine remaining ingredients, and spoon over meat loaf. Microwave at MEDIUM HIGH for 1½ to 2 minutes. Let stand 5 minutes before serving. Yield: 6 servings.

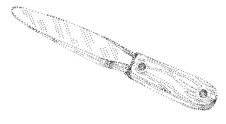

CHILI-SAUCED HAM RING

¾ pound ground fully cooked ham
¾ pound ground pork
1 cup soft breadcrumbs
¼ cup finely chopped onion
2 eggs, beaten
¼ cup chili sauce
1 teaspoon dry mustard
½ cup chili sauce
2 tablespoons brown sugar
1 teaspoon dry mustard
⅛ teaspoon garlic powder

Combine first 7 ingredients, and mix well. Shape mixture into a ring in a 10-inch square baking dish; place a 6-ounce custard cup in center of ring. Cover with waxed paper. Microwave at MEDIUM HIGH for 14 to 16 minutes or until firm to the touch, giving dish a half-turn after 7 minutes. Remove custard cup. Drain off excess drippings.

Combine remaining ingredients, and spoon over loaf. Microwave at MEDIUM HIGH for 2 to 3 minutes. Let stand 5 minutes before serving. Yield: 6 servings.

Bake The Classic Brioche

Brioche—that buttery French yeast roll with a topknot—is easier to make than you might have imagined.

Our recipe specifies individual brioche pans. We tried both 4- and 4½-inch pans with equally good results. If you use much larger or smaller pans, adjust the size of the rolls and the baking time.

BRIOCHE

½ cup milk
1 package dry yeast
¼ cup warm water (105° to 115°)
½ cup butter or margarine, softened
⅓ cup sugar
½ teaspoon salt
4 cups all-purpose flour
3 eggs, slightly beaten
1 egg yolk, slightly beaten
1 egg white
1 tablespoon sugar

Scald milk; let cool to 105° to 115°. Dissolve the yeast in warm water, and set aside.

Cream butter; gradually add ⅓ cup sugar and salt, beating until smooth. Add milk and 1 cup flour to creamed mixture; beat well. Stir in 3 eggs, egg yolk, and the yeast mixture. Gradually stir in remaining flour.

Place dough in a greased bowl, turning to grease top. Cover and let rise in a warm place (85°), free from drafts, 1½ hours or until doubled in bulk. Cover tightly with aluminum foil, and refrigerate overnight.

Punch dough down. Divide dough into 4 equal portions; set 1 portion aside. Divide each of the 3 remaining portions into 8 pieces; shape each piece into a ball (total of 24 balls). Place in greased 4- or 4½-inch individual brioche pans or muffin pans. Using a floured finger, make a deep indentation in center of each.

Divide reserved portion of dough into 24 pieces, and shape into balls. Press one into each indentation. Cover and let rise in a warm place (85°), free from drafts, about 45 minutes or until doubled in bulk.

Combine egg white and 1 tablespoon sugar; mix well, and lightly brush on top of each brioche. Bake at 375° about 15 to 20 minutes or until golden brown. Yield: 2 dozen.

Step 1—*Divide dough into 4 equal portions. Shape 3 portions into 24 balls, and place in greased individual brioche pans. Make a deep indentation in center of each with a floured finger.*

Step 2—*Shape remaining portion of dough into 24 balls. Press one ball into each indentation. Cover and let rise in a warm place until doubled in bulk.*

Step 3—*Brush each brioche with egg white-sugar glaze before baking.*

June

Southerners migrate outdoors in June, and grilled kabobs are a fun way to cook and eat while enjoying nature. The kabobs are loaded with meat and vegetables, so just a salad and bread round out the meal.

While some folks reach for the grill, others head for blackberry patches. Southern Blackberry Cobbler and Blackberry Cream Pie are two delicious rewards for the latter. And if your garden or market is full of fresh corn, we offer everything from fritters to barbecued corn on the cob.

Dining is just as tasty on the Chesapeake Bay—several of our editors visited the region and brought back recipes from favorite restaurants for you to enjoy in your own home. Don't overlook the Black Forest Cake!

Kabobs Mean Dinner On A Stick

Wisps of smoke curl up and over fences, and a smoky aroma floats through the air as Southerners fire up their grills for the long cookout season. And if guests are coming, nothing could be more convenient or colorful than kabobs: chunks of marinated meat or poultry skewered with bits of fresh vegetables and fruits and seared over the hot coals.

For a beefy kabob, try our Skewered Steak With Vegetables: Chunks of sirloin marinated in wine and herbs are threaded with vegetables. Ham kabobs are unusual and quick to prepare: bits of ham, Swiss cheese, and pineapple are basted with an orange glaze while grilling. You'll also love our Overnight Shish Kabobs, typically Greek in seasoning, or Chicken Kabobs Supreme —chicken, pineapple, and vegetables, all brushed with a sweet-and-sour sauce.

SKEWERED STEAK WITH VEGETABLES

½ cup Chablis or other dry white wine
1 clove garlic, crushed
½ teaspoon salt
½ cup vegetable oil
1 teaspoon Worcestershire sauce
2 tablespoons chili sauce
1 tablespoon vinegar
½ teaspoon dried whole oregano
½ teaspoon dried whole thyme
2 pounds (1½-inch-thick) boneless sirloin steak, cut into 1-inch cubes
½ pound fresh mushroom caps
2 large green peppers, cut into 1½-inch pieces
1 pint cherry tomatoes
4 small yellow squash, cut into 1-inch-thick slices

Combine first 9 ingredients. Add meat; cover and marinate at least 2 hours in the refrigerator, turning meat occasionally.

Remove meat from marinade, reserving marinade. Alternate meat and vegetables on skewers. Grill over medium coals 10 to 15 minutes or until desired degree of doneness, basting with marinade. Yield: 4 to 5 servings.

Tip: To slice mushrooms quickly and uniformly, use an egg slicer or a food processor fitted with the slicing blade.

OVERNIGHT SHISH KABOBS

2 pounds boneless lamb
1 onion, finely diced
⅓ cup finely diced green pepper
½ cup Burgundy or other dry red wine
¼ cup olive oil
½ teaspoon pepper
¼ teaspoon rubbed sage
⅛ teaspoon dry mustard
⅛ teaspoon dried whole oregano

Remove fell (tissue-like covering) from lamb, if necessary; cut meat into 1-inch cubes, and set aside.

Combine the remaining 8 ingredients in a 13- x 9- x 2-inch baking dish. Add lamb; cover and marinate overnight in refrigerator.

Remove meat from marinade, reserving marinade. Cook marinade in a small saucepan until thoroughly heated. Place meat on skewers. Grill about 6 inches from medium coals for 15 to 20 minutes or until done, turning and basting frequently with the marinade. Yield: 6 servings. *Margaret W. Cotton, Franklin, Virginia.*

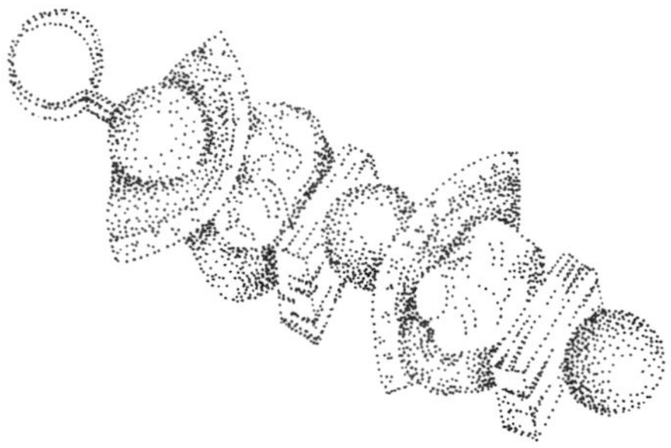

CHICKEN KABOBS SUPREME

2 whole chicken breasts, skinned and boned
½ cup vegetable oil
¼ cup soy sauce
¼ cup Chablis or other dry white wine
¼ cup light corn syrup
1 tablespoon sesame seeds
2 tablespoons lemon juice
¼ teaspoon garlic powder
¼ teaspoon ground ginger
1 small pineapple, cut into 1-inch cubes
1 large green pepper, cut into 1-inch pieces
2 medium onions, quartered
3 small zucchini, cut into 1-inch pieces
½ pound fresh mushroom caps
1 pint cherry tomatoes (optional)

Cut the chicken breasts into 1-inch pieces; set aside.

Combine next 8 ingredients; mix well. Add chicken; cover and marinate at least 2 hours in the refrigerator.

Remove chicken from marinade, reserving marinade. Alternate chicken, pineapple, and vegetables on skewers. Grill about 6 inches from medium-hot coals for 15 to 20 minutes or until done, turning and basting often with marinade. Yield: 6 servings.
Mildred Sherrer, Bay City, Texas.

SWISS-HAM KABOBS

1 (20-ounce) can unsweetened pineapple chunks
½ cup orange marmalade
1 tablespoon prepared mustard
¼ teaspoon ground cloves
1 pound fully cooked ham
½ pound Swiss cheese

Drain pineapple, reserving 2 tablespoons juice. Combine juice, marmalade, mustard, and cloves; mix well.

Cut ham and cheese into 1½- x ½- x ½-inch pieces. Thread ham, cheese, ham, then pineapple on 12-inch skewers (cheese must be between and touching 2 pieces of ham to prevent rapid melting); repeat procedure until all the ingredients are used.

Place kabobs 4 to 5 inches from hot coals. Brush with sauce; grill 3 to 4 minutes until cheese is partially melted and ham is lightly browned, turning and brushing frequently with the sauce. Yield: 6 servings. *Charlene Keebler, Savannah, Georgia.*

Sail Away On Chesapeake Menus

The winds of the Chesapeake Bay caress a land so fertile that it must have been paradise to the Britons who sailed here 350 years ago. They built tiny clustered villages along its inlets, towns like the towns they had left. Gifted with an extraordinary abundance of animals and fish and plants new to them, they set about learning to cook in new ways. Oh, how they cooked: blue crabs and clams and oysters and shad, geese and ducks and turkeys and quail, terrapins and chickens and sweet potatoes and strawberries, and all the other ingredients of culinary heaven.

Today, when those winds are gentle, they stir the masts and chains of sailboats to wind-chime music. They put snap into a flag, send a midshipman's cap scooting across Annapolis' parade grounds. They carry warmth to the Eastern Shore, and with it abundance; they twist the branches of the Wye Oak and give life to its leaves. When the winds stiffen, they send clouds across the sky and stir the shallow, blue-black waters of the Chesapeake Bay into a frothy white spray. The same breezes bring a hint of those early settlers' delight: the aroma of Chesapeake Bay cooking.

J. D. Mallory in the *Baltimore Sun* had the right idea in 1890. His subject was an oyster recipe, but his words mean more. "This may be a little trouble to the cook," he wrote, "but the persons who eat the oysters never get through talking about them." It's impossible to sample the goodness of the Bay's food and stay quiet about it.

Of course, there's more to the Bay than wonderful food. Historical markers are more common than stop signs along the region's backroads, and you'll have to share the pavement with tractors. Sculptured lawns touch the Bay's shores; fences run wild across its gentle hills. Barns of every design are a testament to past and present wealth. Food and history and the Bay are inexorably linked at every stop, and that's the way visitors and natives like it.

Try Some Chesapeake Cooking Yourself

One of a cook's most generous acts is to share his or her secrets. Chefs all along the Chesapeake Bay have their own ways of preparing regional specialties, which they've shared with our test kitchens staff. We've tested each of them and found them all terrific. Your final product may not be an exact duplication of the Bay's intricate cuisine, but we predict you'll come close. Try any of these recipes for a taste of the Chesapeake at home.

■ Wild game is the reigning motif at Easton, Maryland's, **Tidewater Inn.** Their version of Roast Duckling With Orange Sauce flavors the special bird

with just a hint of citrus to add piquancy. Try the inn's recipe for Clams Casino (the recipe is also adaptable to oysters) for a dish that is simple yet magnificent.

CLAMS CASINO

1 dozen clams in shells
¼ cup chopped onion
¼ cup chopped green pepper
1 tablespoon butter or margarine, melted
¼ cup chopped pimiento
3 slices bacon, cut into fourths
Lemon half
Parsley

Wash clams, discarding any open (dead) clams. Pry open shells; discard top shell, and loosen meat from bottom shell. Drain shells and meat on paper towels.

Sauté onion and green pepper in butter; stir in pimiento. Return clams to shell, and arrange in a shallow baking pan. Spoon 1 tablespoon vegetable mixture onto each clam; top with bacon. Bake at 375° for 15 to 20 minutes or until bacon is browned. Garnish with lemon and parsley. Yield: 12 appetizer servings.

Note: Oysters may be substituted for the clams.

ROAST DUCKLING WITH ORANGE SAUCE

1 (3½- to 4-pound) dressed duckling
Salt
1 tablespoon vinegar
1 tablespoon sugar
¼ cup currant jelly
¼ cup orange juice
1 tablespoon cornstarch
Pitted dark sweet cherries
Orange rind strips
Orange slices
Parsley

Remove giblets and neck from duckling; sprinkle cavity with salt. Prick skin with a fork at intervals. Fold neck skin under and place duckling, breast side up, on a rack in roasting pan. Bake, uncovered, at 325° for 2 to 2½ hours or until drumsticks and thighs move easily.

Combine ¼ cup pan drippings, vinegar, sugar, jelly, orange juice, and cornstarch in a small saucepan; stir well. Cook over medium heat, stirring constantly, until thickened and bubbly.

Cut duckling in half or quarters; garnish each with cherries, orange rind strips, orange slices, and parsley. Serve with sauce. Yield: 2 to 4 servings.

■ Captain James Dodson isn't choosy about which kind of fish to use in Captain's Spicy One, since he'll use whatever he caught that day. This is a favorite of diners at his **Captain's Galley,** a waterside restaurant in Crisfield, Maryland.

CAPTAIN'S SPICY ONE

6 (8- to 10-ounce) sea trout or red snapper fillets
½ teaspoon salt
1 tablespoon plus ½ teaspoon Old Bay Seasoning
1 tablespoon plus ½ teaspoon paprika
About ½ cup lemon juice
½ teaspoon parsley flakes
¼ cup plus 2 tablespoons butter or margarine
Lemon slices

Place fish fillets in two 13- x 9- x 2-inch baking dishes. Sprinkle salt, Old Bay Seasoning, and paprika evenly over fish. Sprinkle with lemon juice, and top with parsley. Dot fish with butter. Broil 12 to 15 minutes or until fish flakes easily. Garnish with lemon slices. Yield: 6 servings.

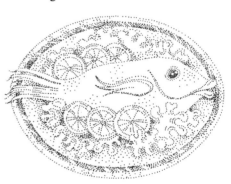

■ From the informal setting of **Town Creek Restaurant & Marina** in Oxford, Maryland, comes this basic recipe for crab cakes—"a lot of crab and not much else." These are terrific for a picnic by the water.

CRAB CAKES

1 pound fresh crabmeat, drained and flaked
½ to ¾ cup mayonnaise
½ cup fine dry breadcrumbs
1 egg, beaten
1 teaspoon prepared mustard
¾ to 1 teaspoon white pepper (optional)
¼ teaspoon parsley flakes
Pinch of salt

Combine all ingredients; stir well. Shape mixture into 10 patties. Fry in deep hot oil (375°) until patties are golden brown. Drain on paper towels. Yield: 10 (2-inch) patties.

■ If you take the relaxing afternoon ferry to Smith Island, Maryland, be sure to visit the **Bayside Inn** for a sweet slice of Sweet Potato Meringue Pie. You'll remember the flavor long after the return trip to the mainland.

SWEET POTATO MERINGUE PIE

1 (30-ounce) can sweet potatoes, drained
 and mashed
1 cup sugar
1 tablespoon all-purpose flour
¼ cup butter or margarine, melted
⅓ cup evaporated milk
½ cup milk
Dash of salt
⅛ teaspoon lemon extract
1½ teaspoons vanilla extract
3 eggs, separated
1 unbaked 10-inch pastry shell
¼ teaspoon cream of tartar
½ teaspoon vanilla extract
⅓ cup sugar

Combine first 9 ingredients and egg yolks; beat until combined. Pour mixture into pastry shell, and bake at 400° for 10 minutes. Reduce heat to 350°, and bake for 30 additional minutes or until set.

Beat egg whites with cream of tartar and vanilla until soft peaks form. Gradually add ⅓ cup sugar, 1 tablespoon at a time, beating until stiff peaks form. Spread meringue over filling, sealing to edge of pastry.

Bake at 350° for 10 to 12 minutes or until golden. Cool completely before serving. Yield: one 10-inch pie.

■ A region is as rich as its desserts, and the Chesapeake is rich. So are Black Forest Cake and Strawberry Napoleons, which are created at the Easton Pastry Shop and served at **Longfellow's** in St. Michaels, Maryland.

BLACK FOREST CAKE

2 cups plus 2 tablespoons all-purpose
 flour
2 cups sugar
¾ cup cocoa
1½ teaspoons baking powder
¾ teaspoon soda
¾ teaspoon salt
½ cup shortening
3 eggs
1 cup milk
1 tablespoon vanilla extract
3 cups whipping cream
¼ cup plus 2 tablespoons powdered sugar
1 (21-ounce) can cherry pie filling

Combine first 6 ingredients in a large mixing bowl; stir until well mixed. Add shortening, eggs, milk, and vanilla; beat mixture 3 minutes at low speed of electric mixer, scraping bowl occasionally.

Grease two 9-inch cakepans; line bottom with waxed paper. Pour batter into pans. Bake at 350° for 30 to 35 minutes or until a wooden pick inserted in center comes out clean. Cool cake in pans 10 minutes; remove from pans, and cool completely.

Split cake layers in half horizontally to make 4 layers. Make fine crumbs using 1 cake layer; set crumbs aside.

Beat whipping cream until foamy; gradually add powdered sugar, beating until soft peaks form. Place 1 cake layer on cake platter; spread with 1 cup whipped cream, and top with ¾ cup cherry pie filling. Repeat with second layer, and then top with third cake layer. Frost sides and top with whipped cream, reserving a small amount for garnish. Pat cake crumbs generously around sides of cake. (There may be leftover cake crumbs.) Spoon dollops of whipped cream around top of cake; spoon remaining pie filling on center of top. Chill well. Yield: one 9-inch cake.

STRAWBERRY NAPOLEONS

2¼ cups all-purpose flour
1 cup plus 1½ teaspoons sifted cake flour
1 cup water
1½ cups butter, softened
¼ teaspoon salt
2 cups whipping cream
½ cup sifted powdered sugar
2 cups sliced fresh strawberries
Whole strawberries (optional)

Combine flour, water, ¼ cup butter, and salt in a large mixing bowl; beat 4 minutes at medium speed of electric mixer. Shape dough into a ball; wrap in aluminum foil. (Dough will be slightly sticky.) Chill for 15 minutes.

Stir 1¼ cups butter with a wooden spoon until smooth. Shape on aluminum foil into a 4-inch square. Chill for 5 minutes.

Roll dough into a 12-inch circle on a lightly floured surface; place butter in center of dough. Fold left side of dough over butter; fold right side of dough over left. Fold upper and lower edges of dough over butter making a thick square.

Place dough, folded side down, on a lightly floured surface; roll dough into a 16- x 8-inch rectangle. Fold rectangle into thirds, beginning with short side. Roll dough into another 16- x 8-inch rectangle; again fold rectangle into thirds. Wrap dough in aluminum foil, and chill about 45 minutes.

Repeat rolling and folding process 2 additional times. Chill 45 minutes.

Divide dough into three equal portions; chill 2 portions. Roll dough into a 14- x 6-inch rectangle. Sprinkle a cookie sheet with water and shake off excess. Place dough on cookie sheet; prick dough with a fork. Bake at 425° for 20 to 25 minutes or until golden brown and puffed. Cool on a rack.

Repeat rolling, baking, and cooling process for other 2 portions of dough. Trim edges of pastry, if necessary, to make a uniform rectangle.

Carefully cut each pastry rectangle in half lengthwise to make two 14- x 3-inch strips. Divide each of the six 14- x 3-inch strips into 3 equal portions to make eighteen 4½- x 3-inch rectangles.

Beat whipping cream until foamy; gradually add powdered sugar, beating until soft peaks form. Spread about one-third of whipped cream on 6 pastry rectangles; place half of sliced strawberries on top of whipped cream. Repeat pastry, whipped cream, and sliced strawberries. Top with pastry. Garnish with a generous portion of whipped cream and a whole strawberry, if desired. Yield: 6 servings.

■ Folks from all over talk about the **Robert Morris Inn** in Oxford, usually followed by a mention of Oysters à la Gino. Fresh oysters are a must. The result is lightly browned, piping hot, and will disappear in a hurry.

OYSTERS A LA GINO

2 dozen unshucked oysters
2 tablespoons butter or margarine
¼ cup plus 2 tablespoons all-purpose
 flour
1 cup milk
3 tablespoons paprika
½ teaspoon garlic powder
½ teaspoon salt
½ teaspoon white pepper
½ teaspoon Old Bay Seasoning
2 tablespoons Worcestershire sauce
2 tablespoons dry sherry
1 (6-ounce) package frozen lump
 crabmeat, thawed and drained
6 slices bacon, cut into fourths

Wash and rinse oysters thoroughly in cold water. Shuck oysters, reserving deep half of shells. Place oysters in colander to drain; set aside.

Melt butter in a heavy saucepan over low heat; add flour, stirring until smooth. Cook 1 minute, stirring constantly. Gradually add milk; cook over medium heat, stirring constantly, until thickened. (Mixture will be very thick.) Add next 6 ingredients; stir until smooth. Stir in sherry; cool 20 minutes. Add crabmeat, and stir until combined.

Place oysters in half shells; arrange in a shallow baking dish. Spoon 1 tablespoon crabmeat mixture on each oyster; top with bacon. Bake at 350° for 15 to 20 minutes or until browned. Yield: 4 servings.

■ The **Steamboat Landing** in Galesville, Maryland, insists on fresh crabmeat as the basis for Steamboat's Cream of Crab Soup, served in a picturesque glass-walled dining room. And Steamboat's Stuffed Soft-Shell Crabs are especially good.

STEAMBOAT'S STUFFED SOFT-SHELL CRABS

16 fresh or frozen soft-shell crabs
   (thawed)
1 pound backfin crabmeat
½ cup soft breadcrumbs
1 egg, beaten
¼ cup mayonnaise
1 teaspoon dry mustard
1 teaspoon Worcestershire sauce
½ teaspoon salt
¼ teaspoon pepper
⅛ teaspoon Old Bay Seasoning
All-purpose flour
Vegetable oil

To clean crabs, remove spongy substance (gills) that lies under the tapering points on either side of back shell. Place crabs on back, and remove the small piece at lower part of shell that terminates in a point (the apron). Wash crabs thoroughly; drain well.

Remove any cartilage or shell from backfin crabmeat. Combine crabmeat and next 8 ingredients; mix well. Stuff about 1 tablespoon crabmeat mixture into cavity of each crab; dredge crabs in flour. Fry crabs in deep hot oil (380°) for 1 to 2 minutes. Drain on paper towels, and serve immediately. Yield: 16 crabs.

Note: Remaining crab mixture may be shaped into patties and fried in shallow, hot oil (360°) until golden brown. Turn once. Drain on paper towels.

STEAMBOAT'S CREAM OF CRAB SOUP

1 pound fresh backfin crabmeat
¼ cup butter
¼ cup all-purpose flour
1 cup chicken broth
1 quart plus 1 cup half-and-half
½ cup dry sherry
1 teaspoon salt
¼ teaspoon white pepper

Remove and discard cartilage from crabmeat; set aside.

Melt butter in a Dutch oven over low heat; add flour, stirring until smooth. Cook 1 minute, stirring constantly. Gradually add broth; cook over medium heat, stirring constantly, until thickened and bubbly. Add crabmeat and remaining ingredients; cook over low heat 10 to 15 minutes (do not boil), stirring frequently. Yield: about 2 quarts.

Summer's Corn Makes Sweet Eating

One of summer's long-anticipated treats is the sheer delight of biting into an ear of fresh corn with those plump, sweet kernels brushed with melting butter. That's not to say that corn on the cob is the best or only way to enjoy fresh corn. For along with the harvest of fresh corn comes a great variety of other dishes, some of the finest of the season.

Those who must have their corn on the cob will be delighted with our foil-baked version. Before baking, the ears are spread with an herb-flavored butter. A perfect recipe for those summer cookouts.

When cut from the cob, the possibilities for corn are endless. The traditional spoonbread is made with cornmeal, but Corn and Bacon Spoonbread adds extra flavor with fresh corn, bacon, and Cheddar cheese. You'll also want to enjoy fresh corn in another Southern classic, a custard-like Corn Pudding.

Corn also takes to being combined with other summer vegetables. In both Corn and Tomato Casserole and Creole Corn, green pepper, tomatoes, and corn are delicious, colorful companions. With the addition of pimiento, celery, onion, and a tangy marinade, corn becomes a crisp summer relish.

The key to success with these and other corn dishes is using the freshest corn possible. The less time between garden and table, the better. Here are some other pointers.

—When buying corn, select ears with snug, green husks and tender, milky kernels. The kernels should be evenly spaced on the ear and firm, yet tender enough to puncture with a slight amount of pressure.

—If you must store corn, buy it in the husks; then store in the refrigerator. This will help prevent the sugar in the corn from turning to starch and tasting pasty rather than sweet.

—Here's a good rule of thumb when you need only kernels: Two average-size ears of corn will generally yield about 1 cup of kernels.

CORN AND TOMATO CASSEROLE

8 slices bacon, cut in half
2 cups soft breadcrumbs
2 cups peeled, chopped fresh tomatoes
1 medium-size green pepper, chopped
3 cups fresh corn cut from cob
¼ teaspoon salt
¼ teaspoon sugar
¼ teaspoon pepper
¼ cup butter or margarine, melted

Place half of bacon in a shallow 2-quart casserole, and top with 1 cup breadcrumbs. Layer half of tomatoes, green pepper, and corn over breadcrumbs; sprinkle with half of salt, sugar, and pepper. Repeat layers of the vegetables and the seasonings.

Combine the melted butter and remaining 1 cup breadcrumbs, stirring well; spoon evenly over casserole. Top with remaining bacon; bake at 375° for 40 to 45 minutes or until breadcrumbs are golden. Yield: 8 servings.

Mrs. Wilson Connell,
Nashville, Georgia.

CREOLE CORN

2 slices bacon, chopped
1 large onion, sliced and separated into rings
1 medium-size green pepper, finely chopped
2½ cups chopped fresh tomatoes
1 small bay leaf
2 cups fresh corn cut from cob
¼ teaspoon salt
⅛ teaspoon pepper

Fry bacon until crisp; remove from skillet, reserving drippings. Drain bacon on paper towels. Add onion and green pepper to drippings in skillet; cook over medium heat, stirring constantly, until crisp-tender.

Add tomatoes and bay leaf to onion mixture; simmer 10 minutes, stirring occasionally. Stir in corn, and simmer 10 minutes. Discard bay leaf; stir in salt, pepper, and bacon. Yield: 6 to 8 servings.   *Ruby Bonelli,*
Pearland, Texas.

CORN AND CHEESE CASSEROLE

2 cups fresh corn cut from cob
1 cup (4 ounces) shredded sharp Cheddar cheese
1 cup soft breadcrumbs
¼ cup chopped green pepper
⅓ cup milk
2 tablespoons butter or margarine, melted
1 tablespoon instant minced onion
1 teaspoon salt
¼ teaspoon ground ginger
⅛ teaspoon pepper

Combine all ingredients, stirring well. Spoon into a lightly greased 1-quart casserole. Cover and bake at 350° for 30 to 40 minutes or until the corn is tender. Yield: 4 servings.   *Alan Pollock,*
Saskatchewan, Canada.

CORN PUDDING

2 cups fresh corn cut from cob
¼ cup all-purpose flour
2 to 3 tablespoons sugar
1 teaspoon salt
2 cups milk
2 eggs, beaten
2 tablespoons butter or margarine, melted

Combine corn, flour, sugar, and salt; stir well. Combine remaining ingredients, mixing well; stir into the corn mixture.

Pour into a lightly greased 1½-quart casserole. Bake at 350° for 1 hour, stirring twice during first 30 minutes. Yield: 6 to 8 servings.   *Dana Peck,*
Clinton, Tennessee.

SCALLOPED CORN

¼ cup cornmeal
3 tablespoons brown sugar
1½ teaspoons salt
¾ cup milk, scalded
3 tablespoons butter or margarine, melted
4 cups fresh corn cut from cob
¼ cup diced pimiento
1 egg, beaten

Combine cornmeal, sugar, and salt; add milk and butter, mixing well. Stir in remaining ingredients. Pour mixture into a lightly greased 1-quart shallow casserole.

Bake at 325° for 1 hour or until knife inserted in center comes out clean; stir twice during first 20 minutes of baking. Yield: 6 servings.   *Linda Clark,*
Elizabethton, Tennessee.

BARBECUED CORN ON THE COB

6 ears fresh corn
½ cup butter or margarine, melted
½ (3-ounce) package instant tomato soup mix (2 envelopes)
½ cup water
1 medium onion, finely chopped

Remove husks and silks from corn just before cooking. Combine remaining ingredients, stirring well. Place each ear on a piece of aluminum foil, and spoon 2 tablespoons sauce over each. Wrap foil tightly around corn. Bake at 425° for 12 to 15 minutes. Yield: 6 servings.
Ann Elsie Schmetzer,
Madisonville, Kentucky.

FOIL-BAKED CORN ON THE COB

12 ears fresh corn
½ cup butter or margarine, softened
½ teaspoon salt
½ teaspoon dried whole rosemary
½ teaspoon dried whole marjoram
⅛ teaspoon pepper

Remove husks and silks from corn just before cooking. Combine remaining

ingredients, stirring well. Spread herb butter on corn, and place each ear on a piece of aluminum foil; wrap tightly.

Bake at 450° for 25 minutes, turning several times. Yield: 12 servings.
Sandra Russell,
Maitland, Florida.

CORN CHOWDER

2 slices bacon
½ cup chopped onion
1 (10¾-ounce) can cream of chicken soup, undiluted
1 cup milk
⅔ cup water
1 cup diced cooked chicken
½ cup cooked fresh corn cut from cob

Place bacon in a medium saucepan, and cook until crisp. Remove bacon, reserving drippings in saucepan; drain and crumble bacon; set aside.

Sauté onion in bacon drippings until transparent; stir in bacon and remaining ingredients. Cook over low heat until thoroughly heated, stirring occasionally. Yield: 4 cups.   *Mrs. Roy Dawson,*
Campbell, Texas.

GOLDEN CORN FRITTERS

1 cup all-purpose flour
1 teaspoon baking powder
1 teaspoon sugar
½ teaspoon salt
2 eggs, beaten
1 cup fresh corn cut from cob
⅔ cup milk
1 teaspoon butter or margarine, melted
Vegetable oil
Powdered sugar

Combine flour, baking powder, sugar, and salt; mix well. Combine eggs, corn, milk, and butter; mix well, and stir into dry ingredients.

Drop mixture by tablespoonfuls into vegetable oil heated to 375°; cook until golden, turning once. Drain on paper towels; sprinkle with powdered sugar. Serve hot. Yield: about 2½ dozen.
Mrs. Martin E. Grosh,
Columbus, Ohio.

CORN AND BACON SPOONBREAD

¾ cup yellow cornmeal
1½ cups water
2 cups (8 ounces) shredded Cheddar cheese
1½ cups cooked fresh corn cut from cob
¼ cup butter or margarine
1 or 2 cloves garlic, minced
1 teaspoon salt
1 cup milk
4 eggs, separated
10 slices bacon, cooked and crumbled

Combine cornmeal and water; boil 1 minute or until thickened, stirring constantly. Remove from heat. Add cheese, corn, butter, garlic, and salt; stir until the cheese melts. Stir in milk.

Beat egg yolks until thick and lemon colored; add bacon. Stir into cornmeal mixture. Beat egg whites until stiff, but not dry; gently fold into the cornmeal mixture.

Pour into a lightly greased 2½-quart casserole or soufflé dish. Bake at 325° for 1 hour or until a knife inserted in the center comes out clean. Yield: about 10 to 12 servings.

Mrs. Donald C. Vanhoy,
Salisbury, North Carolina.

CORN RELISH

1 cup vinegar
½ cup sugar
1½ teaspoons mustard seeds
½ teaspoon salt
3½ cups cooked fresh corn cut from cob
½ cup chopped green pepper
½ cup diced pimiento
¼ cup chopped celery
¼ cup chopped onion
1 small clove garlic, minced

Combine first 4 ingredients in a Dutch oven; boil 2 minutes, stirring to dissolve sugar.

Add remaining ingredients to sugar mixture, and boil 3 minutes. Cool. Store in refrigerator in an airtight container. Yield: 3½ to 4 cups.

Betty Jane Morrison,
Lakewood, Colorado.

Tip: Store spices in a cool place and away from any direct source of heat as the heat will destroy their flavor. Red spices (chili powder, paprika, and red pepper) will maintain flavor and retain color longer if refrigerated.

These almond-flavored Swedish Heirloom Cookies are pretty enough for a party.

Treasures For The Cookie Jar

Everyone loves cookies, and everyone has a favorite. Chocolate chip, oatmeal, and brownies seem to be at the top of everyone's list, and here are some versions to try. Chocolate Chip Bars, quicker than drop cookies, are baked in a layer and cut into squares. One bite of Swedish Heirloom Cookies, and you'll add them to your list of favorites; they're crisp and buttery, filled with ground almonds, and rolled in powdered sugar.

To keep cookies at their best, store crisp ones in a loosely covered container, soft ones in a tightly covered container. Most can be frozen up to 6 months.

SWEDISH HEIRLOOM COOKIES

½ cup shortening
½ cup butter or margarine, softened
1 cup sifted powdered sugar
½ teaspoon salt
2 cups all-purpose flour
1 tablespoon water
1 tablespoon vanilla extract
1¼ cups ground almonds
Powdered sugar

Cream shortening and butter until light and fluffy. Add 1 cup powdered sugar and salt; mix well. Stir in flour. Stir in water, vanilla, and almonds. Shape dough into 1-inch balls; place on ungreased baking sheets, and flatten slightly. Bake at 325° for 12 to 15 minutes or until done. Dredge cookies in powdered sugar while they're still warm. Yield: about 8 dozen.

Mrs. J. W. Montgomery,
Kinston, North Carolina.

CHOCOLATE-NUT BROWNIES

½ cup butter or margarine, softened
1 cup sugar
2 eggs, beaten
1 teaspoon vanilla extract
¼ teaspoon salt
⅔ cup all-purpose flour
2 (1-ounce) squares unsweetened chocolate, melted
⅔ cup black walnuts, chopped

Cream butter; add sugar, and beat until light and fluffy. Add eggs, vanilla, salt, and flour; mix well. Stir in chocolate and nuts. Pour into a greased 8-inch square pan. Bake at 325° for 20 minutes or until done. Cut into 1½-inch squares. Yield: about 2 dozen.

Myrtle Green,
Martinsville, Virginia.

CHOCOLATE CHIP BARS

⅓ cup shortening
⅓ cup butter or margarine, softened
½ cup sugar
½ cup firmly packed brown sugar
1 egg
1 teaspoon vanilla extract
1½ cups all-purpose flour
½ teaspoon salt
1 (6-ounce) package semisweet chocolate morsels
1 (6-ounce) package butterscotch morsels
½ cup chopped pecans

Cream shortening and butter; add sugar, and beat until light and fluffy. Beat in egg and vanilla. Add remaining ingredients, and mix well. Pour into an ungreased 13- x 9- x 2-inch pan. Bake at 375° for 20 to 25 minutes. Cut into 1½-inch squares. Yield: about 4½ dozen.
Vickie Hedrick,
Gretna, Virginia.

NUTTY OATMEAL COOKIES

¾ cup shortening
1¼ cups sugar
2 eggs, well beaten
1½ cups all-purpose flour
1 teaspoon ground cinnamon
1 teaspoon ground nutmeg
¼ teaspoon salt
¼ cup plus 2 tablespoons milk
1 teaspoon soda
2 cups regular oats, uncooked
1¼ cups pecans or walnuts, chopped

Cream shortening; add sugar, and beat until light and fluffy. Add eggs, and mix well. Combine flour, cinnamon, nutmeg, and salt; mix well. Combine milk and soda. Add dry ingredients and milk mixture alternately to creamed mixture, beating well after each addition. Stir in oats and pecans. Drop dough by teaspoonfuls onto greased baking sheets, and bake at 350° for 10 to 12 minutes or until brown. Yield: about 7 dozen. *Mrs. William R. Boies,*
Mangham, Louisiana.

Tip: Always measure ingredients accurately. For liquids, use a glass measuring cup; this allows you to see that you are measuring correctly. Use metal or plastic dry measuring cups for solids; fill cups to overflowing, and level off with a knife or metal spatula.

Chilled Soups Are Meant For Summer

For summer dining, consider serving a refreshing cold soup. Try light and creamy cucumber or yellow squash, beef consommé with curry, colorful raspberry topped with whipped cream—they're all quickly prepared with the help of an electric blender.

The secret to preparing cold soups is to make them well in advance of serving, allowing plenty of time for the soup to chill and the flavors to blend.

For a creative touch, serve cold soups in unusual containers—perhaps a tall stemmed glass with a large bowl or a smaller soup bowl nestled in an icy liner.

COLD CUCUMBER SOUP

2 medium cucumbers, peeled and sliced
3 cups chicken broth
¼ cup chopped onion
1 tablespoon all-purpose flour
1 medium bay leaf
½ teaspoon salt
1 medium cucumber, peeled and seeded
1 cup half-and-half
⅓ cup commercial sour cream
2 tablespoons lemon juice
Chopped fresh parsley
Additional cucumber slices (optional)

Combine first 6 ingredients in a medium saucepan. Cover and simmer 20 minutes. Press the cucumber mixture through a sieve into a medium bowl; discard seeds and pulp. Chill.

Shred remaining cucumber. Combine chilled broth mixture and shredded cucumber in container of electric blender; blend until smooth, and pour into a large bowl. Stir in half-and-half, sour cream, and lemon juice. Garnish with parsley and cucumber slices, if desired. Yield: about 6 cups. *Elizabeth Terry,*
Birmingham, Alabama.

COLD CREAM OF SQUASH SOUP

2 cups sliced yellow squash
2 tablespoons butter or margarine
4 cups chicken broth
1 thin slice of onion
½ teaspoon salt
3 to 4 drops of hot sauce
1 (8-ounce) carton commercial sour cream

Combine squash, butter, and ½ cup chicken broth in a medium saucepan;

cover and cook 10 minutes or until squash is tender. Pour squash mixture into container of electric blender. Add remaining chicken broth, onion, salt, and hot sauce; blend until smooth. Pour into a large bowl; cover and chill several hours. Stir in sour cream just before serving. Yield: about 5½ cups.
Betty Morrow,
Birmingham, Alabama.

CURRIED SOUP

1 (10½-ounce) can beef consommé, diluted
4 (3-ounce) packages cream cheese, softened
¾ teaspoon curry powder
½ clove garlic, minced
Chopped fresh parsley (optional)

Combine first 4 ingredients in container of electric blender; blend 30 seconds or until smooth. Cover and chill several hours. Sprinkle with chopped parsley, if desired, before serving. Yield: about 4 cups.
Mrs. Peter Rosato III,
Memphis, Tennessee.

CHILLED RASPBERRY SOUP

2 (10-ounce) packages frozen raspberries, thawed
2 cups Burgundy or other dry red wine
2½ cups water
1 (3-inch) stick cinnamon
¼ cup plus 1 tablespoon sugar
1½ to 2 tablespoons arrowroot
Whipped cream

Combine first 5 ingredients in a deep, ceramic, heatproof casserole or stainless steel saucepan (mixture will discolor aluminum). Bring mixture to a boil; reduce heat, and simmer 15 minutes.

Press raspberry mixture through a sieve or food mill and return to casserole or saucepan; discard seeds. Combine ¼ cup raspberry liquid and arrowroot; stir well. Bring remaining liquid to a boil. Reduce heat to low, and stir in arrowroot mixture. Cook, stirring constantly, until slightly thickened. Chill 6 to 8 hours. Serve soup with a dollop of whipped cream. Yield: about 6 cups.

He Makes The Most Of Fresh Ingredients

Jeff Twardy of Alexandria, Virginia, quickly admits that his wife, Mary Pat, prepares most of their meals; occasionally, however, he likes to take over the kitchen. Sunday brunch is one of those times, but he enjoys cooking even more when his garden comes in. That's because Jeff believes that really great meals should include as many fresh ingredients as possible.

While a student in law school, Jeff worked in a natural foods restaurant. "I guess this type of food was sort of faddish at the time, but I still try to cook with fresh, naturally grown foods when possible," he explained. "This year, I have a vegetable and herb garden with over 20 types of herbs, and I enjoy using the fruits of my labor, especially in casseroles and salads."

One of Jeff's specialties is Veal au Madeira, which is deftly seasoned with garlic, basil, and fresh parsley. With it, he serves a salad made of garden-fresh greens and other vegetables tossed with Rosemary Dressing.

Following Jeff's recipes are specialties from other men who enjoy cooking.

FRESH GARDEN SALAD WITH ROSEMARY DRESSING

2 cups torn red leaf lettuce
2 cups torn green leaf lettuce
2 cups torn fresh spinach
1 cucumber, peeled and chopped
10 radishes, thinly sliced
½ cup fresh parsley sprigs
½ lemon, thinly sliced and quartered
Rosemary Dressing

Combine first 7 ingredients in a large bowl, tossing well. Add dressing, and toss lightly. Yield: 8 servings.

Rosemary Dressing:

3 tablespoons red wine vinegar
1 tablespoon olive oil
1 tablespoon water
1 to 1½ teaspoons dried whole rosemary, crushed
1 teaspoon lemon juice
¾ teaspoon Dijon mustard
¼ teaspoon salt
⅛ teaspoon white pepper

Combine all of the ingredients in a jar. Cover tightly, and shake jar vigorously. Chill for several hours. Yield: about ⅓ cup.

VEAL AU MADEIRA

1 to 1½ pounds (¼-inch-thick) veal scallops or cutlets
⅓ cup whole wheat pastry flour
¼ cup butter or margarine
1 (28-ounce) can whole tomatoes, undrained
½ pound fresh mushrooms, sliced
¼ cup sweet Madeira or Marsala
1 to 2 tablespoons chopped fresh parsley
1 clove garlic, minced
1 teaspoon dried whole basil
4 to 6 ounces provolone cheese, shredded
Parsley sprigs
Lemon slices

Flatten veal to ⅛-inch thickness, using a meat mallet or rolling pin; dredge in flour. Melt butter in a large skillet over medium heat; add veal, and cook about 1 minute on each side or until lightly browned. Remove veal from skillet, and set aside.

Drain liquid from tomatoes, reserving ¾ cup; chop tomatoes. Combine tomatoes, mushrooms, Madeira, chopped parsley, garlic, and basil in skillet; stir well, and heat until simmering. Arrange veal over tomato mixture, and pour reserved tomato liquid over all. Cover and simmer 4 minutes.

Sprinkle cheese over veal; cover and cook 4 additional minutes. Garnish with parsley sprigs and lemon slices. Yield: 4 to 6 servings.

SHRIMP AND SIRLOIN SUPREME

¾ pound boneless sirloin steak
1½ cups water
2 tablespoons cornstarch
3 tablespoons soy sauce
2 tablespoons oyster-flavored sauce
1 teaspoon sugar
2 tablespoons vegetable oil
1 large onion, thinly sliced and separated into rings
1 cup diagonally sliced celery
1 medium-size green pepper, cut into ¼-inch strips
½ cup chopped water chestnuts
½ cup bamboo shoots
½ pound fresh mushrooms, sliced
1 (6-ounce) package frozen Chinese pea pods, thawed and drained
½ pound shrimp, peeled and deveined
Hot cooked rice

Partially freeze steak; slice across grain into 2- x ¼-inch strips.

Combine water, cornstarch, soy sauce, oyster-flavored sauce, and sugar; stir well, and set aside.

Pour oil around top of preheated wok, coating sides; allow to heat at medium high (325°) for 2 minutes. Add steak, and stir-fry about 2 minutes. Remove steak from wok, and set aside.

Add all vegetables except pea pods to wok; stir-fry 2 to 3 minutes. Add pea pods, shrimp, and steak; stir-fry for 1 to 2 minutes.

Stir in soy sauce mixture. Cook, stirring constantly, until thickened and bubbly (about 2 to 3 minutes). Serve over rice. Yield: 4 servings.

Tom Hawthorne,
Roanoke, Virginia.

CLASSIC QUICHE LORRAINE

Pastry for 9-inch pie
12 slices bacon, cooked and crumbled
1 cup (4 ounces) shredded Swiss cheese
4 eggs, beaten
2 cups half-and-half
¾ teaspoon salt
⅛ teaspoon pepper

Line a 9-inch quiche dish or piepan with pastry; trim excess pastry around edges. Prick bottom and sides of shell with a fork, and bake at 425° for 6 to 8 minutes. Let cool on wire rack.

Sprinkle bacon and cheese evenly into pastry shell. Combine eggs, half-and-half, salt, and pepper; mix well, and pour into shell.

Bake the quiche at 425° for 15 minutes. Reduce heat to 300°, and bake an additional 40 minutes or until set. Yield: one 9-inch quiche. *Ron Barker,*
Mesquite, Texas.

EASY SAUTEED MUSHROOMS

2 tablespoons butter or margarine
½ pound fresh mushrooms, sliced
3 green onions, finely chopped
1 medium-size green pepper, diced
Dash of salt
Dash of pepper

Melt 1 tablespoon butter in a medium skillet. Add vegetables; sauté 5 minutes, stirring occasionally. Add remaining butter; cook an additional 5 minutes or until vegetables are just tender. Stir in salt and pepper. Yield: 2 to 4 servings.

Note: Easy Sautéed Mushrooms may also be served as a topping for steak, chicken, or hamburgers.

Terrence Heinen,
Nashville, Tennessee.

FAVORITE POUND CAKE

1 cup butter, softened
1 tablespoon shortening
2¾ cups sugar
5 eggs
½ teaspoon soda
1 tablespoon warm water
1¼ cups buttermilk
3 cups all-purpose flour
¼ teaspoon salt
1 teaspoon vanilla extract

Combine butter and shortening, mixing well; gradually add sugar, creaming until light and fluffy. Add eggs, one at a time, beating well after each addition.

Dissolve soda in warm water, and stir into buttermilk. Combine flour and salt, stirring well; add to creamed mixture alternately with buttermilk, beginning and ending with flour mixture. Mix well after each addition. Stir in vanilla.

Pour batter into a greased and floured 10-inch tube pan. Bake at 325° for 1 hour and 30 minutes or until wooden pick inserted in center comes out clean. Cool in pan 10 to 15 minutes; remove from pan, and let cool completely. Yield: one 10-inch cake.

Odin Williams, Jr.
Pineville, Louisiana.

Cobblers And Other Rewards Of Blackberry Picking

The best thing about picking fresh blackberries is what comes afterward—juicy cobblers, rich pies, moist cakes. So fill your pail, and head for the kitchen to reap the sweet rewards.

SOUTHERN BLACKBERRY COBBLER

5 cups fresh blackberries
¾ cup sugar
1 tablespoon cornstarch
⅛ teaspoon salt
2 tablespoons butter or margarine
Pastry for 9-inch pie
1 tablespoon milk
1 tablespoon sugar

Place blackberries in a 9-inch square baking dish. Combine sugar, cornstarch, and salt, mixing well; sprinkle over blackberries. Dot with butter.

Roll pastry out on a lightly floured surface to a 9-inch square. Place pastry on top of blackberries; trim edges and seal. Make several slits in top to allow steam to escape. Brush pastry with milk; sprinkle with sugar. Bake at 425° for 30 minutes. Yield: 6 to 8 servings.

Charlotte Pierce,
Greensburg, Kentucky.

BLACKBERRY-ALMOND COBBLER

1 cup all-purpose flour
⅓ cup ground almonds
1 tablespoon powdered sugar
¼ cup plus 1 tablespoon butter
3 cups fresh blackberries
1 cup water
1 cup sugar
2 tablespoons butter or margarine
Sugar

Combine first 3 ingredients, mixing well. Cut in ¼ cup plus 1 tablespoon butter with pastry blender until mixture resembles coarse meal. Chill mixture 15 minutes.

Combine blackberries, water, 1 cup sugar, and 2 tablespoons butter in saucepan; place over medium heat, and bring to a boil. Remove from heat, and pour into a 2-quart casserole.

Roll out pastry on a lightly floured surface to fit the top of the casserole; place pastry over blackberries. Brush pastry with water and sprinkle lightly with sugar. Bake at 375° for 35 minutes or until golden. Yield: 6 servings.

Mrs. William S. Bell,
Chattanooga, Tennessee.

DELUXE BLACKBERRY COBBLER

½ (8-ounce) package cream cheese, softened
¼ cup plus 1 tablespoon butter or margarine, softened
1½ cups all-purpose flour
½ teaspoon salt
3 tablespoons orange juice
4 cups fresh blackberries
1½ cups sugar
1 cup thinly sliced, peeled apples
1 tablespoon lemon juice
2½ teaspoons grated lemon rind
1 teaspoon vanilla extract
1 tablespoon butter or margarine
Vanilla ice cream (optional)

Combine cream cheese and softened butter in a mixing bowl; stir well. Combine flour and salt; add to cream cheese

mixture, stirring until well blended. Sprinkle orange juice over surface; stir with a fork until dry ingredients are moistened. Shape into a ball. Chill 1 hour.

Press half of dough onto bottom and sides of a lightly greased 1½-quart casserole to within 1 inch of top.

Combine blackberries, sugar, apples, lemon juice, lemon rind, and vanilla in medium saucepan. Bring to a boil; boil 10 minutes. Pour over prepared crust.

With floured hands, shape remaining dough into irregular pieces about ¼ inch thick; place on top of fruit in a patchwork fashion. Dot with remaining butter. Bake at 425° for 40 minutes or until golden. Serve with vanilla ice cream, if desired. Yield: about 6 to 8 servings.

Allegre Parker,
Bessemer, Alabama.

FRESH BLACKBERRY CAKE

3 cups all-purpose flour
2 cups sugar
1 teaspoon salt
1 teaspoon ground nutmeg
1 teaspoon ground cinnamon
1 teaspoon ground cloves
3 eggs, beaten
1 cup butter or margarine, melted
1 cup buttermilk
1½ cups fresh blackberries
1 tablespoon soda
½ cup chopped pecans or walnuts
½ cup raisins

Combine first 6 ingredients in a large mixing bowl; add eggs, butter, buttermilk, and blackberries. Beat 1 minute on medium speed of an electric mixer. Stir in soda, pecans, and raisins; spoon batter into a greased and floured 10-inch Bundt pan. Bake at 350° for 55 to 60 minutes or until cake tests done. Yield: one 10-inch cake.

Rhonda Harrell,
Titusville, Florida.

BLACKBERRY CREAM PIE

1 cup sugar
1 (8-ounce) carton commercial sour cream
3 tablespoons all-purpose flour
⅛ teaspoon salt
4 cups fresh blackberries
1 unbaked 9-inch pastry shell
1 tablespoon sugar
¼ cup fine dry breadcrumbs
1 tablespoon sugar
1 tablespoon butter or margarine, melted

Combine first 4 ingredients; stir well. Place blackberries in pastry shell; sprinkle 1 tablespoon sugar over berries. Spread sour cream mixture over berries. Combine breadcrumbs, 1 tablespoon sugar, and butter; sprinkle over top. Bake at 375° for 45 to 50 minutes or until center of pie is firm. Yield: one 9-inch pie. *Marsha Hayes, McKenzie, Tennessee.*

Two Can Eat As Cheaply As One

Whether newly married or newly retired, budget-minded couples often have trouble planning well-balanced, yet economical, meals for two. Using leftover and less expensive meats, these main dish recipes inspire menus that satisfy both the appetite and the pocketbook.

Chicken livers, a top nutritional buy, are sautéed and served over toast points for Chicken Livers With Mushrooms. Ham and Broccoli Casserole finishes off the last few slices of leftover ham by combining them with broccoli spears and a creamy cheese sauce.

For Chicken-Almond Salad, fresh tomatoes form the base for a generous scoop of chicken salad topped with crumbled bacon and toasted almonds.

CHICKEN CROQUETTES

2 tablespoons butter or margarine
2 tablespoons all-purpose flour
½ cup milk
¼ teaspoon salt
Dash of pepper
1 cup minced cooked chicken
1 egg, beaten
1 tablespoon milk
2 tablespoons all-purpose flour
⅓ cup soft breadcrumbs

Melt butter in a heavy saucepan over low heat; add 2 tablespoons flour and cook 1 minute, stirring constantly. Gradually add milk; cook over medium heat, stirring constantly, until sauce is thickened and bubbly. Stir in salt and pepper. Remove from heat; stir in chicken. Cover and chill about 1 hour.

Shape chicken mixture into 2 balls or rolls. Combine egg and milk; mix well, and set aside. Dredge each croquette in 2 tablespoons flour; then dip into egg and milk mixture, and coat each croquette with breadcrumbs.

Fry croquettes in deep hot oil (370°) for 3 to 5 minutes or until golden brown. Drain on paper towels. Yield: 2 servings. *Mrs. James L. Twilley, Macon, Georgia.*

CHICKEN-ALMOND SALAD

1 cup chopped cooked chicken
½ cup chopped celery
1½ teaspoons lemon juice
½ teaspoon salt
¼ teaspoon pepper
2 hard-cooked eggs, chopped
¼ cup mayonnaise
2 large tomatoes
Lettuce leaves
5 slices bacon, cooked, drained, and crumbled
2 tablespoons chopped slivered almonds, toasted

Combine first 5 ingredients; toss lightly. Fold in eggs and mayonnaise; cover and chill 2 hours.

With stem end up, cut each tomato into 6 wedges, cutting to, but not through, base of tomato. Spread wedges slightly apart; sprinkle inside of wedges with salt. Cover and chill 1½ hours.

Place each tomato on lettuce leaves; spoon chicken mixture into wedges. Sprinkle with bacon and almonds. Yield: 2 servings. *Nell Hodges, Guntersville, Alabama.*

CHICKEN LIVERS WITH MUSHROOMS

½ pound chicken livers
2 tablespoons butter or margarine, melted
1 (2-ounce) can mushroom stems and pieces
¼ cup water
1 tablespoon all-purpose flour
1 teaspoon dried parsley flakes
1 teaspoon instant chicken-flavored bouillon granules
¼ teaspoon salt
⅛ teaspoon pepper
Toast points

Sauté chicken livers in butter for 5 minutes. Stir in remaining ingredients, except toast; bring to a boil. Reduce heat and simmer, uncovered, for 10 to 15 minutes. Serve over toast points. Yield: 2 servings.

Mrs. Arthur E. Mitchell, Longboat Key, Florida.

BAKED STUFFED EGGPLANT

1 medium eggplant
½ pound ground beef
1 medium tomato, peeled and chopped
2 tablespoons chopped onion
2 tablespoons chopped green pepper
2 tablespoons chopped celery
½ cup cooked regular rice
½ teaspoon seasoned salt
¼ teaspoon dried whole basil
Dash of pepper
½ cup (2 ounces) shredded Cheddar cheese

Wash eggplant, and cut in half lengthwise. Remove pulp, leaving a ¼-inch shell; set shells aside. Dice pulp, and set aside.

Cook ground beef in a large skillet over medium heat until browned. Add eggplant pulp, tomato, onion, green pepper, and celery. Cook 5 minutes, stirring occasionally. Remove from heat; stir in rice, salt, basil, and pepper. Place eggplant shells in a 10- x 6- x 2-inch baking dish. Spoon meat mixture into shells; sprinkle Cheddar cheese on each eggplant half. Bake at 350° for 30 minutes. Yield: 2 servings.

Mrs. J. C. Kiles, Lewisville, Texas.

HAM AND BROCCOLI CASSEROLE

1 (10-ounce) package frozen broccoli spears
2 slices cooked ham
2 tablespoons butter or margarine
2 tablespoons all-purpose flour
1 cup milk
2 tablespoons shredded medium Cheddar cheese
1 teaspoon minced onion
1 teaspoon prepared mustard
½ teaspoon salt

Cook broccoli according to package directions, omitting salt; drain. Arrange broccoli in a lightly greased 1-quart casserole. Place ham slices over broccoli. Set casserole aside.

Melt butter in a heavy saucepan over low heat; add flour and cook 1 minute, stirring constantly. Gradually add milk; cook over medium heat, stirring constantly, until sauce is thickened and bubbly. Add remaining ingredients, stirring until cheese is melted.

Pour cheese sauce over broccoli and ham. Bake at 350° for 30 minutes. Yield: 2 servings. *Grace Padilla, Virginia Beach, Virginia.*

Fresh Basil, A Flavor Enhancer

Herb connoisseurs capture the truest flavor of basil by cooking it when it's fresh, rather than dried. So if you have access to fresh basil, snip off a few leaves and enjoy its mild, sweet flavor in these recipes.

Buttery Baked Perch Fillets reveal the flavor of fresh basil since few other seasonings are used. Skillet Vegetable Medley offers a different side dish in only minutes with eggplant and zucchini flavored with basil. And you're sure to enjoy Italian Tomato Sauce for Spaghetti, a reminder that basil is one of the key seasonings in Italian cooking.

If your garden produces a bumper crop of basil, harvest and dry your own for later use. Simply spread the freshly picked basil over a wire screen or similar device that allows the air to circulate around it, or hang it in bunches upside down. Cover with paper towels, and store in a warm, preferably dark place. When completely dry, store basil in airtight containers, away from heat and sunlight.

When substituting dried basil leaves for fresh, remember that 1 tablespoon minced fresh basil equals 1 teaspoon dried crushed leaves.

BUTTERY BAKED PERCH FILLETS

2 pounds fresh or frozen perch fillets, thawed
¼ cup butter or margarine
½ teaspoon paprika
1 tablespoon minced fresh basil
Salt and pepper
Fresh basil leaves
Lemon wedges
Tartar sauce (recipe follows)

Place fillets, skin side down, in a greased 13- x 9- x 2-inch baking dish; dot with butter. Sprinkle paprika, minced basil, salt, and pepper over fillets. Bake at 350° for 20 to 30 minutes or until fish flakes easily when tested with a fork. Arrange fish on a platter, and garnish with basil leaves and lemon wedges. Serve with tartar sauce. Yield: 6 servings.

Tartar Sauce:
½ cup mayonnaise
2 tablespoons chopped sweet pickle
1 teaspoon instant minced onion
Juice of 1 lemon

Combine all ingredients, and mix well; chill before serving. Yield: about ⅔ cup. *Gloria Pedersen, Brandon, Mississippi.*

ITALIAN TOMATO SAUCE FOR SPAGHETTI

1 small onion, chopped
4 cloves garlic, minced
¼ cup olive oil
½ pound lean ground beef
1 (28-ounce) can tomatoes
1 (15-ounce) can tomato puree
½ teaspoon salt
½ teaspoon pepper
1 teaspoon dried whole oregano
3 tablespoons minced fresh basil
1 teaspoon sugar
1 teaspoon dried Italian seasoning
Hot cooked spaghetti
Grated Parmesan cheese

Sauté onion and garlic in hot oil in a large skillet. Add ground beef; cook until browned, stirring to crumble. Add next 8 ingredients; cover and simmer 1 hour, stirring occasionally.

Serve over spaghetti, and sprinkle with Parmesan cheese. Yield: 4 servings. *Leonora Pickering, Berclair, Texas.*

SKILLET VEGETABLE MEDLEY

1 large onion, sliced and separated into rings
2 small cloves garlic, minced
2 tablespoons olive oil
1 small eggplant, peeled and cut into ½-inch cubes
2 small zucchini, sliced
1 medium-size green pepper, cut into strips
½ head fennel, sliced (optional)
1 (14½-ounce) can Italian-style tomatoes, drained and coarsely chopped
1½ teaspoons minced fresh basil
¾ teaspoon salt
¼ teaspoon minced fresh parsley
Freshly ground pepper to taste

Sauté onion and garlic in oil in a large skillet. Add remaining ingredients; cover and cook over low heat 5 to 7 minutes or until tender. Yield: 6 servings. *Anna Hoosack, Knob Noster, Missouri.*

A Pitcherful Of Refreshment

Combine fresh fruit or fruit juices, rum, and crushed ice; the result is two terrific ways to cool off on a hot summer day. Enjoy Luscious Piña Colada, thick and creamy, with a south-of-the-border accent. Pour Tart Caribbean Cooler over crushed ice for a special lemonade.

LUSCIOUS PINA COLADAS

1 (8-ounce) can crushed pineapple, undrained
1 (8½-ounce) can cream of coconut
1 large banana, peeled and sliced
½ cup nonfat dry milk powder
¼ cup water
¼ cup light rum
1 teaspoon lemon juice
1 tablespoon sugar
15 ice cubes
Shredded coconut (optional)

Combine first 9 ingredients in an electric blender; blend until ice is finely crushed. Top with coconut, if desired. Yield: 4 cups. *Mrs. Gary Ferguson, Corsicana, Texas.*

TART CARIBBEAN COOLER

¼ cup lemonade-flavor drink mix
1 tablespoon sugar
¾ cup pineapple juice
¼ cup light rum
1 cup crushed ice

Combine all ingredients in an electric blender; blend well. Serve over crushed ice. Yield: 2 cups. *Heather Riggins, Nashville, Tennessee.*

Tip: Read labels to learn the weight, quality, and size of food products. Don't be afraid to experiment with new brands. Store brands can be equally good in quality and nutritional value, yet lower in price. Lower grades of canned fruits and vegetables are as nutritious as higher grades. Whenever possible, buy most foods by weight or cost per serving rather than by volume or package size.

Tuna Makes The Zippiest Burgers, The Creamiest Salads

Tuna, a rich source of protein, is so versatile you could consider it a convenience food—an ideal substitute for more expensive meats. So open a can of tuna, and try some of our new ideas. They're sure to become family favorites.

Shape tuna into fat burgers flavored with catsup, mustard, and pickle relish for Zippy Tuna Burgers. Mold it into a creamy salad with Cheddar cheese, or serve it in a vegetable casserole that's thick and nutritious enough for a one-dish meal.

ZIPPY TUNA BURGERS

3 slices bread, crusts removed
1 (5.33-ounce) can evaporated milk
1 tablespoon catsup
1 tablespoon prepared mustard
1 tablespoon pickle relish
2 (6½-ounce) cans tuna, drained and flaked
6 hamburger buns
6 slices tomato

Tear bread into small pieces. Pour milk over bread in a mixing bowl; add catsup, mustard, and relish. Stir with a fork until smooth; stir in tuna.

Toast cut sides of buns; set top halves aside. Spoon tuna mixture on each bottom half, carefully spreading to edges. Broil about 6 inches from heat 5 to 6 minutes or until lightly browned. Place a tomato slice on each. Cover with bun tops. Yield: 6 sandwiches.
Mrs. Charles W. Kelly,
Somerville, New Jersey.

TUNA VEGETABLE CASSEROLE

1 cup canned English peas, drained
1½ cups cooked cubed carrots
1½ cups cooked cubed potatoes
½ cup chopped onion
1 (9¼-ounce) can tuna, drained and flaked
2 tablespoons butter or margarine
2 tablespoons all-purpose flour
2 cups milk
2 tablespoons butter or margarine, melted
½ cup soft breadcrumbs

Combine vegetables; spoon half into a greased 2-quart shallow casserole. Cover with half of tuna; repeat layers, and set mixture aside.

Melt 2 tablespoons butter in a heavy saucepan over low heat; add flour, stirring until smooth. Cook 1 minute, stirring constantly. Gradually add milk; cook over medium heat, stirring constantly, until thickened and bubbly. Spread white sauce over casserole. Combine 2 tablespoons melted butter and breadcrumbs; mix well and sprinkle over casserole. Bake at 350° about 30 minutes. Yield: 6 servings.
Mrs. Russell T. Shay,
Murrells Inlet, South Carolina.

CREAMY TUNA-CHEESE MOLD

1 envelope unflavored gelatin
⅓ cup cold water
½ cup boiling water
1 (9¼-ounce) can tuna, drained and flaked
¾ cup chopped celery
½ cup (2 ounces) shredded sharp Cheddar cheese
⅓ cup mayonnaise
¼ cup finely chopped onion
¼ cup chopped green pepper
½ teaspoon salt
½ teaspoon lemon pepper seasoning
Lettuce leaves

Soften gelatin in cold water. Add boiling water, stirring until gelatin is dissolved. Stir in remaining ingredients except lettuce leaves, mixing well. Spoon into a lightly oiled 4-cup mold; chill until firm. Unmold on a lettuce-lined plate. Serve with crackers. Yield: about 3 cups.
Mrs. J. M. Hamilton,
Fort Mill, South Carolina.

LUNCHEON TUNA SALAD

1 (3-ounce) package lemon-flavored gelatin
1¼ cups boiling water
2 teaspoons vinegar
½ teaspoon salt
1 cup mayonnaise
1 (9¼-ounce) can tuna, drained and flaked
1 hard-cooked egg, chopped
2 tablespoons sliced pimiento-stuffed olives
1 tablespoon chopped green pepper

Dissolve gelatin in boiling water. Add vinegar and salt; mix well and chill until slightly thickened. Add remaining ingredients, stirring well. Spoon mixture into a lightly oiled 9-inch square pan; chill until firm. Cut into squares to serve. Yield: 9 servings.
Irene Murry,
Herculaneum, Missouri.

TUNA-EGG SALAD

4 hard-cooked eggs
1 tablespoon lemon juice
1 (9¼-ounce) can tuna, drained and flaked
1 cup sliced celery
¼ cup finely chopped onion
¼ cup sliced pimiento-stuffed olives
½ cup mayonnaise
Dash of pepper

Slice one egg in half; remove yolk. Press yolk through a sieve; set aside for garnish. Coarsely chop egg white and 2 eggs. Set aside.

Sprinkle lemon juice over tuna. Add celery, onion, olives, mayonnaise, pepper, chopped egg, and egg white; mix well, and chill. Slice remaining egg. Garnish salad with egg slices and sieved yolk before serving. Yield: 6 servings.
Mrs. C. D. Marshall,
Culpeper, Virginia.

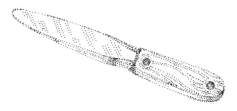

Oyster Lover Invents A New Trick

Here is a recipe developed for those who love raw oysters but also enjoy the crunchiness of fried oysters. First bread the oysters, then freeze them until firm. Quick-frying crisps the cracker-crumb coating but only thaws the oyster. Your "fried raw" oysters will be a hit with any oyster lover.

FRIED RAW OYSTERS

½ cup fine cracker crumbs
⅛ teaspoon salt
¼ teaspoon pepper
1 (12-ounce) can fresh Select oysters, drained
Vegetable oil

Combine cracker crumbs, salt, and pepper; dredge oysters in crumbs. Place on a baking sheet, and freeze until firm.

Heat 1 inch of oil to 350°. Fry frozen oysters in oil until golden brown; drain on paper towels. Yield: 4 servings.
Dr. D. P. Hightower,
York, Alabama.

We Have The Pies For You

Whether your favorite is chocolate, coconut, lemon, or fruit, do we have some pies for you. Listen to some of the names: Luscious Peach, Lemon Cheese, Coconut Cream, Chocolate-Mocha Crunch—and all taste just as good as they sound. There's no last-minute rush with these pies, either, for they're prepared and chilled well in advance of serving.

For that picture-perfect look, garnish your pies with a recipe ingredient. A dollop of whipped cream, a slice of fruit, or a sprinkling of chocolate shavings can work wonders.

CHOCOLATE MOUSSE PIE

½ cup butter or margarine, softened
¾ cup sugar
2 (1-ounce) squares unsweetened chocolate, melted and cooled
2 eggs
1 (4-ounce) carton frozen whipped topping, thawed
1 baked 9-inch pastry shell
Whipped cream (optional)
Shaved chocolate (optional)

Cream butter and sugar until light and fluffy; stir in chocolate. Add eggs, one at a time, beating 5 minutes after each addition. Fold in whipped topping.

Spoon filling into pastry shell. Chill until firm (about 2 hours), or freeze. Garnish with whipped cream and shaved chocolate before serving, if desired. Yield: one 9-inch pie.
Marie Raney,
Dogpatch, Arkansas.

CHOCOLATE-MOCHA CRUNCH PIE

½ cup butter or margarine, softened
¾ cup firmly packed brown sugar
1 (1-ounce) square unsweetened chocolate, melted and cooled
2 teaspoons instant coffee granules
2 eggs
Mocha Pastry Shell
2 cups whipping cream
½ cup sifted powdered sugar
1½ tablespoons instant coffee granules
½ (1-ounce) square semisweet chocolate, grated (optional)

Beat butter until creamy; gradually add brown sugar, beating well. Then beat at medium speed of electric mixer 2 to 3 minutes, scraping sides of bowl occasionally. Stir in 1 square melted chocolate and 2 teaspoons coffee granules. Add eggs, one at a time, beating 5 minutes after each addition.

Pour filling into pastry shell. Refrigerate at least 6 hours.

About 1 or 2 hours before serving, combine whipping cream, powdered sugar, and 1½ tablespoons coffee granules in a large, chilled mixing bowl. Beat until stiff peaks form (do not overbeat); spoon over chilled filling. Sprinkle with grated chocolate, if desired. Chill. Yield: one 9-inch pie.

Mocha Pastry Shell:

1 stick piecrust, crumbled, or ½ (11-ounce) package piecrust mix
1 (1-ounce) square unsweetened chocolate, grated
¾ cups finely chopped walnuts or pecans
¼ cup firmly packed brown sugar
1 tablespoon water
1 teaspoon vanilla extract

Combine crumbled piecrust stick and chocolate with a fork; stir in walnuts and brown sugar. Combine water and vanilla; sprinkle over pastry. Mix with fork until mixture forms a ball.

Line a 9-inch pieplate with aluminum foil; place a circle of waxed paper over foil in bottom of pieplate. Press pastry mixture evenly into pieplate. Bake at 375° for 15 minutes; cool completely. Carefully invert crust on back of an 8½-inch pieplate; remove foil and waxed paper. Return to 9-inch pieplate. Yield: one 9-inch shell.
Mrs. Warren D. Davis,
Yulee, Florida.

COCONUT CREAM PIE

¾ cup sugar
3 tablespoons cornstarch
¼ teaspoon salt
2 cups milk
3 eggs, separated
2 tablespoons butter or margarine
1 teaspoon vanilla extract
1 (3½-ounce) can flaked coconut
1 baked 9-inch pastry shell
½ teaspoon vanilla extract
¼ teaspoon cream of tartar
¼ cup plus 2 tablespoons sugar

Combine ¾ cup sugar, cornstarch, and salt; gradually stir in milk. Cook mixture over medium heat, stirring constantly, until thickened.

Beat egg yolks until thick and lemon colored. Gradually stir about one-fourth of hot mixture into yolks; add to remaining hot mixture, stirring constantly. Cook 2 minutes, stirring constantly. Remove from heat; stir in butter, 1 teaspoon vanilla, and 1 cup coconut. Spoon into pastry shell.

Combine egg whites, ½ teaspoon vanilla, and cream of tartar; beat until foamy. Gradually add ¼ cup plus 2 tablespoons sugar, 1 tablespoonful at a time, beating until stiff peaks form. Spread meringue over pie, being careful to seal edges; sprinkle with remaining coconut. Bake at 350° about 10 minutes or until lightly browned. Cool; then refrigerate until time to serve. Yield: one 9-inch pie.
Rita Zimmerle,
Bunnell, Florida.

LEMON CHEESE PIE

1 (3-ounce) package lemon-flavored gelatin
1 cup boiling water
3 tablespoons lemon juice
1 (8-ounce) package cream cheese, softened
1 cup sugar
1 teaspoon vanilla extract
1 (13-ounce) can evaporated milk, chilled
2 (9-inch) graham cracker crusts

Dissolve gelatin in boiling water; stir in lemon juice, and set aside to cool.

Combine cream cheese, sugar, and vanilla; beat until light and fluffy. Add gelatin mixture, mixing until smooth.

Pour evaporated milk into a large, chilled mixing bowl, and beat until stiff peaks form. Stir in the cream cheese mixture.

Spoon filling into graham cracker crusts. Chill at least 3 hours. Yield: two 9-inch pies.
Elaine Bell,
Dexter, New Mexico.

LUSCIOUS PEACH PIE

2 (3-ounce) packages cream cheese, softened
¾ cup sifted powdered sugar
¼ teaspoon almond extract
¾ cup whipping cream, whipped
1 (16-ounce) can sliced peaches, drained
1 (9-inch) graham cracker crust

Combine first 3 ingredients; beat until smooth. Fold in whipped cream, and gently stir in peaches.

Pour filling into graham cracker crust. Chill well. Yield: one 9-inch pie.
Carolyn Gammon,
Tignall, Georgia.

Enjoy cornbread in a variety of shapes and flavors. Try a ring of Corn Lightbread, Tomato Corn Muffins, or spicy Mexican Cornbread.

Cornbread–All Kinds And Shapes

There are about as many kinds of cornbread as there are regions of the country, and most cooks seem to be pretty adamant about the superiority of their own particular versions.

Southern cooks generally prefer white cornmeal, milder in flavor than the yellow used more in the Southwest. Sugar is an unheard-of ingredient in cornbread to many cooks, while others insist that sugar brings out a special flavor. Some cooks like to add special ingredients such as corn, cheese, or tomatoes.

And when it comes to shaping cornbread, some insist on squares or muffins; some prefer a cakelike ring or a casserole of spoonbread. Whatever the shape or flavor, plenty of butter is a must to top off the hot-from-the-oven result.

MEXICAN CORNBREAD

1 (17-ounce) can cream-style corn
1 cup buttermilk
½ cup vegetable oil
2 eggs, beaten
1 cup cornbread mix
1 (4-ounce) can chopped green chiles, drained
1½ cups (6 ounces) shredded sharp Cheddar cheese, divided

Combine corn, buttermilk, oil, and eggs; mix well. Stir in cornbread mix. Pour half of batter into a greased 9-inch square pan; sprinkle with green chiles and half of cheese. Pour remaining half of batter over top, and sprinkle with remaining cheese. Bake at 350° for 45 to 50 minutes or until done. Cut into squares. Yield: 9 servings.

Mrs. Jack Hampton,
Elizabethton, Tennessee.

TOMATO CORN MUFFINS

⅓ cup shortening
⅓ cup sugar
1 egg, beaten
1 cup milk
1 cup all-purpose flour
½ teaspoon salt
1 tablespoon plus 1 teaspoon baking powder
1 cup cornmeal
½ cup canned tomatoes, drained and chopped

Cream shortening and sugar. Add egg, milk, and dry ingredients; stir only enough to combine. Fold in tomatoes. Fill greased muffin tins two-thirds full. Bake at 425° for 25 minutes or until done. Yield: 1 dozen.

Mrs. Ansel L. Todd,
Royston, Georgia.

CORN LIGHTBREAD

3 cups cornmeal
1 cup all-purpose flour
¾ cup sugar
1 teaspoon salt
1 teaspoon soda
1 teaspoon baking powder
½ cup shortening, melted
3 cups buttermilk

Combine all ingredients, and mix well. Spoon into a well-greased 10-inch tube pan; let stand 10 minutes.

Bake at 350° for 1 hour or until done. Cool 5 minutes before removing from pan. Yield: 12 to 15 servings.

Verla Sullivan,
Nashville, Tennessee.

SOUR CREAM CORNBREAD

1 (8½-ounce) can cream-style corn
1 cup commercial sour cream
2 eggs
½ cup vegetable oil
1 cup self-rising cornmeal
2 teaspoons baking powder

Combine corn, sour cream, eggs, and oil; beat well. Combine cornmeal and baking powder; stir into corn mixture. Pour into a greased 10-inch iron skillet. Bake at 400° for 30 minutes or until done. Yield: 8 servings.

Gail Thompson,
Montgomery, Alabama.

SPOONBREAD

1 cup cornmeal
3 cups milk, divided
1 teaspoon salt
1 teaspoon baking powder
2 tablespoons vegetable oil
3 eggs, separated

Combine cornmeal and 2 cups milk in a saucepan, stirring until blended; cook over low heat until the consistency of mush. Remove from heat; add salt, baking powder, oil, and remaining 1 cup milk. Beat egg yolks well; stir into warm mixture. Beat egg whites until stiff peaks form; fold into cornmeal mixture.

Spoon into a greased 2-quart casserole. Bake at 325° for 1 hour. Serve hot with butter. Yield: about 6 servings.

Debra Lancaster,
Hawkinsville, Georgia.

Microwave Cookery

This Picnic Is Microwave Easy

A picnic is one of the best ways we know to enjoy a long, lazy summer day. And with the help of your microwave oven, the food can be special, yet simple to prepare. To make sure your picnic is a memorable occasion, we've put together the following menu—with all five recipes developed in the *Southern Living* test kitchens.

We think you'll agree that Spicy Party Mix is an excellent choice for all-day munching. Crunchy with cereal, nuts, and pretzel sticks, it's easy to mix up and microwaves in about 5 minutes.

A well-seasoned mixture of cracker crumbs, Parmesan cheese, and lemon juice is the coating for our Lemon Chicken. To ensure even cooking, arrange the chicken pieces with meatier portions to the outside of the dish.

For Marinated Fresh Broccoli, broccoli and onion are microwaved just until crisp-tender, plunged into ice water to stop the cooking process, then marinated overnight in a tangy sauce.

The microwave oven makes quick work of cooking the potatoes, eggs, and bacon for Chunky Potato Salad. Cooking time is based on using three medium

potatoes. If you use large or small potatoes, adjust the microwaving time.

With our Cinnamon-Chocolate Cupcake recipe, you can have 10 cupcakes in 6 minutes or less. They're microwaved in paper-lined custard cups; to ensure even cooking, remember to arrange them in a circle about 1 inch apart. Since turning is necessary during microwaving, we recommend placing the cups on a glass pizza plate; that way, the plate can be turned rather than turning each cup. If you place the cups directly in the oven, you may need to slightly reduce cooking time.

Spicy Party Mix
Lemon Chicken
Chunky Potato Salad
Marinated Fresh Broccoli
Cinnamon-Chocolate Cupcakes

SPICY PARTY MIX

6 tablespoons butter or margarine
1 (1-ounce) envelope cheese Italian salad dressing mix
1 teaspoon Worcestershire sauce
⅛ teaspoon garlic powder
⅛ teaspoon hot sauce
4 cups bite-size crispy corn or wheat square cereal
3 cups pretzel sticks
1 cup mixed salted nuts

Place butter in a large glass mixing bowl; microwave at HIGH for 45 seconds to 1 minute or until butter melts. Stir in next 4 ingredients.

Add cereal, pretzel sticks, and nuts to butter mixture; toss gently. Microwave at MEDIUM for 3 to 5 minutes or until thoroughly heated, stirring after 2 minutes. Let cool, and store in an airtight container. Yield: 8 cups.

LEMON CHICKEN

1 cup fine cracker crumbs
⅓ cup grated Parmesan cheese
½ cup butter or margarine
2 tablespoons lemon juice
1 (2½- to 3-pound) broiler-fryer, cut up and skinned
Celery salt
Lemon pepper

Combine cracker crumbs and cheese in a pieplate; mix well, and set aside.

Place butter in a glass pieplate; microwave at HIGH for 45 seconds to 1 minute or until melted. Stir in lemon juice.

Sprinkle chicken with celery salt and lemon pepper. Dip chicken pieces in butter, and roll each in crumb mixture; arrange on a microwave roasting rack set in a 12- x 8- x 2-inch baking dish, placing meatier portions to outside of dish. Cover with waxed paper, and microwave at HIGH for 8 to 10 minutes.

Rearrange chicken pieces (do not turn) so uncooked portions are to outside of dish. Cover and microwave at HIGH for 9 to 12 minutes or until done. Yield: 4 servings.

CHUNKY POTATO SALAD

3 medium potatoes, peeled and cut into ¾-inch cubes
1 cup water
2 eggs
4 slices bacon
¼ cup chopped green onion
¼ cup sliced celery
¼ cup mayonnaise
¼ cup commercial sour cream
1 tablespoon vinegar
½ teaspoon dry mustard
½ teaspoon Italian seasoning
½ teaspoon salt
¼ teaspoon pepper
Leaf lettuce (optional)

Combine potatoes and water in a 2-quart casserole; cover with heavy-duty plastic wrap. Microwave at HIGH for 10 to 12 minutes or until tender, stirring after 5 minutes. Drain well, and set aside.

Gently break each egg into a 6-ounce custard cup and pierce yolks with a wooden pick. Cover each cup with heavy-duty plastic wrap, and arrange about 2 inches apart in microwave oven. Microwave at MEDIUM for 1½ to 3 minutes or until eggs are almost set, giving cups a half-turn after 1 minute.

Test eggs with a wooden pick (yolks should be just firm and whites almost set). Let eggs stand, covered, for 1 to 2 minutes to complete cooking. (If eggs are not desired degree of doneness after standing, cover and continue microwaving briefly.) Let eggs cool. Remove yolks and mash; chop whites.

Place bacon on a microwave bacon rack, and cover with paper towel. Microwave at HIGH for 4 to 5 minutes or until crisp. Crumble bacon.

Combine potatoes, egg whites, bacon, onion, and celery; mix well. Combine egg yolks, mayonnaise, sour cream, vinegar, and seasonings; mix well, and stir into potato mixture. Chill at least 2 hours. Serve in a lettuce-lined bowl, if desired. Yield: 4 servings.

MARINATED FRESH BROCCOLI

¾ cup sugar
½ cup vinegar
½ cup water
⅓ cup vegetable oil
1 teaspoon poppy seeds
1 medium head broccoli (about 1¾ pounds)
1 medium onion, thinly sliced and separated into rings
¼ cup water
3 tablespoons chopped pimiento

Combine first 5 ingredients in a 4-cup glass measure; mix well. Microwave at HIGH for 3 to 4 minutes or until boiling, stirring after 1 minute. Let cool to room temperature.

Trim off large leaves of broccoli. Wash broccoli, and break off flowerets; reserve stalks for another use.

Combine broccoli, onion, and ¼ cup water in a 2-quart casserole; cover with heavy-duty plastic wrap. Microwave at HIGH for 4 to 6 minutes or until vegetables are crisp-tender, giving dish a half-turn after 2 minutes. Immediately plunge vegetables into ice water; let stand in water for 4 minutes. Drain; stir in pimiento.

Pour marinade over vegetables; cover and chill 8 hours or overnight. Yield: 4 servings.

CINNAMON-CHOCOLATE CUPCAKES

¾ cup all-purpose flour
½ cup sugar
2 tablespoons cocoa
½ teaspoon soda
½ teaspoon ground cinnamon
¼ teaspoon salt
½ cup water
¼ cup vegetable oil
1½ teaspoons vinegar
½ teaspoon vanilla extract
Buttery Cinnamon Frosting

Combine first 6 ingredients; mix well. Add water, oil, vinegar, and vanilla; stir until smooth.

Place paper liners in five 6-ounce custard cups; fill half full with batter. Place

custard cups in a circle, about 1 inch apart, on a glass pizza plate. Microwave at HIGH for 2 to 3 minutes or until surface is almost dry, giving plate a half-turn at 1-minute intervals. Place on wire rack to cool. Repeat with remaining batter. Frost with Buttery Cinnamon Frosting. Yield: 10 cupcakes.

Buttery Cinnamon Frosting:

3 tablespoons butter or margarine
1½ cups sifted powdered sugar
¼ teaspoon ground cinnamon
Pinch of salt
1 tablespoon milk
½ teaspoon vanilla extract

Place butter in a medium-size glass mixing bowl; microwave at LOW for 30 to 45 seconds or until softened. Add ½ cup powdered sugar, cinnamon, and salt; beat with electric mixer until light and fluffy. Add remaining sugar alternately with milk, beating until smooth. Add vanilla, beating well. Yield: enough for 10 cupcakes.

Good Eating From The Vegetable Patch

Okra, corn, tomatoes, squash—all fresh from your garden. There's no better way to enjoy them than right now as they are freshly picked.

Fill large, ripe tomatoes with a cheesy rice stuffing, or add them to freshly cut okra for a favorite combination. If you're lucky enough to have both zucchini and yellow squash growing in your garden, be sure to try Squash Medley.

Whatever your garden bears, these recipes should start you off on a summer full of vegetable enjoyment.

CORN SALAD

6 ears fresh corn
1 cup diced green pepper
⅓ cup minced onion
2 tablespoons diced pimiento
½ cup mayonnaise
½ teaspoon curry powder
½ teaspoon salt
⅛ teaspoon pepper
Lettuce leaves

Remove husks and silks from corn. Drop corn into boiling water to cover, and cook 7 minutes. Drain and let cool

completely. Cut corn from cob; set aside.

Combine next 7 ingredients in a large bowl, mixing well. Add corn and toss lightly. Chill about 1 hour; serve on lettuce leaves. Yield: 8 to 10 servings.
Mrs. Don Jamerson,
Selmer, Tennessee.

OKRA AND TOMATOES

2 pounds okra
2 cups water
1 medium onion, sliced
1 tablespoon vinegar
1 teaspoon salt
2 tablespoons bacon drippings
1 (16-ounce) can stewed tomatoes, undrained
½ teaspoon sugar
½ teaspoon salt
⅛ teaspoon pepper

Wash okra well. Cut off tips and stem ends; cut okra into ½-inch slices.

Combine okra, water, onion, vinegar, and 1 teaspoon salt. Cover and cook over medium-high heat for 15 minutes. Drain off liquid; cook over low heat until all moisture evaporates. Add remaining ingredients; cook over medium heat, turning frequently, until brown. Yield: 6 to 8 servings. *C. Jobe,*
Tahlequah, Oklahoma.

SQUASH MEDLEY

2 slices bacon, diced
1 medium onion, chopped
3 medium-size yellow squash, cut into ¼-inch slices
1 medium zucchini, cut into ¼-inch slices
2 medium tomatoes, cut into eighths
1 teaspoon salt
¼ teaspoon pepper
½ teaspoon dried whole basil
½ teaspoon sugar

Fry bacon in a large skillet until almost crisp. Add onion, squash, and tomatoes; sprinkle with remaining ingredients. Cover and cook over low heat 15 minutes, stirring several times. Yield: about 5 to 6 servings.
Jane Crum,
North Little Rock, Arkansas.

TOMATO DELIGHTS

6 firm, ripe tomatoes
Salt to taste
1 medium-size green pepper, chopped
1 small onion, chopped
¼ cup butter or margarine, melted
1 cup (4 ounces) shredded Cheddar cheese
1 cup cooked regular rice
1 egg, well beaten
¼ teaspoon dried whole oregano
¼ teaspoon dried whole basil
½ teaspoon salt
4 slices bacon, cooked and crumbled
Parsley

Cut a slice from top of each tomato; scoop out pulp, leaving shells intact and reserving pulp. Sprinkle inside of tomato shells lightly with salt; invert to drain. Chop tomato pulp.

Sauté green pepper and onion in butter. Add tomato pulp and remaining ingredients except parsley; stir well. Spoon mixture into tomato shells, and place in a shallow baking dish. Bake at 350° for 25 to 30 minutes. Garnish with parsley. Yield: 6 servings.

Dorothy Adams,
Minden, Louisiana.

Serve Ground Beef Texas Style

Texans are fond of beef. And these recipes from Texas readers prove there is good reason. Each is a hearty entrée that stretches a pound of ground meat to serve at least six. We recommend them for flavor as well as economy.

Taco Beef-Noodle Bake is flavored with taco seasoning mix and baked under a layer of mozzarella cheese. A cornmeal pastry tops ground beef and pork for Sombrero Pie; and in El Dorado Casserole, ground beef is cooked with onion, ripe olives, and tomato sauce, then layered with crisp corn chips, Monterey Jack cheese, and a sour cream mixture; watch out for the green chiles when you bite into this one.

EL DORADO CASSEROLE

1 pound ground beef
1 medium onion, chopped
½ teaspoon garlic powder
2 (8-ounce) cans tomato sauce
1 cup ripe olives, sliced
1 (8-ounce) carton commercial sour cream
1 cup small-curd cottage cheese
¾ cup chopped green chiles
1 (7-ounce) package tortilla corn chips, crushed
2 cups (8 ounces) shredded Monterey Jack cheese

Cook ground beef until browned, stirring often to crumble; drain off drippings. Add next 4 ingredients; cook over low heat until onion is transparent.

Combine sour cream, cottage cheese, and chiles.

Layer half the chips, meat mixture, sour cream mixture, and cheese in a greased 2½-quart casserole; repeat the layers. Bake at 350° for 30 minutes. Yield: 8 servings.

Judy Garrett,
Austin, Texas.

SOMBRERO PIE

½ pound ground beef
½ pound ground lean pork
1 large onion, thinly sliced
2½ cups tomato juice
1 (10-ounce) package frozen whole kernel corn
1 to 2 tablespoons chili powder
1 teaspoon salt
¼ teaspoon pepper
Cornmeal Pastry

Cook ground beef, pork, and onion in a large skillet until meat is browned, stirring often to crumble meat; drain. Add tomato juice, corn, chili powder, salt, and pepper, mixing well. Bring to a boil; reduce heat, and simmer for 10 minutes.

Spoon mixture into a greased 12- x 8- x 2-inch baking dish; top with Cornmeal Pastry. Seal and flute edges. Cut slits in top for steam to escape. Bake at 400° for 30 to 35 minutes or until golden brown. Yield: 6 servings.

Cornmeal Pastry:

1 cup all-purpose flour
¼ cup cornmeal
½ teaspoon salt
⅓ cup plus 1 tablespoon shortening
3 tablespoons cold water

Combine flour, cornmeal, and salt; cut in shortening until mixture resembles coarse meal. Sprinkle evenly with

cold water, and stir with a fork until dry ingredients are moistened. On a lightly floured surface, roll pastry to a 12- x 8-inch rectangle. Yield: pastry for one 12- x 8- x 2-inch casserole.

Phyllis Owens,
Arlington, Texas.

FIVE-LAYER MEAL

1 (28-ounce) can whole tomatoes
1 pound ground beef
⅔ cup chopped onion
1 teaspoon salt
2 teaspoons chili powder
¼ teaspoon pepper
3 large potatoes, thinly sliced
1 cup uncooked regular rice
⅔ cup chopped green pepper
⅓ cup catsup

Drain tomatoes, reserving juice. Chop tomatoes; set aside.

Cook ground beef and onion until beef is browned, stirring often to crumble meat; drain off drippings. Add salt, chili powder, and pepper. Place potatoes in a greased 13- x 9- x 2-inch baking dish; sprinkle with rice. Top with ground beef mixture and green pepper. Combine reserved tomato juice and catsup; pour over casserole. Top with tomatoes. Cover and bake at 350° for about 1 hour or until the potatoes are tender. Yield: 6 to 8 servings.

Debbie Cornett,
Murchison, Texas.

HAMBURGER-NOODLE BAKE

1 pound ground beef
1 (16-ounce) can tomatoes
2 teaspoons sugar
1 teaspoon salt
1 (8-ounce) can tomato sauce
1 (5-ounce) package medium egg noodles
1 (3-ounce) package cream cheese, cubed and softened
1 (8-ounce) carton commercial sour cream
6 green onions, chopped
½ cup (2 ounces) shredded Cheddar cheese

Cook ground beef in a large skillet until browned, stirring often to crumble; drain off drippings.

Drain tomatoes, reserving juice; cut tomatoes into quarters. Add tomatoes, tomato juice, sugar, salt, and tomato sauce to ground beef; heat to boiling. Reduce heat, and simmer 20 minutes.

Cook noodles according to package directions; drain. Add cream cheese to hot noodles, mixing well. Add sour cream and green onion, stirring well. Alternate layers of meat mixture and noodle mixture in a lightly greased 2½-quart casserole, beginning and ending with meat mixture. Top with cheese. Bake at 350° for 30 minutes. Yield: 6 to 8 servings. *Mrs. Ray Pearce, Winnsboro, Texas.*

TACO BEEF-NOODLE BAKE

1 pound ground beef
½ cup chopped onion
1 (15-ounce) can tomato sauce
½ cup water
1 (1¼-ounce) package taco seasoning mix
2 (5-ounce) packages medium egg noodles
2 cups small curd cottage cheese
¼ cup commercial sour cream
1 tablespoon all-purpose flour
2 teaspoons beef-flavored bouillon granules
¼ cup chopped green onion
1 cup (4 ounces) shredded mozzarella cheese

Cook ground beef and onion until meat is browned, stirring often to crumble meat; drain off drippings. Add tomato sauce, water, and taco seasoning mix; bring to a boil. Reduce heat, and simmer 10 minutes.

Cook noodles according to package directions; drain. Combine noodles, cottage cheese, sour cream, flour, bouillon granules, and green onion; mix well. Spoon noodle mixture into a greased 2½-quart casserole. Top with meat mixture. Bake at 350° for 25 minutes; sprinkle with mozzarella cheese, and bake 5 additional minutes or until cheese melts. Let stand 10 minutes before serving. Yield: about 8 servings. *Sue Kercher, Richardson, Texas.*

Enchiladas, Hot And Saucy

If you like your enchiladas hot and saucy, this recipe is just what you may be looking for. The fried tortillas are wrapped around an onion-flavored meat filling, then baked in a cheese sauce that's spicy with green chiles.

These enchiladas also offer the convenience of advance preparation, just store in the refrigerator.

HOT AND SAUCY ENCHILADAS

1 pound ground beef
1 medium onion, chopped
1½ dozen frozen corn tortillas, thawed
Vegetable oil
1 (10¾-ounce) can cream of chicken soup, undiluted
1 (5.33-ounce) can evaporated milk
1 (8-ounce) package American process cheese slices
1 (4-ounce) can chopped green chiles, drained
1 (0.56-ounce) package green onion dip mix
1 teaspoon garlic salt
½ cup (2 ounces) shredded Cheddar cheese

Combine ground beef and onion in a large skillet; cook until the meat is browned, stirring to crumble. Drain well.

Fry tortillas, one at a time, in ¼ inch of hot oil; cook about 5 seconds on each side or just until softened. Drain well on paper towels. Spoon meat mixture evenly in center of each tortilla, and roll them up. Place tortillas, seam side down, in a jellyroll pan.

Combine remaining ingredients except Cheddar cheese in a small saucepan; cook over medium heat until the slices of American cheese melt. Pour evenly over enchiladas, and sprinkle with Cheddar cheese. Bake at 350° for 20 minutes or until bubbly. Yield: 6 to 9 servings.

Note: May be prepared ahead and stored in refrigerator. When ready to serve, bake enchiladas as directed.
Thelma Moore, Alexandria, Louisiana.

Fresh Fruit Means Fresh Dessert

Summer's best desserts start with fresh fruit at the moment of ripeness. Pick from Strawberry-Glaze Pie topped with whipped cream or hot peach cobbler for sweet treats. And you can mix summer's bounty for easy fruit cups, which can be either salad or dessert.

FRESH FRUIT MEDLEY

2 oranges, peeled and sectioned
2 apples, cubed
2 bananas, sliced
Orange Dressing

Combine orange sections, apples, and bananas. Serve with Orange Dressing. Yield: 4 to 6 servings.

Orange Dressing:

1 cup orange juice
½ cup sugar
2 teaspoons cornstarch

Combine all ingredients in a small saucepan. Cook, stirring constantly, until mixture is thickened. Cool. Yield: about 1 cup. *Mrs. Galen Johnson, Transylvania, Louisiana.*

FRUIT CUP

1 large cantaloupe
1 (11-ounce) can mandarin oranges, undrained
1 (20-ounce) can pineapple chunks, drained
3 to 4 fresh peaches, sliced
½ cup sugar
⅓ cup lemon juice

Peel cantaloupe, and cut into chunks. Combine with remaining ingredients. Chill. Keeps in refrigerator 4 to 5 days. Yield: about 6 servings. *Mabel Clarke, Martinsville, Virginia.*

STRAWBERRY-GLAZE PIE

1 cup sugar
2 tablespoons cornstarch
1 cup water
¼ cup strawberry-flavored gelatin
2 cups strawberries, halved
1 baked 9-inch pastry shell
Whipped cream

Combine sugar and cornstarch in a saucepan; stir in water. Cook over medium heat, stirring constantly, until thickened and clear. Remove from heat; stir in gelatin. Cool. Place strawberries in cooled pastry shell. Pour glaze over berries. Refrigerate pie before serving. Top with whipped cream. Yield: one 9-inch pie. *Mrs. Dennis Black, McCool, Mississippi.*

QUICK PEACH COBBLER

½ cup butter or margarine
1 cup self-rising flour
2 cups sugar, divided
1 cup milk
4 cups sliced fresh peaches

Melt butter in a 13- x 9- x 2-inch pan. Combine flour, 1 cup sugar, and milk; mix well. Pour over melted butter; do not stir. Combine peaches and remaining cup sugar in a saucepan; bring to a boil. Pour over batter; do not stir. Bake at 375° for 30 minutes or until browned. Yield: about 10 servings.

Sylvia Stephens,
New Hill, North Carolina.

Using too much flour when rolling pastry results in a tough crust. To reduce the amount of flour needed, use a stockinette rolling pin cover.

Mix Up Perfect Pastry

The home economists in our test kitchens have discovered an easy way to have tender, flaky pastry for every pie filling they test. They keep a batch of Perfect Pastry Mix in the refrigerator; then when a pastry shell is needed, it's simply a matter of taking out the amount of mix needed, adding cold water, and rolling out the dough.

Our home economists also offer these recommendations for working with pastry.

—Roll pastry on a lightly floured surface, but remember that too much flour toughens the crust. A stockinette rolling pin cover will minimize the amount of flour needed during rolling.

—Roll pastry lightly; too much handling will result in a tough crust.

—To transfer rolled pastry to pieplate, fold it into quarters and place in pan. Unfold pastry, being careful not to stretch it; if stretched, the crust will shrink during baking.

in a covered container, and store in refrigerator (keeps up to 1 month). Yield: seven 9-inch pastry shells.

PERFECT PASTRY SHELL

1¼ cups Perfect Pastry Mix
3 to 4 tablespoons cold water

Place pastry mix in a large mixing bowl. With a fork, stir in enough cold water (1 tablespoon at a time) to moisten dry ingredients. Shape dough into a ball.

Roll out dough to ⅛-inch thickness on a lightly floured surface. Place in a 9-inch pieplate; trim off excess pastry around edges. Fold edges under and flute; prick bottom and sides of shell with a fork. Bake at 425° for 12 to 15 minutes or until golden brown. Yield: one 9-inch pastry shell.

Note: Double the recipe for a double-crust pie. Do not prick shell if it will be filled before baking.

other protein-rich foods. But its delicate flavor and creamy texture also make cottage cheese a valuable addition to a variety of dishes.

For a quick and easy breakfast, stir cottage cheese into scrambled eggs along with Cheddar cheese, bacon, and mushrooms; the fluffy eggs come out extra special. Mixed with whipped cream, cottage cheese transforms congealed salad into a layered delight.

You can also bake cottage cheese into a ground beef casserole, or blend it into Lemon Cottage Cheese Pie, spiced with cinnamon and nutmeg.

CREAMY GROUND BEEF CASSEROLE

1½ pounds ground beef
1 (15-ounce) can tomato sauce
1 (8-ounce) package elbow macaroni
1 (8-ounce) package cream cheese, softened
1 (12-ounce) carton cottage cheese
1 (8-ounce) carton commercial sour cream
½ cup chopped onion
2 (6-ounce) packages sliced mozzarella cheese

Cook ground beef until browned, stirring to crumble. Drain off pan drippings, and stir in tomato sauce. Simmer the mixture about 20 minutes, stirring occasionally.

Cook macaroni according to package directions; drain and set aside.

Combine cream cheese, cottage cheese, sour cream, and onion; stir well. Layer half each of the macaroni, cottage cheese mixture, mozzarella cheese, and meat sauce in a lightly greased 13- x 9- x 2-inch baking dish; repeat layers, except for mozzarella cheese. Bake at 350° for 15 to 20 minutes; place remaining mozzarella cheese on top. Bake an additional 10 minutes or until cheese melts. Yield: 8 to 10 servings.

Kathy Greever,
Mountain City, Tennessee.

PERFECT PASTRY MIX

7 cups all-purpose flour
1 tablespoon salt
2 cups vegetable shortening

Combine flour and salt. Cut in shortening with pastry blender until mixture resembles coarse meal. Place pastry mix

Cottage Cheese Makes Eggs Fluffy, Pie Creamy

Those watching their weight rely on cottage cheese as a good source of protein that's lower in calories than many

COTTAGE CHEESE SCRAMBLED EGGS

6 eggs
½ cup cottage cheese
½ cup (2 ounces) shredded Cheddar cheese
½ cup sliced fresh mushrooms
1 tablespoon minced onion
6 slices bacon

Beat eggs; stir in cheese, mushrooms, and onion. Set aside.

Cook bacon in a medium skillet over low heat until crisp. Drain bacon; crumble and set aside. Pour off drippings, reserving 1 tablespoon in skillet. Add egg mixture; cook over medium heat, stirring often, until eggs are firm but still moist. Stir in bacon. Yield: 6 servings. *Mrs. E. J. Hughes, Jr., Falkner, Mississippi.*

SPINACH AND BACON SALAD

1 pound fresh spinach, torn
½ head iceberg lettuce, torn
4 slices bacon, cooked and crumbled
½ cup vegetable oil
¼ cup cider vinegar
2 tablespoons sugar
1 tablespoon poppy seeds
1 tablespoon onion juice
1 teaspoon salt
1 teaspoon dry mustard
¾ cup large-curd cottage cheese

Combine spinach, lettuce, and bacon in a large salad bowl; toss lightly.

Combine next 7 ingredients in a jar. Cover tightly, and shake vigorously. Stir in cottage cheese.

Pour dressing over spinach, and toss lightly. Yield: 8 to 10 servings.
Amelia M. Brown, Pittsburgh, Pennsylvania.

HAM AND SPINACH ROLL-UPS

1 (10-ounce) package frozen chopped spinach
2 cups small-curd cottage cheese
½ cup chopped green onion
½ teaspoon dry mustard
2 eggs, beaten
2 (16-ounce) packages thinly sliced cooked ham
1 (10¾-ounce) can cream of mushroom soup, undiluted
½ cup commercial sour cream

Cook spinach according to package directions; drain and press dry. Combine spinach, cottage cheese, onion, mustard, and eggs; mix well. Spread 1½ tablespoons spinach mixture on each ham slice. Roll up ham slices; place seam side down in a 13- x 9- x 2-inch baking dish. Set aside.

Combine mushroom soup and sour cream; mix well, and spread over ham rolls. Bake at 325° for 15 to 20 minutes or until well heated. Yield: 12 servings.
Mrs. Ralph Dillon, Boone, North Carolina.

EMERALD SALAD

1 (3-ounce) package lime-flavored gelatin
¾ cup boiling water
¾ cup shredded cucumber
2 tablespoons grated onion
1 (8-ounce) carton cream-style cottage cheese
1 cup mayonnaise
⅓ cup toasted slivered almonds (optional)

Dissolve gelatin in boiling water; chill until consistency of unbeaten egg white. Place cucumber and onion on paper towels, and squeeze out moisture.

Combine cottage cheese, mayonnaise, almonds, if desired, and vegetables; add to gelatin, stirring well. Pour into a lightly oiled 4-cup mold; chill until firm. Yield: 6 to 8 servings. *Sandy Preston, Biloxi, Mississippi.*

LAYERED CONGEALED SALAD

1 (3-ounce) package lemon-flavored gelatin
1 cup boiling water
1½ cups cottage cheese
1 cup whipping cream, whipped
1 (20-ounce) can crushed pineapple
1 (3-ounce) package lime-flavored gelatin
1 cup boiling water
⅓ cup chopped pecans
⅓ cup pimiento-stuffed olives, sliced (optional)
Leaf lettuce (optional)
Lime slices (optional)

Dissolve lemon gelatin in 1 cup boiling water; chill until consistency of unbeaten egg white. Beat on medium

speed of electric mixer until light and fluffy. Fold in cottage cheese and whipped cream. Pour into a lightly oiled 8-cup mold; refrigerate until firm.

Drain pineapple, reserving juice; add enough water to juice to make 1 cup. Set mixture aside.

Dissolve lime gelatin in 1 cup boiling water; stir in pineapple juice. Chill until consistency of unbeaten egg white. Stir in pineapple, pecans, and olives, if desired. Pour over first layer in mold. Chill until firm. Unmold on lettuce leaves; garnish with lime slices, if desired. Yield: 10 to 12 servings.
Mrs. H. G. Drowdy, Spindale, North Carolina.

LEMON COTTAGE CHEESE PIE

1 unbaked 10-inch pastry shell
1 (8-ounce) carton cottage cheese
1¼ cups sugar
1 tablespoon all-purpose flour
¼ teaspoon ground nutmeg
Grated rind and juice of 1 lemon
2 tablespoons melted butter or margarine
1 teaspoon vanilla extract
½ teaspoon salt
4 eggs, separated
2 teaspoons sugar
½ teaspoon ground cinnamon

Prick bottom of pastry shell with a fork. Bake at 350° for 8 minutes; cool on a wire rack.

Place cottage cheese in blender; blend until smooth. Pour into a large mixing bowl. Add next 7 ingredients and egg yolks; stir well.

Beat egg whites until stiff peaks form; fold into cottage cheese mixture. Pour into pastry shell. Combine 2 teaspoons sugar and cinnamon; mix well and sprinkle over pie. Bake at 350° for 30 to 35 minutes or until center is set. Yield: one 10-inch pie.

Note: Pie separates into two layers while baking. *Mrs. Harold Wagner, Hendersonville, North Carolina.*

Tip: Save lemon and orange rinds. Store in the freezer, and grate as needed for pies, cakes, breads, and cookies. Or the rinds can be candied for holiday uses.

Microwave Cookery

Process, Then Microwave

A food processor and a microwave oven are a natural team. That's how Pat Hodgson of Montgomery, Alabama, feels about it, and she's adapted many of her favorite recipes and created some new ones for quick preparation with these time-saving appliances.

For her Strawberry Soup Supreme, Pat purees the berries and mixes the soup in the food processor, then cooks it in the microwave oven. After chilling, it's served in melon halves.

She slices fresh squash in the processor for Jiffy Squash Casserole and microwaves it with only 3 tablespoons water to preserve nutrients. After mixing the casserole in the processor, it only takes 8 to 10 minutes to complete cooking in the microwave oven.

Pat also finds that these two appliances really come in handy when the vegetable garden is at its peak. She and her husband pick the fresh produce each night, slice it in the processor, blanch it in the microwave, and it's ready for freezing.

JIFFY SQUASH CASSEROLE

4 medium-size yellow squash
3 tablespoons water
1½ ounces Parmesan cheese
1 tablespoon butter or margarine
⅓ cup milk
3 slices bread, torn in pieces
1 egg
¼ teaspoon garlic salt
¼ teaspoon pepper
⅛ teaspoon salt
Dash of red pepper
Paprika

Position slicing disc in processor bowl, and top with cover. Arrange squash in food chute (cut large squash to fit); slice, applying firm pressure with food pusher.

Spoon squash into a 1½-quart casserole; add water. Cover and microwave at HIGH for 6 to 8 minutes or until squash is crisp-tender.

Position shredding blade in processor bowl. Cut Parmesan cheese (at room temperature) to fit food chute; shred, applying firm pressure with food pusher.

Microwave butter at HIGH for 30 to 40 seconds or until melted. Position knife blade in processor bowl. Combine squash, Parmesan, butter, and remaining ingredients except paprika in processor bowl; top with cover. Process 5 seconds or until squash is in small pieces. Return to casserole, and sprinkle with paprika.

Microwave at MEDIUM HIGH for 7 to 10 minutes or until firm but moist. Yield: 4 servings.

STRAWBERRY SOUP SUPREME

2 pints fresh strawberries
1 cup orange juice
1½ teaspoons quick-cooking tapioca
⅛ teaspoon ground cinnamon
⅛ teaspoon ground allspice
1 cup buttermilk
½ cup sugar
1 tablespoon lemon juice
1 teaspoon grated lemon rind
3 cantaloupe or honeydew melons, halved
Plain yogurt
Lemon zest

Wash strawberries, and reserve 6 berries for garnish. Hull remaining strawberries. Position knife blade in processor bowl, and top with cover; puree strawberries. Add orange juice, tapioca, cinnamon, and allspice; process 10 seconds.

Pour strawberry mixture into a 3-quart casserole. Microwave at HIGH for 5 to 6 minutes or until tapioca is transparent. Stir in buttermilk, sugar, lemon juice, and lemon rind. Cover and chill several hours or overnight.

Serve soup in melon halves; garnish with yogurt, lemon zest, and reserved strawberries. Yield: 4½ cups.

Let the food processor do the mixing for Strawberry Soup Supreme, a blend of fresh strawberries, orange juice, buttermilk, and spices. Then cook it in the microwave oven.

After a thorough chilling, the soup is spooned into melon halves and garnished with whole strawberries, plain yogurt, and lemon zest.

Ice Cream Makes This Pie

Imagine this for a frozen pie: vanilla ice cream laced with crème de menthe and crème de cacao, piled into a chocolate crust, and topped with whipped cream. Sound delicious? It is. Not only that, but Chocolate-Mint Ice Cream Pie is easy to assemble, and you keep it in the freezer until you need it.

CHOCOLATE-MINT ICE CREAM PIE

20 chocolate cream-filled cookies, crushed
¼ cup butter or margarine, softened
1 quart vanilla ice cream, softened
¼ cup plus 2 tablespoons green crème de menthe
2 tablespoons crème de cacao
1 cup whipping cream
2 tablespoons powdered sugar
Chocolate shavings
Chocolate curls

Combine chocolate cookie crumbs and butter; mix well, and press into a buttered 9-inch pieplate.

Combine ice cream, crème de menthe, and crème de cacao; mix until smooth. Spread ice cream mixture evenly over crust; cover and freeze.

Beat whipping cream until foamy; gradually add powdered sugar, beating until soft peaks form. Spread on pie. Garnish with chocolate shavings and curls, if desired; freeze until firm.

Let frozen pie stand at room temperature 5 minutes before slicing. Yield: one 9-inch pie.   *Millie Fetzer, Jacksonville, Florida.*

July

Nothing cools off the long hot days of July better than a slice of juicy melon, unless maybe it is Light Watermelon Sherbet or Minted Melon Cocktail. We describe how to pick that perfect melon and present tempting new ways to serve it.

If you don't want to heat up your house by cooking, turn to our no-cook menu. We also have vegetables that microwave in a fraction of the time they cook on the range.

And whether you are picnicking in the park or your own backyard, we have the pack-and-go favorites you will need. But who serves chilled soup in cantaloupe shells at the park? Our hostess—and she has other unique ideas that save time and make the meal special. Read on for other entertaining ideas in our special *Summer Suppers* section.

Melon Is A Taste Of Summer

The flavor of melon says summer. It's just that simple. Perhaps you remember barefoot trips into the patch to pick just the right-size melon, or maybe your talents include a thumping-thumb that picks the ripe one every time. One thing is for sure, any kind of melon is a cool, delicious treat when the weather gets hot.

True melon lovers agree that it's hard to improve upon the flavors of cantaloupes, honeydews, or watermelons just as they come from the patch. They keep spears or chunks of the fresh fruit in the refrigerator for a delicious snack. A little imagination works wonders; consider mixing melon with a minty syrup, pureeing it for a frosty beverage, freezing it in a creamy sherbet, or tossing some into a salad. The secret is picking a ripe melon.

Watermelon: Opinions vary on how to choose a ripe watermelon, with the different points of view generally divided into two groups: the "pluggers" and the "thumpers." The "pluggers" maintain that you should cut a small section of the melon and take a look. The "thumpers" insist that all that's really needed is a knuckle tap on the center of the melon; if it's ripe, you'll hear a dull sound.

Then there are those who disagree with both theories and prefer to choose a watermelon by outside color, with ripeness indicated by a dull, velvety rind color and a yellowish underside. On one method, however, all agree: The only foolproof way to always choose a ripe watermelon is to buy one that's cut so you can see for yourself what you're getting.

Cantaloupe: The guidelines for selecting a ripe cantaloupe seem more dependable. First of all, the stem should not be attached; instead, there should be a slight cavity at that end of the melon. If the cantaloupe is reasonably mature, the stem of the melon will have completely slipped away during harvest. This is the condition that experienced produce men look for when making their purchases.

Aroma is the other major factor to check for when selecting a cantaloupe. If a pronounced, fruity aroma is not evident, try gently mashing the stem cavity with your fingernail. If the characteristic aroma still isn't apparent, the cantaloupe probably is not ready to be eaten.

Honeydew: Aroma is also a sign of ripeness when choosing honeydew melons. A distinct and pleasing fragrance should be present at the stem end of the melon. A mature honeydew will also have a creamy-white or pale-yellow rind.

FRUITED HAM SALAD

2 cups diced cooked ham
1 cup diced celery
1 cup cubed honeydew melon
½ cup diced peeled apple
½ cup drained pineapple chunks
½ cup raisins
½ cup mayonnaise or salad dressing
Lettuce leaves

Combine first 7 ingredients, and toss gently. Chill. Serve on lettuce leaves. Yield: 6 to 8 servings. *Eva G. Key, Isle of Palms, South Carolina.*

MELON COOLER

2 cantaloupes, halved
1 to 1½ cups watermelon balls
½ cup seedless green grapes
½ cup fresh blueberries

Scallop edges of cantaloupe halves. Combine remaining ingredients, tossing gently. Spoon into cantaloupe halves. Yield: 4 servings.

MARINATED FRUIT DELUXE

1½ cups cantaloupe balls
1½ cups honeydew balls
1 (15¼-ounce) can pineapple chunks, drained
1 (11-ounce) can mandarin oranges, drained
1 cup fresh strawberries
1 (6-ounce) can frozen lemonade, thawed and undiluted
¼ cup orange marmalade
2 tablespoons Cointreau or other orange-flavored liqueur

Combine fruit in a large serving bowl. Cover and chill 2 hours.
Combine lemonade, marmalade, and liqueur; stir well, and pour over fruit. Toss gently. Yield: 6 to 8 servings.
Mrs. Harvey Kidd, Hernando, Mississippi.

MINTED MELON COCKTAIL

1 cup sugar
2 cups water
4 mint leaves
¼ cup lemon juice
2 cups cantaloupe balls
2 cups watermelon balls
2 cups honeydew balls
Mint sprigs

Combine sugar, water, and mint leaves in a saucepan; stir well. Bring to a boil over medium heat, and boil 2 minutes. Discard mint leaves. Add lemon juice to syrup mixture, stirring well. Chill thoroughly.
Combine melon balls in serving dish; pour syrup mixture over fruit, and toss gently. Garnish fruit with mint sprigs. Yield: 8 servings. *Kathleen D. Stone, Houston, Texas.*

ROYAL FRUIT CUPS

½ cup mayonnaise
1 tablespoon lemon juice
2 teaspoons sugar
1 cup cubed fresh pineapple
1 cantaloupe, peeled and cubed
½ cup seedless green grapes
1 cup fresh strawberries, halved
2 bananas, sliced
1 cup cubed watermelon
1 medium avocado, cubed
1 medium peach, peeled and cubed
1 cup miniature marshmallows (optional)
Lettuce leaves
Cottage cheese
6 to 8 maraschino cherries (optional)

Combine mayonnaise, lemon juice, and sugar; stir well, and set aside.
Combine the next 8 ingredients; add marshmallows, if desired. Toss gently. Spoon fruit into lettuce-lined sherbet or champagne glasses, and top each with a dollop of cottage cheese. Spoon mayonnaise mixture over each; top with a cherry, if desired. Yield: 6 to 8 servings.
Note: To prepare ahead, toss fruit (omitting marshmallows until serving time) with an ascorbic-citric mixture prepared according to the package directions. *Shirley Hodge, Delray Beach, Florida.*

Tip: To ripen cantaloupe or honeydew melons quickly, place them in a brown paper bag, close the top, and let sit a couple of days.

HONEYDEW FRUIT BOATS

1 (8-ounce) package cream cheese, softened
1 (7-ounce) jar marshmallow creme
1 tablespoon grated orange rind
1 tablespoon orange juice
Dash of ground ginger
1 cup seedless green grapes
1 cup fresh strawberries, halved
¾ cup mandarin orange sections
1¼ cups watermelon balls
2 large honeydew melons
Orange rind curls (optional)

Beat cream cheese until smooth; gradually add marshmallow creme, beating at medium speed of electric mixer until well blended. Add grated orange rind, orange juice, and ginger; beat mixture until light and fluffy.

Combine grapes, strawberries, orange sections, and watermelon balls.

Cut each honeydew into quarters, and scoop out seeds. Fill each melon quarter with mixed fruit, and top with a large dollop of cream cheese mixture. If desired, garnish each with an orange rind curl. Yield: 8 servings. *Janet Benton, Monroe, Georgia.*

CANTALOUPE COMPOTE

½ cup sugar
¼ cup water
¼ cup Cointreau
5 cups cantaloupe balls, chilled
Mint leaves (optional)

Combine sugar and water; bring to a boil. Remove from heat, and add Cointreau; chill. Combine cantaloupe balls and Cointreau mixture; chill. Serve in sherbet glasses; garnish with mint, if desired. Yield: 6 servings.

CANTALOUPE PUNCH

3½ cups cubed cantaloupe, chilled
3 cups pineapple juice, chilled
2 cups orange juice, chilled
⅓ cup sugar
2 tablespoons lemon juice
2 tablespoons lime juice
Maraschino cherries
Orange slices

Place cantaloupe in container of electric blender, and process until smooth; pour into pitcher or punch bowl. Stir in next 5 ingredients. Garnish with cherries and orange slices. Yield: about 7½ cups. *Mrs. Bud Holtum, Charlotte, North Carolina.*

LIGHT WATERMELON SHERBET

2 cups cubed watermelon
2 eggs
¾ cup sugar
⅛ teaspoon salt
1 quart half-and-half
1 tablespoon vanilla extract

Place watermelon in container of electric blender; process until smooth. Pour the watermelon puree through a strainer, reserving 1 cup juice; discard the pulp.

Beat eggs at medium speed of electric mixer until frothy. Combine sugar and salt; gradually add to eggs, beating until thick. Stir in half-and-half, vanilla, and watermelon juice.

Pour juice mixture into freezer can of a 1-gallon hand-turned or electric freezer. Freeze according to manufacturer's instructions. Let ripen at least 1 hour before serving. Yield: about ½ gallon. *Rosanne Bragwell, Pensacola, Florida.*

Give Jams And Jellies A New Twist

Grandma's fresh preserves were always a treat, but we've found some new ideas for jams and jellies that may have grandma begging for your recipes.

Some fruits naturally contain enough pectin to make the mixture gel, while others depend on the addition of commercial pectin. Your recipe will indicate if additional pectin is needed. For information to aid your jellymaking, refer to the tips on page 148.

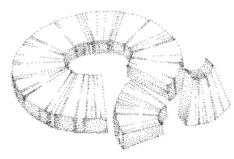

PINEAPPLE JAM

2 small fresh pineapples
2½ cups sugar
1 cup water
½ lemon, unpeeled and chopped

Remove leaf and stem ends from pineapples. Peel and trim all pineapple eyes; remove core. Finely chop pineapple, and measure 1 quart; reserve remaining pineapple for other uses.

Combine 1 quart pineapple and remaining ingredients. Gradually bring to a boil, stirring occasionally, until sugar dissolves. Boil until thick, about 30 minutes; stir frequently to prevent sticking.

Quickly pour jam into hot sterilized jars, leaving ¼-inch headspace. Cover at once with metal lids, and screw metal bands tight. Process 15 minutes in boiling-water bath. Yield: 2 half-pints.

STRAWBERRY JELLY

About 6 pints strawberries
7½ cups sugar
2 (3-ounce) packages liquid fruit pectin

Wash and hull strawberries. Place strawberries, one pint at a time, in a large clean cloth; gather edges of cloth up and over strawberries. Squeeze enough strawberries through cloth to extract 4 cups juice. Discard pulp.

Combine 4 cups juice and sugar in a large Dutch oven; bring to a rolling boil. Cook 1 minute, stirring frequently. Add pectin to strawberry mixture. Bring to a boil and continue boiling 1 minute, stirring frequently. Remove from heat.

Skim off foam with a metal spoon. Pour jelly into hot sterilized jars, leaving ½-inch headspace; seal with a ⅛-inch layer of paraffin. Cover with lids. Yield: about 8 half-pints.

PEACH PRESERVES

3½ cups sugar
2 cups water
5 cups sliced peaches (about 5 large)

Combine sugar and water in a large Dutch oven; cook over medium heat, stirring constantly, until sugar dissolves. Add peaches, and bring to a boil. Cook 20 minutes or until peaches are clear, stirring occasionally. Remove from heat; cover and let stand 12 to 18 hours in a cool place.

Drain peaches, reserving liquid in pan. Spoon peaches into hot sterilized jars; set aside. Bring liquid to a boil. Cook 2 to 3 minutes, stirring often; pour liquid over peaches, leaving ¼-inch headspace. Cover at once with metal lids, and screw metal bands tight. Process in a boiling-water bath 15 minutes. Yield: 5 half-pints.

CARROT-CITRUS MARMALADE

About 6 cups water
Grated rind of 1 large orange
Grated rind of 2 large lemons
4 cups grated carrots
Juice of 2 large oranges
Juice of 4 large lemons
About 3 cups plus 3 tablespoons sugar

Combine 3 cups water and rind in a heavy 5-quart Dutch oven. Bring to a boil; boil about 25 minutes or until about ½ cup liquid remains.

Add carrots and 3 cups water to rind mixture; boil 20 minutes. Combine fruit juices; add water, if necessary, to measure 1 cup. Add 1 cup fruit juice to carrot mixture. Measure amount of carrot and liquid; then add ⅔ cup sugar per 1 cup carrot and liquid. Stir well; bring mixture to a boil, and boil until mixture registers 220° on a candy thermometer (about 1 hour), stirring mixture frequently.

Quickly pour marmalade into hot sterilized jars, leaving ¼-inch headspace; cover at once with metal lids, and screw metal bands tight. Process in boiling-water bath 10 minutes. Yield: about 4 half-pints.

Tips For Jams And Jellies

Jams and jellies, as well as preserves, marmalades, and conserves, are some of the best ways to enjoy the fresh fruit of summer. To ensure your success with jellymaking, here are some pointers you need to know.

■ Follow your recipe exactly, and measure ingredients accurately. Jellymaking is not the time to cut back on sugar since it, along with pectin, promotes gel formation. Reducing sugar will make a syrup instead of a jam.

■ Start with a kettle large enough to allow the fruit mixture to double or triple in size as it boils.

■ Jelly glasses may be used for jelly only. For jam and other products containing pieces of fruit, standard canning jars and lids must be used for proper processing.

■ Have all glasses, jars, lids, and bands ready before starting to make the jelly. Wash them in warm sudsy water and rinse in hot water. Then boil them 10 minutes to sterilize, and leave in hot water until ready to use.

■ Canning jars and metal bands may be reused, but the lids must be new.

■ Use a funnel to pour the product into hot jars to keep rims of jars clean and promote a good seal.

■ To seal, using standard canning jars and lids, fill each hot jar to within ¼ inch of the top with hot fruit mixture. Wipe the jar rim clean, and place a hot metal lid on the jar with the sealing compound next to the glass; screw the metal band firmly in place.

■ After sealing with lids, process all jams, or products with pieces of fruit, in a boiling-water bath for time that recipe specifies. Jellies sealed with lids do not have to be processed.

■ When making jelly, you may prefer to seal the glasses or jars with paraffin. Pour the hot jelly mixture immediately into hot glasses, filling to within ½ inch of top. Melt paraffin in a double boiler, and spoon enough paraffin in each glass to make a layer ⅛ inch thick. Prick air bubbles in the paraffin before it gets firm. Cover with lids.

■ Let sealed jars stand overnight to make sure that seal has been made. If the seal has not been made, store jars in refrigerator.

Too Hot To Cook? Try Our No-Cook Meal

While July temperatures are soaring, take a break from cooking and serve this delicious cold meal. Built around a light, refreshing salmon salad, it's a perfect menu for lunch or a light dinner.

Crunchy Salmon Salad
Easy Marinated Asparagus
Breadsticks
Chocolate Almond Velvet
Chablis

CRUNCHY SALMON SALAD

1 (15½-ounce) can red salmon
1 cup diced celery
2 tablespoons chopped sweet pickle
1 tablespoon chopped green pepper
1 teaspoon chopped fresh chives
½ cup mayonnaise
2 tablespoons lemon juice
Lettuce leaves
Tomato wedges

Drain salmon, and remove skin and bones; flake salmon with a fork. Add celery, sweet pickle, green pepper, and chives; mix well. Combine mayonnaise and lemon juice; add to salmon, stirring well. Chill 2 to 3 hours. Serve salad on lettuce leaves with tomato wedges. Yield: 6 servings.   *Sarah Watson,*
Knoxville, Tennessee.

EASY MARINATED ASPARAGUS

2 (14½-ounce) cans asparagus spears, drained
1 green pepper, chopped
1 small bunch green onions with tops, chopped
1 stalk celery, finely chopped
¾ cup vegetable oil
½ cup red wine vinegar
½ cup sugar
½ clove garlic, minced
¼ teaspoon paprika
Pimiento strips

Place asparagus in a 13- x 9- x 2-inch baking dish. Combine next 8 ingredients; mix well and pour over asparagus; chill 4 hours or overnight. Drain marinade before serving; garnish with pimiento. Yield: 6 to 8 servings.
Betty Rabe,
Plano, Texas.

CHOCOLATE ALMOND VELVET

⅓ cup chocolate syrup
⅓ cup sweetened condensed milk
¼ teaspoon vanilla extract
1 cup whipping cream, whipped
¼ cup toasted slivered almonds

Combine chocolate syrup, condensed milk, and vanilla; chill. Fold whipped cream into chocolate mixture; pour into sherbet dishes. Sprinkle with almonds. Freeze 3 to 4 hours or until firm. Yield: 6 to 8 servings.   *Martha M. Dooley,*
Chattanooga, Tennessee.

summer Suppers

Southern Hospitality Moves Outdoors

As the afternoon sun slips over the horizon and the breezes blow a little cooler, Southerners take to the outdoors to enjoy the warm-weather season with friends and family. The activity generally centers around food, whether a complete meal or just appetizers and frosty beverages.

A salad-bar party is an excellent way to take advantage of the garden-fresh produce that's so plentiful now. The possibilities for stocking the salad bar are endless. For salad greens, there's spinach, along with many kinds of lettuce—Bibb, iceberg, romaine, Boston, escarole, and leaf. Select two or three that are in season.

When preparing the greens, remember to tear the greens rather than cut them, as a knife can bruise the leaves. Thoroughly wash the greens, and wrap them in a damp paper towel; place in a plastic bag, and store in the crisper section of the refrigerator.

For the salad fixings, emphasize variety. Include the classics—tomatoes, cucumbers, mushrooms, and carrots—but add unusual ingredients, such as sliced squash, broccoli, and marinated artichokes. Other possibilities are strips of ham, turkey, and cheese.

The crowning touch to any salad is the dressing. Our delicious homemade dressings—a spicy French, creamy blue cheese, and Greek Goddess—can be made well in advance of serving.

A light meal is the perfect opportunity to serve heavier appetizers and a rich dessert. We suggest Baked Chicken Nuggets and zesty Salmon Spread. Also Amaretto Cheesecake, garnished with toasted almonds and grated chocolate, is a delicious way to end the festivities.

Let our menu and recipes guide you in planning your own salad-bar party.

Baked Chicken Nuggets
Salmon Spread
Hot Five-Bean Salad
Assorted Salad Ingredients
Creamy Blue Cheese Dressing
Greek Goddess Dressing
Spicy French Dressing
Herb Croutons
Sesame-Cheddar Sticks
Amaretto Cheesecake
Wine   Beer   Iced Tea

BAKED CHICKEN NUGGETS

7 to 8 whole chicken breasts, boned
2 cups fine, dry breadcrumbs
1 cup grated Parmesan cheese
1½ teaspoons salt
1 tablespoon plus 1 teaspoon dried whole thyme
1 tablespoon plus 1 teaspoon dried whole basil
1 cup butter or margarine, melted

Cut chicken into 1½-inch pieces.
Combine breadcrumbs, cheese, salt, and herbs; mix well. Dip chicken pieces in butter, and coat with breadcrumb mixture. Place on a baking sheet in a single layer. Bake at 400° for 20 minutes or until done. Yield: 14 to 16 appetizer servings. *Don R. Ammerman, Orlando, Florida.*

SALMON SPREAD

2 (15½-ounce) cans red salmon
2 (8-ounce) packages cream cheese, softened
2 tablespoons lemon juice
1 tablespoon plus 1 teaspoon grated onion
2 teaspoons celery seeds
2 teaspoons prepared horseradish
½ teaspoon salt
Coarsely ground black pepper to taste
1 cup finely chopped pecans or walnuts
Fresh parsley

Drain salmon; remove skin and bones. Flake salmon with a fork.
Combine next 7 ingredients; mix well, and gently stir in salmon.
Spoon mixture into a well-oiled 5-cup mold. Chill several hours or overnight. Unmold on serving platter, and gently pat pecans over surface; garnish with parsley sprigs. Serve with assorted crackers. Yield: about 14 to 16 appetizer servings. *Marge Killmon, Annandale, Virginia.*

HOT FIVE-BEAN SALAD

8 slices bacon
⅔ cup sugar
2 tablespoons cornstarch
1½ teaspoons salt
Dash of pepper
¾ cup vinegar
½ cup water
1 (15½-ounce) can red kidney beans, drained
1 (16-ounce) can cut green beans, drained
1 (16-ounce) can lima beans, drained
1 (16-ounce) can wax beans, drained
1 (15-ounce) can garbanzo beans, drained
1 medium onion, sliced and separated into rings

Cook bacon in a large Dutch oven until crisp; drain well, reserving ¼ cup drippings in Dutch oven. Crumble the bacon, and set aside.
Add sugar, cornstarch, salt, and pepper to drippings; stir until smooth. Gradually add vinegar and water; cook over medium heat, stirring constantly, until thickened and bubbly.
Add beans to Dutch oven; cover and simmer 15 to 20 minutes. Add onion, tossing gently. Spoon salad into a 2½-quart serving dish, and sprinkle with bacon. Serve immediately. Yield: 14 to 16 servings. *Mrs. W. P. Chambers, Louisville, Kentucky.*

CREAMY BLUE CHEESE DRESSING

1½ cups cream-style cottage cheese
1 cup mayonnaise or salad dressing
½ cup crumbled blue cheese
¼ cup vinegar
½ teaspoon salt
6 drops of hot sauce

Combine all ingredients, mixing well. Chill thoroughly. Yield: 3 cups.

Mrs. Bruce Fowler,
Woodruff, South Carolina.

GREEK GODDESS DRESSING

1 (8-ounce) carton commercial sour cream
2 cups mayonnaise or salad dressing
½ cup finely chopped fresh parsley
¼ cup tarragon vinegar
1 green onion, minced
1 tablespoon lemon juice
½ teaspoon garlic powder

Combine all ingredients, mixing well. Chill overnight. Yield: 3⅓ cups.

Mrs. William S. Bell,
Chattanooga, Tennessee.

SPICY FRENCH DRESSING

1 cup vegetable oil
1 cup mayonnaise or salad dressing
1 (10¾-ounce) can tomato soup, undiluted
½ cup firmly packed brown sugar
⅓ cup vinegar or dry white wine
1 teaspoon dry mustard
1 teaspoon garlic salt
½ teaspoon onion salt
½ teaspoon celery salt
¼ teaspoon paprika
¼ teaspoon Worcestershire sauce
Dash of hot sauce

Combine all ingredients in container of electric blender; process on low speed until thoroughly blended. Chill at least several hours. Yield: about 4 cups.

Margaret Cotton,
Franklin, Virginia.

HERB CROUTONS

1½ cups butter or margarine, melted
1 tablespoon garlic powder
3 tablespoons parsley flakes
¼ teaspoon dried whole oregano
36 slices day-old bread, cut into ½-inch cubes

Combine first 4 ingredients, mixing well; pour over bread cubes. Gently toss until bread cubes are well coated. Place on baking sheet in a single layer. Bake at 275° for 1 hour, stirring occasionally. Yield: 4½ cups.

Mrs. William J. Morris,
Titusville, Florida.

SESAME-CHEDDAR STICKS

1½ cups all-purpose flour
2 teaspoons sesame seeds
½ teaspoon salt
1 cup (4 ounces) shredded sharp Cheddar cheese
½ cup butter or margarine
3 tablespoons Worcestershire sauce
2 teaspoons cold water

Combine flour, sesame seeds, and salt; stir well. Cut in cheese and butter until mixture resembles coarse meal. Combine Worcestershire sauce and water; sprinkle evenly over flour mixture, and stir with a fork until all ingredients are moistened. Shape into a ball.

Roll dough to ¼-inch thickness on a lightly floured surface, and cut into 3- x ½-inch strips.

Place strips on ungreased cookie sheets. Bake at 450° for 6 to 8 minutes or until golden. Place on wire racks to cool. Yield: about 6 dozen.

Linda Clark,
Charlottesville, Virginia.

AMARETTO CHEESECAKE

1½ cups graham cracker crumbs
2 tablespoons sugar
1 teaspoon ground cinnamon
¼ cup plus 2 tablespoons butter or margarine, melted
3 (8-ounce) packages cream cheese, softened
1 cup sugar
4 eggs
⅓ cup amaretto
1 (8-ounce) carton commercial sour cream
1 tablespoon plus 1 teaspoon sugar
1 tablespoon amaretto
¼ cup toasted sliced almonds
1 (1.2-ounce) chocolate candy bar, grated

Combine graham cracker crumbs, 2 tablespoons sugar, cinnamon, and butter; mix well. Firmly press mixture into bottom and ½ inch up the sides of a 9-inch springform pan.

Beat cream cheese with electric mixer until light and fluffy. Gradually add 1 cup sugar, mixing well. Add eggs, one at a time, beating well after each addition. Stir in ⅓ cup amaretto; pour into prepared pan. Bake at 375° for 45 to 50 minutes or until set.

Combine sour cream, 1 tablespoon plus 1 teaspoon sugar, and 1 tablespoon amaretto; stir well, and spoon over the cheesecake. Bake at 500° for 5 minutes. Let cool to room temperature; refrigerate 24 to 48 hours. (Cheesecake is best when thoroughly chilled and flavors have time to ripen.) Garnish with almonds and the grated chocolate. Yield: about 12 servings.

Mildred Williams,
Roanoke, Virginia.

Right: *Layered Salad Deluxe, Marinated Summer Salad, and Dilled Cucumber and Tomato Salad (recipes on page 153) are everything summer salads should be—cool, colorful, and prepared well in advance of serving.*

Page 152: *An array of summer's tastiest desserts and beverages comes from fresh lemons and limes. Clockwise: Lemon Zephers (page 172), Lemon Custard in Meringue Cups (page 173), Luscious Lime Mousse Freeze (page 173), Deluxe Lemon Meringue Pie (page 172), and Fresh Squeezed Lemonade (page 172).*

Salads To Make Now, Serve Later

Cool, colorful salads are as much a part of summertime menus as hamburgers cooked on the grill and homemade ice cream ripening in the freezer. And these are everything a warm-weather salad should be, yet they offer something more—that luxury of advance preparation that gives you a headstart on tomorrow's meal.

You can't think of make-ahead salads without marinated vegetables coming to mind. In both Dilled Cucumber and Tomato Salad and Marinated Summer Salad, the season's best produce chills overnight in a tangy marinade lightly seasoned with herbs. Layered Salad Deluxe takes crisp salad greens and layers them with bacon, water chestnuts, and hard-cooked eggs. After being spread with a sour cream dressing and thoroughly chilled, it's ready to toss and serve.

For those menus that call for a fruit salad, choose from two molded specialties: Frosted Orange Salad and Orange Sherbet Salad.

MACARONI-CRABMEAT SALAD

1 (8-ounce) package shell macaroni
1 (6½-ounce) can lump crabmeat, drained and flaked
½ cup chopped celery
1 small onion, chopped
2 hard-cooked eggs, finely chopped
3 slices bacon, cooked and crumbled
½ cup mayonnaise
1 tablespoon sweet pickle relish
1½ teaspoons lemon juice
½ teaspoon salt
¼ teaspoon dried parsley flakes
¼ teaspoon pepper
Paprika (optional)

Cook macaroni according to package directions; drain and cool. Add remaining ingredients except paprika, stirring gently. Cover and chill at least 2 hours. Sprinkle with paprika before serving, if desired. Yield: 8 to 10 servings.
Eunice C. Hudgins,
Salem, Virginia.

LAYERED SALAD DELUXE

1 pound fresh spinach, torn
1 medium head lettuce, torn
6 hard-cooked eggs, sliced
1 pound bacon, cooked and crumbled
1 (8-ounce) can water chestnuts, drained and sliced
1 (10-ounce) package frozen English peas, thawed
1 cup mayonnaise or salad dressing
½ cup commercial sour cream
½ (0.4-ounce) package buttermilk-mayonnaise dressing mix
Chopped fresh parsley (optional)

Layer first 6 ingredients in order listed in a large salad bowl.

Combine salad dressing, sour cream, and dressing mix; mix well. Spread over top of vegetables, sealing to edge of bowl. Garnish with chopped parsley, if desired. Cover tightly, and refrigerate several hours or overnight. Toss gently before serving. Yield: 12 to 15 servings.
Cheryl Smith,
Valdosta, Georgia.

MARINATED SUMMER SALAD

1 cup cauliflower flowerets
1 cup thinly sliced carrots
1 cup sliced fresh mushrooms
1 cup sliced brussels sprouts
1 cup thinly sliced yellow squash
1 cup broccoli flowerets
1½ cups thinly sliced zucchini
¾ cup lemon juice
¾ cup vegetable oil
3 tablespoons sugar
1 to 1½ teaspoons dried whole oregano
1 tablespoon salt
½ teaspoon pepper
½ cup thinly sliced radishes

Combine first 7 ingredients in a large shallow container. Combine remaining ingredients except radishes, mixing well. Pour marinade over vegetables, and toss salad lightly.

Cover and chill at least 12 hours or overnight, stirring occasionally. Stir in radishes just before serving. Yield: 10 to 12 servings.
Mrs. Carl Ramay,
Englewood, Colorado.

DILLED CUCUMBER AND TOMATO SALAD

1 large cucumber, thinly sliced
⅓ cup vegetable oil
3 tablespoons vinegar
½ teaspoon dried dillweed
¼ teaspoon sugar
½ teaspoon salt
⅛ teaspoon pepper
3 large tomatoes
Boston or leaf lettuce

Place cucumber in a shallow container. Combine next 6 ingredients in a small jar; cover tightly, and shake vigorously. Pour marinade over cucumber, and chill 6 hours or overnight.

Just before serving, slice tomatoes; remove cucumber from marinade. Arrange the vegetables on lettuce leaves, and spoon on the remaining marinade. Yield: 6 servings.
Claire Bastable,
Chevy Chase, Maryland.

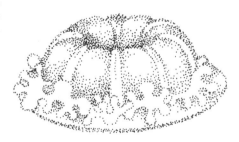

PERFECTION MOLDS

1 envelope unflavored gelatin
¼ cup sugar
½ teaspoon salt
1¼ cups cold water, divided
¼ cup vinegar
1 tablespoon lemon juice
1 cup chopped celery
½ cup finely shredded cabbage
2 tablespoons chopped green pepper
1 whole pimiento, diced

Combine gelatin, sugar, and salt in a small saucepan. Add ½ cup water; bring to a boil, and stir until gelatin is dissolved. Stir in remaining water, vinegar, and lemon juice. Chill until consistency of unbeaten egg white.

Stir vegetables into thickened gelatin mixture. Pour into 4 lightly oiled ½-cup molds. Chill until mixture is firm. Yield: 4 servings.
Cathy Darling,
Grafton, West Virginia.

ORANGE SHERBET SALAD

1 (6-ounce) package orange-flavored gelatin
1 cup boiling water
1 pint orange sherbet, softened
1 (8¼-ounce) can crushed pineapple, drained
1 (11-ounce) can mandarin orange sections, drained
1 cup miniature marshmallows
1 cup whipping cream, whipped

Dissolve gelatin in boiling water; add sherbet, stirring until melted. Chill until consistency of unbeaten egg white. Fold in remaining ingredients. Spoon into a lightly oiled 6-cup mold. Chill until firm. Yield: 8 servings.
Mrs. James T. Orrell,
Hot Springs, Arkansas.

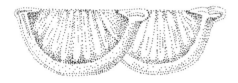

FROSTED ORANGE SALAD

1 (20-ounce) can pineapple chunks
1 (16-ounce) can sliced peaches
1 (6-ounce) package orange-flavored gelatin
1¼ cups boiling water
¾ cup ginger ale
1 cup whipping cream
½ cup mayonnaise or salad dressing
1 cup miniature marshmallows
3 tablespoons toasted coconut (optional)

Drain fruit, reserving juice; add enough water to juice to make 1¾ cups. Set fruit aside.

Dissolve gelatin in boiling water; stir in reserved juice and ginger ale. Chill until consistency of unbeaten egg white. Fold in fruit, and spoon into a lightly oiled 12- x 8- x 2-inch dish. Chill until firm.

Beat whipping cream until soft peaks form; fold in salad dressing and marshmallows. Spread topping over salad; sprinkle with coconut, if desired. Chill well. Yield: 12 servings.
Bettye Cartner,
Cerulean, Kentucky.

Cookouts & Summer Go Hand In Hand

Perhaps it's the tantalizing aroma of food cooking on the grill or the fellowship the occasion offers, but whatever the reason, cooking out is the rule of summer around the South.

Whether you grill chicken or ribs (we've included one of each), you can round out the menu with Make-Ahead Coleslaw, Three-Bean Bake, or Any Day Potato Salad. For dessert, we suggest Very Strawberry Ice Cream.

ANY DAY POTATO SALAD

5 to 6 medium-size new potatoes
½ cup chopped celery
½ cup chopped sweet pickle
¼ cup chopped onion
¼ cup chopped green pepper
¼ cup vinegar
1 tablespoon sugar
¾ teaspoon salt
¼ teaspoon pepper
½ cup mayonnaise
2 tablespoons prepared mustard
2 tablespoons sweet pickle juice
½ teaspoon sugar
Leaf lettuce (optional)
Chopped fresh parsley (optional)
Sliced hard-cooked eggs
Pimiento strips

Cook potatoes in boiling water about 30 minutes or until tender. Drain well, and cool. Peel potatoes, and cut into ½-inch cubes.

Combine potatoes, celery, pickle, onion, and green pepper in a large bowl; toss lightly.

Combine vinegar, 1 tablespoon sugar, salt, and pepper; stir until sugar and salt are dissolved. Pour over potato mixture; stir to coat vegetables. Chill.

Combine mayonnaise, mustard, pickle juice, and ½ teaspoon sugar; stir well. Pour over potato mixture; stir to coat vegetables. Chill thoroughly. Serve potato salad in a lettuce-lined bowl, and garnish with chopped parsley, if desired.

Top with egg slices and pimiento strips. Yield: 6 servings. *Lynette Walther,*
Palatka, Florida.

GRILLED BARBECUED CHICKEN

1 cup red wine vinegar
½ cup vegetable oil
1½ teaspoons hot sauce
Dash of garlic salt
1 (2½- to 3-pound) broiler-fryer, quartered
Salt to taste
Parsley (optional)

Combine first 4 ingredients in a jar; cover tightly, and shake vigorously.

Sprinkle chicken with salt, and place skin side down on grill. Brush with sauce. Grill over medium coals 50 to 60 minutes or until tender, turning chicken and brushing with sauce about every 10 minutes. Garnish with parsley, if desired, before serving. Yield: 4 servings.
Sara A. McCullough,
Broaddus, Texas.

LEMON GRILLED RIBS

½ cup water
1 chicken-flavored bouillon cube
1 cup pineapple juice
3 tablespoons brown sugar
2 cloves garlic, minced
¼ cup minced onion
¼ cup catsup
¼ cup lemon juice
2 tablespoons cornstarch
Salt and pepper
3 pounds spareribs or country-style spareribs

Combine first 9 ingredients in a saucepan, and season to taste with salt and pepper. Bring to a boil, stirring well. Lower heat, and simmer 5 minutes; set aside.

Cut ribs into serving-size pieces (3 to 4 ribs per person). Place ribs, bone side down, on grill over slow coals. Grill about 20 minutes; turn meaty side down, and cook until browned. Turn meaty side up again, and grill about 20 minutes longer. Brush meaty side with sauce mixture. Continue to grill, without turning, 20 to 30 minutes; baste occasionally. Brush sauce on both sides of the ribs, and let cook 2 to 3 minutes on each side. Yield: 4 to 6 servings.

Peggy Fowler Revels,
Woodruff, South Carolina.

MAKE-AHEAD COLESLAW

1 large head cabbage, shredded
2 green onions, finely chopped
2 stalks celery, chopped
2 large carrots, shredded
1 large green pepper, chopped
1 cucumber, thinly sliced
½ cup red or white wine vinegar
½ cup vegetable oil
½ cup sugar
½ teaspoon salt
¼ teaspoon pepper
1 teaspoon dry mustard
Additional cucumber slices (optional)

Combine first 6 ingredients in a large bowl; mix well, and set aside.

Combine next 6 ingredients in a small saucepan, mixing well. Bring to a boil and cook 3 minutes, stirring occasionally. Pour over vegetables, tossing well. Cover and refrigerate overnight. Garnish with cucumber slices, if desired, before serving. Yield: 8 to 10 servings.

Fay Crow,
Clinton, Arkansas.

THREE-BEAN BAKE

3 slices bacon
1 medium onion, chopped
1 medium-size green pepper, chopped
2 (16-ounce) cans baked beans
1 (16-ounce) can lima beans, drained
1 (15½-ounce) can kidney beans, undrained
½ cup chili sauce
2 tablespoons brown sugar
3 tablespoons vinegar
½ teaspoon dry mustard
¼ teaspoon pepper

Cook bacon in a medium skillet until crisp; drain, reserving 2 tablespoons drippings in skillet. Crumble bacon, and set aside. Sauté onion and green pepper in drippings until tender.

Combine onion mixture, bacon, and remaining ingredients; stir well. Spoon mixture into a greased 2½-quart casserole. Bake, uncovered, at 350° for 1 hour. Yield: about 8 to 10 servings.

Mrs. Frank Tetrault,
Southlake, Texas.

VERY STRAWBERRY ICE CREAM

2 (3-ounce) packages strawberry-flavored gelatin
2 cups boiling water
2 eggs
1½ cups sugar
1 (13-ounce) can evaporated milk
6 cups milk
1 teaspoon vanilla extract
1 quart strawberries, mashed

Dissolve gelatin in boiling water; cool slightly. Set aside.

Beat eggs with electric mixer at medium speed until frothy. Gradually add sugar, beating until thick. Add gelatin mixture, milk, and vanilla; mix well. Stir in strawberries.

Pour mixture into freezer can of a 1-gallon hand-turned or electric freezer. Freeze according to manufacturer's directions. Let ripen at least 1 hour. Yield: about 1 gallon.

Mrs. Gerard R. Franz, Jr.,
Jacksonville, Florida.

Something Frosty To Sip

The only thing more refreshing than relaxing in the shade on a hot summer afternoon is relaxing in the shade while sipping one of these frosty drinks.

Peach ice cream, rum, and fresh peaches are whirled in the blender for refreshing Peach Frosty. Orange juice and fruit flavor Banana-Orange Slush and Peachy Orange Shake. And frozen lemonade gives a different twist to the all-time favorite strawberry daiquiri. And what could be more Southern than an ice-cold mint julep?

BANANA-ORANGE SLUSH

3 cups water
1 (6-ounce) can frozen orange juice concentrate, undiluted
10 to 12 ice cubes
1 banana
1 (12-ounce) can ginger ale, chilled

Combine water, orange juice, ice cubes, and banana in container of electric blender; process until smooth. Combine orange juice mixture and ginger ale; stir gently. Yield: about 5 cups.

Mrs. Charles Price,
Houston, Texas.

MINT JULEPS

12 cups bourbon
2 tablespoons sugar
3 cups water
Fresh mint leaves
Finely crushed ice
Fresh mint sprigs

Place bourbon in freezer 24 hours prior to preparing mint juleps (the bourbon won't freeze, but it will acquire a syrup-like consistency).

For each serving, place ¼ teaspoon sugar in a julep cup; add 2 tablespoons water and 7 fresh mint leaves. Stir gently until sugar is dissolved.

Add ½ cup bourbon to each cup, stirring gently. Add enough finely crushed ice to fill cup; stir gently. Place in freezer, and freeze at least 3 hours.

Before serving, break the ice with a spoon; then garnish each julep with fresh mint sprigs. Yield: 24 servings.

Quentin Crommelin,
Wetumpka, Alabama.

FROSTY SOURS

⅓ cup bourbon
1 (6-ounce) can frozen lemonade
   concentrate, undiluted
1 tablespoon frozen orange juice
   concentrate, undiluted
Cracked ice

Combine first 3 ingredients in container of electric blender; process until smooth. Gradually add ice, processing until mixture reaches desired consistency. Yield: 4 cups.
Walter W. Wickstrom,
Pelham, Alabama.

PEACHY ORANGE SHAKE

1 (8-ounce) can sliced peaches
2 cups orange juice
2 tablespoons peach yogurt
1 pint vanilla ice cream, softened and
   cut into pieces
2 tablespoons milk

Drain peaches, reserving 2 tablespoons syrup. Combine peaches, reserved syrup, and remaining ingredients in the container of electric blender; process until smooth. Yield: about 5 cups.
Linda E. Whitt,
Missouri City, Texas.

PEACH FROSTY

1 cup peach ice cream
½ cup light rum
3 tablespoons powdered sugar
3 fresh peaches, unpeeled and sliced
Cracked ice

Combine ice cream, rum, sugar, and peaches in container of electric blender; process until smooth. Add ice to within 1 inch of container top; blend well. Yield: about 5 cups. *Jeane Baughan,*
Birmingham, Alabama.

STRAWBERRY DAIQUIRI

4 cups frozen strawberries, thawed
1 (6-ounce) can frozen pink lemonade
   concentrate, thawed and undiluted
¾ cup light rum
Cracked ice

Combine half each of strawberries, lemonade, and rum in container of electric blender; process until smooth. Gradually add ice, processing until mixture reaches desired consistency. Pour into serving glasses.
Repeat the process with the remaining ingredients. Yield: about 6 cups.
Larry A. Bonorato,
Huntsville, Alabama.

This Picnic Matches The Performance

Suzanne and Randy Nuckolls of Arlington, Virginia, take a picnic to Wolf Trap Farm Park for the Performing Arts and share it with friends before the evening's entertainment.

Suzanne's menu reflects the careful attention she gives to keeping foods hot or cold. Along with flavor and variety, the menu offers simplicity in both preparation and serving.

Once a picnic site is selected, guests sip sangría while the last-minute touches are put on the meal. The first course is cantaloupe soup served icy cold in the scooped-out melon halves.

The Dijon Chicken is "perfect picnic fare," Suzanne says, "whether served hot, warm, or cold." Spinach-and-Onion Salad Bowl is easily packed for the picnic in a plastic bag with a zip seal, and the dressing is taken in a jar.

Other dishes carefully selected to round out the menu are Squash-Carrot Casserole, Sally Lunn served with zesty Tomato-Cheese Spread, and Old-Fashioned Gingerbread for dessert.

Quick Sangría
Chilled Cantaloupe Soup
Dijon Chicken
Squash-Carrot Casserole
Spinach-and-Onion Salad Bowl
Sally Lunn   Tomato-Cheese Spread
Old-Fashioned Gingerbread

QUICK SANGRIA

2 (12-ounce) cans frozen pink lemonade
   concentrate, thawed and undiluted
1 (33.8-ounce) bottle rosé, chilled
1 (33.8-ounce) bottle Burgundy, chilled
Juice of 2 limes
2 (33.8-ounce) bottles club soda, chilled
1 lemon, thinly sliced
1 lime, thinly sliced
1 orange, thinly sliced

Combine first 4 ingredients, mixing well. Slowly stir in club soda. Garnish with lemon, lime, and orange slices. Serve over ice. Yield: about 5 quarts.

CHILLED CANTALOUPE SOUP

6 medium cantaloupes, halved
¾ cup dry sherry
¾ cup sugar
1½ cups orange juice
Mint leaves

Scoop pulp from each cantaloupe, leaving shells ½ inch thick. Cut a thin slice from bottom of each shell, being careful not to cut a hole in shell.

Combine cantaloupe pulp and next 3 ingredients in the container of electric blender; process until smooth. Chill thoroughly. Serve soup in cantaloupe shells, and garnish with mint. Yield: 12 servings.

DIJON CHICKEN

6 whole chicken breasts, halved
Salt and pepper to taste
Garlic powder to taste
1½ cups commercial sour cream
1½ cups Dijon mustard
1 (8-ounce) package Italian-style fine
   breadcrumbs
Parsley

Lightly sprinkle chicken with salt, pepper, and garlic powder.
Combine the sour cream and mustard in a shallow dish, mixing well. Dip each

chicken breast into mustard mixture, and dredge in breadcrumbs. Arrange chicken in a single layer in baking pans. Bake at 375° for 50 minutes or until tender. Garnish with parsley. Yield: 12 servings.

SQUASH-CARROT CASSEROLE

2 dozen round buttery crackers
1 (8-ounce) package cream cheese, softened
2 (10¾-ounce) cans cream of chicken soup, undiluted
2 eggs, beaten
½ cup butter or margarine, melted
8 cups (about 2½ pounds) sliced yellow squash, cooked
6 small carrots, grated
1 cup finely chopped onion
1 cup herb-seasoned stuffing mix

Place crackers in a greased 13- x 9- x 2-inch baking dish; set aside.

Combine cream cheese, soup, eggs, and butter; beat well. Stir in squash, carrot, and onion. Spoon into prepared baking dish; sprinkle with stuffing mix. Bake at 350° for 30 to 40 minutes. Yield: 10 to 12 servings.

SPINACH-AND-ONION SALAD BOWL

3 large oranges
1 medium-size purple onion, thinly sliced and separated into rings
1 pound fresh spinach, torn
Dressing (recipe follows)
6 slices bacon, cooked and crumbled

Peel and slice oranges; cut slices in half. Combine oranges, onion, and spinach in a large bowl; add dressing, tossing gently. Sprinkle with bacon. Yield: 10 to 12 servings.

Dressing:

2 to 3 tablespoons cider vinegar
1 tablespoon sugar
½ teaspoon salt
¼ teaspoon dry mustard
⅓ cup vegetable oil

Combine all ingredients in container of electric blender; process well. Yield: about ⅓ cup.

SALLY LUNN

1 cup milk, scalded
½ cup butter
3 tablespoons sugar
1 teaspoon salt
2 eggs
1 package dry yeast
⅓ cup warm water (105° to 115°)
4 cups all-purpose flour
2 tablespoons butter, melted

Combine milk, ½ cup butter, sugar, and salt in a large mixing bowl; stir until butter melts. Let cool to 105° to 115°. Add eggs, beating well.

Dissolve yeast in warm water, and stir into milk mixture. Add flour, stirring until smooth. Cover and let rise in a warm place (85°), free from drafts, 1 hour or until doubled in bulk.

Punch dough down, and pour into a greased Bundt pan. Cover and let rise in a warm place (85°), free from drafts, 35 minutes or until doubled in bulk.

Brush top of dough with melted butter. Bake at 350° for 45 to 55 minutes. Remove bread from pan, and place on wire rack to cool. Yield: one 10-inch loaf.

TOMATO-CHEESE SPREAD

2 cups (8 ounces) shredded Cheddar cheese
1 cup peeled, chopped fresh tomatoes
1 (8-ounce) package cream cheese, softened
½ cup butter or margarine, softened
⅓ cup finely chopped onion
1 teaspoon salt
⅛ teaspoon red pepper
Dash of garlic powder
1½ cups chopped pecans
Parsley
Cherry tomatoes

Combine first 8 ingredients, mixing well; shape into a log (mixture will be soft). Roll log in pecans, coating well.

Carefully place log on serving platter, bringing ends together to form a ring. Cover and chill 2 hours. Garnish with parsley and cherry tomatoes. Yield: 1 cheese ring.

OLD-FASHIONED GINGERBREAD

1 cup molasses
½ cup sugar
½ cup butter or margarine, softened
½ cup boiling water
1 egg
1 teaspoon soda
1 teaspoon ground ginger
1 teaspoon ground cinnamon
½ teaspoon salt
½ teaspoon ground allspice
3 cups all-purpose flour
Lemon-Cream Cheese Frosting
Lemon twists

Combine molasses and sugar; mix well. Add next 9 ingredients in order listed, mixing well. Pour batter into a greased and floured 13- x 9- x 2-inch baking pan.

Bake at 350° for 25 to 30 minutes or until wooden pick inserted in center comes out clean. Do not remove from pan. Let cool completely; spread top of gingerbread with the Lemon-Cream Cheese Frosting. Cut into squares, and garnish with lemon twists. Yield: 15 to 18 servings.

Lemon-Cream Cheese Frosting:

1 (3-ounce) package cream cheese, softened
¼ cup butter, softened
2 cups sifted powdered sugar
1 teaspoon grated lemon rind
½ teaspoon lemon extract

Combine cream cheese and butter, beating until light and fluffy. Add sugar, and beat well. Stir in lemon rind and lemon extract. Yield: about 1 cup.

Tip: Lightly oil the cup or spoon used to measure honey or molasses. No-stick cooking spray works well for this.

Vegetables With The Garden-Freshest Flavor

In summer, nutrition comes easily in delicious red, green, and yellow packages of garden-fresh vegetables. Take advantage of their abundance, and try one of these new ideas.

Thread corn, zucchini, and onions on skewers, and broil them with an herb-butter sauce for Fresh Vegetable Kabobs. Top zucchini and yellow squash with cheese for Green-and-Gold Scallop, and prepare Okra-Corn-Tomato Medley—the vegetables are sautéed with onion in bacon drippings.

These Fresh Vegetable Kabobs are basted with an herb butter sauce.

SWEET-AND-SOUR GREEN BEANS

1½ pounds fresh green beans
1 quart water
Salt to taste
4 slices bacon
2 medium onions, thinly sliced
1 tablespoon dry mustard
1 teaspoon salt
2 tablespoons brown sugar
2 tablespoons sugar
¼ cup vinegar

Remove strings from beans; cut beans into 1½-inch pieces. Wash thoroughly. Place water, salt, and beans in a medium saucepan, and bring to a boil. Reduce heat; cover and simmer 10 to 15 minutes or until beans are crisp-tender. Drain the beans, reserving 1 cup liquid; set aside.

Cook bacon in a large skillet until crisp; remove bacon, reserving drippings in skillet. Crumble bacon, and set aside. Sauté onion in bacon drippings until tender; gradually stir in mustard.

Combine 1 teaspoon salt, sugar, reserved bean liquid, and vinegar; pour over onion. Bring to a boil, stirring to blend well. Add beans and bacon; cover and simmer about 15 minutes. Yield: 6 servings.   *Ann Elsie Schmetzer,*
Madisonville, Kentucky.

FRESH VEGETABLE KABOBS

2 medium ears fresh corn
2 medium zucchini
8 boiling onions
½ cup butter or margarine, melted
2 tablespoons minced fresh chives
2 tablespoons chopped fresh parsley
½ teaspoon garlic salt

Remove shucks and silk from corn. Slice corn and zucchini into 1-inch pieces (an electric knife works well with corn). Peel onions. Thread the vegetables, alternately, on 4 large skewers.

Combine butter, chives, parsley, and garlic salt, stirring well.

Place skewers on a 13- x 9- x 2-inch baking pan (skewers may rest on edges of pan); broil about 8 minutes, turning and brushing vegetables with butter sauce at 2-minute intervals. Yield: 4 servings.

Tip: Wash or chop vegetables and open cans before you begin preparing any recipe. It is also a good idea to have most ingredients measured before beginning to cook.

OKRA-POTATO FRY

1 pound okra
⅓ cup cornmeal
¼ cup all-purpose flour
1 teaspoon salt
½ teaspoon pepper
Vegetable oil
2 medium potatoes, peeled and cut into
  ½-inch cubes

Wash okra well; drain. Cut off tip and stem ends; cut okra into ½-inch slices, and set aside.

Combine cornmeal, flour, salt, and pepper, mixing well. Dredge the okra in the cornmeal mixture; cook in ½ inch oil over high heat until golden, stirring occasionally. Add potatoes; cook until potatoes are golden and okra is light brown. Drain; serve immediately. Yield: 6 servings. *Mrs. Harry Lay, Jr.,
Fairmount, Georgia.*

OKRA-CORN-TOMATO MEDLEY

1 medium onion, chopped
3 tablespoons bacon drippings or
  margarine
2 cups sliced fresh okra
2 cups fresh corn cut from cob
3 cups peeled and chopped tomatoes
1 teaspoon sugar
1 teaspoon salt
¼ teaspoon pepper

Sauté onion in bacon drippings until tender; add okra and cook 5 minutes, stirring occasionally. Add remaining ingredients; stir well. Cover and simmer 15 minutes or until corn is tender. Yield: 6 servings. *Dorsella Utter,
Columbia, Missouri.*

PEPPERS DELUXE

6 large green peppers
1 cup cooked rice
½ cup peeled chopped tomato
1 cup (4 ounces) shredded Cheddar cheese
½ teaspoon curry powder
1 teaspoon lemon pepper seasoning
1 cup soft breadcrumbs
2 tablespoons butter or margarine

Cut off tops of green peppers; remove seeds. Cook peppers 5 minutes in boiling salted water to cover; drain and set aside.

Combine rice, tomato, cheese, curry powder, and lemon pepper; mix well, and spoon into peppers. Place in a lightly greased 8-inch square baking dish; bake at 350° for 15 minutes. Spoon breadcrumbs on top of each pepper; dot with butter. Bake an additional 15 minutes. Yield: 6 servings.
*Mrs. William Bell,
Chattanooga, Tennessee.*

POSH SQUASH

2 pounds yellow squash, sliced
1 cup mayonnaise
1 cup grated Parmesan cheese
1 small onion, chopped
2 eggs, beaten
½ teaspoon salt
¼ teaspoon pepper
½ cup soft breadcrumbs
1 tablespoon butter or margarine, melted

Cook squash, covered, in boiling salted water 10 to 15 minutes or until tender. Drain and cool slightly.

Combine mayonnaise, cheese, onion, eggs, salt, and pepper; stir until well combined. Add squash, stirring gently. Pour squash mixture into a lightly greased 1½-quart casserole.

Combine breadcrumbs and butter; spoon over squash mixture. Bake at 350° for 30 minutes. Yield: 6 servings.
*Linda Radomski,
Birmingham, Alabama.*

GREEN-AND-GOLD SCALLOP

1 medium onion, chopped
2 tablespoons vegetable oil
2 medium zucchini, grated
2 medium-size yellow squash, grated
1 cup unsalted cracker crumbs
3 eggs, slightly beaten
2 tablespoons chopped fresh parsley
½ teaspoon salt
½ teaspoon dried whole oregano
¼ teaspoon pepper
1 cup (4 ounces) shredded Cheddar cheese

Sauté onion in oil until tender. Remove from heat; stir in remaining ingredients, except cheese. Spoon one-third of mixture into a 1½-quart casserole. Sprinkle ¼ cup cheese over squash. Repeat layers, ending with squash mixture. Sprinkle remaining ½ cup cheese in a crisscross design over squash. Bake at 325° for 45 minutes. Yield: about 4 to 6 servings. *Sara B. Tucker,
Arlington, Texas.*

TOMATO MEDLEY

3 tablespoons vegetable oil
2 large onions, cut into eighths
2 large green peppers, cut into eighths
4 firm tomatoes, cut into eighths
1 tablespoon brown sugar
1 tablespoon cornstarch
1 tablespoon soy sauce
½ cup water

Heat oil in a skillet over medium heat; add onion and sauté 5 minutes, stirring frequently. Add green peppers and tomatoes to skillet.

Combine brown sugar and cornstarch; stir in soy sauce and water. Add mixture to skillet, and cook until thickened, stirring constantly. Cover and cook until vegetables are crisp-tender, stirring occasionally. Yield: 6 servings.
*Mrs. Cecil R. Lemley,
Little Rock, Arkansas.*

Tip: Chopped onions have the best flavor if they are browned in shortening before being added to casserole dishes.

CHEESE-TOPPED TOMATOES

5 medium tomatoes
¼ cup soft breadcrumbs
¼ cup grated Parmesan cheese
1 tablespoon butter or margarine, melted
⅛ teaspoon salt
⅛ teaspoon sugar
⅛ teaspoon garlic powder
Dash of dried whole basil
Dash of ground oregano

Remove stems from tomatoes, and cut a ¼-inch slice from top of each.

Combine remaining ingredients, stirring well. Press about 2 tablespoons cheese mixture on top of each tomato. Place tomatoes in a greased 9-inch square baking pan. Bake at 350° for 20 minutes. Yield: 5 servings.
*M. L. Wessels,
Carlisle, Pennsylvania.*

Have A Party With Fruit And Cheese

Bring out the fruit and cheese, add a glass of wine, and even the simplest gathering becomes a festive occasion.

Some of our appetizers combine both the fruit and cheese in one. Pineapple Cheese Ball combines cream cheese and crushed pineapple, while Gruyère-Apple Spread features the nutty flavor of Gruyère with cream cheese and grated apple.

For our Heavenly Fruit Dip, whipped cream is folded into a pineapple sauce and served with fresh fruit for dipping.

Don't miss Bear Claws—they're an unusual version of cheese straws.

HEAVENLY FRUIT DIP

½ cup sugar
2 tablespoons all-purpose flour
1 cup pineapple juice
1 egg, beaten
1 tablespoon butter or margarine
1 cup whipping cream, whipped

Combine first 5 ingredients in a heavy saucepan; cook over medium heat, stirring constantly, until smooth and thickened. Let cool completely; fold in whipped cream. Serve with fresh fruit. Yield: about 2 cups.
*Mrs. John R. Allen,
Dallas, Texas.*

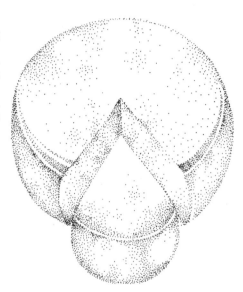

SIX-LAYER DIP

2 large avocados
⅛ teaspoon garlic powder
⅛ teaspoon garlic salt
1 tablespoon lemon juice
2 tablespoons mayonnaise
1 (8-ounce) carton commercial sour cream
2 (8-ounce) jars picante sauce
¾ cup chopped ripe olives
3 cups (about 3 medium) peeled and chopped tomatoes
1½ cups (6 ounces) shredded Cheddar cheese

Peel, seed, and mash avocados; stir in garlic powder, garlic salt, lemon juice, and mayonnaise. Spread evenly in a 12- x 8- x 2-inch baking dish. Carefully spread the sour cream over avocado mixture.

Drain picante sauce well; spoon over sour cream. Top with layers of olives and tomatoes; sprinkle with cheese. Serve with large corn chips. Yield: about 6 cups. *Janet Revels,
Dallas, Texas.*

GRUYERE-APPLE SPREAD

1 (8-ounce) package cream cheese, softened
1 cup (4 ounces) shredded Gruyère cheese
1 tablespoon milk
2 teaspoons prepared mustard
⅓ cup shredded peeled apple
2 tablespoons finely chopped pecans
2 teaspoons chopped chives

Combine first 4 ingredients; beat at medium speed of electric mixer 3 minutes. Stir in remaining ingredients. Cover and chill at least 1 hour. Serve with crackers. Yield: about 2¼ cups.
*Janet M. Filer,
Arlington, Virginia.*

BEER CHEESE SPREAD

2 cups (8 ounces) shredded sharp Cheddar cheese
2 cups (8 ounces) shredded Swiss cheese
1 teaspoon Worcestershire sauce
1 teaspoon dry mustard
½ cup beer

Combine Cheddar and Swiss cheese (at room temperature), Worcestershire sauce, and mustard; gradually add beer, beating constantly on medium speed of an electric mixer until mixture is of spreading consistency.

Serve spread with assorted crackers. Yield: about 2 cups. *Doris Amonette,
Tulsa, Oklahoma.*

PINEAPPLE CHEESE BALL

2 (8-ounce) packages cream cheese, softened
2 tablespoons finely chopped green pepper
2 tablespoons finely chopped onion
¼ cup drained crushed pineapple
2 teaspoons seasoned salt
2 cups chopped pecans, divided
Fresh fruit

Beat cream cheese until smooth; add green pepper, onion, pineapple, seasoned salt, and 1 cup pecans, mixing well. Shape into a ball; roll in remaining pecans. Chill 1 to 2 hours; garnish with fresh fruit, and serve with assorted crackers. Yield: 1 cheese ball.

Sara A. McCullough,
Broaddus, Texas.

BEAR CLAWS

3 slices bacon, cooked and crumbled
2 tablespoons chopped green onion
3 tablespoons mayonnaise
¾ cup (3 ounces) shredded Cheddar cheese
Dash of red pepper
Pastry for a 9-inch pie

Combine first 5 ingredients; stir well.

Roll pastry into a 12- x 9-inch rectangle on a lightly floured board; cut in half lengthwise.

Spread each rectangle with cheese mixture; roll jellyroll fashion, beginning at long side. Press edges lightly to seal; turn seam side down. Cut each roll into 1-inch slices.

Make 2 cuts to center of each slice, making them about ½ inch apart; spread to create a claw effect. Bake on an ungreased baking sheet at 375° for about 10 to 15 minutes. Yield: 2 dozen.

Merrily Miller,
Morristown, Tennessee.

Pack The Desserts To Go

For many, summer means countless picnics in the park. No matter how much you may pack in that picnic basket, your hungry picnickers will be clamoring for dessert. With that in mind, we've tested some sweets that are both easy to transport and easy to serve.

Consider our Praline Cake with a brown sugar topping or our Spice Cake

filled with raisins or pecans—no messy frostings but lots of flavor.

Pies can also be easy to carry along with you; just avoid those with delicate toppings like meringue or whipped cream, and choose pies with firm fillings. Our delicious Coconut Pecan Pie or Chocolate Chess Pie will do nicely.

FRIED APPLE TURNOVERS

3 medium cooking apples, peeled and chopped
1 tablespoon water
⅔ cup sugar
1 tablespoon all-purpose flour
⅛ teaspoon ground cinnamon
⅛ teaspoon ground nutmeg
Pastry (recipe follows)
Vegetable oil

Combine apples and water in a saucepan; cover and cook over low heat about 10 to 15 minutes or until tender. Drain off any liquid that accumulates.

Combine sugar, flour, and spices; stir well. Add to apples, and cook over medium heat 10 minutes or until mixture is thickened.

Roll pastry to ⅛-inch thickness; cut out 8 (5-inch) circles. Spoon about 2½ tablespoons apple filling on each pastry circle. Moisten edges of circles; fold pastry in half, making sure edges are even. Using a fork dipped in flour, press edges together to seal.

Heat 1 inch of oil to 375°. Fry pies in hot oil until golden, turning once. Drain on paper towels. Yield: 8 turnovers.

Pastry:

2 cups all-purpose flour
1 teaspoon salt
½ cup milk
½ cup vegetable oil

Combine flour and salt. Combine milk and oil, stirring well. Pour milk mixture into flour mixture, and stir just until blended. Shape dough into a ball. Yield: pastry for 8 turnovers.

Barbara Boies,
Mangham, Louisiana.

CHOCOLATE CHESS PIE

1½ cups sugar
3½ tablespoons cocoa
Pinch of salt
2 eggs, beaten
¼ cup butter or margarine, melted
1 (5.33-ounce) can evaporated milk
1 teaspoon vanilla extract
1 unbaked 9-inch pastry shell

Combine sugar, cocoa, and salt. Add eggs, butter, milk, and vanilla; mix thoroughly. Pour into pastry shell, and bake at 350° for 45 to 50 minutes. Yield: one 9-inch pie.

Mrs. Robert C. Henson,
Benton, Kentucky.

COCONUT PECAN PIE

3 eggs
¾ cup sugar
¾ cup dark corn syrup
1 teaspoon vanilla extract
⅛ teaspoon salt
¼ cup butter or margarine, melted
1 tablespoon cocoa
2 cups pecan halves
½ cup flaked coconut
1 unbaked 9-inch pastry shell

Combine eggs, sugar, syrup, vanilla, and salt in a large mixing bowl; mix well. Combine butter and cocoa, and stir into egg mixture. Add pecans and coconut, mixing well.

Pour mixture into pastry shell. Bake at 350° about 50 minutes or until pie is set. Yield: one 9-inch pie.

C. Wayne Woodard,
Dillwyn, Virginia.

Tip: To prevent a soggy crust in custard pies or quiche, brush slightly beaten egg white on the uncooked pie shell; bake at 425° for 5 to 10 minutes. Add filling, and bake according to recipe directions.

PRALINE CAKE

½ cup butter or margarine, softened
2 cups firmly packed brown sugar
2 eggs
2 cups all-purpose flour
2 tablespoons cocoa
1 teaspoon soda
¼ teaspoon salt
1 cup buttermilk
1 tablespoon vanilla extract
Brown sugar topping (recipe follows)

Cream butter; gradually add sugar, beating until light and fluffy. Add eggs, one at a time, beating mixture well after each addition.

Combine flour, cocoa, soda, and salt; add to creamed mixture alternately with buttermilk, beginning and ending with flour mixture. Stir in vanilla.

Pour the batter into a greased and floured 13- x 9- x 2-inch baking pan. Bake at 350° for 25 to 30 minutes or until wooden pick inserted in center comes out clean.

Pour brown sugar topping evenly over cake. Broil 5 inches from broiler element about 1 minute. Cool and cut into squares. Yield: 15 to 18 servings.

Brown Sugar Topping:

1 cup firmly packed brown sugar
1 cup chopped pecans or walnuts
⅓ cup evaporated milk

Combine all ingredients in a saucepan; boil 1 minute, stirring constantly. Yield: about 1⅔ cups.

Carolyn McKittrick,
Easley, South Carolina.

SPICE CAKE

1 cup butter or margarine, softened
2 cups sugar
4 eggs, separated
3½ cups all-purpose flour
1 teaspoon soda
¼ teaspoon salt
1 teaspoon ground nutmeg
1 teaspoon ground cinnamon
1 teaspoon ground cloves
1 teaspoon ground allspice
1 cup buttermilk
1 cup raisins
1 cup chopped pecans

Cream butter; gradually add sugar, beating until light and fluffy and sugar is dissolved. Add egg yolks, beating well.

Combine flour, soda, salt, and spices; mix well. Add flour mixture to creamed mixture alternately with buttermilk, beginning and ending with flour mixture. Stir in raisins and pecans.

Beat egg whites (at room temperature) until stiff peaks form; fold into batter.

Pour the batter into a greased and floured 10-inch tube pan. Bake at 350° for 1 hour and 20 minutes or until wooden pick inserted in cake comes out clean. Cool in pan 10 minutes; remove from pan, and cool completely. Yield: one 10-inch cake. *Dora Farrar,*
Gadsden, Alabama.

CHOCOLATE CHIP BROWNIES

¼ cup butter or margarine, softened
¾ cup sugar
¼ cup light corn syrup
2 eggs, beaten
1 teaspoon vanilla extract
2 (1-ounce) squares unsweetened
 chocolate, melted
1 cup all-purpose flour
½ teaspoon baking powder
½ teaspoon salt
½ cup semisweet chocolate morsels
½ cup chopped walnuts

Cream butter; gradually add sugar, and beat until light and fluffy. Add corn syrup, eggs, and vanilla; beat well. Stir in melted chocolate.

Combine flour, baking powder, and salt; stir into creamed mixture. Stir in chocolate morsels and walnuts.

Spread mixture into a lightly greased 9-inch square pan. Bake at 350° for 25 to 30 minutes. Cool and cut into squares. Yield: about 25 servings.

Judy Cunningham,
Roanoke, Virginia.

Bake In The Flavors Of Summer

Bite into one of these plump, hot muffins or a slice of steaming cornbread. You'll be surprised to discover that each of these breads has a secret ingredient that's fresh from the garden. We've added squash to muffins, carrots to cornbread, and zucchini to fritters. The bounty of summer is baked into each delicious bite.

EASY ONION BREAD

1 large Spanish onion, thinly sliced
¼ cup butter or margarine
4 eggs
1½ cups commercial sour cream
1 teaspoon caraway seeds (optional)
½ teaspoon salt
2 tablespoons butter or margarine, melted
½ cup milk
1¾ cups biscuit mix

Sauté onion in ¼ cup butter 10 minutes or until golden brown. Set aside.

Slightly beat 3 eggs; add onion, sour cream, caraway seeds, if desired, and salt. Stir well and set aside.

Combine 2 tablespoons butter, 1 egg, and milk; stir well. Add to biscuit mix, and stir just until moistened (dough will be slightly lumpy).

Spread dough in a lightly greased 12- x 8- x 2-inch baking pan; spread onion mixture over dough. Bake bread at 375° for 30 minutes or until top is set. Yield: 10 to 12 servings. *Grace L. Grogaard,*
Baltimore, Maryland.

CARROT CORNBREAD

1 cup self-rising cornmeal
1 tablespoon light brown sugar
1 teaspoon salt
1 cup shredded carrot
2 eggs, separated
2 tablespoons water
2 tablespoons vegetable oil
¾ cup boiling water

Combine first 4 ingredients in a large bowl. Combine egg yolks, 2 tablespoons water, and oil; mix well. Stir egg mixture into cornmeal mixture. Add boiling water, and stir well.

Beat egg whites (at room temperature) until stiff peaks form. Fold egg whites into cornmeal mixture. Spoon batter into a lightly greased 8-inch square pan. Bake at 450° for 20 minutes or until bread is golden brown. Yield: 9 servings.
Annie Hopkins,
Cedartown, Georgia.

The bounty of summer is baked into each bite of Banana-Blueberry Bread, Carrot Cornbread, and Yellow Squash Muffins.

BANANA-BLUEBERRY BREAD

½ cup shortening
1 cup sugar
2 eggs
1 cup mashed banana
½ cup quick-cooking oats, uncooked
½ cup chopped pecans or walnuts
1½ cups all-purpose flour
1 teaspoon soda
¼ teaspoon salt
½ cup fresh blueberries

Cream shortening; gradually add sugar, beating until light and fluffy. Add eggs, one at a time, beating well after each addition. Stir in banana.

Combine remaining ingredients, stirring gently. Add blueberry mixture to creamed mixture; stir just until moist.

Spoon batter into a greased and floured 9- x 5- x 3-inch loafpan. Bake at 350° for 50 to 55 minutes or until wooden pick inserted in center comes out clean. Cool in pan 10 minutes; remove from pan, and cool completely on a wire rack. Yield: 1 loaf.
Margaret Corn,
Lonoke, Arkansas.

ZUCCHINI FRITTERS

1 pound zucchini (about 3 medium), unpeeled and grated
1 tablespoon minced fresh parsley
1 teaspoon minced fresh chives
1 cup buttermilk pancake mix
1 egg, beaten
¼ teaspoon salt
¼ teaspoon pepper
½ cup vegetable oil

Combine first 7 ingredients, stirring well. Drop mixture by tablespoonfuls into hot oil (375°); cook until golden brown, turning once. Drain on paper towels; serve immediately. Yield: about 1 dozen fritters.
Aimee A. Goodman,
Knoxville, Tennessee.

Tip: Place a few halved cloves of garlic in a cup of vegetable oil and allow to stand overnight. Use oil to add garlic flavor to a dish.

YELLOW SQUASH MUFFINS

2 pounds yellow squash (about 8 medium)
2 eggs
1 cup butter or margarine, melted
1 cup sugar
3 cups all-purpose flour
1 tablespoon plus 2 teaspoons baking powder
1 teaspoon salt

Wash squash thoroughly; trim off ends. Cut squash into 1-inch slices. Cook in a small amount of boiling water 15 to 20 minutes or until tender. Drain well, and mash. Measure enough of the squash to equal 2 cups.

Combine squash, eggs, and butter; stir well, and set aside.

Combine remaining ingredients in a large bowl; make a well in center of mixture. Add squash mixture to dry ingredients, stirring just until moistened. Spoon into greased muffin pans, filling three-fourths full. Bake at 375° for 20 minutes or until wooden pick inserted in center of muffin comes out clean. Yield: 1½ dozen.
Mrs. Bennie Cox,
Clinton, Tennessee.

Bake Fresh Blueberries Into Something Sweet

When baskets of plump, juicy blueberries start appearing in markets and on roadside trucks, it's time to pull out recipes for old favorites like blueberry pancakes and blueberry coffee cake as well as some new treats like Deluxe Blueberry Buns. These sweet rolls are baked in a spiral form and filled with butter, sugar, cinnamon, and lots of fresh blueberries. Don't miss them!

SOUR CREAM BLUEBERRY PANCAKES

1 cup milk
1 egg
¼ cup commercial sour cream
1 cup all-purpose flour
1 tablespoon baking powder
1 tablespoon sugar
¼ teaspoon salt
2 tablespoons butter or margarine, melted
½ cup fresh blueberries
Blueberry syrup (optional)

Combine milk, egg, and sour cream; beat well. Stir together flour, baking powder, sugar, and salt; add to milk mixture. Beat just until large lumps disappear. Stir in the butter. Fold in the blueberries.

For each pancake, pour about ¼ cup batter onto a hot, lightly greased griddle or skillet. Turn pancakes when tops are covered with bubbles and edges are slightly dry. Serve with blueberry syrup, if desired. Yield: 12 (4-inch) pancakes.
Carole Tebay,
Pensacola, Florida.

DELUXE BLUEBERRY BUNS

3½ to 4 cups all-purpose flour, divided
1 package dry yeast
1⅓ cups evaporated milk
¼ cup plus 2 tablespoons butter or margarine
¼ cup sugar, divided
1 teaspoon salt
1 egg
¼ cup butter or margarine, melted
½ cup sugar
2 teaspoons ground cinnamon
1 teaspoon grated lemon rind
2 cups fresh blueberries
Powdered sugar glaze (recipe follows)

Combine 1½ cups flour and yeast in a large mixing bowl; mix well and set aside.

Combine evaporated milk, ¼ cup plus 2 tablespoons butter, ¼ cup sugar, and salt in a small saucepan; cook over medium heat, stirring constantly, until butter melts. Cool to 105° to 115°; stir into flour mixture. Add egg; beat on low speed of an electric mixer 3 minutes; gradually stir in enough of the remaining flour to make a moderately stiff dough.

Place dough in a greased bowl; turning to grease top. Cover and let rise in a warm place (85°), free from drafts, 1½ hours or until doubled in bulk. Punch dough down; divide in half. Cover and let rest 10 minutes.

Turn half of dough out on a lightly floured surface. Roll out to a 14- x 8-inch rectangle (about ¼ inch thick); brush 2 tablespoons melted butter over dough, leaving a narrow margin on all sides. Combine ½ cup sugar, cinnamon, and lemon rind; sprinkle half of mixture over dough. Sprinkle 1 cup blueberries evenly over dough. Roll up dough, jellyroll fashion, beginning at long side; moisten edges with water to seal. Cut roll into 12 slices; place slices in a greased 9-inch round baking pan.

Repeat procedure with remaining dough, butter, sugar mixture, and blueberries. Cover and let rise in a warm place (85°) about 1 hour or until doubled in bulk. Bake at 375° for 18 to 20 minutes or until rolls are browned. Drizzle powdered sugar glaze over warm rolls. Yield: 2 dozen.

Powdered Sugar Glaze:

1 cup sifted powdered sugar
½ teaspoon vanilla extract
1 tablespoon plus 1 teaspoon milk

Combine all ingredients. Yield: about ½ cup.
Susan Settlemyre,
Raleigh, North Carolina.

HOT BLUEBERRY BREAD

2 eggs
1 cup sugar
1 cup milk
¼ cup butter or margarine, melted
3 cups all-purpose flour
1 tablespoon plus 1 teaspoon baking powder
1 teaspoon salt
2 cups fresh blueberries
2 tablespoons all-purpose flour

Combine eggs and sugar in a large bowl; beat with electric mixer until thoroughly blended. Add milk and butter, mixing well.

Combine 3 cups flour, baking powder, and salt; add to liquid ingredients, stirring just until all ingredients are thoroughly moistened.

Combine blueberries and 2 tablespoons flour; stir well to coat blueberries. Fold into batter.

Spoon batter into 2 greased and floured 7½- x 3- x 2-inch loafpans. Bake at 350° for 55 to 60 minutes or until bread tests done. Remove from pans; serve hot. Yield: 2 loaves.
Susan Leftwich,
DeSoto, Texas.

FRESH BLUEBERRY COFFEE CAKE

1¼ cups fresh blueberries
⅓ cup sugar
2 tablespoons cornstarch
½ cup butter or margarine, softened
1 cup sugar
2 eggs
2 cups all-purpose flour
1 teaspoon baking powder
1 teaspoon soda
½ teaspoon salt
1 (8-ounce) carton commercial sour cream
1 teaspoon almond extract
½ cup finely chopped pecans
Powdered sugar glaze (recipe follows)

Combine blueberries, ⅓ cup sugar, and cornstarch in a small saucepan; cook over low heat 2 to 3 minutes or until sauce is thickened, stirring constantly. Set sauce aside.

Cream butter; gradually add 1 cup sugar, beating until well blended. Add the eggs, one at a time, beating well after each addition.

Combine flour, baking powder, soda, and salt; add to creamed mixture alternately with sour cream, beginning and ending with the flour mixture. Stir in almond extract.

Spoon half of batter into a greased 8-inch Bundt pan or tube pan; spoon on half the blueberry sauce, swirling partially through batter with a knife. Repeat with the remaining batter and blueberry sauce. Sprinkle with pecans. Bake at 350° for 50 minutes or until done. Let stand 5 minutes before removing from pan. Place coffee cake on serving plate, and drizzle powdered sugar glaze over top. Yield: one 8-inch coffee cake.

Powdered Sugar Glaze:
¾ cup sifted powdered sugar
1 tablespoon warm water
½ teaspoon almond extract

Combine all ingredients, mixing well. Yield: about ½ cup.   *Mack Herring, Mount Olive, North Carolina.*

Microwave Cookery

Southern-Style Vegetables From The Microwave

Southerners are rather partial to that simmered-all-day flavor that conventional cooking gives to vegetables, yet much nutritional value is lost when using this method. With microwaving, you can still have this characteristic flavor without the nutrient loss because microwaves cook fast and use the natural moisture of the vegetable as most of the cooking liquid.

The recipes featured here are products of our test kitchens and include such regional favorites as cream-style corn, okra and tomatoes, and fresh black-eyed peas. Each recipe gives a time range to allow for the difference in wattage of microwave ovens. To avoid overcooking, check for doneness at the lower end of the range. If you're cooking a different amount of vegetables than specified in the recipe, be sure to adjust the cooking time accordingly.

ORANGE-GLAZED CARROTS

6 medium carrots, sliced
¾ cup orange juice, divided
1 tablespoon sugar
2 teaspoons cornstarch
½ teaspoon salt

Combine carrots, ¼ cup orange juice, and sugar in a 2-quart casserole; cover with heavy-duty plastic wrap. Microwave at HIGH for 9 to 11 minutes or until desired degree of doneness.
Combine cornstarch and salt, mixing well; add remaining orange juice, and beat with a wire whisk until cornstarch

is dissolved. Gradually add orange juice mixture to carrots, mixing well. Cover and microwave at HIGH for 1½ to 2½ minutes or until thickened and bubbly, stirring at 1-minute intervals. Yield: about 4 servings.

SOUTHERN-STYLE CREAMED CORN

6 medium ears fresh corn
¼ cup butter or margarine
¼ cup water
1 teaspoon sugar
½ cup half-and-half
2 teaspoons cornstarch
½ teaspoon salt
½ teaspoon coarsely ground pepper

Cut corn from cob, scraping cobs well to remove all milk.
Place butter in a 2-quart casserole, and microwave at HIGH for 1 minute or until melted; stir in corn, water, and sugar. Cover with heavy-duty plastic wrap. Microwave at HIGH for 3 minutes; stir well, and give dish a half-turn. Cover and microwave at HIGH for 5 to 7 minutes or until corn is done.
Combine remaining ingredients, and beat with a wire whisk until cornstarch is dissolved; add to corn, mixing well. Cover and microwave at HIGH for 2 to 2½ minutes or until thickened and bubbly, stirring at 1-minute intervals. Yield: 4 to 6 servings.

FRESH OKRA AND TOMATOES

4 medium-size ripe tomatoes, peeled
3 cups sliced fresh okra
¼ cup chopped onion
¼ cup chopped green pepper
½ cup water
1 teaspoon sugar
1 teaspoon salt
½ teaspoon pepper
1 tablespoon all-purpose flour
2 tablespoons water

Puree 2 tomatoes in electric blender or food processor; chop remaining 2 tomatoes.
Combine okra, onion, green pepper, and ½ cup water in a 2-quart casserole; mix well. Cover with heavy-duty plastic wrap. Microwave at HIGH for 9 to 11 minutes or until okra is done, stirring and turning dish every 3 minutes. Drain and rinse vegetables well, reserving vegetables in dish.
Add chopped tomatoes, tomato puree, sugar, salt, and pepper to okra mixture; mix well. Cover casserole with

heavy-duty plastic wrap, and microwave at HIGH for 3 minutes.
Combine flour and 2 tablespoons water, beating with a wire whisk until flour is dissolved; gradually stir into okra mixture. Cover and microwave at HIGH for 1½ to 2½ minutes or until mixture is thickened and bubbly, stirring at 1-minute intervals. Yield: about 4 to 6 servings.

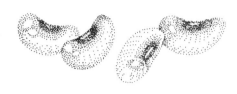

FRESH BLACK-EYED PEAS

4 cups shelled fresh black-eyed peas
3 slices bacon, coarsely chopped
1 cup water
1 medium onion, chopped
¾ teaspoon salt
½ teaspoon ground red pepper
1 bay leaf

Combine all ingredients in a 2-quart casserole, mixing well. Cover with heavy-duty plastic wrap. Microwave at HIGH for 4 minutes; stir well. Cover and microwave at MEDIUM for 25 to 30 minutes, stirring every 5 minutes. Let stand, covered, for 5 minutes. Discard bay leaf. Yield: 4 servings.

FRESH SQUASH MEDLEY

1 medium-size yellow squash, sliced
1 medium zucchini, sliced
1 medium onion, sliced and separated into rings
¼ cup water
1 medium tomato, chopped
2 tablespoons chopped fresh parsley
¼ teaspoon dried whole oregano
¼ teaspoon salt
¼ teaspoon pepper
½ cup grated Parmesan cheese

Combine first 4 ingredients in a 2-quart casserole; cover with heavy-duty plastic wrap. Microwave at HIGH for 5½ to 7½ minutes or until squash is crisp-tender; stir and give dish a half-turn after 3 minutes. Drain well.
Add remaining ingredients, except cheese, to squash; mix well. Cover and microwave at HIGH for 2 to 3 minutes or until thoroughly heated and squash is desired degree of doneness. Sprinkle with cheese, tossing gently. Yield: 4 servings.

Texas Ribs And Chicken Boast A Feisty Flavor

When Texans serve ribs and chicken, they like them hot, hearty, and saucy. These recipes promise to deliver all the feisty flavor that's expected, for each comes directly from a Texas kitchen.

Saucy-Sweet Ribs and Smoky Oven Ribs are two outstanding examples of how Texans liven up spareribs; pineapple marmalade is the special ingredient in one, and liquid smoke flavors the other. And chicken gets a Texas stamp of approval when it's Mexican Fried Chicken.

SMOKY OVEN RIBS

4 pounds spareribs
3½ cups catsup
½ cup butter or margarine, melted
¼ cup liquid smoke
¼ cup plus 2 tablespoons firmly packed brown sugar
2 tablespoons sugar
2 tablespoons lemon juice
2 teaspoons garlic powder

Cut ribs into serving-size pieces; place in a large Dutch oven. Add enough water to cover ribs; cover and simmer 45 minutes. Drain ribs and place in a 13- x 9- x 2-inch baking pan.

Combine remaining ingredients in a medium saucepan; cook over medium heat, stirring until heated through. Pour sauce over ribs; cover and bake ribs at 325° for 1 to 1½ hours or until done. Yield: 4 servings. *Mrs. V. O. Walker, Pennington, Texas.*

LEMON BAKED RIBS

1½ cups water
1 cup catsup
⅓ cup Worcestershire sauce
1 teaspoon chili powder
1 teaspoon salt
2 dashes of hot sauce
3 to 4 pounds spareribs
1 lemon, thinly sliced
1 onion, thinly sliced

Combine first 6 ingredients in a small saucepan; mix well. Bring sauce to a boil; reduce heat and simmer 5 minutes.

Cut ribs into serving-size pieces; place in a 13- x 9- x 2-inch baking pan. Bake, uncovered, at 425° for 30 minutes; drain off pan drippings. Place lemon and onion slices over ribs; top with sauce. Reduce heat to 325°; bake an additional 1½ hours or until done, basting every 20 minutes with sauce. Yield: 3 to 4 servings. *Carolyn Look, El Paso, Texas.*

SAUCY-SWEET RIBS

4 pounds spareribs
1 (12-ounce) bottle chili sauce
1 (12-ounce) jar pineapple preserves or marmalade
2 tablespoons water
2 tablespoons vinegar
1 tablespoon Worcestershire sauce
⅓ cup finely chopped onion
½ teaspoon celery seeds

Cut ribs into serving-size pieces; place in a large Dutch oven. Add enough water to cover ribs; cover and simmer over low heat 45 minutes. Drain the ribs and place in a 13- x 9- x 2-inch baking pan.

Combine remaining ingredients; stir well. Spoon sauce over ribs; cover and bake at 325° for 1 to 1½ hours or until done. Yield: 4 servings.

Norene Brundige, Amarillo, Texas.

MEXICAN FRIED CHICKEN

¼ cup all-purpose flour
1½ teaspoons chili powder
½ teaspoon salt
1 (2½- to 3-pound) broiler-fryer, cut up and skinned
⅓ cup vegetable oil
¼ cup chopped onion
¾ cup chopped green pepper
¾ cup uncooked regular rice
1 (10-ounce) can tomatoes and green chiles, undrained
1½ cups water
1 teaspoon chili powder
½ teaspoon salt

Combine first 3 ingredients, stirring well. Dredge chicken pieces in flour mixture, and brown in hot oil (375°) in a large skillet.

Remove chicken from skillet. Add onion and green pepper to skillet; sauté until tender. Stir in rice, tomatoes, water, 1 teaspoon chili powder, and ½ teaspoon salt. Arrange chicken over rice and vegetables; cover and simmer 35 to 40 minutes or until chicken is tender and rice is done. Yield: 4 servings.

Vertie Vandervort, Austin, Texas.

SAN ANTONIO-STYLE CHICKEN

3 pounds chicken pieces (breasts, thighs, and legs)
½ cup all-purpose flour
Salt and pepper
3 tablespoons vegetable oil
1 large green pepper, cut into thin strips
1 large onion, coarsely chopped
1 to 2 cloves garlic, minced
3 medium tomatoes, peeled and coarsely chopped
½ teaspoon salt
⅛ teaspoon pepper
Pinch of ground cumin
2 cups hot water
Hot cooked rice

Dredge chicken in flour seasoned with salt and pepper; brown in hot oil. Transfer chicken to a shallow 2½-quart casserole, reserving pan drippings.

Add green pepper, onion, and garlic to pan drippings; sauté until tender. Stir in tomatoes, ½ teaspoon salt, ⅛ teaspoon pepper, cumin, and water. Pour mixture over chicken; cover and bake at 350° for 1 hour or until chicken is tender. Serve over rice. Yield: 4 to 6 servings. *Mrs. Hilmer Haegelin, Hondo, Texas.*

CHICKEN TORTILLA CASSEROLE

1 (8-ounce) package frozen corn tortillas, thawed
Vegetable oil
1 large onion, chopped
2 small cloves garlic, minced
¼ cup vegetable oil
1 (10-ounce) can tomatoes and green chiles, undrained
1 (7½-ounce) can whole tomatoes, undrained and chopped
1½ teaspoons dried whole cilantro or 1½ tablespoons fresh coriander leaves, minced
¼ to ½ teaspoon salt
2 cups chopped, cooked chicken
4 cups (16 ounces) shredded Monterey Jack cheese
1 (8-ounce) carton commercial sour cream

Using tongs, carefully arrange 3 tortillas in ⅛-inch-deep hot oil in a large skillet; cook 3 to 5 seconds on each side. Drain tortillas on paper towels. Repeat cooking procedure with remaining tortillas; add oil to skillet if necessary. Tear each tortilla into 4 pieces, and set aside.

Sauté onion and garlic in ¼ cup oil until tender. Stir in tomatoes and green chiles, chopped tomatoes, cilantro, and salt; simmer mixture, uncovered, 10 to 15 minutes.

Spread tortillas in a 13- x 9- x 2-inch baking dish. Pour tomato mixture over tortillas; arrange chicken over sauce. Top with cheese. Bake at 350° for 20 to 30 minutes or until bubbly. Serve with sour cream. Yield: 8 servings.

Mrs. Don H. Eldridge,
Houston, Texas.

Fresh Beets Belong On The Menu

Give summertime meals a lift by adding fresh beets to the menu. Served with a simple glaze, they make wonderful side dishes. Should there be any leftovers, use them as a colorful addition to a tossed salad.

When buying fresh beets, choose those that are a rich, deep-red color. They should be firm, round, and smooth over most of the surface and have a slender taproot (the large main root). Although badly wilted or decayed tops indicate a lack of freshness, the roots may still be satisfactory, provided they are firm.

ORANGE-GLAZED BEETS

12 medium beets
2 tablespoons all-purpose flour
¼ cup sugar
½ teaspoon salt
½ cup orange juice
1 tablespoon butter or margarine

Leave root and 1 inch of stem on beets; scrub well with vegetable brush. Place beets in a saucepan; add water to cover. Bring to a boil; cover and cook 35 to 40 minutes or until tender. Drain. Pour cold water over beets, and drain.

Let cool. Trim off beet stems and roots, and rub off skins. Cut beets into ¼-inch slices.

Place sliced beets in a 1½-quart casserole. Combine remaining ingredients except butter, stirring until smooth; pour over beets, and dot with butter. Bake at 400° for 30 minutes. Yield: 8 servings. *Mrs. M. L. Sandy, Sr.,*
Corinth, Mississippi.

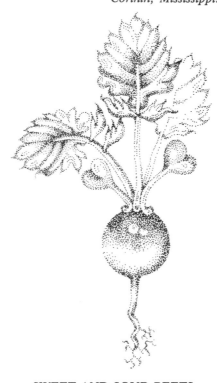

SWEET-AND-SOUR BEETS

9 medium beets
½ cup sugar
1 tablespoon cornstarch
½ teaspoon salt
2 whole cloves
½ cup vinegar
3 tablespoons orange marmalade
2 tablespoons butter or margarine

Leave root and 1 inch of stem on beets; scrub well with vegetable brush. Place beets in a saucepan, and add water to cover. Bring to a boil; cover and cook 35 to 40 minutes or until tender. Drain. Pour cold water over beets; drain. Let cool. Trim off stems and roots, and rub off skins. Cut beets into ¼-inch slices.

Combine sugar, cornstarch, salt, and cloves in a heavy saucepan; stir in vinegar. Cook over medium heat, stirring constantly, until thickened and bubbly.

Add beets to sauce, and cook 15 minutes; stir in marmalade and butter. Yield: 6 servings.

Mrs. Charles R. Simms,
Palestine, Illinois.

GLAZED FRESH BEETS

9 medium beets
⅓ cup vinegar
3 tablespoons all-purpose flour
2 tablespoons sugar
1 teaspoon salt
Dash of pepper

Leave root and 1 inch of stem on beets; scrub well with vegetable brush. Place beets in a saucepan, and add water to cover. Bring to a boil; cover and cook 35 to 40 minutes or until tender. Drain, reserving 1 cup juice; pour cold water over beets, and drain. Let cool. Trim off beet stems and roots, and rub off skins. Dice beets.

Combine vinegar and dry ingredients, stirring well; add to beets along with reserved juice. Cook over medium heat, stirring occasionally, until sauce is thickened and bubbly. Yield: 6 servings.

B. A. McGuire,
Norris, South Carolina.

Iced Tea–The Southern Cooler

Nothing quenches a summertime thirst like a tall, frosty glass of freshly brewed iced tea. And for many Southerners, it's a tradition to add mint sprigs and a wedge of lemon.

Some of our readers add more than that. Summertime Tea is full of orange juice and lemonade, and Bubbly Iced Tea sparkles with ginger ale. If you'd like to try a version of solar-produced tea, we've included Southern Sun Tea.

SUMMERTIME TEA

1½ cups sugar
6 small tea bags
1 quart boiling water
1 (6-ounce) can frozen lemonade
  concentrate, thawed and undiluted
1 (6-ounce) can frozen orange juice
  concentrate, thawed and undiluted
2 quarts cold water

Add sugar and tea bags to boiling water; stir well. Cover and steep 5 minutes. Remove tea bags, squeezing gently. Stir in all of the remaining ingredients; serve tea over ice. Yield: about 3½ quarts. *Patricia Flint,*
Staunton, Virginia.

SOUTHERN SUN TEA

8 small tea bags with paper tags removed
1 quart cold water
¼ cup sugar
1 tablespoon lemon juice
Fresh mint sprigs

Combine tea bags and water in a glass jar or pitcher; cover top with a lid or plastic wrap, and place outside in the sun 7 to 10 hours (until tea is desired strength).

Remove tea bags, squeezing gently. Add sugar and lemon juice to tea, stirring to dissolve sugar. Serve tea over ice, garnishing each serving with mint. Yield: about 1 quart.

Mrs. Antone Callaway,
Decatur, Georgia.

BUBBLY ICED TEA

8 small tea bags
3 quarts boiling water
½ cup sugar
1 (12-ounce) can frozen lemonade concentrate, thawed and undiluted
1 (33.8-ounce) bottle ginger ale, chilled

Add tea bags to boiling water; cover and steep 5 minutes. Remove tea bags, squeezing gently; stir in sugar and lemonade. Set tea aside to cool; stir in ginger ale just before serving. Serve tea over ice. Yield: about 4½ quarts.

Florence L. Costello,
Chattanooga, Tennessee.

Zesty Side Dishes From Tomatoes

Fried Ripe Tomatoes, Baked Tangy Tomatoes, and Scalloped Tomato Slices are some of the best ways we know to make the most of those vine-ripened tomatoes. There's even a recipe using cherry tomatoes—they're sautéed with herbs in a brown butter sauce.

You'll find that the fried tomatoes included here aren't the usual version; in this one, the crispy slices are served on toast and topped with a milk-base sauce. Our other recipes also vary from the everyday. The scalloped tomatoes are seasoned with basil and topped with croutons before baking, while our baked tomatoes owe their zesty flavor to the mustard and onion stirred into the filling.

BAKED TANGY TOMATOES

4 large tomatoes
2 tablespoons chopped green pepper
2 tablespoons chopped celery
1 tablespoon chopped onion
1 tablespoon prepared mustard
¼ teaspoon salt
⅔ cup soft breadcrumbs
2 tablespoons melted butter or margarine

Cut tomatoes in half crosswise. Scoop out pulp, leaving shells intact. Chop tomato pulp.

Combine tomato pulp, green pepper, celery, onion, mustard, and salt; stir well. Spoon into tomato shells, and place in a 13- x 9- x 2-inch baking dish.

Combine breadcrumbs and butter; sprinkle over tomatoes. Bake at 350° for 25 to 30 minutes. Yield: 8 servings.

Mrs. George Lance,
Madison, Tennessee.

SCALLOPED TOMATO SLICES

4 medium-size firm tomatoes, cut into ¼-inch slices
1 cup diced celery
½ cup chopped onion
¼ cup butter or margarine
1 teaspoon salt
1 teaspoon sugar
1 teaspoon dried whole basil
⅛ teaspoon pepper
1 cup seasoned croutons

Arrange tomatoes in a buttered 12- x 8- x 2-inch baking dish. Sauté celery and onion in butter 2 minutes; stir in seasonings. Set aside ¼ cup of celery mixture, and spoon the remainder over tomatoes.

Combine reserved celery mixture and croutons, tossing gently; spoon over tomatoes. Cover and bake at 350° for 30 minutes. Yield: 4 to 6 servings.

Cindy Fields,
Courtland, Virginia.

CHERRY TOMATOES IN BROWN BUTTER SAUCE

3 tablespoons butter or margarine
¼ cup finely chopped fresh parsley
1 tablespoon lemon juice
1 teaspoon dried whole tarragon
1 pint cherry tomatoes

Melt butter over low heat; let cook until browned, stirring constantly. Add remaining ingredients; cook about 3 minutes or until tomato skins pop, stirring constantly. Yield: 6 servings.

Jodie McCoy,
Tulsa, Oklahoma.

FRIED RIPE TOMATOES

2 cups all-purpose flour
2 tablespoons sugar
½ teaspoon salt
¼ teaspoon pepper
3 large firm-ripe tomatoes
½ cup butter or margarine
6 slices bread, toasted
1 tablespoon butter or margarine
1 cup milk

Combine flour, sugar, salt, and pepper; mix well. Set 2 tablespoons flour mixture aside. Cut tomatoes into ½-inch slices, and dredge in remaining flour mixture.

Melt ½ cup butter in a large skillet over medium heat, and add tomatoes; cook until golden brown, turning once. Arrange toast on a serving platter; top with tomatoes, and keep warm.

Add 1 tablespoon butter to pan drippings, and heat until melted. Add the reserved flour mixture, stirring until smooth. Cook 1 minute, stirring constantly. Gradually add milk; cook over medium heat, stirring constantly, until thickened. Spoon over tomatoes. Serve immediately. Yield: 4 to 6 servings.

William Groseclose,
Fallston, Maryland.

Tip: Keep butter, margarine, and fat drippings tightly covered in the refrigerator. Vegetable shortening can be kept covered at room temperature. Homemade salad dressing should be kept in the refrigerator; mayonnaise and commercial salad dressings should be refrigerated after opening. Foods mixed with mayonnaise, such as potato salad or egg salad, should be refrigerated and used within a couple of days.

Fry An Orange Fritter

A light and airy batter is the secret to Puffy Orange Fritters. The recipe combines the sunny flavor of orange juice and orange rind in a sweet batter that is fried until golden. These orange-flavored puffs are best when served hot and sprinkled with powdered sugar.

PUFFY ORANGE FRITTERS

2 eggs
½ cup sugar
2 tablespoons butter or margarine, melted
1 tablespoon grated orange rind
2 cups all-purpose flour
2 teaspoons baking powder
½ teaspoon salt
½ cup orange juice
Hot vegetable oil
Powdered sugar

Beat eggs in a large bowl; gradually add sugar, mixing well. Stir in butter and orange rind.

Combine flour, baking powder, and salt; mix well. Add to egg mixture alternately with orange juice, beginning and ending with flour mixture. Let batter stand 15 minutes.

Drop mixture by rounded teaspoonfuls into hot vegetable oil (350°); cook fritters until golden, turning once. Drain well on paper towels. Sprinkle with powdered sugar. Yield: about 3 dozen.
Helen Harris,
Orlando, Florida.

These orange-flavored fritters are just right for breakfast, snack, or dessert.

Never Cooked Lobster? Here's How

Boiling a live lobster is a lot easier than you might think. Along with a few tips on buying fresh lobster, we give you a step-by-step cooking procedure.

Always purchase live lobsters on the day they are to be served. It may be helpful to take a large container with you so the lobster can be iced down at the store and covered until you get home. Allow about 1 to 1¼ pounds of lobster per person. Remember that Florida lobster (also called spiny lobster) is prepared like any other; the only difference is that the Florida lobster doesn't have large meat-filled claws.

Step 1—In a large kettle, bring 4 quarts of water (sufficient for cooking two 1-pound lobsters) to a boil. Grasp the lobster just behind the eyes, and quickly rinse under cold water. Plunge the lobster headfirst into the boiling water.

Step 2—Return the water to boiling; then reduce heat, and simmer as follows: 12 minutes for one 1-pound lobster; add 3 minutes for each additional pound of lobster. At the end of the cooking period, remove lobster from water with kitchen tongs, and rinse under cold water.

Step 3—Position lobster on its back on a cutting board. With a sharp knife or kitchen shears, cut the entire length of the lobster from head to tail; leave back intact, if desired.

Step 4—Cut down the outside edges of tail to remove membranous covering and expose meat.

Step 5—Remove the organs (in the body section) and the vein that runs through body to tail. You may prefer to save the reddish-colored coral roe (found only in female lobsters) and the greenish-colored liver, as they are considered delicacies.

Step 6—Serve the lobster with a seafood fork, as well as a nutcracker so the claws can be cracked. The appropriate accompaniment for lobster is melted or clarified butter.

Make Your Own Ice Cream Toppings

Take a bowl of ice cream, top it with one of these rich sauces, and you've got a fabulous dessert with very little effort.

STRAWBERRY SAUCE WITH CRUNCHY TOPPING

1 (10-ounce) package frozen strawberries, thawed
1 teaspoon sugar
1 tablespoon cornstarch
2 teaspoons strawberry-flavored liqueur (optional)
Crunchy Topping

Place strawberries in a liquid measuring cup; add water to make 2 cups.

Combine sugar and cornstarch in a saucepan. Gradually add strawberry mixture, stirring until combined; cook over low heat, stirring constantly, until smooth and thickened. Stir in liqueur, if desired. Chill. Spoon over ice cream, and sprinkle with Crunchy Topping. Yield: 2 cups.

Crunchy Topping:

2 tablespoons butter or margarine, melted
⅔ cup flaked coconut
¼ cup chopped almonds or pecans
3 tablespoons brown sugar

Combine all ingredients in a 9-inch square baking pan. Place under broiler, 4 inches from heat; broil, stirring occasionally, only until slightly browned. Yield: about 1 cup. *Betty Chason, Tallahassee, Florida.*

PEACH-BLUEBERRY SAUCE

1 cup sliced fresh peaches, divided
1 cup fresh blueberries, divided
¾ cup sugar
½ cup water
Dash of ground nutmeg

Combine ½ cup peaches, ½ cup blueberries, and remaining ingredients in a small saucepan. Bring to a boil, reduce heat, and simmer 15 to 20 minutes. Add remaining fruit; stir well. Serve warm over ice cream. Yield: about 2 cups.
Note: Also good over pancakes, waffles, and pound cake.
Mrs. Carlysle Sayre, Lexington, Kentucky.

BOURBON PRALINE SAUCE

½ cup butter or margarine, melted
1 cup firmly packed brown sugar
1 cup pecan pieces
1 tablespoon light corn syrup
¼ cup bourbon

Combine first 4 ingredients in a heavy skillet; bring mixture to a boil, stirring constantly. Reduce heat; cook for 1 minute (do not overcook). Stir in bourbon. Serve immediately. Yield: about 1½ cups.

Ground Beef Goes A Long Way

When it comes to economical main dishes, nothing stretches quite so far as ground beef. And here are three more ways you can enjoy it: a meatloaf with a spicy topping, cheesy American Enchiladas, and a deluxe version of Salisbury steak.

When serving ground beef, count on 4 servings per pound. It's best to store ground beef in the refrigerator no more than 24 to 48 hours. In the freezer, it will keep at zero-degree storage about three months with little loss of quality.

MEAT LOAF

1½ pounds ground beef
1 medium onion, chopped
1 egg
1 teaspoon salt
½ teaspoon pepper
1 cup dry breadcrumbs
½ cup catsup
1½ cups tomato juice
Catsup Topping

Combine all ingredients except Catsup Topping; mix well. Pack into a lightly greased 9- x 5- x 3-inch loafpan. Spoon Catsup Topping over mixture. Bake meatloaf at 400° for 1½ hours or until done. Yield: 6 servings.

Catsup Topping:

½ cup catsup
3 tablespoons light brown sugar
2 teaspoons prepared mustard
¼ teaspoon chili powder

Combine all ingredients; mix well. Yield: about ⅔ cup. *Vickie Hedrick, Gretna, Virginia.*

SALISBURY STEAK DELUXE

1 (10¾-ounce) can cream of mushroom soup, undiluted
1 tablespoon prepared mustard
2 teaspoons Worcestershire sauce
1 teaspoon prepared horseradish
1½ pounds ground beef
1 egg, slightly beaten
¼ cup dry breadcrumbs
¼ cup finely chopped onion
½ teaspoon salt
Dash of pepper
½ cup water
2 tablespoons chopped parsley

Combine soup, mustard, Worcestershire sauce, and horseradish; blend well.

Combine beef, egg, breadcrumbs, onion, salt, pepper, and ¼ cup soup mixture. Shape into 6 patties; brown in skillet. Drain drippings from pan. Combine remaining soup mixture, ½ cup water, and parsley; pour over patties. Cook over low heat 20 minutes, stirring occasionally. Yield: 6 servings.
Mrs. Lawrence E. Nilson, El Campo, Texas.

AMERICAN ENCHILADAS

1 pound ground beef
½ cup quick-cooking oats, uncooked
1 teaspoon salt
⅛ teaspoon garlic powder
Dash of pepper
12 corn tortillas
Vegetable oil
2 (10-ounce) cans enchilada sauce
2 cups cream-style cottage cheese
1 cup (4 ounces) shredded Cheddar cheese

Brown ground beef in a skillet; drain and stir in oats, salt, garlic powder, and pepper. Set aside. Fry tortillas, one at a time, in ½ inch oil for 1 second on each side or just until tortillas are softened. Drain on paper towels; dip each tortilla in enchilada sauce.

On each tortilla, place about 2 tablespoons meat mixture and 2 tablespoons cottage cheese; roll up tightly, and place in a lightly greased 13- x 9- x 2-inch baking dish. Pour remaining enchilada sauce over top; sprinkle with cheese. Bake enchiladas at 350° for 30 minutes. Yield: 6 to 8 servings. *Dolores Lamb, Dryden, Texas.*

August

Southerners pickle much more than cucumbers, as their recipes for such vegetables as corn, yellow squash, okra, and zucchini attest. Our home economists thoroughly enjoyed preparing the favorite recipes you submitted, and we share with you a rainbow of pickles almost too pretty to bite into!

You will also find among these pages a kitchenful of new ideas for lemons and limes—beverages and desserts have never been so refreshing.

Entrées range from elegant to easy with our new ideas for fresh salmon, and don't miss gorgeous cakes you can mix up in minutes. No one will ever know you started with a mix.

Squeeze Lemons And Limes For Flavor

The cool green of limes and the sparkling yellow of lemons only hint at the goodness contained inside. It's the juice that makes these fruits so welcome in desserts and beverages.

Enjoy their zippy flavor in time-tested favorites, such as Fresh Squeezed Lemonade and our Deluxe Lemon Meringue Pie. Or choose an elegantly different selection like lime mousse served in lime shells, lemon custard in crisp meringue cups, or bubbling Lime Fizz.

For best quality, choose lemons that have a fine-textured skin and are heavy for their size. Deep-yellow lemons are usually more mature than lighter ones and aren't quite as acid. Lemons will keep up to a month in the refrigerator.

Select limes that feel firm and have a smooth, shiny skin that's deep green in color. Limes will keep in the refrigerator for six to eight weeks.

LEMON CUSTARD IN MERINGUE CUPS

3 egg whites (at room temperature)
½ teaspoon vinegar
¼ teaspoon vanilla extract
⅛ teaspoon salt
1 cup sugar
Lemon custard (recipe follows)

Combine egg whites, vinegar, vanilla, and salt; beat until frothy. Gradually add sugar, 1 tablespoonful at a time, beating until stiff peaks form. (Do not underbeat the mixture.)

Spoon meringue into 6 equal portions on unglazed brown paper. (Do not use recycled paper.) Using back of spoon, shape meringue into circles about 4 inches in diameter; then shape each circle into a shell (sides should be about 1½ inches high).

Bake at 300° for 45 minutes. Cool away from drafts. Spoon lemon custard into shells. Yield: 6 servings.

Lemon Custard:

1 cup sugar
¼ cup plus 1 tablespoon cornstarch
⅛ teaspoon salt
1½ cups boiling water
3 egg yolks
¼ cup lemon juice
2 tablespoons grated lemon rind

Combine sugar, cornstarch, and salt in a heavy saucepan; mix well. Stir in boiling water; cook over low heat, stirring constantly, until thickened.

Combine egg yolks, lemon juice, and lemon rind; beat well. Gradually stir about one-fourth of hot mixture into yolks; add to remaining hot mixture, stirring constantly. Cook custard, stirring constantly, 10 minutes or until smooth and thickened. Chill thoroughly. Yield: about 2½ cups.

Mrs. Paul Raper,
Burgaw, North Carolina.

DELUXE LEMON MERINGUE PIE

1½ cups sugar
⅓ cup cornstarch
¼ teaspoon salt
1½ cups cold water
½ cup lemon juice
5 eggs, separated
2 tablespoons butter or margarine
1 to 3 teaspoons grated lemon rind
1 baked 9-inch pastry shell
¼ teaspoon cream of tartar
½ cup plus 2 tablespoons sugar
½ teaspoon vanilla extract

Combine 1½ cups sugar, cornstarch, and salt in a large heavy saucepan; mix well. Gradually add water and lemon juice, stirring until mixture is smooth.

Beat egg yolks until thick and lemon colored; gradually stir into lemon mixture. Add butter. Cook over medium heat, stirring constantly, until thickened and bubbly. Cook 1 minute, stirring constantly. Remove from heat, and stir in lemon rind. Pour into pastry shell.

Combine egg whites (at room temperature) and cream of tartar; beat until foamy. Gradually add remaining sugar, 1 tablespoonful at a time, beating until stiff peaks form. Beat in vanilla. Spread meringue over filling, sealing to edge of pastry. Bake at 350° for 12 to 15 minutes or until golden brown. Cool to room temperature. Yield: one 9-inch pie.

LEMON ZEPHERS

1 cup butter or margarine, softened
½ cup sifted powdered sugar
2 cups all-purpose flour
⅛ teaspoon salt
1 teaspoon lemon extract
Lemon filling (recipe follows)
Powdered sugar

Cream butter; gradually add ½ cup powdered sugar, beating until light and fluffy. Combine flour and salt; add to creamed mixture, beating well. Stir in lemon flavoring.

Flour hands, and shape dough into ¾-inch balls. Place about 2 inches apart on ungreased cookie sheets, and flatten each slightly. Bake at 400° for 8 to 10 minutes or until browned. Remove to wire racks to cool.

Spoon ¼ to ½ teaspoon lemon filling onto half the cookies; spread evenly. Place a second cookie on top of filling, and sprinkle with powdered sugar. Yield: about 3 dozen.

Lemon Filling:

1 egg, beaten
⅔ cup sugar
3 tablespoons lemon juice
2 tablespoons butter or margarine, softened
1½ teaspoons grated lemon rind

Combine all ingredients in top of double boiler, and bring water to a boil. Reduce heat to low; cook, stirring constantly, until thickened. Chill about 1 hour. Yield: about ⅔ cup.

Mabel Clarke,
Martinsville, Virginia.

FRESH SQUEEZED LEMONADE

1½ cups sugar
½ cup boiling water
1 tablespoon grated lemon rind
1½ cups fresh lemon juice
5 cups cold water
Lemon or lime slices
Fresh mint sprigs

Combine sugar and boiling water, stirring until sugar dissolves. Add lemon rind, lemon juice, and cold water; mix well. Chill.

Serve over ice. Garnish with lemon or lime slices and fresh mint sprigs. Yield: about 7¼ cups.

LIME FIZZ

¼ cup crème de menthe
¼ cup lime juice
2 teaspoons commercial sweetened lime juice
1 pint vanilla ice cream
1 quart carbonated lemon-lime beverage, chilled
Lime slices (optional)

Combine first 3 ingredients, stirring well; pour equal amounts into 4 large glasses. Spoon ½ cup ice cream into each glass, and pour 1 cup carbonated lemon-lime beverage over ice cream; stir gently. Garnish with lime slices, if desired. Yield: 4 servings.

Brenda Yazel,
Kiowa, Kansas.

LUSCIOUS LIME MOUSSE FREEZE

12 limes
½ cup butter or margarine
1¾ teaspoons grated lime rind
1½ cups sugar
Dash of salt
3 eggs, beaten
3 egg yolks, beaten
1 cup whipping cream
Additional whipped cream
Additional grated lime rind
Fresh mint sprigs

Cut a thin slice from bottom of each lime so they will sit flat. Cut a ¾-inch slice from top of each lime.

Carefully juice limes, preserving shape of shell. Set aside ¼ cup juice (save remainder for other uses). Clip membranes inside lime shells, and carefully remove the pulp (do not puncture bottom).

Melt butter in top of a double boiler; stir in 1¾ teaspoons lime rind, ¼ cup lime juice, sugar, and salt. Gradually add eggs and egg yolks, stirring constantly. Cook over hot water, stirring constantly, until very thick and smooth. Remove from heat, and let mixture cool completely.

Beat 1 cup whipping cream until soft peaks form, and fold into lime mixture; spoon into lime shells, mounding mixture on top. Freeze for 6 hours or until firm.

To serve, top with additional whipped cream and lime rind; garnish with fresh mint sprigs. Yield: 12 servings.

Jane Walcott,
Fort Smith, Arkansas.

Pickle The Pick Of The Summer Garden

Seasons come and go, but the marvelous flavors of a summertime garden are definitely worth preserving. Imagine the cold winter day when you open that first jar of pickles. Whether you crunch into a crisp cucumber slice or savor a juicy pod of well-spiced okra, you'll taste your garden once again.

Pickling was a necessity in times gone by, one of the ways to preserve food for the winter months. Today, this almost-forgotten art is being revived—not out of necessity, but for flavor, economy, and the satisfaction of preserving fresh fruits and vegetables. Included here are pointers on ingredients and techniques, along with some special recipes.

The Ingredients

Almost anything that grows in the garden can be pickled. To name a few choices besides cucumbers, there's corn, okra, tomatoes, squash, watermelon, and all sorts of combinations. Just remember that good pickles begin with good-quality produce. This means tender vegetables and firm fruit; the more uniform in size, the better. Uniformity is also something you'll need to keep in mind when chopping or slicing fruit and vegetables for pickling.

One way to make your homemade pickles extra special is to use fresh herbs. A sprig of fresh dillweed and a fresh bay leaf will make dill pickles taste better and look prettier. Hot red peppers, cloves of garlic, and sprigs of fresh tarragon may be added to tangy pickles for an extra touch of zest.

We suggest that you purchase fresh spices for each pickling season, as spices tend to deteriorate and lose their flavor during storage.

Besides good-quality produce and fresh herbs and spices, you'll want to use vinegar with 5% acetic acid. For best color, distilled vinegar is usually recommended. The cider type can be substituted, however, as long as it's 5% acidity.

You'll also need to buy pickling salt; it acts as a preservative, as well as adds flavor and crispness to the pickles. Do not use regular table salt; the additives in this type of salt can cause pickles to be cloudy and discolored.

Some older recipes call for soaking the vegetables to be pickled in powdered alum or lime to add crispness and firmness to the pickles. If all the other proper ingredients are used, these products will not be necessary.

About the Containers

Glass canning jars are the most popular containers for pickles. They come in a wide choice of sizes and styles, and many people especially like the look of the old-style jars equipped with glass lids and wire-bail closures.

One problem with these old-style jars and also with the newer reproductions is that they sometimes do not seal properly. Always check them carefully for leakage. If leaks do occur, repeat the sealing process immediately.

By far, the most popular and reliable closure for jars is the two-piece vacuum lid and cap.

Processing and Storing

The final heat processing of a boiling-water bath is needed for all home-canned goods, including pickles. The processing doesn't affect the flavor or texture of the pickles, but it does help ensure safety by killing micro-organisms that could cause food spoilage.

After processing pickles, let the jars cool. Then check to see if each is properly sealed. Turn the jars upside down, and look for leakage or bubbles that start at the seal or cap and rise through the contents. If either is the case, an improper seal is indicated; re-process that jar of pickles immediately or refrigerate and use as soon as possible.

To keep your pickles at their best, store them in a cool, dark, dry place. In most cases, the pickles should be stored at least several weeks before eating to let the flavors fully develop.

OKRA PICKLES

3½ pounds small okra pods
5 cloves garlic
5 small fresh hot peppers
1 quart water
1 pint vinegar (5% acidity)
⅓ cup pickling salt
2 teaspoons dillseeds

Pack okra tightly into hot sterilized jars, leaving ¼-inch headspace. Place a clove of garlic and a hot pepper in each of the jars.

Combine remaining ingredients in a medium saucepan; bring to a boil. Pour vinegar mixture over okra, leaving ¼-inch headspace.

Cover at once with metal lids, and screw bands tight. Process in boiling-water bath for 10 minutes. Yield: 4 to 5 pints.

MIXED PICKLES

¾ cup pickling salt
4 quarts cold water
1 quart sliced small cucumbers
(1-inch slices)
2 cups sliced carrots (1½-inch slices)
2 cups sliced celery (1½-inch slices)
2 cups small boiling onions
2 sweet red peppers, cut into ½-inch
strips
1 small cauliflower, broken into flowerets
6½ cups vinegar (5% acidity)
2 cups sugar
1 fresh hot red pepper, sliced crosswise
¼ cup mustard seeds
2 tablespoons celery seeds

Dissolve salt in water; pour over vegetables in a large crock or plastic container. Cover and let stand in a cool place 12 to 18 hours. Drain well.

Combine vinegar, sugar, hot red pepper, and spices in a 10-quart Dutch oven; bring to a boil, and boil 3 minutes. Add vegetables; reduce heat, and simmer until thoroughly heated.

Pack into hot sterilized jars, leaving ¼-inch headspace. Cover at once with metal lids, and screw bands tight. Process in boiling-water bath for 15 minutes. Yield: about 6 pints.

DILL PICKLES

30 to 40 medium cucumbers, sliced
lengthwise
Fresh dill sprigs
Bay leaves
Garlic cloves
Fresh hot red pepper, thinly sliced
Mustard seeds
¾ cup sugar
½ cup pickling salt
1 quart vinegar (5% acidity)
1 quart water
3 tablespoons mixed pickling spices

Pack cucumbers into hot sterilized jars, leaving ¼-inch headspace. Place 1 sprig dill, 1 bay leaf, 1 clove garlic, 1 slice red pepper, and ½ teaspoon mustard seeds in each jar.

Combine sugar, salt, vinegar, and water in a medium saucepan. Tie pickling spices in cheesecloth; add to vinegar mixture. Bring to a boil, and simmer 15 minutes. Remove spice bag, and return mixture to a boil; pour over cucumbers, leaving ¼-inch headspace.

Cover at once with metal lids, and screw bands tight. Process in boiling-water bath for 15 minutes. Yield: about 8 pints.

CUCUMBER SANDWICH PICKLES

6 cups sliced medium cucumbers
(¼-inch slices)
½ cup pickling salt
2 quarts water
5 cups vinegar (5% acidity), divided
4 cups water, divided
1 cup firmly packed brown sugar
1 cup sugar
½ teaspoon celery seeds
½ teaspoon mustard seeds
½ teaspoon ground turmeric

Place cucumbers in a large Dutch oven; sprinkle with salt, and add 2 quarts water. Cover and let stand 2 to 3 hours. Drain cucumbers well.

Combine 3 cups vinegar and 3 cups water in a large Dutch oven; bring to a boil. Add cucumbers, and simmer about 8 minutes. (Do not allow cucumbers to become soft.) Drain well.

Combine 2 cups vinegar and 1 cup water in a large Dutch oven; add remaining ingredients except cucumbers. Simmer 10 minutes; add cucumbers, and bring to a boil.

Pack cucumbers into hot sterilized jars, leaving ¼-inch headspace. Cover at once with metal lids, and screw bands tight. Process in boiling-water bath for 10 minutes. Yield: about 3 pints.

SQUASH PICKLES

4 medium-size yellow squash, sliced ¼
inch thick
½ cup pickling salt
2 small onions, thinly sliced
½ cup sugar
1½ cups vinegar (5% acidity)
3 tablespoons dry mustard
1 tablespoon ground ginger
1 tablespoon curry powder
6 whole peppercorns

Layer squash and salt in a large glass or plastic container. Cover and let stand about 4 hours. Rinse squash several times in cold water; drain well.

Place squash and onion in a large Dutch oven. Combine remaining ingredients in a small, heavy saucepan, mixing well. Bring to a boil; boil 5 minutes, stirring often.

Pour vinegar mixture over squash; bring mixture to a boil, and cook 5 minutes or just until squash is crisp-tender.

Pack into hot sterilized jars, leaving ¼-inch headspace. Cover at once with metal lids, and screw bands tight. Process in boiling-water bath for 15 minutes. Yield: about 2 pints.

DILLED FRESH ZUCCHINI

6 pounds medium zucchini, thinly sliced
2 cups thinly sliced celery
2 cups chopped onion
½ cup sugar
2 tablespoons dillseeds
2 cups vinegar (5% acidity)
6 cloves garlic, halved

Combine vegetables in a large bowl; cover with ice cubes. Cover and let stand about 3 hours. Drain well.

Combine sugar, dillseeds, and vinegar in a large Dutch oven; bring to a boil over medium heat, stirring constantly. Add vegetables, and bring to a boil.

Pack into hot sterilized jars, leaving ¼-inch headspace. Add 1 to 2 pieces of garlic per jar. Cover at once with metal lids, and screw bands tight. Process in boiling-water bath for 15 minutes. Yield: about 10 pints.

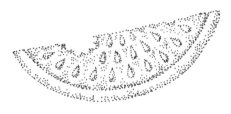

WATERMELON RIND PICKLES

1 large watermelon, quartered
Pickling salt
2 tablespoons plus 2 teaspoons whole
cloves
16 (1½-inch) sticks cinnamon
½ teaspoon mustard seeds
8 cups sugar
1 quart vinegar (5% acidity)

Peel watermelon, and remove flesh; cut rind into 1-inch cubes.

Place rind in a large crock or plastic container. Add water by the quart until it covers the rind; add ¼ cup pickling salt for each quart water, stirring until salt dissolves. Cover and let stand in a cool place overnight. Drain well.

Place rind in a 10-quart Dutch oven; cover with cold water. Bring to a boil, and boil until rind is almost tender. Drain and set aside.

Tie cloves, cinnamon, and mustard seeds in cheesecloth. Combine spice bag, sugar, and vinegar in a Dutch oven. Bring to a boil; remove from heat, and let stand 15 minutes. Add rind to syrup. Bring to a boil; reduce heat to low, and cook until rind is transparent. Remove spice bag.

Pack rind into hot sterilized jars, leaving ½-inch headspace. Cover at once with metal lids, and screw bands tight. Process in boiling-water bath for 5 minutes. Yield: about 6 pints.

CHILI SAUCE

4 quarts peeled, cored, and chopped ripe
   tomatoes
2 cups chopped onion
2 cups chopped sweet red pepper
1 fresh hot red pepper, minced
1 cup sugar
3 tablespoons pickling salt
3 tablespoons mixed pickling
   spices
1 tablespoon celery seeds
1 tablespoon mustard seeds
2½ cups vinegar (5% acidity)

Combine first 6 ingredients in a heavy 10-quart Dutch oven. Simmer, uncovered, 45 minutes.

Tie pickling spices, celery seeds, and mustard seeds in cheesecloth; add to tomato mixture. Simmer, uncovered, about 1½ hours or until thick. Stir in vinegar, and simmer 1 additional hour or until mixture reaches desired thickness. Remove spice bag.

Pour chili sauce into hot sterilized jars, leaving ¼-inch headspace. Cover at once with metal lids, and screw bands tight. Process in boiling water bath for 15 minutes. Yield: about 4 pints.

CORN RELISH

About 18 ears fresh corn
7 quarts water
1 small head cabbage, chopped
1 cup chopped onion
1 cup chopped green pepper
1 cup chopped sweet red pepper
1 to 2 cups sugar
2 tablespoons dry mustard
1 tablespoon celery seeds
1 tablespoon mustard seeds
1 tablespoon salt
1 tablespoon ground turmeric
1 quart vinegar (5% acidity)
1 cup water

Remove husks and silks from corn just before cooking. Bring 7 quarts water to a boil; add corn. Bring water to a second boil; boil 5 minutes. Cut corn from cob, measuring about 2 quarts of kernels.

Combine corn kernels and remaining ingredients in a large saucepan; simmer over low heat 20 minutes. Bring mixture to a boil.

Pack into hot sterilized jars, leaving ¼-inch headspace. Cover at once with metal lids, and screw bands tight. Process in boiling-water bath for 15 minutes. Yield: about 6 pints.

The sweet, refreshing flavor of Orange Rice is just right for a party menu; it's an elegant dish that's easy to prepare.

Three Rich Ideas For Rice

Fluffy rice is hospitable to a host of other ingredients in these three recipes. Plain rice becomes party fare when it's simmered with orange juice and orange rind. Cheese, rice, and pimiento combine for Cheese-Rice Strata, while Far East Fruited Rice calls for pineapple, ham, and chicken.

ORANGE RICE

2 cups water
½ cup orange juice
1 tablespoon grated orange rind
1 teaspoon salt
1 cup uncooked regular rice

Combine first 4 ingredients in a medium saucepan. Bring to a boil; add rice. Reduce heat and simmer, covered, 25 minutes or until liquid is absorbed. Yield: about 4 to 6 servings.

Mrs. Francis Blanchard,
St. Martinville, Louisiana.

FAR EAST FRUITED RICE

¼ cup butter or margarine, softened
3 cups hot cooked rice
1 cup cubed cooked ham
1 cup cubed cooked chicken
1 cup pineapple chunks, drained
1 cup thinly sliced green pepper
½ cup sliced water chestnuts
½ teaspoon pepper
2 tablespoons soy sauce
¼ teaspoon garlic powder
1 teaspoon onion powder

Stir butter into hot rice; add remaining ingredients, mixing well. Spoon rice mixture into a lightly greased 2-quart casserole. Cover and bake at 350° for 30 minutes. Yield: 6 servings.

Doris Amonette,
Tulsa, Oklahoma.

CHEESE-RICE STRATA

3 cups cooked regular rice
2 cups (8 ounces) shredded Cheddar or
American cheese
¼ cup diced pimiento
2½ cups milk
4 eggs, slightly beaten
½ teaspoon seasoned pepper
½ teaspoon dry mustard
¼ teaspoon hot sauce

Place half the rice in a lightly greased 13- x 9- x 2-inch baking dish; top with half the cheese, and sprinkle with pimiento. Repeat layers. Combine remaining ingredients, mixing well; pour milk mixture over rice layers. Cover and refrigerate overnight. Bake at 325° for 45 minutes or until firm. Yield: 10 to 12 servings.

Mrs. J. Russell Buchanan,
Prospect, Kentucky.

Try A Versatile Crab Stuffing

This moist crabmeat stuffing is exceptional for its flavor—and its versatility. You can use it mounded between fresh jumbo shrimp, wrapped in bacon, and baked. It's also an outstanding stuffing for fresh flounder.

CRAB-STUFFED SHRIMP BUNDLES

1 pound fresh crabmeat, drained and
flaked
45 (2-inch) saltine crackers, crushed
½ cup mayonnaise
½ cup catsup
¼ cup butter or margarine, melted
2 tablespoons prepared mustard
1 egg, beaten
1 teaspoon Worcestershire sauce
Dash of hot sauce
30 to 40 jumbo shrimp, peeled and
deveined
10 slices bacon

Combine first 9 ingredients; mix well and set aside.

Place 2 shrimp side by side in the center of a slice of bacon. Spoon 3 tablespoons crab stuffing over shrimp; top with 1 or 2 additional shrimp. Wrap ends of bacon over crab stuffing and shrimp, securing with a wooden pick.

Repeat procedure with the remaining ingredients.

Place bundles in a 13- x 9- x 2-inch baking dish. Bake, uncovered, at 350° for 40 minutes. (Any extra crab stuffing may be spooned into a lightly greased ½-quart casserole and baked at 350° for 30 minutes.)

Baste bundles with drippings; place under broiler, and broil 1 to 2 minutes or until lightly browned. Yield: about 5 servings.

Note: Crab stuffing may also be used to stuff flounder. Lay flounder on a cutting board, light side down; slit lengthwise, beginning ¾ inch from head and cutting down center of fish to tail. Make a crosswise slit in flounder near head. Cut flesh along both sides of backbone to the tail, allowing the knife to run over the rib bones to form a pocket for stuffing.

Stuff flounder loosely with crabmeat mixture, and place on a greased baking sheet. Bake at 350° for 40 to 60 minutes (depending on size of fish) or until fish flakes easily when tested with a fork.

Donald R. Smith,
Panacea, Florida.

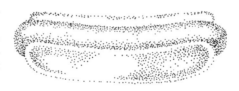

Microwave Cookery

Serve Lunch In A Jiffy

Busy schedules call for lunches that are quick and easy to prepare. With this in mind, we've adapted four favorite lunch ideas for simplified preparation in a microwave oven.

Chili-Cheese Dogs are sure to make a hit with youngsters. For a soup meal, we suggest our tomato-vegetable combination topped with a dollop of sour cream. Equally delicious are the Cheddary Egg Medley and Macaroni-Ham Casserole.

A time range is given in each recipe to allow for the difference in wattage of microwave ovens. To prevent overcooking, always check for doneness at the lower end of the range.

CHILI-CHEESE DOGS

8 hot dog buns
Spicy brown mustard
1 (15-ounce) can chili with beans
8 frankfurters
1 cup (4 ounces) shredded process
American cheese

Spread hot dog buns with mustard; set aside.

Place chili in a small bowl; cover with heavy-duty plastic wrap. Microwave at HIGH for 3 to 4 minutes or until thoroughly heated, stirring and giving dish a half-turn after 2 minutes. Set aside, and keep warm.

Pierce frankfurters with a fork in several places. Place frankfurters on a glass pizza plate or microwave-safe platter; cover with paper towels. Microwave at HIGH for 2 to 3 minutes or until thoroughly heated, giving dish a half-turn after 1 minute.

Place frankfurters in buns; spoon on chili, and sprinkle with cheese. Microwave at HIGH for 1 to 1½ minutes or until hot and cheese begins to melt. Yield: 8 servings.

CHEDDARY EGG MEDLEY

6 slices bacon
¼ cup finely chopped green pepper
¼ cup finely chopped onion
1 tablespoon butter or margarine
4 eggs
2 tablespoons milk
¼ teaspoon celery salt
Dash of pepper
2 tablespoons chopped pimiento
½ cup (2 ounces) shredded Cheddar
cheese

Place bacon on a microwave bacon rack; cover with paper towels. Microwave at HIGH for 5½ to 6½ minutes or until crisp. Crumble and set aside.

Place green pepper, onion, and butter in a 9-inch glass pieplate. Microwave at HIGH for 1 minute or until butter melts.

Combine eggs, milk, celery salt, and pepper; mix well, and stir in pimiento and bacon. Pour mixture into pieplate. Microwave at HIGH for 1½ minutes; stir to break up cooked portions. Microwave at HIGH for 1 to 2 minutes or until eggs are almost set but still moist, stirring at 1-minute intervals.

Sprinkle egg mixture with cheese; microwave at MEDIUM for 30 to 45 seconds or until cheese begins to melt. Let stand about 3 minutes before serving. Yield: 2 servings.

MACARONI-HAM CASSEROLE

1¼ cups elbow macaroni
4 cups hot water
½ teaspoon salt
1 cup diced fully cooked ham
2 tablespoons butter or margarine
2 tablespoons all-purpose flour
¼ teaspoon salt
¼ teaspoon dry mustard
1 cup milk
1½ cups (6 ounces) shredded Cheddar
   cheese
Paprika

Combine first 3 ingredients in a deep 3-quart casserole. Cover and microwave at HIGH for 10 to 12 minutes or until macaroni is done, stirring after 5 minutes. Drain well; stir in ham, and set aside.

Place butter in a 4-cup glass measure, and microwave at HIGH for 45 seconds or until melted. Add flour, ¼ teaspoon salt, and dry mustard; stir until smooth. Gradually stir in milk; microwave at HIGH for 1½ minutes, and stir well. Microwave at HIGH for 2 to 3 minutes or until thickened and bubbly, stirring at 1-minute intervals. Stir in cheese.

Combine macaroni mixture and cheese sauce in a 1½-quart casserole, mixing well. Sprinkle with paprika, and cover with heavy-duty plastic wrap. Microwave at HIGH for 3 to 4 minutes or until thoroughly heated, giving dish a half-turn after 2 minutes. Let stand 3 minutes before serving. Yield: about 4 servings.

TOMATO-VEGETABLE SOUP

2 tablespoons butter or margarine
¼ cup chopped celery
¼ cup chopped onion
1 (10¾-ounce) can condensed tomato
   soup, undiluted
1¼ cups water
1 tablespoon chopped fresh parsley
⅛ teaspoon pepper
Commercial sour cream

Place butter in a deep 1½-quart casserole. Microwave at HIGH for 45 seconds or until melted; stir in celery and onion. Cover with heavy-duty plastic wrap. Microwave at HIGH for 2 to 3 minutes or until onion is tender.

Stir soup, water, parsley, and pepper into onion mixture. Cover and microwave at HIGH for 5 to 7 minutes or until thoroughly heated, stirring after 3 minutes. Spoon into serving bowls, and top each with a dollop of sour cream. Yield: 2 servings.

Freeze A Fruit Ice Or Sherbet

One of the best ways to cool off on a warm afternoon is with a fruit sherbet or ice. Fruit and fruit juices are the basic ingredients for these frosty refreshers. Some are made for sipping, while others may be eaten with a spoon. For a special dessert, try Apricot Yogurt Ice topped with a fruit sauce and toasted almonds.

APRICOT SHERBET

2 (17-ounce) cans apricot halves, drained
½ cup sugar
⅓ cup orange juice
3 tablespoons lemon juice
2 tablespoons apricot brandy (optional)
2 egg whites
1 tablespoon sugar
½ cup whipping cream, whipped

Combine apricots, ½ cup sugar, orange juice, lemon juice, and brandy in container of an electric blender; process until smooth.

Pour mixture into freezer can of a 1-gallon hand-turned or electric freezer. Freeze according to manufacturer's instructions for 10 to 15 minutes or until mixture has thickened.

Beat egg whites (at room temperature) until foamy. Gradually add 1 tablespoon sugar, beating until stiff peaks form; fold into whipped cream. Fold whipped cream mixture into apricot mixture. Continue to freeze according to manufacturer's instructions. Let ripen at least 1 hour before serving. Yield: about 1 quart.
Elizabeth Kraus,
Louisville, Kentucky.

APRICOT YOGURT ICE

1 (30-ounce) can apricot halves
2 envelopes unflavored gelatin
2 (8-ounce) cartons plain yogurt
2 tablespoons sugar
2 tablespoons dark rum
2 tablespoons honey
Fruit sauce (recipe follows)
Toasted slivered almonds

Drain apricots, reserving liquid. Soften gelatin in ⅓ cup of reserved liquid; bring remaining liquid to a boil. Add gelatin to boiling liquid; stir until completely dissolved. Cool.

Place apricots in container of food processor or electric blender; process until smooth. Add yogurt, sugar, rum, and honey; process until thoroughly blended. Combine gelatin mixture and apricot mixture; stir well. Pour into a 9-inch square pan; freeze. Beat mixture with electric mixer two or three times during freezing process. Let stand at room temperature 10 minutes before serving. To serve, spoon into serving bowls and top with fruit sauce; sprinkle with almonds. Yield: about 6½ cups.

Fruit Sauce:

1 cup dried apricots
¼ cup water
1 (8¼-ounce) can crushed pineapple,
   undrained
½ cup sugar

Combine apricots and water in a small saucepan. Cover and cook over low heat, stirring frequently, until fruit becomes soft (about 30 minutes); add water as needed. Add pineapple and sugar; bring mixture to a boil, stirring until sugar dissolves. Chill. Yield: 2 cups.
Mrs. Harvey Kidd,
Hernando, Mississippi.

PINEAPPLE SHERBET

2½ cups buttermilk
⅔ cup sugar
½ cup light corn syrup
½ cup lemon juice
½ cup orange juice
1 (8-ounce) can crushed pineapple,
   undrained
2 tablespoons honey

Combine all ingredients, mixing well. Pour mixture into freezer can of a 1-gallon hand-turned or electric freezer. Freeze according to manufacturer's instructions. Let ripen at least 1 hour before serving. Yield: 1¼ quarts.
Mrs. William S. Bell,
Chattanooga, Tennessee.

MIXED FRUIT ICE

3 cups water
1½ cups sugar
½ cup lemon juice
1¼ cups orange juice
3 bananas, mashed

Combine water and sugar in a medium saucepan; place over medium heat and cook, stirring constantly, until sugar dissolves. Cool.

Combine syrup and remaining ingredients in a large bowl, mixing well. Cover and freeze until firm. Let stand at room temperature 30 minutes before serving. Yield: about 7 cups.

Mrs. Brenda Preston,
Greensboro, North Carolina.

PEACH ICE

1 cup sugar
½ cup light corn syrup
2 cups water, divided
1 (29-ounce) can peaches, drained
¼ cup lemon juice

Combine sugar, corn syrup, and 1 cup water in a small saucepan. Bring mixture to a boil, stirring constantly until sugar dissolves; reduce heat, and simmer 3 minutes. Cool.

Place peaches in container of food processor or electric blender; process until smooth. Add remaining cup of water, and process until thoroughly combined.

Combine syrup, peach mixture, and lemon juice; stir well. Pour into an 8-inch square pan; freeze. Stir a few times during freezing process. Let stand at room temperature 10 minutes before serving. Yield: about 6½ cups.

Kathleen McWilliams,
Midway, Kentucky.

HAWAIIAN FRAPPE

1 cup water
¾ cup sugar
2 cups unsweetened pineapple juice
1 cup orange juice
Mint sprigs (optional)

Combine water and sugar in a small saucepan. Bring to a boil, stirring constantly until sugar dissolves; reduce heat, and simmer 5 minutes. Cool.

Combine syrup, pineapple juice, and orange juice; stir well. Pour into an 11- x 7- x 2-inch pan; freeze. Let stand at room temperature 10 minutes before serving. Garnish with mint sprigs, if desired. Yield: about 4 cups.

Mrs. Sidney I. McGrath,
Hopkinsville, Kentucky.

Add Extras To That Cake Mix

When you don't have time to bake a cake from scratch, reach for a cake mix. By adding a few extra ingredients to the mix, you can bake a cake that rivals grandmother's favorite without the fuss of measuring, creaming, and mixing.

Miniature marshmallows, pecans, and chocolate chips transform a chocolate macaroon ring cake mix into Rocky Road Cake. Baked in a Bundt pan, then lightly glazed, this cake is ideal to take along on a picnic. Angel food cake mix, lemon pudding mix, and whipped cream short-cut the preparation time of Lemon-Coconut Cream Cake—layers of angel food cake spread with lemon filling and frosted with whipped cream and coconut.

ROCKY ROAD CAKE

1 (27¼-ounce) package chocolate
    macaroon ring cake mix
1¼ cups water
¼ cup butter or margarine, softened
2 eggs
½ cup miniature marshmallows
½ cup finely chopped pecans
1 (6-ounce) package semisweet chocolate
    morsels, divided
⅓ cup water
1 tablespoon plus 1 teaspoon water

The package of cake mix should include separate envelopes: cake mix, macaroon mixture, and glaze mix.

Combine cake mix, 1¼ cups water, butter, and eggs in a large mixing bowl; beat 2 minutes at highest speed of electric mixer. Stir in the marshmallows,

pecans, and ½ cup chocolate morsels. Spoon batter into a greased and floured 10-inch Bundt pan or tube pan.

Combine macaroon mix, ⅓ cup water, and remaining chocolate morsels; mix well. Spoon over chocolate batter without touching sides of pan.

Bake at 350° for 40 to 45 minutes or until cake tests done. Cool in pan 25 minutes; remove from pan, and complete cooling on a wire rack.

Combine glaze mix and 1 tablespoon plus 1 teaspoon water; mix until smooth. Spoon over cake. Yield: one 10-inch cake.

Sandra Russell,
Maitland, Florida.

CREME DE MENTHE CAKE

1 (18.5-ounce) package regular white cake
    mix (not pudding type)
2 egg whites
1 cup plus 3 tablespoons water
¼ cup crème de menthe, divided
1 (16-ounce) can chocolate fudge topping
1 (8-ounce) carton frozen whipped
    topping, thawed
Mint leaves (optional)
Maraschino cherries (optional)

Combine cake mix, egg whites, water, and 2 tablespoons crème de menthe. Beat 2 minutes at highest speed of electric mixer. Reduce speed to low; beat for 1 minute. Pour batter into a greased and floured 13- x 9- x 2-inch baking pan. Bake at 350° for 25 minutes or until a wooden pick inserted in center comes out clean. Let cake cool completely in pan.

Spread fudge topping over cake. Combine whipped topping with remaining 2 tablespoons crème de menthe; mix well, and spread over fudge topping. Cover and chill at least 2 hours. Cut into squares to serve. Garnish with mint leaves and maraschino cherries, if desired. Yield: 15 to 18 servings.

Mrs. Thomas R. Cherry,
Birmingham, Alabama.

Tip: If a recipe calls for egg whites, use leftover yolks to make mayonnaise, thicken soups or cream sauces, make eggnog, or enrich scrambled eggs or omelets.

COCONUT CREAM CAKE

1 (18.5-ounce) package regular white cake
    mix (not pudding type)
1 (3½-ounce) can flaked coconut, divided
1⅓ cups water
2 egg whites
1 (8½-ounce) can cream of coconut
1 (12-ounce) carton frozen whipped
    topping, thawed

Combine cake mix, 1 cup coconut, water, and egg whites; beat 2 minutes at highest speed of electric mixer. Reduce speed to low; beat for 1 minute. Pour batter into a greased and floured 13- x 9- x 2-inch baking pan. Bake at 350° for 25 to 30 minutes or until a wooden pick inserted in center comes out clean. Cool cake in pan for 10 minutes.

Punch holes in top of cake with a wooden pick. Pour cream of coconut over cake while still warm. Spread whipped topping over cake; sprinkle with remaining coconut. Cover and chill at least 4 hours. Cut cake into squares to serve. Yield: 15 to 18 servings.
Diana Curtis,
Albuquerque, New Mexico.

LEMON-COCONUT CREAM CAKE

1 (16-ounce) package white angel food
    cake mix
1 (4½-ounce) package lemon pudding and
    pie filling mix
2 egg yolks, beaten
½ cup sugar
2 cups water
1 tablespoon grated lemon rind
2 tablespoons lemon juice
2½ cups whipping cream, divided
1 (3½-ounce) can flaked coconut, divided

Prepare and bake cake mix according to package directions. Invert pan on funnel or bottle until cake is completely cooled (approximately 2 hours).

Combine lemon pudding mix, egg yolks, sugar, and 2 cups water in a heavy saucepan; mix well. Cook over medium heat, stirring constantly, until thickened and bubbly. Remove from heat; stir in lemon rind and lemon juice. Cover and chill completely (about 1 hour).

Loosen cake from sides of pan using a small metal spatula. Remove from pan. Split cake horizontally into 4 layers.

Beat 1 cup whipping cream until stiff peaks form. Fold whipped cream and ⅔ cup coconut into lemon filling.

Place bottom layer of cake on a cake plate; spread with 1¼ cups lemon mixture. Repeat with second and third layers. Place remaining layer, cut side down, on top of cake. Cover and chill cake overnight.

Beat remaining whipping cream until stiff peaks form; frost sides and top of cake. Sprinkle with remaining coconut. Chill at least 2 hours before serving. Yield: one 10-inch cake. *Deann Reed,*
Staunton, Virginia.

Cook Supper In A Skillet

If a busy schedule leaves you short of time and ideas for family meals, try one of these skillet suppers. They require little attention while cooking, and you have only one pan to clean.

Economical ground beef is featured in Beef-Cabbage Dinner and Beefy Noodle Dinner. Skillet Chicken is cooked with wine and currant jelly and served with a sour cream sauce. And for Pork Chop Dinner, meat and vegetables simmer together, with the drippings used for making gravy.

BEEF STROGANOFF

1 (3-pound) round steak, ½ inch thick
¼ cup all-purpose flour
¼ cup butter or margarine
1 large onion, thinly sliced
1 (10½-ounce) can consommé, undiluted
1 (10¾-ounce) can tomato soup, undiluted
1 (4-ounce) can sliced mushrooms,
    drained
½ teaspoon salt
¼ teaspoon pepper
½ cup commercial sour cream
Hot cooked egg noodles

Partially freeze steak; then slice across grain into 2- x ¼-inch strips. Dredge steak in flour.

Melt butter in a large skillet; add meat and onion, and cook until meat is browned. Stir in consommé, soup, mushrooms, salt, and pepper. Reduce heat to low; cover and simmer 30 to 45 minutes or until meat is tender. Stir in sour cream, and cook just until thoroughly heated. Serve over noodles. Yield: 8 servings. *Phyllis H. William,*
Salemburg, North Carolina.

BEEFY NOODLE DINNER

½ pound ground beef
1 medium onion, chopped
1 small clove garlic, crushed
2 tablespoons minced fresh parsley
1 (6-ounce) can tomato paste
2¼ cups water
1 teaspoon sugar
¾ teaspoon salt
½ teaspoon pepper
2 cups medium egg noodles
Grated Parmesan cheese (optional)

Combine ground beef, onion, garlic, and parsley in a large skillet; cook over medium heat until meat is browned, stirring frequently. Drain well. Stir in tomato paste, water, sugar, salt, and pepper. Reduce heat to low; cover and cook 10 minutes. Add noodles; cover and cook about 20 minutes or until noodles are done, stirring occasionally. Serve with Parmesan cheese, if desired. Yield: 4 servings. *Cindy Murphy,*
Cleveland, Tennessee.

BEEF-CABBAGE DINNER

1 teaspoon butter or margarine
4 to 5 cups coarsely shredded cabbage
1 medium onion, chopped
2 cups thinly sliced potatoes
1 teaspoon caraway seeds
1 pound lean ground beef
½ teaspoon salt
¼ teaspoon pepper
1 (15-ounce) can tomato sauce

Melt butter in a large skillet; add cabbage and onion, mixing well. Arrange potatoes over cabbage; sprinkle with caraway seeds. Crumble ground beef over potatoes; sprinkle with salt and pepper. Pour tomato sauce over ground beef. Cover skillet, and cook over low heat 30 to 35 minutes or until meat is done. Yield: 4 servings.
Margaret Peterson,
Birmingham, Alabama.

PORK CHOP DINNER

4 pork chops
1 tablespoon vegetable oil
4 to 6 potatoes, quartered
4 large carrots, cut into 1-inch thick
  slices
¼ cup chopped onion
¼ cup chopped celery
1 chicken-flavored bouillon cube
1 cup boiling water
1 teaspoon salt
⅛ teaspoon pepper
2 tablespoons all-purpose flour
1 cup water

Sauté pork chops in hot oil in an electric skillet set at 300° for 15 minutes, turning once; drain. Top pork chops with vegetables. Dissolve bouillon cube in boiling water; pour over vegetables, and sprinkle with salt and pepper. Reduce heat to 220°; cover and cook 30 minutes or until vegetables are tender. Remove meat and vegetables to serving platter, reserving drippings in skillet.

Combine flour and 1 cup water, mixing until smooth. Gradually add mixture to drippings; cook over medium heat until thickened and bubbly, stirring constantly. Serve sauce with meat and vegetables. Yield: 4 servings.

Carolyn Sorrells,
Ozark, Missouri.

SKILLET CHICKEN

2 whole chicken breasts, split and skinned
Salt to taste
¼ cup butter or margarine
¼ cup Chablis or other dry white wine
½ cup red currant jelly
½ cup commercial sour cream

Sprinkle chicken with salt. Melt butter in a large skillet. Add chicken and cook until golden brown. Reduce heat to low; add wine. Cover and cook 30 minutes.

Remove chicken; add jelly to pan drippings, stirring until blended. Return chicken to skillet, meaty side down; cover and cook 15 minutes or until done, basting frequently. Remove chicken to serving platter. Stir sour cream into sauce, and cook just until heated. Pour sauce over chicken. Yield: 4 servings. *Mrs. W. J. Scherffius,*
Mountain Home, Arkansas.

Texans Cool It With Dessert

Hot and spicy is one way Texans like their main dishes, but they like their desserts cool and creamy. That's what these recipes tell us, for all are specialties of Texas readers.

Two of the desserts feature fruit. We found Strawberry-Banana Glazed Pie particularly appealing. Bananas are also the basis for Banana Cream Dessert, with the sliced fruit tucked between layers of coconut and a creamy filling.

Sinfully delicious is the best way we know to describe Texas Cream Pie, and it's all because of the richness of the custard filling. A similar custard is the filling for Captivating Cream Puffs.

BANANA CREAM DESSERT

½ cup butter or margarine, softened
1 cup all-purpose flour
1 cup finely chopped pecans, divided
1 (8-ounce) package cream cheese,
  softened
1 cup sifted powdered sugar
1 (12-ounce) carton frozen whipped
  topping, thawed and divided
1 (3½-ounce) can flaked coconut
2 (3¾-ounce) packages vanilla instant
  pudding and pie filling mix
3 cups cold milk
3 bananas, sliced

Cut butter into flour until mixture resembles coarse meal; stir in ½ cup pecans. Press flour mixture into a 13- x 9- x 2-inch baking pan. Bake at 350° for 20 minutes; let cool completely.

Combine cream cheese and powdered sugar, beating until fluffy; stir in 1 cup whipped topping. Spread over crust, and sprinkle with coconut.

Combine pudding mix and milk; beat 2 minutes at medium speed of electric mixer. Spread over coconut layer, and top with bananas. Spread remaining whipped topping over bananas; sprinkle with remaining pecans. Store in refrigerator. Yield: 15 servings.

Frances Ewing,
Dallas, Texas.

Tip: Stale cake or cookies can be made into crumbs in a blender. Sprinkle over ice cream or puddings for a delicious topping.

CREAMY GRASSHOPPER FREEZE

2 cups finely crushed chocolate sandwich
  cookies (about 25)
¼ cup butter or margarine, melted
1 (7-ounce) jar marshmallow creme
¼ cup green crème de menthe
2 cups whipping cream, whipped

Combine cookie crumbs and butter; set aside ¼ cup crumb mixture for garnish. Press remaining mixture into bottom of a 9-inch springform pan. Chill 1 hour before filling.

Combine marshmallow creme and crème de menthe, mixing well; fold in whipped cream. Pour into prepared crust, and sprinkle with the reserved crumbs. Freeze mixture 8 hours. Yield: 8 servings. *Eleanor K. Brandt,*
Arlington, Texas.

CAPTIVATING CREAM PUFFS

1 cup water
½ cup butter or margarine
½ teaspoon salt
1 cup all-purpose flour
4 eggs
Creamy Custard Filling
Chocolate-flavored syrup

Combine water and butter in a medium saucepan; bring to a boil. Add salt and flour, all at once, stirring vigorously over low heat until mixture leaves sides of pan and forms a smooth ball. Remove from heat, and cool slightly.

Add eggs, one at a time, beating with a wooden spoon after each addition; then beat until batter is smooth.

Drop batter by rounded tablespoonfuls 3 inches apart on ungreased baking sheets. Bake at 450° for 10 minutes; reduce heat to 375° and bake an additional 30 minutes or until golden brown and puffed. Cool away from drafts.

Cut top off cream puffs; pull out and discard soft dough inside. Fill bottom halves with Creamy Custard Filling, and cover with top halves. Drizzle chocolate syrup over top. Serve immediately or refrigerate. Yield: 1 dozen.

Creamy Custard Filling:

3 tablespoons all-purpose flour
3 tablespoons cornstarch
1 cup sugar
¾ teaspoon salt
3 cups milk
3 egg yolks
1 teaspoon vanilla extract
1 tablespoon butter or margarine

Combine flour, cornstarch, sugar, and salt in a heavy saucepan; gradually stir in milk. Cook over medium heat, stirring constantly, until thickened and bubbly.

Beat egg yolks until thick and lemon colored. Gradually stir about one-fourth of hot mixture into yolks; add to remaining hot mixture, stirring constantly. Cook over medium heat, stirring constantly, about 2 minutes or until thickened. Stir in vanilla and butter; let cool. Yield: about 3 cups. *Diana McConnell, Arlington, Texas.*

FAVORITE BOILED CUSTARD

3 eggs
⅓ cup sugar
⅛ teaspoon salt
2 cups milk, scalded
1 teaspoon vanilla extract

Place eggs in top of a double boiler; beat at medium speed of electric mixer until frothy. Combine sugar and salt; gradually add to eggs, beating until thick.

Gradually stir about one-fourth of hot milk into egg mixture; add remaining milk, stirring constantly.

Bring water in bottom of double boiler to a boil. Reduce heat to low; cook custard over hot water, stirring occasionally, 20 to 25 minutes or until it thickens and coats a metal spoon. Stir in vanilla. Pour into serving bowl, and chill thoroughly. Yield: 4 servings.
Mrs. Don Rogers, Irving, Texas.

TEXAS CREAM PIE

2 cups milk
2 cups sugar, divided
2 tablespoons butter or margarine
¼ cup all-purpose flour
3 eggs, well beaten
1 teaspoon vanilla extract
3 cups whipping cream, whipped
2 baked 8-inch pastry shells
Grated chocolate

Combine milk, 1½ cups sugar, and butter in top of a double boiler. Cook over boiling water, stirring occasionally, until butter melts.

Combine flour and ½ cup sugar, mixing well; stir in eggs. Gradually stir about one-fourth of hot mixture into egg mixture; stir into remaining hot mixture. Cook over boiling water, stirring constantly, until smooth and thickened. Let cool, and stir in vanilla.

Fold about one-third of whipped cream into custard mixture; pour into pastry shells. Spread remaining whipped cream evenly on each pie; sprinkle with grated chocolate. Chill until serving time. Yield: two 8-inch pies.
Idella Cowan, Littlefield, Texas.

STRAWBERRY-BANANA GLAZED PIE

1 pint strawberries
¾ cup sugar
3 tablespoons cornstarch
Dash of salt
1 cup water
1 tablespoon butter or margarine
2 to 3 drops red food coloring
2 bananas, sliced
1 baked 9-inch pastry shell
1 cup frozen whipped topping, thawed

Wash and hull strawberries; cut in half, and set aside.

Combine sugar, cornstarch, and salt in a saucepan; mix well, and stir in water. Add butter; cook glaze over low heat until thickened, stirring constantly. Stir in food coloring.

Arrange strawberries and bananas in pastry shell, alternating layers of each. Pour glaze evenly over fruit; refrigerate 2 to 3 hours or until well chilled. Spread with whipped topping before serving. Yield: one 9-inch pie.
Jill Rorex, Dallas, Texas.

Have You Tried Fresh Salmon?

Fresh salmon is becoming a more familiar sight in supermarkets across the South. It's being sold whole or cut into steaks, fillets, or roasts.

Like most fish, salmon is simple to prepare. Our Oven-Fried Salmon Steaks, for example, marinate in a lemon juice-oil mixture, then are dredged in a seasoned coating and bake in only 15 minutes. For Salmon Kabobs, cubes of salmon are threaded on skewers along with bacon, pineapple, and vegetables and then brushed with a sauce while they cook.

Keep in mind that salmon purchased fresh needs to be prepared right away, while frozen salmon will keep up to five or six months.

BARBECUED SALMON

¾ cup firmly packed brown sugar
2 tablespoons lemon juice
2 tablespoons butter or margarine
4 (½-pound) salmon steaks, 1 inch thick

Combine brown sugar, lemon juice, and butter in a saucepan; cook mixture over low heat, stirring constantly, just until sugar dissolves.

Place salmon steaks in a well-greased, hinged fish basket. Place on grill about 3 to 4 inches from coals. Cook salmon 12 to 15 minutes on each side or until fish flakes easily, brushing often with sauce. Yield: 4 servings.

OVEN-FRIED SALMON STEAKS

½ cup vegetable oil
2 tablespoons lemon juice
2 cloves garlic, finely chopped and divided
4 (½-pound) salmon steaks, 1 inch thick
1 cup crushed herb-seasoned stuffing
½ cup grated Parmesan cheese
¼ cup chopped fresh parsley

Combine oil, lemon juice, and half the chopped garlic. Place salmon steaks in a shallow pan, and pour marinade over steaks. Cover and marinate 30 minutes in refrigerator, turning once.

Remove salmon from marinade, reserving 2 tablespoons of marinade. Combine herb-seasoned stuffing, cheese, parsley, and remaining garlic; dredge salmon in stuffing mixture. Place salmon in a greased 13- x 9- x 2-inch baking dish. Sprinkle reserved marinade over salmon, and bake at 500° for 15 minutes or until fish flakes easily. Yield: 4 servings.

Tip: Fish and onion odors can be removed from the hands by rubbing them with a little vinegar, followed by washing in soapy water.

SALMON KABOBS

¼ cup butter or margarine, melted
1 tablespoon minced onion
1 tablespoon lemon juice
1 teaspoon Worcestershire sauce
⅛ teaspoon dried whole thyme
1½ pounds salmon, cut into 1-inch cubes
2 slices bacon, cut into 1-inch pieces
12 pineapple chunks
1 medium onion, cut in half and quartered
12 fresh mushroom caps
2 medium dill pickles, cut into ½-inch slices
12 cherry tomatoes
1 medium-size green pepper, cut into 1-inch pieces
½ teaspoon salt
⅛ teaspoon pepper

Combine first 5 ingredients in a small saucepan. Cook over low heat just until heated; set aside.

Alternate salmon, bacon, pineapple, and vegetables on skewers. Place skewers in a 13- x 9- x 2-inch baking dish. Sprinkle with salt and pepper. Brush kabobs with sauce. Broil 3 inches from heat 3 to 4 minutes on each side, brushing often with sauce. Yield: 6 servings.

FRESH SALMON SOUFFLE

3 tablespoons butter or margarine
3 tablespoons all-purpose flour
1 cup milk
Salt
⅛ teaspoon coarsely ground black pepper
Dash of red pepper
Dash of ground nutmeg
4 eggs, separated
2 cups flaked, cooked salmon

Preheat oven to 400°.

Lightly grease bottom of a 1½-quart soufflé dish. Cut a piece of aluminum foil long enough to circle the dish, allowing a 1-inch overlap; fold lengthwise into thirds. Wrap foil around dish so it extends 3 inches above rim; secure with string tied around dish.

Melt butter in a heavy saucepan over low heat; add flour, stirring until smooth. Cook 1 minute, stirring constantly. Gradually add milk; cook over medium heat, stirring constantly, until thickened and bubbly. Stir in ½ teaspoon salt, pepper, red pepper, and nutmeg.

Beat egg yolks until thick and lemon colored. Gradually stir about one-fourth of white sauce into yolks; add to remaining white sauce, stirring constantly. Add salmon, and stir well.

Beat egg whites (at room temperature) and a pinch of salt until stiff but not dry; gently fold into salmon mixture. Spoon into prepared soufflé dish. Place dish in preheated oven, and immediately reduce heat to 375°. Bake for 50 minutes or until golden brown. Remove collar and serve immediately. Yield: 6 servings.

Fresh Vegetables For The Two Of You

If you think cooking just enough fresh vegetables for two servings sounds difficult, think again. It's just a matter of buying small or—if you're lucky enough to have a garden—harvesting in small quantities. Preparation is quick and easy; the rewards, delicious fresh flavors.

GREEN BEANS PROVENCAL

½ pound green beans
2 slices bacon
¼ cup chopped onion
¼ cup chopped celery
½ teaspoon salt
⅛ teaspoon pepper
1 medium tomato, peeled and cut into 8 wedges

Remove strings from beans; wash and cut diagonally into 2-inch pieces.

Fry bacon in a large skillet until crisp; drain well, reserving 2 tablespoons bacon drippings in skillet. Crumble bacon, and set aside.

Add onion and celery to skillet, and sauté until tender; add beans, salt, and pepper. Cover and simmer 10 minutes, stirring occasionally. Add tomato; cover and cook an additional 5 minutes. Sprinkle with crumbled bacon before serving. Yield: 2 servings.

Geneva P. Tobias,
Albemarle, North Carolina.

Tip: Freshen wilted vegetables by letting them stand about 10 minutes in cold water to which a few drops of lemon juice have been added; drain well, and store in a plastic bag in the refrigerator.

CREOLE OKRA

¾ cup sliced okra
2 tablespoons minced onion
2 tablespoons minced green pepper
1 tablespoon butter or margarine
¾ cup chopped tomato
1 teaspoon sugar
¼ teaspoon salt
⅛ teaspoon pepper

Sauté okra, onion, and green pepper in butter 5 minutes, stirring constantly. Stir in remaining ingredients; cook over low heat 10 to 15 minutes, stirring occasionally. Yield: 2 servings.

Darlene George,
Dickson, Tennessee.

STIR-FRY SPINACH

1 tablespoon peanut oil
½ pound fresh spinach, washed and drained
½ teaspoon salt
¼ teaspoon sugar
1 hard-cooked egg, diced

Pour oil around top of preheated wok or skillet; allow to heat at high for 2 minutes. Add half of spinach; stir-fry until leaves are coated with oil. Repeat procedure with remaining spinach. Add salt and sugar; stir-fry 1 minute. Sprinkle with egg. Yield: 2 servings.

Mrs. H. G. Drowdy,
Spindale, North Carolina.

ZIPPY BAKED TOMATO HALVES

2 tablespoons minced onion
1 tablespoon butter or margarine
½ teaspoon prepared mustard
¼ teaspoon Worcestershire sauce
1 large tomato, cut in half crosswise
1 tablespoon melted butter
½ cup soft breadcrumbs
1 teaspoon chopped fresh parsley

Sauté onion in 1 tablespoon butter until tender but not browned. Remove from heat; stir in mustard and Worcestershire sauce. Spread onion mixture over cut surface of tomato.

Combine 1 tablespoon melted butter, breadcrumbs, and parsley; mix well. Spoon over cut surface of tomato.

Place tomato halves in a baking dish. Bake at 350° for 15 minutes or until tomato is thoroughly heated and breadcrumbs are golden. Yield: 2 servings.

Norma Patelunas,
St. Petersburg, Florida.

ZUCCHINI SAUTE

2 medium zucchini
1 tablespoon chopped onion
1 tablespoon chopped green pepper
2 tablespoons olive oil
¼ teaspoon salt
⅛ teaspoon pepper
Pinch of sugar

Wash zucchini, and trim ends; cut into ½-inch slices. Sauté onion and green pepper in hot oil (375°) until tender. Reduce heat, and add zucchini; cook until crisp-tender and lightly browned, stirring frequently. Stir in salt, pepper, and sugar. Yield: 2 servings.

Nora Joyce Roach,
Conway, South Carolina.

ZUCCHINI ITALIANO

3 small zucchini, thinly sliced
1½ tablespoons butter or margarine, melted
1 large tomato, peeled, cored, and chopped
½ teaspoon sugar
½ teaspoon salt
¼ teaspoon dried Italian seasoning
⅛ teaspoon pepper

Sauté zucchini in butter 5 minutes; add remaining ingredients, stirring gently. Cover and simmer 5 to 7 minutes. Yield: 2 servings.

Marya M. James,
Seneca, South Carolina.

Squash Offers Some Of Summer's Best Dishes

Versatile yellow squash and zucchini go into some of the most popular dishes around. Serve delicate yellow squash filled and baked with a flavorful sausage stuffing or grated and fried into patties. Zucchini is delicious sliced into strips, battered, and fried until crispy.

When buying, select squash that are firm and smooth skinned. Choose small to medium squash since they are more likely to have tender skin.

Sausage and herb-seasoned stuffing make a delicious filling for yellow squash.

SAUSAGE-STUFFED SQUASH

6 medium-size yellow squash
½ pound bulk pork sausage
¼ cup finely chopped onion
½ cup herb-seasoned stuffing
¼ teaspoon salt
2½ tablespoons grated Parmesan cheese

Wash squash thoroughly; cook in boiling salted water to cover 8 to 10 minutes or until tender but still firm. Drain and cool slightly. Trim off stems. Cut squash in half lengthwise; remove and reserve pulp, leaving a firm shell.

Cook sausage and onion in a skillet over medium heat until sausage is browned, stirring to crumble. Remove from heat, and drain off pan drippings. Stir in squash pulp, herb-seasoned stuffing, and salt.

Place squash shells in a 13- x 9- x 2-inch baking dish. Spoon sausage mixture into shells; sprinkle with Parmesan cheese. Bake at 350° for 30 minutes or until lightly browned. Yield: 6 servings.

Marion Dunn Wagstaff,
Jacksonville, Florida.

Tip: Lightly mix and shape ground meat or meatloaf mixtures. Excessive handling results in a compact mixture.

COMPANY SQUASH CASSEROLE

1 pound (about 3 medium-size) yellow squash, chopped
1 medium onion, chopped
5 tablespoons butter or margarine, divided
2 tablespoons all-purpose flour
1 cup milk
5 slices process American cheese, chopped
1 (3-ounce) can sliced mushrooms, drained
½ cup cracker crumbs
½ cup chopped pecans

Place squash and onion in boiling salted water to cover. Cover and cook 5 minutes; drain well, and set aside.

Melt 3 tablespoons butter in a heavy saucepan over low heat; add flour and cook 1 minute, stirring constantly. Gradually add milk; cook over medium heat, stirring constantly, until thickened and bubbly. Add cheese and stir until melted.

Combine the squash mixture, cheese sauce, and mushrooms; spoon into a lightly greased 1½-quart casserole.

Melt 2 tablespoons butter in a small saucepan; stir in cracker crumbs and pecans. Sprinkle mixture over squash. Bake casserole at 350° for 30 minutes. Yield: 6 servings.

Jo Ann Johnson,
Fordyce, Arkansas.

SUMMER SQUASH PATTIES

1¼ cups self-rising flour
½ teaspoon sugar
¾ teaspoon salt
½ cup commercial sour cream
1 egg
1 tablespoon vegetable oil
3 cups coarsely grated yellow squash
1 medium onion, coarsely grated
Pepper to taste (optional)

Combine first 6 ingredients, beating until smooth. Stir in squash and onion; add pepper, if desired.

Drop mixture by tablespoonfuls into a hot, greased skillet. Cook until golden brown, turning once. Drain on paper towels. Yield: about 2 dozen.
*Frances Presnell,
Atlanta, Georgia.*

SUMMER SQUASH CASSEROLE

4 cups cubed yellow squash
1 cup chopped green onion
3 tablespoons butter or margarine
1 cup (4 ounces) shredded medium
  Cheddar cheese
1 cup soft breadcrumbs
1 cup milk
3 eggs, slightly beaten
½ teaspoon salt
¼ teaspoon pepper

Arrange squash and onion in steaming rack. Steam 5 to 10 minutes or to desired degree of doneness.

Combine squash mixture, butter, and cheese; stir until butter and cheese melt.

Combine remaining ingredients, and stir into squash mixture. Spoon into a lightly greased 2-quart casserole. Bake at 350° for 30 to 35 minutes or until casserole is set. Yield: 6 servings.
*Mrs. G. Pedersen,
Brandon, Mississippi.*

FRIED ZUCCHINI STRIPS

3 medium zucchini
¼ cup all-purpose flour
½ teaspoon salt
⅛ teaspoon pepper
2 eggs, slightly beaten
1 cup fine, dry breadcrumbs
½ cup vegetable oil

Cut zucchini into finger-size strips. Combine flour, salt, and pepper; mix well. Dredge zucchini in flour mixture; dip in egg, and coat with breadcrumbs. Fry zucchini in hot oil (375°) until golden brown. Drain on paper towels. Yield: 4 to 6 servings. *Cathy Darling,
Grafton, West Virginia.*

Peaches Bring A Sweet Taste Of Summer

Nothing says summer more than a basket of fresh, ripe peaches. Enjoy them baked into a golden cobbler, folded into a rich and creamy ice cream, or baked into a creamy pie.

Select peaches that are free of blemishes. A rosy color alone isn't a sign of maturity; the best clue to ripeness is the golden undercolor of the skin.

One pound of peaches equals 3 medium peaches or 2 cups sliced. To prevent the sliced fruit from darkening, sprinkle with ascorbic acid, fruit-freeze powder, or lemon juice.

PEACH COBBLER SUPREME

About 8 cups sliced fresh peaches
2 cups sugar
2 to 4 tablespoons all-purpose flour
½ teaspoon ground nutmeg
1 teaspoon almond extract
⅓ cup melted butter or margarine
Pastry for double-crust 9-inch pie

Combine peaches, sugar, flour, and nutmeg; set aside until syrup forms. Bring peaches to a boil, and cook over low heat 10 minutes or until tender. Remove from heat; add almond extract and butter, stirring well.

Roll out half of pastry to ⅛-inch thickness on a lightly floured board; cut into a 10- x 8-inch rectangle. Spoon half of peaches into a lightly buttered 10- x 8-inch baking dish; top with pastry. Bake at 475° for 12 minutes or until pastry is golden brown. Spoon remaining peaches over baked pastry.

Roll out remaining pastry, and cut into ½-inch strips; arrange in lattice design over peaches. Return to oven for 10 to 15 minutes or until lightly browned. Yield: 8 to 10 servings.

PEACHES-AND-CREAM PIE

6 fresh peaches
1 unbaked 9-inch pastry shell
½ cup sugar
¼ cup all-purpose flour
½ teaspoon ground cinnamon
1 cup commercial sour cream
2 tablespoons sugar
½ teaspoon ground cinnamon

Peel peaches and cut in half; place in pastry shell, cut side up. Combine ½ cup sugar, flour, and ½ teaspoon cinnamon in a small mixing bowl; sprinkle evenly over peaches. Spread sour cream over top. Combine 2 tablespoons sugar and ½ teaspoon cinnamon; sprinkle over sour cream. Bake at 450° for 10 minutes; lower heat to 350°, and continue baking 30 minutes. Yield: one 9-inch pie.
*Mrs. Don Jamerson,
Selmer, Tennessee.*

PEACH ICE CREAM

2 tablespoons unflavored gelatin
3 cups milk, divided
2 cups sugar
¼ teaspoon salt
6 eggs
1½ cups half-and-half
1 (3¾-ounce) package vanilla instant
  pudding and pie filling mix
1 tablespoon plus 2 teaspoons vanilla
  extract
4 cups crushed peaches

Soften gelatin in ½ cup milk. Scald 1½ cups milk; stir in gelatin mixture until dissolved. Add sugar, salt, and remaining 1 cup milk. Beat eggs at high speed of electric mixer 5 minutes. Add half-and-half, pudding mix, vanilla, and gelatin mixture; blend well. Stir in peaches. Pour into freezer can of a 1-gallon freezer. Freeze according to manufacturer's instructions. Let ripen 2 hours before serving. Yield: 1 gallon.
*Laura L. Allen,
Jay, Oklahoma.*

Right: *Fresh mushrooms are marinated for Fabulous Mushroom Salad (page 190), then served on a bed of spinach and garnished with tomato wedges and crisp bacon.*

Page 186: *Full of ham, chicken, sausage, and specialties from the sea, these gumbos are waiting to be ladled over hot rice. From top: Combo Gumbo (page 198), Crab and Shrimp Gumbo (page 200), and Chicken Gumbo With Smoked Sausage (page 199).*

Flavor It With Coffee

If your coffee enjoyment is limited to one cup in the morning, you may be missing the flavor potential of this time-honored beverage. Take a tip from these recipes, which feature coffee in lavish desserts and a rich beverage.

FROZEN MOCHA SQUARES

16 large marshmallows
½ cup strong coffee
1 cup whipping cream, whipped
Chocolate shavings

Combine marshmallows and coffee in a medium saucepan; cook over low heat until marshmallows melt, stirring occasionally. Cool.

Fold whipped cream into coffee mixture. Spoon into an 8-inch square pan. Freeze about 3 hours or until firm. Sprinkle top with chocolate shavings, and cut into squares to serve. Yield: 9 servings.   *Alberta Pinkston,
Knoxville, Tennessee.*

MEXICAN-STYLE CHOCOLATE

1½ cups water
3 (1-ounce) squares unsweetened chocolate
½ cup sugar
3 tablespoons instant coffee powder
1 teaspoon ground cinnamon
½ teaspoon ground nutmeg
¼ teaspoon salt
4 cups milk
Whipped cream

Combine first 7 ingredients in a large saucepan; bring to a boil over medium heat, stirring occasionally. Reduce heat to low; simmer 4 minutes, stirring constantly. Stir in milk; heat thoroughly.

Beat hot chocolate with rotary beater until foamy, about 1 minute. Garnish each serving with whipped cream. Yield: 1½ quarts.
*Mrs. Roderick W. McGrath,
Orlando, Florida.*

JAVA CREAM PUFFS

½ cup water
¼ cup butter or margarine
½ cup all-purpose flour
⅛ teaspoon salt
2 eggs
⅓ cup finely chopped pecans
Mocha Cream Filling
Commercial chocolate fudge sauce

Combine water and butter in saucepan; bring to a boil. Combine flour and salt; add all at once, stirring vigorously over low heat for approximately 1 minute or until mixture leaves sides of pan and forms a smooth ball. Remove from heat, and allow to cool slightly.

Add eggs, one at a time, beating with a wooden spoon after each addition; beat until batter is smooth. Stir in pecans, and drop tablespoonfuls of batter 2 inches apart on an ungreased baking sheet.

Bake at 400° for 35 to 40 minutes or until puffed and golden brown. Cool away from drafts. Cut top off cream puffs; pull out and discard soft dough inside. Fill cream puffs with Mocha Cream Filling; replace tops of cream puffs and drizzle fudge sauce over top. Yield: 10 servings.

Mocha Cream Filling:

1 cup strong coffee
24 large marshmallows
1½ cups whipping cream, whipped

Combine coffee and marshmallows in a saucepan; cook over low heat, stirring constantly, until marshmallows melt. Chill just until mixture is thickened.

Beat coffee mixture in a large bowl until light in color; fold in whipped cream. Yield: enough filling for 10 cream puffs.   *T. O. Davis,
Waynesboro, Mississippi.*

Tip: Check the accuracy of meat, candy, or deep-fat thermometers by placing in boiling water. If thermometer reads 212°, it is accurate. If not, add or subtract number of degrees above or below 212° in future recipes.

Bacon Brings On The Flavor

If the thought of bacon sizzling in the skillet starts your taste buds tingling, don't wait until breakfast for this mouth-watering temptation. Just try our bacon-filled recipes, and you'll have the flavor of crisp, fried bacon any time.

DILLICIOUS POT ROAST

4 slices bacon
1 (3- to 4-pound) boneless chuck roast
1 teaspoon lemon-pepper marinade
1 (10¾-ounce) can golden mushroom soup, undiluted
½ cup chopped dill pickle
2 teaspoons Worcestershire sauce

Fry bacon in a large Dutch oven until crisp; remove bacon, reserving 2 tablespoons drippings. Crumble bacon, and set aside.

Sprinkle roast with lemon-pepper marinade. Brown roast on all sides in hot bacon drippings.

Combine remaining ingredients; mix well. Pour mixture over roast. Cover and simmer 2½ to 3 hours or until the roast is tender.

Remove roast to warm platter; sprinkle with bacon. Skim fat from pan drippings. Serve roast with pan drippings. Yield: 8 servings.   *Eleanor K. Brandt,
Arlington, Texas.*

CHICKEN-CELERY SALAD

4 cups diced cooked chicken
2 cups diced celery
1 (4½-ounce) jar whole mushrooms, drained
4 slices bacon, cooked and crumbled
½ cup mayonnaise
½ cup commercial sour cream
1 tablespoon lemon juice
Salt to taste
Lettuce leaves
⅓ cup chopped pecans, toasted

Combine first 8 ingredients; stir gently. Cover and chill 2 hours. Serve salad on lettuce, and sprinkle with pecans. Yield: 8 servings.
*Mrs. Phillip E. Maffett,
Canton, Georgia.*

CHUCKWAGON BEANS

10 slices bacon, diced
2 medium onions, chopped
1 medium-size green pepper, chopped
1 (28-ounce) can pork and beans
¾ cup catsup
½ cup firmly packed brown sugar
½ cup molasses
1 teaspoon liquid smoke

Combine bacon, onion, and green pepper in a 10-inch skillet; cook over medium heat until bacon is lightly browned and onion and pepper are tender. Drain.

Combine bacon mixture and remaining ingredients; mix well. Spoon mixture into a lightly greased 12- x 8- x 2-inch baking dish. Bake, uncovered, at 425° for 30 to 45 minutes or until mixture is bubbly. Yield: 6 servings.

Jane Grace,
Cyril, Oklahoma.

OVERNIGHT LAYERED SALAD

1 large head cauliflower
1 head iceberg lettuce, torn
1 (10-ounce) package frozen English peas, thawed
1 (8-ounce) carton commercial sour cream
1 cup mayonnaise
1 to 2 tablespoons sugar
1 cup grated Parmesan cheese
1 pound bacon, cooked and crumbled

Remove outer leaves, and break cauliflower into flowerets; wash thoroughly.

Layer lettuce, cauliflower, and peas in a 3-quart bowl (in that order). Combine sour cream and mayonnaise, mixing well; spread evenly over top, sealing to edge of bowl. Sprinkle with remaining ingredients in the order listed. Cover bowl tightly, and chill overnight. Yield: 8 to 10 servings. *Carolyn Sorrells,*
Ozark, Missouri.

Tip: New cast-iron cookware should always be seasoned before using. Rub the interior of the utensil with oil or shortening, and place in a 250° or 300° oven for several hours. Wipe off oily film, and store. If scouring is necessary after using the utensil, re-season the surface immediately to prevent rusting.

If utensils are to be stored for any length of time between use, rub a light film of oil over interior. Wipe off film before using, and wash in clear water.

COWBOY CORNBREAD

1½ cups cornmeal
½ cup all-purpose flour
½ teaspoon soda
½ teaspoon salt
1 cup milk
2 eggs, beaten
2 tablespoons vegetable oil
2 cups (8 ounces) shredded medium Cheddar cheese
1 (8-ounce) can cream-style corn
1 small onion, chopped
12 to 14 slices bacon, cooked and crumbled
2 tablespoons chopped pimiento

Combine first 4 ingredients; mix well. Add milk, eggs, and vegetable oil, stirring well. Stir in remaining ingredients. Pour into a greased 9-inch square baking pan. Bake at 350° for 40 to 45 minutes or until lightly browned. Yield: 9 servings. *Jane Chappell,*
New Braunfels, Texas.

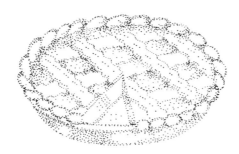

Make It Pie For Dessert

Flaky double-crust pies are a treasured dessert among Southerners, and everyone seems to have a favorite. This one combines mincemeat, peach pie filling, and orange rind.

MINCEMEAT-PEACH PIE

1 (9-ounce) package dry mincemeat
½ cup water
1 (16-ounce) can peach pie filling
1 tablespoon grated orange rind, divided
Pastry for double-crust 9-inch pie
2 teaspoons half-and-half
1 tablespoon sugar

Combine mincemeat and water in a saucepan; bring to a boil, and boil 1 minute. Remove from heat; stir in pie filling and 2 teaspoons orange rind. Pour into a pastry-lined 9-inch pieplate; top with remaining pastry. Trim edges;

then seal and flute. Cut slits in crust for steam to escape. Brush with half-and-half.

Combine remaining orange rind and sugar; sprinkle over pastry. Bake at 425° for 30 to 35 minutes or until browned. Yield: one 9-inch pie.

Mrs. Roland P. Guest, Jr.,
Jackson, Mississippi.

Speed Up The Lasagna

The thought of homemade lasagna suggests hours of work in the kitchen. However, our recipe for Simple Lasagna proves that it's possible to cut corners on the preparation and not come up short on flavor.

SIMPLE LASAGNA

1 pound ground beef
1 clove garlic, minced
3 tablespoons minced fresh parsley, divided
1 tablespoon minced fresh basil
1 teaspoon salt
1 (16-ounce) can tomatoes, undrained
2 (6-ounce) cans tomato paste
1 (8-ounce) package lasagna noodles
2 (12-ounce) cartons cream-style cottage cheese
2 eggs, beaten
½ teaspoon salt
½ teaspoon pepper
½ cup grated Parmesan cheese
1 pound sliced mozzarella cheese

Cook ground beef in a large skillet until browned, stirring to crumble; drain off pan drippings. Add garlic, 1 tablespoon parsley, basil, 1 teaspoon salt, tomatoes, and tomato paste; simmer, uncovered, 30 minutes or until thick, stirring occasionally.

Cook lasagna noodles according to package directions; drain.

Combine cottage cheese, eggs, ½ teaspoon salt, pepper, 2 tablespoons parsley, and Parmesan cheese, mixing well.

Spread about ½ cup meat sauce in a greased 13- x 9- x 2-inch baking dish. Layer half each of the noodles, cottage cheese mixture, mozzarella cheese, and meat sauce. Repeat layers. Bake at 375° for 30 minutes; let stand 10 minutes before serving. Yield: 6 to 8 servings.

Mrs. T. J. Compton,
Austin, Texas.

September

Children head back to school in September and you will find our drop cookies quick to make and easy to pack in their lunch boxes. While the young ones are gone, stir up a pot of hearty gumbo—it made the Cajuns famous, and you will be, too.

September also heralds our second annual *Mexican Food Fest*, featuring recipes submitted by Southwest readers. We now offer that colorful mélange of flavors to all our readers. The Chimichangas will quickly become a favorite at your house.

For those green tomatoes left on your vines, we show you crispy ways to fry them. And mushrooms are anything but ordinary as you can see when you try our recipes and our tricks for slicing and carving.

Work Magic With Mushrooms

Fresh mushrooms transform even the simplest dish into something special. That's the magic of mushrooms. Besides enjoying the tender morsels in soups and sauces, try marinating some for a salad or stuffing the caps with a tasty filling. Here are some things you should know about buying fresh mushrooms, as well as their storage and preparation.

Examine fresh mushrooms from cap to stem. Check beneath the cap for a thin membrane called the veil; it appears on young mushrooms, disappearing or opening up to expose the mushroom gills a few days after harvest. If the veil is apparent, the mushroom tends to have a delicate flavor; an open veil means more robust flavor. Either is fine, so choose the type you enjoy most.

Also check color. Fresh mushrooms should be off-white to cream colored; avoid stark-white mushrooms, for their color is due to a bleaching and washing process that reduces their flavor and texture as well as keeping quality.

Store fresh mushrooms in the refrigerator, choosing a container that will let them breathe, such as a cotton bag or a brown paper sack, rather than an airtight container.

Never soak or wash mushrooms prior to storage; they will absorb water and deteriorate quickly. Just before using the mushrooms, clean them by simply wiping with a damp cloth or paper towel.

One other hint: Avoid cooking mushrooms in aluminum cookware. The mushrooms react with aluminum and turn the containers dark. Instead, we suggest preparing mushrooms in cookware that is made of steel.

CRAB-STUFFED MUSHROOMS

20 to 24 large fresh mushrooms (about 1 pound)
1 cup commercial Italian salad dressing
¾ cup soft breadcrumbs, divided
1 (6½-ounce) can crabmeat, drained and flaked
2 eggs, beaten
¼ cup salad dressing or mayonnaise
¼ cup minced onion
1 teaspoon lemon juice

Clean mushrooms with damp paper towels. Remove mushroom stems, and reserve for use in another recipe. Combine mushroom caps and Italian salad dressing; cover and refrigerate 1 to 2 hours. Drain well.

Combine ½ cup breadcrumbs and remaining ingredients; mix well. Spoon crabmeat mixture into mushroom caps, and sprinkle with the remaining breadcrumbs. Place in an 8-inch square baking dish; bake at 375° for 15 minutes. Yield: about 2 dozen appetizer servings.
Mrs. H. S. Wright,
Leesville, South Carolina.

HOT MUSHROOM SPREAD

4 slices bacon
½ pound fresh mushrooms, chopped
1 medium onion, finely chopped
1 clove garlic, minced
2 tablespoons all-purpose flour
¼ teaspoon salt
⅛ teaspoon pepper
1 (8-ounce) package cream cheese, cubed
2 teaspoons Worcestershire sauce
1 teaspoon soy sauce
½ cup commercial sour cream

Fry bacon until crisp, and drain on paper towels. Crumble bacon, and set aside. Drain off bacon drippings, reserving 2 tablespoons in skillet.

Add mushrooms, onion, and garlic to skillet; cook, stirring often, until liquid is evaporated. Stir in flour, salt, and pepper. Add cream cheese, Worcestershire sauce, and soy sauce; cook, stirring constantly, until cheese melts.

Stir sour cream and bacon into mushroom mixture; cook until thoroughly heated, stirring constantly. (Do not boil.) Serve warm with assorted crackers. Yield: about 2½ cups.
Grace Bravos,
Timonium, Maryland.

CREAMED MUSHROOMS ON TOAST

¼ cup butter or margarine
1 pound fresh mushrooms, thinly sliced
½ cup chopped green onion
1 tablespoon all-purpose flour
½ cup beef broth
1 teaspoon dried dillweed
¼ teaspoon salt
⅛ teaspoon pepper
1 (8-ounce) carton commercial sour cream
6 slices rusk
6 (½-inch-thick) slices tomato
3 tablespoons grated Parmesan cheese
Fresh parsley (optional)

Melt butter in a heavy saucepan over low heat. Add mushrooms and green onion; sauté 3 minutes. Add flour, stirring until smooth; cook 1 minute, stirring mixture constantly.

Gradually add broth to mushroom mixture; cook over medium heat, stirring constantly, until thickened and bubbly. Reduce heat; stir in dillweed, salt, and pepper. Simmer 10 minutes, stirring often. Remove from heat, and stir in the sour cream.

Place slices of rusk on a large baking sheet; top each with a tomato slice, and cover with mushroom sauce. (Reserve any remaining mushroom sauce and keep warm.) Sprinkle each serving with cheese; bake at 350° for 10 minutes. Remove to serving platter, and serve with any remaining sauce. Garnish with parsley, if desired. Yield: 6 servings.
Mrs. B. F. Turner,
West Palm Beach, Florida.

FABULOUS MUSHROOM SALAD

2 pounds fresh mushrooms
1 cup commercial Italian salad dressing
½ teaspoon garlic powder
½ teaspoon dried whole basil
½ teaspoon onion salt
1 teaspoon dried parsley flakes
½ pound spinach, torn
3 tomatoes, cut into wedges
3 slices bacon, cooked and crumbled

Clean mushrooms with damp paper towels. Combine with next 4 ingredients, tossing gently; sprinkle with parsley. Cover and refrigerate 8 hours or overnight. Drain well, and serve on spinach; garnish with tomatoes and bacon. Yield: 6 to 8 servings.
Anita McLemore,
Knoxville, Tennessee.

BRISK MUSHROOM BISQUE

¼ cup butter
4 green onions, thinly sliced
1 pound fresh mushrooms, thinly sliced
1 tablespoon all-purpose flour
2 cups chicken broth
1 pint half-and-half
Dash of ground nutmeg
1 cup fresh crabmeat, drained and flaked
Dash of red pepper
Pinch of white pepper
½ teaspoon salt

Melt butter in a heavy Dutch oven; add onion and mushrooms, and sauté until tender. Add flour, stirring until smooth; cook 1 minute, stirring mixture constantly.

Combine chicken broth, half-and-half, and nutmeg; gradually add to mushroom mixture, stirring constantly. Stir in remaining ingredients, and reduce heat. Cook until thoroughly heated, stirring frequently. (Do not boil.) Yield: about 8 cups.
Joanne C. Champagne,
Covington, Louisiana.

Store fresh mushrooms in the refrigerator, choosing a container that will let them breathe, such as a cotton bag or brown paper sack. Just before using, wipe them off with a damp cloth or paper towel.

You can make quick work of slicing fresh mushrooms by doing the job with an egg slicer.

For a special dish or garnish, flute mushrooms with a paring knife. Simply cut thin wedges from each cap, using a circular motion.

Breads That Say "The South"

Flaky biscuits dripping with butter, golden-brown cornsticks piping hot from the oven, and hush puppies sizzling in the skillet represent Southern cooking at its best. For breads, from corn muffins to old-fashioned dumplings, are among the most cherished recipes of the Southern cook, and our recipes provide a classic collection of the region's finest.

Two Southern favorites, cornsticks and corn muffins, can be prepared from our Quick Cornstick recipe by changing baking pans and adjusting baking times.

And for a basic biscuit recipe, Favorite Buttermilk Biscuits is a delicious choice. Leavened by soda and baking powder, these biscuits can be prepared quickly, yet look and taste like you've been baking for hours.

EASY HUSH PUPPIES

2¼ cups cornmeal
½ cup finely chopped onion
¾ teaspoon soda
½ teaspoon salt
½ teaspoon garlic salt
1½ cups buttermilk
Vegetable oil

Combine first 5 ingredients; stir well. Add buttermilk, stirring until dry ingredients are moistened. Drop batter by tablespoonfuls into deep hot oil (375°); fry only a few at a time, turning once. Cook until hush puppies are golden brown (3 to 5 minutes). Drain on paper towels. Yield: about 5 dozen.
Martha Rabon,
Stapleton, Alabama.

FAVORITE BUTTERMILK BISCUITS

2 cups all-purpose flour
1 tablespoon baking powder
2 teaspoons sugar
½ teaspoon salt
½ teaspoon cream of tartar
½ cup shortening
¾ cup buttermilk
½ teaspoon soda

Combine first 5 ingredients, mixing well; cut in shortening until mixture resembles coarse meal.

Combine buttermilk and soda; add to dry ingredients, stirring until dry ingredients are moistened. Turn dough out on a lightly floured surface; knead lightly 10 to 12 times.

Roll dough to ½-inch thickness; cut with a 2¾-inch biscuit cutter. Place biscuits on a lightly greased baking sheet. Bake at 450° for 10 minutes or until golden brown. Yield: 10 biscuits.
Jill Cox,
Charlottesville, Virginia.

OLD-FASHIONED DUMPLINGS

1½ cups all-purpose flour
2 teaspoons baking powder
½ teaspoon salt
½ cup chicken broth
2 tablespoons vegetable oil
2 quarts broth or soup

Combine flour, baking powder, and salt. Add ½ cup chicken broth and oil, stirring until dry ingredients are moistened. Turn dough out on a floured surface, and form into a ball.

Roll dough to a 1/16-inch thickness; cut into 5- x 1-inch strips. Drop dumplings into boiling broth; cover and cook 15 minutes or until dumplings are tender. Yield: 8 servings.

Note: Cooked chicken may be added to dumpling mixture, if desired.
Frances R. Dickson,
Tucker, Georgia.

QUICK CORNSTICKS

1 cup self-rising cornmeal
1 (8-ounce) carton commercial sour cream
1 (8½-ounce) can cream-style corn
½ cup vegetable oil
2 eggs, beaten

Combine all ingredients; mix well. Place a well-greased cast-iron cornstick pan in a 400° oven for 3 minutes or until hot. Remove pan from oven; spoon batter into pan, filling two-thirds full. Bake at 400° for 20 minutes or until cornsticks are lightly browned. Yield: 24 cornsticks.

Note: Corn muffins may be prepared from this recipe. Substitute muffin pans for cornstick pans, filling pans two-thirds full. Bake at 400° for 25 to 30 minutes. Yield: 16 corn muffins.

Frances Hazle,
Cross Hill, South Carolina.

No Slicing Or Shaping With These Cookies

Nothing could be easier than drop cookies—the dough is simply mixed up and dropped by spoonfuls onto cookie sheets. While they may not look as perfect as shaped or rolled cookies, drop cookies taste just as delicious and will disappear just as fast.

FROSTED APRICOT COOKIES

½ cup butter or margarine, softened
1 (3-ounce) package cream cheese,
  softened
1¼ cups all-purpose flour
¼ cup sugar
1 teaspoon baking powder
½ cup apricot preserves
½ cup chopped pecans
Apricot Frosting

Combine butter and cream cheese, beating until smooth. Combine flour, sugar, and baking powder; stir into creamed mixture. Add the apricot preserves and chopped pecans, mixing well. Drop dough by tablespoonfuls onto greased cookie sheets. Bake at 350° for 12 to 15 minutes. Cool slightly on wire racks. Frost with Apricot Frosting while warm. Yield: about 3½ dozen.

Apricot Frosting:
1 cup sifted powdered sugar
1 tablespoon butter or margarine,
  softened
¼ cup apricot preserves

Combine all ingredients, and beat until smooth. Yield: about ½ cup.

Irene Haverland,
Deepwater, Missouri.

CANDY BIT COOKIES

⅔ cup butter or margarine, softened
1½ cups firmly packed brown sugar
1 egg, slightly beaten
1 teaspoon vanilla extract
1½ cups all-purpose flour
1½ teaspoons baking powder
¼ teaspoon salt
1 (8-ounce) package candy-coated
  chocolate-covered peanut butter pieces
½ cup chopped pecans

Cream butter; gradually add sugar, beating well. Add egg and vanilla; beat mixture well.

Combine next 3 ingredients; stir into creamed mixture. Add peanut butter pieces and chopped pecans, stirring well.

Drop dough by rounded teaspoonfuls onto ungreased cookie sheets; bake at 350° for 10 to 12 minutes (cookies will still be soft). Remove to wire racks to cool. Yield: about 5½ dozen.

Carol Forcum,
Marion, Illinois.

CHOCOLATE SANDWICH COOKIES

½ cup butter or margarine, softened
1 cup sugar
1 egg yolk
2 cups all-purpose flour
½ teaspoon soda
½ teaspoon baking powder
½ teaspoon salt
¼ cup cocoa
½ cup buttermilk
Fluffy Filling

Cream butter; gradually add sugar, beating until light and fluffy. Add egg yolk, and beat well.

Combine dry ingredients. Add to creamed mixture alternately with buttermilk, beginning and ending with dry ingredients; mix well after each addition.

Drop dough by rounded teaspoonfuls onto greased cookie sheets; bake at 375° for 10 minutes. Cool on wire racks.

Spread about 1 tablespoon Fluffy Filling on bottom of half the cookies. Place remaining cookies, bottom side down, on top of filling. Yield: about 2 dozen.

Fluffy Filling:
1 egg white
½ cup butter or margarine, softened
2 tablespoons all-purpose flour
2 tablespoons whipping cream
1 teaspoon vanilla extract
1 cup plus 1 tablespoon sifted powdered
  sugar

Combine all ingredients; beat at medium speed of electric mixer until smooth and fluffy. Yield: about 1½ cups.

Ellen Hanna,
England, Arkansas.

CINNAMON WAFERS

⅔ cup butter or margarine, softened
1 cup sugar
1 teaspoon ground cinnamon
1 egg, slightly beaten
1 teaspoon vanilla extract
2 cups all-purpose flour
2 teaspoons baking powder
½ teaspoon salt
¼ cup milk

Cream butter; gradually add sugar and cinnamon, beating until light and fluffy. Add egg and vanilla; beat well. Combine flour, baking powder, and salt. Add to creamed mixture alternately with milk, beginning and ending with flour mixture; mix well after each addition.

Drop dough by rounded teaspoonfuls onto greased cookie sheets. Flatten with a fork; bake at 375° for 8 minutes or until edges are lightly browned. Cool on wire racks. Yield: about 6½ dozen.

Mrs. Donald C. Vanhoy,
Salisbury, North Carolina.

Tip: Use shiny cookie sheets and cakepans for baking rather than darkened ones. Dark pans absorb more heat and can cause baked products to overbrown.

MEXICAN FOOD FEST™

Sharing The Best Mexican Main Dishes

Mexican cuisine offers a wide variety of colorful, spicy main dishes. Whether it be authentic Mexican or Tex-Mex, each dish is part of a unique style of cooking that originated south-of-the-border.

Pollo Almendrado, chicken cooked in almond sauce, is one of the milder, more elegant dishes of the Mexican cuisine. Mexicali Meat Pie, a Tex-Mex creation, is a terrific way to serve dinner in a pie; the crust is made of flour and cornmeal, and there's a beefy filling topped with cheese, jalapeño peppers, and bacon.

CHICKEN MOLE

1 (2½- to 3-pound) broiler-fryer, cut up and skinned
Salt and pepper
¼ cup butter or margarine, melted
¼ cup minced onion
¼ cup minced green pepper
1 clove garlic, minced
1 (8¼-ounce) can tomatoes, undrained and chopped
½ cup beef broth
2 teaspoons sugar
½ teaspoon chili powder
⅛ teaspoon ground cinnamon
⅛ teaspoon ground nutmeg
Dash of ground cloves
5 to 6 drops of hot sauce
¼ (1-ounce) square unsweetened chocolate
1 tablespoon cornstarch
2 tablespoons cold water

Sprinkle chicken with salt and pepper; sauté on both sides in melted butter until brown. Remove chicken from skillet, and set aside.

Add onion, green pepper, and garlic to skillet; sauté until tender. Stir in next 9 ingredients; add chicken. Reduce heat and cook, covered, 45 minutes or until chicken is tender. Remove chicken to serving platter.

Combine cornstarch and water; mix well. Add to sauce in skillet; cook, stirring constantly, until thickened and bubbly. Spoon the sauce over chicken. Yield: 4 servings. *Sandra Kondora, Harrison, Arkansas.*

CHORIZO AND EGG TORTILLAS

8 flour tortillas
½ pound chorizo (recipe follows)
8 to 10 eggs, scrambled
Commercial picante sauce

Wrap tortillas tightly in foil; bake at 350° for 15 minutes.

Cook chorizo over medium heat in a large skillet until browned, stirring to crumble. Drain well, and set aside.

Spoon an equal amount of eggs in center of each warm tortilla. Top with an equal amount of chorizo. Roll up tortillas; serve immediately with picante sauce. Yield: 3 to 4 servings.

Chorizo (Spicy Spanish Sausage):

1 (1-pound) boneless pork roast, ground
½ pound ground beef
½ cup Burgundy or other dry red wine
¼ cup plus 2 tablespoons chili powder
½ teaspoon salt
½ teaspoon dried whole oregano
¼ teaspoon ground cumin
1 to 2 cloves garlic, crushed

Combine all ingredients, mixing well. Cover and refrigerate overnight. Cook desired amount of chorizo according to recipe instructions. Freeze remaining chorizo in ¼- to ½-pound portions for future use. Yield: 1½ pounds chorizo.
Mrs. D. W. Sanford, San Antonio, Texas.

POLLO ALMENDRADO

1 teaspoon salt
¼ teaspoon coarsely ground black pepper
1½ tablespoons lime juice
1 (2½- to 3-pound) broiler-fryer, cut up and skinned
3 tablespoons shortening
½ cup blanched whole almonds
1 (1½-inch-thick) slice stale French bread
2 small tomatoes, peeled and seeded
3 peppercorns
1 whole clove
1 bay leaf
2 tablespoons water
¼ teaspoon salt
Tomato wedges
Parsley

Combine first 3 ingredients; drizzle mixture over chicken. Let stand 1 hour in refrigerator.

Melt shortening in a heavy skillet. Add almonds; cook, stirring constantly, until lightly browned. Remove almonds with a slotted spoon, and place in container of electric blender.

Add bread to pan drippings; cook until lightly browned, turning once. Drain on paper towels and crumble. Place in container of electric blender; process until smooth. Add tomatoes, peppercorns, clove, bay leaf, water, and ¼ teaspoon salt to bread and almonds in blender; process until smooth.

Spread about one-third of almond sauce in a lightly greased 13- x 9- x 2-inch baking dish. Arrange chicken on top in a single layer; spread remaining almond sauce over chicken. Bake at 350° for 1 hour or until tender. Garnish with tomato wedges and parsley. Yield: 4 servings. *Mrs. John A. Eckhart, Rocksprings, Texas.*

Tip: Use baking soda on a damp cloth to shine up your kitchen appliances.

MEXICAN FOOD FEST

MEXICALI MEAT PIE

1 cup all-purpose flour
¾ cup cornmeal, divided
⅓ cup shortening
⅓ cup cold water
1 pound ground beef
1 (8-ounce) can tomato sauce
1 (8-ounce) can whole kernel corn, drained
¼ cup chopped green pepper
¼ cup chopped onion
1 teaspoon salt
½ teaspoon dried whole oregano
½ teaspoon chili powder
⅛ teaspoon pepper
1 egg, beaten
¼ cup milk
½ teaspoon dry mustard
½ teaspoon Worcestershire sauce
1½ cups (6 ounces) shredded medium Cheddar cheese
1 canned jalapeño pepper, seeded and chopped
4 to 6 slices bacon, cooked and crumbled

Combine flour and ½ cup cornmeal in bowl; cut in shortening with pastry blender. Sprinkle cold water evenly over surface; stir with a fork until all dry ingredients are moistened. Shape into a ball. Roll dough on a lightly floured surface to a circle 1½ inches larger than an inverted 9-inch pieplate. Fit pastry into the pieplate, and flute edge of pastry as desired; set aside.

Cook ground beef until browned; drain well. Stir in next 8 ingredients and remaining cornmeal; mix well. Spoon into pastry shell.

Bake at 425° for 20 minutes. Combine egg, milk, mustard, Worcestershire, and cheese; mix well and spread over meat mixture. Sprinkle pie with jalapeño pepper and bacon. Bake an additional 10 minutes; let pie stand 10 minutes before serving. Yield: one 9-inch pie.

Brenda Kainer,
Victoria, Texas.

Tip: Before starting a recipe, make sure you have the equipment needed to prepare it. Be sure to use the correct pan size, especially when preparing cakes, pies, or breads.

TOSTADA COMPUESTAS

1 pound ground beef
½ cup chopped onion
1 clove garlic, minced
½ teaspoon chili powder
½ teaspoon salt
1 (8½-ounce) can kidney beans
6 (10-inch) flour tortillas
Vegetable oil
1 large tomato, chopped
1 small head iceberg lettuce, shredded
1 large avocado, peeled and chopped
1 cup (4 ounces) shredded sharp Cheddar cheese
Taco sauce
Commercial sour cream

Combine ground beef, onion, and garlic in a skillet; cook until beef is browned, stirring to crumble meat. Drain off pan drippings. Stir in chili powder and salt; set aside.

Heat beans in a small saucepan over medium heat; drain off liquid, and set beans aside.

Fry tortillas, one at a time, in ¼ inch hot oil (375°) 20 to 30 seconds on each side or until crisp and golden brown. Drain on paper towels.

Spoon meat mixture, beans, tomato, lettuce, avocado, and cheese on warm tortillas. Serve with taco sauce and sour cream. Yield: 6 servings. *Joanne Land,*
Round Rock, Texas.

MEAT-AND-BEAN BURRITOS

¾ pound boneless beef, cut into ½-inch cubes
¾ pound boneless pork, cut into ½-inch cubes
1 cup chopped onion
3 tablespoons vegetable oil, divided
1 clove garlic, crushed
1 teaspoon salt
1½ cups water
1 (4-ounce) can chopped green chiles, drained
1 (15-ounce) can refried beans
¼ cup (1 ounce) shredded Cheddar cheese
12 flour tortillas
Commercial taco sauce

Cook beef, pork, and onion in 2 tablespoons vegetable oil in a small Dutch oven until meat is no longer pink. Stir in garlic, salt, and water; bring to a boil over medium heat. Reduce heat to low; cover and simmer about 1½ to 2 hours or until meat is tender. Shred meat with a fork. Add chiles; cook, uncovered, about 10 minutes or until any remaining liquid evaporates. Set aside.

Heat refried beans in remaining oil in a medium skillet; add cheese, and stir until cheese melts. Set aside.

Wrap tortillas tightly in foil; bake at 350° for 15 minutes. Spread 2 tablespoons bean mixture on each tortilla. Spoon 2 heaping tablespoons of meat mixture off center of each tortilla. Fold the edge nearest meat filling up and over filling just until mixture is covered. Fold in sides of each tortilla to center; roll up.

Place burritos on a baking sheet; cover with aluminum foil. Bake at 325° for 15 minutes. Serve immediately with taco sauce. Yield: 6 servings.

Ellen Krause,
Spicewood, Texas.

CHEESE ENCHILADAS

1 (14-ounce) package corn tortillas
Vegetable oil
3 cups (12 ounces) shredded Monterey Jack cheese, divided
1 onion, minced
Enchilada sauce (recipe follows)

Fry tortillas, one at a time, in ¼ inch hot oil about 5 seconds on each side or just until softened. Drain thoroughly on paper towels.

Sprinkle 2 cups cheese evenly over tortillas. Sprinkle onion over cheese. Roll up each tortilla; place seam side down in a lightly greased 13- x 9- x 2-inch baking dish. Top with enchilada sauce and remaining cheese. Bake the enchiladas at 350° for 15 minutes. Serve immediately. Yield: 6 servings.

Enchilada Sauce:
⅓ cup vegetable oil
1 clove garlic, crushed
3 tablespoons all-purpose flour
2 tablespoons chili powder
1½ cups hot water, divided
½ teaspoon salt

MEXICAN FOOD FEST

Combine oil, crushed garlic, and flour in a medium saucepan; cook over low heat, stirring constantly, until mixture is lightly browned.

Dissolve chili powder in ¼ cup hot water; stir into flour mixture. Add remaining 1¼ cups hot water, stirring constantly. Stir in salt. Cook sauce over low heat 5 minutes, stirring often. Yield: about 1¾ cups.   *Carol Boaz,*
Lindale, Texas.

Taste The Brilliant Colors Of Mexico

Mexico is painted with a lively palette of hot reds, sun-soaked yellows, cool greens, and deep-blue skies. This brilliance is the heart of Mexican cooking—the bold colors can be tasted, as well as seen—and subtlety of preparation is the element that adds elegance. We have chosen and tested recipes of both the distinctive, original Mexican style and the spicier Tex-Mex flavors.

A menu blending both these styles just may make your next party a south-of-the-border success. To begin, we favor the traditional—tortilla chips dipped in cheesy Chile Con Queso.

Spiced Fruited Chicken With Almond Rice may surprise you, but it's a main course we like a lot. It's carefully seasoned with cinnamon and cloves, and simmered in orange juice.

For the side, try our Avocado Salad, combining the classic salad makings of Mexico: avocado, tomato, and lettuce. To round out the main course, choose either Calabaza Mexicana—a squash casserole with corn and green chiles—or Chimichangas, burritos filled with a jazzy bean mixture, then deep fried.

Nothing could end a spicy meal more delicately than Mexican Tea Cakes, a sweet confection often reserved for weddings and other festive celebrations. We think you'll find this menu a dazzling array of colors and colorful tastes, from start to finish.

Chile Con Queso   Tortilla Chips
**Spiced Fruited Chicken
With Almond Rice
Avocado Salad
Calabaza Mexicana or Chimichangas
Mexican Tea Cakes
Sangría**

CHILE CON QUESO

1 (16-ounce) can tomatoes
1 tablespoon bacon drippings
1 large onion, finely chopped
1 (4-ounce) can whole green chiles, drained and coarsely chopped
1 pound process American cheese, cut into ½-inch cubes
½ teaspoon salt
⅛ teaspoon pepper

Drain tomatoes, reserving juice; coarsely chop tomatoes, and set aside.

Heat bacon drippings in a large skillet; add onion, and sauté until tender. Add tomatoes and chiles, and cook over low heat 15 minutes. Add reserved tomato juice, cheese, salt, and pepper; cook over low heat, stirring frequently, until cheese is melted. Serve warm with tortilla chips. Yield: about 4 cups.   *Fran Albrecht,*
Portland, Texas.

SPICED FRUITED CHICKEN WITH ALMOND RICE

1½ teaspoons salt
¼ teaspoon ground cinnamon
¼ teaspoon ground cloves
¼ teaspoon pepper
2 (2½- to 3-pound) broiler-fryers, cut up
¼ cup vegetable oil
2 cups orange juice
½ cup raisins
½ cup drained crushed pineapple
½ cup chopped onion
2 cloves garlic, minced
1 orange, thinly sliced
¼ cup dry sherry
Parsley sprigs
Orange slices
Almond Rice

Combine first 4 ingredients; rub into chicken pieces. Heat oil in an electric skillet, and brown chicken on both sides. Drain off excess oil.

Combine orange juice, raisins, pineapple, onion, and garlic; pour over chicken. Top with orange slices. Cover and simmer 45 minutes or until chicken is tender.

Pour sherry over chicken, and simmer 5 minutes. Arrange chicken on a serving platter; garnish with parsley and orange slices. Serve with Almond Rice. Yield: 8 servings.

Almond Rice:

1 (10¾-ounce) can chicken broth
1¼ cups water
¾ teaspoon salt
1 cup uncooked regular rice
2 tablespoons butter or margarine
½ cup slivered almonds

Combine broth, water, and salt in a heavy saucepan; bring to a boil, and add rice. Reduce heat; cover and simmer 20 minutes or until the liquid is absorbed.

Melt butter in a small skillet. Sauté almonds in butter until lightly browned. Stir into rice. Yield: 8 servings.
Kathleen Stone,
Houston, Texas.

AVOCADO SALAD

½ cup olive oil
¼ cup white wine vinegar
¼ teaspoon freshly ground pepper
2 tablespoons lemon juice
1 teaspoon salt
1 large avocado, chopped
1 medium onion, chopped
1 large tomato, chopped
1 small head iceberg lettuce, shredded

Combine first 5 ingredients in a jar. Cover tightly, and shake vigorously.

Combine avocado, onion, and tomato; add dressing, and marinate in refrigerator at least 30 minutes. Spoon salad onto a bed of lettuce using a slotted spoon. Yield: 6 to 8 servings.
Anita Cox,
Fort Worth, Texas.

MEXICAN FOOD FEST

CALABAZA MEXICANA (MEXICAN SQUASH)

2 tablespoons butter or margarine
2 small calabaza or 3 medium zucchini, thinly sliced
1 medium onion, finely chopped
2 cloves garlic, minced
1 (17-ounce) can whole kernel corn, drained
1 (4-ounce) can green chiles, drained, seeded, and chopped
½ to ¾ cup (2 to 3 ounces) shredded sharp Cheddar cheese

Melt butter in a large skillet. Add calabaza, onion, and garlic; sauté about 8 minutes or until squash is crisp-tender. Stir in corn and chiles; spoon into a 1-quart casserole. Top with cheese; bake, uncovered, at 350° for 10 minutes or until cheese is melted. Yield: 6 servings.
Anita Cox,
Fort Worth, Texas.

CHIMICHANGAS (FRIED BURRITOS)

1 quart water
1 cup dried kidney beans
1 medium onion, chopped
1 dried hot chile pepper, seeded and minced
1 tablespoon shortening
1 clove garlic, minced
1 bay leaf
1 teaspoon salt
¼ cup plus 1 tablespoon shortening
1 medium onion, minced
3 cloves garlic, minced
Tomato sauce with green chiles (recipe follows)
1 (4-ounce) can whole green chiles, drained, seeded, and minced
1 tablespoon chili powder
1 teaspoon ground cumin
⅓ cup (1⅓ ounces) shredded Monterey Jack cheese
10 (8-inch) flour tortillas
Vegetable oil
½ cup (2 ounces) shredded Monterey Jack cheese
Commercial sour cream

Combine first 7 ingredients in a Dutch oven; cover and simmer 2½ hours, stirring occasionally. Discard bay leaf. Stir in salt and refrigerate beans overnight, partially covered.

Melt ¼ cup plus 1 tablespoon shortening in a medium saucepan; add onion and garlic, and sauté until tender. Stir in ⅔ cup tomato sauce with green chiles, minced chiles, chili powder, and cumin; simmer 3 minutes.

Mash beans. Stir sauce into beans, and cook 8 to 10 minutes or until thick. Add ⅓ cup cheese, stirring mixture until melted. Cool.

Spoon ⅓ cup of bean mixture off center of a tortilla. Fold the edge nearest bean filling up and over filling, just until mixture is covered. Fold in opposite side of tortilla to center; roll up. Secure with wooden picks. Repeat with the remaining bean mixture and tortillas.

Fry burritos in deep hot oil (375°) 2 to 3 minutes or until golden brown, turning once. Drain well on paper towels.

Remove wooden picks. Arrange burritos in a 13- x 9- x 2-inch baking dish. Sprinkle with ½ cup cheese. Broil 30 seconds or until cheese melts. Serve with sour cream and remaining tomato sauce with chiles. Yield: 10 servings.

Tomato Sauce With Green Chiles:

1 medium onion, minced
1 clove garlic, minced
2 tablespoons vegetable oil
2 cups tomato sauce
1 (4-ounce) can whole green chiles, drained, seeded, and minced
¼ teaspoon salt
¼ teaspoon dried whole oregano
¼ teaspoon ground cumin

Sauté onion and garlic in oil in a medium saucepan until tender. Stir in the remaining ingredients; simmer, uncovered, 20 minutes, stirring occasionally. Serve warm. Yield: 2⅓ cups.
Ella C. Stivers,
Abilene, Texas.

Tip: Recycle oil used in French-frying by draining through cheesecloth or a fine strainer and storing in refrigerator.

MEXICAN TEA CAKES

2¼ cups all-purpose flour
¼ teaspoon salt
¼ teaspoon ground cinnamon
1 cup butter, softened
¾ cup finely chopped pecans
½ cup sifted powdered sugar
1 teaspoon vanilla extract
Powdered sugar

Combine flour, salt, and cinnamon in a large mixing bowl. Add butter, pecans, ½ cup powdered sugar, and vanilla; stir until well blended. Shape dough into 1-inch balls, and place on ungreased cookie sheets. Bake at 400° for 10 to 12 minutes.

Roll cookies in additional powdered sugar while hot. Remove to wire racks to cool completely, and reroll cookies in powdered sugar. Yield: 5 dozen.
Maxine Cates,
Del City, Oklahoma.

SANGRIA

1 (25.4-ounce) bottle Burgundy or other dry red wine, chilled
½ cup sugar
1 orange, thinly sliced
1 lemon, thinly sliced
1 (10-ounce) bottle club soda, chilled

Combine first 4 ingredients in a large pitcher, stirring to dissolve sugar. Add club soda just before serving. Serve over ice. Yield: about 1 quart.
Marylee Martin,
Alexandria, Louisiana.

All Aboard For Brunch

Half the fun of going to a University of Tennessee football game is getting there, especially if you're aboard one of the boats that travel up the Tennessee River and dock beside the Vols' stadium in Knoxville. When Alabama's Crimson Tide takes on the Volunteers, Mr. and Mrs. Rolla E. Beck, Jr., of Birmingham cruise from Guntersville, Alabama, to Knoxville.

Saturday morning Sara Alice's menu is centered around finger foods, such as biscuits filled with country ham and sausage. Melon balls served with a poppy seed dressing, cheese grits, and blueberry muffins round out the main course. By the time the boat nears the stadium, dessert is completed and guests turn their attention to the activity around the stadium.

> Ham Biscuits   Sausage Biscuits
> Garlic Cheese Grits
> Melon Balls
> Touchdown Salad Dressing
> Easy Blueberry Muffins
> Lemon Squares
> Chocolate-Butterscotch Bars
> Spicy Oatmeal Cookies
> Bloody Marys   Coffee

GARLIC CHEESE GRITS

1 cup uncooked regular grits
½ cup butter or margarine
1 (6-ounce) roll process cheese food with garlic
2 eggs, beaten

Cook grits according to package directions. Add butter and cheese to grits; stir until completely melted. Add a small amount of hot grits to eggs, stirring well; stir egg mixture into remaining grits. Pour mixture into a lightly greased 1½-quart casserole. Bake at 350° for 1 hour. Yield: 6 to 8 servings.

TOUCHDOWN SALAD DRESSING

1 cup olive oil
¼ cup distilled vinegar
¼ cup lemon juice
2 tablespoons powdered sugar
1¼ teaspoons poppy seeds
½ teaspoon salt
½ teaspoon dry mustard

Combine all ingredients in a jar; cover jar tightly, and shake vigorously. Chill. Shake well before serving. Serve over melon balls. Yield: 1½ cups.

EASY BLUEBERRY MUFFINS

1 cup fresh blueberries or 1 cup canned blueberries, drained
2 cups plus 2 tablespoons all-purpose flour, divided
¼ cup sugar
1 tablespoon plus 1 teaspoon baking powder
½ teaspoon salt
1 cup milk
1 egg
2 tablespoons vegetable oil

Dredge blueberries in 2 tablespoons flour; set aside.

Combine remaining 2 cups flour, sugar, baking powder, and salt. Beat together milk, egg, and oil; add to dry ingredients, and stir just until moistened. Fold in blueberries. Fill greased muffin pans two-thirds full. Bake at 400° for 20 to 25 minutes. Remove from pan immediately. Yield: 1 dozen.

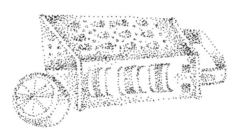

LEMON SQUARES

1 cup all-purpose flour
¼ cup sifted powdered sugar
½ cup butter or margarine, melted
2 tablespoons all-purpose flour
½ teaspoon baking powder
2 eggs, beaten
1 cup sugar
Grated rind of 1 lemon
3 tablespoons lemon juice
Powdered sugar

Combine 1 cup flour and ¼ cup powdered sugar; add butter, mixing well. Spoon into a 9-inch square baking pan; press into pan evenly. Bake at 350° for 18 to 20 minutes or until lightly browned.

Combine 2 tablespoons flour and baking powder; set aside. Combine eggs, sugar, lemon rind, and lemon juice; beat well. Stir dry ingredients into egg mixture, and pour over baked crust. Bake at 350° for 25 minutes or until lightly browned and set. Sprinkle lightly with powdered sugar. Let cool, and cut into 1½-inch squares. Yield: 3 dozen.

CHOCOLATE-BUTTERSCOTCH BARS

1½ cups graham cracker crumbs
½ cup butter or margarine, melted
1 (6-ounce) package semisweet chocolate morsels
1 (6-ounce) package butterscotch morsels
1¼ cups flaked coconut
1 cup chopped pecans
1 (14-ounce) can sweetened condensed milk

Combine crumbs and butter; stir well, and press into a 9-inch baking pan. Layer chocolate morsels, butterscotch morsels, coconut, and pecans over crumb mixture. Pour milk evenly over top. Bake at 350° for 35 to 40 minutes. Cool, and cut into 1½-inch squares. Yield: 3 dozen.

SPICY OATMEAL COOKIES

1 cup all-purpose flour
½ teaspoon soda
½ teaspoon salt
1 teaspoon ground cinnamon
¾ teaspoon ground nutmeg
½ cup shortening
½ cup firmly packed brown sugar
¼ cup sugar
1 egg
2 tablespoons water
2 cups regular oats, uncooked
½ cup chopped pecans
½ cup raisins

Combine first 5 ingredients; stir well, and set aside. Cream shortening; add sugar, beating well. Beat in egg and water. Add flour mixture, mixing well. Stir in oats, pecans, and raisins. Drop by rounded teaspoonfuls onto ungreased cookie sheets. Bake at 375° for 10 to 12 minutes. Yield: about 6 dozen.

Tip: If muffins are done ahead of serving time, loosen them from their cups, tilt slightly, then slide the pan back into the oven to stay warm. This keeps the muffins from steaming on the bottom.

PITCHER BLOODY MARYS

1 (46-ounce) can tomato juice
1 cup vodka
2 tablespoons Worcestershire sauce
½ teaspoon hot sauce
¼ teaspoon pepper
⅛ teaspoon celery salt
Juice of 2 lemons
Celery sticks

Combine first 7 ingredients; stir well. Serve over ice; garnish with celery sticks. Yield: 1¾ quarts.

Great Gumbos In The Cajun Tradition

It's lucky for Southerners that the French who settled in South Louisiana lacked the ingredients they needed to make their favorite fish stew, bouillabaisse. It was the Cajuns who learned to substitute available seafood, local herbs, and new vegetables for the traditional ingredients of bouillabaisse. The result was a dish that made the Cajuns famous—gumbo.

Most Cajuns agree that the secret to a good gumbo is the roux, a mixture of flour and oil that is the foundation of the gumbo. After that, you won't likely find anything else on which Cajuns agree.

Some insist that the roux must be cooked in an iron pot to develop proper flavor. The iron will darken any okra in the recipe, however, so many use pots made of other materials. Whichever you use, cook the roux over low heat and stir it constantly until it is the color of a copper penny.

Ask five Cajuns what kind of meat or fish makes the best gumbo, and you'll hear as many different answers. They most often opt for different combinations of shrimp, crabmeat, oysters, and fish, while others have found that ham, sausage, or chicken can also enhance the flavor. Just what seasonings to add stirs up equal controversy.

Gumbo is thickened with either okra or filé, which is ground sassafras leaves. Okra gives the gumbo a rich, earthy flavor and thickens the stew as it simmers. Filé imparts a delicate taste similar to that of thyme.

Add filé only after the gumbo has finished cooking, for it becomes stringy if it is allowed to boil. A small amount can thicken a whole pot of gumbo, so

add it sparingly. Or pass the filé at the table so each person can thicken the gumbo to his own preference.

While South Louisianians might know gumbo best, these recipes prove that folks along the Gulf Coast and other areas of the South can also stir up a good pot of the stew.

COMBO GUMBO

1 (3-pound) broiler-fryer
2 quarts water
½ cup bacon drippings
½ cup all-purpose flour
4 stalks celery, chopped
2 medium onions, chopped
1 large green pepper, chopped
2 cloves garlic, minced
½ cup chopped fresh parsley
2 pounds shrimp
1 pound okra, sliced
2 tablespoons bacon drippings
4 medium tomatoes, peeled, seeded, and coarsely chopped
2 tablespoons Worcestershire sauce
¼ teaspoon hot sauce
1 large bay leaf
2 teaspoons dried whole thyme
½ teaspoon dried whole rosemary
1 teaspoon salt
½ teaspoon pepper
1 teaspoon paprika
1 ham hock
1½ cups cubed cooked ham
4 soft-shell crabs
2 teaspoons molasses
Juice of 1 large lemon
Hot cooked rice
Gumbo filé (optional)

Combine chicken and water in a Dutch oven. Bring to a boil; cover and simmer 1½ hours or until chicken is tender. Remove chicken from broth; cut into 1-inch cubes. Strain broth, reserving 6 cups.

Heat ½ cup bacon drippings in an 8-quart Dutch oven; stir in flour. Cook over medium heat, stirring occasionally, until roux is the color of a copper penny (10 to 15 minutes). Add celery, onion, green pepper, garlic, and parsley; cook over low heat for 45 minutes. (Mixture will be dry.)

Peel shrimp, reserving shells; refrigerate shrimp until needed. Combine shells and enough water to cover in a saucepan. Bring to a boil, and boil 20 minutes. Strain shell stock, reserving 2 cups.

Cook okra in 2 tablespoons bacon drippings until tender, stirring occasionally. Add okra, reserved chicken stock,

shrimp stock, and next 9 ingredients to roux mixture. Bring to a boil; then reduce heat and simmer 2½ hours, stirring mixture occasionally.

Add cooked chicken, ham hock and cubed ham, crabs, and molasses; simmer 30 additional minutes. Add shrimp, and simmer 10 minutes longer. Stir in lemon juice. Serve over rice.

Add a small amount of filé to each serving, if desired. Yield: 3½ quarts.
Julie Josephs,
Pensacola, Florida.

CHICKEN AND OYSTER GUMBO

1 (5-pound) hen
2½ quarts water
1 tablespoon salt
¾ cup vegetable oil
1 cup all-purpose flour
2 large onions, chopped
¼ cup chopped fresh parsley
1 teaspoon whole allspice
1 teaspoon crushed red pepper
5 bay leaves
½ teaspoon pepper
2 pints oysters, undrained
2 teaspoons gumbo filé
Hot cooked rice

Combine hen, water, and salt in a Dutch oven; cook about 1½ hours or until hen is tender. Remove hen from broth, reserving 8½ cups broth. Remove the meat from bones, and cut into pieces. Set aside.

Combine oil and flour in a Dutch oven; cook over medium heat, stirring constantly, until roux is the color of a copper penny (10 to 15 minutes).

Add onion and parsley; cook 10 minutes, stirring frequently. Gradually add reserved broth to roux, stirring constantly. Combine allspice, red pepper, and bay leaves in a cheesecloth bag; add to broth mixture. Add pepper; simmer 2½ hours, stirring occasionally. Add chicken and oysters; simmer 30 minutes. Remove from heat, and discard spice bag. Stir in filé. Serve over rice. Yield: 3¼ quarts. *Nedra Tuttle,*
Pensacola, Florida.

Tip: Pouring a strong solution of salt and hot water down the sink will help eliminate odors and remove grease from drains.

CHICKEN GUMBO WITH SMOKED SAUSAGE

1 (2½- to 3-pound) broiler-fryer, cut into
    pieces
1 pound smoked sausage, cut into ¼-inch
    slices
½ cup bacon drippings
1 large onion, chopped
1 bunch green onions, sliced
1 medium-size green pepper, chopped
¼ cup all-purpose flour
1 quart water
2 chicken-flavored bouillon cubes
½ teaspoon salt
½ teaspoon pepper
Hot cooked rice
Gumbo filé

Brown the chicken and sausage in hot bacon drippings in a Dutch oven. Remove from Dutch oven; drain well, reserving drippings. Sauté onion and green pepper in reserved drippings until tender; drain well, reserving 2 tablespoons drippings.

Add flour to reserved drippings; cook over medium heat, stirring constantly, until roux is the color of a copper penny (about 10 to 15 minutes).

Gradually add water to roux, stirring until well blended. Stir in bouillon cubes, salt, and pepper. Add chicken, sausage, onion, and green pepper; cover and simmer 1 hour, stirring occasionally. Serve over rice. Add a small amount of filé to each serving. Yield: about 2½ quarts. *Grace Owens, Pride, Louisiana.*

DOVE AND SAUSAGE GUMBO

15 dove breasts
1 (10½-ounce) can consommé
1 beef-flavored bouillon cube
½ cup vegetable oil
½ cup all-purpose flour
1½ cups finely chopped onion
2 stalks celery, finely chopped
2 tablespoons Worcestershire sauce
2 cloves garlic, minced
1 to 2 bay leaves
½ teaspoon dried whole basil
¼ teaspoon poultry seasoning
¼ teaspoon freshly ground pepper
⅛ teaspoon ground red pepper
⅛ teaspoon ground allspice
⅛ teaspoon ground cloves
¾ pound smoked sausage, cut into ¼-inch
    slices
¼ cup dry red wine
⅛ teaspoon hot sauce
Hot cooked rice

Place dove breasts in Dutch oven, and cover with water. Boil about 10 minutes. Cool and remove meat from bones. Reserve cooking liquid in Dutch oven, adding water if necessary to make 2¼ cups liquid. Set meat aside.

Add consommé and bouillon cube to Dutch oven. Cook until bouillon cube is dissolved.

Brown dove in hot oil in a large skillet; drain well. Pour off all but ¼ cup oil. Add flour to reserved oil; cook over medium heat, stirring constantly, until roux is the color of a copper penny (about 10 to 15 minutes).

Gradually add about 1½ cups of consommé mixture to roux; cook over medium heat, stirring constantly, until thickened and bubbly. Stir in onion and celery, and cook about 5 minutes or until vegetables are tender. Add roux mixture to remaining consommé mixture, and stir well. Stir in Worcestershire and seasonings.

Brown sausage, and drain well. Stir sausage and dove into roux mixture; simmer 1½ hours, stirring occasionally. Add wine and hot sauce; stir well. Remove bay leaves, and serve gumbo over rice. Yield: about 1¾ quarts.
Warren S. Martin, Birmingham, Alabama.

HAM AND SEAFOOD GUMBO

6 slices bacon
¼ cup plus 1 tablespoon all-purpose flour
5 cups water
2 (16-ounce) cans whole tomatoes,
    undrained
1 cup chopped green onion
¾ cup chopped green pepper
½ cup chopped celery
1 (10-ounce) package frozen cut okra
2 cups diced ham
2 cloves garlic, minced
2½ teaspoons salt
1 teaspoon dried whole thyme
2 bay leaves
¼ to ½ teaspoon hot sauce
1 pound fresh crabmeat
2 pounds shrimp, peeled and deveined
2 pints oysters, undrained
¾ pound fresh snapper, cubed
Hot cooked rice

Cook bacon until crisp in a large Dutch oven; remove bacon. Crumble bacon, and set aside. Add flour to bacon drippings. Cook over medium heat, stirring constantly, until roux is the color of a copper penny (10 to 15 minutes). Gradually stir in water.

Place tomatoes in container of electric blender; process 10 seconds. Add tomatoes and next 10 ingredients to roux mixture, stirring well; simmer 2½ hours, stirring occasionally.

Stir in crabmeat, shrimp, oysters, and snapper; cook over medium heat 30 minutes. Stir in bacon. Serve over rice. Yield: 5 quarts.
Mrs. Jackie Nakamura, Magnolia Springs, Alabama.

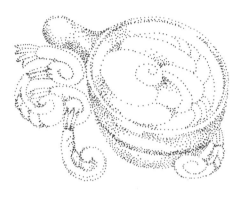

■ The rich and spicy flavor of Shrimp Gumbo would probably fool any Cajun—it's made without a roux.

SHRIMP GUMBO

1 (1- to 1¼-pound) soup bone
6½ cups water
1 tablespoon salt
1 bunch green onions
2 cups sliced okra
2 tablespoons bacon drippings
1 cup peeled chopped tomato
1 pod hot pepper
1 large green pepper, chopped
1 to 2 teaspoons dried whole thyme
1 bay leaf
1 pound shrimp, peeled and deveined
Hot cooked rice

Combine soup bone, water, and salt in a large saucepan; bring to a boil. Reduce heat to low, and simmer 1 hour.

Trim tops from green onions; chop bulbs and tops separately, and set aside.

Sauté onion bulbs and okra in hot bacon drippings 10 minutes. Add tomato, and sauté about 5 minutes. Add 6 cups soup stock, green onion tops, and next 5 ingredients; bring to a boil. Cover, reduce heat, and simmer 1½ hours. Serve over rice. Yield: about 2 quarts.
Mrs. Jack Corzine, St. Louis, Missouri.

CRAB AND SHRIMP GUMBO

⅓ cup vegetable oil
¼ cup plus 2 tablespoons all-purpose
  flour
2 quarts hot water
1 (28-ounce) can whole tomatoes,
  undrained
2 pounds fresh okra, sliced
2 bunches green onions, chopped
4 stalks celery, chopped
1 green pepper, chopped
1 pound fresh crabmeat
2 bay leaves
1 tablespoon salt
1 tablespoon chopped fresh parsley
1½ teaspoons dried whole thyme
1 teaspoon pepper
½ teaspoon garlic powder
¼ teaspoon red pepper
¼ teaspoon liquid crab boil
5 pounds medium shrimp, peeled
Hot cooked rice
Gumbo filé

Combine oil and flour in an 8-quart
Dutch oven. Cook over medium heat,
stirring constantly, until roux is the
color of a copper penny (about 10 to 15
minutes).

Stir in next 15 ingredients, and simmer 1 hour, stirring occasionally.

Add shrimp to gumbo; simmer an ad-
ditional 30 minutes, stirring frequently.
Serve over rice. Add a small amount of
filé to each serving. Yield: 6 quarts.
Betty Patranella,
Bryan, Texas.

Relax With Sunday Night Suppers

Wind down a busy weekend with a
relaxed Sunday night supper. The meal
should be light and special, as well as
simple to prepare. These recipes will get
you out of the kitchen fast. Just add a
salad and bread to complete the meal.

QUICKIE STROGANOFF

1 pound ground beef
1 medium onion, chopped
½ teaspoon salt
¼ teaspoon pepper
1 teaspoon Worcestershire sauce
2 cups uncooked wide egg noodles
2 cups tomato juice
½ cup commercial sour cream
1 tablespoon all-purpose flour

Cook ground beef and onion in a
large skillet until meat is browned, stirring occasionally; drain off pan drippings. Stir in the salt, pepper, and
Worcestershire sauce. Place noodles
evenly over meat. Slowly pour tomato
juice over noodles, moistening all noodles. Cover and simmer 25 to 30 minutes or until noodles are done. Combine
sour cream and flour; stir into meat
mixture. Heat thoroughly (do not boil).
Yield: 4 to 6 servings. *Marcia Kight,*
Paducah, Kentucky.

SLOPPY JOE POCKET SANDWICHES

1 pound ground beef
1 small onion, chopped
½ cup chopped celery or green pepper
1 cup tomato sauce
½ cup catsup
1 tablespoon brown sugar
1 tablespoon vinegar
1 tablespoon Worcestershire sauce
1 teaspoon dry mustard
¼ teaspoon salt
⅛ teaspoon pepper
4 (6-inch) pocket bread rounds

Combine ground beef, onion, and celery in a large skillet; cook until meat is
browned. Drain off pan drippings. Add
next 8 ingredients, and bring to a boil.
Cover; reduce heat and simmer 15 to 20
minutes, stirring occasionally.

Cut pocket bread rounds in half; fill
each half with ⅓ cup of meat sauce.
Yield: 8 sandwiches.
Cheryl Richardson,
Springfield, Virginia.

CREAMY CHICKEN CREPES

1⅓ cups all-purpose flour
1 teaspoon salt
4 eggs, beaten
2 tablespoons vegetable oil
1⅓ cups milk
Vegetable oil
Chicken filling (recipe follows)
Mushroom sauce (recipe follows)
1 cup (4 ounces) shredded Cheddar cheese
Paprika

Combine flour, salt, and eggs; mix
well. Blend in 2 tablespoons oil and
milk, beating until smooth. Refrigerate
batter at least 2 hours. (This allows
flour particles to swell and soften so
crepes are light in texture.)

Brush the bottom of a 10-inch crêpe
pan or heavy skillet with vegetable oil;
place over medium heat until just hot,
not smoking.

Pour 3 tablespoons batter in pan;
quickly tilt pan in all directions so that
batter covers pan in a thin film. Cook
about 1 minute.

Lift edge of crêpe to test for doneness. Crêpe is ready for flipping when it
can be shaken loose from pan. Flip
crêpe, and cook about 30 seconds on
the other side. (This side is rarely more
than spotty brown and is the side on
which the filling should be placed.)

Remove crêpe from pan, and repeat
procedure until all batter is used. Set
aside 10 crêpes; freeze remaining crêpes
for later use.

Spoon ⅓ cup chicken filling in center
of each crêpe; roll up, and place seam
side down in a greased 13- x 9- x 2-inch
baking dish. Spoon mushroom sauce
evenly over crêpes. Bake at 350° for 15
minutes. Sprinkle cheese over crêpes,
and bake 10 additional minutes. Sprinkle with paprika. Yield: 10 crêpes.

Chicken Filling:

2 (10¾-ounce) cans cream of mushroom
  soup, undiluted
1 (8-ounce) carton commercial sour cream
2½ cups chopped cooked chicken

Combine soup and sour cream; stir
well. Combine half of soup mixture and
chicken, stirring well. Reserve remaining soup mixture for mushroom sauce.
Yield: about 3⅓ cups.

Mushroom Sauce:

2 tablespoons butter or margarine
1 small onion, finely chopped
1 chicken bouillon cube
2 tablespoons water
1 (2½-ounce) jar sliced mushrooms,
  drained
Reserved soup mixture

Melt butter in a large skillet; sauté
onion in butter until tender. Add
bouillon cube, water, and mushrooms;
cook, stirring often, until bouillon cube
dissolves. Stir reserved soup mixture
into skillet. Yield: about 2½ cups.
Wanda H. Tripp,
Anderson, South Carolina.

ITALIAN SAUSAGE QUICHE

Pastry for 10-inch pie shell
1 pound Italian sausage, thinly sliced
1 pound fresh mushrooms, sliced
2 cups (8 ounces) shredded Gruyère or
  Swiss cheese
4 eggs, beaten
1 cup whipping cream
¼ teaspoon salt

Line a 10-inch quiche dish or piepan with pastry; trim excess pastry around edges. Prick bottom and sides of quiche shell with a fork; bake at 425° for 6 to 8 minutes. Let cool on a rack.

Cook sausage until browned; drain sausage, reserving 2 tablespoons drippings in pan. Sauté mushrooms in pan drippings 5 minutes or until tender; drain off drippings. Combine sausage, mushrooms, cheese, eggs, whipping cream, and salt; mix well. Pour into pastry shell, and bake at 350° for 45 minutes or until set. Yield: one 10-inch quiche.
Katie Tonore,
Clinton, Mississippi.

Creamed Eggs à la Asparagus and a fruit salad make a light and tempting supper.

CREAMED EGGS A LA ASPARAGUS

1 (10-ounce) package frozen asparagus
  spears
3 tablespoons butter or margarine
3 tablespoons all-purpose flour
1¾ cups milk
½ teaspoon salt
⅛ teaspoon pepper
½ cup (2 ounces) shredded sharp process
  American cheese
5 hard-cooked eggs, sliced
4 slices bread, toasted
Paprika

Cook asparagus according to package directions; drain and set aside.

Melt butter in a heavy saucepan over low heat; add flour and cook 1 minute, stirring constantly. Gradually add milk; cook over medium heat, stirring constantly, until thickened and bubbly. Add salt, pepper, and cheese; stir until cheese melts. Gently fold in hard-cooked eggs.

Arrange one-fourth of asparagus spears on each slice of toast; spoon one-fourth of egg sauce on each. Sprinkle lightly with paprika. Yield: 4 servings.
Evangeline C. Fortner,
Greenville, South Carolina.

SPANISH OMELET

6 eggs
¼ cup plus 2 tablespoons milk
½ teaspoon salt
Dash of pepper
½ cup sliced mushrooms
1 medium-size green pepper, chopped
4 slices bacon, cooked and crumbled
1 medium tomato, diced
2 tablespoons picante sauce
2 tablespoons butter or margarine,
  divided

Combine eggs, milk, salt, and pepper; beat well. Fold in mushrooms, green pepper, bacon, tomato, and picante sauce.

For each omelet, melt 1 tablespoon butter in a 10-inch skillet until just hot enough to sizzle a drop of water; pour in one-half of egg mixture. As mixture starts to cook, gently lift edges of omelet and tilt pan to allow uncooked portion to flow underneath. Fold omelet in half, and place on a warm platter. Repeat procedure with remaining ingredients. Yield: 3 to 4 servings.
Charlie R. Hester,
Austin, Texas.

HOT CHICKEN SALAD

2 cups diced cooked chicken
1 cup finely chopped celery
½ cup sliced almonds, toasted
½ cup round buttery cracker crumbs
2 tablespoons chopped onion
1 (10¾-ounce) can cream of chicken soup,
  undiluted
1 (2-ounce) can mushroom stems and
  pieces, drained
½ cup mayonnaise
½ cup crushed potato chips

Combine all ingredients except potato chips; toss gently. Spoon into a greased 1½-quart casserole. Bake at 375° for 15 minutes. Sprinkle potato chips on top; bake an additional 15 minutes. Yield: 4 to 6 servings.
Mrs. James Collins,
DeFuniak Springs, Florida.

Spaghetti With A Special Sauce

Tender strips of sautéed veal, green peppers, mushrooms, and tomatoes all add up to a delicious spaghetti sauce. Spoon this special sauce over a platter of hot cooked spaghetti, pass the Parmesan cheese, and enjoy.

SPAGHETTI WITH VEAL AND PEPPERS

2 pounds boneless veal cutlets, cut into
  thin strips
¼ cup all-purpose flour
¼ cup olive oil
2 medium-size green peppers, chopped
1 (4-ounce) can sliced mushrooms,
  drained
2 (28-ounce) cans tomatoes, undrained
2 (8-ounce) cans tomato sauce
1 teaspoon dried whole basil
1 teaspoon dried whole oregano
1 teaspoon garlic powder
Hot cooked spaghetti
Grated Parmesan cheese

Dredge veal in flour; sauté in oil in a Dutch oven until no longer pink. Add green peppers and cook, stirring occasionally, until tender. Stir in next 6 ingredients. Cover and simmer 1 hour.

Serve sauce over spaghetti; sprinkle with Parmesan cheese. Yield: about 8 servings.
Ann Marcuccilli,
Louisville, Kentucky.

Budget-Stretching Franks

A family favorite, frankfurters are more appealing than ever as food prices continue to rise. In addition to being economical, they can be prepared in a multitude of ways for variety.

For a one-dish dinner, we offer Hawaiian Franks served over rice. If the traditional hot dog is a favorite at your house, try Hot Dogs Delicious; extra-hot catsup puts the tang in the sauce. For stuffed franks, choose either Bacon-Wrapped Franks or Stuffed Franks and Potatoes.

HAWAIIAN FRANKS

1 (8-ounce) can pineapple chunks
¼ cup butter or margarine
1 large onion, chopped
1 large green pepper, chopped
2 small tomatoes, peeled and chopped
2 tablespoons cornstarch
1 tablespoon vinegar
1 pound frankfurters, cut into
  1-inch pieces
Salt and pepper to taste
Hot cooked rice

Drain pineapple, reserving juice. Add enough water to juice to equal ½ cup, and set aside.

Melt butter in a skillet. Add pineapple, onion, green pepper, and tomato; cook over medium heat until thoroughly heated, stirring occasionally. Combine pineapple juice, cornstarch, and vinegar; add gradually to vegetable mixture, stirring constantly. Add frankfurters, salt, and pepper; cover and simmer 10 minutes, stirring frequently. Serve over rice. Yield: 6 servings.
Mrs. O. V. Elkins,
Raleigh, North Carolina.

STUFFED FRANKS AND POTATOES

3 small potatoes, cooked, peeled, and
  mashed
2 hard-cooked eggs, finely chopped
¼ cup mayonnaise
¼ cup finely chopped celery
2 tablespoons minced onion
2 tablespoons finely chopped sweet pickle
¼ teaspoon salt
⅛ teaspoon pepper
1 pound frankfurters

Combine first 8 ingredients; mix well. Slit frankfurters lengthwise, cutting almost through; stuff with potato mixture. Place frankfurters in a shallow pan, and bake at 400° for 15 to 20 minutes. Yield: 4 to 6 servings.
Kathryn Knight,
Sarasota, Florida.

HOT DOGS DELICIOUS

½ cup chopped onion
1 tablespoon vegetable oil
1 (14-ounce) bottle extra-hot catsup
2 tablespoons pickle relish
1 tablespoon sugar
1 tablespoon vinegar
¼ teaspoon salt
¼ teaspoon pepper
1 pound frankfurters
Warm hot dog buns

Sauté onion in oil in a large saucepan until tender. Stir in next 6 ingredients. Add frankfurters to sauce, and simmer 10 minutes or until frankfurters are thoroughly heated. Serve in warm buns. Yield: 4 to 6 servings. *Vivian Conner,*
Dale, Indiana.

BACON-WRAPPED FRANKS

4 slices bread, cut into ½-inch cubes
2 tablespoons chopped onion
1 tablespoon finely chopped parsley
¼ teaspoon dry mustard
3 to 4 tablespoons water
Salt and pepper
6 frankfurters
6 slices bacon

Combine first 4 ingredients; add enough water to moisten, and mix well. Season to taste with salt and pepper.

Slit frankfurters lengthwise, cutting almost through; stuff with bread mixture. Wrap a bacon slice around each frankfurter, securing with a wooden pick. Place in a shallow pan, and bake at 400° for 15 to 20 minutes. Yield: 6 servings. *Mrs. Paul Raper,*
Burgaw, North Carolina.

Tip: Crumble extra pieces of cooked bacon and freeze. Use as a topping for casseroles or baked potatoes.

SPICY FRANKFURTERS

1 pound frankfurters, cut into thirds
1 small onion, minced
2 tablespoons all-purpose flour
¼ cup water
⅔ cup catsup
¼ cup vinegar
¼ cup sugar
2 tablespoons prepared mustard

Combine frankfurters and onion in a greased 1½-quart casserole; set aside. Combine flour and water; mix well. Add remaining ingredients; stir well, and pour over frankfurters. Cover and bake at 350° for 30 minutes. Yield: 4 to 6 servings. *Mrs. George W. Lee,*
Gadsden, Alabama.

The Difference Is Applesauce

A just-right sweetness and the flavor of fresh apples—that's the difference applesauce makes in a variety of dishes. But don't take our word for it. With these recipes, you can taste the difference applesauce makes in a carrot cake, doughnuts, and a hot fruit casserole.

Applesauce is also the basis for a speedy version of homemade apple butter. It's ready in only 30 minutes.

APPLESAUCE CARROT CAKE

¾ cup butter or margarine, softened
1 cup sugar
1½ cups firmly packed brown sugar
2 eggs
¾ cup shredded carrots
2¼ cups applesauce
3 cups all-purpose flour
1½ cups whole wheat flour
1 tablespoon soda
1½ teaspoons ground nutmeg
1½ teaspoons ground cinnamon
1½ teaspoons ground allspice
1 cup chopped walnuts
1 cup raisins

Cream butter; gradually add sugar, beating well. Add eggs, one at a time, beating well after each addition.

Stir carrots into applesauce. Combine flour, soda, and spices; add to creamed mixture alternately with applesauce mixture, beginning and ending with flour mixture. Mix well after each addition. Fold in walnuts and raisins.

Pour batter into a greased and floured 10-inch tube pan. Bake at 350° for 1 hour and 20 to 25 minutes or until cake tests done. Cool in pan 10 minutes. Remove from pan; let cool. Yield: one 10-inch cake.

Mrs. Farmer L. Burns,
New Orleans, Louisiana.

APPLESAUCE DOUGHNUTS

3⅓ cups all-purpose flour, divided
1 tablespoon baking powder
½ teaspoon salt
¾ teaspoon ground nutmeg
¼ teaspoon ground cloves
1 cup applesauce
¾ cup sugar
2 eggs
2 tablespoons shortening
Vegetable oil
Powdered sugar (optional)

Combine 1⅓ cups flour and next 8 ingredients; beat at low speed of electric mixer until well blended. Increase speed of mixer to medium, and beat 2 additional minutes; stir in remaining flour. Cover dough, and chill at least 1 hour.

Divide dough in half. Working with one portion at a time, place dough on a heavily floured surface; roll out to ½-inch thickness. Cut dough with a floured doughnut cutter.

Heat 2 to 3 inches of oil to 375°; drop in 3 or 4 doughnuts at a time. Cook about 1 minute or until golden on one side; turn and cook other side about 1 minute. Drain on paper towels. Sprinkle with powdered sugar, if desired. Yield: about 2 dozen.

Ann Davis,
Waco, Texas.

HOT FRUIT COMPOTE

1 (16-ounce) can sliced peaches, drained
1 (16-ounce) can pear halves, drained and coarsely chopped
1 (16-ounce) can whole purple plums, drained and pitted
1 (20-ounce) can pineapple chunks, drained
1 (6-ounce) jar maraschino cherries, drained
2 bananas, sliced
¾ cup firmly packed brown sugar
⅓ cup butter or margarine
1 (16-ounce) can applesauce
3 tablespoons brown sugar
½ cup chopped pecans

Combine first 6 ingredients in a 13- x 9- x 2-inch baking dish; set dish aside.

Combine ¾ cup brown sugar, butter, and applesauce in a saucepan; heat thoroughly, stirring occasionally. Spoon applesauce mixture over fruit; sprinkle with 3 tablespoons brown sugar and pecans. Bake at 300° for 1 hour. Serve hot. Yield: 10 to 12 servings.

Note: Compote may be prepared ahead; cover baking dish with plastic wrap and freeze. To serve, let thaw overnight in refrigerator; bake according to directions.

Rita Brady,
Newllano, Louisiana.

HALF-HOUR APPLE BUTTER

1 (25-ounce) jar unsweetened applesauce
½ cup sugar
1½ teaspoons ground cinnamon
¼ teaspoon ground allspice
⅛ teaspoon ground ginger
⅛ teaspoon ground cloves

Combine all ingredients in a heavy saucepan, stirring well; bring to a boil. Then reduce heat and simmer, uncovered, for 30 minutes; stir often. Let cool.

Pour mixture into container of electric blender; process at high speed for 10 seconds or until smooth. Store in refrigerator. Yield: about 2 cups.

Julie Dugan,
Alexandria, Virginia.

Canned Foods Simplify Salad Making

For a quickly assembled salad, whether it be tossed, marinated, or congealed, let the canned fruits and vegetables on your kitchen shelf lend a helping hand.

Turn canned peas and corn into Marinated Pea Salad, kidney beans into Meatless Taco Salad, and cut green asparagus into Tart Asparagus Salad. For Luscious Frozen Fruit Salad, canned pineapple and cherries are added to a creamy mixture, frozen, and served in squares.

CHICKEN-RICE SALAD

3 (6¾-ounce) cans chunk chicken, undrained and flaked
1 (4-ounce) can sliced mushrooms, drained
2 cups cooked regular rice, cooled
1 cup sliced celery
½ cup pitted ripe olives, cut in half
½ cup chopped fresh parsley
¾ cup commercial creamy Italian dressing
¼ cup mayonnaise
2 tablespoons prepared mustard
1 teaspoon seasoned salt
Lettuce leaves (optional)

Combine first 6 ingredients in a large bowl; mix well. Combine dressing, mayonnaise, mustard, and salt; mix well, and stir into chicken mixture. Chill at least 4 hours. Serve on lettuce leaves, if desired. Yield: 4 to 6 servings.

Mrs. J. S. Edwards,
Columbia, South Carolina.

TART ASPARAGUS SALAD

2 envelopes unflavored gelatin
½ cup cold water
¾ cup sugar
½ cup vinegar
1 cup water
1 tablespoon minced onion
2 tablespoons lemon juice
1 (10½-ounce) can cut green asparagus, drained
2 (4-ounce) jars diced pimiento, drained
1 teaspoon salt
1 (8-ounce) can water chestnuts, drained and sliced
1 cup chopped celery

Soften gelatin in ½ cup cold water, and set aside.

Combine sugar, vinegar, and 1 cup water in a medium saucepan; bring to a boil. Remove from heat; stir in gelatin, onion, and lemon juice. Chill until consistency of unbeaten egg white.

Fold in remaining ingredients; spoon into eight ½-cup molds. Chill until firm. Yield: 8 servings.

Mrs. Randy Throneberry,
Shelbyville, Tennessee.

Tip: To save the unused portion of a jar of pimientos or olives, cover with a little vinegar and water; cover tightly and refrigerate.

MEATLESS TACO SALAD

1 small onion, chopped
1 (15-ounce) can kidney beans, drained
    and rinsed
2 avocados, peeled, seeded, and chopped
1 to 2 cups (4 to 8 ounces) shredded
    sharp Cheddar cheese
2 medium tomatoes, diced
1 (3-ounce) jar pimiento-stuffed olives,
    drained and sliced
1 (8-ounce) bottle spicy-sweet French
    dressing
1 small head iceberg lettuce, shredded
1 (10-ounce) package corn chips

Combine first 7 ingredients in a large salad bowl; toss lightly. Just before serving, add lettuce and chips; toss lightly. Yield: 8 to 10 servings.

Mary Nelson,
Richardson, Texas.

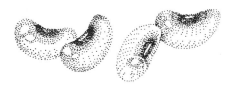

MARINATED PEA SALAD

¾ cup vinegar
¾ cup sugar
1 tablespoon water
1 teaspoon salt
¼ to ½ teaspoon pepper
1 (17-ounce) can small English peas,
    drained
1 (12-ounce) can shoe peg corn, drained
1 (2-ounce) jar diced pimiento, drained
1 cup finely chopped celery
1 cup finely chopped onion

Combine first 5 ingredients in a small saucepan; bring mixture to a boil, and boil 1 minute. Let cool completely.

Combine remaining ingredients in a bowl, and toss lightly. Pour marinade over vegetable mixture; stir gently. Cover salad and refrigerate overnight. Yield: 10 to 12 servings. *Eunice Moss,*
Bloomington, Indiana.

LUSCIOUS FROZEN FRUIT SALAD

½ cup chopped pecans
1 (15¼-ounce) can pineapple chunks,
    drained
1 (16½-ounce) can pitted dark sweet
    cherries, drained
1 (12-ounce) carton frozen whipped
    topping, thawed
1 (8-ounce) carton lemon-flavored yogurt
½ cup mayonnaise

Combine first 3 ingredients, mixing well. Combine remaining ingredients, and fold into fruit mixture. Spoon into a 12- x 8- x 2-inch baking dish, and freeze until firm. Cut into squares to serve. Yield: 12 servings. *Mrs. Jack Veatch,*
Cedartown, Georgia.

Eggplant, The Versatile Side Dish

Versatile eggplant provides a nice break from routine meals because you can serve it in so many ways: stuffed, fried, or baked in a casserole. For a light touch, stir with zucchini for a quick ratatouille.

Although it's available year-round, eggplant is at its peak in both quality and availability during late summer and early fall. When choosing eggplant, select pear-shaped ones that are 3 to 6 inches in diameter and have a glossy purple-black skin.

BEEFY STUFFED EGGPLANT

2 medium eggplant
2 teaspoons salt
1 pound ground beef
½ cup chopped onion
1 (15-ounce) can tomato puree
½ cup water
¼ teaspoon salt
¼ teaspoon pepper
⅛ teaspoon garlic powder
1 cup (4 ounces) shredded Cheddar cheese
½ cup chopped fresh mushrooms
1 tablespoon chopped fresh parsley
1 teaspoon steak sauce
2 tablespoons grated Parmesan cheese

Wash eggplant, and cut in half lengthwise. Remove pulp, leaving a ¼-inch shell. Sprinkle 2 teaspoons salt in shells; drain for 45 minutes, and pat dry. Chop pulp, and set aside.

Cook ground beef and onion in a large skillet until the ground beef is browned; drain. Stir in tomato puree, water, remaining salt, pepper, and garlic powder; simmer 10 minutes. Add chopped eggplant, and cook 15 additional minutes, stirring often.

Stir ½ cup Cheddar cheese, mushrooms, parsley, and steak sauce into ground beef mixture. Spoon mixture

into shells, and place in a lightly greased 13- x 9- x 2-inch baking dish. Bake at 375° for 20 minutes. Sprinkle mixture with Parmesan and remaining Cheddar cheese, and bake 5 additional minutes. Yield: 4 servings.

Marlan Mary Hornburg,
West Melbourne, Florida.

SAUSAGE STUFFED EGGPLANT

2 medium eggplant
1 pound hot bulk sausage
1 large onion, chopped
1 medium-size green pepper, chopped
1 (16-ounce) can tomatoes, undrained and
    coarsely chopped
1 egg, slightly beaten
1 cup (4 ounces) shredded Cheddar cheese

Cut eggplant in half lengthwise; scoop out pulp, leaving a ¼-inch shell. Chop pulp, and set aside.

Cook sausage in a large skillet until browned, stirring to crumble; drain off excess drippings. Add chopped eggplant, onion, green pepper, and tomatoes; cook until most of the liquid evaporates, stirring often.

Gradually stir about one-fourth of sausage mixture into egg; add to remaining sausage mixture, stirring constantly. Stir in cheese. Stuff shells with sausage mixture; place in a 13- x 9- x 2-inch baking dish. Add water to ½-inch depth; cover and bake at 350° for 30 minutes. Yield: 4 servings.

Cindy L. Overall,
Baton Rouge, Louisiana.

FRENCH-FRIED EGGPLANT

1 large eggplant
½ teaspoon salt
⅛ teaspoon pepper
1 egg, beaten
1 tablespoon water
½ cup all-purpose flour
¾ cup fine dry breadcrumbs
Vegetable oil

Peel eggplant, and cut into finger-size strips. Sprinkle with salt and pepper. Combine egg and water; mix well. Dredge strips in flour; then dip in egg mixture, and roll in breadcrumbs. Fry in hot oil (375°) until golden brown. Drain on paper towels. Yield: 4 to 6 servings.

Eloise Haynes,
Greenville, Mississippi.

EGGPLANT-ZUCCHINI RATATOUILLE

1 large onion, thinly sliced
1 large green pepper, chopped
2 cloves garlic, minced
2 tablespoons vegetable oil
1 medium eggplant, peeled and cubed
3 medium zucchini, sliced
3 tomatoes, peeled and chopped
½ teaspoon salt
⅛ teaspoon pepper
Dash of dried whole oregano
2 to 4 tablespoons grated Parmesan
  cheese
2 tablespoons chopped parsley

Sauté onion, green pepper, and garlic in oil until vegetables are crisp-tender. Stir in eggplant and zucchini; cook 5 minutes. Add tomatoes, salt, pepper, and oregano; stir well, and cook just until thoroughly heated.

Sprinkle with cheese and parsley. Yield: 4 to 6 servings.

Charlotte Watkins,
Lakeland, Florida.

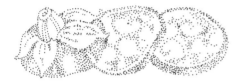

EGGPLANT CASSEROLE

2 medium eggplant
1 onion, chopped
1 green pepper, finely chopped
1 tablespoon bacon drippings
1 egg, beaten
1 cup seasoned dry breadcrumbs
½ teaspoon salt
¼ teaspoon pepper
¾ cup (3 ounces) shredded mild Cheddar
  cheese
1 to 2 tablespoons picante sauce
½ cup grated Parmesan cheese

Peel eggplant, and cut into 1-inch cubes; cook in a small amount of boiling water 10 minutes or until tender. Drain well; mash.

Sauté onion and green pepper in bacon drippings. Remove from heat. Combine eggplant, egg, breadcrumbs, salt, and pepper; mix well, and add onion mixture.

Spoon half of eggplant mixture into a greased 1½-quart casserole; sprinkle with Cheddar cheese. Spoon remaining eggplant over cheese, and top evenly with picante sauce; sprinkle with Parmesan cheese. Bake at 350° for 30 minutes. Yield: 6 servings.

Dorothy Brandon Poston,
Dallas, Texas.

Size Dessert Just For Two

Dessert for two doesn't have to mean the same thing for a week. Try one of our scaled-down favorites from readers who specialize in cooking for two.

CHOCOLATE-ORANGE MOUSSE

2 tablespoons light brown sugar
½ teaspoon grated orange rind
1 egg
1 egg yolk
3 (1-ounce) squares semisweet chocolate,
  melted and cooled
1½ tablespoons orange juice
½ cup whipping cream
Additional whipped cream
Grated orange rind

Combine first 4 ingredients in container of electric blender; process until foamy. Add chocolate, orange juice, and whipping cream, and blend until smooth. Pour mixture into two individual dessert cups; and chill 1 hour or until set. Garnish with whipped cream and orange rind. Yield: 2 servings.

Gaye Wesche,
Memphis, Tennessee.

CREAMY RICE PUDDING

1 cup cooked rice
1 cup milk
2½ tablespoons sugar
Pinch of salt
1 tablespoon butter or margarine
¼ teaspoon vanilla extract

Combine rice, milk, sugar, salt, and butter. Cook over medium heat, stirring constantly, until mixture thickens (about 20 minutes). Stir in vanilla. Serve as is, either hot or cold, or use one of the following variations. Yield: 2 servings.

Velvety Rice Pudding: Fold ½ cup prepared whipped topping into cool pudding. Top with fruit or dessert sauce.

Fruited Rice Pudding: Spoon pudding into serving dishes. Top with fruit preserves, and garnish with whipped cream.

Fudgy Rice Pudding: Pour warm pudding into a baking dish; crumble a chocolate nut candy bar over top. Bake at 350° until chocolate melts.

Wanda Parrish,
Morganfield, Kentucky.

FUDGE CAKE FOR TWO

1 (1-ounce) square unsweetened chocolate
½ cup boiling water
¼ cup butter or margarine
1 cup all-purpose flour
1 cup sugar
¾ teaspoon soda
¼ teaspoon salt
¼ cup buttermilk
1 egg, beaten
½ teaspoon vanilla extract
2 tablespoons powdered sugar (optional)

Combine first 3 ingredients in a medium saucepan. Cook over low heat until chocolate and butter melt; let mixture cool. Stir flour, sugar, soda, and salt into cooled mixture; stir in buttermilk, egg, and vanilla.

Pour batter into a greased and floured 9-inch square pan. Bake at 350° for 35 minutes or until wooden pick inserted in center comes out clean. Cool in pan 10 minutes; remove from pan, and complete cooling on wire rack. Sprinkle cake with powdered sugar, if desired. Yield: one 9-inch cake.

Mrs. David N. Roller,
Louisville, Kentucky.

BANANA-BERRY SUPREME

1 egg, beaten
1 cup milk
2 tablespoons sugar
1 teaspoon cornstarch
⅛ teaspoon vanilla extract
1 large banana, sliced
¾ cup quartered strawberries
1 egg white
⅛ teaspoon salt
2 tablespoons sugar

Combine egg and milk in top of a double boiler. Combine 2 tablespoons sugar and cornstarch; stir into egg mixture. Cook over simmering water until mixture thickens, stirring constantly. Remove from heat; stir in vanilla. Cover and chill.

Divide banana slices and quartered strawberries evenly into two 10-ounce ovenproof dessert cups. Spoon custard over fruit.

Beat egg white (at room temperature) until foamy; add salt and continue beating until soft peaks form. Gradually add 2 tablespoons sugar, beating until stiff peaks form. Spoon meringue into a ring over custards. Bake at 425° for 3 minutes or until the meringue is lightly browned. Chill before serving. Yield: 2 servings.

Peggy Dowdy,
Roanoke, Virginia.

Dressing Makes The Difference

Our readers have discovered that commercial bottled salad dressings will do lots more in the kitchen besides flavor salad greens.

Try pouring Italian dressing straight from the bottle to flavor and tenderize a pot roast. Broccoli and lima beans are turned into delicious cold salads with coleslaw and French dressings. Or use a thick creamy dressing like Thousand Island instead of mayonnaise as a sandwich spread. Just be sure to save a little dressing for the salad.

GRILLED REUBEN SANDWICHES

1 cup commercial Thousand Island
   dressing
18 slices rye bread
12 slices Swiss cheese
½ cup canned sauerkraut
24 slices thinly sliced corned beef
Butter or margarine, softened

Spread Thousand Island dressing on one side of 12 slices of bread; arrange 1 slice cheese, 2 teaspoons sauerkraut, and 2 slices corned beef evenly over each slice. Stack to make six (2-layer) sandwiches; top with remaining bread.

Spread butter on outside of top slice of bread; invert sandwiches onto a hot skillet or griddle. Cook until bread is golden. Spread butter on ungrilled side of bread; carefully turn sandwiches, and cook until bread is golden and cheese is slightly melted. Secure sandwiches with wooden picks; cut crosswise into 3 pieces. Serve hot. Yield: 6 servings.
Peggy F. Revels,
Woodruff, South Carolina.

ZESTY POT ROAST

1 (8-ounce) bottle Italian salad dressing
1 (3- to 4-pound) boneless pot roast
1 (10½-ounce) can condensed beef broth,
   undiluted
1 cup hot water
4 to 6 carrots, cut into 1½-inch pieces
1 (10-ounce) package frozen cut green
   beans
2 tablespoons all-purpose flour

Pour salad dressing over roast in a shallow baking dish; cover and refrigerate 8 hours or overnight, turning roast occasionally.

Remove roast from marinade, reserving marinade. Place roast in a Dutch oven; add beef broth and water. Cover and simmer 2 hours. Add carrots; cook 5 minutes. Add green beans; cook 5 minutes. Add reserved marinade; cook, uncovered, for 10 to 15 minutes or until liquid has decreased to about 2 cups. Add enough water to liquid to measure 2 cups, if necessary.

Remove roast and vegetables to serving platter; keep warm. Combine flour and a small amount of pan juices in a jar. Cover tightly, and shake vigorously. Add to pan juices in Dutch oven; cook, stirring constantly, until gravy is thickened and bubbly. Serve with roast. Yield: 6 to 8 servings. *Lona Bloomer,*
St. Petersburg, Florida.

CHILLY LIMA BEANS

1 cup cooked lima beans, drained
⅓ cup chopped celery
2 green onions, chopped
2 hard-cooked eggs, coarsely chopped
1 tablespoon plus 1 teaspoon chopped
   green pepper
1 tablespoon plus 1 teaspoon chopped
   pimiento
1 tablespoon plus 1 teaspoon chopped
   fresh parsley
¼ cup commercial French dressing
Lettuce leaves

Combine first 7 ingredients; cover and chill 2 hours. Toss with French dressing, and serve on lettuce leaves. Yield: about 4 servings. *Maybelle Pinkston,*
Corryton, Tennessee.

BROCCOLI MEDLEY

1 bunch broccoli
1 bunch green onions, chopped
½ cup chopped celery
½ cup chopped pimiento-stuffed olives
4 hard-cooked eggs, chopped
⅔ to ¾ cup commercial coleslaw dressing

Trim off large leaves of broccoli. Remove tough ends of lower stalks; wash broccoli thoroughly. Cut flowerets from stems, and cut stems into 1-inch pieces. Cook, covered, in a small amount of boiling water 10 minutes or until crisp-tender; drain and cool.

Combine broccoli and remaining ingredients; toss gently. Chill 2 hours. Yield: 6 servings. *Mrs. Robert James,*
Marion, Ohio.

HEARTY SALAD ROLLS

1½ cups cooked chopped chicken or
   turkey
1½ cups diced boiled ham
8 slices bacon, cooked and crumbled
1 cup (4 ounces) shredded Cheddar or
   Swiss cheese
2 hard-cooked eggs, chopped
1½ cups chopped green pepper
¼ cup chopped pimiento, drained
¾ cup commercial green onion dressing
6 large hard rolls
Pickles (optional)
Olives (optional)
Cherry tomatoes (optional)

Combine first 8 ingredients, mixing well; chill at least 1 hour.

Cut a thin slice from the top of each roll; scoop out centers, leaving a ½-inch-thick shell. Spoon salad mixture into rolls; replace top slices. Garnish rolls with pickles, olives, or cherry tomatoes on wooden picks, if desired. Yield: 6 salad rolls. *Lilly B. Smith,*
Richmond, Virginia.

FIESTA DIP

1 (8-ounce) package cream cheese,
   softened
⅓ cup catsup
3 tablespoons commercial French dressing
2 tablespoons half-and-half
1½ tablespoons grated onion
½ teaspoon salt
Red pepper to taste

Combine all ingredients; beat well. Serve dip with raw vegetables. Yield: 1½ cups. *Mrs. Bernie Benigno,*
Gulfport, Mississippi.

Spice Up The Day With Gingerbread

Remember the last time you had homemade gingerbread? If it's been so long you can't remember, it's time to try one of these two recipes and enjoy again its spicy, old-fashioned goodness.

Both have a flavor to match what grandma used to bake.

MOCHA GINGERBREAD

1 (14.5-ounce) package gingerbread mix
1 cup lukewarm coffee
1 egg, beaten
½ cup chopped pecans
Orange Cream Frosting
Grated orange rind

Combine gingerbread mix, coffee, and egg in an ungreased 8-inch square pan. Stir with a fork about 2 minutes or until batter is of uniform color and consistency. Stir in pecans. Bake at 350° for 30 to 35 minutes or until wooden pick inserted in center comes out clean. Cool. Frost with Orange Cream Frosting. Garnish with orange rind. Yield: 9 servings.

Orange Cream Frosting:

2 (3-ounce) packages cream cheese, softened
½ teaspoon grated orange rind
2 tablespoons orange juice
1 cup sifted powdered sugar

Beat cream cheese; add rind and juice. Gradually add sugar, beating until light and fluffy. Yield: about ½ cup.
Mrs. Harvey Kidd,
Hernando, Mississippi.

OLD-FASHIONED GINGERBREAD

½ cup butter or margarine, softened
½ cup sugar
1 egg
1 cup molasses
2½ cups all-purpose flour
1½ teaspoons soda
½ teaspoon salt
1 teaspoon ground cinnamon
1 teaspoon ground cloves
1 teaspoon ground ginger
1 cup hot water

Cream butter; gradually add sugar, mixing well. Add egg and molasses, mixing well.

Combine dry ingredients; add to the creamed mixture alternately with the hot water, beginning and ending with the flour mixture, and beating well after each addition.

Pour batter into a lightly greased and floured 9-inch square pan. Bake at 350° for 35 to 40 minutes or until wooden pick inserted in center comes out clean. Yield: 9 servings.
Evelyn Howell,
Orange, Texas.

Tip: Keep flour in a large shaker for quick and easy flouring of a pan; just shake out the amount needed.

An Everyday Meal, But Not Routine

If your everyday meals could use a little lift, take a look at the menu we've put together. It's an enticing combination of quick-to-prepare dishes that offer a medley of colors, textures, and flavors.

The pork chops that anchor the menu are complemented by an apple salad, herb-seasoned green beans crunchy with toasted almonds, and Celebrity Green Rice. Dessert is Hot Fudge Pudding topped with whipped cream.

Pork Chops and Creamy Gravy
Fresh Apple Salad
Celebrity Green Rice
Italian Green Beans With Almonds
Hot Fudge Pudding

PORK CHOPS AND CREAMY GRAVY

4 to 6 (½-inch-thick) pork chops
Salt and pepper to taste
¼ cup vegetable oil
2 tablespoons all-purpose flour
1½ cups milk
¼ teaspoon salt
⅛ teaspoon pepper
½ teaspoon bottled brown bouquet sauce

Sprinkle pork chops with salt and pepper; brown on both sides in hot oil. Drain chops on paper towels. Reserve 2 tablespoons drippings in skillet.

Add flour to skillet, stirring until smooth. Cook 1 minute, stirring constantly. Gradually add milk; cook over medium heat, stirring constantly, until thickened and bubbly. Stir in ¼ teaspoon salt, ⅛ teaspoon pepper, and brown bouquet sauce. Add pork chops to gravy; cover and simmer 45 minutes. Yield: 4 to 6 servings. *Heather Riggins, Nashville, Tennessee.*

FRESH APPLE SALAD

1½ cups chopped apple
1 cup coarsely chopped celery
½ cup raisins
2 tablespoons mayonnaise
1 tablespoon sugar
⅛ teaspoon salt
Dash of pepper

Combine apple, celery, and raisins. Combine mayonnaise, sugar, salt, and pepper; stir well. Pour over apple mixture; toss gently. Yield: 4 to 6 servings.
Mrs. Malcolm Bowles,
Mableton, Georgia.

CELEBRITY GREEN RICE

1 cup uncooked regular rice
2 cups chicken broth
½ teaspoon salt
⅛ teaspoon pepper
¾ cup chopped celery
¾ cup chopped green onion
¼ cup chopped parsley
¼ cup butter or margarine
1 (8-ounce) can water chestnuts, drained and sliced (optional)

Combine rice, chicken broth, salt, and pepper in a medium saucepan; cover and cook over medium heat 20 minutes or until done. Set rice aside and keep warm.

Sauté celery, green onion, and parsley in butter; stir into rice. Stir in water chestnuts, if desired. Yield: about 6 servings.
Frances V. Skuca,
El Campo, Texas.

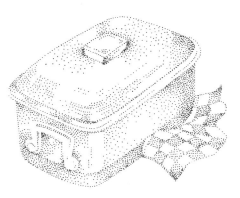

ITALIAN GREEN BEANS WITH ALMONDS

2 (10-ounce) packages frozen Italian green beans or cut green beans
¼ cup sliced almonds
¼ cup butter or margarine
½ teaspoon dried whole oregano

Cook beans according to package directions; drain.

Sauté almonds in butter until toasted. Add almonds and oregano to beans, stirring well. Yield: 6 servings.
Jean Goodwin,
Athens, Georgia.

HOT FUDGE PUDDING

1 cup self-rising flour
1¾ cups sugar, divided
4 tablespoons cocoa, divided
½ cup milk
2 tablespoons butter, melted
1 teaspoon vanilla extract
Pinch of salt
1½ cups hot water
Whipped cream or ice cream (optional)

Combine flour, ¾ cup sugar, and 2 tablespoons cocoa; stir in milk, butter, and vanilla. Pour batter into a 9-inch square baking pan.

Combine 1 cup sugar, 2 tablespoons cocoa, and salt; mix well, and sprinkle over batter. Pour water over top; bake at 350° for 30 minutes. Serve warm; top with whipped cream or ice cream, if desired. Yield: 6 servings.

Pamela Ross,
Louisville, Kentucky.

Microwave Cookery

Slower Cooking Yields A Better Roast

Many cooks have been disappointed with the results when they have cooked a roast in their microwave oven. But the key to success is selecting a roast that's suitable for microwaving and following advanced microwave techniques.

Our two recipes for basic pot roast and pot roast with vegetables give detailed instructions for cooking them in the microwave. The total microwaving time is based on the weight of the roast. We recommend microwaving at MEDIUM LOW (30% power or approximately 200 watts) for 33 to 37 minutes per pound.

Using MEDIUM LOW instead of a higher power prolongs cooking time, but ensures more uniform doneness and reduces shrinkage. If your oven does not have a MEDIUM LOW setting, use 30% of HIGH power. This is setting No. 3 on most ovens with numbered power levels.

The time range in the recipes allows for difference in wattage of microwave ovens. If food is normally done in your oven at the low end of the time range, cook pot roast for 33 minutes per pound. If you usually need to cook to the higher end of the time range, microwave for 37 minutes per pound. If you are unsure of how fast your oven cooks, check for doneness at the lower end of the range.

—To ensure even cooking, select a uniformly shaped chuck roast between 2 and 2½ inches thick and weighing from 1¾ to 3 pounds. If a uniformly shaped roast is not available, trim off the thin ends of roast and freeze for another use.

—Tie cooking bag loosely with string or with a ½-inch-wide strip cut from open end of bag. (Do not use a twist tie.) To tie bag loosely, insert a pencil into bag, and tie around pencil; then remove pencil.

—To promote even cooking of vegetables, slice into uniform pieces.

—Let roast stand in bag for 10 to 15 minutes after microwaving to complete the cooking process.

—Slice roast across the grain to ensure tenderness.

BASIC POT ROAST

1 tablespoon instant beef bouillon
    granules, crushed
1½ teaspoons all-purpose flour
¼ teaspoon paprika
¼ teaspoon pepper
1 (1¾- to 3-pound) boneless chuck roast,
    uniformly shaped and no more than 2
    to 2½ inches thick
¼ cup water
1 medium onion, sliced and separated
    into rings

Combine first 4 ingredients, mixing well. Sprinkle over roast, and rub in gently. Place roast in a roasting bag in a 12- x 8- x 2-inch baking dish; add water and onion. Tie bag loosely with string or a ½-inch-wide strip cut from open end of bag (do not use a twist tie).

Microwave at MEDIUM LOW (30% power or approximately 200 watts) for 33 to 37 minutes per pound or until desired degree of doneness, turning bag over and rotating dish every 30 minutes. Let stand 10 to 15 minutes in bag. To carve, slice across grain of meat. Yield: 4 to 6 servings.

Note: If a gravy is desired, measure drippings and add enough water or broth to equal 2 cups. Microwave ¼ cup butter or margarine in a 4-cup glass measure at HIGH for 1 minute or until melted; stir in ¼ cup all-purpose flour until well blended. Gradually add drippings, stirring constantly. Microwave at HIGH for 1½ minutes; stir well. Microwave at HIGH for 2 to 3 minutes until thickened and bubbly, stirring mixture at 1-minute intervals. Yield: about 2 cups.

POT ROAST WITH VEGETABLES

1 tablespoon instant beef bouillon
    granules, crushed
1½ teaspoons all-purpose flour
¼ teaspoon paprika
¼ teaspoon pepper
1 (1¾- to 3-pound) boneless chuck roast,
    uniformly shaped and no more than 2
    to 2½ inches thick
¼ cup water
1 medium onion, sliced and separated into
    rings
3 medium carrots, cut into 1-inch slices
3 medium potatoes, cut into ½-inch slices
Salt and pepper

Combine first 4 ingredients, mixing well. Sprinkle over roast, and rub in gently. Place roast in a roasting bag in a 12- x 8- x 2-inch baking dish; add water and vegetables. Tie bag loosely with string or a ½-inch-wide strip cut from open end of bag (do not use a twist tie).

Microwave at MEDIUM LOW (30% power or approximately 200 watts) for 33 to 37 minutes per pound or until desired degree of doneness, turning bag over and rotating dish every 30 minutes. Let stand 10 to 15 minutes in bag.

To carve, slice across grain of meat. Serve drippings with roast; for gravy, see instructions in Basic Pot Roast. Season vegetables with salt and pepper to taste. Yield: 4 to 6 servings.

Breakfast Is Big, Texas Style

When it comes to breakfast, Texans start it off big, with hearty main dishes and tempting accompaniments.

A bigger omelet than Tex-Mex Omelet Con Carne has yet to be found; it's so large, it easily serves four. Also proving that eggs are still all-time favorites is Tomato-Cheese Strata. For accompaniments, serve Mexican Breakfast Potatoes or Cinnamon Puffs.

TEX-MEX OMELET CON CARNE

½ pound ground beef
2 cups chopped tomatoes
½ green pepper, cut into ¼-inch strips
1 tablespoon chopped green chiles
1 teaspoon chili powder
½ teaspoon salt
¼ teaspoon sugar
6 eggs, separated
3 tablespoons water
¼ to ½ teaspoon salt
Dash of pepper
1½ tablespoons butter or margarine

Cook ground beef until browned; drain well. Stir in next 6 ingredients; simmer 15 to 20 minutes, stirring occasionally. Set mixture aside.

Beat egg whites (at room temperature) until foamy; add water, salt, and pepper. Continue beating until egg whites are stiff but not dry. Beat egg yolks until thick and lemon colored; fold into egg whites.

Melt butter in a 12-inch ovenproof skillet over medium heat; let heat until just hot enough to sizzle a drop of water. Add egg mixture; spread evenly, making sides slightly higher. Reduce heat to low; cook until mixture appears puffed and golden on sides (about 10 to 12 minutes).

Bake omelet at 325° for 10 minutes or until knife inserted in center comes out clean. Fold in half, and place on a warm platter. Serve omelet with meat sauce. Yield: 4 servings.

Lorraine Keener,
San Angelo, Texas.

TOMATO-CHEESE STRATA

⅓ cup butter or margarine, softened
1 clove garlic, crushed
1 (1-pound) loaf French bread, cut into ½-inch slices
1¾ cups (7 ounces) shredded sharp Cheddar cheese
1½ cups (6 ounces) shredded Swiss cheese
1½ teaspoons salt
1 teaspoon paprika
Dash of pepper
⅓ cup butter or margarine
⅓ cup all-purpose flour
3 cups milk
1 (16-ounce) can stewed tomatoes, undrained
3 eggs, beaten

Combine ⅓ cup butter and garlic, mixing well. Trim crusts from bread; spread each slice with garlic mixture. Place enough bread slices, buttered side down, in a 13- x 9- x 2-inch baking dish

so bottom and sides are covered; set remaining bread slices aside.

Combine cheese, salt, paprika, and pepper; mix well, and sprinkle about 1¼ cups over bread slices. Top with remaining bread slices, placing buttered side up. Sprinkle bread slices with about 1¼ cups cheese mixture.

Melt ⅓ cup butter in a heavy saucepan over low heat; add flour, stirring until smooth. Cook 1 minute, stirring constantly. Gradually add milk; cook over medium heat, stirring constantly, until thickened and bubbly. Stir in tomatoes. Gradually stir about one-fourth of white sauce into eggs; add to remaining sauce, stirring constantly. Pour over casserole, and top with remaining cheese mixture. Cover; chill overnight.

Uncover and bake at 325° for 1 hour and 10 minutes or until golden brown and puffed. Let stand 10 minutes before serving. Yield: 12 servings.

Cecilia Breithaupt,
Boerne, Texas.

SAUCY EGGS ON TOAST

1 (10¾-ounce) can cream of mushroom soup, undiluted
1 cup half-and-half
1 tablespoon chopped pimiento
¼ teaspoon ground nutmeg
6 hard-cooked eggs, chopped
8 slices whole wheat toast, cut diagonally

Combine soup, half-and-half, pimiento, and nutmeg; stir well, and cook over low heat until thoroughly heated. Stir in eggs; heat until warm, stirring constantly. Spoon egg mixture over toast. Yield: 4 servings.

Mrs. A. T. Knight,
Sulphur Springs, Texas.

MEXICAN BREAKFAST POTATOES

5 slices bacon
4 medium potatoes, peeled and cut into ¼-inch slices
2 tablespoons butter or margarine
1 medium onion, sliced and separated into rings
¼ cup chopped green pepper
1 clove garlic, crushed
2 tablespoons chopped pimiento
¼ teaspoon salt

Cook bacon in a large skillet until crisp; drain on paper towels, reserving

drippings in skillet. Crumble bacon. Add potatoes to skillet; cook over medium heat until golden brown. Drain potatoes on paper towels.

Add butter to skillet, and let melt; add onion, green pepper, and garlic. Sauté until tender. Stir in potatoes, bacon, pimiento, and salt. Serve immediately. Yield: 6 servings.

Mary Lou Vaughn,
Dallas, Texas.

FRIED APPLE RINGS

¼ cup all-purpose flour
¼ cup sugar
½ teaspoon ground cinnamon
½ teaspoon ground nutmeg
⅛ teaspoon ground cloves
3 medium unpeeled cooking apples, cored and cut into ½-inch rings
¼ cup bacon drippings

Combine first 5 ingredients, mixing well. Dredge apple rings in sugar mixture. Fry in hot bacon drippings, turning once, until golden brown and tender. Yield: 6 servings.

Kathleen Stone,
Houston, Texas.

CINNAMON PUFFS

1 cup instant corn masa
1 cup all-purpose flour
¼ cup sugar
2 teaspoons baking powder
1 teaspoon salt
1 teaspoon ground cinnamon
½ teaspoon soda
¾ cup buttermilk
2 eggs, slightly beaten
¼ cup vegetable oil
Vegetable oil
½ cup sugar
½ teaspoon ground cinnamon

Combine first 7 ingredients, stirring well. Add buttermilk, eggs, and ¼ cup oil; mix with a wire whisk until smooth.

Drop batter by level tablespoons into deep oil heated to 375°. Fry until golden, turning once. Drain well on paper towels.

Combine ½ cup sugar and cinnamon; stir well. Roll puffs in cinnamon mixture until coated. Serve warm. Yield: about 2½ dozen.

Note: To reheat cinnamon puffs, place in oven preheated to 350°. Turn off heat, and leave puffs in oven 10 minutes.

Edna Chadsey,
Corpus Christi, Texas.

Fry Green Tomatoes For Old-Fashioned Flavor

Ask any Southerner how to prepare green tomatoes and the answer is sure to be "fry them." Dredged in cornmeal and cooked until crisp, fried green tomatoes make a flavorful and nutritious side dish.

FRIED GREEN TOMATOES

4 medium-size green tomatoes, cut into
  ¼-inch slices
½ cup cornmeal
Vegetable oil
½ teaspoon salt
¼ teaspoon sugar
⅛ teaspoon pepper

Dredge tomatoes in cornmeal. Fry tomato slices in hot oil in a skillet until browned, turning once. Drain well on paper towels. Sprinkle tomato slices with salt, sugar, and pepper. Serve hot. Yield: 6 servings. *Ruth Bradley, Olive Hill, Kentucky.*

SAUCY FRIED TOMATOES WITH BACON

8 slices bacon
8 (½-inch-thick) slices green tomato
¼ teaspoon salt
⅛ teaspoon pepper
¼ cup plus 2 tablespoons all-purpose
  flour, divided
1 cup milk

Fry bacon in a large skillet until crisp; remove bacon, reserving drippings. Set bacon aside.

Sprinkle tomato slices with salt and pepper; dredge in ¼ cup flour. Fry in hot bacon drippings until browned, turning once. Drain well on paper towels.

Drain off bacon drippings, reserving 2 tablespoons in skillet. Add 2 tablespoons flour, and cook 1 minute, stirring constantly. Gradually add milk; cook over medium heat, stirring constantly, until thickened and bubbly.

Arrange tomato slices in serving dish; add gravy, and top each tomato slice with bacon. Yield: 4 servings. *Mrs. John R. Taylor, Jr., Jonesboro, Tennessee.*

Bring Your Favorite Dish

Covered dish suppers and dinners-on-the-ground are a way of life in the South. The next time you're invited to bring a favorite dish, choose from one of ours. We offer everything from rolls and chicken pot pie to a special cake.

GARDEN CABBAGE SALAD

1 small cabbage, finely shredded
1 bunch green onions, chopped
1 carrot, shredded
1 small green pepper, finely chopped
6 radishes, thinly sliced
1 cucumber, finely chopped
¾ cup salad dressing or mayonnaise
¼ cup vinegar
¼ cup sugar
1 teaspoon celery seeds
Dash of salt
Dash of pepper

Combine cabbage, onions, carrot, green pepper, radishes, and cucumber in a large salad bowl; cover and chill until serving time.

Combine salad dressing, vinegar, sugar, celery seeds, salt, and pepper; mix well. Toss salad with dressing just before serving. Yield: 8 to 10 servings. *Mrs. Roger L. Fonsler, Mathias, West Virginia.*

BEET PICKLES

8 quarts fresh beets
10 (2-inch) cinnamon sticks
1 tablespoon whole cloves
1½ cups sugar
1 quart vinegar
1 cup water

Leave root and 1 inch of stem on beets; scrub well with vegetable brush. Place beets in a saucepan, and add water to cover. Bring to a boil; cover and cook 35 to 40 minutes or until tender. Drain. Pour cold water over beets, and drain. Let cool. Trim off beet stems and roots, and rub off skins.

Tie spices in a cheesecloth bag. Combine spices, sugar, vinegar, and 1 cup water in a large saucepan or Dutch oven; bring to a boil. Add beets; bring mixture back to boil, and gently boil 5 minutes. Remove spice bag.

Pack beets into hot, sterilized jars, leaving ½-inch headspace. Pour syrup over beets to within ½ inch of top of jar. Top with lids, and screw metal bands tight. Process pints and quarts in boiling-water bath for 30 minutes. Yield: about 8 quarts.
Mrs. Jamie L. Sego, Cloverdale, Alabama.

CHICKEN POT PIE

3 tablespoons butter or margarine
¼ cup all-purpose flour
1¼ cups chicken broth
1 cup milk
2 cups cubed cooked chicken
1⅔ cups cooked peas and carrots
1½ teaspoons salt
¼ teaspoon poultry seasoning
⅛ teaspoon pepper
1 hard-cooked egg, sliced
Flaky Pastry

Melt butter in a large, heavy saucepan; blend in flour. Cook over low heat until bubbly, stirring constantly. Gradually add broth and milk; cook until thickened, stirring constantly. Stir in chicken, peas and carrots, seasonings, and egg; heat.

Spoon chicken mixture into a 1½-quart casserole, and top with Flaky Pastry. Turn pastry edges under, and press firmly to rim of casserole dish. Cut slits in top of pastry to allow steam to escape. Bake at 400° for 30 minutes or until pastry is golden brown. Yield: 6 servings.

Note: Turkey and turkey broth may be used for chicken and chicken broth.

Flaky Pastry:

1 cup all-purpose flour
¾ teaspoon baking powder
½ teaspoon salt
⅓ cup shortening
3 tablespoons ice water

Combine dry ingredients; cut in shortening until mixture resembles coarse meal. Add ice water, and stir lightly. (Dough will be just moist enough to cling together when pressed into a ball.)

Turn dough out on a lightly floured board or cloth. Roll to ¼-inch thickness; trim to ½ inch larger than casserole. Yield: pastry for one 1½-quart casserole. *Betty Witcher, Rocky Mount, Virginia.*

BUTTER-RICH CRESCENT ROLLS

¾ cup milk
1 package dry yeast
¼ cup warm water (105° to 115°)
¼ cup sugar
1 teaspoon salt
¼ cup butter or margarine, softened
1 egg, beaten
3 cups all-purpose flour

Scald milk, and let cool to lukewarm. Dissolve yeast in water in a large bowl. Stir in sugar, salt, butter, and egg. Add milk, stirring well. Add flour, and beat until smooth.

Place dough in a greased bowl, turning to grease top. Cover and let rise in a warm place (85°), free from drafts, until doubled in bulk.

Punch dough down, and divide in half. Roll each half into a circle about 10 inches in diameter and ¼ inch thick; cut into 8 wedges. Roll each wedge tightly, beginning at wide end.

Place rolls on greased baking sheets, point side down. Curve into crescent shape. Cover and let rise until doubled in bulk (about 45 minutes). Bake at 400° for 8 to 10 minutes or until lightly browned. Yield: 16 rolls.

Mrs. Hurley M. Barker,
Milton, North Carolina.

BUTTERMILK SPICE CAKE

¾ cup shortening
¾ cup firmly packed brown sugar
1 cup sugar
3 eggs
1 teaspoon vanilla extract
2¼ cups all-purpose flour
1 teaspoon baking powder
¾ teaspoon soda
1 teaspoon salt
¾ teaspoon ground cloves
¾ teaspoon ground cinnamon
1 cup buttermilk
Sea Foam Frosting

Cream shortening; beat in brown sugar. Gradually add remaining sugar; beat until light and fluffy. Add eggs, one at a time, beating well after each addition; stir in vanilla.

Combine dry ingredients; add to creamed mixture alternately with buttermilk, beginning and ending with dry ingredients. Mix well after each addition.

Grease two 9-inch round cakepans, and line with waxed paper; grease waxed paper. Pour batter into prepared pans; bake at 325° for 35 to 40 minutes or until cake tests done. Cool in pans 5

minutes; turn out on wire rack to finish cooling. Spread Sea Foam Frosting between layers and on top and sides of cake. Yield: one 9-inch layer cake.

Sea Foam Frosting:

1½ cups firmly packed dark brown sugar
2 egg whites
⅓ cup water
1 teaspoon vanilla extract

Combine brown sugar, egg whites (at room temperature), and water in top of double boiler; place over boiling water, and stir constantly until sugar dissolves. Beat with electric mixer for 7 minutes or until frosting is fluffy and holds soft peaks. Remove from heat; beat in vanilla. Yield: enough frosting for one 9-inch layer cake.

Sue Ellis,
Centre, Alabama.

Main Dishes To Stir-Fry

Stir-frying meat and vegetables in a wok cooks the food so rapidly in a small amount of oil that it retains more color, flavor, and nutrients than if cooked in a conventional manner. Combinations of stir-fry ingredients are limited only by what you like.

To make stir-frying easier and more fun, prepare and assemble all ingredients before you begin cooking since the entire stir-frying process is usually completed in a matter of minutes.

BEEF-AND-VEGETABLE STIR-FRY

1 pound boneless round steak
¾ pound small fresh mushrooms
1 small bunch fresh broccoli
2 tablespoons peanut oil or vegetable oil
4 to 5 carrots, diagonally sliced
¼ cup soy sauce
2 tablespoons cornstarch
½ teaspoon sugar
1½ cups beef broth
Hot cooked rice

Partially freeze steak; slice across grain into 3- x ¼-inch strips. Set aside.

Rinse mushrooms, and remove stems; reserve stems for use in another recipe. Set caps aside.

Wash broccoli, and remove flowerets; reserve stalks for use in another recipe. Set flowerets aside.

Heat oil in preheated wok, coating sides; allow to heat at medium high (325°) 1 minute. Add steak; stir-fry until browned. Add mushrooms, carrots, and soy sauce, stirring well. Cover; reduce heat to low (225°), and cook 10 minutes. Add broccoli; cover and cook 5 minutes or until crisp-tender.

Combine cornstarch, sugar, and beef broth, mixing well; add to meat mixture. Cook, stirring constantly until thickened; serve over rice. Yield: 6 servings.

Frances Jean Neely,
Jackson, Mississippi.

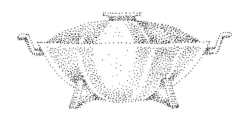

BEEF WITH CHINESE VEGETABLES

1½ pounds flank steak
¼ cup vegetable oil
1½ cups water
1 (0.325-ounce) envelope beef-noodle soup mix
4 carrots, diagonally sliced
3 stalks celery, diagonally sliced
1 (14-ounce) can bean sprouts, drained
1 (8-ounce) can water chestnuts, drained and chopped
2 tablespoons soy sauce
1 tablespoon cornstarch
1 tablespoon water
Hot cooked rice
Soy sauce

Partially freeze flank steak; then slice across grain into 3- x ¼-inch strips, and set aside.

Pour oil around top of preheated wok, coating sides; allow to heat at medium high (325°) 2 minutes. Add steak; stir-fry until browned. Combine 1½ cups water and soup mix, stirring well. Add soup mixture and carrots to steak. Cover and reduce heat to low (225°), and cook 15 minutes.

Stir in celery, bean sprouts, water chestnuts, and 2 tablespoons soy sauce; cook 5 minutes or until vegetables are crisp-tender.

Combine cornstarch and 1 tablespoon water, mixing well; add to meat mixture. Cook, stirring constantly, until thickened; serve over rice with additional soy sauce. Yield: 6 to 8 servings.

Mrs. Dean D. Piercy,
Memphis, Tennessee.

PORK ORIENTAL

1 pound boneless pork
2 tablespoons vegetable oil
2 cups sliced fresh mushrooms
1 cup diagonally sliced celery
1 (8-ounce) can water chestnuts, drained
   and sliced
1 cup water
3 tablespoons dry onion soup mix
2 teaspoons soy sauce
¼ cup water
2 tablespoons cornstarch
Hot cooked rice or chow mein noodles

Partially freeze pork; then slice into 3- x ¼-inch strips. Set pork aside.

Pour oil around top of preheated wok, coating sides; allow to heat at medium high (325°) 2 minutes. Add pork and stir-fry 5 minutes or until browned. Add mushrooms, celery, and water chestnuts; stir-fry 2 minutes. Combine 1 cup water and soup mix, stirring well. Add soup mixture to pork; stir-fry 3 minutes.

Combine soy sauce, ¼ cup water, and cornstarch, mixing well; add to pork mixture. Cook, stirring constantly, until mixture is thickened; serve over rice. Yield: 4 servings.

Mrs. Jack Corzine,
St. Louis, Missouri.

CHINESE CHICKEN AND VEGETABLES

2 whole chicken breasts, skinned and
   boned
⅛ teaspoon garlic powder
¼ cup cornstarch
¼ cup peanut oil
1 (8-ounce) can water chestnuts, drained
   and sliced
1 bunch green onions, cut into ½-inch
   pieces
1 (10-ounce) package frozen Chinese-style
   vegetables, thawed and drained
1 cup diagonally sliced celery
½ medium head cabbage, shredded
¼ cup soy sauce
Hot cooked rice

Cut chicken breasts into 1-inch pieces. Combine garlic powder and cornstarch. Dredge chicken in cornstarch mixture; set aside.

Pour oil around top of preheated wok, coating sides; allow to heat at medium high (325°) 2 minutes. Add chicken, and stir-fry until lightly browned. Add remaining ingredients, except rice; mix well. Cover and reduce heat to low (225°); cook 10 to 12 minutes or until vegetables are crisp-tender. Serve over rice. Yield: 4 servings.

Margot Foster,
Hubbard, Texas.

SZECHWAN CHICKEN WITH CASHEWS

1 pound boneless chicken breasts
2 tablespoons soy sauce
1 teaspoon sherry
2 tablespoons water
1 tablespoon cornstarch
3 tablespoons vegetable oil
2 dried whole red peppers
2 tablespoons chopped fresh ginger
½ cup coarsely chopped fresh mushrooms
1 green pepper, cut into thin strips
4 green onions, cut into ½-inch pieces
2 stalks celery, diagonally sliced
2 tablespoons soy sauce
1 tablespoon sherry
¼ cup plus 1 tablespoon water
1 tablespoon cornstarch
1 tablespoon plus 1 teaspoon sugar
1 teaspoon coarsely ground black pepper
2 teaspoons vinegar
1 teaspoon vegetable oil
1 cup cashews
Hot cooked rice

Place each chicken breast on a sheet of waxed paper; flatten to ¼-inch thickness using a meat mallet or rolling pin. Cut into bite-size pieces. Combine 2 tablespoons soy sauce, 1 teaspoon sherry, 2 tablespoons water, 1 tablespoon cornstarch, and chicken; mix well, and let stand 20 minutes.

Pour oil around top of preheated wok, coating sides; allow to heat at medium high (325°) 2 minutes. Add red peppers; stir-fry 1 minute and discard. Add ginger to hot oil; stir-fry 1 minute and discard. Add chicken, mushrooms, green pepper, onion, and celery. Stir-fry about 5 minutes or until vegetables are crisp-tender.

Combine remaining 2 tablespoons soy sauce, 1 tablespoon sherry, ¼ cup plus 1 tablespoon water, and 1 tablespoon cornstarch, mixing well; stir in sugar, pepper, vinegar, and 1 teaspoon vegetable oil. Pour over chicken mixture; add cashews and cook, stirring constantly, until thickened. Serve over hot cooked rice. Yield: 4 servings.

Jay Jerome,
Charlottesville, Virginia.

Blend Squash For Easy Casserole

Steamed squash and green onion are processed in the blender for this squash casserole. For the finishing touch, sprinkle with crushed potato chips, chopped pecans, and Cheddar cheese.

BLENDER SQUASH CASSEROLE

4 medium-size yellow squash, thinly sliced
2 green onions, sliced
¼ teaspoon celery salt
¼ teaspoon lemon pepper
6 (2-inch-square) saltine crackers
¾ cup milk
3 eggs
¾ cup (3 ounces) shredded Cheddar
   cheese, divided
¼ teaspoon salt
2 tablespoons crushed potato chips
2 tablespoons chopped pecans

Arrange squash and onion in a vegetable steamer; sprinkle with celery salt and lemon pepper. Steam 10 minutes.

Place half of squash mixture in container of electric blender; add crackers, milk, eggs, and ½ cup cheese; process at high speed for 15 to 20 seconds or until well blended. Combine squash puree, remaining squash, and salt in a mixing bowl; stir well.

Spoon into a buttered 1½-quart casserole; sprinkle with potato chips, pecans, and remaining cheese. Bake at 350° for 50 minutes or until center is set. Serve immediately. Yield: about 4 servings.

Betty L. Norman,
Anniston, Alabama.

Tip: Shop alone and after you have eaten. Studies show that people tend to buy more when hungry or when accompanied by others.

October

Whether you are cooking for a household of two, or a porchful of 20 Halloween tricksters, you will find just the treats you need in this chapter.

Then travel with us to Appalachia, a region where food is as rich in tradition as it is in flavor. You will sample such time-honored specialties as homemade Apple Butter and Old-Fashioned Stack Cake. Our home economists tested each recipe, substituting modern standards and ingredients where appropriate.

And if you thought you could only get good pizza at your local pizza parlor, you are wrong—one bite of our Pizza Supreme and you will never settle for bought pizza again. And ours is complete with your choice of thick or thin crusts.

Perfect Your Own Pizza

Italians may have invented pizza, but surely a Southerner perfected the versions laden with fresh vegetables. Take our Pizza Supreme, for example. It's based on a thick homemade tomato sauce full of herbs and chopped vegetables, then crowned with fresh mushrooms, green onion, and green pepper, along with the meat and cheese that make it a meal.

Pizza Supreme even sports your choice of a thick or thin crust. The proportions of ingredients for the two are similar, but the difference is in letting the dough rise twice for the thick type. Our instructions will tell you how.

While baking pizza from scratch takes time, the taste makes the effort worthwhile. If you're short of time but still yen for pizza, our other versions shortcut the preparation but not the flavor.

True to its name, Speedy Pizza takes only minutes to assemble. Although the dough doesn't rise, it still has that favorite yeast taste and aroma. Pizza Cups take on a nontraditional shape but keep the rich and spicy flavor; refrigerator biscuit dough is pressed in muffin pans, then filled with the ingredients.

Unlike many other favorite things to eat, pizza is a nutritionally balanced meal. Its vegetables, meat, cheese, and bread make a taste-tempting way to obtain nutrients needed each day. That's a great excuse to pile on the toppings for a pizza.

SPEEDY PIZZA

1 pound bulk pork sausage
½ cup warm water (105° to 115°)
1 package dry yeast
1 cup all-purpose flour
¼ teaspoon salt
1 (8-ounce) can tomato sauce
½ teaspoon dried whole oregano
¼ teaspoon garlic powder
1½ cups (6 ounces) shredded mozzarella cheese
¼ cup grated Parmesan cheese
¼ cup grated Romano cheese

Cook sausage until browned, stirring to crumble; drain well. Set aside.

Combine water and yeast; let stand 5 minutes. Stir in flour and salt (dough will be soft and sticky). Using the back of a spoon, spread dough on bottom and up sides of a greased 10-inch pizza pan. Bake at 425° for 5 minutes.

Combine tomato sauce, oregano, and garlic powder; spread evenly over crust. Sprinkle with sausage, and bake an additional 15 minutes. Sprinkle with mozzarella, and bake 5 to 10 minutes longer or until crust is browned. Top with Parmesan and Romano cheese. Yield: one 10-inch pizza. *Mary E. Rathburn, Panama City, Florida.*

PIZZA SUPREME

2 tablespoons vegetable oil
1 small green pepper, chopped
1 large onion, chopped
2 small cloves garlic, minced
3 tablespoons chopped fresh parsley
1 (28-ounce) can whole tomatoes, undrained
1 (6-ounce) can tomato paste
2 teaspoons sugar
1½ teaspoons dried whole oregano
½ teaspoon salt
¼ teaspoon pepper
2 (12-inch) thick or thin pizza crusts (recipes follow)
3 cups (12 ounces) shredded mozzarella cheese
2 cups (8 ounces) shredded Cheddar cheese
1½ pounds ground beef
1 teaspoon salt
1 (3½-ounce) package sliced pepperoni
¾ cup sliced ripe olives
1⅓ cups sliced fresh mushrooms
¾ cup sliced green onion
2 small green peppers, sliced into rings
½ to 1 cup grated Parmesan cheese

Heat vegetable oil in a Dutch oven; add chopped green pepper, chopped onion, garlic, and parsley. Sauté until tender, and set aside.

Place tomatoes in container of electric blender or food processor, and process until smooth; add to onion mixture. Stir in next 5 ingredients. Bring to a boil; reduce heat, and simmer 1 hour or until sauce is reduced to about 3½ cups.

Spread sauce evenly over each pizza crust, leaving a ½-inch border around edges. Combine mozzarella cheese and Cheddar, tossing gently; sprinkle 1¼ cups over each pizza.

Combine ground beef and 1 teaspoon salt in a skillet; cook over medium heat until meat is browned, stirring to crumble. Drain well on paper towels. Sprinkle meat over pizzas.

Layer the next 5 ingredients on pizzas, and bake at 450° for 15 minutes.

Sprinkle with remaining shredded cheese, and bake an additional 5 minutes. Top with Parmesan cheese. Yield: two 12-inch pizzas.

Thick Crust:

1½ cups warm water (105° to 115°)
3 tablespoons vegetable oil
1 tablespoon sugar
1 tablespoon salt
2 packages dry yeast
4½ cups all-purpose flour

Combine water, oil, sugar, and salt in a large mixing bowl. Sprinkle yeast over water mixture, stirring until dissolved. Gradually add flour, mixing well after each addition.

Turn dough out on a lightly floured surface, and knead until smooth and elastic. Shape into a ball, and place in a greased bowl, turning once to grease top. Cover and let rise in a warm place (85°), free from drafts, 1 hour or until doubled.

Punch dough down, and divide in half. Lightly grease hands, and pat dough evenly into 2 lightly greased 12-inch pizza pans. Cover and let rise in a warm place (85°), free from drafts, 1 hour or until doubled. Bake at 450° for 5 minutes. Yield: two 12-inch pizza crusts.

Thin Crust:

1 cup warm water (105° to 115°)
2 tablespoons vegetable oil
2 teaspoons sugar
2 teaspoons salt
1 package dry yeast
3 cups all-purpose flour

Combine water, oil, sugar, and salt in a large mixing bowl. Sprinkle yeast over water mixture, stirring until dissolved. Gradually add flour, mixing well after each addition.

Turn dough out on a lightly floured surface, and knead until smooth and elastic. Shape into a ball, and place in a greased bowl; turn once to grease top. Cover and let rise in a warm place (85°), free from drafts, 1 hour or until doubled.

Punch dough down, and divide in half. Lightly grease hands, and pat dough evenly into 2 lightly greased 12-inch pizza pans. Yield: two 12-inch pizza crusts.

Tip: To retain white color of fresh mushrooms, slice just before using or dip in lemon juice.

PIZZA CUPS

¾ pound ground beef
1 (6-ounce) can tomato paste
1 tablespoon instant minced onion
1 teaspoon Italian seasoning
½ teaspoon salt
1 (10-ounce) can refrigerated biscuits
½ to ¾ cup (2 to 3 ounces) shredded
   mozzarella cheese

Cook ground beef in a large skillet until browned, stirring to crumble; drain off drippings. Stir in tomato paste, onion, Italian seasoning, and salt. Cook over medium heat an additional 5 minutes, stirring frequently.

Place each biscuit in a greased muffin cup, pressing to cover bottom and sides. Spoon meat mixture into cups, and sprinkle with cheese. Bake at 400° for 10 to 12 minutes. Yield: 10 to 12 biscuits.
*Becki Lanhardt,
Mechanicsville, Maryland.*

Appalachian Food: Using What They Had

The little boy looks up to the Kentucky sky and catches a glimpse of a rain cloud slipping over the mountain. He drops his toys and runs for the strings of green beans hanging outdoors to dry. He gathers them quickly and runs for shelter, because any moisture would ruin the "shuck beans," an important part of the family's winter food supply.

Farther down the mountains in North Carolina, a woman holds a long paddle and stirs apple butter as it simmers in a large kettle. The sun tells her the children will soon be home from school, eager to take their turns with the paddle. She steps closer to the hot fire and peers into the kettle to check the consistency of the bubbling mixture. It still looks thin. This batch will probably cook into the night.

Time was when such scenes were common from West Virginia to Alabama as Appalachian Mountain families prepared for the winter. It was a way of life born out of their isolation, making them dependent on the produce they could grow and the livestock they could raise for their food supply. And in the process, they developed a wealth of delicious dishes by taking simple foods

and preparing them in imaginative ways.

Improved transportation and modern methods have brought changes in preparation, but many mountain people cling to their traditional foods and customs with pride. Shuck beans continue to be enjoyed, although most people dry them indoors now. Homemade apple butter still layers Old-Fashioned Stack Cake and complements hot herb bread, even though it's usually made in the oven today. And dried apples are still made into a delicious filling for fried pies, although few people dry them over a wood stove any more. It's not fancy food, but the mountain people grew up on these favorites and still find in them something of what they were and are.

Food From The Mountains

These recipes for traditional Appalachian Mountain foods were tested by our home economists, substituting modern preserving methods where appropriate. Old-Fashioned Stack Cake uses apple butter, a mountain favorite for which a recipe is included. Crabapple jelly puts wild fruit to good purpose; cabbage is a good source of vitamin C in land far from oranges, and Kentucky Coleslaw is a tasty way to serve it.

The breakfast of Steak and Gravy With Mush includes a recipe for making mush of cornmeal, salt, and water, a combination our test kitchen staff found "much better than we expected." Imagine yourself snowed in on a mountain, and your interest may be perked.

STEAK AND GRAVY WITH MUSH

1 to 1½ pounds cube steak, cut into
   serving-size pieces
Salt and pepper
½ cup butter
¾ cup water
Mush (recipe follows)

Preheat skillet until a drop of water sizzles. Add steak (it will sear immediately). Season to taste with salt and pepper. Turn steak, and reduce heat. Cook until desired doneness; add butter to skillet. When butter melts, remove steak and keep warm. Add water to skillet; bring to a boil, stirring well. Pour gravy over cube steak. Serve with mush. Yield: 4 to 6 servings.

Mush:

4 cups warm water
1 teaspoon salt
1½ cups cornmeal
2 tablespoons butter or margarine

Combine water, salt, and cornmeal in a heavy saucepan. Cook over high heat, stirring constantly, until boiling. Reduce heat, and cover immediately. Simmer 5 minutes. Pour into a serving bowl, and top with butter. Yield: 4 to 6 servings.

■ These green beans are canned when young and tender. Then before serving, they're simmered with bacon drippings.

APPALACHIAN GREEN BEANS

4 pounds green beans
Salt

Wash beans, trim ends, and remove strings; cut into 2-inch lengths.

Cover beans with boiling water, and boil 3 minutes. Pack beans into hot sterilized jars, leaving 1-inch headspace. Add ½ teaspoon salt to pints and 1 teaspoon salt to quarts. Cover with boiling water, leaving 1-inch headspace. Cover at once with metal lids, and screw bands tight.

Process in pressure canner at 10 pounds pressure (240°); process pints for 20 minutes, quarts for 25 minutes. This processing time applies only to young, tender pods. Beans that have almost reached the "shell-out" stage require 15 to 20 minutes longer. Yield: 8 pints.

Note: To serve, drain beans and discard liquid. Combine beans and bacon drippings (1 tablespoon drippings per pint of beans); cook over low heat for 10 minutes, stirring occasionally.

Tip: Whenever a recipe calls for a reheating process, the dish can be made in advance up to that point.

■ Shuck beans are dried green beans. For generations, the beans were hung on strings and dried outside. Today, many families dry them indoors.

SHUCK BEANS

4 cups shuck beans
½ pound thick-sliced bacon, cut into
    1-inch pieces
2 teaspoons salt

Wash beans several times; cover with cold water, and soak overnight.

Drain beans. Place bacon in a large kettle, and add beans. Cover beans with water, and bring to a boil. Reduce heat; cover and simmer about 4 hours or until tender. Add salt; continue to cook, uncovered, 2 hours or until most of liquid evaporates. Yield: 10 to 12 servings.

PICKLED BEETS

3½ quarts small fresh beets
2 cups sugar
3½ cups vinegar
1½ cups water
1 tablespoon whole allspice
1½ teaspoons salt
2 (4-inch) sticks cinnamon

Wash beets carefully; remove tops, leaving a 1-inch stem. Leave taproot. Place beets in a large kettle, and cover with water. Bring to a boil. Reduce heat; cover and simmer until tender or until skins slip easily. Cool; remove skins, and trim.

Combine remaining ingredients in a large saucepan. Bring to a boil. Reduce heat; cover and simmer 15 minutes.

Pack beets into hot sterilized jars, leaving ½-inch headspace (cut large beets into pieces, if necessary).

Remove cinnamon sticks from syrup. Bring syrup to a boil; pour over beets, leaving ½-inch headspace. Cover with metal lids, and screw bands tight. Process 30 minutes in boiling-water bath. Yield: about 6 pints.

KENTUCKY PICCALILLI

8 pounds cabbage, finely shredded
4 large green peppers, chopped
1 small hot red or yellow pepper, minced
¼ cup plus 3 tablespoons pickling salt

Combine all ingredients in a large mixing bowl; stir well.

Pack solidly into pint-size jars, leaving ½-inch headspace. Fill jars with cold water, leaving ½-inch headspace. Cover at once with metal lids, and screw bands tight.

Allow to ferment at room temperature for 3 to 4 days. (A small amount of liquid will escape from the jars.) Wash outside of jars, and screw bands tight. Process in boiling-water bath for 15 minutes. Yield: 8 pints.

Note: To serve, rinse piccalilli thoroughly; squeeze out liquid. For each pint, heat 2 tablespoons bacon drippings in a large skillet, and add piccalilli. Fry about 10 minutes over low heat, stirring occasionally.

KENTUCKY COLESLAW

2 medium heads cabbage, shredded
3 large carrots, grated
1 large green pepper, chopped
3 cups sugar
1½ cups white vinegar
1½ teaspoons salt
1½ tablespoons celery seeds
1½ teaspoons mustard seeds

Combine cabbage, carrot, and green pepper in a large bowl; set aside.

Combine sugar, vinegar, and salt in a large saucepan; bring to a boil, and boil 2 to 3 minutes. Cool. Stir celery seeds and mustard seeds into vinegar mixture; pour over vegetables, stirring well. Cover and refrigerate 24 hours. Yield: about 5 quarts.

Note: Slaw may be stored several weeks in refrigerator.

HOMEMADE SAUERKRAUT

5 pounds cabbage, finely shredded
3½ tablespoons pickling salt

Combine cabbage and salt in a large mixing bowl; stir well.

Pack cabbage solidly into pint jars, leaving ½-inch headspace. Fill jars with cold water, leaving ½-inch headspace. Cover at once with metal lids, and screw bands tight.

Allow to ferment at room temperature for 3 to 4 days. (A small amount of liquid will escape from the jars.) Wash outside of jars, and screw bands tight. Process in boiling-water bath for 15 minutes. Yield: 5 pints.

Note: To serve, rinse sauerkraut thoroughly; squeeze out liquid. For each pint, heat 2 tablespoons bacon drippings in a large skillet, and add sauerkraut. Fry about 10 minutes over low heat, stirring occasionally.

COLD-PACK CORN

Husk corn, and remove silks; wash well. Cut corn from cob at about two-thirds the depth of the kernel, but do not scrape cob.

Pack corn in hot sterilized jars, leaving 1-inch headspace. Do not shake or press down. Add ½ teaspoon salt to pints, 1 teaspoon to quarts. Cover with boiling water, leaving 1-inch headspace. Cover at once with metal lids, and screw bands tight. Process in pressure canner at 10 pounds pressure (240°); process pints for 55 minutes, quarts for 1 hour and 25 minutes.

■ Thin layers of molasses-flavored cake are spread with apple butter and stacked for this favorite Appalachian dessert.

OLD-FASHIONED STACK CAKE

1 cup firmly packed brown sugar
1 cup shortening
1 cup molasses
1 cup buttermilk
2 eggs, beaten
1 teaspoon soda
1 teaspoon ground ginger
Dash of salt
5½ cups all-purpose flour
About 6⅔ cups apple butter
Additional apple butter (optional)
Dried apples (optional)

Combine sugar, shortening, and molasses; beat until smooth. Add buttermilk, eggs, soda, ginger, and salt; mix well. Add flour, about 1 cup at a time, beating after each addition just until blended (do not overbeat).

Divide dough into 10 portions, and place each on a greased cookie sheet;

pat into a 10-inch circle. Bake at 350° for 5 to 7 minutes. Carefully remove to cooling rack.

Stack the layers, spreading about ⅔ cup apple butter between each. Spoon a mound of apple butter on top of cake and garnish with dried apples, if desired. Yield: one 10-inch cake.

■ Although apple butter was traditionally made outdoors over an open flame, this oven version simplifies the process while preserving the homemade flavor.

APPLE BUTTER

12 to 13 pounds apples
5 pounds sugar
½ cup vinegar
¼ cup cinnamon candies

Core and slice apples (do not peel). Place apples in a large kettle with a small amount of water; cook until soft. Press apples through a sieve.

Combine apples, sugar, and vinegar in a large, deep roasting pan; mix well. Bake at 325° for 5 hours, stirring occasionally. Add cinnamon candies, stirring well. Cook about 1 additional hour or until thickened. Yield: 15 cups.

FRIED APPLE PIES

4 cups or 2 (6-ounce) packages dried
    apples
2 cups water
½ to ¾ cup sugar
Pastry (recipe follows)
Vegetable oil

Combine apples and water in a large saucepan; bring to a boil. Reduce heat; cover and simmer about 30 minutes or until tender. Cool. Mash slightly, if necessary. Stir in sugar, and set aside.

Divide pastry into thirds; roll each portion to ¼-inch thickness on waxed paper. Cut into 5-inch circles.

Place about 2 tablespoons apple mixture on half of each pastry circle. To seal pies: Dip fingers in water, and moisten edges of circles; fold in half, making sure edges are even. Using a fork dipped in flour, press pastry edges firmly together.

Heat ½ inch of oil to 375° in a large skillet. Cook pies until golden brown on both sides, turning only once. Drain well on paper towels. Yield: 1½ dozen.

Pastry:

3 cups all-purpose flour
1 teaspoon salt
¾ cup shortening
1 egg, beaten
¼ cup water
1 teaspoon vinegar

Combine flour and salt; cut in shortening until mixture resembles coarse meal. Combine egg and water; sprinkle over flour mixture. Add vinegar, and lightly stir until mixture forms a ball.

Wrap pastry in waxed paper; chill at least 1 hour or until ready to use. Yield: pastry for about 1½ dozen 5-inch pies.

NO-KNEAD HERB BREAD

2 packages dry yeast
2 cups warm water (105° to 115°)
½ cup sugar
2 teaspoons salt
2 cups whole-wheat flour, divided
4 to 5 cups all-purpose flour, divided
1 egg
¼ cup vegetable oil
¾ teaspoon dried whole sage
¾ teaspoon dried whole basil

Dissolve yeast in water. Combine yeast mixture, sugar, salt, 1 cup whole-wheat flour, and 2 cups all-purpose flour in a large mixing bowl. Beat with electric mixer 2 minutes. Add egg, oil, herbs, and ½ cup all-purpose flour; beat with electric mixer 2 minutes.

Combine remaining flour, stirring well; gradually stir into batter, using enough to form a moderately stiff dough. Divide dough in half; place each portion in a greased bowl, turning to grease top. Cover and let rise in a warm place (85°), free from drafts, until doubled in bulk.

Punch dough down, and shape into 2 loaves. Place in greased 9- x 5- x 3-inch loafpans. Cover and let rise until doubled in bulk. Bake at 375° for 25 to 35 minutes or until loaves sound hollow when tapped. Yield: 2 loaves.

CRABAPPLE JELLY

5 pounds crabapples, stemmed and
    coarsely chopped
5 cups water
1 (1¾-ounce) package powdered fruit
    pectin
9 cups sugar

Combine crabapples and water in a large Dutch oven; bring to a boil. Reduce heat; cover and simmer about 10 minutes. Mash crabapples; simmer for 5 additional minutes. Place in a jelly bag, and squeeze out juice.

Return juice to Dutch oven, and stir in pectin. Quickly bring to a hard boil, stirring occasionally. Add sugar all at once. Cook and stir until mixture returns to a full rolling boil (cannot be stirred down). Cook and stir 1 additional minute. Remove from heat, and skim off foam with a metal spoon.

Pour immediately into hot sterilized jars, leaving ½-inch headspace. Seal with ⅛-inch layer of paraffin. Cover with metal lids, and screw bands tight. Yield: about 5 pints.

Homemade Goodies Are The Best Treats

When doorbells ring and Halloween goblins holler "trick or treat," offer them special goodies from your kitchen. Imagine their delight at filling their bags with Jumbo Chocolate Snappers or walking away munching Candied Red Apples.

CANDIED RED APPLES

10 medium apples
3 cups sugar
⅔ cup water
1 teaspoon lemon juice
15 whole cloves
¼ teaspoon cream of tartar
2 to 3 drops of red food coloring

Wash and dry apples; remove stems. Insert wooden skewers into stem end of each apple. Set aside.

Combine remaining ingredients in a heavy saucepan; stir well. Cook over medium heat, without stirring, until candy thermometer reaches hard crack stage (300°). Remove cloves.

Quickly dip apples in syrup, covering entire surface; allow excess to drip off. Place apples on lightly buttered baking sheets to cool. To store, wrap tightly in plastic wrap. Yield: 10 servings.

Edna A. Peavy,
Atlanta, Georgia.

JUMBO CHOCOLATE SNAPPERS

1 (6-ounce) package semisweet chocolate
   morsels
⅔ cup shortening
½ cup sugar
1 egg
¼ cup corn syrup
1¾ cups all-purpose flour
2 teaspoons soda
¼ teaspoon salt
1 teaspoon ground cinnamon
Sugar

Place chocolate morsels in top of double boiler; bring water to a boil. Reduce heat to low; cook until chocolate is melted. Remove from heat.

Cream shortening; gradually add ½ cup sugar, beating until light and fluffy. Add chocolate, egg, and corn syrup, beating well.

Combine flour, soda, salt, and cinnamon; add to creamed mixture, beating just until blended.

Shape dough into balls, using about 3 tablespoons dough for each ball, and roll in sugar. Place on ungreased cookie sheets about 2½ inches apart; bake at 350° for 18 minutes. Cool on cookie sheets 2 minutes. Remove to wire racks, and cool completely. Yield: about 14 jumbo cookies.

Note: For smaller cookies, shape dough into balls using 1 tablespoon dough. Bake at 350° for 15 minutes. Yield: about 3½ dozen. *Doris Lee, Langdale, Alabama.*

CREAMY FUDGE

2 cups sugar
3 tablespoons cocoa
1 (6-ounce) can evaporated milk
4 (1.05-ounce) bars milk chocolate,
   broken into small pieces
¼ cup butter or margarine
1 teaspoon vanilla extract
½ cup chopped pecans (optional)

Combine sugar, cocoa, and milk; stir well. Cook over medium heat until mixture comes to a boil; boil 3 minutes, stirring occasionally. Remove from heat. Add next 3 ingredients and pecans, if desired; stir until chocolate and butter are melted.

Quickly spread mixture into a lightly greased 8-inch square pan. Allow candy to cool for at least 2 hours. Cut fudge into 1-inch squares. Yield: 30 squares.
Lib Cunningham, Atlanta, Georgia.

BAKED CARAMEL CORN

3 quarts freshly popped popcorn
½ cup chopped pecans
½ cup butter or margarine
1 cup firmly packed brown sugar
¼ cup light corn syrup
½ teaspoon salt
¼ teaspoon soda
½ teaspoon vanilla extract

Combine popcorn and pecans in a lightly greased 15- x 10- x 1-inch jelly-roll pan; mix well and set aside.

Melt butter over low heat in a medium saucepan. Add brown sugar, corn syrup, and salt; bring to a boil, and boil 5 minutes without stirring. Remove from heat; stir in soda and vanilla.

Pour syrup over popcorn mixture, stirring until popcorn is evenly coated. Bake at 300° for 30 minutes, stirring after 15 minutes. Cool completely, and break into pieces. Store in airtight containers. Yield: 9 cups.
Mrs. W. P. Chambers, Louisville, Kentucky.

CRUNCHY GRANOLA

6 cups regular oats, uncooked
¾ cup wheat germ
½ cup flaked coconut
⅓ cup sesame seeds
½ cup shelled sunflower seeds
½ cup raw peanuts
¾ cup whole blanched almonds
½ cup firmly packed brown sugar
½ cup vegetable oil
½ cup honey
1 teaspoon vanilla extract

Combine first 7 ingredients in a large bowl; mix well and set aside.

Combine remaining ingredients in a small saucepan; place over medium heat, stirring until mixture is thoroughly heated. Pour over oats mixture; mix well. Spread mixture evenly into a lightly greased 15- x 10- x 1-inch jelly-roll pan. Bake at 325° for 30 to 45 minutes or until golden brown, stirring often. Cool; then store in an airtight container. Yield: about 9 cups.
Mrs. Charles B. Denson, Little Rock, Arkansas.

PEANUT BUTTER-OATMEAL COOKIES

2 cups sugar
¼ cup butter or margarine
½ cup milk
3 tablespoons cocoa
¾ cup crunchy peanut butter
3 cups quick-cooking oats, uncooked
1 teaspoon vanilla extract

Combine sugar, butter, milk, and cocoa in a heavy saucepan; stir well. Cook over medium heat until mixture comes to a boil; cook 1 minute. Stir in peanut butter, oats, and vanilla; mix well. Drop dough by heaping teaspoonfuls onto lightly greased waxed paper; cool thoroughly. Yield: 4 dozen.
Mrs. Don Heun, Louisville, Kentucky.

COLORFUL MOLDED LOLLIPOPS

Vegetable oil
1 cup sugar
½ cup light corn syrup
¼ cup water
¾ teaspoon peppermint extract
2 drops of red food coloring

Brush inside surfaces of lollipop molds with oil.

Combine sugar, syrup, and water in a medium saucepan; stir well. Cook over low heat without stirring until candy thermometer reaches hard crack stage (310°). Remove from heat; stir in peppermint extract and food coloring. Immediately pour hot mixture into molds. Press sticks in indentations of molds, gently twirling to embed. Cool completely; lift lollipops out of molds, and wrap tightly in plastic wrap. Store in a cool dry place. Yield: about 8 (2-inch) lollipops.
Beckie Webster, Roanoke, Virginia.

Right: *Taste Southern heritage with these delicious cornbread selections. Clockwise: Lacy Corncakes, Southern Corn Sticks, Old Southern Light Cornbread, and Cheesy Beef Cornbread (recipes on page 242).*

Page 222: *These meatless entrées offer a variety of tastes and textures: Mock Meatballs (page 243), Mushroom Quiche (page 244), and Cheesy Macaroni-Mushroom Bake (page 243).*

Far left: *Tostada Compuestas (page 194),
crisp-fried tortillas topped with a spicy meat
mixture and salad, can be served with taco
sauce, sour cream, tortilla chips, and chile
peppers, for a favorite Tex-Mex meal.*

Above: *Sangría (page 196) makes a cooling
accompaniment for Chile Con Queso (page
195) and tortilla chips.*

Left: *Topped with your favorite vegetables,
meats, and cheeses, Pizza Supreme (page
214) is all the reason you need for a party.*

Let Sweet Potatoes Be A Surprise

Part of the excitement of cooking lies in discovering something new. And sweet potato lovers will be pleased to discover Yam Cheesecake, Sweet Potato Loaf Cake (cooked in a can), and Sweet Potato Croquettes.

Those who prefer to keep their sweet potatoes simple should try a batch of French-Fried Sweet Potatoes. They're delightful sliced into thin chips or served up in finger-size strips with a light sprinkling of salt or powdered sugar.

In the South, we know two general types of sweet potatoes—the regular sweet potato and what is called a yam. Though many think of them as being the same, there's actually a difference. The Louisiana Sweet Potato Commission points out that yams have soft, moist flesh that is a deep-orange color. Regular sweet potatoes, on the other hand, have firm, dry, somewhat mealy flesh that is light yellow or pale orange.

The type you choose is really a matter of personal taste. Just remember that plump, medium-size sweet potatoes that taper toward the ends are preferable. Avoid those with any signs of decay, as such deterioration spreads rapidly, affecting the taste of the entire potato.

It's best to buy sweet potatoes in small quantities and use them promptly. If stored, they should be kept in a well-ventilated area at a temperature of about 60° F. Never store sweet potatoes in the refrigerator, as they will lose their flavor and turn black.

For best flavor, cook sweet potatoes in their jackets. This makes the most of the natural sugars found just under their skins. When boiled or baked, these sugars caramelize for a delicious taste.

If flavor isn't reason enough to treasure sweet potatoes, then consider their nutritional value. One of the most all-around nutritious foods, one medium-size sweet potato provides more than twice the recommended daily allowance of vitamin A and about one-third of the vitamin C.

FRENCH-FRIED SWEET POTATOES

3 medium-size sweet potatoes
Vegetable oil
Salt or powdered sugar (optional)

Cook sweet potatoes in boiling water 10 minutes; let cool to touch. Peel sweet potatoes, and cut into finger-size strips or ¼-inch slices. Fry in hot oil (380°) until golden brown; drain on paper towels. Sprinkle with salt or powdered sugar, if desired. Yield: 4 to 6 servings.

ORANGE-GLAZED SWEET POTATOES

4 medium-size sweet potatoes
¼ teaspoon salt
½ cup firmly packed brown sugar
1 tablespoon cornstarch
1 cup orange juice
¼ cup raisins
¼ cup butter or margarine
3 tablespoons chopped walnuts
3 tablespoons dry sherry

Cook sweet potatoes in boiling water 20 to 25 minutes or until tender. Let cool to touch; peel and quarter. Arrange sweet potatoes in a lightly greased 13- x 9- x 2-inch baking dish. Sprinkle with salt.

Combine brown sugar and cornstarch in a small saucepan; stir in orange juice and raisins. Bring to a boil; reduce heat. Cook, stirring constantly, until thickened. Add butter, walnuts, and sherry; stir until butter is melted.

Pour glaze over sweet potatoes. Bake, uncovered, at 350° for 20 minutes. Yield: 6 servings.

Mrs. John W. Stevens,
Lexington, Kentucky.

SWEET POTATO CROQUETTES

2 cups cooked, mashed sweet potatoes
¼ cup minced celery
½ teaspoon salt
1 teaspoon milk
2 tablespoons butter or margarine, melted
¾ cup crushed corn flakes

Combine sweet potatoes, celery, and salt; mix well, and stir in milk. Shape into 6 balls; dip in melted butter, and roll each in corn flakes.

Place croquettes on a broiler pan. Broil 6 to 7 inches from heat for 5 minutes, turning until golden brown on all sides. Yield: about 3 servings.

Ginger Barker,
Mesquite, Texas.

LOUISIANA YAM PIE

½ cup whipping cream
1 teaspoon vinegar
1 teaspoon soda
2 cups cooked, mashed sweet potatoes
3 tablespoons butter, melted
1 cup sugar
1 teaspoon baking powder
½ teaspoon ground cinnamon
½ teaspoon ground nutmeg
3 eggs, beaten
1 unbaked 9-inch pastry shell
Additional whipped cream (optional)
Ground cinnamon (optional)

Combine whipping cream, vinegar, and soda; stir well, and set aside. Combine next 7 ingredients, mixing well; stir in whipping cream mixture. Pour into container of electric blender, and process until smooth.

Pour filling into pastry shell. Bake at 400° for 10 minutes; reduce heat to 300°, and bake 45 to 50 minutes. Serve hot or cold. Garnish pie with dollops of whipped cream and sprinkle with cinnamon before serving, if desired. Yield: one 9-inch pie.
DeLea Lonadier,
Montgomery, Louisiana.

SWEET POTATO-STUFFED ORANGE CUPS

4 medium navel oranges
4 medium-size sweet potatoes
3 tablespoons butter or margarine, melted
¼ cup firmly packed light brown sugar, divided
½ teaspoon grated orange rind
¼ teaspoon salt
2 tablespoons finely chopped pecans
Orange rind curls (optional)

Cut oranges in half crosswise. Clip membranes, and carefully remove pulp (do not puncture bottom). Chop orange pulp; measure ¼ cup, reserving rest for another use. Using kitchen shears, cut edges of orange cups into points.

Cook sweet potatoes in boiling water 20 to 25 minutes or until tender. Let cool to touch; peel and mash. Combine mashed potatoes, butter, 2 tablespoons brown sugar, grated orange rind, ¼ cup orange pulp, and salt; mix well.

Stuff orange cups with potato mixture. Combine remaining brown sugar and pecans; sprinkle over potatoes. Place orange cups in a 13- x 9- x 2-inch baking pan; bake at 375° for 30 to 35 minutes. Top each with an orange rind curl, if desired. Yield: 8 servings.

Billie Taylor,
Afton, Virginia.

SWEET POTATO LOAF CAKE

1½ cups sugar
½ cup vegetable oil
2 eggs
⅓ cup water
1¾ cups all-purpose flour
1½ teaspoons ground cinnamon
1 teaspoon ground nutmeg
1 teaspoon soda
½ teaspoon salt
1 cup cooked, mashed sweet potatoes
½ cup chopped pecans or walnuts
½ cup raisins

Combine sugar, oil, eggs, and water; beat at medium speed of electric mixer just until combined. Combine next 5 ingredients; add to egg mixture, mixing just until moistened. Stir in sweet potatoes, pecans, and raisins.

Spoon batter into 2 greased and floured 1-pound coffee cans; bake at 350° for 1 hour or until a wooden pick inserted in center comes out clean. Let cool in cans 10 minutes; remove from cans to complete cooling. Yield: 2 loaves.
James O. Michelinie,
Louisville, Kentucky.

YAM CHEESECAKE

1⅔ cups graham cracker crumbs
⅓ cup butter or margarine, melted
2 envelopes unflavored gelatin
½ cup cold water
3 eggs, separated
¾ cup sugar
½ teaspoon salt
⅓ cup milk
2 (8-ounce) packages cream cheese, softened
1¼ cups cooked, mashed sweet potatoes
1 cup whipping cream, whipped
½ teaspoon vanilla extract
Additional whipped cream (optional)
Mandarin orange slices (optional)

Combine graham cracker crumbs and butter, mixing well. Press into bottom and 1½ inches up sides of a 9-inch springform pan; chill.

Soften gelatin in cold water in top of a double boiler; stir in egg yolks, sugar, salt, and milk. Place over water, and bring water to a boil. Reduce heat; cook, stirring constantly, until slightly thickened. Add cream cheese and sweet potatoes. Pour mixture into container of electric blender or food processor; blend until smooth.

Beat egg whites (at room temperature) until stiff but not dry. Fold egg whites, whipped cream, and vanilla into sweet potato mixture; spoon into prepared pan. Chill until set. Garnish with dollops of whipped cream and orange slices, if desired. Yield: about 10 servings.
Gail Weeks,
Moultrie, Georgia.

SWEET POTATO MUFFINS

1¾ cups all-purpose flour
¼ cup sugar
1 tablespoon baking powder
1 tablespoon brown sugar
1 teaspoon salt
½ cup coarsely chopped pecans or walnuts
1¼ cups cooked, mashed sweet potatoes
¾ cup milk
¼ cup butter or margarine, melted
2 eggs, slightly beaten
¼ cup sugar
½ teaspoon ground cinnamon

Combine first 6 ingredients in a large bowl, stirring well. Make a well in center of mixture. Combine the next 4 ingredients, stirring well; add to dry ingredients, mixing just until moistened.

Spoon batter into greased muffin pans, filling two-thirds full. Combine ¼ cup sugar and cinnamon; sprinkle over each muffin. Bake at 425° for 20 to 25 minutes. Yield: about 1⅓ dozen.
Betty Butts,
Kensington, Maryland.

Put The Best Of Fall In A Salad

Just because summer is over doesn't mean you can't still have a good variety of salads using fresh fruits and vegetables. Fall markets are brimming with fresh pears, apples, cauliflower, spinach, and celery, all ready to be tossed into crisp, fresh salads.

Apple Snow Salad is a refreshing blend of chopped apples, celery, and crushed pineapple frozen in a light whipped cream mixture. On the heartier side, there's Crunchy Spinach Salad—loaded with hard-cooked eggs, bacon, bean sprouts, and water chestnuts, tossed with a tangy dressing. And those who like to combine fruit and cheese shouldn't miss Blue Cheese-Pear-Apple Salad.

APPLE SNOW SALAD

1 (8¼-ounce) can crushed pineapple
½ cup sugar
3 tablespoons lemon juice
Dash of salt
2 eggs, beaten
2 cups finely chopped apple
½ cup finely chopped celery
1 cup whipping cream, whipped

Drain pineapple, reserving syrup. Add enough water to pineapple syrup to make ½ cup. Combine pineapple syrup, sugar, lemon juice, salt, and eggs in a saucepan; mix well. Cook over low heat, stirring constantly, until smooth and thickened. Chill syrup mixture thoroughly. Fold in pineapple, apple, celery, and whipped cream. Spoon into an 8-inch square pan; freeze until firm. Cut into squares to serve. Yield: about 9 servings.
Mrs. John W. Stevens,
Lexington, Kentucky.

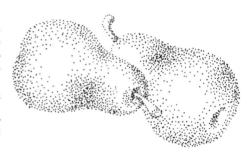

BLUE CHEESE-PEAR-APPLE SALAD

1 medium pear
1 medium apple
About ¼ cup lemon juice
¼ cup crumbled blue cheese
Lettuce leaves
Dressing (recipe follows)

Quarter and core fruit; dip in lemon juice. Slice each quarter into wedges; spread blue cheese on each wedge. Arrange wedges in an attractive pattern on lettuce leaves. Chill; top with salad dressing. Yield: 4 servings.

Dressing:

½ cup commercial sour cream
2 tablespoons chili sauce
1 teaspoon lemon juice
1 teaspoon sugar
¼ teaspoon salt
⅛ teaspoon paprika
Dash of white pepper

Combine all ingredients; blend well. Yield: about ½ cup.
Shirley Hodge,
Delray Beach, Florida.

CAULIFLOWER SALAD

1½ cups sliced raw cauliflower
½ cup thinly sliced celery
¼ cup chopped green pepper
1 cup chopped onion
2 cups chopped tomatoes
⅛ teaspoon salt
⅓ cup spicy sweet French dressing

Combine all ingredients, and toss lightly. Refrigerate before serving. Yield: 6 to 8 servings.

Dora S. Hancock,
Plano, Texas.

CRUNCHY SPINACH SALAD

2 pounds fresh spinach, torn into bite-size
    pieces
1 (8-ounce) can water chestnuts, drained
    and finely chopped
4 hard-cooked eggs, chopped
1 (16-ounce) can bean sprouts, drained
½ pound bacon, cooked and crumbled
Dressing (recipe follows)

Combine all ingredients except dressing in a large bowl and toss well. Serve with dressing. Yield: 12 to 15 servings.

Dressing:

1 cup vegetable oil
¼ cup cider vinegar
½ cup sugar
½ cup catsup
1 tablespoon Worcestershire sauce
1 teaspoon salt

Combine all ingredients in a jar. Cover tightly, and shake vigorously. Chill several hours. Yield: about 2 cups.

Gail Thomas,
White Hall, Maryland.

Two For Brunch

When it comes to brunch dishes, whether for 2 or 20, eggs come to mind: eggs with cheese, eggs with bacon or sausage, eggs in a golden soufflé. If planning for two, these egg dishes will suit you perfectly.

Our version of eggs benedict for two features a slice of Swiss cheese atop the bacon and a cheese sauce atop the eggs. Don't miss our Bacon and Egg Casserole: layers of eggs, bacon, sauce, and seasonings baked in individual custard cups. It's a perfect brunch dish for two.

SAUSAGE EGG BAKE

½ pound bulk pork sausage
1 cup cooked grits
4 eggs
Salt and pepper
½ cup (2 ounces) shredded Cheddar
    cheese

Cook sausage until browned, stirring to crumble; drain well. Place sausage in a lightly greased 1-quart casserole; spoon grits over top. Press 4 indentations in grits with the back of a tablespoon; break one egg into each indentation. Sprinkle casserole with salt and pepper; top with cheese. Bake at 350° for 20 to 25 minutes or until eggs are set. Yield: 2 servings.   *Zoe Newton,*
Fort Smith, Arkansas.

BACON AND EGG CASSEROLE

¾ cup crushed oven-toasted rice cereal
2 tablespoons butter or margarine, melted
½ teaspoon dehydrated chives or
    parsley flakes
⅛ teaspoon onion salt
2 tablespoons butter or margarine
2 tablespoons all-purpose flour
¾ cup milk
½ teaspoon dry mustard
2 hard-cooked eggs, sliced
4 slices bacon, cooked and crumbled

Combine first 4 ingredients; stir well, and set aside.

Melt 2 tablespoons butter in a heavy saucepan over low heat; add flour, and stir until smooth. Cook 1 minute, stirring constantly. Gradually add milk, and cook over medium heat, stirring constantly, until thickened and bubbly. Stir in mustard.

Layer half of eggs, bacon, sauce, and cereal mixture in two greased 10-ounce custard cups. Repeat layering process. Bake at 350° for 15 minutes or until thoroughly heated. Yield: 2 servings.

F. L. Graham,
Lexington, Kentucky.

EGGS BENEDICT WITH CHEESE SAUCE

2 English muffins, halved and buttered
4 slices cooked Canadian bacon
4 (1-ounce) slices Swiss cheese
4 poached eggs
Cheese sauce (recipe follows)

Broil muffins until lightly browned. Place 1 Canadian bacon slice and 1

cheese slice on each muffin half. Top each with a poached egg, and cover with cheese sauce. Serve immediately. Yield: 2 servings.

Cheese Sauce:

1 tablespoon butter or margarine
1 tablespoon all-purpose flour
⅔ cup milk
½ cup (2 ounces) shredded Cheddar
    cheese
¼ teaspoon salt
Dash of pepper

Melt butter in a heavy saucepan over low heat; add flour, and stir until smooth. Cook 1 minute, stirring constantly. Gradually add milk; cook over medium heat, stirring constantly, until thickened and bubbly. Add cheese, salt, and pepper, stirring until cheese is melted. Yield: about ¾ cup.

Mary Boden,
Stuart, Florida.

MEXICAN OMELET

4 eggs, beaten
2 tablespoons chopped green chiles
2 tablespoons chopped green olives
2 teaspoons butter or margarine
¼ cup (1 ounce) shredded Cheddar cheese

Combine eggs, chiles, and olives; blend well. Melt butter in a 10-inch omelet pan or heavy skillet until just hot enough to sizzle a drop of water.

Pour egg mixture into pan. As mixture starts to cook, gently lift edges of omelet and tilt pan to allow uncooked portion to flow underneath.

When egg mixture is set and no longer flows freely, sprinkle cheese over half of omelet. Fold omelet in half, and slide onto plate. Yield: 2 servings.

Peggy Dowdy,
Roanoke, Virginia.

Tip: The reason some hard-cooked eggs have discolored yolks is that the eggs have been cooked at too high a temperature, or they have not been cooled rapidly following cooking. The greenish color comes from sulfur and iron compounds in the eggs. These compounds form at the surface of the yolks when they have been overcooked. This does not interfere with the taste or nutritional value of the eggs, however.

CHEESE SOUFFLE FOR TWO

2 tablespoons grated Parmesan cheese, divided
1 teaspoon butter or margarine
1 teaspoon all-purpose flour
⅓ cup milk
¾ cup (3 ounces) shredded sharp Cheddar cheese
⅛ teaspoon dry mustard
Dash of red pepper
2 eggs, separated

Lightly butter a 2-cup soufflé dish. Cut a piece of aluminum foil long enough to circle the dish, allowing a 1-inch overlap. Fold foil lengthwise into thirds; lightly butter one side. Wrap foil, buttered side against dish, so it extends 2 inches above rim; secure foil with string tied around dish. Sprinkle inside of dish and foil with 1 tablespoon Parmesan cheese.

Melt 1 teaspoon butter in a heavy saucepan over low heat; add flour, and stir until smooth. Cook 1 minute, stirring constantly. Gradually add milk; cook over medium heat, stirring constantly, until thickened and bubbly. Stir in Cheddar cheese, remaining Parmesan cheese, mustard, and red pepper, stirring until cheese is melted.

Beat egg yolks until thick and lemon colored. Gradually stir about one-fourth of cheese sauce into yolks; add to remaining cheese sauce, stirring mixture constantly.

Beat egg whites (at room temperature) until stiff peaks form; fold into cheese mixture. Spoon into prepared soufflé dish.

Bake at 350° for 20 to 22 minutes or until firm. Remove collar before serving. Serve soufflé immediately. Yield: 2 servings.
Linda Q. Kerr,
Auburn, Alabama.

Meat Dishes With A Foreign Accent

What do Indian Kheema and Chicken Chop Suey and Hungarian Goulash have in common? Each carries a special flavor that hints at its foreign origin. The distinctive flavor may come from a particular sauce or a special spice.

Soy sauce, with its distinctive salty taste, brings the East to Chicken Chop Suey, Hot-and-Spicy Pork, and Indonesian Pork Roast. Curry works its magic by giving Indian Kheema a distinctive

The taste of India comes out in curry-flavored Indian Kheema.

golden color and nutty flavor. And Hungarian Goulash gets its appeal by adding Hungarian paprika.

INDIAN KHEEMA

1 pound ground beef
1 medium onion, finely chopped
1 cup water
2 teaspoons curry powder
¾ teaspoon ground turmeric
½ teaspoon salt
½ teaspoon garlic powder
½ teaspoon red pepper
¼ teaspoon ground ginger
¼ teaspoon pepper
1 large potato, peeled and cut into ¾-inch cubes
1 medium tomato, peeled and chopped
1 (17-ounce) can English peas, drained
1 cup water
Hot cooked rice

Cook ground beef and onion in a 10-inch skillet until browned; drain well. Combine next 8 ingredients; add to ground beef mixture, stirring well. Stir in potato, tomato, peas, and remaining water. Bring to a boil; reduce heat and simmer, covered, 20 to 25 minutes or until potatoes are tender. Serve over rice. Yield: about 4 to 6 servings.
Mrs. Carl Ramay,
Englewood, Colorado.

Tip: Wine should be stored at an even temperature of 50 to 60 degrees. It is important that bottles of corked table wines be kept on their side so that the corks are kept moist and airtight. If the bottle has a screw cap, it may remain upright.

HUNGARIAN GOULASH

½ cup all-purpose flour
½ teaspoon salt
½ teaspoon pepper
Pinch of Hungarian paprika
2½ to 3 pounds boneless round steak, cut into 1-inch cubes
3 tablespoons vegetable oil
2 tablespoons butter or margarine, melted
6 large onions, coarsely chopped
2 cups beef broth, divided
3 tablespoons tomato paste
1 tablespoon Hungarian paprika
Grated rind of 1 lemon
½ teaspoon dried whole marjoram
¼ teaspoon caraway seeds
1 clove garlic, crushed
Hot buttered noodles

Combine first 4 ingredients; stir well. Dredge meat in flour mixture, and sauté in oil and butter until browned; drain well, reserving drippings.

Sauté onion in reserved drippings until tender; drain well. Combine onion, ½ cup beef broth, tomato paste, 1 tablespoon paprika, lemon rind, marjoram, caraway seeds, and garlic in a large Dutch oven; simmer 3 minutes. Stir in meat and remaining broth; cover and simmer 1½ hours or until meat is tender. Serve over noodles. Yield: 10 servings. *Geraldine Murphy, Corbin, Kentucky.*

VEAL PARMIGIANA

2 (15-ounce) cans tomato sauce
1 tablespoon butter or margarine, melted
1 tablespoon brown sugar
2 teaspoons Worcestershire sauce
1½ teaspoons Season-All
1 teaspoon dried whole oregano
1 teaspoon dried whole basil
¼ teaspoon garlic powder
¼ teaspoon pepper
2 eggs
1 teaspoon Season-All
¼ teaspoon pepper
2 pounds veal cutlets, cut into serving-size pieces
About 4 cups soft breadcrumbs
½ cup olive oil
¼ cup grated Parmesan cheese
1 (8-ounce) package sliced mozzarella cheese

Combine first 9 ingredients in a saucepan; cook over medium heat, stirring occasionally, about 5 minutes. Set aside.

Combine eggs, remaining Season-All, and pepper; beat well. Dip cutlets into egg mixture, and dredge in breadcrumbs. Sauté cutlets in olive oil 4 to 5 minutes or until brown. Place cutlets in a lightly greased 13- x 9- x 2-inch baking dish. Pour sauce over veal, and sprinkle with Parmesan cheese. Cover and bake at 350° for 30 minutes. Uncover and top with mozzarella cheese; bake 5 minutes or until cheese melts. Yield: 6 servings. *Mrs. Steve Lundquist, Corpus Christi, Texas.*

CHICKEN CHOP SUEY

1 (2½- to 3-pound) broiler-fryer
1 cup fresh mushrooms, sliced
1 medium onion, chopped
1 cup chopped celery
½ cup cornstarch
½ cup water
½ to ¾ cup soy sauce
½ cup bamboo shoots
1 (8-ounce) can water chestnuts, drained and sliced
½ cup bean sprouts
¼ teaspoon pepper
Hot cooked rice or chow mein noodles

Place chicken in a large Dutch oven; add enough water to cover chicken. Heat to boiling; cover and reduce heat. Cook 45 minutes or until tender. Remove chicken; let cool. Bone chicken and chop the meat; set aside. Reserve 4½ cups of the chicken broth.

Bring broth to a boil; add mushrooms, onion, and celery. Reduce heat; cook until vegetables are crisp-tender.

Combine cornstarch and water, stirring until smooth; add to broth mixture. Cook over medium heat, stirring constantly, until thickened and bubbly. Reduce to low heat; stir in chicken, soy sauce, bamboo shoots, water chestnuts, bean sprouts, and pepper; cook, stirring frequently, until thoroughly heated. Serve over rice or chow mein noodles. Yield: 8 to 10 servings. *Karen Rogers, Jonesboro, Arkansas.*

CHICKEN-OLIVE CHALUPAS

6 (10-inch) flour tortillas
2 (16-ounce) cans refried beans
Chicken-Olive Filling
½ medium head lettuce, shredded
2 medium tomatoes, chopped
6 green onions, chopped
2 avocados, peeled and chopped
Commercial taco sauce or commercial sour cream

Fry tortillas, one at a time, in ¼ inch hot oil (375°), 20 to 30 seconds on each side or until crisp and golden brown. Drain on paper towels. Spread an equal amount of beans on each tortilla. Top with equal amounts of Chicken-Olive Filling and the next 4 ingredients. Serve with either taco sauce or sour cream. Yield: 6 servings.

Chicken-Olive Filling:

2 (1.25-ounce) packages taco seasoning mix
2 cups water
3 cups cubed, cooked chicken
1 (6-ounce) can pitted ripe olives, drained and sliced

Combine taco seasoning mix and water in a medium skillet, stirring well; bring to a boil. Reduce heat, and simmer 5 minutes, stirring occasionally. Stir in chicken and olives; simmer 3 additional minutes. Yield: about 4 cups. *Mrs. R. D. Garrett, Austin, Texas.*

INDONESIAN PORK ROAST

1 (4-pound) Boston butt roast
1 tablespoon vegetable oil
1 cup water
½ cup soy sauce
⅓ cup firmly packed brown sugar
¼ cup vinegar
2 cloves garlic, minced
1 chicken-flavored bouillon cube
3 carrots, peeled and cut into 2-inch pieces
6 small potatoes, peeled around middle
6 small onions, peeled

Brown roast on all sides in hot oil in a large Dutch oven; drain off excess oil. Combine next 6 ingredients; add to roast. Cover and simmer 2½ hours. Add carrots; cover and cook 10 minutes. Add potatoes and onions; cover and cook 20 minutes or until all vegetables are tender. Yield: 6 servings.

Mrs. Ralph E. Chase, Hendersonville, North Carolina.

HOT-AND-SPICY PORK

2 pounds boneless pork
½ cup plus 2 tablespoons peanut oil,
  divided
½ cup soy sauce
¼ cup Chablis or other dry white wine
¼ cup cornstarch, divided
¼ cup minced fresh gingerroot, divided
2 tablespoons vinegar
Catsup Sauce
2 cloves garlic, minced
1 bunch green onions, cut into 2-inch
  pieces
2 onions, coarsely chopped
4 carrots, diagonally sliced into ½-inch
  pieces
2 green peppers, cut into 1-inch pieces
1 (8-ounce) can bamboo shoots, drained
1 (8-ounce) can sliced water chestnuts,
  drained
6 dried whole red peppers
Hot cooked rice

Partially freeze pork; slice across grain into 2- x ¼-inch strips. Set aside. Combine 2 tablespoons oil, soy sauce, wine, 2 tablespoons cornstarch, 2 tablespoons gingerroot, and vinegar; mix well, and pour over sliced pork. Cover and marinate overnight in refrigerator.

Combine ¼ cup Catsup Sauce and remaining 2 tablespoons cornstarch; mix well, and set aside.

Pour ¼ cup remaining oil around top of preheated wok, coating sides. Allow to heat at medium high (325°) for 2 minutes. Add pork (undrained); stir-fry about 3 to 5 minutes. Remove pork; drain on paper towels.

Pour remaining ¼ cup oil around top of wok; allow to heat at medium high (325°) for 2 minutes. Add garlic and remaining 2 tablespoons gingerroot; stir-fry 1 minute. Add onion, carrots, and green pepper; stir-fry 2 to 3 minutes. Add bamboo shoots, water chestnuts, and red peppers; stir-fry 1 minute. Add remaining Catsup Sauce, and bring to a boil. Add pork and cornstarch mixture; stir-fry over low heat (225°) for 3 minutes or until thickened and bubbly. Serve over rice. Yield: 8 to 10 servings.

Catsup Sauce:

⅔ cup catsup
⅔ cup chicken bouillon
½ cup soy sauce
½ cup Chablis or other dry white wine
2 tablespoons plus 2 teaspoons brown
  sugar
1 teaspoon hot sauce
2 tablespoons vinegar

Combine all ingredients; mix well. Yield: about 2⅓ cups.
Vickie C. Zambie,
Monroe, Louisiana.

Quiche Served With Flair

Made with ease and served with flair, quiche—the classic pastry filled with cream and eggs—is really a meal in itself. Cheese, meat, seafood, and fresh or frozen vegetables can be baked into the filling for a delicious entrée the whole family will enjoy.

Peppery Quiche Lorraine is delicately spiced with diced green chiles nestled in Swiss cheese. Our whole wheat pastry for Cheese-Vegetable Quiche is a natural complement to the fresh vegetables tucked inside the filling. But if making pastry is a problem, you'll enjoy our crustless Broccoli-Rice Quiche.

PEPPERY QUICHE LORRAINE

Pastry for 9-inch pie
6 thick slices bacon
1 medium onion, chopped
1 (4-ounce) can diced, roasted, and peeled
  green chiles
1 (8-ounce) package Swiss cheese slices
4 eggs, beaten
2 cups half-and-half
1 tablespoon all-purpose flour
½ teaspoon salt
¼ teaspoon ground nutmeg
Dash of red pepper

Line a 9-inch quiche dish with pastry; trim excess pastry around edges and flute. Prick bottom and sides of quiche shell with a fork; bake at 425° for 10 to 12 minutes. Let cool on rack.

Cook bacon and onion in skillet until bacon is transparent and onion is tender. Drain bacon; cut into 1-inch pieces. Sprinkle bacon and onion into pastry shell; top with green chiles and cheese. Set aside.

Combine last 6 ingredients, mixing well. Pour into pastry shell. Bake at 375° for 40 minutes or until set. Yield: one 9-inch quiche.
Gloria A. Cook,
Grants, New Mexico.

Tip: Do not wash eggs before storing; washing removes the coating that prevents the entrance of bacteria. Wash just before using, if desired.

CHEESY SPINACH QUICHE

Pastry for 9-inch deep-dish pie
1 (10-ounce) package frozen spinach
1 (8-ounce) package Swiss cheese slices
2 tablespoons all-purpose flour
3 eggs, beaten
1 cup whipping cream
½ teaspoon salt
Dash of pepper

Line a 9-inch deep-dish pieplate with pastry; trim excess pastry around edges and flute. Prick bottom and sides of quiche shell with a fork; bake at 425° for 10 to 12 minutes. Let cool on rack.

Cook spinach according to package directions; drain well. Cut cheese into ½-inch strips; toss with flour; set aside.

Combine eggs, whipping cream, salt, and pepper, beating well. Stir in spinach and cheese. Pour mixture into pastry shell. Bake at 350° for 1 hour. Yield: one 9-inch quiche.
Rick Mann,
Washington, D.C.

BROCCOLI-RICE QUICHE

1½ cups cooked rice
1 egg, beaten
¾ cup (3 ounces) shredded Cheddar
  cheese, divided
1 (10-ounce) package frozen broccoli
1 tablespoon minced onion
⅓ cup milk
2 eggs, beaten
¼ teaspoon pepper
1 (4-ounce) jar sliced mushrooms, drained

Combine rice, 1 egg, and ½ cup cheese, mixing well. Press mixture into a greased 9-inch pieplate; set aside.

Cook broccoli according to package directions; drain well. Add ¼ cup cheese and remaining ingredients to broccoli; mix well. Pour broccoli mixture into rice-lined pieplate. Bake at 375° for about 50 minutes or until done. Yield: one 9-inch quiche.
Peggy Fowler Revels,
Woodruff, South Carolina.

CHEESE-VEGETABLE QUICHE

1 cup chopped fresh broccoli
1 cup chopped fresh cauliflower
Whole wheat pastry (recipe follows)
3 cups (12 ounces) shredded process
  American cheese
4 egg yolks, beaten
1 cup whipping cream
1½ teaspoons seasoned salt
½ teaspoon white pepper
¼ teaspoon ground nutmeg

Steam vegetables 5 minutes; place in pastry shell, and top with cheese. Combine remaining ingredients, beating well; pour into prepared pastry shell. Bake at 375° for 50 to 60 minutes or until set. Yield: one 9-inch quiche.

Whole Wheat Pastry:
½ cup whole wheat pastry flour
¼ cup cornmeal
½ cup grated Parmesan cheese, divided
2 egg yolks
¼ cup butter, softened
2 tablespoons milk

Combine flour, cornmeal, and ¼ cup cheese; cut in egg yolks and butter with pastry blender until mixture resembles coarse meal. Sprinkle milk evenly over surface; stir with a fork until all ingredients are moistened. Shape dough into a ball; chill. Roll dough to ⅛-inch thickness on a lightly floured surface. Line a 9-inch quiche dish or pieplate with pastry; trim excess pastry around edges and flute. Prick bottom and sides of quiche shell with a fork; bake at 425° for 15 minutes. Let cool on rack. Sprinkle remaining ¼ cup cheese into pastry shell. Yield: pastry for one 9-inch quiche. *Mrs. Jack Cherry, Balsam, North Carolina.*

Breakfast Breads In 30 Minutes Or Less

If you've ever yearned for freshly baked breakfast breads but didn't have the time to prepare them, these convenient breads are just what you're after. They all call for refrigerated biscuits or rolls or a biscuit mix. In 30 minutes or less you'll have a delectable sweet bread to start your day on a happy note.

ORANGE JUICE MUFFINS WITH HONEY SPREAD

2 cups biscuit mix
2 tablespoons sugar
1 egg
1 teaspoon grated orange rind
⅔ cup orange juice
2 tablespoons sugar
¼ teaspoon ground cinnamon
⅛ teaspoon ground nutmeg
Honey Spread

Combine first 5 ingredients in a large bowl, stirring until all ingredients are moistened. Spoon into greased muffin pans, filling two-thirds full.

Combine remaining sugar, cinnamon, and nutmeg; sprinkle over muffin batter. Bake at 400° for 15 minutes or until golden brown. Serve hot with Honey Spread. Yield: 1 dozen.

Honey Spread:
¼ cup butter or margarine, softened
¼ cup honey

Combine butter and honey, mixing well. Yield: about ½ cup.
Mrs. Russell Rehkemper, Tampa, Florida.

ORANGE BREAKFAST RING

1 cup sugar
3 tablespoons grated orange rind
2 (12-ounce) cans refrigerated buttermilk biscuits
⅓ cup butter or margarine, melted
1 (3-ounce) package cream cheese, softened
½ cup sifted powdered sugar
2 tablespoons orange juice

Combine sugar and orange rind. Separate biscuits; dip each in butter, and coat with sugar mixture. Stand biscuits on sides, overlapping edges, in a 9-inch tube pan. Bake at 350° for 30 minutes or until golden brown.

Remove ring from pan, and invert on serving platter. Combine cream cheese and powdered sugar, mixing until smooth. Add orange juice, stirring well; spoon mixture over top while ring is hot. Serve bread warm. Yield: one 9-inch coffee cake. *John C. Patton, Alexandria, Virginia.*

CRESCENT COFFEE CAKE

¼ cup butter or margarine, softened
¾ cup pineapple preserves
½ cup flaked coconut
2 (8-ounce) cans refrigerated crescent dinner rolls
1 tablespoon butter or margarine, melted
Powdered sugar

Combine ¼ cup butter, preserves, and coconut, stirring well. Separate crescent rolls into triangles. Place a heaping tablespoon of preserves mixture

on wide end of each triangle; roll up, starting at wide end. Place rolls, seam side down, in two rows in a lightly greased 9-inch square baking pan; brush with melted butter. Bake at 375° for 30 minutes or until golden brown. Cool in pan 5 minutes. Remove from pan, and invert on a serving platter; sprinkle with powdered sugar. Serve warm. Yield: 8 servings. *Leisa Kilgore, Mount Olive, Alabama.*

Pack A Surprise In The Lunchbox

Carrying a lunch to school or work can be fun, especially if it contains an assortment of special treats. We've compiled two appealing menus for a portable lunch.

Our first menu calls for soup and sandwich, while our second menu packs a marinated vegetable salad and a small serving of chili. Both include a dessert.

Yummy Sandwiches
Savory Vegetable Broth
Cinnamon Brownie Bars

YUMMY SANDWICHES

¼ cup butter or margarine, softened
¼ cup chopped onion
¼ cup prepared mustard
2 tablespoons sesame seeds
Dash of Worcestershire sauce
8 hamburger buns
8 slices cooked ham
8 slices Swiss cheese

Combine first 5 ingredients; mix well. Spread on hamburger buns. Place 1 ham slice and 1 cheese slice on bottom of each bun; cover with tops. Yield: 8 servings.

Note: Sandwiches may be served hot. Wrap each in aluminum foil, and bake at 350° for 25 minutes. *Darlene Dakin, Drakesboro, Kentucky.*

Tip: Small amounts of jelly left in jars may be combined, melted, and used to glaze a ham.

SAVORY VEGETABLE BROTH

4 beef bouillon cubes
4 cups water
1 stalk celery, sliced
1 large carrot, sliced
1 medium onion, chopped
¼ pound fresh mushrooms, chopped
⅓ cup uncooked regular rice
⅛ teaspoon pepper

Soften bouillon cubes in water in a large skillet. Add remaining ingredients, mixing well. Bring to a boil; reduce heat, and simmer gently for 30 to 35 minutes or until vegetables are tender, stirring occasionally. Yield: about 1 quart.   *Mrs. G. Pedersen,*
Brandon, Mississippi.

CINNAMON BROWNIE BARS

½ cup butter or margarine
2½ (1-ounce) squares unsweetened
   chocolate
2 eggs
1 cup sugar
½ cup all-purpose flour
¼ teaspoon baking powder
¼ teaspoon salt
¼ teaspoon ground cinnamon
½ cup chopped pecans or walnuts
5 (1.05-ounce) bars milk chocolate

Combine butter and chocolate in a heavy saucepan; cook over low heat, stirring constantly, until melted. Cool mixture slightly.

Beat eggs; gradually add sugar, beating constantly, until smooth and thickened. Add chocolate mixture; beat well.

Combine dry ingredients; add to chocolate mixture, mixing well. Stir in pecans. Pour into a greased and floured 8-inch square pan. Bake at 350° for 30 minutes or until a wooden pick inserted in center comes out clean. Remove from oven, and immediately arrange milk chocolate bars over brownies; cover loosely with aluminum foil for 3 to 5 minutes or until chocolate melts. Remove foil; spread candy evenly over top. Cool and cut into squares. Yield: 16 (2-inch) squares.   *Cindy Murphy,*
Knoxville, Tennessee.

Lunchtime Chili
Fresh Vegetable Marinate
Easy Pecan Squares

LUNCHTIME CHILI

3 pounds ground beef
6 medium onions, chopped
3 (16-ounce) cans whole tomatoes,
   undrained and chopped
2 (15½-ounce) cans kidney beans, drained
2 (6-ounce) cans tomato paste
3 to 4 tablespoons chili powder
2 teaspoons salt
½ teaspoon hot sauce

Cook ground beef and onion in a Dutch oven until beef is browned, stirring occasionally; drain well.

Add remaining ingredients. Simmer 1 hour, uncovered, stirring occasionally. Yield: about 5 quarts.   *Maggie Sims,*
Homer, Louisiana.

FRESH VEGETABLE MARINATE

1 pound fresh broccoli
1 small head cauliflower
8 large fresh mushrooms, sliced
3 stalks celery, chopped
1½ cups vegetable oil
½ cup sugar
½ cup vinegar
1 small onion, grated
2 tablespoons poppy seeds
2 teaspoons dry mustard
1 teaspoon salt

Trim off large leaves of broccoli. Remove tough ends of lower stalks, and wash broccoli thoroughly. Cut into bite-size pieces.

Wash cauliflower thoroughly, and remove green leaves. Separate cauliflower into flowerets, slicing large flowerets into bite-size pieces.

Combine broccoli, cauliflower, mushrooms, and celery in a large bowl. Combine remaining ingredients; stir well. Add to vegetables, tossing to coat. Cover and refrigerate at least 3 hours. Yield: about 10 servings. *Ginny Shew,*
Wilmington, North Carolina.

Tip: Quick-cooking oats, browned in a small amount of butter or margarine, makes an economical substitute for chopped nuts in cookie recipes.

EASY PECAN SQUARES

½ cup butter or margarine, melted
2 cups firmly packed light brown sugar
2 eggs
1 cup all-purpose flour
2 teaspoons baking powder
¼ teaspoon salt
1 teaspoon vanilla extract
1 cup chopped pecans
Powdered sugar

Combine butter and brown sugar; beat with electric mixer until well blended. Add eggs, beating well.

Combine flour, baking powder, and salt; add to sugar mixture, and mix well. Stir in vanilla and pecans. Spoon batter into a greased and floured 13- x 9- x 2-inch baking dish. Bake at 350° for 25 minutes; sprinkle immediately with powdered sugar. Let cool completely, and cut into 2-inch squares. Yield: about 2 dozen.

Mrs. Delbert R. Snyder,
Williamsburg, Virginia.

Microwave Cookery

Winter Squash, The Easy Way

Winter squash is a natural for microwave cooking. In addition to reducing the cooking time, microwaves preserve the natural flavor of the squash as well as the color and texture.

To show you how easy it is to microwave squash, we've developed five recipes for butternut and acorn squash in our test kitchens. Each recipe gives a time range for microwaving to allow for the difference in wattage of microwave ovens and sizes of squash. The times given are based on medium squash; for larger or smaller squash, adjust the microwaving time accordingly.

Some Tips

—When microwaving whole squash, pierce rind deeply with a knife or tines of fork to allow steam to escape.

—Winter squash cooks faster when cut in half; also remove seeds and fibers. If squash is hard to cut, microwaving at HIGH for 1 to 2 minutes will make it easier. Cover each half of squash with heavy-duty plastic wrap before microwaving.

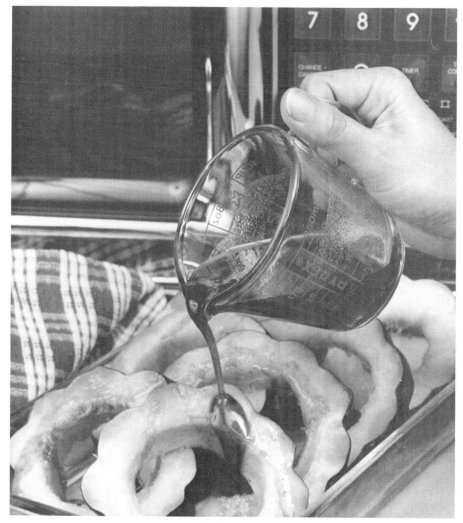

For Easy Glazed Acorn Rings, the squash is microwaved whole, then cut into rings and glazed. Total cooking time is less than 20 minutes.

EASY GLAZED ACORN RINGS

2 medium acorn squash
⅛ teaspoon salt
3 tablespoons butter or margarine
⅓ cup maple syrup
¼ teaspoon ground cinnamon

Pierce squash 4 or 5 times with knife or tines of fork, and place on paper towels about 3 inches apart in microwave oven. Microwave at HIGH for 10 to 12 minutes or until soft to the touch, rearranging and turning squash over after 5 minutes. Let stand 5 minutes.

Cut squash crosswise into 1-inch-thick rings; discard ends and seeds. Overlap rings in a 12- x 8- x 2-inch baking dish. Sprinkle with salt.

Place butter in a 1-cup glass measure; microwave at HIGH for 1 minute or until melted. Add maple syrup and cinnamon, mixing well; pour over squash. Cover with waxed paper; microwave at HIGH for 4 to 6 minutes or until done, basting and rearranging squash after 2 minutes. Yield: 4 servings.

CRANBERRY-FILLED ACORN SQUASH

1 medium acorn squash
1½ cups cranberries
¼ cup plus 2 tablespoons apple juice, divided
¼ cup plus 2 tablespoons sugar
⅛ teaspoon ground cloves
¼ teaspoon ground nutmeg
1 teaspoon cornstarch
1 tablespoon chopped walnuts

Cut squash in half; remove seeds and fibers. Cover each half with heavy-duty plastic wrap, and arrange about 1 inch apart in microwave oven. Microwave at HIGH for 6 to 9 minutes or until soft to the touch, rearranging after 4 minutes. Remove from oven.

Combine cranberries, ¼ cup apple juice, sugar, and spices in a 1-quart casserole. Cover with heavy-duty plastic wrap. Microwave at HIGH for 4 to 6 minutes or until cranberry skins pop. Combine 2 tablespoons apple juice and cornstarch, mixing well. Gradually stir into cranberry mixture, mixing well. Microwave at HIGH for 45 seconds to 1½ minutes or until thickened.

Spoon cranberry mixture into squash shells, and sprinkle with chopped walnuts. Microwave at HIGH for 1 to 2 minutes or until squash is thoroughly heated. Yield: 2 servings.

—To promote even cooking, rearrange squash halves after half the cooking time has elapsed. Whole squash should be rearranged and turned over during the microwaving process.

—The squash will continue to cook after the microwaving cycle is completed. To allow for this, let it stand as indicated in the recipe.

SAUSAGE-STUFFED ACORN SQUASH

2 medium acorn squash
½ pound bulk pork sausage
¼ cup chopped celery
¼ cup chopped onion
¼ cup sliced fresh mushrooms
¼ cup commercial sour cream
3 tablespoons grated Parmesan cheese

Cut squash in half; remove seeds and fibers. Cover each half with heavy-duty plastic wrap. Arrange about 1 inch apart in microwave oven. Microwave at HIGH for 10 to 12 minutes or until soft to the touch, rearranging after 7 minutes. Let stand 3 minutes. Scoop out pulp, leaving shells intact; chop pulp, and set aside.

Crumble sausage into a 1½-quart casserole; add celery and onion. Cover with heavy-duty plastic wrap. Microwave at HIGH for 3 minutes; add mushrooms, mixing well. Cover and microwave at HIGH for 2 to 3 minutes or until sausage is done. Drain well.

Combine sour cream, cheese, and squash pulp; mix well. Stir into sausage mixture, and spoon into squash shells. Arrange squash in a 12- x 8- x 2-inch microwave-safe baking dish. Microwave at HIGH for 2 to 3 minutes or until thoroughly heated. Yield: 4 servings.

BUTTERNUT SQUASH RING

3 medium butternut squash
2 tablespoons butter or margarine
½ cup sugar
1 teaspoon ground cinnamon
¼ teaspoon ground nutmeg
½ teaspoon salt
3 eggs
1 teaspoon vanilla extract

Cut squash in half; remove seeds and fibers. Cover each half with heavy-duty plastic wrap. Arrange about 1 inch apart in microwave oven. Microwave at HIGH for 18 to 22 minutes or until soft to the touch, rearranging after 10 minutes. Let stand 3 minutes. Scoop out pulp; discard shells. Beat pulp at medium speed of electric mixer until smooth.

Place butter in a 1-cup glass measure. Microwave at HIGH for 1 minute or until melted; pour over squash pulp. Combine sugar, spices, and salt; mix well. Add sugar mixture, eggs, and vanilla to squash; mix well.

Pour into a microwave-safe 1-quart ring mold. Microwave at HIGH 9 to 11 minutes or until set, rotating dish a quarter-turn every 3 minutes. Let the squash stand for 8 minutes before unmolding. Yield: 6 servings.

APPLE-STUFFED BUTTERNUT SQUASH

2 medium butternut squash
2 medium cooking apples, chopped
2 tablespoons orange juice
½ teaspoon ground cinnamon, divided
¼ cup plus 2 tablespoons firmly packed
  brown sugar, divided
1 tablespoon butter or margarine
2 tablespoons chopped pecans
1 teaspoon all-purpose flour

Cut squash in half; remove seeds and fibers. Cover each half with heavy-duty plastic wrap, and arrange about 1 inch apart in microwave oven. Microwave at HIGH for 12 to 15 minutes or until soft to the touch, rearranging after 7 minutes. Let squash stand 3 minutes. Scoop out pulp, leaving shells intact; chop pulp, and set aside.

Combine apples, orange juice, and ¼ teaspoon cinnamon in a 1-quart casserole. Cover with heavy-duty plastic wrap. Microwave at HIGH for 3 to 5 minutes or until apples are tender, stirring after 2 minutes. Add squash pulp and 2 tablespoons brown sugar, mixing

well. Spoon into squash shells, and place in a 12- x 8- x 2-inch baking dish.

Place butter in a small microwave-safe bowl. Microwave at LOW for 30 to 45 seconds or until softened. Add ¼ cup brown sugar, pecans, flour, and ¼ teaspoon cinnamon; mix well. Sprinkle topping evenly over apple filling. Microwave at HIGH for 2 to 3 minutes or until topping melts, turning dish after 1 minute. Yield: 4 servings.

Fruit Rounds Out The Menu

One way to spruce up everyday meals is to add fruit to the menu—not just as a salad or dessert, but as a substantial side dish. The natural goodness of fruit complements meat well, and our recipes offer both flavor and the convenience of canned foods.

Spices help perk up the flavor of canned fruits: cinnamon with pears in our Maple-Sugared Pears, and ginger with a variety of fruits in Gingered Baked Fruit. You'll also want to try Fried Pineapple—pineapple rings fried in a crisp coating.

GINGERED BAKED FRUIT

1 (20-ounce) can pineapple chunks,
  drained
1 (16-ounce) can pear halves, drained
1 (16-ounce) can peach halves, drained
1 (6-ounce) jar maraschino cherries,
  drained
¼ cup butter or margarine
¾ cup firmly packed brown sugar
1 tablespoon ground ginger

Combine fruit in a 1½-quart casserole. Melt butter; add sugar and ginger, stirring until smooth. Pour ginger mixture over fruit. Bake at 325° for 30 minutes. Yield: 8 servings.

Lilly S. Bradley,
Salem, Virginia.

Tip: Use leftover liquid from canned or cooked fruits and vegetables in frozen desserts, gelatin molds, soups, stews, and casseroles.

FRIED PINEAPPLE

¼ cup all-purpose flour
1 teaspoon sugar
1 egg, beaten
2 tablespoons milk
¼ teaspoon salt
1 (15½-ounce) can pineapple slices,
  drained
½ cup soft breadcrumbs
Vegetable oil

Combine flour and sugar. Combine egg, milk, and salt; mix well.

Dredge pineapple slices in flour mixture; dip in milk mixture, and coat with breadcrumbs. Fry pineapple in a small amount of hot oil until golden brown, turning once. Drain on paper towels. Yield: 8 slices. *Geraldine Hurst,*
Shreveport, Louisiana.

MAPLE-SUGARED PEARS

1 (15-ounce) can pear halves
¼ cup firmly packed brown sugar
1 tablespoon vegetable oil
1 teaspoon lemon juice
½ teaspoon maple flavoring
½ teaspoon ground cinnamon
2 tablespoons chopped pecans
¼ cup commercial sour cream

Drain pears, reserving ¼ cup syrup. Combine syrup, brown sugar, and oil in a small saucepan; bring to a boil. Remove from heat; stir in lemon juice, maple flavoring, and cinnamon.

Arrange pear halves, cut side up, in a small shallow baking dish; sprinkle with pecans. Pour brown sugar mixture over pears, and bake at 350° for 30 minutes. Before serving, top each pear with a dollop of sour cream. Yield: about 4 servings. *Mrs. H. J. Sherrer,*
Bay City, Texas.

A Sportsman Takes To The Kitchen

Chip Melton of Tallahassee, Florida, is a sportsman who takes hunting seriously. So seriously, in fact, that he has developed some delicious recipes for cooking wild game.

"I didn't like to see wild game go to waste, so I came up with a variety of recipes to utilize it properly," says

Chip. "Venison can be substituted in many dishes that call for beef. Most people who say they don't like the taste of venison have never had it prepared properly." Proper preparation, as Chip went on to explain, is the whole secret to making wild game appealing. He recommends that preparation begin even before the kill. "If the deer is run with dogs, there's sure to be a distinct tainted or wild flavor in the meat. If so, try soaking it in milk."

Chip also points out that cleaning of the venison is important. "Careful attention should be given to completely removing all muscles and fatty tissues because they can add a wild taste. Any small pieces of meat that are left over can be ground up and used to make burgers or chili."

Not only has Chip perfected his preparation of venison, but he also serves a special dessert—Make-Ahead Cheesecake Pie. "I like this recipe because it makes three pies. We can eat one and freeze the other two for later."

In addition to Chip's specialties and his tasty Peanut Butter Barbecue Sauce, we've also included recipes from other men who enjoy cooking.

COUNTRY-FRIED VENISON

1½ pounds (¾-inch-thick) venison
1 cup all-purpose flour
Salt and pepper
¼ teaspoon seasoned salt
¼ cup bacon drippings
2 cloves garlic, minced
4 cups water
⅓ cup all-purpose flour
1½ teaspoons bottled brown bouquet
   sauce
1 medium onion, thinly sliced
½ pound fresh mushrooms, sliced
Hot cooked rice

Prepare venison by trimming all fat and removing connective tissues. Cut meat into serving-size pieces, and pound each piece to ¼- to ½-inch thickness. Combine 1 cup flour, ¼ teaspoon salt, ⅛ teaspoon pepper, and seasoned salt; dredge the venison in flour mixture.

Heat 1 tablespoon bacon drippings in a large, heavy skillet; add garlic, and sauté until golden. Remove garlic, and set aside. Add remaining bacon drippings to skillet; cook venison until it is lightly browned on both sides. Remove from skillet, and set aside.

Gradually stir about ½ cup water into ⅓ cup flour; mix until smooth, and add the remaining water. Stir flour mixture into pan drippings; cook over medium heat, stirring constantly, until thickened. Stir in bouquet sauce, ½ teaspoon salt, and ⅛ teaspoon pepper.

Return venison and garlic to skillet; reduce heat. Cover and simmer 30 minutes. Add onion; cover and simmer 15 minutes. Add mushrooms; cover and simmer 15 minutes. Serve over rice. Yield: 6 servings.

PEANUT BUTTER BARBECUE SAUCE

¼ cup butter
1 teaspoon celery seeds
1 teaspoon salt
1 teaspoon pepper
1 tablespoon creamy peanut butter
½ cup vinegar
Juice of 1 lime

Melt butter in a small saucepan over low heat. Add celery seeds, salt, and pepper; mix well. Stir in the peanut butter, vinegar, and lime juice; simmer 20 minutes, stirring mixture occasionally. Yield: about ½ cup.

MAKE-AHEAD CHEESECAKE PIE

3¾ cups graham cracker crumbs
¾ cup sugar
¾ cup butter or margarine, melted
5 (8-ounce) packages cream cheese,
   softened
1¾ cups sugar
3 tablespoons all-purpose flour
1½ teaspoons grated lemon rind
1½ teaspoons grated orange rind
1 teaspoon grated lime rind
¼ teaspoon vanilla extract
5 eggs
2 egg yolks
¼ cup whipping cream
Fresh strawberries (optional)
Frozen whipped topping, thawed
   (optional)

Combine graham cracker crumbs, ¾ cup sugar, and butter; stir well. Press mixture into three 9-inch pieplates.

Beat cream cheese until soft and creamy. Gradually add 1¾ cups sugar, beating until fluffy. Add flour, citrus rind, and vanilla; mix well. Add eggs and yolks, one at a time, beating well after each addition. Stir in whipping cream.

Pour filling into crusts; bake at 400° for 5 minutes. Reduce heat to 250°, and bake 30 minutes or until set. Cool; two of the cooled cheesecakes may be covered with plastic wrap and frozen. Chill remaining cheesecake for 8 hours or overnight.

Top cheesecake with strawberries and dollops of whipped topping before serving, if desired. Yield: three 9-inch pies.

REAL ITALIAN SPAGHETTI

½ pound ground beef
½ pound Italian sausage
1 (15-ounce) can tomato sauce
1 (6-ounce) can tomato paste
1 (16-ounce) can whole tomatoes, drained
1 large onion, chopped
3 large green peppers, chopped
1 (4½-ounce) jar whole mushrooms,
   drained
1½ teaspoons chopped fresh parsley
1 teaspoon dried whole thyme
1 teaspoon cumin seeds
1 teaspoon dried whole basil
¾ teaspoon ground oregano
½ teaspoon chili powder
¼ teaspoon ground turmeric
3 tablespoons garlic powder, divided
1 cup (4 ounces) shredded mozzarella
   cheese
1 (7-ounce) package thin spaghetti
Grated Parmesan cheese (optional)

Cook ground beef and sausage over medium heat until browned, stirring to crumble; drain off drippings. Stir in next 13 ingredients. Add 1 tablespoon garlic powder, stirring well. Cover and simmer 20 minutes. Stir in an additional tablespoon of garlic powder; cover and simmer 15 minutes. Add remaining garlic powder and mozzarella cheese, stirring well. Cover sauce and simmer 15 additional minutes.

Prepare spaghetti according to package directions. Serve sauce over spaghetti. Sprinkle with Parmesan cheese, if desired. Yield: 6 servings.

Erett Falkie,
Marion, Virginia.

PARMESAN ZUCCHINI

1 (12-ounce) can tomato paste
1½ cups water
2 tablespoons minced fresh basil
½ teaspoon dried whole oregano
1 clove garlic, crushed
1 bay leaf
¾ cup wheat germ
¾ cup sesame seeds
2 to 3 medium zucchini, sliced
2 eggs, beaten
Sunflower or vegetable oil
1 green pepper, chopped
2 onions, sliced and separated into rings
½ cup grated Parmesan cheese
½ pound (about 8 slices) thinly sliced
   mozzarella cheese

Combine first 6 ingredients in a saucepan; simmer, uncovered, 10 minutes. Discard bay leaf, and set sauce aside.

Combine wheat germ and sesame seeds. Dip zucchini slices in egg; then coat with wheat germ mixture. Cook in small amount of hot oil until browned.

Layer half each of zucchini, green pepper, and onion in a greased 9-inch square pan; top with half each of the tomato sauce, Parmesan cheese, and mozzarella cheese. Repeat layers. Bake at 375° for 20 minutes. Let stand 10 minutes before cutting. Yield: 6 to 8 servings.   *William Reid,*
Raleigh, North Carolina.

Pork Chops Make Meaty Meals

Everybody knows how good pork chops can taste. And they can taste even better by enhancing their flavor with sauces and seasonings.

Soy sauce and brown sugar form the marinade for Oven-Barbecued Pork Chops; before baking, they are coated with a tangy mixture of catsup and chili sauce. And Orange-Glazed Pork Chops gets its name from pork chops simmering in a simple orange juice and marmalade sauce.

When selecting fresh pork chops, look for those that have a delicate rose or grayish pink color. Remember to store the meat in the coldest part of the refrigerator and prepare it within one or two days after purchase. For freezer storage, the pork chops should be securely wrapped and frozen for a maximum period of three to six months.

APPLE-CRUMB STUFFED PORK CHOPS

4 (1-inch-thick) pork chops, cut with
   pockets
Apple-Crumb Stuffing
Salt and pepper to taste
1 tablespoon butter or margarine
3 tablespoons water

Stuff pockets of pork chops with Apple-Crumb Stuffing, and secure with wooden picks. Sprinkle pork chops with salt and pepper.

Melt butter in a large, heavy skillet; brown pork chops on both sides. Add water; reduce heat. Cover and simmer 50 to 55 minutes or until pork chops are tender. Yield: 4 servings.

Apple-Crumb Stuffing:

1 cup soft breadcrumbs
½ cup diced apple
3 tablespoons minced onion
3 tablespoons raisins, chopped
½ teaspoon salt
½ teaspoon sugar
Pinch of pepper
Pinch of ground sage
1½ tablespoons butter or margarine,
   melted

Combine all ingredients; mix well. Yield: about 1¾ cups.
Mrs. Sidney I. McGrath,
Hopkinsville, Kentucky.

ORANGE-GLAZED PORK CHOPS

4 (¾-inch-thick) pork chops
Salt and pepper to taste
All-purpose flour
1 tablespoon vegetable oil
½ cup orange juice
2 tablespoons orange marmalade
2 tablespoons brown sugar
1 tablespoon vinegar

Sprinkle pork chops lightly with salt and pepper; dredge in flour.

Heat oil in a heavy skillet; brown pork chops on both sides. Combine remaining ingredients, mixing well; pour over pork chops. Reduce heat; cover and simmer 40 to 45 minutes. Yield: 4 servings.   *Mrs. Russell Spear,*
Hilliard, Florida.

OVEN-BARBECUED PORK CHOPS

2 cups soy sauce
1 cup water
½ cup firmly packed brown sugar
1 tablespoon molasses
1 teaspoon salt
6 (¾- to 1-inch-thick) pork chops
1 tablespoon dry mustard
½ cup firmly packed brown sugar
⅓ cup water
1 (14-ounce) bottle catsup
1 (12-ounce) bottle chili sauce

Combine first 5 ingredients in a large shallow container; mix well. Add pork chops, and turn once to coat; cover container, and marinate overnight.

Remove pork chops from marinade, reserving marinade for use with other meat recipes. Place pork chops in a 13- x 9- x 2-inch baking pan. Cover and bake at 350° for 1½ hours.

Combine remaining ingredients in a heavy saucepan; bring to a boil, stirring constantly. Pour over pork chops; bake, uncovered, an additional 20 to 25 minutes. Yield: 6 servings.

Note: Any remaining sauce may be stored in the refrigerator and used later with other recipes.   *Mina DeKraker,*
Holland, Michigan.

PORK CHOPS RISOTTI

¾ cup uncooked brown rice
1 (10½-ounce) can beef broth, undiluted
¼ cup water
2 medium carrots, peeled and diagonally
   sliced
½ cup thinly sliced onion
½ cup Sauterne or other dry white wine
½ teaspoon salt
Dash of pepper
¼ teaspoon ground marjoram
⅛ teaspoon ground oregano
1 tablespoon vegetable oil
4 (½-inch-thick) pork chops

Combine rice, broth, and water in a heavy saucepan; bring to a boil. Reduce heat; cover and simmer 50 minutes or until rice is done. Add carrots, onion, wine, and seasonings; mix thoroughly. Spoon rice mixture into a lightly greased 12- x 8- x 2-inch baking dish; set aside.

Heat oil in a skillet; brown pork chops on both sides. Drain well; arrange on top of rice mixture. Cover and bake at 350° for 1 hour. Yield: 4 servings.   *Mrs. Ralph E. Chase,*
Hendersonville, North Carolina.

PEPPERED PORK CHOP CASSEROLE

6 (½-inch-thick) pork chops
Salt and pepper to taste
2 medium-size green peppers, cut into ¼-inch rings
1½ cups uncooked regular rice
2 (8-ounce) cans tomato sauce
1 cup water
½ cup chopped onion
1 teaspoon salt
¼ teaspoon pepper

Sprinkle pork chops with salt and pepper, and arrange in a lightly greased 13- x 9- x 2-inch baking dish. Top each pork chop with one green pepper ring; spoon rice into and around pepper rings.

Chop remaining green pepper rings; stir in remaining ingredients, and pour mixture over rice. Cover and bake at 350° for 55 to 60 minutes or until done. Yield: 6 servings.
*Cindy Murphy,
Cleveland, Tennessee.*

You'll Win With These Appetizers

When the football season is in full swing, so are parties before and after the game. If you're planning a party to honor your favorite team, serve our collection of appetizers, and you'll be the real winner. Just provide an assortment of crackers and chips, or serve raw vegetables with Superb Crab Spread and Deviled Cream Cheese Spread. Most of these appetizers can be made ahead and chilled until serving time; only South-of-the-Border Dip has to bake before serving, but we found it to be well worth the effort.

CHICKEN LIVER PATE

¾ pound chicken livers
¾ cup butter or margarine, softened
3 tablespoons minced onion
1 teaspoon dry mustard
¼ teaspoon salt
¼ teaspoon ground nutmeg
¼ teaspoon anchovy paste
Dash of red pepper
Dash of ground cloves

Cook chicken livers in a small amount of boiling water about 5 minutes or

until tender; drain well. Place livers in container of food processor; process with metal blade until smooth. Add remaining ingredients; process until combined. Spoon mixture into an oiled 1½-cup mold; chill several hours or overnight. Invert onto platter, and serve with crackers. Yield: 1½ cups.
*Cherie L. Pentecost,
Gulfport, Mississippi.*

SUPERB CRAB SPREAD

1 (8-ounce) package cream cheese, softened
½ cup mayonnaise
½ cup (2 ounces) shredded Cheddar cheese
1 teaspoon garlic salt
1 teaspoon Worcestershire sauce
¼ teaspoon pepper
1 (6-ounce) package frozen crabmeat, thawed and drained

Combine cream cheese and mayonnaise; beat until creamy, using an electric mixer or food processor. Stir in remaining ingredients. Serve with crackers or vegetables. Yield: 2 cups.
*Tilly W. Mizzell,
Charleston, South Carolina.*

DEVILED CREAM CHEESE SPREAD

1 (3-ounce) package cream cheese, softened
1 (2¼-ounce) can deviled ham
1½ to 2 tablespoons commercial Thousand Island dressing
1 teaspoon lemon juice
1 teaspoon dried parsley flakes
1 tablespoon minced onion
2 drops of hot sauce
Dash of garlic powder

Combine all ingredients, mixing well. Serve with crackers, or use to stuff celery. Yield: about ¾ cup.
*Patsy M. Smith,
Lampasas, Texas.*

SOUTH-OF-THE-BORDER DIP

2 (16-ounce) cans refried beans
1 (1.25-ounce) package taco seasoning mix
1 (16-ounce) carton commercial sour cream
2 cups (8 ounces) shredded Cheddar cheese

Combine refried beans and taco seasoning mix; spoon mixture into a 12- x 8- x 2-inch baking dish. Spread sour cream over bean mixture, and top with cheese. Bake at 350° for 30 minutes. Serve hot with corn chips or tortilla chips. Yield: about 5½ cups.
*Sue Smith,
Rockport, Texas.*

PARTY PECAN CHEESE BALL

1 (8-ounce) package cream cheese, softened
1 (2-ounce) package blue cheese, crumbled
1 cup (4 ounces) shredded extra-sharp Cheddar cheese
1½ teaspoons Worcestershire sauce
½ teaspoon red pepper
¼ teaspoon salt
¼ teaspoon garlic powder
¼ teaspoon onion powder
½ cup finely chopped pecans, divided

Combine all ingredients except ¼ cup pecans; mix well. Shape into a ball, and coat with remaining pecans. Yield: 1 cheese ball.
*Kathryn Elmore,
Demopolis, Alabama.*

Ladle Up The Soup

Celebrate the beginning of cooler weather with one of these hot and hearty soups. Either can be mixed up in minutes with ingredients you'll likely have on hand. Just add a sandwich or salad to complete the meal.

HOT BROCCOLI SOUP

1 (10-ounce) package frozen chopped broccoli
1 (10¾-ounce) can cream of mushroom soup, undiluted
1½ cups milk
2 tablespoons butter or margarine
¼ teaspoon dried whole tarragon, crushed
Dash of pepper

Cook broccoli according to package directions in a large saucepan; drain well. Add remaining ingredients. Cook over medium heat, stirring constantly, until thoroughly heated. Yield: about 1 quart.
*Mary Pappas,
Richmond, Virginia.*

TOMATO SOUP

1 tablespoon butter or margarine
¼ cup finely chopped celery
2 tablespoons chopped onion
1 (8-ounce) can stewed tomatoes, undrained
1 cup water
¼ cup dry white wine
1 chicken-flavored bouillon cube
2 slices bacon, cooked, drained, and crumbled

Melt butter in a 1-quart saucepan; add celery and onion. Sauté over low heat until onion is tender. Add tomatoes, water, wine, and bouillon cube, stirring well; heat to boiling. Reduce heat and simmer 15 minutes, stirring occasionally. Spoon soup into serving bowls; top with bacon. Yield: about 2 cups.
Alice McNamara, Eucha, Oklahoma.

Make The Most With Oats

Mention oatmeal, and visions of homemade cookies or hot cereal come to mind. Yet this cereal has a lot more to offer. Its flavor and whole-grain goodness can be enjoyed in a number of dishes, including muffins and a meat loaf.

Oatmeal can stretch meat loaf inexpensively. In our Cheeseburger Loaf, for example, 2 pounds of ground beef mixed with oats are layered with Cheddar cheese for 8 to 10 servings. And for dessert, our not-so-sweet Oatmeal Bread and our lemon-flavored oatmeal cookies are an inviting change of pace.

CHEESEBURGER LOAF

2 pounds ground beef
1 (1⅜-ounce) envelope onion soup mix
½ cup quick-cooking oats, uncooked
⅛ teaspoon pepper
1 egg, beaten
½ cup milk
½ pound Cheddar cheese, sliced
¼ cup chili sauce
½ teaspoon dry mustard

Combine first 6 ingredients in a large mixing bowl; mix well. Pack half of meat mixture into a 9- x 5- x 3-inch loafpan. Place cheese slices on top of meat mixture. Spoon remaining meat mixture over cheese, covering cheese layer and pressing lightly on sides to seal; set aside.

Combine chili sauce and mustard; mix well. Spread sauce mixture over top of loaf. Bake at 350° for 1 hour and 20 minutes. Yield: 8 to 10 servings.
Linda Jones, Austin, Texas.

OATMEAL BREAD

1½ cups boiling water
1 cup quick-cooking oats, uncooked
½ cup butter or margarine, softened
1 cup sugar
1 cup firmly packed brown sugar
2 eggs
1 teaspoon vanilla extract
1¾ cups all-purpose flour
1 teaspoon soda
½ teaspoon salt
1 teaspoon ground cinnamon

Pour boiling water over oats; set aside. Cream butter; gradually add sugar, beating well. Add eggs, one at a time, beating well after each. Add vanilla; beat well. Combine flour, soda, salt, and cinnamon; gradually add to creamed mixture, beating well. Stir in oats mixture.

Spoon batter into a greased and floured 9- x 5- x 3-inch loafpan. Bake at 350° for 1 hour or until bread tests done. Let cool in pan 10 minutes. Remove to wire rack, and cool. Yield: 1 loaf.
Mary Dishon, Stanford, Kentucky.

OATMEAL BRAN MUFFINS

¾ cup quick-cooking oats, uncooked
¼ cup bran
½ cup all-purpose flour
½ cup whole wheat flour
1 teaspoon baking powder
½ teaspoon soda
1 teaspoon salt
⅓ cup shortening
⅓ cup firmly packed brown sugar
1 egg
1 cup buttermilk

Combine first 7 ingredients, stirring well; set aside.

Cream shortening; gradually add sugar, beating well. Add egg and beat well. Add oats mixture to creamed mixture alternately with buttermilk, beginning and ending with oats mixture; stir just until moistened. Spoon into greased muffin pans, filling three-fourths full. Bake at 400° for 20 to 25 minutes. Yield: about 1 dozen. *Karen Fulghum, Chattanooga, Tennessee.*

SPECIAL OATMEAL COOKIES

1½ cups all-purpose flour
1 teaspoon soda
1 teaspoon salt
2 teaspoons ground cinnamon
½ teaspoon ground nutmeg
1 cup shortening
1 cup sugar
1 cup firmly packed brown sugar
2 eggs
1 teaspoon lemon extract
3 cups quick-cooking oats, uncooked
1 cup chopped pecans

Combine first 5 ingredients; set aside.

Cream shortening and sugar until light and fluffy; beat in eggs and lemon extract. Add flour mixture, mixing well. Stir in oats and pecans.

Shape dough into 1-inch balls, and place on lightly greased cookie sheets. Bake at 350° for 10 to 12 minutes. Yield: 5 dozen. *Kathryn Elmore, Demopolis, Alabama.*

Celebrate Autumn With A Picnic

Autumn brings a cool breeze to Southern days and paints the countryside with rich, warm hues. This relaxed season is a perfect time to pack a picnic and move outdoors. Whether you head for the woods or just to your backyard, we think you'll enjoy this special picnic menu, which is easy to prepare and easy to transport.

Golden Chicken Nuggets
Sweet-and-Sour Slaw
Stuffed Cucumbers
Peanut Butter Snaps
Orange Sangría

GOLDEN CHICKEN NUGGETS

6 whole chicken breasts, skinned and
   boned
1 cup all-purpose flour
1½ teaspoons salt
1 tablespoon plus 1 teaspoon sesame seeds
2 eggs, slightly beaten
1 cup water
Vegetable oil

Cut chicken into 1- x 1½-inch pieces; set aside. Combine next 5 ingredients. Dip chicken into batter, and fry in hot oil (375°) until golden brown. Drain on paper towels. Yield: 8 to 10 servings.
*Rene Ralph,
Newkirk, Oklahoma.*

SWEET-AND-SOUR SLAW

1 large head cabbage, coarsely shredded
1 green pepper, finely chopped
1 medium onion, finely chopped
1 cup sugar
1 cup vinegar
¾ cup vegetable oil
1 tablespoon salt
1 teaspoon celery salt
1 teaspoon mustard seeds

Combine shredded cabbage, green pepper, and onion in a large bowl. Sprinkle with sugar.

Combine remaining ingredients in a small saucepan; bring to a boil. Pour over cabbage mixture; cover and refrigerate at least 4 hours. Toss just before serving. Yield: about 8 servings.
*Mrs. James L. Twilley,
Macon, Georgia.*

STUFFED CUCUMBERS

2 medium cucumbers
1 (3-ounce) package cream cheese,
   softened
1 (2¼-ounce) can deviled ham

Peel cucumbers and cut in half lengthwise; scoop out seeds.

Combine cream cheese and deviled ham; beat until smooth. Spoon into cucumber halves; cover and refrigerate 3 to 4 hours.

Cut each cucumber half in half lengthwise; cut crosswise into quarters. Chill. Yield: 32 pieces.
*Florence L. Costello,
Chattanooga, Tennessee.*

PEANUT BUTTER SNAPS

1 cup butter or margarine, softened
1 cup sugar
1 cup firmly packed brown sugar
2 eggs
2⅔ cups all-purpose flour
2 teaspoons soda
½ teaspoon salt
⅔ cup peanut butter
2 teaspoons vanilla extract
Additional sugar

Cream butter; gradually add sugar, beating until light and fluffy. Add eggs, mixing well.

Combine flour, soda, and salt. Add to creamed mixture; beat until smooth. Stir in peanut butter and vanilla; chill 1 to 2 hours. Shape into 1-inch balls; roll in additional sugar. Place on ungreased baking sheets; bake at 375° for 10 minutes. Let cool slightly before removing from baking sheets. Yield: about 7 dozen.
*Kathy Christensen,
Martinez, Georgia.*

ORANGE SANGRIA

1 orange
¼ cup sugar
2 cups orange juice
1 (25.4-ounce) bottle Burgundy or other
   dry red wine, chilled
½ cup Triple Sec or other orange-flavored
   liqueur

Slice orange in half. Cut one half into 3 or 4 slices; quarter each slice, and reserve for garnish.

Carefully cut off the thin outer peel of the remaining orange half with a vegetable peeler. Combine orange peel and sugar in a large bowl; mash peel with a spoon. Stir in remaining ingredients. Cover and chill for 15 minutes. Remove peel. Serve sangría over ice, and garnish with quartered orange slices. Yield: 6 to 8 servings.
*Flo Kikkman,
Balch Springs, Texas.*

Sheet Cakes: Easy To Bake, Easy To Serve

Sheet cakes are popular with busy Southern cooks for some very good reasons. For one, there are no layers to stack, and you can frost them right in the pan—and serve them from the pan. Also, sheet cakes are easy to pack and carry for a picnic or pot-luck supper. But as these recipes show, you don't sacrifice flavor to convenience.

QUEEN BEE CAKE

1 cup boiling water
1 cup dates, chopped
1 teaspoon soda
¼ cup butter or margarine, softened
1 cup sugar
1 egg
1 teaspoon vanilla extract
1⅓ cups all-purpose flour
1 teaspoon baking powder
¼ teaspoon salt
½ cup chopped pecans or walnuts
Topping (recipe follows)
Frozen whipped topping, thawed
   (optional)
Maraschino cherries with stems (optional)

Pour boiling water over dates; stir in soda. Set aside to cool.

Cream butter; gradually add sugar, beating well. Add egg and vanilla; mix well. Combine dry ingredients; add to creamed mixture alternately with date mixture. Stir in pecans. Pour into a greased and floured 13- x 9- x 2-inch baking pan; bake at 350° for 30 minutes or until a wooden pick inserted in center comes out clean.

Spread topping over warm cake; cut into squares. Garnish each with a dollop of whipped topping and a cherry, if desired. Yield: 15 servings.

Topping:

½ cup plus 2 tablespoons firmly packed
   dark brown sugar
½ cup plus 2 tablespoons whipping cream
½ cup butter or margarine
2 cups flaked coconut
1 cup chopped pecans or walnuts

Combine first 3 ingredients in a heavy saucepan; bring to a boil and cook 4 to 5 minutes, stirring constantly. Stir in coconut and pecans; spread over warm cake. Yield: enough for one sheet cake.
*Mrs. Walter H. Miller,
Birmingham, Alabama.*

COLA CAKE

2 cups all-purpose flour
2 cups sugar
1 teaspoon soda
1 cup cola-flavored carbonated beverage
1 cup butter or margarine
2 tablespoons cocoa
½ cup buttermilk
2 eggs, beaten
1 teaspoon vanilla extract
1½ cups miniature marshmallows
Cola Frosting
1 cup finely chopped pecans or walnuts

Combine flour, sugar, and soda; mix well, and set aside.

Combine cola, butter, and cocoa in a heavy saucepan; bring to a boil, stirring constantly. Gradually stir into flour mixture. Stir in buttermilk, eggs, vanilla, and marshmallows. Pour into a greased and floured 13- x 9- x 2-inch baking pan; bake at 350° for 30 to 35 minutes or until a wooden pick inserted in center comes out clean. Spread Cola Frosting over warm cake; sprinkle with pecans. Yield: 15 servings.

Cola Frosting:

½ cup butter or margarine
¼ cup plus 2 tablespoons cola-flavored carbonated beverage
3 tablespoons cocoa
1 (16-ounce) package powdered sugar, sifted
1 teaspoon vanilla extract

Combine butter, cola, and cocoa in a heavy saucepan; bring to a boil, stirring constantly. Remove from heat; stir in sugar and vanilla. Yield: enough for one sheet cake.   *Dorothy Whitman, West Columbia, South Carolina.*

CHOCOLATE CANDY CAKE

2 cups all-purpose flour
2 cups sugar
1 teaspoon soda
1 cup water
1 cup butter or margarine
¼ cup cocoa
½ cup buttermilk
2 eggs, slightly beaten
1 teaspoon vanilla extract
Chocolate Candy Frosting

Combine flour, sugar, and soda; mix well, and set aside.

Combine water, butter, and cocoa in a heavy saucepan; bring to a boil, stirring constantly. Gradually stir into flour mixture. Stir in buttermilk, eggs, and vanilla. Pour into a greased and floured 13- x 9- x 2-inch baking pan; bake at 350° for 30 minutes or until a wooden pick inserted in center comes out clean. While warm, prick cake surface at 1-inch intervals with a meat fork; spread with Chocolate Candy Frosting. Yield: 15 servings.

Chocolate Candy Frosting:

½ cup butter or margarine
¼ cup plus 2 tablespoons evaporated milk
¼ cup cocoa
1 (16-ounce) package powdered sugar, sifted
1 teaspoon vanilla extract
½ cup chopped pecans or walnuts

Combine butter, milk, and cocoa in a heavy saucepan; bring to a boil, stirring constantly. Stir in sugar; return to a boil, stirring constantly. Immediately remove from heat. Add vanilla and pecans; stir constantly 3 to 5 minutes or until frosting begins to lose its gloss. Yield: enough for one sheet cake.
Mrs. Walter Reese, Birmingham, Alabama.

NUTMEG FEATHER CAKE

¼ cup butter or margarine, softened
¼ cup shortening
1½ cups sugar
3 eggs
2 cups all-purpose flour
1 teaspoon baking powder
1 teaspoon soda
2 teaspoons ground nutmeg
¼ teaspoon salt
1 cup buttermilk
½ teaspoon vanilla extract
¼ cup plus 2 tablespoons butter or margarine, softened
⅔ cup firmly packed brown sugar
1 cup flaked coconut
¼ cup whipping cream
½ teaspoon vanilla extract

Cream ¼ cup butter and shortening; gradually add sugar, beating until light and fluffy. Add eggs, one at a time, beating well after each addition.

Combine flour, baking powder, soda, nutmeg, and salt; add to creamed mixture alternately with buttermilk, beginning and ending with flour mixture. Stir in ½ teaspoon vanilla. Pour into a greased and floured 13- x 9- x 2-inch baking pan; bake at 350° for 30 to 35 minutes or until a wooden pick inserted in center comes out clean. Cool.

Combine remaining ingredients; mix well. Spread on cake; broil 2 to 3 minutes or until golden brown. Yield: 15 servings.
Mrs. Roger Williams, Arden, North Carolina.

QUICK CHERRY CAKE

1 (18.5-ounce) package regular yellow cake mix
1 (16-ounce) can pitted tart red cherries
¼ cup sugar
2 teaspoons cornstarch
⅓ cup water
½ teaspoon almond extract

Prepare cake mix according to package directions; pour batter into a greased and floured 13- x 9- x 2-inch baking pan.

Drain cherries, reserving liquid; place cherries on top of batter. Bake at 350° for 35 to 40 minutes or until wooden pick inserted in center comes out clean.

Combine sugar and cornstarch in a small saucepan; stir well. Add cherry liquid and water; cook over medium heat, stirring constantly, until smooth and thickened. Stir in almond extract. Serve warm sauce over cake. Yield: 15 servings.   *Mrs. Edward E. Woodruff, Charlottesville, Virginia.*

Rally Game Spirit With This Menu

Nothing adds more to the fun of a football game than gathering with family and friends for a meal before the game. Whether served from your car at the stadium or buffet style in your home, this colorful menu will be as popular as your favorite team.

**Imperial Chicken
Marinated Vegetables
Tomato-Cucumber-Onion Salad
Marble Chocolate Chip Cupcakes
Iced Tea**

IMPERIAL CHICKEN

½ cup plus 2 tablespoons butter or margarine, melted
1 small clove garlic, crushed
¾ cup dry breadcrumbs
½ cup grated Parmesan cheese
1½ tablespoons minced parsley
1 teaspoon salt
Pepper to taste
3 whole chicken breasts, split, boned, and skinned
Juice of 1 lemon
Paprika

Combine butter and garlic; set aside. Combine breadcrumbs, cheese, parsley, salt, and pepper; stir well. Dip each chicken breast in butter mixture, and coat with breadcrumb mixture; roll tightly, starting at narrow end, and secure with a wooden pick. Arrange rolls in a shallow baking pan; drizzle with remaining butter and lemon juice. Sprinkle with paprika. Bake at 350° for 45 to 55 minutes. Yield: 6 servings.

Mrs. Dale Taylor,
Beaverdam, Virginia.

MARINATED VEGETABLES

1 (17-ounce) can small English peas, drained
1 (17-ounce) can white shoe peg corn, drained
1 (15½-ounce) can French-style green beans, drained
1 (2-ounce) jar diced pimiento, drained
½ cup diced celery
½ to 1 cup chopped onion
½ cup chopped green pepper
1 cup sugar
1 teaspoon salt
½ teaspoon pepper
½ cup vegetable oil
¾ cup vinegar

Combine vegetables, tossing lightly. Combine remaining ingredients in a medium saucepan; bring to a boil over low heat, stirring occasionally. Pour over vegetables, stirring gently to blend well. Cover and refrigerate 24 hours. Yield: 6 to 8 servings. *Mrs. Roger L. Grace,*
White Plains, Kentucky.

TOMATO-CUCUMBER-ONION SALAD

2 tablespoons vegetable oil
1 tablespoon vinegar
1 tablespoon sugar
½ teaspoon salt
¼ teaspoon pepper
1 teaspoon minced parsley
1 medium cucumber, peeled and thinly sliced
2 medium tomatoes, sliced
1 large onion, sliced and separated into rings

Combine first 6 ingredients in a jar; shake well. Pour marinade over vegetables; refrigerate 2 hours before serving. Yield: 4 servings. *Mary Ann Turk,*
Joplin, Missouri.

MARBLE CHOCOLATE CHIP CUPCAKES

1 (8-ounce) package cream cheese, softened
1½ cups sugar, divided
1 egg, slightly beaten
⅛ teaspoon salt
1 (6-ounce) package semisweet chocolate morsels
1½ cups all-purpose flour
1 teaspoon soda
½ teaspoon salt
¼ cup cocoa
1 cup water
½ cup vegetable oil
1 tablespoon vinegar
1 teaspoon vanilla extract

Combine cream cheese and ½ cup sugar; beat until smooth. Add egg, ⅛ teaspoon salt, and chocolate morsels, stirring well. Set aside.

Combine flour, remaining 1 cup sugar, soda, ½ teaspoon salt, and cocoa; stir until blended. Add water, oil, vinegar, and vanilla; stir until batter is smooth. Spoon batter into paper-lined muffin pans, filling half full. Spoon a tablespoonful of cream cheese mixture into center of each cupcake. Bake at 350° for 25 to 30 minutes or until cupcakes test done. Yield: 1½ dozen cupcakes. *Mrs. Jack O'Bryan,*
Moberly, Missouri.

Look What's Gotten Into Vegetables

Mushrooms, green peppers, and acorn squash are natural containers for a variety of stuffings. After tasting these stuffed vegetables, you'll agree that flavor is what's gotten into them.

HAM-STUFFED ACORN SQUASH

2 medium acorn squash
2 tablespoons butter or margarine
½ cup chopped celery
⅓ cup chopped onion
1½ cups chopped cooked ham
2 tablespoons light brown sugar
⅛ teaspoon ground allspice

Cut squash in half lengthwise, and remove seeds. Place cut side down in a greased baking dish; add ½ inch water. Cover and bake at 350° for 30 minutes. Melt butter in a small saucepan. Add celery and onion; cook until tender. Add ham, sugar, and allspice; stir well. Cook over medium heat until thoroughly heated. Stuff squash with ham mixture. Cover and bake at 350° for 15 minutes. Remove cover, and bake an additional 15 minutes. Yield: 4 servings. *Mrs. James Barden,*
Suffolk, Virginia.

STUFFED PEPPERS

6 large green peppers
1 pound ground beef
1 large onion, minced
1 clove garlic, minced
3 tomatoes, peeled and chopped
1 teaspoon Worcestershire sauce
½ teaspoon ground allspice
1 teaspoon salt
¼ teaspoon pepper
1 cup bread cubes or cooked rice
½ cup buttered breadcrumbs

Cut off top of each green pepper; remove seeds. Cover peppers in boiling salted water, and cook 5 minutes; drain.

Cook beef, onion, and garlic in skillet over medium heat, stirring to crumble meat. Add tomatoes; simmer 10 minutes. Add remaining ingredients except breadcrumbs, and stir well. Stuff peppers with beef mixture, and place in a shallow baking dish. Top with breadcrumbs. Bake at 350° for 25 minutes. Yield: 6 servings. *Mrs. Carlton James,*
New Orleans, Louisiana.

STUFFED MUSHROOMS

1 pound fresh medium mushrooms
¼ cup butter or margarine
¼ cup chopped onion
¼ cup chopped celery
1 teaspoon Worcestershire sauce
½ teaspoon salt
⅛ teaspoon pepper
Melted butter or margarine
¼ cup (1 ounce) shredded process American cheese

Clean mushrooms with damp paper towels. Remove stems and chop, reserving caps. Melt ¼ cup butter in a skillet; add onion, celery, and mushroom stems. Sauté until celery is tender. Stir in Worcestershire sauce and seasonings.

Brush mushroom caps with melted butter; fill with mixture. Arrange mushrooms in a greased baking dish; sprinkle with cheese. Bake at 350° for 15 minutes or until cheese is melted. Yield: 4 servings. *Mrs. W. P. Chambers,*
Louisville, Kentucky.

Build A Sandwich For Lunch

These recipes prove that a sandwich lunch can be as satisfying as any meal. For our Chicken-Almond Pocket Sandwiches, rounds of pocket bread are cut in half and stuffed with shredded lettuce, alfalfa sprouts, and yogurt-flavored chicken filling.

Equally satisfying are Eggs-Tra Special Sandwiches, a combination of chopped bologna, hard-cooked eggs, and celery that's spread on onion rolls. And in our version of those hearty, classic Reubens, the sandwiches are broiled rather than grilled.

BROILED REUBEN SANDWICHES

½ cup mayonnaise
1 tablespoon chili sauce
About 3 tablespoons butter or margarine, softened
12 slices rye bread
6 slices Swiss cheese
2 (4-ounce) packages thinly sliced
   corned beef
1 (16-ounce) can sauerkraut, well drained

Combine mayonnaise and chili sauce, stirring well.

Spread butter on one side of each slice of bread; spread other side with mayonnaise mixture. Arrange cheese, corned beef, and sauerkraut on mayonnaise side of 6 bread slices. Top with remaining bread, buttered side out.

Place sandwiches on a cookie sheet, and broil each side until browned. Yield: 6 servings. *Mrs. Ron Bain, Nashville, Tennessee.*

CHICKEN-ALMOND POCKET SANDWICHES

3 cups cubed cooked chicken
½ cup plain yogurt
½ cup chopped toasted almonds
1½ tablespoons lemon juice
½ teaspoon salt
¼ teaspoon pepper
⅛ teaspoon dried dillweed
4 (6-inch) pocket bread rounds
2 cups shredded lettuce
1 cup alfalfa sprouts

Combine first 7 ingredients, mixing well; set aside.

Cut bread rounds in half; fill each about half full with lettuce and alfalfa sprouts. Spoon in chicken mixture. Chill at least 1 hour. Yield: 8 sandwiches. *Martha Edington, Oak Ridge, Tennessee.*

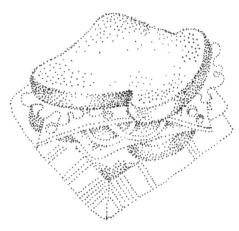

TEMPTING TWOSOME

1 (3-ounce) package cream cheese, softened
2 tablespoons sliced green onion
1 tablespoon soy sauce
1 tablespoon dry sherry
About 3 tablespoons butter or margarine, softened
12 slices rye bread
Lettuce leaves
2 (3-ounce) packages thinly sliced
   roast beef
4 (3-ounce) packages thinly sliced
   smoked pork

Combine cream cheese, onion, soy sauce, and sherry; mix well.

Spread butter on one side of each slice of bread; spread cream cheese mixture over butter. On 6 bread slices, arrange lettuce, roast beef, and pork evenly over cream cheese mixture. Top with remaining bread. Yield: 6 servings. *Mrs. Parke LaGourgue Cory, Neosho, Missouri.*

EGGS-TRA SPECIAL SANDWICHES

4 slices bologna, chopped
4 hard-cooked eggs, chopped
1 stalk celery, chopped
¼ cup sweet pickle relish, drained
¼ cup mayonnaise
1 teaspoon instant minced onion
Leaf lettuce
4 onion rolls, split horizontally

Combine first 6 ingredients, stirring well. Chill. Arrange lettuce on bottom half of each onion roll; top with filling, and cover with roll top. Yield: 4 servings. *Peggy Fowler Revels, Woodruff, South Carolina.*

The Best Stir-Fried Steak

When you get out the wok, cook something special. And special is exactly how to describe Pepper Stir-Fry Steak—thinly sliced steak, broccoli, green pepper, and onion stir-fried in a sherry and soy sauce mixture.

PEPPER STIR-FRY STEAK

2 pounds sirloin steak
½ cup soy sauce
2 tablespoons sherry
3 cloves garlic
1 bunch fresh broccoli
½ cup peanut oil
1 medium-size green pepper, sliced into
   thin strips
2 medium onions, thinly sliced and
   separated into rings
2 tablespoons cornstarch
1 cup water
Hot cooked rice

Partially freeze steak; slice across grain into 3- x ¼-inch strips. Set aside. Combine soy sauce, sherry, and garlic; mix well. Add steak and marinate 30 minutes.

Trim off large outer leaves of broccoli, and remove tough ends of stalks. Wash broccoli thoroughly; cut stalks diagonally into 1-inch pieces. If stalks are more than 1 inch in diameter, cut in half lengthwise. Separate flowerets into small pieces.

Pour oil around top of preheated wok, coating sides; allow to heat at medium high (325°) for 2 minutes. Add broccoli, green pepper, and onion; stir-fry about 2 minutes. Remove vegetables from wok, and set aside.

Add steak and marinade to wok; stir-fry 5 minutes. Combine cornstarch and water, stirring well. Add cornstarch mixture and vegetables to meat; stir-fry over low heat (225°) until mixture becomes thickened and bubbly. Serve over rice. Yield: 8 servings.

Thomas Pittenger, Winchester, Tennessee.

November

November marks the start of festivities that run throughout the holidays, and our fourth annual *Holiday Dinners* special section sports some of our snappiest ways yet to entertain. You will find spirited beverages, delightful appetizers, and side dishes as special as carved potato roses.

In between those heavy holiday meals, our meatless main dishes will save on your food budget and still satisfy your appetite. In fact, one member of our staff snitched a Mock Meatball prior to our formal testing and discussion, and we had a hard time convincing him the meatballs didn't contain meat! They will equally satisfy your cravings.

If you have problems making homemade frosting, you may want to bookmark our story on the topic. Our recipes and tips can make your frosting virtually foolproof!

Cornbread: Break Off A Piece Of Southern Heritage

Mark Twain is said to have once remarked, "The North thinks it knows how to make corn bread, but this is mere superstition."

Surely this crusty bread is as Southern as fried chicken and grits. Even so, the quickest way to stir up a controversy is to ask a group of Southerners how to make it. In some regions of the South yellow cornmeal is used, while in others anything but white is considered an abomination. Then, there are other debates. Should you include sugar? Buttermilk or sweet milk?

Traditionally, cornbread recipes were never written down. They were simply passed by word of mouth in the vaguest terms—a handful of cornmeal, some eggs, a pinch of salt. Today's versions are often varied with the addition of other ingredients, such as cheese and peppers, but the common objective is to make cornbread as mouth-watering as that remembered from childhood.

Just the thought of cornbread conjures up the smell of bacon drippings sizzling in a cast-iron skillet. That familiar aroma signals that supper will soon be on the table, for every Southerner knows you eat cornbread piping hot from the oven. Except, of course, for the leftovers, which go into cornbread dressing or get crumbled up in milk.

Regardless of what kind of cornbread you grew up on, we think you'll want to try these recipes. Some specify yellow cornmeal, others white. You can use either. But, remember, cornmeal mix has the leavening added and should not be substituted for plain cornmeal.

CHEESY BEEF CORNBREAD

1 tablespoon yellow cornmeal
½ pound ground beef
1 cup yellow cornmeal
¾ teaspoon salt
½ teaspoon soda
1 cup milk
1 (17-ounce) can cream-style corn
2 eggs, well beaten
¼ cup vegetable oil
2 cups (8 ounces) shredded hoop cheese
1 large onion, finely chopped
2 to 4 jalapeño peppers, seeded and chopped

Sprinkle 1 tablespoon cornmeal in the bottom of a well-greased 10-inch cast-iron skillet. Cook over medium heat until cornmeal is lightly browned; then set skillet aside.

Cook ground beef until browned, stirring to crumble; drain well, and set aside.

Combine 1 cup cornmeal, salt, and soda; mix well. Add milk, corn, eggs, and oil; mix well. Pour half of batter into prepared skillet; sprinkle with cheese, onion, peppers, and ground beef. Top with remaining batter. Bake at 350° for 50 to 55 minutes. Yield: 6 servings.
Mildred Sherrer,
Bay City, Texas.

QUICK MEXICAN CORNBREAD

1 cup self-rising cornmeal
¼ teaspoon salt
¼ teaspoon red pepper
½ cup chopped onion
½ cup chopped green pepper
½ cup (2 ounces) shredded process American cheese
¼ cup vegetable oil
1 cup milk
2 eggs, beaten
1 (8¾-ounce) can cream-style corn

Combine first 3 ingredients; add remaining ingredients, mixing well. Spoon into a greased 8-inch square baking pan. Bake at 450° for 20 to 25 minutes or until golden. Yield: 6 servings.
Bertha Stutts,
Waynesboro, Tennessee.

LACY CORNCAKES

2 eggs, well beaten
2 cups milk
¼ cup vegetable oil
1⅓ cups yellow cornmeal
¾ teaspoon salt

Combine eggs, milk, and oil, mixing well. Combine cornmeal and salt; stir into egg mixture.

Drop batter by 2 tablespoonfuls onto a hot, lightly greased griddle or skillet. (Stir mixture well each time to prevent cornmeal from settling.) Turn cakes when tops are covered with bubbles and edges look cooked. Serve hot with butter. Yield: about 2½ dozen.
Mrs. B. R. Dasher,
Guyton, Georgia.

SOUTHERN CORN STICKS

1½ cups white cornmeal
3 tablespoons all-purpose flour
1 teaspoon salt
1 tablespoon sugar
1 teaspoon soda
2 cups buttermilk
1 egg, beaten
2 tablespoons melted shortening

Combine first 5 ingredients; mix well. Stir in buttermilk and egg just until dry ingredients are moistened. Stir shortening into batter.

Place a well-greased cast-iron corn-stick pan in a 400° oven for 3 minutes or until hot. Remove from oven; spoon batter into pan, filling two-thirds full. Bake at 450° for 15 minutes or until lightly browned. Yield: about 2½ dozen corn sticks.
Mrs. Bruce Fowler,
Woodruff, South Carolina.

OLD-FASHIONED CORNBREAD

2 cups cornmeal
1 teaspoon soda
1 teaspoon salt
2 eggs, beaten
2 cups buttermilk
¼ cup bacon drippings

Combine cornmeal, soda, and salt; stir in eggs and buttermilk. Heat bacon drippings in an 8-inch cast-iron skillet until very hot. Add drippings to batter and mix well.

Pour batter into hot skillet, and bake at 450° about 25 minutes or until bread is golden brown. Yield: 8 to 10 servings.

OLD SOUTHERN LIGHT CORNBREAD

2 cups yellow cornmeal
1 cup all-purpose flour
½ cup sugar
1 teaspoon soda
1 teaspoon salt
3 tablespoons bacon drippings
2 cups buttermilk

Combine first 5 ingredients; add bacon drippings and buttermilk, mixing well. Pour into a greased 9- x 5- x 3-inch loafpan. Bake at 300° for 1 hour and 10 minutes or until brown. Yield: 1 loaf.
René Harper,
Calvert City, Kentucky.

You'll Never Miss The Meat In These Main Dishes

If hearty holiday meals leave your pocketbook empty, your schedule jumbled, and your appetite yearning for a change, our meatless main dishes may be just what you're looking for. They're protein packed—with enough eggs, cheese, beans, nuts, or pasta to please even the most determined meat and potatoes fan.

Take Mock Meatballs, for example. Full of nuts, cracker crumbs, and cheese, and baked in a spicy tomato sauce, they taste like the real thing.

Or try Cheesy Macaroni-Mushroom Bake. This recipe is a regal version of macaroni and cheese topped with mushroom and tomato slices.

If you are ready for a change, join the growing number of Southerners who frequently go meatless with their meals.

MOCK MEATBALLS

¾ cup cracker crumbs
½ cup (2 ounces) shredded Cheddar
　cheese
½ cup finely chopped walnuts or pecans
1 small onion, finely chopped
2 teaspoons chopped fresh parsley
1 clove garlic, minced
½ teaspoon salt
Pinch of ground sage
2 eggs, beaten
1 tablespoon vegetable oil
1 (32-ounce) jar mushroom-flavored
　spaghetti sauce
Hot cooked spaghetti
Grated Parmesan cheese

Combine first 9 ingredients, mixing well; shape into 1-inch balls. Sauté in a medium skillet in hot oil, turning frequently, until browned; drain. Place meatballs in a shallow 2-quart casserole; pour sauce over top. Cover and bake at 350° for 45 minutes. Serve over spaghetti; top with Parmesan cheese. Yield: 4 servings. *Virginia Mathews, Jacksonville, Florida.*

SPINACH LASAGNA

1 (1½-ounce) package spaghetti sauce mix
1 (6-ounce) can tomato paste
1 (8-ounce) can tomato sauce
1¾ cups water
2 eggs, beaten
1 (16-ounce) carton ricotta or cottage
　cheese
½ teaspoon salt
1 (10-ounce) package frozen chopped
　spinach, thawed and drained
½ cup grated Parmesan cheese, divided
1 (8-ounce) package uncooked lasagna
　noodles
1 (8-ounce) package sliced mozzarella
　cheese

Combine spaghetti sauce mix, tomato paste, tomato sauce, and water in a medium saucepan; bring to a boil over low heat. Remove from heat.

Combine eggs, ricotta cheese, salt, spinach, and ¼ cup Parmesan cheese, mixing well. Set aside.

Spread ½ cup tomato sauce in a greased 13- x 9- x 2-inch baking dish. Place half the lasagna noodles over sauce; spread with half the spinach mixture, half the mozzarella cheese, and half the tomato sauce. Repeat layers using remaining ingredients. Sprinkle with remaining Parmesan cheese.

Cover dish securely with aluminum foil, and bake at 350° for 1 hour. Let stand 10 minutes before serving. Yield: 8 to 10 servings. *Shirley Hodge, Delray Beach, Florida.*

CHEESY MACARONI-MUSHROOM BAKE

1 (8-ounce) package elbow macaroni
1 (10¾-ounce) can cream of celery soup,
　undiluted
1 cup milk
½ cup chopped onion
1 teaspoon salt
¼ teaspoon pepper
¼ teaspoon ground oregano
2 cups (8 ounces) shredded Cheddar
　cheese
1 (3-ounce) can sliced mushrooms,
　drained and divided
3 tablespoons grated Parmesan cheese
2 small tomatoes, cut into wedges

Cook macaroni according to package directions; drain. Rinse macaroni, and set aside.

Combine next 6 ingredients, mixing well. Layer one-half each of macaroni, soup mixture, Cheddar cheese, and mushrooms in a lightly greased 2-quart casserole. Repeat layers with remaining macaroni, soup mixture, and cheese, reserving remaining mushrooms. Sprinkle with Parmesan cheese; bake, uncovered, at 350° for 30 minutes.

Remove from oven, and line edges of casserole with tomato wedges. Arrange reserved mushrooms on top of casserole; bake 5 minutes. Yield: 6 servings. *Glyna Meredith Gallrein, Anchorage, Kentucky.*

BROCCOLI-CHEESE FRITTATA

3 eggs
3 tablespoons milk
¼ teaspoon salt
Dash of red pepper
2 tablespoons margarine
1 (10-ounce) package frozen chopped
　broccoli, thawed and well drained
1 small onion, finely chopped
1 small clove garlic, crushed
2 cups (8 ounces) shredded Swiss or
　Cheddar cheese

Combine eggs, milk, salt, and pepper; beat well, and set aside.

Melt margarine in a 10-inch skillet. Add broccoli, onion, and garlic; sauté until tender. Remove from heat; stir in egg mixture. Sprinkle with cheese; cover and cook over low heat about 10 minutes or until egg mixture is set and cheese is melted. Cut into wedges and serve immediately. Yield: 4 servings. *Kay Castleman, Nashville, Tennessee.*

BEAN SALAD SANDWICHES

2 cups cooked, drained pinto beans
3 hard-cooked eggs, chopped
½ cup chopped sweet pickle
2 tablespoons chopped onion
¾ teaspoon salt
¼ cup mayonnaise
5 (6-inch) pocket bread rounds, halved
Leaf lettuce

Drain beans, and mash well. Add eggs, pickle, onion, salt, and mayonnaise; mix well, and chill 1 to 2 hours.

Line bread rounds with lettuce; spoon about 2 rounded tablespoons filling mixture into each. Yield: 5 servings. *Mrs. Bill Hodges, Guntersville, Alabama.*

CHEESY EGG CASSEROLE

½ cup butter or margarine
½ cup all-purpose flour
4 cups milk
1 teaspoon salt
½ teaspoon pepper
2 cups (8 ounces) shredded American
  cheese
6 hard-cooked eggs, separated
3 tablespoons butter or margarine
1 small onion, chopped
1 (4½-ounce) jar sliced mushrooms,
  drained
1 tablespoon chopped fresh parsley
1 (4-ounce) jar diced pimiento, drained
½ teaspoon celery salt
1 tablespoon sherry
Toast points or toasted English muffins

Melt ½ cup butter in a heavy sauce-pan over low heat; add flour, stirring until smooth. Cook 1 minute, stirring constantly. Gradually add milk; cook over medium heat, stirring constantly, until thickened and bubbly. Stir in salt, pepper, and cheese. Chop egg whites, and stir into sauce; set aside.

Melt 3 tablespoons butter in a skillet; add onion, mushrooms, parsley, and pimiento. Sauté until tender. Stir mushroom mixture, celery salt, and sherry into cheese sauce. Pour into a greased 2-quart shallow baking dish. Bake at 325° for 35 minutes. Grate egg yolks; sprinkle over casserole. Serve over toast points. Yield: 8 servings. *Ruth Butts, Fulton, Kentucky.*

MUSHROOM QUICHE

Pastry for 9-inch pie shell
2 tablespoons butter or margarine
2 tablespoons chopped green onion
½ pound fresh mushrooms, sliced
½ teaspoon lemon juice
½ teaspoon salt
3 eggs, beaten
1½ cups whipping cream
⅛ teaspoon ground nutmeg
⅛ teaspoon pepper
1 cup (4 ounces) shredded Swiss cheese

Line a 9-inch quiche dish or piepan with pastry; trim excess pastry around edges. Prick bottom and sides of pastry with a fork. Bake at 400° for 3 minutes; remove from oven, and gently prick with a fork. Bake 5 minutes longer. Let cool on rack.

Melt butter in a medium skillet over low heat; add onion, mushrooms, lemon juice, and salt. Cook until liquid evaporates; set aside.

Combine eggs, whipping cream, nutmeg, pepper, and cheese in a medium mixing bowl. Stir in mushroom mixture. Pour into pastry shell; bake at 375° for 30 minutes. Let stand 15 minutes before serving. Yield: one 9-inch quiche.
Mrs. Gene Crow, Dallas, Texas.

CREAMY VEGETABLE-CHEESE SOUP

¼ cup plus 1 tablespoon butter or
  margarine, divided
1 cup chopped onion
2 cups hot water
2 cups shredded cabbage
1 (10-ounce) package frozen baby limas
1 cup sliced carrots
1 cup cubed potatoes
1 tablespoon chicken-flavored bouillon
  granules
3 tablespoons all-purpose flour
3 cups milk
¼ teaspoon paprika
¼ teaspoon pepper
1½ cups (6 ounces) shredded Cheddar
  cheese

Melt 2 tablespoons butter in a large heavy skillet; add onion. Sauté 5 minutes or until tender; add hot water, vegetables, and bouillon granules. Bring to a boil; reduce heat and simmer, covered, 20 minutes or until vegetables are tender. Cool completely.

Melt remaining butter in a heavy Dutch oven over low heat; add flour, stirring until smooth. Cook 1 minute, stirring constantly. Gradually add milk; cook over medium heat, stirring constantly, until thickened and bubbly. Stir in paprika, pepper, and cheese. Gradually stir in vegetable mixture; cook, stirring constantly, just until heated. Yield: about 2½ quarts. *Mary Pappas, Richmond, Virginia.*

Tip: Keep leftover soup by freezing in an ice cube tray. When frozen, remove the cubes, and store in an airtight container in the freezer. Thaw and heat the cubes as needed.

Jazz Up Your Coffee

Next time you serve coffee, don't just pass the cream and sugar. Jazz up your favorite beverage with ice cream, brandy, chocolate syrup, and whipped cream.

BRANDIED COFFEE

3 cups boiling water
2 tablespoons instant coffee granules
1 tablespoon plus 1 teaspoon sugar
½ cup brandy
1 pint vanilla ice cream, softened
Whipped cream (optional)

Combine water, coffee granules, and sugar; stir until sugar dissolves. Stir in brandy. Scoop ice cream evenly into six coffee cups. Fill cups with coffee mixture; garnish with whipped cream, if desired. Yield: 6 servings. *Edna Chadsey, Cleveland, Tennessee.*

FROSTED COFFEE

1 pint vanilla ice cream
1½ cups strong coffee, chilled
1½ cups milk
⅓ cup chocolate-flavored syrup
2 tablespoons sugar
Vanilla ice cream

Combine first 5 ingredients in container of electric blender; process on low speed until frothy. Pour in serving glasses, and top with a scoop of ice cream. Yield: about 5½ cups.
Mabel Baldwin Couch, Chelsea, Oklahoma.

CREAMY COFFEE

3½ cups milk
¼ cup instant coffee granules
¼ cup firmly packed brown sugar
Dash of salt

Heat milk in a heavy saucepan. Add coffee granules, brown sugar, and salt; stir over low heat until dry ingredients dissolve and the mixture is well heated. Serve immediately. Yield: 3½ cups.
Charlotte Pierce, Greensburg, Kentucky.

Presenting The Best Of The Holidays

One of the most cherished times of the year is when the home is decorated for the holidays and the scent of evergreens mingles with tantalizing kitchen aromas. For this is when Southerners gather their family and friends to share special times and to feast upon favorite foods.

We are pleased to share this special section of festive recipes, menus, and entertaining ideas to help brighten the season.

To begin our holiday extravaganza we feature a special dinner party menu, a favorite of Walli and Louis Beall of Tallahassee, Florida. Nothing pleases this couple more than inviting close friends for an evening of gracious holiday dining.

When guests arrive, they congregate around the living room fire, and everyone is served tart Cranberry Daiquiris. Crackers are spread with generous portions of Oyster Mousse, and rye bread is lavished with a fruit and cheese mixture served from a pineapple shell. Also enjoyed by the warmth of the fire is the first course, Cream of Squash Soup. Walli says she enjoys serving soup in the living room because everyone can settle back and anticipate the dinner to come.

With crystal sparkling and candles casting their inviting shadows, dinner is served from an elegant buffet. Guests help themselves to Marinated Beef Tenderloin delightfully garnished with Potato Roses. A light and airy broccoli casserole, stuffed mushrooms, and a tomato and feta cheese salad complete the selections.

As special to this feast as the tenderloin are the dessert choices: Apricot Bars and Sherried Mousse. Walli proudly claims the mousse as an old family recipe, and the Apricot Bars are a Christmas favorite with her children.

Cranberry Daiquiris
Fruit and Cheese Spread
Oyster Mousse
Cream of Squash Soup
Marinated Beef Tenderloin
Potato Roses
Vegetable Mushroom Caps
Broccoli Bake
Tomato-Feta Salad
Apricot Bars   Sherried Mousse
Wine   Coffee

CRANBERRY DAIQUIRIS

1 (8-ounce) can cranberry jelly
1 tablespoon sweetened lime juice
3 tablespoons liquid daiquiri mix
½ cup plus 2 tablespoons light rum

Combine all ingredients in container of an electric blender; blend well. Add crushed ice to fill blender; blend well. Yield: about 3½ cups.
Note: Recipe may be doubled or tripled, if desired.

FRUIT AND CHEESE SPREAD

1 (17-ounce) can fruit cocktail, drained and crushed
1 (8-ounce) package cream cheese, softened
2 tablespoons minced green onion tops
2 tablespoons mayonnaise
4 slices bacon, cooked and crumbled
1 medium pineapple
Chopped fresh parsley

Combine first 5 ingredients, mixing well. Chill.

Cut a lengthwise slice from pineapple, removing one-third of the pineapple.

Scoop pulp from slice; discard rind. Scoop pulp from remaining portion of pineapple, leaving the shell ½ to ¼ inch thick. Reserve the pulp for use in another recipe.

Spoon cream cheese mixture into pineapple shell, and garnish with parsley. Serve with party-size slices of rye bread. Yield: 2½ cups.

OYSTER MOUSSE

2 envelopes unflavored gelatin
½ cup water
1 (8-ounce) package cream cheese
1 cup mayonnaise
2 (3.66-ounce) cans smoked oysters, drained and minced
2 tablespoons chopped fresh parsley
1 tablespoon Worcestershire sauce
½ teaspoon garlic powder
Dash of hot sauce
Fresh parsley sprigs (optional)
Lemon twists (optional)
Ripe olives (optional)

Soften gelatin in water, and set aside.

Combine cream cheese and mayonnaise in a saucepan; cook over low heat, stirring constantly, until cream cheese melts and mixture is smooth. Stir in next 5 ingredients and softened gelatin; spoon into a well-greased 3½-cup fish-shaped mold. Cover and chill overnight or until mousse is firm.

Unmold mousse; if desired, garnish with parsley, lemon twists, and olives. Serve with crackers. Yield: about 3 cups.

Tip: Bent or dented measuring utensils give inaccurate measures. Use only standard measuring cups and spoons that are in good condition.

CREAM OF SQUASH SOUP

¼ cup butter or margarine, melted
2 tablespoons vegetable oil
1 large onion, minced
2 cloves garlic, minced
3 pounds yellow squash, thinly sliced
3½ to 4 cups chicken broth
1 cup half-and-half
1½ teaspoons salt
½ teaspoon white pepper
Chopped fresh parsley

Combine butter and oil in a large Dutch oven. Add onion and garlic; sauté until tender. Stir in squash and chicken broth; cover and simmer 15 to 20 minutes or until squash is tender.

Spoon a third of squash mixture into container of electric blender, and process until smooth. Repeat with remaining squash mixture.

Return squash mixture to Dutch oven; stir in half-and-half, salt, and pepper. Cook over low heat, stirring constantly, until well heated. Serve hot or chilled. Garnish with parsley. Yield: 10 cups.

MARINATED BEEF TENDERLOIN

1 (5-pound) beef tenderloin, trimmed
Marinade (recipe follows)
Endive (optional)
Cherry tomatoes (optional)

Place tenderloin in a large baking dish; pour marinade over top, and cover tightly. Refrigerate 2 hours, turning after 1 hour.

Uncover tenderloin, and place dish on bottom rack of oven (do not drain off marinade). Broil 20 minutes on each side. Cover and bake at 350° for 10 to 15 minutes. Garnish with endive and cherry tomatoes, if desired. Yield: 8 to 10 servings.

Marinade:

½ cup Burgundy
¼ cup olive oil
¼ cup soy sauce
1 tablespoon dried parsley flakes
1 tablespoon paprika
⅓ cup tarragon vinegar
1½ teaspoons Beau Monde seasoning

Combine all of the ingredients in a small mixing bowl, and mix well. Yield: about 1½ cups.

POTATO ROSES

8 large potatoes
3 chicken-flavored bouillon cubes
¼ cup butter or margarine, melted

Peel potatoes; beginning at the bottom, carve petal shapes onto sides of each. Place potatoes in water until ready to cook to prevent discoloration.

Drain potatoes, and gently place in a large Dutch oven; cover with water, and add bouillon cubes. Cover and bring to a boil; uncover and cook 30 to 35 minutes or until potatoes are tender.

Using a slotted spoon, remove potatoes from cooking liquid and place on serving dish. Drizzle melted butter over top of each. Yield: 8 servings.

VEGETABLE MUSHROOM CAPS

2 pounds large fresh mushrooms
½ cup butter or margarine
½ cup minced onion
½ cup minced celery
2 teaspoons Worcestershire sauce
½ teaspoon salt
⅛ teaspoon pepper
Melted butter or margarine
Fresh parsley sprigs (optional)

Rinse mushrooms, and pat dry; remove and chop stems. Set mushroom caps aside.

Melt ½ cup butter in a large skillet; stir in mushroom stems, onion, celery, Worcestershire sauce, salt, and pepper. Sauté for 5 or 10 minutes or until vegetables are tender.

Brush mushroom caps with melted butter; spoon in vegetable mixture. Place caps, stuffed side up, in skillet; cover and simmer 5 minutes. Garnish with parsley, if desired. Yield: about 8 servings.

BROCCOLI BAKE

2½ bunches fresh broccoli
2 tablespoons butter, melted
1 tablespoon vegetable oil
½ pound fresh mushrooms, finely chopped
¼ cup minced onion
2 shallots, minced
4 eggs, beaten
2 egg yolks, beaten
½ cup fine dry breadcrumbs
½ cup whipping cream
Dash of ground nutmeg
Salt and pepper to taste

Trim off large leaves of broccoli, and remove tough ends of lower stalks. Wash broccoli thoroughly, and separate into spears. Cook broccoli, covered, in a small amount of boiling water 10 minutes or until tender. Drain well, and set aside 1 cup flowerets for garnish.

Place broccoli spears, a small amount at a time, in container of electric blender; process until smooth.

Combine butter and oil in a medium saucepan; add mushrooms, onion, and shallots; sauté until all liquid has evaporated. Stir in pureed broccoli. Add remaining ingredients, mixing well.

Spoon broccoli mixture into a lightly greased 1½-quart casserole. Set casserole in a large shallow pan filled with 1 inch hot water. Bake at 325° about 35 minutes or until set. Garnish with reserved flowerets. Yield: 8 servings.

TOMATO-FETA SALAD

2 cloves garlic
2 pints cherry tomatoes, halved
½ cup pitted ripe olives
1½ cups crumbled feta cheese
½ to 1 cup olive oil
½ cup plus 2 tablespoons wine vinegar
1 teaspoon dried whole oregano
1 teaspoon dried whole thyme
Salt and pepper to taste

Rub inside of salad bowl with garlic; discard garlic. Combine tomatoes, olives, and cheese in salad bowl. Combine remaining ingredients in a jar. Cover tightly; shake vigorously. Pour over tomato mixture, tossing gently; refrigerate at least 4 hours. Yield: 8 servings.

APRICOT BARS

2 (6-ounce) packages dried apricots
¾ cup sugar
¾ cup butter or margarine, softened
1 cup sugar
2 cups all-purpose flour
½ teaspoon salt
½ teaspoon soda
1 (3-ounce) can flaked coconut
½ cup chopped pecans or walnuts

Cover apricots with water, and bring to a boil; reduce heat. Simmer, uncovered, 15 minutes or until tender. Drain, reserving ¼ cup liquid. Coarsely chop apricots, and set aside. Combine reserved apricot liquid and ¾ cup sugar in a saucepan; simmer 5 minutes. Stir in the chopped apricots.

Cream butter; gradually add 1 cup sugar, beating until light and fluffy. Combine flour, salt, and soda; stir well. Add to creamed mixture, mixing well (mixture will be crumbly). Stir in coconut and pecans. Pat three-fourths of coconut mixture into an ungreased 13- x 9- x 2-inch baking pan. Bake at 350° for 10 minutes.

Spread apricot mixture evenly over crust; sprinkle with remaining coconut mixture. Bake an additional 30 minutes. Let cool in pan, and cut into 2-inch squares. Yield: 2 dozen.

SHERRIED MOUSSE

1 envelope unflavored gelatin
⅓ cup cold water
3 tablespoons cream sherry
5 egg whites
⅔ cup sugar, divided
1 cup whipping cream
Candied cherries (optional)
Ground cinnamon (optional)

Combine gelatin and cold water in top of a double boiler; let stand 5 minutes. Place over boiling water; cook, stirring constantly, until gelatin is dissolved. Remove from heat, and let cool (do not allow mixture to become firm). Stir in the sherry.

Beat egg whites (at room temperature) until foamy. Gradually add ⅓ cup sugar, 1 tablespoon at a time, beating until stiff peaks form.

Beat whipping cream until foamy; gradually add remaining sugar, beating until soft peaks form.

Fold whipped cream and gelatin mixture into egg whites. Spoon into serving bowl. Cover and chill 4 to 5 hours or until set. Garnish with cherries and cinnamon, if desired. Yield: 8 servings.

Let The Dessert Be Lavish

If there's anything that captures the spirit of the holidays, it's lavish desserts beautifully garnished and served with a flair. Grasshopper Soufflé, Chocolate-Rum Dessert, and Brandied Apples are just a sampling of what we have to offer. As festive as the names sound, they only hint at the wonderful flavors.

Chocolate-Rum Dessert is a rich cousin of chocolate pudding, just more delicious. When served in cordial glasses or demitasse cups and topped with whipped cream and chocolate curls, this rum-laced delight is sure to stir up the holiday spirit.

For something as cool and refreshing as it looks, we suggest Grasshopper Soufflé. The flavor is owed to crème de menthe, and even the cheerful green color is in keeping with the season. Its finishing touch is a mound of whipped cream crowned with curls of chocolate.

Or delight your guests with apples served in a special way. For Brandied Apples, the fruit is flambéed and smothered in Vanilla Cream.

CHOCOLATE-RUM DESSERT

1 (6-ounce) package semisweet chocolate morsels
3 eggs, separated
2 tablespoons light rum
¼ teaspoon almond extract
¼ teaspoon ground nutmeg
Whipped cream
Chocolate curls

Melt chocolate over hot water in top of double boiler.

Beat egg yolks until thick and lemon colored. Gradually stir about one-fourth of chocolate into yolks; add to remaining chocolate, stirring constantly. Remove from heat; stir in rum, almond extract, and nutmeg.

Beat egg whites (at room temperature) until stiff peaks form; gently fold into chocolate mixture. Spoon into cordial glasses or demitasse cups. Chill. Before serving, top with whipped cream and chocolate curls. Yield: 4 servings.
Janet M. Filer,
Arlington, Virginia.

APPLE-CREAM CHEESE PIE

Pastry for 9-inch pie
4 cups peeled, thinly sliced apples
1 (8-ounce) package cream cheese, softened
¼ cup sugar
1 egg, beaten
¼ teaspoon vanilla extract
⅛ teaspoon salt
2 teaspoons grated lemon rind
⅓ cup sugar
½ teaspoon ground cinnamon
½ cup sliced almonds

Line a 9-inch pieplate with pastry, and trim excess from around edges; flute. Prick bottom and sides of pastry shell with a fork; bake at 425° for 10 to 12 minutes. Let cool on rack.

Arrange apples evenly on a baking sheet, and bake at 400° for 15 minutes or until tender.

Beat cream cheese until smooth; gradually add ¼ cup sugar, beating well. Add egg, vanilla, salt, and lemon rind; beat well. Spread mixture evenly in prepared pastry shell, and top with apples.

Combine ⅓ cup sugar and ½ teaspoon cinnamon; sprinkle over apples. Bake at 400° for 35 minutes.

Sprinkle almonds on top of pie; bake 10 more minutes or until almonds are toasted. Let cool on rack. Yield: one 9-inch pie.
Mrs. O. V. Elkins,
Chattanooga, Tennessee.

BRANDIED APPLES

8 large cooking apples
½ cup lemon juice
⅓ cup butter or margarine
½ cup brandy
⅔ cup firmly packed brown sugar
1 tablespoon grated lemon rind
1 teaspoon ground cinnamon
⅓ cup brandy
Vanilla Cream

Peel and core apples; cut into ½-inch-thick wedges. Sprinkle with lemon juice, tossing gently.

Melt butter in chafing dish; drain apples, and stir into butter. Cook apples over medium heat, stirring gently, about 3 minutes.

Combine ½ cup brandy, brown sugar, lemon rind, and cinnamon; mix well, and pour over apples. Cook over medium heat about 5 to 7 minutes or until apples appear glazed.

Heat ⅓ cup brandy in a small saucepan over medium heat. Ignite brandy, and pour over apples. After flames die down, spoon brandied apples into individual serving dishes, and top with Vanilla Cream. Yield: 10 servings.

Vanilla Cream:

1 cup whipping cream
1½ tablespoons lemon juice
½ teaspoon vanilla extract

Combine all ingredients, mixing well. Chill. Yield: about 1 cup.
*Mrs. Harvey Kidd,
Hernando, Mississippi.*

APPLE-WALNUT COBBLER

4 cups sliced apples
1½ cups sugar, divided
½ teaspoon ground cinnamon
½ cup coarsely chopped walnuts
1 cup all-purpose flour
1 teaspoon baking powder
¼ teaspoon salt
1 egg, beaten
½ cup half-and-half
⅓ cup melted butter or margarine
¼ cup finely chopped walnuts

Spread apples evenly in a greased 9-inch square baking pan. Combine ½

cup sugar, cinnamon, and coarsely chopped walnuts; sprinkle over apples.

Combine flour, 1 cup sugar, baking powder, and salt; stir well, and set aside. Combine egg, half-and-half, and butter; mix well. Add flour mixture, beating until smooth; pour over apples. Sprinkle with finely chopped walnuts. Bake at 325° for 1 hour. Yield: 6 servings.
*Charlotte A. Pierce,
Greensburg, Kentucky.*

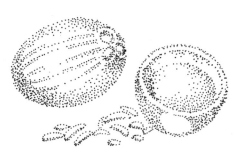

COCONUT-PECAN CHESS PIE

3 eggs
1 cup sugar
¼ cup plus 1 tablespoon buttermilk
2 tablespoons butter or margarine, melted
1 tablespoon cornmeal
1 teaspoon coconut flavoring
¾ cup flaked coconut
¼ cup chopped pecans
Pastry (recipe follows)

Beat eggs with a wire whisk or fork; add next 5 ingredients, mixing well. Stir in coconut and pecans; pour into prepared pastry shell. Bake at 400° for 10 minutes. Reduce heat to 350°, and bake an additional 30 minutes. Yield: one 9-inch pie.

Pastry:

1⅓ cups all-purpose flour
½ teaspoon salt
⅛ teaspoon ground nutmeg
⅓ cup vegetable oil
3 tablespoons cold milk

Combine flour, salt, and nutmeg; add oil and milk, stirring until mixture forms a ball.

Roll dough to ⅛-inch thickness on a lightly floured surface. Fit pastry into a 9-inch pieplate. Yield: one 9-inch pastry shell.
*Gayle Wallace,
Memphis, Tennessee.*

CRANBERRY COBBLER ROLL

2 cups fresh cranberries
1¾ cups all-purpose flour
½ teaspoon salt
⅓ cup shortening
7 to 8 tablespoons cold water
1½ cups sugar, divided
½ cup plus 1 tablespoon butter or margarine, divided
1 cup hot water
½ teaspoon vanilla extract

Wash and sort cranberries; drain well.

Combine flour and salt; cut in shortening with pastry blender until mixture resembles coarse meal. Sprinkle with cold water, stirring with a fork until all dry ingredients are moistened. Divide dough in half.

Roll half of dough into a 9-inch circle on a lightly floured surface. Place 1 cup cranberries in center; sprinkle with ½ cup sugar, and dot with 3 tablespoons butter. Fold pastry over berries, and press ends together to seal; place seam side down in a well-greased 12- x 8- x 2-inch baking dish. Repeat with remaining dough, and place beside first roll.

Slightly flatten each roll with hand. Sprinkle remaining ½ cup sugar over top, and dot with remaining butter.

Bake at 325° for 45 minutes; combine hot water and vanilla, and pour in baking dish around edges of rolls. Bake an additional 15 minutes. Serve warm. Yield: 8 servings. *Mrs. R. S. Barnes,
Birmingham, Alabama.*

GRASSHOPPER SOUFFLE

2 envelopes unflavored gelatin
2 cups water
4 eggs, separated
1 cup sugar, divided
1 (8-ounce) package cream cheese, softened
¼ cup crème de menthe
1 cup whipping cream, whipped
Additional whipped cream
Chocolate curls

Cut a piece of aluminum foil or waxed paper long enough to fit around a 1½-quart soufflé dish, allowing a 1-inch overlap; fold lengthwise into thirds. Lightly oil one side of foil; wrap around

outside of dish, oiled side against dish, allowing it to extend 3 inches above rim to form a collar. Secure foil with tape.

Combine gelatin and 1 cup water in top of a double boiler. Cook over low heat, stirring constantly until gelatin dissolves; gradually stir in remaining water.

Beat egg yolks until thick and lemon colored; gradually add ¾ cup sugar, beating well. Stir into gelatin mixture. Cook over low heat until thickened, stirring constantly; let cool.

Beat cream cheese until smooth; gradually add yolk mixture, beating well. Stir in crème de menthe.

Beat egg whites (at room temperature) until foamy; gradually add ¼ cup sugar, beating until stiff peaks form. Gently fold whipped cream and beaten egg whites into yolk mixture.

Spoon into prepared dish, and chill until firm. Remove collar from dish. Garnish with whipped cream and chocolate curls. Yield: 8 servings.

Tammy Smith,
Talbott, Tennessee.

Spice The Bread With Fruit

Southerners are noted for their bread-baking, and keeping that tradition growing are those who toss a few cranberries into the batter or spoon crushed pineapple over the top. In fact, it's the flavor of fruit that makes each of the breads included here so special—special enough for holiday snacking and giving.

Apple Coffee Cake and Cranberry Muffins take their flavor from the fresh fruit of the season, while Cranberry-Nut Coffee Cake and Pineapple Muffins rely on the speed and convenience of canned fruit.

The flavors are wonderful, yet all of these breads offer something more: the convenience of quick preparation. That's because they depend on baking powder or soda for leavening rather than yeast.

CRANBERRY MUFFINS

1 cup fresh cranberries
2 tablespoons sugar
2 cups all-purpose flour
¼ cup sugar
1 tablespoon plus 1 teaspoon baking powder
½ teaspoon salt
1 egg, beaten
¾ cup milk
¼ cup butter or margarine, melted

Toss cranberries with 2 tablespoons sugar; set aside.

Combine flour, ¼ cup sugar, baking powder, and salt; stir well. Combine egg, milk, and butter. Make a well in center of dry ingredients; add liquid ingredients and cranberries, stirring just until dry ingredients are moistened. Spoon into greased muffin pans, filling two-thirds full. Bake at 400° for 25 to 30 minutes. Yield: 1 dozen.

Becky Burnett,
Concord, Tennessee.

TANGY APRICOT BREAD

1 (8-ounce) package dried apricots
½ cup chopped pecans
¼ cup all-purpose flour
1 cup sugar
2 tablespoons butter or margarine, softened
1 egg, beaten
1¾ cups all-purpose flour
2 teaspoons baking powder
¼ teaspoon soda
¼ teaspoon salt
½ cup orange juice
¼ cup water

Soak apricots in warm water to cover for 30 minutes; drain well, and cut into ¼-inch pieces.

Combine the apricot pieces and pecans; dredge with ¼ cup flour, and set aside.

Combine sugar and butter, mixing well. Add egg, and beat well.

Combine 1¾ cups flour, baking powder, soda, and salt. Combine orange juice and water. Add flour mixture to creamed mixture alternately with liquid ingredients, beginning and ending with

flour mixture. Mix lightly after each addition. Stir in apricots and pecans.

Spoon batter into a waxed paper-lined and greased 9- x 5- x 3-inch loaf-pan. Let batter stand at room temperature for 20 minutes. Bake at 350° for 1 hour or until wooden pick inserted in center comes out clean. Remove from pan, and place on wire rack to cool. Yield: 1 loaf. *Mrs. R. P. Hotaling,*
Martinez, Georgia.

APPLE COFFEE CAKE

¼ cup butter or margarine, softened
¾ cup sugar
1 egg
1½ cups all-purpose flour
2 teaspoons baking powder
½ teaspoon ground nutmeg
¼ teaspoon salt
⅔ cup milk
1 teaspoon vanilla extract
1 cup finely chopped cooking apples
⅓ cup sugar
1 teaspoon ground cinnamon

Cream butter; gradually add ¾ cup sugar, beating well. Add egg; mix well.

Combine flour, baking powder, nutmeg, and salt; add to creamed mixture alternately with milk, beginning and ending with the flour mixture. Mix well after each addition. Stir in vanilla. Pour batter into a greased and floured 9-inch square pan.

Combine apples, ⅓ cup sugar, and cinnamon; mix well. Sprinkle over batter. Bake at 375° for 25 to 30 minutes or until wooden pick inserted in center comes out clean. Yield: one 9-inch coffee cake. *Wanda Bishop,*
Little Rock, Arkansas.

CRANBERRY-NUT COFFEE CAKE

¼ cup firmly packed brown sugar
½ cup chopped walnuts
¼ teaspoon ground cinnamon
2 cups biscuit mix
2 tablespoons sugar
1 egg
⅔ cup water
⅔ cup whole-berry cranberry sauce
Powdered Sugar Glaze

Combine brown sugar, walnuts, and cinnamon; mix well, and set aside.

Combine biscuit mix, sugar, egg, and water; beat 30 seconds at medium speed of electric mixer. Pour batter into a greased 9-inch square pan. Sprinkle batter with prepared walnut mixture, and spoon cranberry sauce evenly over top.

Bake at 400° for 25 to 30 minutes or until wooden pick inserted in center comes out clean. Drizzle glaze over warm cake. Yield: one 9-inch coffee cake.

Powdered Sugar Glaze:

1 cup sifted powdered sugar
1 tablespoon plus 1 teaspoon water
½ teaspoon vanilla extract

Combine all ingredients, stir well. Yield: about ½ cup.
Mrs. Russell Rehkemper,
Tampa, Florida.

GLAZED ORANGE-PECAN BREAD

¼ cup butter or margarine, softened
¾ cup sugar
2 eggs, beaten
2 teaspoons grated orange rind
2 cups all-purpose flour
2½ teaspoons baking powder
1 teaspoon salt
¾ cup orange juice
½ cup chopped pecans
2½ teaspoons orange juice
½ cup sifted powdered sugar

Cream butter; gradually add ¾ cup sugar, beating well. Add the beaten eggs and grated orange rind; mix well.

Combine flour, baking powder, and salt; add to creamed mixture alternately with ¾ cup orange juice, beginning and ending with flour mixture. Mix well after each addition. Stir in pecans.

Pour batter into a greased 9- x 5- x 3-inch loafpan. Bake at 350° for 50 to 55 minutes or until a wooden pick inserted in center comes out clean. Cool loaf in pan 10 minutes. Remove from pan, and cool completely.

Combine 2½ teaspoons orange juice and powdered sugar; drizzle over loaf. Wrap and store overnight before serving. Yield: 1 loaf.
Mrs. William R. Zollman,
Houston, Texas.

PINEAPPLE MUFFINS

1 (8-ounce) can crushed pineapple
½ cup all-purpose flour
⅓ cup firmly packed brown sugar
¼ teaspoon ground cinnamon
½ cup butter or margarine, melted and divided
2 cups all-purpose flour
½ cup sugar
1 tablespoon baking powder
½ teaspoon salt
1 egg, beaten
¾ cup milk

Drain pineapple, reserving ¼ cup juice. Combine ½ cup flour, brown sugar, cinnamon, and ¼ cup butter; stir well.

Combine next 4 ingredients. Combine egg, milk, remaining ¼ cup butter, and reserved pineapple juice; stir well. Make a well in center of dry ingredients; add liquid ingredients, stirring just until moistened.

Spoon batter into greased and floured muffin pans, filling half full. Spoon pineapple over batter, and sprinkle with cinnamon mixture. Bake at 375° for 30 minutes. Yield: 16 muffins.
Mrs. Bennie Cox,
Clinton, Tennessee.

Tip: If you grease more muffin cups than you need, fill the empty cups with water to keep grease from baking on.

STRAWBERRY BREAD

3 cups all-purpose flour
1 teaspoon soda
½ teaspoon salt
1 tablespoon ground cinnamon
2 cups sugar
3 eggs, beaten
1 cup vegetable oil
2 (10-ounce) packages frozen sliced strawberries, thawed

Combine first 5 ingredients; mix well. Combine eggs, oil, and strawberries; add to dry ingredients, mixing well.

Pour batter into 2 greased and floured 9- x 5- x 3-inch loafpans. Bake at 350° for 1 hour or until a wooden pick inserted in the center comes out clean. Yield: 2 loaves.
Mrs. James M. Cavender,
Memphis, Tennessee.

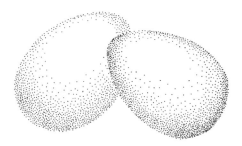

Springerle—The Carved Cookies

Sometime during the holiday season, chances are you're going to bake a batch of special cookies. If the cookies are made into decorative shapes, the preparation is half the fun.

One such decorative cookie is springerle. Originally brought to this country from Europe, springerle are pressed with a carved mold or rolling pin before baking to give them their distinctive embossed design. Along with the design, they have a firm texture and strong anise flavor that distinguish them from other cookies.

In addition to eating springerle, you can also use them as tree or package ornaments. Simply punch holes in the cookies with a wooden pick before baking; then tie ribbons through the holes after baking.

Cookie molds and rolling pins are available in a variety of designs at kitchen specialty shops and department stores.

Salads Make Fancy Fare

If a plain tossed salad seems a little too everyday for holiday menus, use your imagination and some different ingredients to add that needed sparkle.

For Carrot-Ambrosia Salad, for example, pineapple, raisins, marshmallows, and coconut are added to the shredded carrots and tossed with sour cream and honey. It's a combination that's sure to bring glowing color to your table. A tossed green salad can be just as colorful, especially if it's Mandarin Orange Salad.

APRICOT SALAD

2 (3-ounce) packages orange-flavored
   gelatin
2 cups boiling water
⅓ cup miniature marshmallows
1 (30-ounce) can apricots
1 (8¼-ounce) can crushed pineapple
2 tablespoons butter or margarine
2 tablespoons all-purpose flour
½ cup sugar
1 egg, beaten
1 cup frozen whipped topping, thawed
Chopped pecans (optional)

Dissolve gelatin in boiling water. Add marshmallows; stir until dissolved.

Drain apricots and pineapple, reserving juice. Set aside ½ cup apricot juice and ½ cup pineapple juice for topping. Combine remaining juice, and add water to measure 2 cups; stir into gelatin. Chill until consistency of unbeaten egg white.

Chop apricots; fold apricots and pineapple into gelatin. Pour into a 13- x 9- x 2-inch dish. Chill until firm.

Melt butter; add flour, stirring well. Add sugar, egg, and reserved apricot and pineapple juice. Cook over medium heat until thickened. Chill. Fold in whipped topping. Spread over gelatin mixture. Sprinkle with pecans, if desired. Yield: about 15 servings.

Rachel Youree,
Murfreesboro, Tennessee.

SPRINGERLE

3 eggs
2 cups sugar
2 teaspoons grated lemon rind
3¼ cups all-purpose flour, divided
¼ teaspoon baking powder
2 teaspoons anise seeds, crushed

Beat eggs with electric mixer on medium speed until thick and lemon colored; gradually add sugar, and continue beating 5 minutes. Add lemon rind, mixing well.

Combine 2¾ cups flour and baking powder. Add to egg mixture, beating well. Chill dough at least 3 hours or overnight.

Remove dough from refrigerator; let stand at room temperature for 15 minutes. Turn dough out onto a floured board; knead in remaining ½ cup flour to make a stiff dough.

Roll dough to ¼-inch thickness. Using a floured cookie mold or springerle rolling pin, press firmly to imprint dough. Cut the cookie squares apart. Place cookies on a rack, and let stand uncovered in a cool, dry place 12 hours or overnight to set the design.

Sprinkle the crushed anise seeds onto well-greased cookie sheets. Top with cookies. Bake at 300° for 15 to 20 minutes or until light yellow, but not golden. Yield: about 5 dozen.

HOLIDAY JEWEL SALAD

1 (3-ounce) package pineapple-flavored
  gelatin
1 cup boiling water
1 (8-ounce) can crushed pineapple
1 cup fresh cranberries, chopped
½ cup diced celery
½ cup chopped walnuts
Lettuce leaves (optional)
Mayonnaise (optional)

Dissolve gelatin in boiling water.
Drain pineapple, reserving juice. Add
water to juice to measure 1 cup; add to
gelatin mixture, stirring well. Chill until
consistency of unbeaten egg white.

Combine pineapple, cranberries, celery, and walnuts; fold into gelatin. Pour
into a lightly oiled 1-quart mold; chill
until firm.

Unmold on lettuce leaves, and garnish with a dollop of mayonnaise, if desired. Yield: 6 to 8 servings.
  Mrs. William Russell,
  Yazoo City, Mississippi.

LAYERED HOLIDAY SALAD

1 (3-ounce) package cherry-flavored
  gelatin
1½ cups boiling water
1 (3-ounce) package lemon-flavored gelatin
1½ cups boiling water
1 (3-ounce) package cream cheese,
  softened
1 cup whipping cream, whipped
1 (3-ounce) package lime-flavored gelatin
1 cup boiling water
1 (15¼-ounce) can crushed pineapple,
  undrained

Dissolve cherry gelatin in 1½ cups
boiling water. Pour into a 12- x 7½- x
1½-inch dish. Chill until layer is firm.

Dissolve lemon gelatin in 1½ cups
boiling water. Gradually add to cream
cheese, mixing until smooth. Cool. Fold
in whipped cream. Pour over first layer;
chill until firm.

Dissolve lime gelatin in 1 cup boiling
water. Chill until consistency of unbeaten egg white. Stir pineapple into
gelatin; pour over cream cheese layer.
Chill until firm. Yield: 12 servings.
  Marmell O'Brien,
  Clay, West Virginia.

CARROT-AMBROSIA SALAD

1 pound carrots, shredded
1 (8-ounce) carton commercial sour cream
1 (20-ounce) can crushed pineapple,
  drained
¾ cup golden raisins
2 tablespoons honey
¾ cup flaked coconut
¾ cup miniature marshmallows

Combine all ingredients, tossing well.
Chill. Yield: 6 to 8 servings.
  Mrs. Robert H. Kirk,
  Winchester, Virginia.

DELICIOUS FROZEN CHERRY SALAD

2 (3-ounce) packages cream cheese,
  softened
¾ to 1 cup mayonnaise
1 (20-ounce) can crushed pineapple,
  drained
½ cup chopped pecans
2½ cups miniature marshmallows
½ cup red maraschino cherries, halved
½ cup green maraschino cherries, halved
1 cup whipping cream, whipped

Combine cream cheese and mayonnaise, mixing well. Stir in next 5 ingredients. Fold in whipped cream.

Pour into a greased 8-cup ring mold,
and freeze until firm. Unmold just before serving. Yield: 10 to 12 servings.
  Mrs. William B. Moore,
  Selma, Alabama.

HEARTS OF PALM SALAD

¼ cup softened vanilla ice cream
2 tablespoons mayonnaise
2 tablespoons crunchy peanut butter
1 tablespoon pineapple juice
1 (14-ounce) can hearts of palm, drained
  and sliced
½ cup drained pineapple chunks
2 tablespoons chopped dates
1 tablespoon finely chopped crystallized
  ginger
½ cup chopped celery
½ small head lettuce, shredded

Combine first 4 ingredients, stirring
well; refrigerate until serving time.

Combine hearts of palm, pineapple,
dates, ginger, and celery; toss gently.
Serve on a bed of lettuce, and top with
dressing. Yield: 4 servings.
  Mrs. C. C. Stalder,
  Orlando, Florida.

MANDARIN ORANGE SALAD

1 large head romaine, torn
4 small onions, thinly sliced
1 (11-ounce) can mandarin oranges,
  drained
¼ cup chopped celery
Poppy Seed Dressing

Combine first 4 ingredients in a large
salad bowl, and toss with Poppy Seed
Dressing. Yield: 6 to 8 servings.

Poppy Seed Dressing:
½ cup sugar
⅔ cup vegetable oil
1 teaspoon prepared mustard
1 to 2 tablespoons poppy seeds
¼ cup vinegar
1 teaspoon salt

Combine all ingredients in a jar.
Cover tightly, and shake vigorously.
Yield: about 1 cup.
  Betty Jane Morrison,
  Lakewood, Colorado.

HEAVENLY SALAD

1 egg, beaten
1 tablespoon sugar
1 tablespoon orange juice
1 tablespoon vinegar
1½ teaspoons butter or margarine
Dash of salt
1 (8-ounce) carton commercial sour cream
1 cup seedless green grapes
1 cup sliced bananas
1 cup diced pineapple
1 (16-ounce) can pitted Bing cherries,
  drained
1 cup maraschino cherries, drained
1 cup diced orange
1 (10-ounce) package frozen mixed fruit,
  thawed and drained
2 cups miniature marshmallows
Flaked coconut

Combine first 4 ingredients in a saucepan; mix well. Cook over medium heat until thickened, stirring constantly. Remove from heat. Add butter and salt; stir until butter melts. Chill.

Fold in sour cream. Combine remaining ingredients except coconut. Fold in dressing. Sprinkle coconut over top. Chill. Yield: 10 to 12 servings.
Janice Finn,
Greensburg, Kentucky.

COLORFUL RICE SALAD

1 (10-ounce) package frozen English peas
3 cups cooked rice
1 (4-ounce) jar diced pimiento
1 cup diced cooked ham
6 green onions, chopped
4 hard-cooked eggs, chopped
¾ cup sliced pimiento-stuffed olives
½ cup chopped celery
⅓ cup sweet pickle relish
2 cups (8 ounces) shredded Cheddar
    cheese
¼ cup salad dressing or mayonnaise
Lettuce leaves (optional)
Cherry tomatoes (optional)

Cook peas according to package directions; drain and cool. Combine peas and next 9 ingredients; stir well. Add salad dressing, tossing until well mixed. Chill thoroughly. Serve on lettuce leaves and garnish with cherry tomatoes, if desired. Yield: 6 to 8 servings.
Linda Stone,
McGehee, Arkansas.

ITALIAN VEGETABLE SALAD

2 (10-ounce) packages frozen broccoli
    spears
1 (8-ounce) can sliced water chestnuts,
    drained
1 (6-ounce) can ripe olives, drained and
    sliced
½ pound fresh mushrooms, sliced
1 pint cherry tomatoes, halved
1 medium-size green pepper, thinly sliced
1 medium onion, coarsely chopped
2 cups sliced celery
1 (8-ounce) bottle commercial Italian salad
    dressing

Cook broccoli according to package directions, omitting salt; drain well. Cut spears in half crosswise.

Combine broccoli and remaining ingredients, tossing gently. Cover and chill at least 4 hours before serving. Yield: 12 servings.
Mina De Kraker,
Holland, Michigan.

GOURMET MACARONI SALAD

1 (8-ounce) package elbow macaroni
1 (16-ounce) can mixed peas and carrots,
    drained
1 cup chopped kosher dill pickles
1 cup chopped celery
2 tablespoons instant minced onion
1 tablespoon prepared mustard
1½ teaspoons lemon pepper seasoning
⅛ teaspoon anchovy paste
½ teaspoon salt
½ cup mayonnaise
Cherry tomatoes (optional)
Parsley sprigs (optional)

Cook macaroni according to package directions; drain. Rinse macaroni with cold water; drain. Combine macaroni and next 8 ingredients, mixing well. Cover and chill at least 2 hours.

Just before serving, stir in mayonnaise. Garnish with cherry tomatoes and parsley, if desired. Yield: 8 servings.
Mrs. H. G. Drawdy,
Spindale, North Carolina.

Be Your Own Candymaker

Each year about this time, candymakers crowd Southern kitchens to stir up batches of homemade candy—a ritual as much a part of the season as a decorated tree. To satisfy that sweet tooth, try these irresistible treats.

For peanut fans, Nut Clusters fold salted peanuts into a rich chocolate mixture. And those who think all fudge is alike should try Nutty White Fudge, a tasty confection without chocolate.

NUTTY WHITE FUDGE

2 cups sugar
½ cup commercial sour cream
⅓ cup light corn syrup
2 tablespoons butter or margarine
⅛ teaspoon salt
1 cup chopped pecans or walnuts
2 teaspoons vanilla extract

Combine first 5 ingredients in a small Dutch oven; bring to a boil. Cover and boil for 3 minutes. Uncover and cook, without stirring, until mixture registers 230° on candy thermometer. Remove from heat, and let stand 15 minutes.

Add pecans and vanilla; beat with a wooden spoon until fudge is thick and begins to lose its gloss (2 to 3 minutes).

Pour fudge into a buttered 8-inch square pan. Cool and cut into squares. Yield: about 2 dozen.
Helen Dill,
Oklahoma City, Oklahoma.

BUTTERSCOTCH PRALINES

1 (3⅝-ounce) package butterscotch
    pudding and pie filling mix
1 cup sugar
½ cup firmly packed brown sugar
½ cup evaporated milk
1 tablespoon butter
1½ cups chopped pecans

Combine first 5 ingredients in a large heavy saucepan, mixing well; bring to a boil. Stir in pecans; cook over medium heat, stirring occasionally, until mixture reaches soft ball stage (234°). Remove from heat; beat with a wooden spoon 2 to 3 minutes or until mixture is creamy and begins to thicken. Working rapidly, drop by rounded tablespoonfuls onto waxed paper; let cool. Yield: about 2½ dozen.
Mrs. Farmer L. Burns,
New Orleans, Louisiana.

Tip: To ensure success when using the cold-water test in candymaking, always pour the hot syrup into a fresh cup of cold water. Once the water has warmed from having hot syrup added, it's no longer cold enough for an accurate test.

November   253

NUT CLUSTERS

½ cup sugar
½ cup evaporated milk
1 tablespoon light corn syrup
1 (6-ounce) package semisweet chocolate
    morsels
¾ cup roasted salted peanuts

Combine sugar, milk, and corn syrup in a heavy 2-quart saucepan; cook over medium heat, stirring constantly, until mixture reaches soft ball stage (234°).

Remove from heat; add chocolate morsels, and beat with wooden spoon until chocolate melts. Stir in peanuts. Drop by rounded teaspoonfuls onto waxed paper; chill until set. Yield: about 2 dozen.

Note: Coarsely chopped pecans can be substituted for peanuts, if desired.
Mrs. Ted Robertson,
Canton, Texas.

BOURBON BALLS

2 cups vanilla wafer crumbs
2 cups chopped pecans or walnuts
2 cups sifted powdered sugar
¼ cup cocoa
3 tablespoons light corn syrup
¼ cup plus 2 tablespoons bourbon
Sifted powdered sugar

Combine first 4 ingredients; mix well. Combine corn syrup and bourbon; mix well, and stir into crumb mixture. Shape into 1-inch balls, and roll each in powdered sugar. Store in airtight container. Yield: about 6 dozen. *Robin Benjamin, Louisville, Kentucky.*

Nuts Make The Season Munchier

Nutmeats are one of the foods that make holidays special. Enjoy them not just in your traditional baked goods but as an appetizer with drinks or as a crunchy addition to the holiday buffet table.

Start your party with Chinese Fried Walnuts, sweetened with sugar and fried until golden. For a spicier beginning, try Hot Chili Nuts, home-roasted peanuts coated with chili powder and red pepper. The sweet tooths in the crowd will enjoy Glazed Pecans; this version calls for sugar, sour cream, and vanilla.

When you shop for nuts, keep in mind that those in their natural shells store longer and better than shelled nuts. Keep them in a cool, dry place, or you can refrigerate or freeze them. To store shelled nuts, place them in a tightly covered container and refrigerate or freeze.

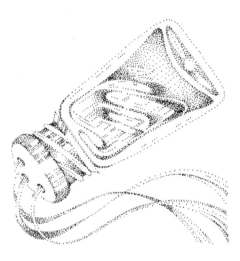

HOT CHILI NUTS

1 pound shelled raw peanuts
¼ cup peanut oil
1 tablespoon chili powder
¾ teaspoon paprika
1 teaspoon salt
½ teaspoon red pepper

Place peanuts in a shallow roasting pan; pour peanut oil over nuts, stirring well. Roast peanuts at 350° for 35 minutes or until light brown. Drain on paper towels. Combine remaining ingredients; sprinkle over peanuts, and stir until well coated. Yield: about 2½ cups.
Lattie Plyler,
Salisbury, North Carolina.

CHINESE FRIED WALNUTS

6 cups water
4 cups walnut halves
½ cup sugar
Vegetable oil
Salt

Pour water into a 4-quart saucepan; bring to a boil. Add walnuts, and allow to return to a boil; cook 1 minute. Drain. Rinse walnuts under hot water; drain well. Combine warm walnuts and sugar in a large mixing bowl; stir until the sugar dissolves.

Heat 1 inch of oil to 350°. Fry walnuts in oil 5 minutes or until golden brown. Drain on paper towels. Sprinkle lightly with salt. Cool. Store walnuts in a tightly covered container. Yield: 4 cups.
Gail Greene,
Birmingham, Alabama.

GLAZED PECANS

3 cups sugar
1 (8-ounce) carton commercial sour cream
2 teaspoons vanilla extract
5 cups pecan halves

Combine sugar and sour cream in a heavy 2½-quart saucepan. Cook over low heat, stirring constantly, until mixture reaches soft ball stage (240°). Remove from heat, and stir in vanilla. Continue stirring until mixture begins to cool. Add pecans, mixing well. Place pecans individually on waxed paper; cool completely. Yield: about 6 cups.
Judy Bonorato,
Huntsville, Alabama.

Right: *Instead of a cheese ball, shape our festive Cheese Ring (page 261); studded with parsley and served with strawberry preserves, it's dressed for the season.*

Page 258: *The flavor of fresh fruit is the key to Cranberry Muffins (page 249), while Cranberry-Nut Coffee Cake (page 250) relies on cranberry sauce for its flavor.*

Above: *Colorful Rice Salad (page 253), a medley of colors and flavors, is filling enough for a main dish. While the cherry tomatoes and lettuce are optional, they add a festive look.*

Right: *Toast the holidays with these festive beverages. Clockwise from top: Party Punch, Hot Apricot Nectar, Holiday Brew, and Syllabub (recipes on page 265).*

Far right: *Beautifully browned and presented on a bed of wild and regular rice, Duck With Orange Gravy (page 259) is an elegant alternative to the traditional roast turkey.*

Entrées Fit For A Feast

For many, choosing the entrée for a special holiday meal means simply selecting a turkey. A festive entrée doesn't have to mean turkey, as these recipes show. Try one, and start a new tradition in your house.

A succulent, crisp-skinned duck served with orange gravy, individual Brandied Cornish Hens, and quail with a mushroom gravy are some offerings.

For a real change of pace, try Rack of Lamb With Herb Mustard Glaze; before roasting, the lamb is coated with a mustard sauce flavored with garlic, rosemary, and soy sauce. Garnished and served on a bed of rice, it's a spectacular entrée.

We've also included a version of country ham that is soaked in wine, baked, then given a mustard and brown sugar glaze during its final baking.

BAKED QUAIL WITH MUSHROOMS

⅓ cup all-purpose flour
1 teaspoon salt
½ teaspoon pepper
6 quail, cleaned
2 tablespoons butter
½ pound fresh mushrooms, sliced
½ cup butter
¼ cup plus 1 tablespoon all-purpose flour
2 cups chicken broth
½ cup sherry
Hot cooked rice

Combine ⅓ cup flour, salt, and pepper. Dredge quail in flour mixture, and set aside.

Melt 2 tablespoons butter in a large skillet; add mushrooms, and sauté 4 minutes. Remove mushrooms from skillet; set aside.

Melt ½ cup butter in skillet; brown quail on both sides. Remove quail to a 1½-quart casserole. Add ¼ cup plus 1 tablespoon flour to drippings in skillet; cook 1 minute, stirring constantly. Gradually add chicken broth and sherry; cook over medium heat, stirring constantly, until gravy is thickened and bubbly. Stir in mushrooms.

Pour mushroom gravy over quail. Cover and bake at 350° for 1 hour. Serve over rice. Yield: 6 servings.

Diane J. Rabon,
Florence, South Carolina.

DUCK WITH ORANGE GRAVY

½ cup orange juice
½ cup apple jelly
1 (4- to 4½-pound) dressed duck
½ teaspoon salt
1 stalk celery, cut into 2-inch pieces
1 small onion, quartered
2 tablespoons butter or margarine
1 cup uncooked regular rice
1 (4-ounce) package wild rice
Chopped fresh parsley
Orange twists
Parsley sprigs
Orange Gravy

Combine juice and jelly in a small saucepan; cook over medium heat, stirring often, until jelly melts. Remove from heat, and set aside.

Rub cavity of duck with salt; stuff with celery and onion. Close cavity of duck with skewers. Place duck, breast side up, on rack in a shallow roasting pan; dot with butter. Bake, uncovered, at 375° for 1 hour, basting often with jelly mixture. Cover duck loosely with aluminum foil; bake 1 to 1½ hours, basting often.

Prepare regular and wild rice according to package directions; stir together, and spoon onto serving platter. Sprinkle with chopped parsley. Place duck on top of rice; garnish with orange twists and parsley sprigs. Serve with Orange Gravy. Yield: 4 servings.

Orange Gravy:

¼ cup butter or margarine
¼ cup all-purpose flour
2 cups milk
½ cup orange juice
½ teaspoon paprika
1 teaspoon salt
¼ teaspoon pepper
⅔ cup raisins

Melt butter in a heavy saucepan over low heat; add flour, stirring until smooth. Cook 1 minute, stirring constantly. Gradually add milk and orange juice; cook over medium heat, stirring constantly, until thickened and bubbly. Remove from heat, and stir in remaining ingredients. Yield: about 3 cups.

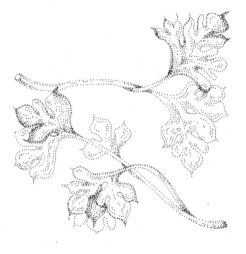

BRANDIED CORNISH HENS

2 (1¼-pound) Cornish hens
⅓ cup finely chopped fresh parsley
½ teaspoon salt
½ cup butter or margarine, softened and divided
½ cup red currant jelly
½ cup brandy

Remove giblets from hens; reserve for another use. Rinse hens with cold water, and pat dry. Combine parsley, salt, and ¼ cup butter; mix well. Stuff cavity of hens with parsley mixture, and truss securely. Place hens breast side up in shallow baking pan. Rub hens with remaining ¼ cup butter. Bake at 375° for 30 minutes.

Combine jelly and brandy in a small saucepan; cook over low heat, stirring often, until jelly melts. Spoon half of jelly mixture over hens, and bake 30 additional minutes; baste every 5 to 10 minutes with remaining jelly mixture and pan drippings. Yield: 2 servings.

Norma Patelunas,
St. Petersburg, Florida.

COUNTRY HAM IN WINE

1 (12- to 14-pound) country ham
8 cups Chablis or other dry white wine
Whole cloves
2½ cups Burgundy or other dry red wine
Ground cloves
¼ cup firmly packed brown sugar
¼ cup dry mustard

Place ham in a very large container; cover with cold water, and add 4 cups Chablis. Soak ham overnight. Scrub ham thoroughly with a stiff brush; then place ham, skin side down, on rack in a large roasting pan. Pour remaining 4 cups Chablis over ham. Cover and bake at 350° for 4 hours, basting every 30 minutes with pan drippings.

Carefully remove ham from pan juices; remove skin. Place ham, fat side up, on a cutting board; score fat in a diamond design, and stud with whole cloves. Return ham to roaster, fat side up. Pour Burgundy over ham; lightly sprinkle with ground cloves. Combine brown sugar and mustard, stirring well. Coat exposed portion of ham with brown sugar mixture. Bake, uncovered, at 325° for 1 hour and 30 minutes.

Remove ham from roaster; discard pan drippings. Cool ham thoroughly; place on a carving board or platter. To serve, thinly slice ham. Yield: 24 to 28 servings.
Griffith S. Clark,
Pennington, New Jersey.

ARISTA OF PORK

1 (4- to 5-pound) pork loin roast
3 cloves garlic, sliced
1½ teaspoons dried whole rosemary, crumbled
½ teaspoon salt
¼ teaspoon coarsely ground black pepper
3 whole cloves
2 cups Chablis or other dry white wine
2 cups water

Trim excess fat from pork; cut small slits in meat, and insert slivers of garlic. Rub meat with rosemary, salt, and pepper, and stud with whole cloves. Place meat, fat side up, on rack in a shallow roasting pan. Pour wine and water into pan.

Roast at 325° until done, allowing 30 to 35 minutes per pound (170° on meat thermometer); baste occasionally. Cut pork into thin slices, and serve with pan drippings. Yield: 8 servings.
Mrs. Ralph E. Chase,
Hendersonville, North Carolina.

RACK OF LAMB WITH HERB MUSTARD GLAZE

½ cup prepared mustard
2 tablespoons soy sauce
1 clove garlic, minced
1 teaspoon dried whole rosemary, crushed
¼ teaspoon ground ginger
1 egg
2 tablespoons olive oil
2 (2½-pound) racks of lamb
Hot cooked rice (optional)

Combine first 6 ingredients in container of electric blender; blend 15 seconds or until smooth. Add oil, one drop at a time, to mustard mixture; blend on low speed of blender until mixture is light and creamy.

Place lamb, fat side up, on rack in a shallow roasting pan; insert meat thermometer in one of the racks, making sure it does not touch fat or bone. Brush mustard mixture on lamb.

Bake at 350° until meat thermometer registers 175° to 180° (about 1 hour and 20 to 30 minutes). Serve over rice, if desired. Yield: 8 servings.
Mary Ellen Shuppert,
Santa Monica, California.

Appetizers Invite A Party

When you open your house for the holidays, you'll want to be ready with a variety of tempting appetizers. Whether you're planning a casual evening with a few friends or a large formal open house, you'll find our selection of appetizers, both hot and cold, suitable to the occasion.

Our Cheese Ring is dressed especially for the season. A center of strawberry preserves adds holiday color and a flavor twist; sprigs of parsley help transform the ring into a colorful wreath.

Other tempting snacks include make-ahead Chafing Dish Meatballs; a large, colorful, and easy-to-assemble casserole of Layered Nacho Dip; and crunchy Candied Nuts, made with an assortment of favorite nuts.

CHAFING DISH MEATBALLS

1 pound ground beef
½ cup fine dry breadcrumbs
⅓ cup minced onion
¼ cup milk
1 egg, beaten
1 tablespoon minced fresh parsley
1 teaspoon salt
½ teaspoon Worcestershire sauce
⅛ teaspoon pepper
¼ cup shortening
1 (12-ounce) bottle chili sauce
1 (10-ounce) jar grape jelly

Combine first 9 ingredients, mixing well; shape into 1-inch meatballs. Cook in hot shortening over medium heat for 10 to 15 minutes or until browned. Drain on paper towels.

Combine chili sauce and grape jelly in a medium saucepan; stir well. Add meatballs; simmer 30 minutes, stirring occasionally. Serve in a chafing dish. Yield: 5 dozen.
Geraldine Murphy,
Corbin, Kentucky.

CHICKEN NUT PUFFS

1 cup chicken broth
½ cup butter or margarine
2 teaspoons Worcestershire sauce
1 cup all-purpose flour
1 tablespoon chopped fresh parsley
2 teaspoons seasoned salt
¾ teaspoon celery seeds
½ teaspoon paprika
⅛ teaspoon red pepper
4 eggs
1 (5-ounce) can boned chicken, drained
¼ cup chopped toasted almonds

Combine broth, butter, and Worcestershire sauce in a saucepan; bring to a boil. Combine next 6 ingredients; add to boiling mixture all at once, stirring vigorously over low heat for approximately 1 minute or until mixture leaves sides of pan and forms a smooth ball. Remove pan from heat, and allow mixture to cool slightly.

Add eggs, one at a time, beating with a wooden spoon after each addition; beat until batter is smooth. Stir in chicken and almonds. Drop teaspoonfuls of batter on ungreased baking sheets. Bake at 400° for 15 to 18 minutes or until golden brown and puffed. Remove from baking sheets immediately. Yield: about 7½ dozen.

Barbara Beacom,
Kernersville, North Carolina.

HOT CHEESE AND CRAB DIP

2½ cups (10 ounces) shredded Cheddar
  cheese
8 (1-ounce) slices American cheese
⅓ cup milk
1 (6½-ounce) can crabmeat, drained and
  flaked
½ cup dry white wine

Combine cheese and milk in a heavy saucepan; cook over low heat, stirring until cheese melts. Stir in crabmeat and wine; cook until heated. Serve with crackers. Yield: 2 cups. *Jayne Perala,*
Salem, Virginia.

LAYERED NACHO DIP

1 (16-ounce) can refried beans
½ (1.25-ounce) package taco seasoning
  mix
1 (6-ounce) carton avocado dip
1 (8-ounce) carton commercial sour cream
1 (4½-ounce) can chopped ripe olives
2 large tomatoes, diced
1 small onion, finely chopped
1 (4-ounce) can chopped green chiles
1½ cups (6 ounces) shredded Monterey
  Jack cheese

Combine beans and seasoning mix; spread bean mixture in a 12- x 8- x 2-inch

dish. Layer remaining ingredients in order listed. Serve with corn chips. Yield: about 8 cups. *Diana Curtis,*
Albuquerque, New Mexico.

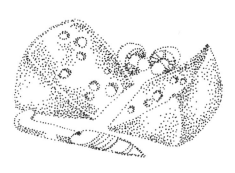

CHEESE RING

1 (16-ounce) package extra sharp Cheddar
  cheese, shredded
1 (16-ounce) package medium Cheddar
  cheese, shredded
1 small onion, grated
1 cup mayonnaise
1 teaspoon red pepper
1 cup chopped pecans
Parsley sprigs
Strawberry preserves (optional)

Combine first 5 ingredients, and mix well. Sprinkle about ¼ cup pecans in an oiled 7-cup ring mold, and press cheese mixture into mold. Chill until firm.

Unmold on platter, and pat remaining pecans onto cheese ring. Garnish with parsley sprigs. Serve on crackers with strawberry preserves on top, if desired. Yield: 1 cheese ring. *Vivian Knox,*
Columbus, Georgia.

CARAWAY WAFERS

1 cup butter, softened
1 (8-ounce) package cream cheese,
  softened
¼ cup whipping cream
2½ cups all-purpose flour
2 teaspoons salt, divided
1 egg white
1 teaspoon water
3 tablespoons caraway seeds

Combine butter and cream cheese; cream until light and fluffy. Add whipping cream, and beat well.

Combine flour and 1 teaspoon salt; stir well. Add flour mixture to creamed mixture, beating well.

Divide dough into 3 equal portions. Shape each portion into a roll, 1 inch in diameter; wrap in waxed paper, and chill 3 hours or until firm.

Unwrap rolls, and cut into ¼-inch slices; place on lightly greased baking sheets. Combine egg white and water; mix well. Brush wafers with egg white mixture, and sprinkle with caraway seeds and remaining salt. Bake at 350° for 25 to 30 minutes or until lightly browned. Yield: about 12 dozen.

Note: To freeze, place sliced dough on baking sheets; freeze until firm. Place in plastic bags, and freeze until needed. To serve, thaw, and bake as directed. *Anne Fezell,*
Bel Air, Maryland.

CANDIED NUTS

2 cups sugar
⅛ teaspoon cream of tartar
½ cup water
⅓ cup whole blanched almonds
⅓ cup pecan halves
⅓ cup walnut halves

Combine sugar, cream of tartar, and water in a heavy medium saucepan; stir well. Boil, without stirring, until mixture reaches soft ball stage (240°). Add nuts; boil until mixture reaches hard crack stage (300°).

Strain nut mixture through a sieve. Quickly turn nuts onto a buttered baking sheet; immediately separate nuts with a fork. Yield: 1 cup.

Note: Do not double this recipe. If additional nuts are desired, prepare two batches. *Edna A. Peavy,*
Atlanta, Georgia.

Tip: Use a pastry tube to stuff eggs, potatoes, or celery to give a decorative look.

Take A Break With This Casual Menu

When the calorie-packed foods and the fast-paced tempo of the holiday season have you longing for a simple, relaxing meal at home, our casual menu is probably just what you had in mind. Built around a soup and sandwich combination, this menu provides welcome relief from the rich entrées and elaborate side dishes of the season.

Start the meal with Curried Dip and an assortment of crisp, raw vegetables such as broccoli, cauliflower, celery, and mushrooms. For the main course, Cheesy Carrot Soup, a combination of carrots, onion, celery, and Cheddar cheese, is delicious and creamy and just right for a chilly evening. With the soup, serve Greek Pocket Steaks, fried beef steaks in pocket bread rounds that are topped with marinated vegetables. Butter Pecan Pie Squares and After-Dinner Coffee offer the perfect ending for this casual meal.

**Curried Dip With Assorted
Raw Vegetables
Cheesy Carrot Soup
Greek Pocket Steaks
Butter Pecan Pie Squares
After-Dinner Coffee**

CURRIED DIP

1 cup mayonnaise
1 teaspoon curry powder
1 teaspoon minced onion
1 teaspoon horseradish
1 teaspoon prepared mustard
1 teaspoon vinegar

Combine all ingredients; mix well. Serve with assorted raw vegetables. Yield: about 1 cup. *Freda Lovelace, Wytheville, Virginia.*

Tip: Cut raw turnips into strips and serve as a snack or hors d'oeuvre. They're good served with a dip.

CHEESY CARROT SOUP

3 carrots, peeled and shredded
1 small onion, chopped
½ cup chopped celery
2 cups chicken broth
2 cups milk
¼ cup all-purpose flour
¼ teaspoon salt
⅛ teaspoon pepper
1½ cups (6 ounces) shredded medium
    Cheddar cheese

Combine first 4 ingredients in a medium saucepan; bring to a boil. Reduce heat, and let simmer for 15 minutes.

Combine milk, flour, salt, and pepper in container of electric blender; blend until frothy. Spoon in one-third of the vegetable-broth mixture; blend 20 seconds. Repeat until all ingredients have been blended. Pour mixture back into the saucepan. Stir in cheese. Cook over medium heat, stirring constantly, until cheese is melted. Yield: about 5 cups.
Mrs. James Tuthill, Virginia Beach, Virginia.

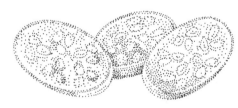

GREEK POCKET STEAKS

2 tablespoons olive oil
1 tablespoon red wine vinegar
½ teaspoon dried whole oregano
¼ teaspoon salt
1 medium cucumber, thinly sliced
1 large tomato, chopped
2 (6-inch) pocket bread rounds
1 medium onion, thinly sliced and
    separated into rings
1 tablespoon vegetable oil
4 (4-ounce) cubed beef steaks
½ teaspoon salt
Pepper to taste
1 cup shredded lettuce

Combine olive oil, vinegar, oregano, and ¼ teaspoon salt; add cucumber and tomato, tossing gently. Chill 2 hours.

Cut pocket bread rounds in half; place on baking sheet. Bake at 250° for 10 minutes or until warm.

Sauté onion in oil until tender. Remove onion and set aside. Cook steaks on each side 3 minutes or until done. Sprinkle steaks with ½ teaspoon salt and pepper.

Place 1 steak and several onion rings in each half. Gently toss lettuce with cucumber mixture; spoon into each half. Yield: 4 sandwiches. *Anne Ringer, Warner Robins, Georgia.*

BUTTER PECAN PIE SQUARES

1¼ cups all-purpose flour
⅓ cup sugar
½ cup butter, softened
2 eggs, beaten
⅔ cup sugar
¾ cup honey
2 tablespoons all-purpose flour
¼ teaspoon salt
2 tablespoons butter, melted
1½ teaspoons vanilla extract
1 cup chopped pecans

Combine 1¼ cups flour and ⅓ cup sugar in a medium bowl; cut in ½ cup butter with a pastry blender until mixture resembles coarse meal. Press mixture evenly into a greased 9-inch square pan. Bake at 375° for 15 minutes.

Combine next 7 ingredients, and beat well. Stir in pecans. Pour filling over prepared crust. Bake at 350° for 25 minutes or until firm. Let cool on rack; cut into squares. Yield: about 3 dozen.
Mrs. R. D. Walker, Garland, Texas.

AFTER-DINNER COFFEE

4 (1-ounce) packages instant cocoa
1 tablespoon plus 1 teaspoon instant
    coffee
4 cups boiling water
¼ cup brandy
Whipped cream

Combine instant cocoa and coffee; add boiling water, stirring until cocoa and coffee dissolve. Stir in brandy. Pour coffee into mugs; top with whipped cream. Yield: 4 servings. *Mary Nelson, Richardson, Texas.*

You're Ahead With These Recipes

What could be more welcome during this busy season than dishes that can be made ahead of time? Whether you're planning a gala dinner party or a quiet family dinner, you'll want to include some foods that can be partially or completely prepared in advance.

For an appetizer, we recommend Tangy Cheese Ball coated with pecans. Brandy Applesauce Loaf goes equally well as an accompaniment or a light dessert. Hot Curried Fruit and Cheesy Spinach Casserole make festive side dishes, and Chicken-and-Dressing Casserole is a delicious, timesaving entrée.

CHICKEN-AND-DRESSING CASSEROLE

4 large chicken breasts or 1 (2½- to 3-pound) broiler-fryer, cut up
1 (10¾-ounce) can cream of chicken soup, undiluted
1 (10¾-ounce) can cream of mushroom soup, undiluted
1 (8-ounce) package herb-seasoned stuffing mix
½ cup butter or margarine, melted

Cook chicken in boiling water until tender. Remove chicken from broth. Strain broth, reserving 2⅔ cups. Bone chicken, and cut meat into small pieces; set aside.

Combine chicken soup with half the broth; mix well and set aside. Combine mushroom soup with remaining broth; mix well and set aside.

Combine stuffing mix and butter; reserve ¼ cup for garnish. Spoon half of remaining stuffing mixture into a lightly greased 13- x 9- x 2-inch baking dish; top with half the chicken. Cover with chicken soup mixture; repeat layers. Pour mushroom soup over layers; sprinkle with reserved stuffing mixture. Cover and refrigerate overnight.

Remove casserole from refrigerator 15 minutes before baking. Uncover and bake at 350° for 30 to 45 minutes. Yield: 8 to 10 servings. *Carol Noble, Burgaw, North Carolina.*

BRANDY APPLESAUCE LOAF

1 cup raisins
¼ cup plus 1 tablespoon brandy
½ cup shortening
1 cup sugar
1 egg, beaten
2 cups all-purpose flour, divided
1 teaspoon soda
½ teaspoon salt
1 teaspoon ground cinnamon
½ teaspoon ground nutmeg
¼ teaspoon ground allspice
¼ teaspoon ground cloves
1 cup applesauce
1 cup chopped pecans

Combine raisins and brandy, stirring well. Cover and refrigerate several hours or overnight.

Line a 9- x 5- x 3-inch loaf pan with waxed paper; grease and set aside.

Cream shortening; gradually add sugar, beating well. Add egg, mixing well. Combine 1⅔ cups flour, soda, salt, and spices; add to creamed mixture alternately with applesauce, beginning and ending with flour mixture.

Dredge pecans and raisins in remaining ⅓ cup flour; stir to coat well. Fold into batter. Spoon batter into prepared pan. Bake at 350° for 1 hour and 15 minutes or until done. Cool in pan 10 minutes; remove from pan, and cool completely. Wrap in aluminum foil, and store in refrigerator. Yield: 1 loaf.
Mrs. Harvey Kidd, Hernando, Mississippi.

TANGY CHEESE BALL

2 (8-ounce) packages cream cheese, softened
1½ cups (6 ounces) shredded sharp Cheddar cheese
1 small onion, minced
2 tablespoons Worcestershire sauce
1½ teaspoons minced garlic
1 teaspoon lemon juice
1 cup chopped pecans

Combine all ingredients, except pecans; mix well. Chill at least 1 hour. Shape into a ball, and roll in pecans; refrigerate overnight. Serve with crackers. Yield: 1 cheese ball. *Jan Lewis, Simpsonville, South Carolina.*

CHEESY SPINACH CASSEROLE

2 (10-ounce) packages frozen chopped spinach
1 (8-ounce) carton commercial sour cream
2 tablespoons dry onion soup mix
1 cup (4 ounces) shredded medium Cheddar cheese

Cook spinach according to package directions, omitting salt; drain well.

Combine spinach, sour cream, and onion soup mix; mix well. Spoon into a lightly greased 1-quart casserole. Sprinkle cheese over spinach mixture. Cover and chill overnight.

Remove casserole from refrigerator 30 minutes before baking. Bake at 350° for 30 minutes. Yield: 6 servings.
Geraldine Murphy, Corbin, Kentucky.

IRISH POTATO CASSEROLE

8 to 10 medium potatoes, peeled
1 (8-ounce) package cream cheese, softened
1 (8-ounce) carton commercial sour cream
½ cup butter or margarine, melted
¼ cup chopped chives
1 clove garlic, minced
2 teaspoons salt
Paprika

Cook potatoes in boiling water about 30 minutes or until tender. Drain potatoes, and mash.

Beat cream cheese with an electric mixer until smooth. Add potatoes and remaining ingredients except paprika; beat just until combined. Spoon mixture into a lightly buttered 2-quart casserole; sprinkle with paprika. Cover and refrigerate overnight.

Remove from refrigerator 15 minutes before baking. Uncover and bake at 350° for 30 minutes or until thoroughly heated. Yield: 8 to 10 servings.
Mrs. E. R. Mosteller, Morganton, North Carolina.

Tip: New potatoes should be cooked in boiling water. Old potatoes should start in cold water and be brought to a boil.

HOT CURRIED FRUIT

1 (16-ounce) can sliced pears
1 (16-ounce) can peach halves
1 (15½-ounce) can pineapple chunks
1 (16-ounce) can apricot halves
1 (6-ounce) jar maraschino cherries
1 (16½-ounce) can pitted dark sweet
  cherries
1 cup firmly packed brown sugar
1 tablespoon curry powder
¼ cup butter or margarine
¼ teaspoon ground cinnamon
⅛ teaspoon ground nutmeg
⅛ teaspoon salt
1 tablespoon lemon juice

Drain fruit and pat dry with paper towels; place in a 13- x 9- x 2-inch baking dish. Sprinkle with brown sugar and curry powder, and mix gently; dot with butter. Sprinkle with remaining ingredients. Bake at 325° for 30 minutes. Refrigerate several hours or overnight.

Remove from refrigerator 15 minutes before baking. Bake at 325° for 30 minutes. Yield: 8 to 10 servings.
Mrs. Thomas D. Pinson,
Coral Springs, Florida.

FESTIVE CRANBERRY SALAD

3½ cups fresh cranberries
1 cup water
1 cup sugar
1 (6-ounce) package cherry-flavored
  gelatin
1½ cups cold water
2 (16-ounce) cans seedless white grapes
1 (20-ounce) can crushed pineapple,
  drained
1 cup chopped pecans
1 (12-ounce) container frozen whipped
  topping, thawed
2 (3-ounce) packages cream cheese,
  softened
2 cups miniature marshmallows

Wash cranberries; combine berries and 1 cup water in a saucepan. Cook 7 to 10 minutes or until all berries pop. Drain berries, reserving juice. Measure juice; add hot water, if necessary, to measure 1½ cups.

Combine cranberries, 1½ cups hot cranberry liquid, sugar, and gelatin; mix well, stirring to dissolve gelatin. Add cold water, and chill until the consistency of unbeaten egg white.

Combine grapes, pineapple, and pecans; mix well. Fold fruit-nut mixture into gelatin mixture. Pour into a 13- x 9- x 2-inch baking dish; cover dish, and refrigerate overnight.

Combine whipped topping and cream cheese; mix well. Fold in marshmallows. Cover and chill overnight.

Remove topping from refrigerator, and let stand about 15 minutes or until slightly softened. Spread topping over salad. Cut into squares to serve. Yield: 15 servings. *Rhonda Matson,*
St. Albans, West Virginia.

Taste The Holidays In These Cakes

You'll really get into the holiday spirit when you bake one of these special cakes. Filled with fruit, nuts, and candies, they're festively flavored for the season.

Our Fruited Pound Cake will remind you of fruitcake and pound cake at the same time. Favorite Holiday Cake is a two-layer beauty with a coconut filling and chocolate frosting. Candy orange slices, coconut, pecans, and dates enrich our Orange-Slice Cake.

ORANGE-SLICE CAKE

3½ cups all-purpose flour
½ teaspoon salt
1 pound candy orange slices, chopped
1 (8-ounce) package chopped dates
2 cups chopped pecans
1 (3½-ounce) can flaked coconut
¾ cup butter or margarine, softened
2 cups sugar
4 eggs
½ cup buttermilk
1 teaspoon soda
½ cup orange juice
½ cup sifted powdered sugar

Combine flour and salt; stir and set aside.

Combine orange slices, dates, pecans, and coconut; stir in ½ cup flour mixture. Set aside.

Cream butter; gradually add sugar, beating until light and fluffy and sugar is dissolved. Add eggs, one at a time, beating well after each addition.

Combine buttermilk and soda, mixing well. Add remaining 3 cups flour mixture alternately with buttermilk to creamed mixture, beginning and ending with flour. Add candy mixture; stir until well blended.

Spoon batter into a greased and floured 10-inch tube pan. Bake at 300° for 2 hours or until cake tests done.

Combine orange juice and powdered sugar. Punch holes in top of cake using a wooden pick; while cake is still hot, spoon glaze over top. Let cake cool before removing from pan. Yield: one 10-inch cake. *Mrs. Raymond Lunsford,*
Hiltons, Virginia.

FAVORITE HOLIDAY CAKE

1 cup shortening
2 cups sugar
5 eggs
1 cup all-purpose flour
1 cup self-rising flour
1 cup milk
2 teaspoons vanilla extract
Coconut Filling
Chocolate Frosting

Cream shortening; gradually add sugar, beating until mixture is light and fluffy and sugar is dissolved. Add eggs, one at a time, beating well after each addition.

Combine flour; add to creamed mixture alternately with milk, beginning and ending with flour mixture. Add the vanilla, mixing well.

Pour into two greased and floured 9-inch cakepans. Bake at 350° for 30 to 35 minutes or until cake tests done. Cool in pans 10 minutes; remove from pans, and cool completely.

Split cake layers in half horizontally. Place half of one cake layer, cut side up, on a cake plate; spread evenly with

one-third Coconut Filling. Repeat procedure with second and third layers. Place remaining layer, cut side down, on top of cake. Frost with Chocolate Frosting. Yield: one 4-layer cake.

Coconut Filling:

1 cup sugar
1 cup milk
1 pound frozen coconut, thawed
12 large marshmallows
1 teaspoon vanilla extract

Combine sugar and milk in a saucepan; bring to a boil. Add coconut and marshmallows; boil over medium heat for 5 minutes. Remove from heat, and stir in vanilla. Yield: about 2½ cups filling.

Chocolate Frosting:

2 cups sugar
½ cup butter or margarine
1 cup evaporated milk
2 to 3 tablespoons cocoa

Combine all ingredients; cook over medium heat almost to soft ball stage (230°), stirring constantly. Remove from heat. Beat until thick enough to spread. Yield: enough frosting for one 4-layer cake.   *Mrs. Bobby Norris,*
Guin, Alabama.

FRUITED POUND CAKE

1 cup butter, softened
1 (8-ounce) package cream cheese, softened
1½ cups sugar
4 eggs
2¼ cups all-purpose flour, divided
1½ teaspoons baking powder
Grated rind of 1 lemon
1 cup chopped mixed candied fruit
½ cup golden seedless raisins
½ cup dates, chopped
½ cup chopped pecans
Powdered sugar
Candied cherries (optional)
Candied pineapple slices (optional)

Cream butter and cream cheese; gradually add sugar, beating until light and fluffy and sugar is dissolved. Add eggs, one at a time, beating well after each addition.

Combine 1¾ cups flour and baking powder; gradually add to creamed mixture, and beat until well blended. Dredge lemon rind, candied fruit, raisins, dates, and pecans with remaining ½ cup flour; stir to coat well. Stir mixture into batter.

Spoon into a greased and floured 10-inch tube pan. Bake at 325° about 1 hour and 20 minutes. Cool cake 10 minutes; remove from pan. Dust top with powdered sugar. Garnish with candied cherries and pineapple slices, if desired. Yield: one 10-inch cake.   *Elaine Bell,*
Dexter, New Mexico.

Toast The Season's Best Beverages

When the holiday celebration turns to toasting the season, we have some delicious ideas for sipping. Holiday Brew lets your guests enjoy eggnog in a version so thick and rich you'll have to serve it with a spoon. For something a little lighter but just as traditional, offer them Syllabub.

HOT APRICOT NECTAR

1 cup water
2 tablespoons sugar
4 whole cloves
1 (3-inch) cinnamon stick
1 (12-ounce) can apricot nectar
2 tablespoons lemon juice
Cinnamon sticks (optional)
Lemon slices (optional)

Combine water, sugar, cloves, and cinnamon stick in a small saucepan; bring to a boil, stirring until sugar is dissolved. Strain the mixture, discarding cloves and cinnamon stick.

Gradually add nectar and juice to hot mixture; heat thoroughly. Garnish with cinnamon sticks and lemon slices, if desired. Yield: about 2½ cups.

Mabel B. Couch,
Chelsea, Oklahoma.

HOLIDAY BREW

4 eggs, separated
½ cup sugar
⅛ teaspoon salt
½ to ¾ cup dark rum
2 cups whipping cream, whipped
Ground nutmeg

Beat egg yolks until thick and lemon colored; gradually add sugar and salt, beating well. Slowly stir in rum. Cover and chill at least 1 hour.

Beat egg whites (at room temperature) until stiff. Fold whipped cream into rum mixture; fold in egg whites. Sprinkle with nutmeg before serving. Yield: 6 cups.   *Tilley W. Mizzell,*
Charleston, South Carolina.

PARTY PUNCH

1 quart orange juice, chilled
1 quart cranberry juice, chilled
2 (33.8-ounce) bottles ginger ale, chilled
1 (32-ounce) bottle champagne, chilled
Fresh strawberries (optional)

Combine orange juice and cranberry juice in punch bowl. Gently stir in ginger ale and champagne. Garnish punch with fresh strawberries, if desired. Yield: about 20 cups. *Geraldine Hurst,*
Shreveport, Louisiana.

SYLLABUB

½ cup sugar
1 cup white wine
1 quart half-and-half
Whipped cream
Ground nutmeg

Combine sugar and wine in a 1½-quart saucepan; place over low heat until sugar dissolves, stirring constantly. Remove from heat, and gradually stir in half-and-half. Beat mixture until frothy, and chill thoroughly. Before serving, top with whipped cream, and sprinkle with nutmeg. Yield: 5 cups.

Mrs. Thad M. Jones,
Houston, Texas.

Be Famous For These Pecan Treats

Southerners can make almost any dessert better simply by adding pecans. We're famous, in fact, for our pecan pies, but don't stop there with fall's bountiful harvest. Try Brown Sugar Pecans, Pecan Clusters, and be sure to make our Heavenly Pecan Torte.

PECAN TARTS

¾ cup firmly packed light brown sugar
1 tablespoon margarine
1 egg
½ teaspoon vanilla extract
Pinch of salt
1 cup pecans, chopped
Cream Cheese Patty Shells

Combine first 6 ingredients in a small saucepan; cook over low heat, stirring frequently, until mixture is melted and well blended. Fill each patty shell half full with filling. Bake at 350° for 30 to 35 minutes. Yield: 15 tarts.

Cream Cheese Patty Shells:

1 (3-ounce) package cream cheese, softened
½ cup margarine, softened
1 cup all-purpose flour

Combine cream cheese and margarine; cream until smooth. Add flour, mixing well. Refrigerate dough at least 2 hours.

Shape the dough into 15 balls; put each ball into a greased 1¾-inch muffin tin, and shape into a shell. Yield: 15 patty shells. *Mrs. Marvin H. White, Pensacola, Florida.*

GOLDEN PECAN PIE

¾ cup sugar
1 tablespoon all-purpose flour
Pinch of salt
3 eggs, well beaten
1 cup light corn syrup
1 teaspoon vanilla extract
2 tablespoons margarine, softened
1 cup pecan halves
1 unbaked 9-inch pastry shell

Combine dry ingredients in large mixing bowl. Add eggs, syrup, vanilla, and margarine; beat with electric mixer until blended. Stir in pecans. Pour mixture into pastry shell. Bake at 350° for 55 to 60 minutes. Yield: one 9-inch pie.
Mrs. J. W. Hutchison, Clarksville, Tennessee.

MAPLE-PECAN PIE

3 eggs, well beaten
½ cup sugar
1 cup maple or maple-flavored syrup
Dash of salt
3 tablespoons butter, melted
1 cup pecan halves
1 unbaked 9-inch pastry shell

Combine first 5 ingredients, mixing well. Sprinkle pecans evenly in pastry shell. Pour syrup mixture over pecans.
Bake at 400° for 12 minutes. Reduce heat to 375°, and bake 35 minutes or until set. Yield: one 9-inch pie.
Maxine Devore, Knob Lick, Kentucky.

HEAVENLY PECAN TORTE

3 cups finely chopped pecans
2 tablespoons all-purpose flour
2 teaspoons baking powder
6 eggs, separated
1½ cups sugar, divided
1½ teaspoons vanilla extract
¼ teaspoon salt
½ cup powdered sugar
1 pint whipping cream
½ cup grated sweet cooking chocolate
Pecan halves

Grease bottoms of three 9-inch round cakepans, line with waxed paper, and grease paper. Combine pecans, flour, and baking powder; set aside.
Combine egg yolks and 1 cup sugar; beat until thick and light colored. Add vanilla, and mix well. Stir into pecan mixture.
Combine egg whites (at room temperature) and salt; beat on high speed of electric mixer until stiff but not dry. Gradually add ½ cup sugar, beating until stiff peaks form. Gently fold in pecan mixture. Pour into prepared pans. Bake at 325° for 30 minutes. Cool 15 minutes. Loosen layers around edges, and turn out of pans onto wire racks; remove waxed paper.
Combine powdered sugar and whipping cream; beat until soft peaks form. Chill. Spread whipped cream and sprinkle grated chocolate between layers and on top of torte. Garnish top with pecan halves. Yield: 12 servings.
Alma Parsons, Springdale, Arkansas.

BROWN SUGAR PECANS

2 egg whites
¾ cup firmly packed brown sugar
1 tablespoon vanilla extract
Pinch of salt
2 cups pecan halves

Beat egg whites (at room temperature) until stiff peaks form. Gradually add sugar, beating until well blended. Fold in remaining ingredients.
Drop by rounded teaspoonfuls onto greased cookie sheets. Bake at 250° for 30 minutes. Remove from sheet to wire racks to cool. Yield: 6 to 7 dozen.
Reba Walley, Purvis, Mississippi.

PECAN CLUSTERS

1 (7-ounce) jar marshmallow creme
1½ pounds milk chocolate kisses
5 cups sugar
1 (13-ounce) can evaporated milk
½ cup butter
6 cups pecan halves

Place marshmallow creme and kisses in a large bowl; set aside. Combine sugar, milk, and butter in a saucepan. Bring mixture to a boil; cook for 8 minutes. Pour over marshmallow creme and kisses, stirring until well blended. Stir in pecans. Drop by teaspoonfuls onto waxed paper. Yield: about 12 dozen.
Margaret H. King, Calhoun, Georgia.

Side Dishes Dressed For The Holidays

Holiday feasting calls for side dishes that are as festive and colorful as the season itself. These side dishes are just that—and more, bringing an elegant look and marvelous flavor to that special meal.

Choices range from Broccoli Elegant to Sweet Potato Surprise (the surprise is a hint of bourbon) and everyone's favorite, Creamy Corn Pudding. Our fruit dishes include Tipsy Fruit Cup, which is flavored with Grand Marnier, and Cheese-Filled Pears.

ACORN SQUASH DELIGHT

2 acorn squash
¼ cup butter or margarine
1 tablespoon plus 1 teaspoon sugar
2 teaspoons ground cinnamon
¾ cup water

Cut squash in half, and remove seeds.

Place 1 tablespoon butter, 1 teaspoon sugar, and ½ teaspoon cinnamon in each squash half.

Place squash, cut side up, in a 13- x 9- x 2-inch baking dish. Pour water into dish. Cover and bake at 400° for about 45 minutes or until squash is tender. Yield: 4 servings.   *Crystal Stimpson, Oklahoma City, Oklahoma.*

SWEET POTATO SURPRISE

10 medium-size sweet potatoes
¾ cup butter or margarine
⅓ cup bourbon
½ teaspoon salt
½ cup coarsely chopped walnuts or pecans
2 tablespoons butter or margarine

Wash sweet potatoes well; rub with vegetable oil. Place potatoes on a baking sheet, and bake at 400° for 1 hour or until tender.

Cool potatoes to touch; remove pulp.

Combine pulp, ¾ cup butter, bourbon, and salt. Beat with electric mixer until light and fluffy. Stir in walnuts, reserving 2 tablespoons for garnish. Spoon potato mixture into a lightly greased 1½-quart casserole; dot with 2 tablespoons butter, and sprinkle with reserved walnuts. Bake at 350° for 20 minutes. Yield: 8 servings.
Lilly S. Bradley, Salem, Virginia.

BROCCOLI ELEGANT

1½ cups water
¼ cup butter or margarine
1 (6-ounce) package cornbread stuffing mix
2 (10-ounce) packages frozen broccoli spears, thawed
2 tablespoons butter or margarine
2 tablespoons all-purpose flour
1 teaspoon chicken-flavored bouillon granules
¾ cup milk
1 (3-ounce) package cream cheese, softened
¼ teaspoon salt
4 green onions, sliced
1 cup (4 ounces) shredded Cheddar cheese
Paprika

Combine water, ¼ cup butter, and packaged seasoning mix; bring to a boil. Remove from heat; stir in stuffing crumbs, and let stand 5 minutes.

Spoon stuffing around inside edge of a lightly buttered 13- x 9- x 2-inch baking dish, leaving a well in the center. Place broccoli in well; set aside.

Melt 2 tablespoons butter in a heavy saucepan over low heat; add flour, stirring until smooth. Cook 1 minute, stirring constantly. Stir in bouillon. Gradually add milk; cook over medium heat, stirring constantly, until thickened and bubbly. Add cream cheese and salt, stirring until smooth. Stir in onion. Spoon mixture over center of broccoli; sprinkle with cheese and paprika. Cover with aluminum foil, and bake at 350° for 35 minutes. Remove foil, and bake an additional 10 minutes. Yield: 8 servings.   *Mrs. Harry Lay, Jr., Fairmount, Georgia.*

CREAMY CORN PUDDING

3 tablespoons butter or margarine
3 tablespoons all-purpose flour
1 tablespoon sugar
¾ teaspoon salt
¾ cup milk
1 (17-ounce) can cream-style corn
3 eggs

Melt butter in a heavy saucepan over low heat; add flour, sugar, and salt, stirring until smooth. Cook 1 minute, stirring constantly. Gradually add milk; cook over medium heat, stirring constantly, until thickened and bubbly. Remove mixture from heat, and stir in corn.

Beat eggs well. Gradually stir about one-fourth of hot mixture into beaten eggs; add to remaining hot mixture, stirring constantly.

Pour into a buttered 1½-quart casserole. Bake at 350° for 1 hour. Yield: 6 servings.   *Norma Sorenson, Birmingham, Alabama.*

DELUXE PEAS AND CELERY

1 (10-ounce) package frozen English peas
2 tablespoons butter or margarine
2 cups sliced celery
2 tablespoons finely chopped onion
1 (4-ounce) can sliced mushrooms, drained
3 tablespoons chopped pimiento
¼ teaspoon salt
¼ teaspoon ground savory
Freshly ground pepper

Cook peas according to package directions; drain and set aside.

Melt butter in a medium saucepan; add remaining ingredients except peas, and cook until celery is crisp-tender. Add peas; heat thoroughly, stirring occasionally. Yield: 4 servings.
Thelma Burch, Decatur, Georgia.

Tip: To easily remove waxed paper or aluminum foil from frozen food, place package in 300° oven for 5 minutes.

VEGETABLE MEDLEY BAKE

1 (10-ounce) package frozen cauliflower
2 (10-ounce) packages frozen peas and
  carrots
1½ cups commercial sour cream
1 tablespoon minced onion
1 teaspoon salt
3 tablespoons fine, dry breadcrumbs
1 medium tomato, sliced
Fresh parsley sprigs

Cook frozen vegetables according to package directions; drain well. Combine cooked vegetables, sour cream, onion, and salt; gently stir until combined. Spoon mixture into a lightly greased 1½-quart casserole; sprinkle with breadcrumbs. Arrange tomato slices on breadcrumbs. Bake at 325° for 20 minutes or until bubbly. Garnish with parsley. Yield: 6 to 8 servings.

Fran Barbrick,
Collierville, Tennessee.

HONEY-BAKED BANANAS

4 firm ripe bananas, peeled and cut in
  half crosswise
2 teaspoons butter or margarine, melted
¼ cup honey
1 tablespoon orange juice
¼ cup chopped pecans

Brush bananas with butter, and place in a shallow baking dish. Combine honey and orange juice; mix well and pour over bananas. Sprinkle with chopped pecans. Bake at 375° for 15 minutes. Yield: 4 to 6 servings.

Nancy Parker,
Rocky Mount, North Carolina.

CHEESE-FILLED PEARS

1 (29-ounce) can pear halves
1 (8-ounce) package cream cheese,
  softened
¼ cup honey
¼ cup vanilla wafer or graham cracker
  crumbs

Drain pear halves, and reserve the juice. Set aside.

Combine cream cheese and honey; beat until blended. Fill pear halves with cream cheese mixture; place in a shallow baking dish. Add reserved juice; sprinkle with crumbs. Bake at 350° for 15 to 20 minutes. Yield: 6 to 8 servings.

Joan B. Piercy,
Memphis, Tennessee.

TIPSY FRUIT CUP

1 (11-ounce) can mandarin oranges,
  drained
1 (8-ounce) can pineapple chunks, drained
1 medium apple, cubed
¼ cup Grand Marnier or other
  orange-flavored liqueur
1 banana, sliced
2 tablespoons flaked coconut

Combine first 4 ingredients in a medium bowl; chill at least 1 hour. Stir in banana and coconut just before serving. Yield: 4 to 6 servings.

Mrs. Bruce Fowler,
Woodruff, South Carolina.

Microwave Cookery

Holiday Pies In Minutes

Microwave cookery reduces the time required to cook traditional holiday pies, yet it yields a product identical in texture, appearance, and flavor to those cooked the conventional way.

Our special microwave recipes give you a choice of several favorite fillings, including pumpkin, pecan, and eggnog, along with a basic microwaved pastry shell. The key to success is a matter of technique. Here are some pointers.

—Conventional recipes for most chiffon, fruit, and cream pies can be adapted to microwave cooking without adjusting the ingredients. However, the liquid in a custard filling should be reduced by about ¼ cup for a 9-inch pie.

—Some pie fillings, such as pumpkin and pecan, should be partially cooked in the microwave oven before being poured into the pastry shell. This promotes even cooking since the filling can be occasionally stirred.

—Custard pies are done when almost set in the center. (The center will continue to cook and become firm after the microwaving cycle is complete.)

—Because microwaving causes pie fillings to boil high, the pastry shell should have a standing rim.

—To ensure doneness, the pastry shell must be microwaved before the filling is added. Use dried beans or peas to keep the sides and bottom from puffing during microwaving (do not use metal pastry weights). To keep the rim from puffing and losing its shape, gently prick it with a fork.

—When done, the pastry shell should appear opaque and dry. If a few wet spots remain after microwaving to the top of the time range given in the recipe, remove the beans or peas and continue microwaving briefly (30 seconds is usually enough time).

—Even though the pastry shell has a standing rim, some fillings may bubble over in spots. To ensure easy cleanup should this happen, set the pieplate on a piece of waxed paper.

BASIC PASTRY

1 cup all-purpose flour
½ teaspoon salt
⅓ cup plus 1 tablespoon shortening
3 to 4 drops of yellow food coloring
  (optional)
2 to 3 tablespoons cold water

Combine flour and salt; cut in shortening with pastry blender until mixture resembles coarse meal. Add food coloring to the water if extra color is desired (pastry will not brown in microwave oven). Sprinkle water evenly over flour

mixture, and stir with a fork until all ingredients are moistened.

Shape dough into a ball, and place on a lightly floured surface; roll dough into a circle 2 inches larger than inverted 9-inch pieplate. Fit pastry loosely into pieplate. Trim edges, and fold under to form a standing rim; flute.

Place a piece of heavy-duty plastic wrap over pastry, and cover with dried beans or peas. Gently prick rim of pastry (this will help maintain fluted shape). Microwave at HIGH for 5½ to 7 minutes or until pastry is opaque and bottom is dry. Yield: one 9-inch pastry shell.

FLUFFY EGGNOG PIE

1 envelope unflavored gelatin
2 tablespoons cold water
1½ cups commercial eggnog, divided
1 tablespoon cornstarch
4 eggs, separated
¼ cup sugar
1 teaspoon vanilla extract
½ teaspoon ground nutmeg
⅛ teaspoon salt
1 microwaved 9-inch pastry shell
Sweetened whipped cream
Additional ground nutmeg for garnish

Soften gelatin in water, and set aside.
Combine ¼ cup eggnog and cornstarch, mixing well. Add egg yolks, sugar, vanilla, ½ teaspoon nutmeg, and salt; mix well, and set aside.

Place remaining eggnog in a large glass mixing bowl. Microwave at HIGH for 2 to 3 minutes or until hot. Stir one-fourth of hot eggnog into egg yolk mixture; then stir into remaining hot eggnog. Microwave at MEDIUM HIGH for 3 to 4 minutes or until slightly thickened, stirring at 1-minute intervals. Stir in gelatin mixture, and refrigerate until the consistency of unbeaten egg white.

Beat egg whites until stiff peaks form; fold into chilled mixture. Pour into pastry shell, and chill until set. Top with whipped cream and sprinkle with additional nutmeg before serving. Yield: one 9-inch pie.

OLD-FASHIONED PECAN PIE

2 tablespoons butter or margarine
3 eggs, slightly beaten
¼ cup firmly packed dark brown sugar
1 cup dark corn syrup
1 tablespoon all-purpose flour
1 cup pecan pieces
1 microwaved 9-inch pastry shell

Place butter in a medium mixing bowl, and microwave at HIGH for 1 minute or until melted. Add next 4 ingredients, mixing well; stir in pecans. Microwave at HIGH for 3 minutes, stirring well after 2 minutes.

Pour filling into pastry shell. Microwave at MEDIUM for 8 to 11 minutes or until filling is almost set in middle, giving dish one half-turn every 4 minutes. Let cool before slicing. Yield: one 9-inch pie.

FESTIVE PUMPKIN PIE

1 cup canned pumpkin
½ cup firmly packed brown sugar
1⅓ cups half-and-half
3 eggs, separated
1 tablespoon all-purpose flour
1 teaspoon ground cinnamon
¼ teaspoon ground nutmeg
⅛ teaspoon salt
1 microwaved 9-inch pastry shell
Sweetened whipped cream
Additional ground cinnamon for garnish

Combine pumpkin, brown sugar, half-and-half, egg yolks, flour, 1 teaspoon cinnamon, nutmeg, and salt in a large glass mixing bowl; mix well, and set aside.

Beat egg whites until stiff peaks form; fold into pumpkin mixture. Microwave

at HIGH for 3 minutes, stirring after 1½ minutes. Microwave at MEDIUM for 6 to 9 minutes or until slightly thickened, stirring with a whisk every 2 minutes.

Pour filling into pastry shell, filling to about ¼ inch of rim. Microwave at MEDIUM for 20 to 25 minutes or until almost set, giving dish one quarter-turn every 4 minutes. Cool. Top with whipped cream and sprinkle with cinnamon before serving. Yield: one 9-inch pie.

CRANBERRY-APPLE HOLIDAY PIE

3 cups peeled and sliced cooking apples
1¾ cups fresh cranberries
¼ cup orange juice
⅔ cup sugar
¼ teaspoon ground cinnamon
1 tablespoon cornstarch
2 tablespoons orange juice
1 microwaved 9-inch pastry shell
½ cup all-purpose flour
3 tablespoons brown sugar
½ teaspoon ground cinnamon
¼ teaspoon salt
¼ cup plus 1 tablespoon butter or
    margarine
¼ cup chopped pecans

Combine first 5 ingredients in a 2-quart casserole, and cover with heavy-duty plastic wrap. Microwave at HIGH for 6 to 8 minutes or until cranberry skins pop, stirring every 2 minutes.

Combine cornstarch and 2 tablespoons orange juice, mixing well; gradually stir into cranberry mixture, mixing well. Microwave, uncovered, at HIGH for 1 minute or until thickened and bubbly. Pour into pastry shell, and set aside.

Combine flour, brown sugar, ½ teaspoon cinnamon, and salt; cut in butter with a pastry blender until mixture resembles coarse crumbs. Add pecans, stirring well. Sprinkle topping over filling. Microwave at HIGH for 2 to 3 minutes or until butter is melted. If necessary, spread topping with a knife to evenly distribute butter. Let cool completely. Yield: one 9-inch pie.

Get An Early Start On Brunch

Brunch doesn't necessarily mean an early morning rush to prepare and serve, with no time left for the host to enjoy the occasion. Here's a menu that's entirely prepared the day before and only requires a quick heating in the oven before serving. Bake the cake the day before, and assemble the main casserole, fruit dish, and grits casserole in the evening. Even the Bloody Marys are ready and awaiting the vodka in the morning.

Overnight Bloody Marys
Sausage Breakfast Casserole
Hot Fruit Bake   Cheesy Grits Casserole
Sour Cream Coffee Cake
Coffee

OVERNIGHT BLOODY MARYS

1 (46-ounce) can cocktail vegetable juice
1 (46-ounce) can tomato juice
1 cup lemon juice
2 tablespoons Worcestershire sauce
1 teaspoon salt
½ teaspoon seasoned salt
3 cups vodka

Combine first 6 ingredients; mix well. Cover and chill overnight. Stir in vodka just before serving. Serve over crushed ice. Yield: about 15½ cups.

Mrs. George Sellers,
Albany, Georgia.

SAUSAGE BREAKFAST CASSEROLE

6 slices bread
Butter or margarine
1 pound bulk pork sausage
1½ cups (6 ounces) shredded longhorn cheese
6 eggs, beaten
2 cups half-and-half
1 teaspoon salt

Remove crusts from bread; spread bread slices with butter. Place in a greased 13- x 9- x 2-inch baking dish, and set aside.

Cook sausage until browned, stirring to crumble; drain well. Spoon over bread slices; sprinkle with cheese. Combine eggs, half-and-half, and salt; mix well, and pour over cheese. Cover casserole and chill overnight.

Remove from refrigerator 15 minutes before baking. Bake casserole, uncovered, at 350° for 45 minutes or until set. Yield: 8 servings.   *Jan Stevens,*
Wichita Falls, Texas.

HOT FRUIT BAKE

1 (20-ounce) can sliced pineapple, drained
1 (17-ounce) can apricot halves, drained
1 (16-ounce) can peach halves, drained
1 (16-ounce) can pear halves, drained
1 (15-ounce) jar spiced apple rings, drained
½ cup butter or margarine
½ cup sugar
2 tablespoons cornstarch
1 cup dry sherry

Layer fruit in a 2-quart casserole, and set aside.

Melt butter in a small saucepan. Combine sugar and cornstarch; stir into butter. Gradually stir in sherry; cook over low heat, stirring constantly, until thickened and smooth. Pour over fruit; cover and refrigerate overnight.

Remove from refrigerator 15 minutes before baking. Bake, uncovered, at 350° for 30 minutes or until bubbly. Yield: 10 servings.   *Alice G. Pahl,*
Raleigh, North Carolina.

CHEESY GRITS CASSEROLE

1½ cups uncooked regular grits
½ cup butter or margarine
3 cups (12 ounces) shredded medium-sharp Cheddar cheese
1 tablespoon Worcestershire sauce
2 teaspoons paprika, divided
3 eggs, beaten

Cook grits according to package directions. Add butter and cheese; stir until melted. Add Worcestershire sauce and 1 teaspoon paprika, mixing well. Add a small amount of hot grits to eggs, stirring well; stir egg mixture into remaining grits. Pour grits into a lightly greased 2-quart baking dish; sprinkle with 1 teaspoon paprika. Cover and refrigerate overnight.

Remove from refrigerator 15 minutes before baking. Bake, uncovered, at 325° for 1 hour. Yield: 8 servings.
Emile Michel,
Richardson, Texas.

SOUR CREAM COFFEE CAKE

½ cup chopped pecans
2 tablespoons firmly packed brown sugar
2 teaspoons ground cinnamon
1 cup butter or margarine
1 cup sugar
2 eggs
2 cups all-purpose flour
1 teaspoon baking powder
1 teaspoon soda
1 (8-ounce) carton commercial sour cream
Powdered Sugar Glaze

Combine pecans, brown sugar, and cinnamon; stir well, and set aside.

Cream butter; gradually add sugar, beating until fluffy. Add eggs; beat well.

Combine flour, baking powder, and soda; add to creamed mixture alternately with sour cream, beginning and ending with flour mixture.

Spoon half of batter into a greased and floured 10-inch Bundt pan; sprinkle half of pecan mixture over batter. Repeat layers. Bake at 375° for 35 to 40 minutes or until cake tests done.

Cool 5 minutes in pan on a wire rack. Invert onto serving plate. Let cool. Drizzle with glaze. Store overnight in airtight container. Yield: one 10-inch coffee cake.

Powdered Sugar Glaze:

1¼ cups powdered sugar, sifted
1 tablespoon water
¼ teaspoon vanilla extract

Combine all ingredients; stir well. Yield: about ⅔ cup.   *Dorsella Utter,*
Louisville, Kentucky.

Give Cabbage Some Special Attention

Add a flavorful touch to fall menus with these deliciously different cabbage dishes. One is a delightful mixture of cabbage, celery, and onion that has the fresh flavor and crisp texture that comes from stir-frying. Another—Chinese Cabbage Salad—is a blend of Chinese cabbage and onion rings chilled in a sour cream dressing.

There are also main-dish possibilities with cabbage, such as our Sausage-Sauced Cabbage. In this dish, wedges of cabbage are served with an Italian-style tomato sauce.

Along with offering flavor and versatility, cabbage is also a bargain when it comes to nutrition. This vegetable is a dependable source of vitamin C and supplies a wide range of other nutrients. Choose heads with fresh, crisp-looking leaves that are free of cuts and bruises. "Weigh" the cabbage in your hand, making sure that it feels solid and heavy for its size.

SAUSAGE-SAUCED CABBAGE

½ pound bulk Italian sausage
½ cup chopped onion
½ cup chopped green pepper
1 cup water
1 (8-ounce) can tomato sauce
1 (6-ounce) can tomato paste
1 tablespoon chopped fresh parsley
2 teaspoons sugar
1 teaspoon garlic salt
½ teaspoon dried whole oregano
1 medium cabbage

Combine sausage, onion, and green pepper; cook over medium heat until sausage is browned and vegetables are tender; drain well. Add next 7 ingredients; cover and simmer 15 minutes.

Cut cabbage into 6 wedges, removing core; cover and cook 10 minutes in a small amount of boiling water. Drain well; place wedges on a serving plate, and spoon on sauce. Yield: 6 servings.
Carol T. Keith,
Roanoke, Virginia.

STIR-FRIED CABBAGE

1 medium cabbage, coarsely chopped
2 stalks celery, thinly sliced
1 medium onion, chopped
2 tablespoons butter or margarine
½ teaspoon salt
⅛ teaspoon pepper

Stir-fry cabbage, celery, and onion in butter in a heavy Dutch oven for 5 minutes over high heat. Cover and remove from heat; let steam until cabbage is tender (about 5 to 7 minutes). Stir in salt and pepper. Yield: 8 servings.
Mrs. A. J. Lee,
Brooklet, Georgia.

COUNTRY-STYLE CABBAGE

2 onions, sliced
3 tablespoons butter or margarine
1 large green pepper, cut into strips
1 small cabbage, cut into 6 wedges
2 large tomatoes, cut into wedges
¾ teaspoon salt
¼ teaspoon pepper

Sauté onion in butter in a large skillet until tender. Add green pepper; cover and cook 5 minutes over low heat. Arrange cabbage and tomatoes over onion mixture; sprinkle with salt and pepper. Cover and cook 20 to 25 minutes. Yield: 6 servings. *Marie Greiner,*
Baltimore, Maryland.

CHINESE CABBAGE SALAD

1 large head Chinese cabbage, coarsely
 chopped
2 small purple onions, sliced and
 separated into rings
1 (8-ounce) carton commercial sour cream
½ cup chopped onion
2 tablespoons vinegar
2 teaspoons celery seeds
1 teaspoon salt
Dash of pepper

Combine chopped cabbage and onion rings; set aside.

Combine sour cream, chopped onion, vinegar, celery seeds, salt, and pepper; stir well. Pour dressing over cabbage mixture; toss well. Chill until serving time. Yield: 6 to 8 servings. *Lily Jo Drake,*
Satellite Beach, Florida.

PICKLED RED CABBAGE

3 tablespoons butter or margarine
6 cups finely shredded red cabbage
¾ cup cranberry juice
2 tablespoons vinegar
¼ teaspoon salt
¼ cup sugar

Melt butter in a large skillet over low heat; add cabbage, stirring well. Cook until cabbage is wilted. Stir in cranberry juice, vinegar, and salt. Cover and simmer 15 to 20 minutes; add sugar, mixing well. Serve pickled cabbage hot or cold. Yield: 6 servings. *Marge Killmon,*
Annandale, Virginia.

Tip: Don't add salt to a green salad until just before serving. Salt wilts and toughens salad greens.

Dried Fruit–Old Flavors With A Fresh Look

If the thought of dried fruit brings to mind specialties from grandmother's kitchen, don't just reminisce about those childhood delights. Prepare a few dried fruit favorites for your own family. Brimming with raisins, prunes, peaches, and pears, our recipes feature some down-home classics along with several new twists for using dried fruit.

For a good old-fashioned fried pie, try our Fried Peach Pies; they have an extra-flaky crust and tart peach filling. (The pastry dough is chilled overnight; we found this made it especially easy to work with.) Pear-Mince Pie, filled with chopped prunes, raisins, and pears, is a delicious variation from the traditional mincemeat pie.

Dried fruit takes on an elegant look in Wine Fruit Compote. This combination of dried fruit, wine, and honey is served warm over a scoop of vanilla ice cream, providing the perfect finale for any special meal.

PEAR-MINCE PIE

6 large pears, peeled, cored, and cubed
¾ cup unsweetened pineapple juice
¾ cup firmly packed brown sugar
½ cup chopped pitted prunes
½ cup golden raisins
½ cup chopped walnuts
½ teaspoon ground cinnamon
¼ teaspoon ground allspice
¼ teaspoon ground nutmeg
¼ teaspoon salt
1 tablespoon all-purpose flour
2 tablespoons brandy or 1 teaspoon
 brandy extract
Pastry for double-crust 9-inch pie

Combine first 11 ingredients in a large heavy saucepan. Bring to a boil; cook, uncovered, over low heat 40 minutes or until thickened, stirring occasionally. Stir in brandy. Pour into a pastry-lined 9-inch pieplate; top with remaining pastry. Trim edges; seal and flute. Cut slits in crust to allow steam to escape.

Bake on lower rack of oven at 425° for 15 minutes; reduce heat to 375°, and continue baking 30 minutes. Yield: one 9-inch pie.
Mary Boden,
Stuart, Florida.

FRIED PEACH PIES

2½ cups all-purpose flour
1 tablespoon sugar
1 tablespoon baking powder
1 teaspoon salt
⅓ cup shortening
1 egg, beaten
¾ cup plus 1 tablespoon evaporated milk
1 (8-ounce) package dried peaches
1¼ cups water
¼ to ⅓ cup sugar
Vegetable oil

Combine flour, sugar, baking powder, and salt; cut in shortening until mixture resembles coarse meal. Combine egg and milk; mix well, and stir into flour mixture just until moistened. Cover mixture, and chill 24 hours.

Cut peaches into quarters. Bring peaches and water to a boil; simmer, uncovered, 15 minutes, stirring occasionally. Stir in sugar.

Divide pastry into 22 to 24 portions. On a lightly floured surface, roll each portion to a 3-inch circle.

Place about 1 tablespoon peach mixture on each pastry circle. Moisten edges of circles; fold pastry in half, making sure edges are even.

Using a fork dipped in flour, press edges of pastry together to seal. Prick pastry 2 or 3 times.

Heat 1 inch of oil to 375°. Cook pies until golden brown, turning only once. Drain well. Yield: about 2 dozen.
Mrs. Blair Cunnyngham,
Cleveland, Tennessee.

WINE FRUIT COMPOTE

2 (8-ounce) packages mixed dried fruit
1 (25.4-ounce) bottle Concord wine
1½ cups water
½ cup honey
½ small lemon, thinly sliced and seeded
Vanilla ice cream (optional)

Combine first 5 ingredients in a large Dutch oven; mix well. Bring to a boil; reduce heat, and simmer 30 minutes. Serve over ice cream, if desired. Yield: about 6 cups.
Note: Wine Fruit Compote may be served with crêpes, if desired.
Cathy Darling,
Grafton, West Virginia.

Tip: Use sharp kitchen shears to quickly snip dates, marshmallows, fresh herbs, or other items that are difficult to cut with a knife.

RAISIN BUTTER

1½ cups raisins
¾ cup orange juice
1 tablespoon sugar
⅛ teaspoon ground cinnamon
Dash of ground cloves

Combine all ingredients in a small saucepan, and bring to a boil. Reduce heat and simmer, uncovered, 10 minutes. Pour raisin mixture into container of electric blender; process until smooth. Store in refrigerator. Yield: about 1¼ cups.
Ruth Butts,
Fulton, Kentucky.

The Flavor Of Pumpkin Delights

It's always a treat to have a warm slice of freshly baked pumpkin pie. But if you're looking for other ways to use pumpkin this fall, try our cool Pumpkin Ice Cream Pie, Pumpkin Cake, or moist Pumpkin Muffins filled with pecans or raisins.

Canned pumpkin makes these recipes delicious possibilities at any time of the year. However, when fresh pumpkin is plentiful, you can substitute 2 cups cooked, mashed pumpkin for 1 (16-ounce) can.

PUMPKIN CAKE

2 cups sugar
1 (16-ounce) can pumpkin
1 cup vegetable oil
4 eggs, beaten
2 cups all-purpose flour
1 teaspoon salt
2 teaspoons soda
2 teaspoons baking powder
2 teaspoons ground cinnamon
½ cup flaked coconut
½ cup chopped pecans
Frosting (recipe follows)

Combine sugar, pumpkin, oil, and eggs; beat 1 minute at medium speed of electric mixer. Combine next 5 ingredients; add to pumpkin mixture. Beat 1 minute at medium speed of an electric mixer. Stir in coconut and pecans. Pour batter into three greased and floured 8-inch round cakepans. Bake at 350° for 25 to 30 minutes or until cake tests done. Cool in pans 10 minutes; remove from pans, and cool completely. Spread frosting between layers and on top of cake. Yield: one 3-layer cake.

Frosting:
½ cup butter or margarine, softened
1 (8-ounce) package cream cheese, softened
1 (16-ounce) package powdered sugar
2 teaspoons vanilla extract
½ cup chopped pecans
½ cup flaked coconut

Combine butter and cream cheese; beat until light and fluffy. Add sugar and vanilla, mixing well. Stir in pecans and coconut. Yield: enough frosting for one 3-layer cake.
Mrs. William A. Caldwell,
Mesa, Arizona.

PUMPKIN MUFFINS

¾ cup firmly packed brown sugar
½ cup butter or margarine, softened
¼ cup molasses
1 egg, beaten
1 cup canned pumpkin
1¾ cups all-purpose flour
1 teaspoon soda
¼ teaspoon salt
½ cup pecans or raisins

Combine sugar, butter, and molasses; beat well. Add egg and pumpkin, beating until smooth. Stir together remaining ingredients; add to pumpkin mixture, stirring just until moistened (the batter will be lumpy).

Fill lightly greased muffin pans half full. Bake at 350° for 20 minutes. Yield: about 15 muffins.
Cher Haile,
Atlanta, Georgia.

PUMPKIN ICE CREAM PIE

1 pint vanilla ice cream, softened
1 baked 9-inch pastry shell, chilled
1 cup canned pumpkin
¾ cup sugar
½ teaspoon salt
½ teaspoon ground ginger
½ teaspoon ground cinnamon
¼ teaspoon ground nutmeg
1 cup whipping cream, whipped

Spread ice cream evenly in chilled pastry shell; freeze.

Combine next 6 ingredients, mixing well. Fold in whipped cream. Spread pumpkin mixture evenly over ice cream; freeze pie.

Remove pie from freezer 15 minutes before serving. Yield: one 9-inch pie.

Eleanor K. Brandt,
Arlington, Texas.

Classic Entrées Just For Two

If there are always two for dinner at your house, you needn't restrict your repertoire to just a few favorites or have lots of repeat meals from large-scale recipes. Here is a whole new range of entrée recipes scaled down for two; they're based on pork, chicken, or beef, and there's one for salmon.

Pork chops appear on a bed of rice and apples. Beef appears deliciously in Swiss Steak With Vegetables—a classic usually based on a family-size roast—and in our not-to-be-missed Pepper Steak, perfectly seasoned and colorful with tomatoes and peppers. Chicken Breasts in Mornay Sauce presents a classic touch for two.

PEPPER STEAK

¾ pound round steak
2 tablespoons vegetable oil
1 large tomato, peeled and coarsely chopped
2 medium-size green peppers, thinly sliced
2 tablespoons soy sauce
¼ teaspoon sugar
¼ teaspoon garlic salt
¼ teaspoon pepper
⅛ teaspoon ground ginger
1 tablespoon cornstarch
½ cup beef consommé
Hot cooked rice

Partially freeze steak; slice across grain into 2- x ¼-inch strips.

Cook steak in oil in a large skillet until brown. Stir in tomato, green pepper, soy sauce, sugar, garlic salt, pepper, and ginger; cover and simmer 15 minutes.

Combine cornstarch and consommé; stir into steak mixture. Cover and simmer 30 minutes, stirring occasionally. Serve over rice. Yield: 2 servings.

Lela Floyd,
Whiteville, North Carolina.

SWISS STEAK WITH VEGETABLES

½ pound boneless round steak
2 tablespoons all-purpose flour
½ teaspoon salt
¼ teaspoon pepper
1 tablespoon vegetable oil
2 carrots, sliced
1 small onion, sliced
1 stalk celery, sliced
1 (8-ounce) can tomato sauce
½ cup water
1 tablespoon butter or margarine
1 beef-flavored bouillon cube
1 teaspoon bottled brown bouquet sauce

Trim excess fat from steak; cut steak into serving-size pieces. Combine flour, salt, and pepper; dredge steak in flour mixture, and pound into steak with a meat mallet. Brown steak in oil in a large skillet; place in a shallow 2-quart casserole. Spoon carrots, onion, and celery over meat.

Combine remaining ingredients in skillet; cook over medium heat until bouillon is dissolved. Pour sauce over vegetables. Cover and bake at 350° for 1 hour and 10 minutes. Yield: 2 servings.

Susie Lavenue,
Ridgely, Tennessee.

CHICKEN BREASTS IN MORNAY SAUCE

1 whole chicken breast, split
1 tablespoon butter or margarine
1 tablespoon all-purpose flour
1 cup milk
¼ cup (1 ounce) shredded Swiss cheese
2 tablespoons grated Parmesan cheese
1 (4-ounce) can sliced mushrooms, drained
¼ teaspoon salt
Dash of pepper
Paprika

Cook chicken in boiling salted water about 20 minutes or until tender; discard skin. Place chicken on a serving dish, and keep warm.

Melt butter in a heavy saucepan over low heat; add flour, stirring until smooth. Cook 1 minute, stirring constantly. Gradually add milk; cook over medium heat, stirring constantly, until thickened and bubbly. Add cheese, mushrooms, salt, and pepper; cook, stirring constantly, until cheese melts and mushrooms are thoroughly heated.

Spoon sauce over chicken. Sprinkle with paprika. Yield: 2 servings.

Mrs. James Tuthill,
Virginia Beach, Virginia.

PORK CHOP MEAL FOR TWO

2 (¾-inch-thick) loin pork chops
1 tablespoon vegetable oil
2 tablespoons chopped onion
⅓ cup uncooked regular rice
1 chicken bouillon cube
1 cup hot water
½ cup chopped apple
1 tablespoon butter or margarine, melted
1 tablespoon brown sugar
¼ teaspoon ground cinnamon
1 small apple, sliced

Brown chops on both sides in hot oil. Remove chops, and drain on paper towels. Reserve drippings in skillet.

Add onion and rice to skillet. Sauté until onion is tender and rice is golden brown, stirring constantly.

Place bouillon cube in hot water; stir until dissolved. Add to onion and rice mixture; bring to a boil. Stir in chopped apple. Pour mixture into a 10- x 6- x 2-inch glass baking dish; arrange pork chops on top. Cover and bake at 325° for 25 to 30 minutes.

Combine butter, brown sugar, and cinnamon. Brush apple slices with sugar mixture; arrange around chops. Return to oven; bake, uncovered, 20 minutes or until rice and apples are tender and pork chops are done. Yield: 2 servings.

Linell Pringle,
Winston-Salem, North Carolina.

SCALLOPED SALMON

2 tablespoons chopped onion
1 tablespoon chopped green pepper
2 tablespoons butter or margarine, melted
1 (7¾-ounce) can salmon, drained and flaked
½ cup evaporated milk
1 tablespoon all-purpose flour
¼ teaspoon salt
2 tablespoons buttered soft breadcrumbs

Sauté onion and green pepper in butter until tender but not brown. Add next 4 ingredients; mix well. Spoon mixture into buttered individual baking shells; top with breadcrumbs. Bake at 400° for 15 minutes. Yield: 2 servings.

J. P. Jackson,
Sarasota, Florida.

Tried Steamed Rutabagas Or Fried Turnips?

If you don't think of turnips or rutabagas when shopping for winter vegetables, then you're missing something good. These vegetables don't have to be served simply boiled and mashed the old-fashioned way, as our readers prove with a variety of exciting ideas. What's more, turnips and rutabagas are low in cost and calories, but high in flavor.

Try a delicious break from fried potatoes with Shoestring Fried Turnips; you'll find them especially good piled high next to your favorite sandwich. And for something really different, why not try steaming a rutabaga? Lemon and fresh parsley top Steamed Rutabagas, a colorful addition to pork chops, roasts, or turkey.

If you've tried preparing these extra-firm vegetables and found them devilishly hard to cut, start by using a very sharp knife to cut a thin slice from the bottom. This will give a flat, steady surface for further slicing. Remove the peel from the individual slices.

GLAZED TURNIPS

8 small turnips, peeled and quartered
2 tablespoons butter or margarine
2 tablespoons sugar
½ teaspoon salt
⅛ teaspoon ground mace

Place turnips in a saucepan; cover with water, and bring to a boil. Cover and cook 15 to 20 minutes or until tender; drain and set aside.

Combine remaining ingredients; cook over medium heat, stirring constantly, until smooth and bubbly. Pour over turnips, and toss gently to coat. Yield: 4 servings. *Mrs. Grant Adkins,*
Wichita Falls, Texas.

SHOESTRING FRIED TURNIPS

½ cup all-purpose flour
¾ teaspoon salt
¼ teaspoon pepper
2 large turnips, peeled and cut into thin strips
Vegetable oil

Combine flour, salt, and pepper; mix well. Dredge turnips in flour mixture; fry in hot oil (375°) until golden brown. Drain turnips on paper towels. Yield: 4 to 6 servings. *Jewel Williamson,*
East Brewton, Alabama.

BUTTERED RUTABAGAS

4 cups peeled and cubed rutabagas
¼ cup sugar
1½ teaspoons Worcestershire sauce
¼ teaspoon onion powder
1 teaspoon salt
4 drops of hot sauce
¼ cup butter or margarine, melted

Combine first 6 ingredients in saucepan; cover with water, and bring to a boil. Cover and cook over low heat about 30 minutes or until rutabaga is tender; drain. Add melted butter to rutabaga, and mash to desired consistency. Yield: 4 servings.
Mrs. Charles R. Simms,
Palestine, Illinois.

SWEET-AND-SOUR TURNIPS

3 medium turnips, peeled and sliced
1 teaspoon salt
4 slices bacon, diced
1 egg, beaten
¼ cup sugar
¼ cup vinegar

Place turnips in a saucepan; cover with water. Add salt, and bring to a boil; cover and cook 15 to 20 minutes, or until turnips are tender. Drain and set aside.

Fry bacon in a skillet until crisp. Combine egg, sugar, and vinegar in a small mixing bowl, mixing well; stir into bacon and drippings. Pour bacon mixture over turnips; toss gently. Yield: about 4 servings. *Elaine Winters,*
College Park, Maryland.

STEAMED RUTABAGAS

2 cups peeled and cubed rutabagas
2 tablespoons butter or margarine, melted
1 tablespoon chopped fresh parsley
1½ teaspoons lemon juice
½ teaspoon salt
⅛ teaspoon pepper

Place rutabaga in a steaming rack; steam 30 to 45 minutes or until tender.

Combine remaining ingredients; stir well, and pour over rutabaga. Toss before serving. Yield: 4 servings.
Rhunella Johnson,
Bay Springs, Mississippi.

There's More To A Cranberry Than Sauce

When the pilgrims received a gift of cranberries from the Indians, who would have guessed the saucy berry would become such an important part of modern holiday celebrations? Over the years, this tart fruit has maintained a long-running record as a popular accompaniment for turkey and ham. The pilgrims may have turned the cranberry into a sauce, but our readers combine it with raspberries in an elegant compote, grind it into tangy relish, and even bake it in a cobbler.

As you might expect, cranberries are at their best when red, ripe, and fresh. Look for plump berries that are uniform in size, avoiding those that are crushed or shriveled. If you're planning to use the berries within a few weeks, you can store them in the refrigerator. To store cranberries for a longer period of time, place them in an airtight container and put in the freezer. The berries will keep for a full year in a large freezer and for about six months in the frozen food compartment of a standard refrigerator.

CRANBERRY GLAZED HAM

1 (5- to 7-pound) uncooked ham
Whole cloves
2 cups fresh cranberries
1 cup water
1 cup firmly packed brown sugar

Score fat on ham in a diamond design; stud with cloves. Place ham, fat side up, on rack in a shallow roasting pan. Insert meat thermometer, making sure it does not touch fat or bone.

Bake ham, uncovered, at 325° until thermometer reaches 160°, about 2½ to 3 hours.

Combine cranberries and water in a medium saucepan; bring to a boil. Reduce heat; simmer 10 minutes or until thickened and bubbly. Stir in sugar, and simmer 5 to 7 additional minutes or until thickened.

Spread cranberry glaze over ham during last 30 minutes of baking. Yield: 10 to 14 servings. *Gary McCalla, Birmingham, Alabama.*

BERRY COMPOTE

1 (10-ounce) package frozen raspberries, thawed
2 cups fresh cranberries
½ cup sugar
3 tablespoons port or sweet red wine
1 (8-ounce) carton vanilla yogurt
½ cup whipping cream, whipped

Combine raspberries and cranberries in a small saucepan; bring to a boil. Reduce heat; cover and simmer 5 minutes or until cranberries pop. Stir in sugar; cool. Stir in port; cover and chill.

Spoon fruit mixture into individual serving dishes. Combine yogurt and whipped cream; spoon over fruit. Yield: 6 servings. *Ruth Cunliffe, Lake Placid, Florida.*

CRANBERRY COBBLER

1 cup sugar
1¼ cups water
1 teaspoon vanilla extract
¼ cup butter or margarine, divided
¾ cup all-purpose flour
1¼ teaspoons baking powder
½ teaspoon salt
⅓ cup sugar
½ cup milk
1 cup fresh cranberries, cut in half
Vanilla ice cream (optional)

Combine 1 cup sugar, water, vanilla, and 2 tablespoons butter in a small saucepan; bring to a boil, stirring constantly. Remove from heat; pour mixture into an 8-inch square baking dish.

Combine flour, baking powder, salt, and ⅓ cup sugar; cut in remaining 2 tablespoons butter. Stir in milk; fold in cranberries. Spoon cranberry mixture evenly over sugar mixture. Bake at 375° for 30 to 35 minutes. Serve warm with ice cream, if desired. Yield: about 9 servings. *Mrs. Harland Stone, Ocala, Florida.*

CRANBERRY RELISH

4 cups fresh cranberries, ground
2 tart cooking apples, peeled, cored, and ground
1 orange, unpeeled, seeded, and ground
1¾ cups sugar
½ cup chopped walnuts
2 to 3 drops of red food coloring

Combine first 3 ingredients, mixing well. Add remaining ingredients, stirring until blended. Chill. Store in airtight container in refrigerator. Yield: 1 quart. *Betty White, Hemet, California.*

Meat Loaf With An Exciting Change Of Taste

Meat loaf takes kindly to a variety of ingredients and seasonings. Our Cheeseburger Loaf capitalizes on the flavor of American cheese, both in and on top of the loaf. Mexicali Meat Loaf bakes under a sauce of corn and cheese, while Chili Meat Loaf, definitely for chili lovers, is flavored with both chili powder and kidney beans.

Always mix meat loaf slightly with a fork to avoid packing the meat. Don't overcook—a good meat loaf should be firm but not dry.

MEXICALI MEAT LOAF

1½ pounds ground beef
¾ cup quick oats, uncooked
½ cup tomato juice
1 egg, beaten
2 tablespoons minced onion
2 teaspoons salt
1 tablespoon chili powder
1 teaspoon pepper
3 tablespoons butter or margarine
3 tablespoons self-rising flour
1½ cups milk
8 slices American cheese, broken into pieces
1 (12-ounce) can whole kernel corn with sweet peppers, drained
2 small green peppers, cut into rings

Combine first 8 ingredients; mix lightly. Put into a shallow 2-quart baking dish, and shape into a loaf. Bake at 350° for 45 minutes. Drain off juice.

Melt butter in a saucepan; add flour and cook over low heat, stirring constantly, until bubbly. Gradually add milk; cook, stirring constantly, until smooth and thickened. Add cheese; stir until cheese melts. Stir in corn; pour over meat mixture. Top loaf with pepper rings. Bake at 350° for 20 minutes. Yield: 6 to 8 servings.
Mrs. F. G. Miller, Poplarville, Mississippi.

CHILI MEAT LOAF

2 pounds ground chuck
2 teaspoons salt
¼ teaspoon pepper
2 eggs, beaten
1 cup canned tomatoes, chopped
¼ cup finely chopped onion
1 teaspoon chili powder
¼ teaspoon garlic powder
½ cup cracker crumbs
1 (15-ounce) can red kidney beans, drained and mashed

Combine all ingredients in a large mixing bowl, and mix lightly. Place mixture in a 9- x 5- x 3-inch loafpan, and shape into a loaf. Bake at 350° for 1½ hours or until done. Yield: 6 to 8 servings. *Mrs. Bill Hodges, Guntersville, Alabama.*

BARBECUED MEAT LOAF

1½ pounds ground beef
1 cup breadcrumbs
1 onion, finely chopped
1 egg, beaten
1½ teaspoons salt
¼ teaspoon pepper
2 (8-ounce) cans tomato sauce, divided
½ cup water
3 tablespoons vinegar
3 tablespoons brown sugar
3 tablespoons Worcestershire sauce

Combine first 6 ingredients in a large mixing bowl; add ½ can tomato sauce, mixing well. Place mixture in a 10- x 6- x 2-inch baking dish, and shape into a loaf. Combine remaining tomato sauce and remaining ingredients in a small mixing bowl, and pour over loaf. Bake at 350° for 1 hour and 15 minutes or until done, basting often. Yield: 8 servings. *Jeri Holcomb, Boaz, Alabama.*

CHEESEBURGER LOAF

1½ pounds ground chuck
1 (5⅓-ounce) can evaporated milk
½ cup cracker crumbs
1 cup (4 ounces) shredded American cheese
1 egg, beaten
¼ cup chopped onion
¼ cup chopped green pepper
¾ teaspoon salt
¼ teaspoon pepper
¼ teaspoon dried basil leaves
2 slices American cheese

Combine all ingredients except cheese slices in a large mixing bowl, and mix lightly. Place mixture in an 8½- x 4½- x 2⅝-inch loafpan, and shape into a loaf. Bake at 375° for 1 hour.

Remove loaf from oven. Cut each cheese slice into 2 triangles, and arrange triangles overlapping on top of loaf. Return meat loaf to oven 2 minutes or until cheese melts. Let stand 10 minutes before slicing. Yield: 6 to 8 servings.

Mrs. Jack L. Huey, Jr.,
Guthrie, Texas.

Potatoes With A Certain Flair

Whether baked, stuffed, or drizzled with a butter sauce, potatoes are an all-time family favorite.

Washing potatoes speeds decay, so never wash before storing. Don't store in the refrigerator because potato starch turns to sugar at lower temperatures.

SAUCY POTATO CASSEROLE

8 medium potatoes, peeled and cubed
1 (3-ounce) package cream cheese
1 (8-ounce) carton commercial sour cream
1 (8-ounce) jar process cheese spread
1 (10¾-ounce) can cream of mushroom soup, undiluted
⅛ teaspoon seasoned salt
Buttered breadcrumbs (optional)

Cook potatoes in boiling water to cover 15 to 20 minutes or until tender. Drain and set aside.

Combine cream cheese, sour cream, cheese spread, soup, and seasoned salt in a saucepan; cook over low heat until mixture is thoroughly heated, stirring often. Pour over potatoes, mixing well.

Spoon into a greased 2½-quart casserole. Sprinkle with breadcrumbs, if desired. Bake at 350° for 20 to 25 minutes or until bubbly. Yield: 10 servings.

Mrs. Terry Parks,
Chattanooga, Tennessee.

BLUE CHEESE STUFFED POTATOES

4 large baking potatoes
Vegetable oil
8 slices bacon
1 cup plain yogurt
½ cup milk
¼ cup chopped green onion
2 to 3 tablespoons crumbled blue cheese
1 teaspoon Dijon mustard
½ to ¾ teaspoon salt
¼ teaspoon pepper
Paprika

Scrub potatoes thoroughly, and rub skins with oil; bake at 400° for 1 hour or until done.

Allow potatoes to cool to touch. Cut potatoes in half lengthwise; carefully scoop out pulp, leaving shells intact. Mash pulp.

Cook bacon until crisp; drain and crumble. Combine potato pulp, bacon, and remaining ingredients except paprika; mix well. Stuff shells with potato mixture; sprinkle with paprika. Place in a 12- x 8- x 2-inch baking dish; bake at 400° for 15 to 20 minutes or until thoroughly heated. Yield: 8 servings.

Sandra Russell,
Maitland, Florida.

HOT POTATO SALAD

6 medium potatoes
1 (10¾-ounce) can cream of celery soup, undiluted
1 (8-ounce) carton commercial sour cream
1 cup (4 ounces) shredded mild Cheddar cheese
½ cup chopped celery
6 hard-cooked eggs, chopped
1 small onion, chopped
1 (2-ounce) jar diced pimiento, drained
2 tablespoons imitation bacon bits

Scrub potatoes. Cook in boiling water about 30 minutes or until tender. Drain and cool slightly. Peel and cut potatoes into ¾-inch cubes.

Combine soup, sour cream, and cheese in a large bowl; mix well. Add potatoes, celery, eggs, onion, and pimiento, mixing well. Spoon mixture into a 13- x 9- x 2-inch baking dish. Sprinkle

with bacon bits. Bake at 350° for 30 minutes. Yield: 8 to 10 servings.

Agnes Harbin Fisher,
Sylva, North Carolina.

POTATOES WITH HERB BUTTER

4 large baking potatoes
½ cup butter or margarine
1 tablespoon lemon juice
1 tablespoon chopped chives
½ teaspoon dried whole chervil
½ teaspoon dried whole tarragon
½ teaspoon dried dillweed
¼ teaspoon hot sauce

Scrub potatoes. Cook in boiling water about 30 minutes or until tender. Drain and cut into ½-inch slices; arrange on a serving platter, and keep warm.

Combine remaining ingredients in a small saucepan; cook over low heat until butter is melted. Pour over potatoes. Yield: 4 servings. *Patty Merritt,*
Jacksonville, North Carolina.

POTATO SLIMS

2 large baking potatoes
½ cup water
2 tablespoons vegetable oil
½ teaspoon hot sauce
1 envelope seasoned coating mix for pork
¼ cup grated Parmesan cheese

Peel potatoes and cut into lengthwise strips, ¼ to ⅜ inch wide. Combine water, oil, and hot sauce in a shallow dish. Combine coating mix and cheese in a plastic bag. Dip potato strips in water mixture, shaking off excess water. Drop 8 to 10 potato strips into coating mix; shake until coated. Repeat with remaining potatoes. Place in a single layer on a greased baking sheet. Bake at 400° for 30 to 35 minutes or until done. Yield: 4 servings.

Lilly S. Bradley,
Salem, Virginia.

A Real Switch For Liver

Liver need no longer have the reputation of being one of those dull, good-for-you dishes. Packed with nutrients (protein, iron, vitamin A, and B vitamins), liver can be an exciting main dish when livened up with a variety of seasonings and ingredients.

When selecting liver, look for a fresh overall appearance, avoiding dried or discolored meat. Be sure to use fresh liver within two days of purchase, or store it in the freezer, keeping it solidly frozen until ready to use.

Many people overcook liver, making it tough and less appealing. For maximum tenderness, brown the meat lightly so that the inside remains a delicate pink. If liquid ingredients are then added and the liver simmers over low heat, the extra moisture preserves the tenderness.

LIVER SAUTE

4 slices bacon
1 pound thinly sliced calves liver
1 tablespoon all-purpose flour
¼ cup dry red wine
1 (10½-ounce) can condensed onion soup, undiluted
1 cup thinly sliced carrots
1 small bay leaf
⅛ teaspoon ground thyme
Fresh parsley sprigs (optional)

Cook bacon in a large skillet until crisp; remove from skillet, reserving 2 tablespoons drippings. Crumble bacon, and set aside. Brown liver in reserved bacon drippings; remove to platter, and set aside.

Blend flour into bacon drippings, and cook 1 minute. Gradually stir in wine and soup. Add bacon, liver, and next 3 ingredients; cover and cook over low heat 10 minutes, stirring occasionally. Garnish with parsley, if desired. Yield: 4 servings.
Sara McCullough,
Broaddus, Texas.

SWEET-AND-SOUR LIVER

6 slices bacon
½ cup chopped onion
¼ cup chopped green pepper
⅓ cup firmly packed brown sugar
3 tablespoons all-purpose flour
½ teaspoon salt
½ teaspoon pepper
⅓ cup vinegar
1½ pounds thinly sliced beef liver
Hot cooked rice (optional)

Cook bacon in a large skillet until crisp; remove from skillet, reserving 1 tablespoon drippings. Crumble bacon, and set aside.

Combine next 7 ingredients in a small mixing bowl, stirring well; set aside.

Cook liver in reserved bacon drippings for 5 minutes, turning once. Pour vinegar mixture over liver; cover and simmer over low heat 10 minutes. Turn liver; cover and simmer an additional 10 minutes. Sprinkle with bacon. Serve with rice, if desired. Yield: 6 servings.
Mrs. B. W. Zeagler,
Baytown, Texas.

BEEF LIVER PATTIES

1½ pounds thinly sliced beef liver
⅔ cup soft breadcrumbs
¼ cup chopped onion
½ teaspoon seasoning salt
¼ teaspoon pepper
2 tablespoons soy sauce
3 eggs
¼ teaspoon coarsely ground red pepper (optional)
Fine breadcrumbs
Vegetable oil

Cook liver 3 to 4 minutes in boiling salted water or just until it loses its pink color. Drain well and cool. Place in food processor or chopper; process until finely chopped.

Combine liver and next 7 ingredients; mix well. Shape into 2½-inch patties; coat in fine breadcrumbs. Brown in oil over medium-low heat, turning once. Yield: 6 servings.
Audrey Skinner,
Texarkana, Texas.

LIVER WITH HERBS

6 slices bacon
½ cup all-purpose flour
1 teaspoon salt
¼ teaspoon pepper
1½ pounds thinly sliced beef liver
1 small onion, chopped
2 tablespoons chopped fresh parsley
2 tablespoons butter or margarine, melted
1 tablespoon lemon juice
1 teaspoon dried whole tarragon

Cook bacon in a large heavy skillet until crisp; remove from skillet, reserving drippings. Crumble bacon, and set aside.

Combine flour, salt, and pepper; dredge liver in flour mixture, and brown in reserved bacon drippings. Remove liver to a warm platter, and top with crumbled bacon.

Sauté onion and parsley in butter in a small skillet; stir in lemon juice and tarragon. Pour over liver. Yield: 6 servings.
Mrs. Ray H. McDuffie,
Morganton, North Carolina.

SAUCY LIVER

3 tablespoons butter or margarine
½ cup chopped onion
1 clove garlic, minced
2 tablespoons chopped fresh parsley
½ cup sliced fresh mushrooms
1½ pounds thinly sliced beef liver
½ cup tomato sauce
¼ teaspoon salt
⅛ teaspoon pepper
¼ teaspoon ground thyme
¼ teaspoon dried whole oregano
1 bay leaf, crushed

Melt butter in a heavy skillet; add next 4 ingredients, and sauté until onion is transparent. Push to side of skillet, and brown liver.

Combine remaining ingredients in a small mixing bowl; add to liver, and simmer 5 minutes over low heat. Yield: 6 servings.
Cindy Fields,
Courtland, Virginia.

Another Way To Enjoy Turkey

Finding new ways to use up all the leftover turkey is sometimes a problem. Try our solution to this dilemma.

LATTICE-TOPPED TURKEY PIE

2 cups chopped cooked turkey
1 (10-ounce) package frozen English peas
1 cup (4 ounces) shredded sharp Cheddar cheese
1 cup diced celery
½ cup soft breadcrumbs
¼ cup chopped onion
¼ teaspoon salt
⅛ teaspoon pepper
1 cup mayonnaise
3 dashes of hot sauce
1 (8-ounce) can crescent dinner rolls
2 teaspoons sesame seeds
Radish slices (optional)
Fresh parsley sprigs (optional)

Combine first 10 ingredients; mix well. Spoon into a 12- x 8- x 2-inch baking dish. Separate crescent dough into 2 rectangles; press perforations to seal. Cut into 4 long strips and 4 short strips. Arrange strips in lattice design across top of casserole. Sprinkle with sesame seeds. Bake at 350° for 35 minutes. Garnish with radish slices and parsley, if desired. Yield: 6 servings.
Hortense Callaway,
Tallahassee, Florida.

Perfect Frosting Every Time

Do you sometimes hesitate to bake a cake because you don't like to make the frosting? Perhaps you've tried to create a light, creamy frosting only to end up with a grainy or sticky mess. What's the secret to making frostings behave?

Actually, fluffy toppings for cakes result not from luck, but from carefully following each step of the procedure described in the recipe. We selected some of the basic icing recipes because they explain in detail how to make perfect frosting. Our test kitchens staff tested each recipe and found them all to be creamy and delicious.

Once the frosting is prepared, follow these hints to help guarantee smooth, even spreading.

—Always spread frosting on a completely cooled cake. Lightly brush the cake to remove loose crumbs.

—To keep the cake plate neat, try placing strips of waxed paper underneath the edges of the cake. After cake is frosted, carefully remove the paper.

SEVEN-MINUTE DOUBLE BOILER FROSTING

1½ cups sugar
2 egg whites
1 tablespoon light corn syrup
Dash of salt
⅓ cup cold water
1 teaspoon vanilla extract

Combine sugar, egg whites, corn syrup, and salt in top of a large double boiler; add cold water, and beat on low speed of electric mixer for 30 seconds or just until blended.

Place over boiling water; beat constantly on high speed about 7 minutes or until stiff peaks form. Remove from heat. Add vanilla; beat 2 additional minutes or until frosting is thick enough to spread. Spread on cooled cake. Yield: enough for one 3-layer cake.

Frances Robison,
Mobile, Alabama.

CARAMEL FROSTING

1½ cups butter, softened
3 cups sugar
1½ teaspoons soda
1½ cups buttermilk
1 teaspoon vanilla extract

Cream butter; gradually add sugar, beating well with electric mixer.

Dissolve soda in buttermilk. Add to creamed mixture, beating well.

Cook mixture in a large Dutch oven over medium heat, stirring constantly, until candy thermometer registers 234° (soft ball stage). Remove from heat, and add vanilla (do not stir); cool 10 minutes.

Beat on medium speed of electric mixer until thick enough to spread (about 10 minutes). Spread immediately on cooled cake. Yield: enough for one 3-layer cake.

Fran Collier,
Jacksonville, Florida.

FLUFFY WHITE FROSTING

1 cup sugar
½ cup light corn syrup
¼ cup water
2 egg whites
1 teaspoon vanilla extract

Combine sugar, corn syrup, and water in a medium-size heavy saucepan. Cook over medium heat, stirring frequently, until mixture comes to a boil and sugar is dissolved. Continue cooking, stirring frequently, until the candy thermometer reaches 240° (soft ball stage).

Beat egg whites until foamy. While beating at medium speed of electric mixer, slowly pour hot syrup in a thin stream over egg whites. Turn mixer to high speed, and continue beating until stiff peaks form and frosting is thick enough to spread. Add vanilla; beat until blended. Spread immediately on cooled cake. Yield: enough for one 2-layer cake.

Christine Reeves,
Hillsboro, Alabama.

QUICK FUDGE FROSTING

1 cup firmly packed brown sugar
3 tablespoons cocoa
3 tablespoons shortening
1 tablespoon butter or margarine
¼ teaspoon salt
⅓ cup milk
1½ cups sifted powdered sugar
1 teaspoon vanilla extract

Combine first 6 ingredients in a medium saucepan. Cook over medium heat, stirring frequently until mixture comes to a boil. Boil 3 minutes, stirring constantly. Remove from heat; cool.

Add powdered sugar and vanilla; beat on medium speed of electric mixer until smooth and creamy (about 1 minute). If necessary, add a small amount of milk to obtain spreading consistency. Use immediately on cooled cake. Yield: enough for one 2-layer cake.

Florence L. Costello,
Chattanooga, Tennessee.

Sweet Breakfast Ideas

On a cool fall morning, nothing beats fresh hot bread for breakfast. We recommend Apple Toast and Breakfast Pullapart.

BREAKFAST PULLAPART

1 cup chopped pecans
⅔ cup sugar
2 to 3 teaspoons ground cinnamon
1 (1-pound) loaf frozen bread dough, thawed
¼ cup plus 2 tablespoons butter or margarine, melted

Sprinkle pecans evenly in bottom of a lightly greased 9-inch pieplate. Set aside. Combine sugar and cinnamon, and set aside.

Cut bread into quarters, and cut each quarter into 6 pieces. Dip each dough piece into butter; coat in sugar mixture. Arrange dough pieces over pecans. Cover, and let rise in a warm place (85°), free from drafts, for 1 hour. Bake at 350° for 30 minutes or until done. Immediately invert on a serving plate. Yield: one 9-inch coffee cake.

Evelyn Pollard,
Sainte Genevieve, Missouri.

APPLE TOAST

2 large cooking apples, peeled and thinly sliced
2 tablespoons water
1 tablespoon sugar
¼ teaspoon ground cinnamon
¼ teaspoon ground nutmeg
¼ cup butter, divided
4 (1-inch-thick) slices French bread

Combine apples, water, sugar, cinnamon, nutmeg, and 2 tablespoons butter in a saucepan; bring to a boil. Reduce heat, cover and simmer 5 minutes or until tender, stirring occasionally.

Melt remaining 2 tablespoons butter in an electric skillet at 350°; place bread in skillet, and cook 4 minutes on each side or until browned. Spoon apple mixture over toast. Serve hot. Yield: 4 servings.
G. Pedersen,
Brandon, Mississippi.

Enjoy Kiwi For A Change

Kiwi, a delicious newcomer to the Southern fruit market, is bound to attract a following. The dark, fuzzy covering of this egg-size fruit camouflages the delightful taste that's found inside. Its lime-green flesh dotted with tiny black seeds has an unusual flavor that reminds you of watermelon with a dash of strawberry. Rich in vitamin C with only 30 calories per fruit, kiwi can be eaten plain or added to salads, entrées, and desserts.

To prepare kiwi, chill first; then simply peel and thinly slice for use in recipes or as an eye-catching garnish. When preparing, slice the fruit crosswise for the most attractive appearance.

KIWI AND CREAM IN MERINGUE CUPS

2 egg whites
¼ teaspoon vinegar
⅛ teaspoon vanilla extract
Dash of salt
⅔ cup sugar
1 cup whipping cream
¼ cup powdered sugar
2 to 3 kiwis, peeled and thinly sliced

Combine egg whites (at room temperature), vinegar, vanilla, and salt; beat until frothy. Gradually add sugar, 1 tablespoon at a time, beating until stiff peaks form. (Do not underbeat the mixture.)

Spoon meringue into 4 equal portions on unglazed brown paper. (Do not use recycled paper.) Using back of spoon, shape meringue into circles about 4 inches in diameter; shape each circle into a shell (sides should be about 1½ inches high). Bake at 300° for 45 minutes. Cool away from drafts.

Beat whipping cream until foamy; gradually add powdered sugar, beating until soft peaks form. Spoon whipped cream into meringue shells. Arrange kiwi over cream. Yield: 4 servings.

Freezing Ahead Is Easy–And Smart

Wouldn't it be nice to be able to go to the freezer and take out a whole meal that's already prepared and waiting for you? These recipes let you do just that.

INDIVIDUAL MEAT LOAVES

2 pounds ground beef
1 cup round buttery cracker crumbs
1 egg, beaten
½ cup finely chopped green pepper
½ cup finely chopped onion
½ cup evaporated milk
1 teaspoon salt
¼ teaspoon pepper
1 teaspoon seasoned meat tenderizer
1¼ cups catsup, divided
3 tablespoons dark corn syrup

Combine first 9 ingredients and ¼ cup catsup; mix well. Shape mixture into 6 loaves, and wrap individually in freezer paper or aluminum foil. Freeze. To serve, thaw in refrigerator; bake at 350° for 35 minutes. Combine corn syrup and remaining 1 cup catsup; brush on tops of meat loaves. Bake 10 minutes longer. Yield: 6 servings.
Mary H. Gillian,
Cartersville, Virginia.

SLOPPY JOES

3 pounds ground beef
1 medium onion, finely chopped
1 cup finely chopped celery
1 (10¾-ounce) can tomato soup, undiluted
1 cup catsup
1 teaspoon salt
⅛ teaspoon pepper
8 hamburger buns, halved
Shredded Cheddar cheese

Brown meat in a large skillet. Add onion and celery; cook until tender. Drain off drippings. Stir in tomato soup, catsup, salt, and pepper; simmer 30 minutes.

Freeze in a plastic freezer container.

To serve, thaw in refrigerator, and heat in a saucepan. Spoon over warm bun halves, and sprinkle with cheese. Yield: 16 servings.
Nell Little,
Jonesboro, Tennessee.

FREEZER SLAW

1 large head cabbage
½ green pepper
6 large carrots
1 teaspoon salt
2 cups sugar
1 teaspoon dry mustard
½ cup water
1 cup vinegar
1 teaspoon celery seeds

Shred the vegetables. Sprinkle with salt; let stand 1 hour. Drain mixture, if water accumulates.

Combine remaining ingredients in a saucepan. Bring to a boil; boil 3 minutes. Cool. Pour over cabbage mixture, and let stand 3 minutes. Stir well. Freeze in plastic freezer bags or containers. To serve, thaw in refrigerator. Yield: 10 servings.
Mrs. Ken Keller,
Alcoa, Tennessee.

STRAWBERRY FROST

½ cup butter
1 cup all-purpose flour
¼ cup firmly packed brown sugar
½ cup finely chopped pecans
2 egg whites
1 (10-ounce) package frozen sliced strawberries, slightly thawed
⅔ cup sugar
2 tablespoons lemon juice
1 cup whipping cream
Whole fresh strawberries (optional)

Melt butter in a 13- x 9- x 2-inch baking pan. Add flour, brown sugar, and pecans; mix well. Pat out evenly in pan. Bake at 350° for 10 minutes. Stir and bake 10 minutes longer. Cool; remove one-third of crumbs for topping. Pat remaining crumbs smoothly in pan.

Beat egg whites, sliced strawberries, sugar, and lemon juice on high speed of an electric mixer for 15 minutes.

Beat whipping cream until light and fluffy; fold into strawberry mixture. Spread mixture over crust in pan, and sprinkle with remaining crumbs.

Cover tightly with aluminum foil, and freeze. Cut into squares, and garnish with whole strawberries, if desired. Yield: 12 to 16 servings.
Mrs. W. G. Greenlee,
Inverness, Florida.

Keep Right On Serving Salads

The end of summer's fresh garden vegetables does not necessarily mean the end of your salad making. You can still serve an attractive salad by taking advantage of the produce now available at the supermarket, as well as canned or frozen vegetables. Marinated Vegetable Salad, for example, provides a colorful and tasty combination of cooked carrots, cucumber, and cauliflower, covered in a sweet but tangy marinade.

If you prefer a tossed salad, try Mexican Tossed Salad: lettuce, kidney beans, tomatoes, and Cheddar cheese with a salad dressing and corn chips. Remember to add the corn chips last so they'll remain fresh and crunchy.

OVERNIGHT BLACK-EYED PEA SALAD

2 (15-ounce) cans black-eyed peas with snaps, drained
½ cup red onions, thinly sliced and separated into rings
½ cup chopped green pepper
½ clove garlic
¼ cup sugar
¼ cup vinegar
¼ cup vegetable oil
½ teaspoon salt
Dash of pepper
Dash of hot sauce

Combine peas, onion, and green pepper in a medium bowl. Stick a wooden pick through garlic; add to vegetables. Combine remaining ingredients, stirring well. Add to vegetable mixture, and toss lightly to coat. Cover; refrigerate at least 12 hours. Remove the wooden pick with garlic before serving. Yield: 6 to 8 servings.

Mrs. J. W. Hopkins,
Abilene, Texas.

BROCCOLI AND CAULIFLOWER SALAD

1 pound fresh cauliflower, chopped
1 pound fresh broccoli, chopped
1 small onion, chopped
⅓ cup vinegar
⅓ cup sugar
⅔ cup mayonnaise
1 teaspoon salt

Combine cauliflower, broccoli, and onion; toss well. Combine remaining ingredients, mixing well; pour over vegetables. Cover and refrigerate overnight. Yield: 6 to 8 servings.

Mrs. Forest Lundy,
Choctaw, Oklahoma.

SAVORY CAULIFLOWER AND PEA SALAD

1 medium head cauliflower, broken into flowerets
1 (10-ounce) package frozen English peas, cooked and drained or 1 (16-ounce) can English peas, drained
¾ cup sliced radishes
3 stalks celery, thinly sliced
2 green chili peppers, finely chopped
1 cup mayonnaise
¼ cup milk
1 small onion, grated
1½ teaspoons seasoned salt
½ teaspoon seasoned pepper

Combine first 5 ingredients in a medium bowl. Combine remaining ingredients, and pour over the cauliflower mixture; toss lightly to coat. Cover and chill. Yield: 8 to 10 servings.

Mrs. Roger Buelow,
Desdemona, Texas.

VEGETABLE SLAW

1 envelope unflavored gelatin
¼ cup cold water
⅔ cup sugar
⅔ cup vinegar
1 teaspoon celery seeds
1½ teaspoons salt
¼ teaspoon pepper
⅔ cup vegetable oil
8 cups shredded cabbage
2 carrots, shredded
1 green pepper, finely chopped
½ cup onion, finely chopped

Soften gelatin in cold water; set aside. Combine sugar, vinegar, celery seeds, salt, and pepper in a small saucepan. Bring to a boil; stir in softened gelatin. Cool until slightly thickened.

Beat mixture well; gradually add vegetable oil, beating constantly. Refrigerate dressing until needed.

Combine cabbage, carrots, green pepper, and onion; toss with dressing. Yield: about 8 servings.

Mrs. Robert W. McNeil,
Ronceverte, West Virginia.

ENGLISH PEA SALAD

1 (17-ounce) can English peas, drained
3 hard-cooked eggs, chopped
½ cup sweet pickle, chopped
½ cup pimiento, chopped
¼ teaspoon celery seeds
¼ cup mayonnaise
Lettuce leaves
Pimiento strips

Combine first 6 ingredients; mix well, and chill. Serve on lettuce leaves; garnish salad with pimiento strips. Yield: 4 to 6 servings.

Sara A. McCullough,
Louisville, Mississippi.

MARINATED VEGETABLE SALAD

1 pound carrots, sliced and cooked
1 green pepper, cut into rings
2 onions, cut into rings
1 cucumber, sliced
2 stalks celery, sliced
1 cup sliced cauliflower
1 (10¾-ounce) can tomato soup, undiluted
1 cup sugar
¾ cup vinegar
¼ cup vegetable oil
1 tablespoon Worcestershire sauce
1 teaspoon pepper
1 teaspoon prepared mustard
¼ teaspoon salt

Combine vegetables in a large bowl. Stir together remaining ingredients; pour over vegetables. Cover and chill overnight. Yield: 10 to 12 servings.

Lucille Blankenship,
Hawkinsville, Georgia.

MEXICAN TOSSED SALAD

1 head lettuce, torn into bite-size pieces
1 (15½-ounce) can kidney beans, drained
2 to 3 medium tomatoes, cut into wedges
½ cup sliced green onion
Salt and pepper to taste
1 cup (4 ounces) shredded Cheddar cheese
½ cup commercial Russian salad dressing
3 cups regular size corn chips, crushed

Place lettuce in a large bowl; top with beans, tomatoes, and onion. Add salt, pepper, and cheese. Just before serving, add dressing and chips. Toss lightly to combine. Yield: 6 to 8 servings.

Mrs. Thomas Clayton,
Baton Rouge, Louisiana.

Six Choices For Chicken

Any way you prepare it, chicken is a family favorite. And it makes sense to take advantage of chicken's low cost and versatility. Ranging from savory chicken pie to creamed chicken served over rice, these selections will satisfy your family and please the pocketbook.

CHICKEN AND PINEAPPLE

2 chicken legs
2 chicken thighs
2 whole chicken breasts, split
½ cup all-purpose flour
⅓ cup vegetable oil
1 teaspoon salt
¼ teaspoon pepper
1 (20-ounce) can sliced pineapple
1 cup sugar
2 tablespoons cornstarch
¾ cup cider vinegar
1 tablespoon soy sauce
¼ teaspoon ground ginger
1 chicken-flavored bouillon cube
1 large green pepper, sliced into ¼-inch rings
Hot cooked rice

Dredge chicken pieces in flour, coating well; brown in hot oil over medium heat. Place chicken in a 13- x 9- x 2-inch baking pan; sprinkle with salt and pepper. Set aside.

Drain pineapple, reserving juice. Add enough water to pineapple juice to make 1¼ cups liquid. Combine sugar and cornstarch in a saucepan; add pineapple juice mixture, vinegar, soy sauce, ginger, and bouillon cube. Bring sauce to a boil; reduce heat and simmer 2 minutes, stirring constantly. Pour sauce over chicken.

Bake, uncovered, at 350° for 30 minutes. Place pineapple and green pepper slices over chicken; bake an additional 30 minutes. Serve with rice. Yield: 4 to 6 servings.   *Louise Denmon,*
Silsbee, Texas.

Tip: An uncooked or cooked stuffed turkey or chicken should never be refrigerated. The stuffing should be thoroughly removed and refrigerated in a separate container.

CHICKEN-VEGETABLE POT PIE

1 (2½- to 3-pound) broiler-fryer
1 teaspoon salt
½ teaspoon pepper
4 to 5 medium potatoes, pared
5 stalks celery
½ pound carrots
1 (17-ounce) can English peas
½ cup butter or margarine
⅔ cup all-purpose flour
1 cup milk
1 chicken-flavored bouillon cube
2 teaspoons salt
½ teaspoon pepper
Pastry for a double-crust 9-inch pie

Place chicken, 1 teaspoon salt, ½ teaspoon pepper, and water to cover in a Dutch oven. Bring to a boil; cover and simmer 1 hour or until tender. Remove chicken from broth; cool. Remove chicken from bone, and cut into bite-size pieces.

Cut potatoes, celery, and carrots into 1-inch chunks. Place in broth; simmer until tender. Drain vegetables, reserving 3 cups broth. Combine chicken, potatoes, celery, carrots, and peas; spoon into a 13- x 9- x 2-inch pan.

Melt butter in a heavy saucepan over low heat; add flour, stirring until smooth. Cook 1 minute, stirring constantly. Gradually stir in milk, 3 cups chicken broth, and bouillon cube; cook over medium heat, stirring constantly, until thickened and bubbly. Stir in 2 teaspoons salt and ½ teaspoon pepper. Pour the sauce evenly over chicken-vegetable mixture.

Prepare pastry; roll to fit a 13- x 9- 2-inch pan. Place crust over chicken mixture; cut 4 to 6 small slits in crust to allow steam to escape. Bake at 400° for 45 to 55 minutes or until crust is golden brown. Yield: 6 to 8 servings.
Mrs. Bob Whitmire,
Burleson, Texas.

CHICKEN PIE

1 (2½- to 3-pound) broiler-fryer
1 stalk celery, cut into large pieces
Salt
½ cup margarine, melted
1 cup all-purpose flour
1 tablespoon baking powder
¼ teaspoon salt
½ teaspoon pepper
1 cup milk
1 (10¾-ounce) can cream of celery soup, undiluted

Combine chicken, celery, salt to taste, and water to cover in a Dutch oven. Bring to a boil; cover and simmer 1 hour or until chicken is tender. Remove chicken from Dutch oven, reserving 1¼ cups chicken broth.

Remove chicken from bone; dice meat. Place in a lightly greased 11- x 7- x 2-inch baking dish. Drizzle chicken with margarine.

Combine flour, baking powder, salt, pepper, and milk; beat until smooth. Pour over chicken.

Combine celery soup and reserved chicken broth in a small saucepan; bring to a boil over medium heat. Pour over chicken mixture. Bake at 425° about 50 minutes or until top is golden brown. Yield: 6 servings.   *Fay Newsom,*
Madison, North Carolina.

TOMATO-BAKED CHICKEN

1 (2½- to 3-pound) broiler-fryer, cut into serving-size pieces
Salt and pepper
2 tablespoons vegetable oil
½ cup chopped onion
1 clove garlic, pressed
1 (16-ounce) can whole tomatoes, undrained and quartered
¼ cup grated Parmesan cheese
3 tablespoons all-purpose flour
½ cup commercial sour cream

Sprinkle chicken with salt and pepper; sauté in oil until brown. Remove chicken from skillet, and set aside. Sauté onion and garlic in drippings until onion is tender. Stir in tomatoes; bring to a boil.

Place chicken in a 13- x 9- x 2-inch baking dish. Pour tomato mixture over chicken. Cover and bake at 350° for 1 hour or until done. Remove chicken to a serving platter, reserving the drippings; sprinkle chicken with Parmesan cheese.

Combine flour, sour cream, and drippings in a saucepan; mix well. Cook over low heat, stirring constantly, until mixture thickens. Spoon sauce over chicken. Yield: 4 to 6 servings.
Gwen Granderson,
Kingsland, Arkansas.

CREAMED CHICKEN OVER CONFETTI RICE SQUARES

3 cups cooked rice
1 cup (4 ounces) shredded Swiss cheese
½ cup chopped parsley
⅓ cup chopped onion
⅓ cup chopped pimiento
1 teaspoon salt
3 eggs, beaten
1½ cups milk
2 tablespoons butter or margarine
3 tablespoons all-purpose flour
2 cups milk
½ teaspoon salt
¼ teaspoon ground marjoram
3 cups cubed cooked chicken
Paprika

Combine first 8 ingredients; spoon into a buttered 8-inch baking dish. Bake at 325° for 1 hour or until a knife inserted in center comes out clean.

Melt butter in a heavy saucepan over low heat; add flour, and stir until smooth. Cook 1 minute, stirring constantly. Gradually add 2 cups milk; cook over medium heat, stirring constantly until thickened and bubbly. Stir in salt and marjoram. Stir in chicken; sprinkle with paprika. Cut rice into squares. Spoon creamed chicken over rice squares. Yield: 4 to 6 servings.

Mrs. James Barden,
Suffolk, Virginia.

PEANUT BUTTER-MARMALADE CHICKEN

1 teaspoon salt
¼ teaspoon pepper
⅛ teaspoon ground ginger
2 whole chicken breasts, split and skinned
⅓ cup peanut butter
⅓ cup orange marmalade
3 tablespoons orange juice
1 tablespoon lemon juice
1 cup round buttery cracker crumbs
¼ cup vegetable oil

Combine salt, pepper, and ginger; rub into chicken. Combine peanut butter, marmalade, orange juice, and lemon juice. Dip chicken in peanut butter mixture; coat well with cracker crumbs.

Pour oil into a 13- x 9- x 2-inch baking dish; arrange chicken in dish. Bake at 350° for 30 minutes. Turn chicken, and cook 30 additional minutes or until done. Yield: 4 servings.

Bonnie Baumgardner,
Sylva, North Carolina.

Talk Of Texas Chili

When the subject of Texas chili comes up, the talk never ends for there seems to be as many varieties of the spicy red as there are cooks in the Lone Star State. Here are several samplings from our Texas readers.

CHUCK WAGON CHILI

1 (2-pound) boneless chuck blade steak, cut into ½-inch cubes
2 tablespoons vegetable oil
1 cup chopped onion, divided
1 large green pepper, diced
2 cloves garlic, crushed
1 (28-ounce) can whole tomatoes, undrained and chopped
1 (6-ounce) can tomato paste
1 cup water
3 tablespoons chili powder
1 tablespoon salt
1 teaspoon dried whole oregano
½ teaspoon pepper
½ cup (2 ounces) shredded Monterey Jack cheese

Brown meat in oil in a Dutch oven. Remove meat, reserving drippings. Sauté ¾ cup onion, green pepper, and garlic in reserved drippings until tender. Add meat and next 7 ingredients, mixing well. Bring to a boil. Reduce heat; cover and simmer 1½ hours, stirring chili occasionally.

Transfer to serving bowls, and sprinkle with remaining onion and cheese. Yield: about 9 cups.

Mrs. Gary Ferguson,
Corsicana, Texas.

MEATY CHILI

3 pounds ground beef
1 medium onion, chopped
3 small cloves garlic, minced
1 (15-ounce) can tomato sauce
5½ cups water
¼ cup plus 2 tablespoons chili powder
1 tablespoon paprika
1 tablespoon cumin seeds
1 teaspoon salt

Combine ground beef, onion, and garlic in a Dutch oven; cook until beef is browned, stirring to crumble meat. Drain off pan drippings. Add remaining ingredients, mixing well. Cook over low heat 3 to 4 hours, stirring occasionally. Yield: about 9½ cups.   *Judy Irwin,*
Mabank, Texas.

CHILI WITH NOODLES

3 pounds ground beef
1 medium onion, chopped
2 (1.25-ounce) packages chili seasoning mix
1 (5-ounce) package fine egg noodles
1 (46-ounce) can tomato juice
2 (15½-ounce) cans chili beans
1 tablespoon Worcestershire sauce
½ teaspoon garlic salt
½ teaspoon onion salt
¼ teaspoon pepper

Combine ground beef, onion, and chili seasoning mix in a Dutch oven; cook until beef is browned, stirring to crumble meat. Drain off pan drippings. Add remaining ingredients, mixing well. Cook over low heat 1 hour, stirring occasionally. Yield: about 12 cups.
Mrs. J. A. Satterfield,
Fort Worth, Texas.

QUICK AND SIMPLE CHILI

1 pound ground beef
1 cup chopped onion
1 clove garlic, crushed
2 (8-ounce) cans tomato sauce
Salt and pepper to taste
2 to 4 tablespoons chili powder
2 cups water

Combine ground beef, onion, and garlic in a large saucepan; cook until beef is browned, stirring to crumble meat. Drain off pan drippings. Add remaining ingredients; simmer 45 minutes to 1 hour. Yield: about 6 cups.

Becky Reynolds,
Rio Vista, Texas.

CHILI HOMINY BAKE

1 pound ground beef
½ cup chopped onion
2 tablespoons all-purpose flour
1 teaspoon salt
1 teaspoon chili powder
1 (14½-ounce) can hominy, undrained
1 (16-ounce) can tomatoes, undrained and chopped
¼ cup (1 ounce) shredded Cheddar cheese

Combine ground beef and onion; cook until beef is browned, stirring to crumble meat. Drain off pan drippings.

Add remaining ingredients except cheese; stir well. Spoon mixture into a greased 2-quart casserole. Bake, uncovered, at 350° for 25 minutes; sprinkle with Cheddar cheese, and bake 5 additional minutes. Yield: 4 servings.

Mrs. R. A. Dibrell,
Dallas, Texas.

December

Christmas in the South is not complete without the traditional holiday dinner. To make your feast the merriest ever, we have put together a menu complete with traditions you might expect and new ideas sure to become favorites.

Give your December gift-giving a new twist, too, by sharing goodies from your kitchen. The following pages are brimming with recipe ideas for gifts as well as novel ways to package them. How about a carafe of Hot Wine Mix capped with gaily printed fabric?

And warm those chilly winter evenings with hearty stroganoffs served over steaming noodles. Teamed with one of our make-ahead salads and fresh yeast breads, a stroganoff makes a meal as special as the season.

Crafting Gifts In The Kitchen

More special than any gift you can purchase is a gift you've made yourself. And at this time of year, you'll find Southerners crafting their special holiday remembrances in the kitchen: dipping cherries in chocolate, kneading and shaping yeast dough, cooking and stirring marmalade to just the right temperature. This holiday season, why not get out your apron, roll up your sleeves, and turn your kitchen into a workshop for preparing some of these tasty gifts.

Keep a supply of Spiced Pecans or Chocolate-Covered Cherries in your pantry—you'll have something special on hand to share with that last-minute visitor who surprises you with a gift. Bring friends and family in other cities a little closer to home with a box of Lemon Crinkle Cookies or Cherry Nut Nuggets, which can be wrapped and mailed. On your way to holiday parties, tuck a bottle of homemade Orange Liqueur in your pocket to give as a hostess gift.

Express those neighborly feelings with a small gift of Hot Cocoa Mix or a jar of Christmas Brunch Jam. Send a special neighbor a loaf of Old-Fashioned White Bread teamed with a crock of Strawberry Butter.

Just as much fun as making food gifts is selecting pretty and practical containers to hold them. These can be as simple as a cardboard box covered with wrapping paper or as elaborate as a crystal candy dish. Check supermarkets, florists, antique shops, and discount houseware stores for boxes, wide-mouthed jars, and decorative tins.

Baskets lined with dainty napkins or tea towels are perfect for homemade breads and cookies, while canisters make just the right airtight container for assorted candies.

For containers without added expense, save old bottles and small wine carafes for giving homemade liqueurs and our Hot Wine Mix. Cap the liqueurs with a cork, and top the carafes with plastic wrap and scraps of cloth. Transform fabric into bonnets for jams and jellies; simply clip the edges with pinking shears, or lace the edges with rickrack and tie with a ribbon.

After you've filled the container with homemade goodies, attach a label, instructions for serving, and a recipe for making more. For the final touch, attach a printed, plaid, or striped bow and a sprig of holly.

CHOCOLATE DATE-NUT BREAD

2 (1-ounce) squares unsweetened chocolate
1 cup hot water
1 cup chopped dates
½ cup chopped pecans or walnuts
1 teaspoon soda
¼ cup shortening
1 cup sugar
1 egg
2 cups all-purpose flour
½ teaspoon salt
1 teaspoon vanilla extract

Combine chocolate and water in top of a double boiler; bring water to a boil. Reduce heat to low; cook until chocolate is melted. Stir in dates, pecans, and soda; set aside to cool.

Cream shortening; gradually add sugar, beating well. Add egg, and beat well.

Combine flour and salt; add to creamed mixture alternately with chocolate mixture, beginning and ending with flour mixture. Stir in vanilla.

Pour batter into 2 greased and floured 28-ounce fruit cans. Bake at 350° for 1 hour or until wooden pick inserted in center comes out clean. Cool in cans 10 minutes; remove from cans, and cool completely. Yield: 2 loaves.

Mrs. Gene Foster,
Whitesboro, Texas.

HOLIDAY WREATH

Pinch of dried whole saffron
1¼ cups buttermilk
2 packages dry yeast
½ cup warm water (105° to 115°)
6½ to 7 cups all-purpose flour, divided
½ cup sugar
2 teaspoons baking powder
2 teaspoons salt
½ cup butter or margarine, softened
2 eggs, slightly beaten
½ cup finely chopped candied citron
¼ cup chopped blanched almonds
1 tablespoon grated lemon rind
Glaze (recipe follows)
Candied citron
Candied red cherries
Grated lemon rind
Whole blanched almonds, toasted

Combine saffron and buttermilk; let stand 10 to 15 minutes, stirring mixture occasionally.

Dissolve yeast in warm water in a large bowl, set aside.

Combine 2½ cups flour, sugar, baking powder, and salt; stir well. Add buttermilk mixture, butter, eggs, and flour mixture to yeast; beat at low speed of electric mixer 30 seconds, scraping sides of bowl constantly with a spatula.

Combine ½ cup additional flour and ½ cup candied citron, stirring well; stir citron mixture, chopped almonds, and 1 tablespoon lemon rind into dough. Gradually add enough of remaining flour to make a soft dough (dough should remain soft and slightly sticky).

Turn dough out onto a heavily floured surface, and knead 5 minutes or until dough is elastic. Cover and let rest 10 minutes.

Divide dough in half; shape each portion into a ball. Divide 1 ball of dough into 3 equal portions, and shape each into a 24-inch rope.

Transfer ropes to a large greased baking sheet. Firmly pinch ends of the 3 ropes together at one end to seal. Braid ropes together; firmly pinch ends together to seal. Shape braid into a circle with a 5-inch diameter hole. Join ends of braid; firmly pinch ends to seal. Invert a well-greased 3½-inch custard cup in center of wreath. Repeat procedure with remaining dough.

Cover and let rise in a warm place (85°), free from drafts, until doubled in bulk.

Bake at 375° for 25 to 30 minutes or until golden brown and braids sound hollow when tapped with finger. Carefully transfer to wire rack to cool.

Spread half of glaze over each wreath. Garnish each with candied citron, candied cherries, lemon rind, and almonds. Yield: 2 loaves.

Glaze:

4 cups sifted powdered sugar
¼ cup water

Combine sugar and water; mix until smooth. Yield: about 2 cups.

Marjorie L. Chase,
Midland, Texas.

THREE-C BREAD

2½ cups all-purpose flour
1 cup sugar
1 teaspoon baking powder
1 teaspoon soda
½ teaspoon salt
1 teaspoon ground cinnamon
½ cup milk
½ cup vegetable oil
3 eggs, beaten
1 (3½-ounce) can flaked coconut
½ cup chopped maraschino cherries
2 cups shredded carrot
½ cup chopped pecans
½ cup raisins (optional)

Combine first 6 ingredients in a large bowl; make a well in center of mixture. Combine milk, oil, and eggs, stirring well; add to dry ingredients, stirring just until moistened. Stir in remaining ingredients. Spoon into three greased 7- x 3- x 2-inch loafpans. Bake at 350° for 30 to 35 minutes or until wooden pick inserted in center comes out clean. Yield: 3 loaves.
Mrs. J. A. Satterfield,
Fort Worth, Texas.

MEXICAN SWEET ROLLS

3¾ to 4 cups all-purpose flour, divided
1 package dry yeast
1 cup milk
¼ cup sugar
¼ cup shortening
1 teaspoon salt
2 eggs
⅔ cup all-purpose flour
½ cup sugar
¼ cup butter or margarine
2 egg yolks, beaten
¼ teaspoon vanilla extract

Combine 2 cups flour and yeast in a large mixing bowl; stir well and set aside.

Combine milk, ¼ cup sugar, shortening, and salt in a small saucepan; place over low heat, stirring constantly, until shortening melts. Remove from heat; let cool to lukewarm (105° to 115°). Stir milk mixture and eggs into flour mixture. Beat at low speed of electric mixer for 30 seconds. Stir in 1¾ to 2 cups additional flour to make a stiff dough.

Turn dough out on a lightly floured surface; knead until smooth and elastic (about 8 to 10 minutes). Place dough in a greased bowl, turning to grease top. Cover and let rise in a warm place (85°), free from drafts, about 1 hour and 15 minutes or until doubled in bulk.

Punch dough down, and shape into 16 balls; flatten each with fingers to about ¼-inch thickness. Place rolls 2 inches apart on greased baking sheets.

Combine ⅔ cup flour and ½ cup sugar; cut in butter until mixture resembles coarse meal. Stir in egg yolks and vanilla. Press mixture together with hands, and shape into 16 balls; roll each out on a lightly floured surface to about ⅛-inch thickness. Using a spatula, place each circle on top of a roll on baking sheets.

Score through topping and halfway through roll with a sharp knife to form a swirl design, being careful not to cut through outer edges. Cover and let rise in a warm place (85°), free from drafts, 1 hour or until doubled in bulk. Bake at 375° for 15 to 18 minutes or until lightly browned. Yield: about 16 rolls.
Martha T. Leoni,
New Bern, North Carolina.

GINGERBREAD MUFFINS

1 cup shortening
1 cup sugar
4 eggs
1 cup molasses
1 (8-ounce) carton commercial sour cream
4 cups all-purpose flour
2 teaspoons soda
1 teaspoon baking powder
2 teaspoons ground ginger
¼ teaspoon ground allspice
¼ teaspoon ground cinnamon
½ cup raisins
½ cup chopped pecans or walnuts

Cream shortening; gradually add sugar, beating until light and fluffy. Add eggs, one at a time, beating well after each addition. Stir in molasses and sour cream.

Combine remaining ingredients, stirring well; add to batter, and stir just until moistened. Spoon into greased muffin pans, filling one-half full. Bake at 375° for 12 to 15 minutes. Yield: about 1½ dozen.
Mrs. Billie Taylor,
Afton, Virginia.

OLD-FASHIONED WHITE BREAD

2½ cups milk, scalded
3 tablespoons sugar
1 tablespoon salt
3 tablespoons shortening
1 package dry yeast
¼ cup warm water (105° to 115°)
7 cups all-purpose flour, divided
Melted butter or margarine

Combine scalded milk, sugar, salt, and shortening; stir until shortening melts. Cool to lukewarm (105° to 115°).

Dissolve yeast in warm water in a large mixing bowl. Stir in milk mixture and 4 cups flour; beat 2 minutes at medium speed of electric mixer or until smooth. Cover and let rise in a warm place (85°), free from drafts, 45 minutes. Punch dough down; gradually stir in 2 cups additional flour. Turn dough out on a lightly floured surface, and knead in remaining 1 cup flour. Knead until smooth and elastic, about 8 to 10 minutes (dough will be very soft). Place dough in a well-greased bowl, turning to grease top. Cover and let rise in a warm place (85°), free from drafts, about 20 minutes.

Knead dough in bowl 2 minutes. Turn dough over; let rise 20 minutes (dough will be sticky). Repeat kneading and rising procedure. Punch dough down; turn out onto a lightly floured surface. Let dough rest 10 minutes.

Divide dough in half, and shape each half into a loaf. Place loaves in two greased 9- x 5- x 3-inch loafpans. Cover and let rise in a warm place (85°), free from drafts, 45 minutes or until doubled in bulk. Bake at 350° for 45 to 50 minutes or until golden brown.

Remove loaves from pans; brush with melted butter, and cool on wire racks. Yield: 2 loaves.
Carol Forcum,
Marion, Illinois.

DELICIOUS FRUIT MARMALADE

3 oranges
1 lemon
2 cups drained crushed pineapple
6¾ cups sugar
½ cup hot water
1 (6-ounce) jar maraschino cherries, drained and chopped

Wash oranges and lemon; cut in half crosswise. Remove seeds and membrane in center of each. Cut fruit into quarters; grind unpeeled fruit in meat grinder or food processor.

Combine ground fruit, pineapple, sugar, and water in a Dutch oven; bring to a boil over high heat. Reduce heat and boil 30 minutes, stirring often. Remove from heat; stir in cherries. Pour into hot sterilized jars, leaving ¼-inch headspace. Cover at once with metal lids, and screw bands tight. Process in boiling-water bath 10 minutes. Yield: 7 half-pints.
Mrs. Bruce Fowler,
Woodruff, South Carolina.

CHRISTMAS BRUNCH JAM

3 cups fresh cranberries
1 (20-ounce) can crushed pineapple, undrained
1 cup peeled and diced cooking apple
3 cups sugar
1½ cups water
1¾ teaspoons grated lemon rind
2 tablespoons lemon juice

Combine all ingredients in a Dutch oven. Cook, uncovered, over medium-low heat, stirring frequently, until mixture registers 221° on a candy thermometer (this will take about 1½ hours).

Spoon cranberry mixture into hot sterilized jars, leaving ¼-inch headspace; cover at once with metal lids, and screw bands tight. Process in boiling-water bath 15 minutes. Yield: 5 pints.
Bonnie S. Baumgardner,
Sylva, North Carolina.

STRAWBERRY BUTTER

1 (10-ounce) carton frozen strawberries, thawed
1 cup unsalted butter, softened
½ cup powdered sugar

Combine all ingredients in a mixing bowl; mix until blended and smooth. Store in refrigerator. Yield: 1¾ cups.
Mrs. Doug Hail,
Moody, Texas.

CANDIED ORANGE PEEL

1 quart orange peel strips (¼ inch wide)
2 cups sugar
1 cup water
Sugar

Place orange peel in salted water to cover in a Dutch oven; bring to a boil and boil 20 minutes. Drain. Repeat boiling procedure twice without salt, and set peel aside.

Combine 2 cups sugar and 1 cup water in a small saucepan; bring to a boil and cook, stirring often, until candy thermometer registers soft ball stage (235°). Add peel; simmer 30 minutes, stirring often. Drain well.

Roll peel, a few pieces at a time, in sugar. Arrange in a single layer on wire racks; let dry 4 to 5 hours. Store in an airtight container. Yield: about 1 pound.
Edna A. Peavy,
Atlanta, Georgia.

SPICED PECANS

1 cup sugar
⅓ cup whipping cream
½ teaspoon salt
Dash of ground cinnamon
1 teaspoon grated orange rind
2 teaspoons orange juice
1½ cups pecan pieces

Combine first 4 ingredients in a large saucepan; stir well. Place over medium high heat, stirring constantly, and cook to soft ball stage (235°). Stir in rind and juice. Remove from heat; add pecans, and stir until coated.

Spread pecans on waxed paper, and immediately separate into clusters with a spoon. Let cool. Yield: about 2 dozen pieces.
Louise Holmes,
Winchester, Tennessee.

CHRISTMAS DIVINITY

2 cups sugar
½ cup water
½ cup light corn syrup
2 egg whites
1 teaspoon vanilla extract
¾ cup chopped pecans
¾ cup candied cherries, coarsely chopped
Candied cherry halves

Combine sugar, water, and syrup in a 3-quart saucepan; cook over low heat, stirring constantly, until sugar dissolves. Cook over high heat, without stirring, until mixture reaches hard ball stage (260°).

Beat egg whites (at room temperature) in a large mixing bowl until stiff peaks form. Pour hot sugar mixture in a very thin stream over egg whites while beating constantly at high speed of an electric mixer. Add vanilla, and continue beating until mixture holds its shape (5 to 10 minutes). Stir in pecans and chopped cherries.

Drop by teaspoonfuls onto waxed paper. Garnish tops with candied cherry halves. Cool. Yield: about 3 dozen.
Mrs. William B. Moore,
Selma, Alabama.

Tip: For easy chopping of dried fruit, place fruit in freezer 2 hours before chopping. Cut with knife or kitchen shears dipped frequently in hot water to prevent sticking.

CHOCOLATE-COVERED CHERRIES

¼ cup plus 2 tablespoons butter, softened
2½ cups sifted powdered sugar
1½ teaspoons milk
¼ teaspoon vanilla extract
About 48 maraschino cherries with stems
1 (12-ounce) package semisweet chocolate morsels
1 tablespoon shortening

Cream butter; gradually add sugar, beating well. Blend in milk and vanilla. Chill mixture 2 hours or until firm.

Drain cherries; dry on absorbent paper towels. Place bowl of sugar mixture in a bowl of ice to keep mixture chilled. Shape a small amount of sugar mixture around each cherry. Place on waxed paper-lined cookie sheet; chill about 2 hours or until firm.

Melt chocolate and shortening in top of a double boiler. Dip each cherry by the stem into chocolate. Place on a waxed paper-lined cookie sheet; chill until firm. Store in a cool place. Yield: about 4 dozen.
Martin A. Davis, Sr.,
Durham, North Carolina.

CHERRY NUT NUGGETS

1 cup shortening
1 (3-ounce) package cream cheese, softened
1 cup sugar
1 egg
1 teaspoon almond extract
2½ cups all-purpose flour
½ teaspoon salt
¼ teaspoon soda
1⅓ cups finely chopped pecans
Maraschino cherries, drained and halved

Cream shortening and cream cheese; gradually add sugar, beating until light and fluffy. Add egg and almond extract; beat well.

Combine flour, salt, and soda; stir into creamed mixture. Chill dough at least 1 hour.

Shape dough into 1-inch balls. Roll in pecans, and place on ungreased cookie sheets. Gently press a cherry half into center of each cookie. Bake at 350° for 16 to 18 minutes. Yield: about 4 dozen.
Judy Irwin,
Mabank, Texas.

LEMON CRINKLE COOKIES

½ cup shortening
1 cup firmly packed brown sugar
1 egg
1 tablespoon grated lemon rind
1½ cups all-purpose flour
½ teaspoon soda
½ teaspoon cream of tartar
¼ teaspoon ground ginger
Pinch of salt
About 2 tablespoons sugar

Cream shortening and brown sugar until fluffy; add egg and lemon rind, beating well. Combine flour, soda, cream of tartar, ginger, and salt; stir into creamed mixture.

Roll dough into 1-inch balls; roll each in sugar. Place 2 inches apart on ungreased cookie sheets. Bake at 350° for 10 to 12 minutes. Yield: about 3½ dozen. *Virginia Mathews,*
Jacksonville, Florida.

TANGY CHEESE BALL

2 cups (8 ounces) shredded sharp
    Cheddar cheese
6 (3-ounce) packages cream cheese,
    softened
1 medium onion, grated
3 tablespoons Worcestershire sauce
2 drops of hot sauce
½ to 1 clove garlic, minced
1 cup chopped pecans

Combine all ingredients except pecans; mix well. Chill overnight. Shape into a ball, and roll in pecans. Serve with crackers. Yield: 1 cheese ball.
Donna Fargis,
Reidsville, North Carolina.

ORANGE LIQUEUR

3 medium-size oranges
3 cups brandy
1 cup honey

Peel oranges, leaving inner white skin on fruit. Cut rind into 2- x ¼-inch strips. Reserve oranges for use in another recipe.

Combine brandy and rind in a jar. Cover tightly, and let stand at room temperature for 3 weeks.

Remove rind; stir in honey. Let stand 3 days. Strain off clear portion, and store in airtight containers; reserve cloudy portion for use as a liquid or flavoring in other recipes. Yield: about 3 cups.

ALMOND-FLAVORED LIQUEUR

3 cups sugar
2¼ cups water
Finely grated rind of 3 lemons
1 quart vodka
3 tablespoons almond extract
2 tablespoons vanilla extract

Combine first 3 ingredients in a Dutch oven; bring to a boil. Reduce heat and simmer 5 minutes, stirring occasionally; cool completely. Stir in remaining ingredients; store in airtight containers. Yield: about 2 quarts.

HOT WINE MIX

6 cups sugar
2 tablespoons ground cinnamon
2 tablespoons ground cloves
1 tablespoon ground allspice
¾ teaspoon ground nutmeg
Burgundy or other dry red wine
Cinnamon sticks (optional)

Combine first 5 ingredients in a large bowl; stir well. Store mix in an airtight container.

To serve, combine 2 teaspoons mix and ½ cup water in a small saucepan; bring to a boil. Reduce heat; add 1 cup wine and heat thoroughly (do not boil). Serve with a cinnamon stick, if desired. Yield: about 72 servings. *Diana Curtis,*
Albuquerque, New Mexico.

HOT COCOA MIX

2 cups nondairy coffee creamer
1½ cups sugar
¾ cup cocoa
½ cup instant nonfat dry milk powder
¼ teaspoon salt
1 cup boiling water
Marshmallows or whipped cream
    (optional)

Combine first 5 ingredients in a large bowl, and mix well. Store mix in an airtight container.

To serve, place 2 tablespoons mix in a cup. Add 1 cup boiling water, and stir well. Top with a marshmallow or whipped cream, if desired. Yield: about 36 servings. *Peggy H. Amos,*
Martinsville, Virginia.

Begin Christmas With A Family Breakfast

If breakfast is the least-thought-of meal at your house on a busy Christmas morning, you and your family may be missing a treat. Our test kitchens staff has assembled a complete breakfast menu that's just as festive as the day. The dishes include everyone's favorites—eggs, sausage, biscuits, and fruit in a delicious combination. But most important, much of the preparation can be done ahead.

The menu centers around an extra-creamy version of scrambled eggs. The accompanying Crunchy Sausage Casserole and Ruby Pears can be started the evening before. While baking the biscuits in the morning (grate the cheese the evening before), let the punch perk; its delightful cinnamon fragrance will tell your family that breakfast is almost ready.

Topping off this generous menu, for anyone still hungry, is a sugar-glazed Banana Coffee Cake.

Cream Cheese Scrambled Eggs
Crunchy Sausage Casserole
Ruby Pears   Cheese Biscuits
Banana Coffee Cake
Hot Percolator Punch

CREAM CHEESE SCRAMBLED EGGS

12 eggs
1 cup half-and-half or milk
2 (3-ounce) packages cream cheese, cubed
¾ teaspoon salt
¼ teaspoon pepper
¼ cup plus 2 tablespoons butter or
    margarine
Chopped fresh parsley (optional)

Combine first 5 ingredients in container of electric blender; cover and blend at medium speed until frothy (7 to 10 seconds).

Melt butter in a large heavy skillet over medium heat; add egg mixture. Cook over low heat until eggs are partially set, lifting edges gently to allow uncooked eggs to flow underneath. Cook until eggs are set but still moist (9 to 12 minutes). Garnish with parsley, if desired. Yield: 8 to 10 servings.
Mrs. Bennie Cox,
Clinton, Tennessee.

CRUNCHY SAUSAGE CASSEROLE

1 (6-ounce) package long grain and wild
　rice mix
1 pound bulk pork sausage
1 pound ground beef
1 large onion, chopped
1 (8-ounce) can sliced mushrooms,
　drained
1 (8-ounce) can water chestnuts, drained
　and sliced
3 tablespoons soy sauce
1 (2¾-ounce) package sliced almonds
Lemon slice (optional)
Parsley sprigs (optional)

Cook rice mix according to package directions; set aside.

Cook sausage, ground beef, and onion over medium heat in a large skillet until meat is brown, stirring to crumble. Drain off drippings. Add rice, mushrooms, water chestnuts, and soy sauce; stir well. Spoon into an ungreased 2-quart casserole. Cover and refrigerate overnight.

Remove from refrigerator, and allow to sit at room temperature 30 minutes. Sprinkle almonds over top. Bake, uncovered, at 325° for 50 minutes or until thoroughly heated. Garnish with a lemon slice and parsley sprigs, if desired. Yield: 8 to 10 servings.

Note: Casserole may be baked without refrigeration. Bake, uncovered, at 300° for 20 minutes or until thoroughly heated. *Mrs. Carroll L. Oliver,*
Dillwyn, Virginia.

RUBY PEARS

2 (29-ounce) cans pear halves, drained
2 cups ginger ale
Juice of 1 orange
Juice of ½ lemon
2 tablespoons butter, melted
1 (4-inch) stick cinnamon
3 whole cloves
1½ cups red currant jelly
Mock Devonshire Cream

Arrange pears, cut side up, in a 13- x 9- x 2-inch baking dish. Combine next 6 ingredients, and pour over pears; cover dish and refrigerate overnight.

Remove from refrigerator, and allow to sit at room temperature 30 minutes. Cover and bake at 350° for 30 minutes or until pears are hot.

Melt jelly in a small saucepan over low heat; add 3 tablespoons pan juices and beat well.

Remove pears from liquid using a slotted spoon. Place pears in a serving dish; pour jelly mixture over pears. Serve with Mock Devonshire Cream. Yield: 8 to 10 servings.

Mock Devonshire Cream:

1 cup whipping cream
½ cup commercial sour cream
2 tablespoons powdered sugar
1 teaspoon vanilla extract
Ground cinnamon (optional)

Whip cream until soft peaks form; fold in next 3 ingredients. Garnish with cinnamon, if desired. Yield: 2½ cups.

Note: Pears may be served cold. Prepare as directed omitting butter; chill before serving. *Mrs. Arthur A. Olson,*
Knoxville, Tennessee.

CHEESE BISCUITS

2 cups self-rising flour
¼ cup plus 2 tablespoons shortening
1 cup (4 ounces) shredded sharp Cheddar
　cheese
¾ cup buttermilk
1 teaspoon dry mustard
¼ teaspoon soda

Combine flour and shortening in a medium bowl; cut in shortening with pastry blender until mixture resembles coarse meal. Stir in cheese.

Combine buttermilk, mustard, and soda; pour into flour mixture, and stir well. Turn dough out onto floured surface, and knead lightly 3 or 4 times.

Roll dough to 1-inch thickness; cut into rounds with a 2-inch cutter. Place biscuits on a lightly greased baking sheet; bake at 450° for 10 to 15 minutes. Yield: about 1 dozen.

Mrs. Kenneth L. Decker,
Clearwater, Florida.

BANANA COFFEE CAKE

½ cup butter or margarine, softened
1 (8-ounce) package cream cheese,
　softened
1¼ cups sugar
2 eggs
1 cup mashed banana
1 teaspoon vanilla extract
2¼ cups all-purpose flour
1½ teaspoons baking powder
½ teaspoon soda
¾ cup chopped pecans
2 tablespoons sugar
1 teaspoon ground cinnamon
Glaze (recipe follows)

Cream butter and cream cheese; gradually add 1¼ cups sugar, beating until light and fluffy. Add eggs, one at a time, beating well after each addition. Stir in banana and vanilla.

Combine flour, baking powder, and soda; gradually add to banana mixture, stirring well.

Combine pecans, 2 tablespoons sugar, and cinnamon; stir half of pecan mixture into batter. Pour half of batter into a greased and floured 10-inch Bundt pan; sprinkle with remaining nut mixture. Pour remaining batter into pan. Bake at 350° for 40 to 45 minutes or until wooden pick inserted in center comes out clean. Cool in pan 10 minutes; remove from pan, and cool completely. Spoon glaze over coffee cake. Yield: one 10-inch cake.

Glaze:

¾ cup sifted powdered sugar
1 tablespoon warm water

Combine ingredients; stir until smooth. Yield: about ½ cup.

Mrs. Bob Renfro,
Louisville, Kentucky.

HOT PERCOLATOR PUNCH

3 cups unsweetened pineapple juice
3 cups cranberry juice
1½ cups water
⅓ cup firmly packed brown sugar
2 lemon slices
1 or 2 (4-inch) sticks cinnamon, broken
1½ teaspoons whole cloves
Cinnamon sticks (optional)

Pour juices and water into a 12-cup percolator. Place remaining ingredients, except whole cinnamon sticks, in percolator basket. Perk through complete cycle of electric percolator. Serve with cinnamon stick stirrers, if desired. Yield: about 7 cups. *Sherry Tickling,*
Greenville, North Carolina.

Microwave Cookery

Gifts From The Microwave

If a demanding holiday schedule leaves you little time to spend in the kitchen preparing homemade gifts, then let your microwave come to the rescue. Here is a selection of treats for everyone on your list, and preparation time for each is a maximum of 15 minutes.

The choices of microwave-quick gifts from our kitchen to yours include something for everyone—sweets like Pineapple Ice Cream Sauce and Jam Squares, as well as snacks like Peppery Cheese Sticks and Spicy Pecans.

Each recipe gives a time range for microwaving to allow for the difference in wattage of microwave ovens. Check for doneness at the lower end of the range to avoid overcooking.

JAM SQUARES

¼ cup butter or margarine
½ cup sugar
2 eggs
¼ cup milk
½ teaspoon vanilla extract
¾ cup all-purpose flour
½ teaspoon soda
¾ teaspoon ground cinnamon
¼ teaspoon ground cloves
¼ teaspoon ground nutmeg
½ cup raspberry or blackberry jam
½ cup chopped walnuts
Caramel Frosting

Place butter in a glass bowl. Microwave at LOW (10% power) 1½ minutes or until softened. Cream with electric mixer; gradually add sugar, beating until light and fluffy. Add eggs, milk, and vanilla; beat well.

Combine flour, soda, and spices; stir well. Add dry ingredients to creamed mixture, mixing well. Add jam and walnuts; stir gently.

Spread mixture in a lightly greased 8-inch square baking dish. Shield corners with triangles of foil, keeping foil smooth and close to dish. Microwave at MEDIUM HIGH (70% power) for 4 minutes. Give dish one half-turn, and microwave at HIGH for 3½ to 7½ minutes or until top is dry. Cool. Spread with frosting. Yield: 16 squares.

Caramel Frosting:

1½ tablespoons butter or margarine
¼ cup firmly packed brown sugar
1 tablespoon light corn syrup
1¼ cups sifted powdered sugar
2 teaspoons milk
¼ teaspoon vanilla extract

Place butter in a 1½-quart casserole; microwave at HIGH for 30 seconds or until melted. Stir in brown sugar and corn syrup; cover with heavy-duty plastic wrap. Microwave at HIGH for 1 to 1½ minutes or until boiling. Add powdered sugar, milk, and vanilla; beat until creamy. Yield: enough frosting for 8-inch cake.

CRANBERRY-ORANGE RELISH

4 cups fresh cranberries
2 oranges, peeled, seeded, and sectioned
½ cup raisins
½ cup chopped walnuts
1¼ cups sugar
¼ teaspoon ground ginger
¼ teaspoon ground cinnamon
2 tablespoons orange juice
2 tablespoons vinegar

Combine all ingredients in a 3-quart casserole, mixing well. Cover with waxed paper. Microwave at HIGH for 9 to 11 minutes or until berries burst and liquid is slightly thickened, stirring at 4-minute intervals.

Ladle into hot sterilized jars, leaving ¼-inch headspace; cover at once with metal lids, and screw metal bands tight. Process in boiling-water bath 10 minutes. Yield: about 4 cups.

PEPPERY CHEESE STICKS

½ cup butter or margarine
1 cup (4 ounces) shredded sharp Cheddar cheese
1 tablespoon water
1 teaspoon Worcestershire sauce
1½ cups all-purpose flour
¼ teaspoon salt
½ teaspoon red pepper

Place butter in a small glass mixing bowl. Microwave at LOW (10% power) for 2 minutes or until softened. Add cheese, water, and Worcestershire sauce; stir until well blended. Add flour, salt, and pepper, mixing well (mixture should resemble soft cookie dough).

Turn dough out onto a floured board; roll to ⅛-inch thickness. Cut into 2½- x ½-inch strips, and place on a waxed paper-lined glass pizza plate. Place pizza plate on an inverted saucer in microwave oven. Microwave at HIGH for 4½ to 5½ minutes or until cheese sticks are firm, rotating dish one half-turn after 2 minutes. Yield: about 8 dozen.

SPICY PECANS

2 cups sugar
2 teaspoons ground cinnamon
1¼ teaspoons salt
1 teaspoon ground nutmeg
½ teaspoon ground cloves
½ cup water
4 cups pecans halves

Combine first 6 ingredients in a deep 3-quart casserole, mixing well. Cover with waxed paper. Microwave at HIGH for 4 minutes; stir well. Microwave at HIGH for 2½ to 4½ minutes or until mixture reaches soft ball stage (a small amount dropped in cold water forms a soft ball but flattens when removed from water). Add pecans; stir until well coated. Spread pecans on waxed paper, and separate with a fork. Cool. Yield: about 4 cups.

PINEAPPLE ICE CREAM SAUCE

3 (20-ounce) cans crushed pineapple packed in its own juice
1 tablespoon cornstarch
¾ cup chopped pecans
¼ cup flaked coconut
3 tablespoons Grand Marnier or other orange-flavored liqueur

Drain pineapple, reserving ¾ cup juice. Combine cornstarch and ¼ cup reserved juice in a 3-quart casserole; mix until cornstarch is dissolved. Add remaining juice and pineapple. Microwave at HIGH for 2 minutes; stir well. Microwave at HIGH for 2 to 3 minutes or until thickened, stirring at 1-minute intervals. Stir in pecans, coconut, and Grand Marnier. Spoon into ½-pint jars; refrigerate.

To reheat in microwave; remove metal lid, and microwave at HIGH for 1 to 2 minutes or until warm, stirring after 1 minute. To reheat conventionally: Spoon into a small saucepan, and cook over low heat 3 to 4 minutes or until warm, stirring constantly. Yield: about 5 cups.

New Ideas For Your Open House

In December, the emphasis is on entertaining, and for many Southerners this means planning a festive open house. Even the best of cooks may exhaust their supply of recipes for appetizers, snacks, and beverages during this busy month. Here are some delicious new ideas to try at your open house this season.

Any party, formal or informal, will benefit from Sparkling Holiday Punch, a blend of cranberry and citrus juices and white wine. Champagne adds the sparkle. Our Cheesy Ham Nuggets, ham cubes baked in a wrapping of Cheddar cheese pastry, are equally good served hot or cold. For something sweet, serve our Cream Cheese Pound Cake filled with chopped pecans.

CHEESY HAM NUGGETS

1 cup (4 ounces) shredded Cheddar cheese
2 tablespoons butter or margarine, softened
½ cup all-purpose flour
½ teaspoon paprika
⅛ teaspoon salt
2 tablespoons water
1 pound cooked ham

Combine first 6 ingredients; mix well with a fork. Cut ham into 20 (1-inch) cubes. Shape a thin layer of cheese mixture around each ham cube; place on a greased cookie sheet. Bake at 400° for 15 minutes or until lightly browned. Serve hot or cold. Yield: 20 appetizers.
Judy Cunningham,
Roanoke, Virginia.

CHICKEN-PECAN LOG

2 (8-ounce) packages cream cheese, softened
1 tablespoon commercial steak sauce
½ teaspoon curry powder
1½ cups minced cooked chicken
⅓ cup minced celery
¼ cup finely chopped toasted pecans

Combine first 3 ingredients; beat until smooth. Stir in chicken and celery. Shape into a log; chill 4 hours or overnight. Coat with pecans. Serve with crackers. Yield: 1 chicken log.
Pauline Lester,
Saluda, South Carolina.

CREAMY OLIVE SPREAD

2 (3-ounce) packages cream cheese, softened
½ cup mayonnaise
1 cup salad olives, chopped
½ cup chopped pecans
2 tablespoons olive liquid
Dash of pepper

Beat cream cheese well; stir in mayonnaise. Add remaining ingredients, and stir well. Cover and chill 24 hours. Serve on party rye bread. Yield: 2 cups.
Mrs. Bernie Benigno,
Gulfport, Mississippi.

CREAM CHEESE POUND CAKE

1½ cups chopped pecans, divided
1½ cups butter, softened
1 (8-ounce) package cream cheese, softened
3 cups sugar
6 eggs
3 cups sifted cake flour
Dash of salt
1½ teaspoons vanilla extract

Sprinkle ½ cup pecans in a greased and floured 10-inch tube pan; set aside.

Cream butter and cream cheese; gradually add sugar, beating until light and fluffy. Add eggs, one at a time, beating well after each addition. Add flour and salt, stirring until combined. Stir in vanilla and remaining 1 cup pecans.

Pour batter into prepared pan. Bake at 325° for 1½ hours or until a wooden pick inserted in center comes out clean. Cool in pan 10 minutes; remove from pan, and cool completely on a rack. Yield: one 10-inch cake.
Gail T. Brown,
Screven, Georgia.

SPARKLING HOLIDAY PUNCH

1 (32-ounce) bottle cranberry juice cocktail, chilled
1 quart orange juice, chilled
½ cup lemon juice, chilled
1 cup sugar
1 (25.4-ounce) bottle Chablis or other dry white wine, chilled
2 (25.4-ounce) bottles champagne, chilled
Orange slices (optional)

Combine cranberry juice cocktail, orange juice, lemon juice, and sugar; stir until sugar dissolves. Add wine, and pour over ice in punch bowl; stir in champagne just before serving. Garnish with orange slices, if desired. Yield: about 5 quarts.
Cathy Darling,
Grafton, West Virginia.

A Jelly Flavored For The Holidays

Cranberry-Wine Jelly is perfect for Christmastime. It's easily prepared with cranberry juice—no cranberries to grind—sugar, spices, and port wine. Just be sure to make enough of this tart jelly for your own family to enjoy as well as for gifts.

CRANBERRY-WINE JELLY

7 cups sugar
3 cups cranberry juice
¼ teaspoon ground cinnamon
¼ teaspoon ground cloves
1 cup port wine
2 (3-ounce) packages liquid fruit pectin

Combine first 4 ingredients in a Dutch oven; bring to a boil, stirring to dissolve sugar. Boil 1 minute, stirring frequently. Remove from heat; stir in wine and fruit pectin. Skim off foam with a metal spoon.

Quickly pour jelly into sterilized jars, leaving ½-inch headspace. Cover at once with a ⅛-inch layer of paraffin. Cover with lids. Yield: 7 cups.
Elizabeth R. Geitz,
Columbia, South Carolina.

Right: *When the candymaking begins, try your hand at these confections. Clockwise: Bourbon Balls (page 254), Butterscotch Pralines (page 253), Nut Clusters (page 254), and Nutty White Fudge (page 253).*

Page 294: *Be imaginative in your choice of decorative containers. Here colorfully packaged in baskets are Gingerbread Muffins (page 285) and Three-C Bread (page 284); in canisters are Lemon Crinkle Cookies (page 287) and Cherry Nut Nuggets (page 286). Spiced Pecans (page 286) are ready to be "bagged," and Chocolate-Covered Cherries (page 286) sit on their own special board.*

Above left: *Holiday Pecan Pie, German Chocolate Cake, and Macaroon Charlotte (recipes on page 296) add up to an irresistible choice of desserts.*

Above: *Chocolate-Rum Dessert (page 247) isn't your everyday chocolate pudding. It's laced with rum and attractively garnished with whipped cream and curls of chocolate.*

Right: *While our bounteous Christmas Day feast centers around Cranberry-Orange Glazed Ham (page 295), we give you a choice of accompaniments: Apricot-Glazed Sweet Potatoes (page 295), Baked Fruit Medley (page 297), Broccoli With French Sauce (page 295), and Festive Cranberry Salad (page 296).*

Trim The Table With A Christmas Feast

The traditional Christmas feast generates much of the excitement surrounding the holiday season—each recipe is carefully selected, each ingredient searched out in bustling markets, each dish meticulously prepared to make the meal a spectacular occasion.

Those wonderful smells that come with baking fill the kitchen for days as cakes, pies, bread, and finally the holiday ham are readied for the feast. Rosy cranberries, plump sweet potatoes, and baskets of other fresh produce promise accompaniments that are too delicious to pass up. The refrigerator brims with chilled desserts, congealed salads, and other dishes made ahead and waiting to be sampled.

With the silver polished and the linens pressed, the feast goes onto the table. There's always more food than can possibly be eaten in a single sitting, and everyone's favorite is sure to be included.

To help make this Christmas one of your merriest ever, our foods staff has compiled a complete holiday menu using some of our readers' favorite recipes. We started with a cranberry-glazed ham, then added all the trimmings, giving you several choices of salads, side dishes, and desserts.

CRANBERRY-ORANGE GLAZED HAM

1 (12- to 15-pound) uncooked ham
Whole cloves
2½ cups firmly packed brown sugar, divided
1⅓ cups cranberry juice cocktail
½ cup honey
¼ cup cider vinegar
1 tablespoon plus 1½ teaspoons all-purpose flour
3 tablespoons prepared mustard
3 tablespoons butter or margarine
2 to 3 oranges, sliced
About 6 maraschino cherries, halved

Remove skin from ham; place fat side up. Score fat in a diamond design, and stud with cloves. Place ham, fat side up, on a rack in a shallow roasting pan. Insert meat thermometer, making certain end of thermometer does not touch fat or bone. Bake at 350° for 3½ to 4 hours.

Combine ½ cup sugar and next 6 ingredients in a saucepan; mix well. Bring to a boil, and cook 1 minute.

Coat exposed portion of ham with remaining sugar. Place orange slices on ham, securing in center with a wooden pick; leave tip of pick exposed. Place cherry half on pick.

Pour hot cranberry mixture over ham; bake an additional 30 minutes or until thermometer registers 160°. Yield: 24 to 30 servings.

Note: A larger or smaller ham may be substituted. Cooking is complete when thermometer registers 160° (about 18 to 20 minutes per pound).

Mrs. Earl L. Faulkenberry,
Lancaster, South Carolina.

BROCCOLI WITH FRENCH SAUCE

2 pounds fresh broccoli
2 tablespoons butter or margarine
2 tablespoons all-purpose flour
1 cup chicken broth
½ teaspoon Worcestershire sauce
¼ teaspoon salt
Dash of pepper
4 hard-cooked eggs, sliced
½ cup sliced pimiento-stuffed olives

Trim off large leaves of broccoli. Remove tough ends of lower stalks, and wash broccoli thoroughly; separate into spears. Cook broccoli, covered, in a small amount of boiling salted water for 10 minutes or until crisp-tender. Arrange in a serving dish.

Melt butter in a heavy saucepan over low heat; add flour, stirring until smooth. Cook 1 minute, stirring constantly. Gradually add broth; cook over medium heat, stirring constantly, until thickened and bubbly. Stir in Worcestershire, salt, and pepper. Pour sauce over broccoli, and garnish with egg slices and olives. Yield: 8 servings.

Roberta E. McGrath,
Hopkinsville, Kentucky.

FRUIT-STUFFED ACORN SQUASH

2 medium acorn squash
Salt
2 cups chopped unpeeled cooking apple
¾ cup fresh cranberries
¼ cup firmly packed brown sugar
¼ teaspoon ground nutmeg
¼ teaspoon ground cinnamon
2 tablespoons butter or margarine, melted

Cut squash in half, and remove seeds. Place cut side down in a shallow baking dish. Add water to 1-inch depth. Bake at 350° for 30 minutes.

Turn cut side up, and sprinkle cavity with salt. Combine remaining ingredients; spoon evenly into squash halves. Bake at 350° for 30 to 40 minutes or until squash is tender. Yield: 4 servings.

Carole Garner,
Little Rock, Arkansas.

APRICOT-GLAZED SWEET POTATOES

3 pounds sweet potatoes
1 cup firmly packed brown sugar
1 tablespoon plus 1½ teaspoons cornstarch
¼ teaspoon salt
⅛ teaspoon ground cinnamon
1 cup apricot nectar
½ cup hot water
2 tablespoons butter or margarine
½ cup chopped pecans

Cook sweet potatoes in boiling salted water about 10 minutes or until fork-tender. Cool to touch. Peel, and cut into ½-inch slices. Arrange slices in a 2-quart casserole.

Combine brown sugar, cornstarch, salt, and cinnamon in a saucepan; stir well. Add nectar and water; cook over medium heat, stirring constantly, until thickened and bubbly. Stir in butter and pecans. Pour sauce over sweet potato slices, and bake at 350° for 25 minutes. Yield: about 6 servings.

Mrs. Kenneth Bailey,
Paris, Texas.

OLD-FASHIONED WALDORF SALAD

5 cups chopped unpeeled apple
2½ cups chopped celery
1¼ cups chopped pecans or walnuts
½ to 1 cup mayonnaise
Lettuce leaves
Apple wedges
Pecan halves

Combine first 4 ingredients; toss gently to coat, and chill 1 to 2 hours. Spoon salad into a lettuce-lined serving bowl. Garnish with apple wedges and pecan halves. Yield: 10 servings.

Mrs. Joe DeJournette,
Thurmond, North Carolina.

MAKE-AHEAD LAYERED SALAD

1 pound spinach, torn
1 small head red leaf lettuce
1 (8-ounce) carton commercial sour cream
1 cup mayonnaise
1 (1.18-ounce) package creamy Italian salad dressing mix
2 hard-cooked eggs, sliced
1 (10-ounce) package frozen English peas, thawed
½ cup chopped green onion
6 slices bacon, cooked and crumbled
Additional chopped green onion
Additional cooked and crumbled bacon

Combine spinach and lettuce; place half of salad greens in a large salad bowl. Combine sour cream, mayonnaise, and salad dressing mix; stir well, and spread half of mixture evenly over salad greens. Layer in order egg slices, peas, ½ cup onion, 6 slices crumbled bacon, and remaining salad greens. Spread remaining sour cream mixture over top, sealing to edge of bowl. Cover; chill overnight. Garnish with additional onion and bacon. Yield: 8 to 10 servings.
Kathleen D. Stone,
Houston, Texas.

FESTIVE CRANBERRY SALAD

2 (3-ounce) packages lemon-flavored gelatin
1 cup sugar
1 cup boiling water
4 cups fresh cranberries, ground
1 orange, unpeeled, seeded, and ground
2 large apples, unpeeled, cored, and ground
½ cup chopped pecans
Lettuce leaves
Mayonnaise or salad dressing
Orange slices

Dissolve gelatin and sugar in boiling water. Add next 4 ingredients; stir well. Pour into a lightly oiled 6-cup ring mold; chill until set. Unmold on lettuce leaves. Fill center of ring with mayonnaise; garnish with orange slices. Yield: 6 to 8 servings. *Mrs. E. R. Hendrix,*
Augusta, Georgia.

REFRIGERATOR YEAST ROLLS

1 package dry yeast
¼ cup warm water (105° to 115°)
¼ cup shortening
¼ cup sugar
1 egg, slightly beaten
1 cup warm water (105° to 115°)
1 to 1½ teaspoons salt
4 cups all-purpose flour

Dissolve yeast in ¼ cup warm water; set aside. Cream shortening; gradually add sugar, and beat until light and fluffy. Stir in egg, 1 cup warm water, and yeast mixture; beat until smooth. Stir in salt and flour to make a soft dough.

Place dough in a well-greased bowl, turning to grease top. Cover and chill 24 hours.

Lightly grease muffin pans. Shape dough into 1-inch balls; place 3 balls in each muffin cup. Cover and let rise in a warm place (85°), free from drafts, 1 hour or until doubled in bulk. Bake at 400° for 12 to 15 minutes or until golden brown. Yield: 1½ dozen rolls.
Rena C. Nixon,
Mount Airy, North Carolina.

GERMAN CHOCOLATE CAKE

1 (4-ounce) package sweet baking chocolate
½ cup water
1 teaspoon vanila extract
1 cup butter or margarine, softened
2 cups sugar
4 eggs, separated
3 cups sifted cake flour
1 teaspoon soda
½ teaspoon salt
1 cup buttermilk
Coconut-Pecan Frosting

Combine chocolate and water; bring to a boil, and stir until chocolate melts. Cool; stir in vanilla, and set aside.

Cream butter; gradually add sugar, beating until light and fluffy. Add egg yolks, one at a time, beating well after each addition. Add chocolate mixture; beat until blended.

Combine flour, soda, and salt; add to creamed mixture alternately with buttermilk, beginning and ending with flour mixture. Beat egg whites (at room temperature) until stiff peaks form; fold into batter.

Pour batter into 3 greased and floured 9-inch round cakepans. Bake at 350° for 30 to 35 minutes or until a wooden pick inserted in center comes out clean. Cool in pans 10 minutes; remove from pans, and cool completely.

Spread Coconut-Pecan Frosting between layers and on top and sides of cake. Yield: one 9-inch layer cake.

Coconut-Pecan Frosting:

1⅓ cups evaporated milk
1⅓ cups sugar
4 egg yolks
⅔ cup butter or margarine
1½ teaspoons vanilla extract
1⅓ cups flaked coconut
1⅓ cups chopped pecans

Combine milk, sugar, egg yolks, and butter in a heavy saucepan; bring to a boil and cook over medium heat for 12 minutes, stirring constantly. Add vanilla, coconut, and pecans; stir until frosting is cool and of spreading consistency. Yield: enough for one 9-inch cake.
Mrs. Walter Wickstrom,
Pelham, Alabama.

HOLIDAY PECAN PIE

½ cup sugar
1 cup light corn syrup
2 eggs
2 tablespoons all-purpose flour
1½ teaspoons shortening, melted
1 teaspoon vanilla extract
¼ teaspoon salt
1 cup coarsely chopped pecans
1 unbaked 9-inch pastry shell

Combine first 7 ingredients; beat well. Stir in pecans. Pour into pastry shell. Bake at 450° for 10 minutes. Reduce oven temperature to 350°, and continue to bake for 25 minutes. Yield: one 9-inch pie. *Mrs. Maston Rowe,*
Jacksonville, Florida.

MACAROON CHARLOTTE

1 envelope unflavored gelatin
3 tablespoons milk
3 eggs, separated
1 cup sugar
2 cups milk
2 cups whipping cream, whipped
3 or 4 coconut or almond macaroons, crumbled

Soften gelatin in 3 tablespoons milk; set aside.

Beat egg yolks; gradually add sugar, beating until thick and lemon-colored. Stir in remaining milk. Cook in top of double boiler, stirring constantly, until thickened (15 to 20 minutes). Remove from heat, and stir in gelatin mixture; cool.

Beat egg whites (at room temperature) until stiff peaks form. Fold egg whites into custard. Chill overnight.

Beat custard mixture with electric mixer until smooth. Fold whipped cream into custard mixture, and spoon into individual serving dishes. Sprinkle with macaroons. Chill overnight. Yield: 14 servings. *Elizabeth Hicks, Talladega, Alabama.*

BAKED FRUIT MEDLEY

1 orange
1 lemon
1 (16-ounce) can sliced peaches, drained
1 (16-ounce) can pear halves, drained
1 (16-ounce) can apricots, drained
1 (15¼-ounce) can sliced pineapple, drained
1 (6-ounce) jar maraschino cherries, drained
1 cup firmly packed brown sugar
1 tablespoon all-purpose flour
1 tablespoon angostura bitters

Grate rind of orange and lemon; peel and slice. Layer orange and lemon slices and remaining fruit in a 13- x 9- x 2-inch baking dish. Combine orange and lemon rind, brown sugar, flour, and angostura bitters; mix well, and sprinkle over fruit. Bake at 325° for 30 minutes or until bubbly. Serve hot or chilled. Yield: 12 to 14 servings.
Ann C. Maffett, Canton, Georgia.

For A Saucy Main Dish, Serve Stroganoff

Looking for a main dish that can be prepared with a variety of ingredients and will suit almost every taste preference and budget? Then turn to stroganoff, and take your pick of basics: strips of sirloin steak, ground beef, chicken livers, shrimp, or even mushrooms. Flavored with herbs, thickened with sour cream, and served over steaming noodles, stroganoff is a main dish you can always count on to be impressive.

If you like seafood, you'll want to try the Oven-Baked Shrimp Stroganoff. It adds a different twist to stroganoff by combining the herb-seasoned shrimp mixture with the cooked noodles and baking it in a casserole.

OVEN-BAKED SHRIMP STROGANOFF

1 (8-ounce) package medium egg noodles
1 (8-ounce) carton commercial sour cream
1 (10¾-ounce) can cream of mushroom soup, undiluted
1 teaspoon dried whole dillweed
¼ cup sliced green onion
¼ cup sliced ripe olives
1 cup (4 ounces) shredded Cheddar cheese, divided
1 (16-ounce) package frozen shrimp, thawed and drained

Cook noodles according to package directions; drain and set aside.

Combine sour cream, soup, and dillweed in a large bowl, mixing well. Add onion, olives, ½ cup cheese, and shrimp; stir well. Stir in noodles.

Spoon mixture into a lightly greased shallow 2-quart casserole. Cover and bake at 350° for 30 minutes. Uncover and sprinkle with remaining ½ cup cheese. Bake an additional 5 minutes or until the cheese melts. Yield: 6 to 8 servings. *Mrs. R. M. Lancaster, Brentwood, Tennessee.*

SIRLOIN STROGANOFF

½ cup minced onion
¼ cup butter or margarine, melted
2 (4-ounce) cans sliced mushrooms, drained
3 pounds boneless sirloin steak, cut into ½-inch strips
1 (10¾-ounce) can cream of chicken soup, undiluted
1 (10½-ounce) can beef broth, undiluted
⅓ cup all-purpose flour
½ teaspoon salt
½ teaspoon paprika
¼ teaspoon pepper
2 (8-ounce) cartons commercial sour cream
Minced fresh parsley
Hot cooked noodles

Sauté onion in butter 3 to 5 minutes or until transparent; stir in mushrooms. Add beef, and cook until browned. Add next 6 ingredients to beef mixture, stirring well. Reduce heat; simmer 10 to 12 minutes. Remove from heat, and stir in sour cream; cook over low heat just until thoroughly heated. Sprinkle with parsley and serve over hot cooked noodles. Yield: 8 to 10 servings.
Martha Ann Rabon, Stapleton, Alabama.

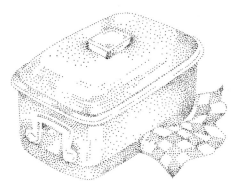

MEATBALL STROGANOFF

1 pound ground beef
¼ cup fine dry breadcrumbs
½ cup milk
¼ cup catsup
1 teaspoon salt
¼ teaspoon dry mustard
¼ teaspoon pepper
¼ cup chopped onion
2 (4-ounce) cans sliced mushrooms, drained
2 tablespoons all-purpose flour
1 cup beef bouillon
1 teaspoon Worcestershire sauce
¼ cup commercial sour cream
Hot cooked noodles

Combine first 7 ingredients, mixing well. Shape mixture into 1-inch meatballs; brown over medium heat in a large skillet. Remove meatballs from skillet, and drain on paper towels. Add onion and mushrooms to pan drippings; cook over medium heat until onion is tender. Add flour, stirring constantly. Gradually stir in bouillon and Worcestershire. Add meatballs; cover and simmer 20 minutes. Remove from heat, and add sour cream, stirring well. Cook over low heat just until thoroughly heated. Serve over noodles: Yield: 6 servings. *Mrs. William Poole, Jr., Jarrettsville, Maryland.*

Tip: Break up stale bread and whirl in blender to make breadcrumbs; store in freezer. (No need to thaw the crumbs before using.)

CHICKEN LIVERS SUPREME

1 medium onion, thinly sliced
1 (2½-ounce) jar sliced mushrooms, drained
2 tablespoons butter or margarine, melted
½ pound chicken livers
1 (8-ounce) carton commercial sour cream
1 teaspoon salt
1 teaspoon pepper
1 teaspoon paprika
Hot cooked noodles

Sauté onion and mushrooms in butter in a large skillet until onion is tender. Add chicken livers, and brown on all sides. Reduce heat; cover and simmer 10 minutes, stirring occasionally.

Remove from heat and add sour cream, salt, pepper, and paprika, stirring well. Cover and simmer 5 additional minutes, stirring occasionally. Serve over noodles. Yield: 4 servings.
Mrs. H. J. Sherrer,
Bay City, Texas.

MUSHROOM STROGANOFF

2 pounds fresh mushrooms, sliced
¼ cup butter, melted
3 green onions, thinly sliced
1 tablespoon all-purpose flour
2 tablespoons water
1 (8-ounce) carton commercial sour cream
1 teaspoon salt
½ teaspoon pepper
4 slices bacon, cooked and crumbled
1 tablespoon minced fresh parsley
Hot cooked noodles

Sauté mushrooms in butter for 2 minutes; add onions. Reduce heat; cover and simmer 15 minutes.

Combine flour and water, stirring well. Stir flour mixture into mushroom mixture; cook over medium heat until bubbly. Remove from heat and add sour cream, salt, and pepper, stirring well. Cook over low heat just until thoroughly heated. Sprinkle with bacon and parsley. Serve over noodles. Yield: 8 servings. *Mrs. Charles R. Simms,*
Palestine, Illinois.

Tip: When preparing a recipe, follow directions carefully. Avoid substituting items: for example, soft margarine for butter or margarine, or whipped cream cheese for cream cheese.

Put Variety In The Pot Roast

When it comes to pot roast, the variations are many. Choose the traditionally seasoned Simple Roast or go elegant with Pot Roast in White Wine Gravy.

Larger, less tender cuts of meat are excellent choices for the slow, moist-heat cooking of a pot roast. In most recipes, the meat is browned in oil first. Liquid is then added as the tenderizing agent, along with a selection of herbs, spices and vegetables for flavor, and the roast simmers until tender.

COLA ROAST

1 teaspoon salt
½ teaspoon pepper
½ teaspoon garlic salt
1 (4- to 5-pound) bottom round roast
3 tablespoons vegetable oil
1 (10-ounce) bottle cola-flavored beverage
1 (12-ounce) bottle chili sauce
2 tablespoons Worcestershire sauce
2 tablespoons hot sauce

Combine salt, pepper, and garlic salt; rub over surface of roast. Brown roast on all sides in vegetable oil in a Dutch oven. Drain off drippings.

Combine remaining ingredients; pour over roast. Cover and bake at 325° for 3 hours or until tender. Yield: 8 to 10 servings. *Mrs. Farmer L. Burns,*
New Orleans, Louisiana.

SIMPLE ROAST

1 (4- to 5-pound) shoulder or chuck roast
2 tablespoons vegetable oil
½ cup catsup
½ cup water
¼ cup red wine vinegar
2 tablespoons Worcestershire sauce
1 teaspoon dried whole rosemary
1 teaspoon salt
2 medium onions, thinly sliced
5 to 6 medium potatoes, peeled and halved

Brown roast on all sides in hot oil in a large Dutch oven. Combine next 6 ingredients; pour over roast. Add onion; cover and simmer 2 hours. Add potatoes; cover and cook 30 to 45 minutes or until potatoes are tender. Yield: 8 to 10 servings.
Mrs. James Branham, Jr.,
Andrews, South Carolina.

POT ROAST WITH GRAVY

1 (4-pound) shoulder roast
2 tablespoons bacon drippings
1 clove garlic, minced
2 (8-ounce) cans tomato sauce
½ teaspoon salt
¼ teaspoon pepper
¼ teaspoon ground oregano
¼ cup cider vinegar
½ cup apple juice
¼ cup chopped fresh parsley
½ cup water
2 tablespoons cornstarch
3 tablespoons water

Brown roast on all sides in bacon drippings in a Dutch oven. Combine next 8 ingredients; pour over roast. Cover and simmer 3 hours or until tender.

Remove roast to serving platter, and keep warm. Stir ½ cup water into pan drippings. Combine cornstarch and 3 tablespoons water, mixing well; stir into pan drippings. Cook the mixture over medium-high heat, stirring constantly, until thickened and bubbly. Serve gravy with roast. Yield: 8 servings.
Mrs. Robert Bryce,
Fairport, New York.

HAWAIIAN POT ROAST

1 (3- to 4-pound) boneless chuck roast
3 tablespoons shortening, melted
1 medium onion, sliced
½ cup water
¼ cup soy sauce
¼ teaspoon ground ginger
¼ teaspoon pepper
1 (8-ounce) can pineapple chunks, undrained
1 (4½-ounce) jar sliced mushrooms, drained
⅓ cup sliced celery
Pineapple slices, halved (optional)
Parsley (optional)
Hot cooked rice (optional)

Brown roast on all sides in shortening in a Dutch oven. Drain off drippings. Place onion on top of roast. Combine next 4 ingredients; pour over roast. Cover and bake at 250° for 2 hours and 45 minutes or until tender.

Add pineapple, mushrooms, and celery; cover and bake an additional 30 minutes. Remove roast, pineapple, and vegetables to a warm platter. Ladle pan drippings over roast. Garnish with pineapple and parsley, and serve with rice, if desired. Yield: 6 to 8 servings.
Mrs. John Fitts,
Birmingham, Alabama.

ITALIAN POT ROAST

¼ cup all-purpose flour
½ teaspoon salt
¼ teaspoon pepper
1 (3- to 4-pound) boneless chuck roast
2 tablespoons vegetable oil
2 medium onions, sliced
2 (4-ounce) cans sliced mushrooms, drained
½ cup water
¼ cup catsup
¼ cup dry sherry
1 clove garlic, crushed
¼ teaspoon dry mustard
¼ teaspoon dried whole rosemary
¼ teaspoon dried whole thyme
¼ teaspoon dried whole marjoram
1 bay leaf
1 tablespoon all-purpose flour
¼ cup cold water

Combine first 3 ingredients; dredge roast in flour mixture. Brown roast on all sides in hot oil in a large Dutch oven. Place onion on top of roast. Combine next 10 ingredients; pour over roast. Cover and bake at 325° for 2½ to 3 hours or until tender.

Remove roast and vegetables to serving platter; reserve pan drippings. Combine 1 tablespoon flour and ¼ cup water; stir until smooth. Pour flour mixture into pan drippings; cook, stirring constantly, until thickened and bubbly. Serve gravy with roast. Yield: 6 to 8 servings.
Diana McConnell, Arlington, Texas.

POT ROAST IN WHITE WINE GRAVY

2 tablespoons butter or margarine
3 to 4 large onions, sliced
1 (3-pound) boneless chuck or shoulder roast
1 (16-ounce) can tomatoes, undrained
½ teaspoon dried whole basil
1 teaspoon salt
½ teaspoon pepper
1 cup Chablis or other dry white wine
3 large carrots, cut into 1-inch pieces
3 stalks celery, cut into 1-inch pieces
2 tablespoons cornstarch
½ cup water

Melt butter in a Dutch oven; add one-third of onion slices, and sauté until tender. Add roast, and brown on all sides. Stir in tomatoes, basil, salt, pepper, and wine; cover and simmer 1½ hours. Add carrots, celery, and remaining onion slices; cover and simmer 1 hour. Remove roast and vegetables to serving platter; keep warm.

Measure pan drippings, and add enough water to make 1½ cups liquid. Combine cornstarch and ½ cup water, mixing well; stir into pan drippings. Cook over medium-high heat, stirring constantly, until thickened and bubbly. Serve gravy with roast and vegetables. Yield: 6 servings.
Dorothy Apgar, Flagler Beach, Florida.

The Best Breads Are Homemade

Piping hot rolls just out of the oven, a warm loaf waiting to be sliced, sweet buns topped with a sugary glaze. Anyone who has ever taken the time to prepare homemade yeast breads knows that the flavors and aromas are well worth the extra effort of preparation.

To start, try our rich Rum Buns. Sweetened with brown sugar and raisins and spiced with rum flavoring and cinnamon, these irresistible buns make a luscious breakfast roll or double as dessert. Hurry-Up Cheese Buns, with process cheese spread providing the cheesy taste, are an excellent partner to any meal.

If you enjoy making loaf breads, try our hearty Oatmeal Bread and Light Yeast Bread; both make two generous loaves, one for yourself and maybe one to share with a neighbor at gift-giving time.

RUM BUNS

2 packages dry yeast
½ cup warm water (105° to 115°)
½ cup milk, scalded
½ cup butter or margarine, softened
½ cup sugar
2 eggs
1 teaspoon salt
1 teaspoon rum flavoring
About 5 cups all-purpose flour
¼ cup butter or margarine, melted
1 cup firmly packed brown sugar
¼ cup raisins
¾ teaspoon ground cinnamon
1½ cups sifted powdered sugar
1½ tablespoons milk
¾ teaspoon rum flavoring

Dissolve yeast in warm water; set aside.

Combine scalded milk, ½ cup butter, ½ cup sugar, eggs, salt, and 1 teaspoon rum flavoring; beat until well blended. Stir in yeast mixture. Add flour, and beat until mixture leaves sides of bowl.

Turn dough out onto a floured surface; knead until dough is smooth and elastic (about 5 minutes).

Place dough in a greased bowl, turning to grease top. Cover and let rise in a warm place (85°), free from drafts, 1½ hours or until doubled in bulk.

Punch dough down, and divide in half. Roll each half into a 13- x 8-inch rectangle; brush with melted butter. Combine brown sugar, raisins, and cinnamon; stir well. Sprinkle half of brown sugar mixture evenly over each dough rectangle.

Starting at widest end, roll up each rectangle in jellyroll fashion; seal edges. Cut each roll into 1½-inch slices. Grease a 13- x 9- x 2-inch pan and an 8-inch square pan. Place slices, cut side down, 1 inch apart in prepared pans. Cover and let rise in a warm place (85°), free from drafts, 30 minutes or until doubled in bulk.

Bake at 400° for 15 to 20 minutes or until golden brown. Remove from pans to cooling racks. Combine remaining ingredients in a small bowl; drizzle glaze over hot buns. Yield: about 2 dozen buns.

LIGHT YEAST BREAD

2 packages dry yeast
½ cup warm water (105° to 115°)
¾ cup milk, scalded
¼ cup sugar
1 teaspoon salt
⅓ cup vegetable oil
2 eggs, beaten
About 4½ cups all-purpose flour

Dissolve yeast in warm water; let stand 5 minutes. Combine milk, sugar, and salt in a large bowl; mix well. Cool to 105° to 115°. Add oil, eggs, 1 cup flour, and yeast mixture, mixing well. Gradually stir in enough remaining flour to make a soft dough.

Turn dough out on a floured surface, and knead until smooth and elastic (about 8 to 10 minutes). Place in a well-greased bowl, turning to grease top. Cover and let rise in a warm place, free from drafts, 50 to 60 minutes or until doubled in bulk. Bake at 400° for 30 minutes or until loaves sound hollow when tapped. Yield: 2 loaves.

Bobbie Wells, Ackerman, Mississippi.

POTATO ROLLS

2 medium potatoes, peeled and quartered
2 packages dry yeast
1 teaspoon sugar
½ cup butter or margarine, melted
¼ cup shortening, melted
½ cup honey
2 eggs, beaten
2 teaspoons salt
About 6½ cups all-purpose flour

Cook potatoes in boiling water to cover 15 to 20 minutes or until tender. Drain, reserving 1 cup water; set potatoes aside. Cool water to 105° to 115°. Stir yeast and sugar into water; set aside.

Mash potatoes to measure 1 cup; add butter, shortening, honey, eggs, salt, yeast mixture, and 2½ cups flour. Beat on medium speed of electric mixer for 2 minutes. Gradually stir in enough remaining flour to make a soft dough.

Turn dough out on a floured surface, and knead until smooth and elastic (about 8 to 10 minutes). Place in a well-greased bowl, turning to grease top. Cover and let rise in a warm place (85°), free from drafts, 1 hour or until doubled in bulk.

Punch dough down; shape dough into 1½-inch balls. Place in 3 greased 9-inch cakepans. Cover and let rise in a warm place, free from drafts, 40 to 50 minutes or until doubled in bulk. Bake at 400° for 25 minutes. Yield: about 2½ dozen. *Mrs. Robert Collins, Fairfax, Missouri.*

HURRY-UP CHEESE BUNS

1 package dry yeast
2 cups all-purpose flour, divided
1 (5-ounce) jar sharp process cheese spread
½ cup water
¼ cup shortening
2 tablespoons sugar
¾ teaspoon salt
1 egg, beaten

Combine yeast and 1 cup flour in a medium mixing bowl; set aside. Combine cheese spread, water, shortening, sugar, and salt in a small saucepan; heat to 105° to 115°, stirring constantly. Add cheese mixture and egg to yeast mixture; beat ½ minute on low speed of electric mixer, scraping sides of bowl. Beat 3 minutes on high speed. Stir in remaining flour.

Turn out on a lightly floured surface, and knead 1 to 2 minutes. Shape dough into 1¼-inch balls. Place in well-greased muffin cups. Let rise in a warm place

(85°), free from drafts, 1½ hours or until doubled in bulk. Bake at 350° for 15 to 18 minutes. Yield: 1 dozen.
Judy Cunningham, Roanoke, Virginia.

OATMEAL BREAD

1 cup regular oats, uncooked
½ cup molasses
⅓ cup vegetable oil
1 teaspoon salt
1½ cups boiling water
2 packages dry yeast
½ cup warm water (105° to 115°)
1 cup whole wheat flour
About 5 cups all-purpose flour
2 eggs, beaten

Combine first 5 ingredients, mixing well; cool to 105° to 115°. Dissolve yeast in warm water in a large bowl; let stand 5 minutes. Add oats mixture, whole wheat flour, 2 cups all-purpose flour, and eggs; mix well. Stir in enough remaining flour to make a soft dough.

Turn dough out on a floured surface, and knead until smooth and elastic (about 8 to 10 minutes). Place in a well-greased bowl, turning to grease top. Cover tightly with plastic wrap, and refrigerate overnight.

Punch dough down; divide in half. Shape each into a loaf. Place in well-greased 9- x 5- x 3-inch loafpans. Cover; let rise in a warm place, free from drafts, about 45 minutes or until doubled in bulk. Bake at 375° for 40 minutes or until loaves sound hollow when tapped. Yield: 2 loaves. *Saralyn Lundy, Tallahassee, Florida.*

CHOCOLATE STICKY BUNS

1 package dry yeast
⅓ cup warm water (105° to 115°)
⅓ cup sugar
1 teaspoon salt
½ cup butter or margarine
¾ cup milk, scalded
About 3½ cups all-purpose flour, divided
1 egg, beaten
½ cup butter
1 cup firmly packed brown sugar
¼ cup light corn syrup
3 tablespoons cocoa
1 cup chopped pecans
1 cup sugar
2 tablespoons cocoa
2 teaspoons ground cinnamon
¼ cup butter or margarine, melted

Dissolve yeast in warm water; set aside. Combine ⅓ cup sugar, salt, ½ cup butter, and scalded milk in a mixing bowl; stir until butter melts. Cool to 105° to 115°. Stir in 1½ cups flour, egg, and yeast mixture. Beat on medium speed of electric mixer 2½ minutes. Stir in enough remaining flour to make a soft dough.

Place dough in a greased bowl, turning to grease top. Cover and let rise in a warm place (85°), free from drafts, about 1 hour or until doubled in bulk.

Melt ½ cup butter in a small saucepan. Add brown sugar, syrup, and 3 tablespoons cocoa; bring to a boil and cook, stirring constantly, 1 minute. Pour sugar mixture evenly into two greased 9-inch cakepans. Sprinkle pecans over sugar mixture. Set aside.

Combine 1 cup sugar, 2 tablespoons cocoa, and cinnamon; mix well, and set aside.

Punch dough down, and divide in half. Roll each half into a 14- x 9-inch rectangle; brush with melted butter; sprinkle half of cinnamon mixture over each dough rectangle. Starting at widest end, roll up each strip in jellyroll fashion; pinch edges together to seal.

Cut each roll into 1-inch slices. Place 9 slices in each prepared cakepan. Cover and let rise in a warm place (85°), free from drafts, about 1 hour or until doubled in bulk. Bake at 375° for 25 minutes. Invert pans on serving plates; serve warm. Yield: 1½ dozen.
Mrs. Robert W. Caldwell, Birmingham, Alabama.

Bake Lots Of These Cookies

Whether mixed with fruit or chocolate, dropped from a spoon or shaped into small balls, filled with jam or topped with a candied cherry—cookies are irresistible, and there never seem to be enough of them. To help keep your cookie jar filled, here is a sampling of favorites from our test kitchens.

Don't miss Strawberry Bars; they're easy and have a delectable filling of strawberry jam. Double Chip Cookies are doubly good with peanut butter chips as well as chocolate chips. And Holiday Fruitcake Cookies, made with buttermilk and all the goodies usually found in fruitcakes, are just right for the season.

AMBROSIA COOKIES

½ cup butter or margarine, softened
½ cup shortening
1 cup firmly packed brown sugar
1 cup sugar
2 eggs
1 tablespoon grated orange rind
2 cups all-purpose flour
1 teaspoon baking powder
½ teaspoon salt
½ teaspoon soda
3 tablespoons orange juice
1½ cups regular oats, uncooked
3 cups flaked coconut

Cream butter and shortening; gradually add sugar, beating until light and fluffy. Add eggs and orange rind; beat well.

Combine dry ingredients; add to creamed mixture alternately with orange juice, beginning and ending with dry ingredients. Stir in oats and coconut. Chill dough 1 hour.

Drop dough by heaping teaspoonfuls onto ungreased cookie sheets. Bake at 375° for 12 minutes. Cool on wire racks. Yield: about 8 dozen.
Mrs. J. A. Satterfield,
Fort Worth, Texas.

HOLIDAY FRUITCAKE COOKIES

4 cups all-purpose flour
1 teaspoon soda
1 teaspoon salt
1 cup shortening
2 cups firmly packed brown sugar
2 eggs
⅔ cup buttermilk
1 (8-ounce) package pitted dates, chopped
1 cup candied cherries, quartered
⅓ cup chopped candied pineapple
1 cup chopped pecans
Red or green whole candied cherries, halved (optional)

Combine flour, soda, and salt; set aside.

Cream shortening; gradually add sugar, beating until light and fluffy. Add

eggs, and beat well. Add dry ingredients alternately with buttermilk, beating until well blended. Stir in next 4 ingredients. Chill dough at least 1 hour.

Drop dough by heaping teaspoonfuls onto lightly greased cookie sheets. Top each cookie with a cherry half. Bake at 375° for 8 to 10 minutes or until lightly browned. Cool on wire racks. Yield: about 10 dozen.
Mrs. Parke LaGourgue Cory,
Neosho, Missouri.

LEMON YUMMIES

1 cup shortening
½ cup sugar
½ cup firmly packed brown sugar
1 egg, well beaten
1 tablespoon lemon rind
2 tablespoons lemon juice
2 cups all-purpose flour
¼ teaspoon soda
½ teaspoon salt
½ cup chopped pecans or walnuts

Cream shortening; gradually add sugar, beating until light and fluffy. Add egg, lemon rind, and juice; beat well.

Combine dry ingredients; add to creamed mixture, and mix well. Stir in pecans.

Drop by teaspoonfuls onto lightly greased cookie sheets. Bake at 400° for 8 to 10 minutes. Cool on cookie sheet about 1 minute; remove to wire racks, and cool completely. Yield: 3½ dozen.
Carolyn Epting,
Leesville, South Carolina.

STRAWBERRY BARS

¾ cup butter or margarine, softened
1 cup sugar
2 egg yolks
1 teaspoon vanilla extract
2 cups self-rising flour
1 cup pecans, chopped
½ cup strawberry jam

Cream butter; gradually add sugar, beating until light and fluffy. Add egg yolks and vanilla, beating well. Gradually stir in flour and pecans.

Pat half of dough evenly in a greased 9-inch square baking pan. Spread strawberry jam evenly over dough in pan. Drop remaining dough by tablespoonfuls over jam; spread evenly. Bake at 325° for 1 hour. Cool. Cut into bars. Yield: 2 dozen.   *Charlotte A. Pierce,*
Greensburg, Kentucky.

DOUBLE CHIP COOKIES

¾ cup butter or margarine, softened
¼ cup shortening
1 cup sugar
½ cup firmly packed brown sugar
2 eggs
1 teaspoon vanilla extract
2¼ cups all-purpose flour
1 teaspoon soda
½ teaspoon salt
1 (6-ounce) package peanut butter morsels
1 (6-ounce) package semisweet chocolate morsels

Cream butter and shortening; gradually add sugar, beating until light and fluffy. Add eggs and vanilla, beating well. Combine flour, soda, and salt; add to creamed mixture, beating well. Stir in peanut butter and chocolate morsels.

Drop dough by heaping teaspoonfuls onto ungreased cookie sheets. Bake at 350° for 12 to 14 minutes. Cool slightly on cookie sheets; remove to wire racks to cool completely. Yield: about 5½ dozen.
Mariel S. Fails,
Temple Hills, Maryland.

WALNUT COOKIES

½ cup butter or margarine, softened
½ cup sugar
1 egg, separated
¾ teaspoon grated lemon rind
1 cup all-purpose flour
¼ teaspoon salt
¼ teaspoon ground cinnamon
⅛ teaspoon ground cloves
1¾ cups finely chopped walnuts, divided
½ cup apricot preserves

Cream butter; gradually add sugar, beating until light and fluffy. Add egg yolk and lemon rind; beat well.

Combine dry ingredients and 1 cup walnuts; stir into creamed mixture. Cover dough; chill at least 30 minutes.

Shape dough into 1-inch balls. Beat egg white lightly. Dip balls in egg white; roll in remaining ¾ cup walnuts, and place on greased cookie sheets. Make an indentation in center of each cookie; fill with preserves. Bake at 350° for 20 minutes. Cool on wire racks. Yield: 3 dozen.   *Mrs. Earl L. Faulkenberry,*
Lancaster, South Carolina.

Tip: A clean toothbrush is a handy gadget to aid in removal of all bits of grated rind from grater.

CHOCOLATE MELTAWAYS

¾ cup butter or margarine, softened
1 cup sugar
1 egg
2 (1-ounce) envelopes liquid baking
   chocolate
2 tablespoons milk
1 teaspoon vanilla extract
2 cups all-purpose flour
¼ teaspoon salt
½ cup chocolate drink mix
½ cup chopped pecans or walnuts

Cream butter; gradually add sugar, beating until light and fluffy. Add next 4 ingredients, and beat well.

Combine flour and salt; gradually add to creamed mixture, beating just until smooth. Chill dough 1 to 2 hours.

Shape dough into ¾-inch balls. Combine drink mix and pecans; roll balls in mixture. Place on ungreased cookie sheets. Bake at 350° for 10 minutes. Cool on wire racks. Yield: about 6½ dozen.
Mrs. Ed Holby,
Birmingham, Alabama.

Salads For Every Taste And Occasion

Whether it's a plump, juicy tomato stuffed with guacamole or a congealed salad filled with crunchy chopped vegetables, there's a salad to suit every taste and every menu.

Fresh fruit and vegetables give these salads their unsurpassed flavor. And regardless of which one you choose, these brilliantly colored salads will enliven any meal.

TOMATO-VEGETABLE RING

3½ cups tomato juice
1 tablespoon finely chopped onion
1 bay leaf
½ teaspoon salt
Dash of red pepper
2 envelopes unflavored gelatin
¼ cup cold water
1 tablespoon Worcestershire sauce
1 teaspoon lemon juice
1 cup diced celery
1 cup grated carrots
1 green pepper, chopped

Combine tomato juice, onion, bay leaf, salt, and red pepper in a large

saucepan; bring to a boil. Reduce heat, and simmer 15 minutes. Remove bay leaf.

Soften gelatin in cold water; add to hot tomato mixture, stirring until gelatin dissolves. Add Worcestershire sauce and lemon juice; chill until partially set.

Fold vegetables into gelatin. Pour mixture into an 8-inch ring mold; chill until firm. Yield: about 8 servings.
Mary Avery,
McGehee, Arkansas.

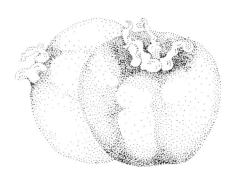

GUACAMOLE-TOMATO SALAD

3 large tomatoes
Salt
¼ cup chopped onion
2 hot green chiles, chopped
1 teaspoon lemon juice
¾ teaspoon salt
1 ripe avocado
2 slices cooked bacon, crumbled
Lettuce leaves

Cut tomatoes in half crosswise, scoop out pulp; chop and set aside. Sprinkle tomato shells with salt. Turn upside down to drain; chill.

Combine tomato pulp with onion, chiles, lemon juice, and salt; chill.

Just before serving, peel avocado and mash well; stir into pulp mixture. Spoon filling into tomato shells; top with bacon. Serve on lettuce leaves. Yield: 6 servings.
Beverly Scheppke,
Carlsbad, New Mexico.

FRUIT MELANGE DELIGHT

1 large fresh pineapple
2 to 3 oranges
2 pears, peeled, cored, and diced
1 cup seedless grapes, halved
Ginger-Yogurt Dressing

Cut pineapple (including leafy top) in half lengthwise. Hollow out pineapple, leaving shell ½ inch thick. Remove

core, and cut pineapple into chunks. Reserve juice that collects when pineapple is being prepared.

Peel and section oranges, reserving juice. Combine pineapple juice and orange juice to make ¼ cup; set juice mixture aside for dressing.

Combine pineapple chunks, oranges, pears, and grapes; spoon into pineapple shells. Top with Ginger-Yogurt Dressing. Yield: about 6 servings.

Ginger-Yogurt Dressing:

1 (8-ounce) carton plain yogurt
¼ cup reserved fruit juice
Dash of ground ginger

Stir together yogurt and juice; add ginger. Chill. Yield: about 1 cup.
Karen Cromer,
Anderson, South Carolina.

MIXED VEGETABLE SALAD

1 medium cabbage, shredded
2 cucumbers, thinly sliced
1 large onion, thinly sliced
1 cup diced celery
2 carrots, thinly sliced
½ red pepper, thinly sliced
½ green pepper, thinly sliced
¾ cup vinegar
¾ cup sugar
¼ cup water
¼ cup vegetable oil
1 tablespoon salt

Combine vegetables in a large bowl; set aside.

Combine remaining ingredients; stir until sugar dissolves. Pour marinade over vegetable mixture, and toss well. Chill at least 12 hours. Yield: 10 to 12 servings.
Mrs. Teal Therrell,
Bennettsville, South Carolina.

On Cooking Quail

As a Southern game bird and entrée, the quail is legendary. Subtly flavored and full fleshed, these tiny birds serve as the main attraction at a hearty breakfast or wild game dinner.

Since quail meat tends to be dry, it is best when sautéed or baked in a saucy covering. Quail Superb enhances the flavor and tenderness of quail by marinating and then basting them during the cooking process. Plan on serving two quail per person.

QUAIL SUPERB

12 quail, cleaned
Salt and pepper
1 medium onion, sliced
1 cup dry sherry
½ cup butter or margarine, melted
½ cup currant jelly, melted
1 to 2 teaspoons garlic powder
1 tablespoon cornstarch
2 tablespoons cold water

Sprinkle quail with salt and pepper; place in baking pan, breast side down. Top with onion slices. Combine next 4 ingredients; pour over quail. Cover and marinate in the refrigerator 1 hour.

Drain quail, reserving marinade.

Combine cornstarch and cold water stirring until smooth. Stir cornstarch mixture into marinade, mixing well. Bake quail, uncovered, at 350° for 45 minutes or until done, basting often with marinade. Yield: 6 servings.

Mildred Morrow,
Portersdale, Georgia.

Surprise your guests with the distinct flavor of Kahlúa in this luscious, easy-to-prepare cake.

There's Kahlúa In The Cake

Kahlúa, a coffee-flavored liqueur of Mexican origin, and grated orange rind are added to a basic cake mix for a delectable dessert. Kahlúa is also stirred into the thick, creamy date-nut filling. Finally, the liqueur dresses up the canned fudge frosting used to top it off.

KAHLUA CHOCOLATE CAKE

1 (18.5-ounce) package German chocolate
  cake mix
1 tablespoon grated orange rind
⅔ cup orange juice
½ cup Kahlúa or other coffee-flavored
  liqueur
⅓ cup vegetable oil
3 eggs
Date Cream Filling
Fudge Frosting
Pecan halves (optional)

Combine first 6 ingredients in a large mixing bowl; beat 2 minutes at highest speed of an electric mixer. Line bottom of two greased 9-inch round cakepans with waxed paper. Pour the batter into cakepans. Bake at 350° for 30 to 35 minutes or until a wooden pick inserted in center comes out clean. Cool in pans 10 minutes; remove from pans, and peel off paper. Cool completely.

Spread Date Cream Filling between layers; spread top and sides of cake with Fudge Frosting. Garnish outer edge of cake with pecan halves, if desired. Yield: one 9-inch layer cake.

Date Cream Filling:

⅔ cup chopped dates
½ cup whipping cream or half-and-half
½ cup Kahlúa or other coffee-flavored
  liqueur
1 egg, beaten
¼ cup sugar
1 tablespoon all-purpose flour
½ cup chopped pecans
1 tablespoon grated orange rind

Combine dates, whipping cream, and Kahlúa in a heavy saucepan; cook over medium heat until mixture bubbles. Gradually stir about one-fourth of hot mixture into egg; add to remaining hot mixture, stirring constantly. Combine sugar and flour; mix well, and stir into date mixture. Cook over medium heat, stirring constantly, until mixture thickens. Remove from heat; stir in pecans and orange rind. Cool completely. Yield: about 1 cup.

Fudge Frosting:

1 (16-ounce) can chocolate fudge frosting
1 tablespoon grated orange rind
1 teaspoon Kahlúa or other
  coffee-flavored liqueur

Combine all ingredients; mix well. Yield: enough frosting for one 9-inch layer cake.

Marie H. Webb,
Roanoke, Virginia.

Roll Your Own Tortillas

Tortillas are most often enjoyed as the wrapping for a taco or burrito, but you'll praise their melt-in-your-mouth goodness when they're homemade and served plain, hot off the griddle.

FLOUR TORTILLAS

4 cups all-purpose flour
2 teaspoons salt
⅛ teaspoon baking powder
⅔ cup shortening
1 cup plus 3 tablespoons hot water

Combine flour, salt, and baking powder; stir well. Cut in shortening with a pastry blender until mixture resembles coarse meal. Gradually stir in water, mixing well.

Shape dough into 1½-inch balls; roll each out on a lightly floured surface into a very thin circle. Circles should be about 6 inches in diameter.

Heat an ungreased electric skillet to 375°; cook tortillas about 2 minutes on each side or until lightly browned. Pat tortillas lightly with spatula while browning the second side if they puff during cooking. Serve hot. Yield: about 2 dozen.

Note: Tortillas may also be cooked on an ungreased griddle or in a skillet over medium heat.

Fran Albrecht,
Portland, Texas.

Setting Two Places For Dinner

Preparing a dinner for two opens up a wealth of menu and serving possibilities. Because the quantity of food is small, extra care can be taken to make the dinner special.

Our menu centers around Chicken Cordon Bleu. Preparing this dish for a crowd requires hours of pounding, stuffing, and rolling chicken breasts, but assembling it for two is relatively fast. Extra time can then be spent on the accompaniments and dessert we suggest to round out the menu.

Chicken Cordon Bleu
Spinach Soufflé   Glazed Carrots
Popovers for Two
Lemon-Sour Cream Tarts
White Wine

CHICKEN CORDON BLEU

1 whole chicken breast, split, boned, and skinned
1 (1-ounce) slice Swiss cheese, cut into thin strips
1 (1-ounce) slice cooked ham, cut into thin strips
1 egg, beaten
¼ cup milk
½ cup soft breadcrumbs
¼ cup all-purpose flour
¼ cup grated Parmesan cheese
1 tablespoon parsley flakes
⅛ teaspoon salt
Dash of pepper
3 tablespoons all-purpose flour
¼ cup butter or margarine
4 ounces fresh mushrooms, sliced
¼ cup Chablis or other dry white wine

Place each chicken breast half on a sheet of waxed paper; flatten to ¼-inch thickness, using a meat mallet or rolling pin. Place half the cheese strips and half the ham strips in the center of each chicken piece. Fold ends over ham and cheese; roll up, beginning with a long side, and secure with wooden picks, if desired.

Combine egg and milk, mixing well; set aside. Combine breadcrumbs, ¼ cup flour, Parmesan cheese, parsley, salt, and pepper; mix well. Dredge chicken rolls in 3 tablespoons flour; dip in egg mixture; coat well with breadcrumb mixture. Cover and chill at least 30 minutes.

Melt butter in a heavy skillet; brown chicken on all sides. Reduce heat, cover, and simmer 5 minutes. Remove chicken from pan, reserving drippings.

Sauté mushrooms in drippings until tender; add wine. Cook over medium heat, stirring constantly, until mixture is reduced one-half. Add chicken, and simmer 1 to 2 minutes. Yield: 2 servings. *Mrs. Robert L. Amsler, Signal Mountain, Tennessee.*

SPINACH SOUFFLE

1 (10-ounce) package frozen chopped spinach
3 tablespoons butter or margarine
1 small onion, finely chopped
2 tablespoons all-purpose flour
¼ teaspoon dry mustard
⅔ cup milk
¼ teaspoon salt
Pepper to taste
2 eggs, separated
⅔ cup shredded sharp Cheddar cheese
¼ teaspoon cream of tartar

Cook spinach according to package directions; drain and press dry.

Melt butter in a heavy saucepan over low heat; add onion and cook until tender. Blend in flour, stirring until smooth. Cook 1 minute, stirring constantly. Stir in mustard. Gradually stir in milk; cook over medium heat, stirring constantly, until thickened and bubbly. Stir in salt and pepper.

Beat egg yolks. Add one-fourth of hot white sauce to yolks, stirring well; return to hot mixture. Add spinach and cheese; stir well.

Combine egg whites (at room temperature) and cream of tartar; beat until stiff but not dry. Fold into spinach mixture. Spoon into a 1-quart soufflé dish. Place in a shallow pan containing about 1 inch water. Bake at 350° for 55 to 60 minutes or until golden brown. Yield: 2 servings. *Sandra Souther, Gainesville, Georgia.*

GLAZED CARROTS

4 medium carrots, peeled and sliced into thin strips
1 tablespoon butter or margarine
¼ cup sugar

Cook carrots in a small amount of boiling salted water until crisp-tender; drain, reserving 2 tablespoons liquid.

Melt butter; stir in sugar and reserved liquid. Cook over low heat until sugar dissolves. Add carrots; cook over low heat, stirring occasionally, 8 to 10 minutes or until glazed and lightly browned. Yield: 2 servings. *Lauvonda M. Young, Charlottesville, Virginia.*

POPOVERS FOR TWO

½ cup all-purpose flour
½ cup milk
1 egg
¼ teaspoon salt

Combine all ingredients; beat with an electric mixer just until smooth.

Place 4 well-greased 4-ounce custard cups in oven at 425° for 3 minutes or until water sizzles when dropped in them. Remove cups from oven; fill half full with batter. Bake at 425° for 20 minutes; reduce heat to 300°, and bake an additional 20 minutes. Serve immediately. Yield: 4 popovers.
Mrs. Ben M. Beasley, Orlando, Florida.

LEMON-SOUR CREAM TARTS

⅓ cup sugar
1 tablespoon cornstarch
Dash of salt
⅓ cup milk
1 egg yolk, slightly beaten
1 tablespoon butter or margarine
¼ teaspoon grated lemon rind
1 tablespoon plus 1 teaspoon lemon juice
⅓ cup commercial sour cream
4 baked 3-inch pastry shells
1 egg white
Pinch of cream of tartar
2 tablespoons sugar
¼ teaspoon vanilla extract

Combine sugar, cornstarch, and salt in a small saucepan. Gradually add milk, stirring well. Cook over low heat, stirring constantly, until thickened and bubbly.

Gradually stir about one-fourth of hot mixture into yolk; add to remaining hot mixture, stirring constantly. Cook over low heat, stirring constantly, 2 minutes.

Remove from heat. Add butter, lemon rind, and juice; stir until butter dissolves. Cover and chill.

Fold sour cream into lemon mixture; spoon into pastry shells.

Beat egg white (at room temperature) and cream of tartar until foamy. Gradually add sugar 1 tablespoon at a time; add vanilla, beating until stiff peaks form. Spread meringue over filling, sealing to edge of pastry. Bake at 425° for 4 to 5 minutes or until golden. Chill before serving. Yield: four 3-inch tarts.

Mrs. C. D. Marshall,
Culpeper, Virginia.

Texans Have A Holiday With Bread

Hushpuppies made with potatoes? Wampus Bread, an unusual variation of a Southern favorite, is great not only with fish but other meats as well. Discover another delicious use of potatoes in Feathery Light Potato Rolls.

Also included in this collection of Texas recipes are some fruit and nut breads. Why not take advantage of fresh cranberries while they're still available and stir them into Raisin-Cranberry Bread. Slice into a moist loaf of Cherry Nut Bread and discover colorful chunks of maraschino cherries sprinkled throughout.

SPICY ZUCCHINI BREAD

3 cups all-purpose flour
1 teaspoon baking powder
1 teaspoon soda
1 teaspoon ground cinnamon
1 teaspoon ground nutmeg
1 cup chopped pecans or walnuts
¾ cup vegetable oil
3 eggs
2 cups sugar
2 teaspoons vanilla extract
3 cups unpeeled shredded zucchini

Combine first 6 ingredients in a mixing bowl; make a well in center of mixture. Combine oil, eggs, sugar, and vanilla; mix well. Stir in zucchini. Add mixture to dry ingredients, stirring just until moistened.

Spoon mixture into 2 greased and floured 8½- x 4½- x 3-inch loafpans. Bake at 350° for 1 hour. Cool 10 minutes in pans; remove to wire rack, and cool completely. Yield: 2 loaves.

Mrs. Ellis D. Weathermon,
Comanche, Texas.

WAMPUS BREAD

2 cups cornmeal
1 cup all-purpose flour
1 tablespoon baking powder
1 teaspoon sugar
1 teaspoon salt
1 cup minced onion
1 cup peeled shredded potato
1 cup evaporated milk
Vegetable oil

Combine first 5 ingredients, mixing well; stir in onion, potato, and milk. Drop by tablespoonfuls into hot oil (375°). Cook until golden brown (3 to 5 minutes), turning once. Drain on paper towels. Yield: about 1½ dozen.

Mrs. Ted Robertson,
Canton, Texas.

FEATHERY LIGHT POTATO ROLLS

1 (2-ounce) package instant potato flakes or 1½ cups mashed potatoes
1 cup milk
⅔ cup shortening
½ cup sugar
1 teaspoon salt
1 package dry yeast
½ cup warm water (105° to 115°)
2 eggs
7½ cups all-purpose flour
Melted butter or margarine

Prepare instant potatoes according to package directions.

Scald milk; remove from heat and add shortening, potatoes, sugar, and salt. Stir until shortening is melted; cool to lukewarm.

Dissolve yeast in water in a large bowl; let stand 5 minutes. Add milk mixture and eggs, beating well. Gradually beat in 2 cups flour; add remaining flour to form a moderately stiff dough, beating well after each addition.

Turn dough onto a lightly floured surface; knead until smooth and elastic (about 7 minutes). Place in a well-greased bowl, turning to grease top. Cover and let rise in a warm place (85°), free from drafts, 1½ hours or until doubled in bulk.

Punch dough down. Shape into 1½-inch balls; arrange in a lightly greased jellyroll pan. Cover and let rise in a warm place, free from drafts, 1 hour or until doubled in bulk. Bake at 350° for 20 to 25 minutes; brush tops with melted butter. Yield: about 8 dozen rolls.

Lexie Freeman,
Fort Worth, Texas.

APPLESAUCE NUT BREAD

1 cup sugar
1 cup applesauce
⅓ cup vegetable oil
2 eggs
3 tablespoons milk
2 cups all-purpose flour
1 teaspoon soda
½ teaspoon baking powder
½ teaspoon ground cinnamon
¼ teaspoon salt
¼ teaspoon ground nutmeg
1 cup chopped pecans, divided
2 tablespoons brown sugar
½ teaspoon ground cinnamon

Combine first 5 ingredients in a large mixing bowl; beat at medium speed of electric mixer 1 minute. Set aside.

Combine flour, soda, baking powder, ½ teaspoon cinnamon, salt, and nutmeg; add to applesauce mixture, beating until smooth. Stir in ¾ cup pecans.

Spoon batter into a greased and floured 9- x 5- x 3-inch loafpan. Combine remaining pecans, brown sugar, and ½ teaspoon cinnamon; sprinkle over batter, and bake at 350° for 30 minutes.

Remove from oven, and cover loosely with foil; return to oven for 40 additional minutes. Uncover and cool 10 minutes in pan; remove from pan, and cool on a wire rack. Yield: 1 loaf.

Eleanor K. Brandt,
Arlington, Texas.

RAISIN-CRANBERRY BREAD

2 cups all-purpose flour
1 cup sugar
1½ teaspoons baking powder
½ teaspoon soda
½ teaspoon salt
¼ cup butter or margarine
1 teaspoon grated orange rind
¾ cup orange juice
1 egg, beaten
1½ cups raisins
1½ cups fresh cranberries, chopped

Combine first 5 ingredients; cut in butter until mixture resembles coarse crumbs. Combine orange rind, juice, and egg; add to dry ingredients and stir just until moistened. Fold in raisins and cranberries. Spoon batter into a greased and floured 9- x 5- x 3-inch loafpan. Bake at 350° for 1 hour and 10 minutes or until wooden pick inserted in center comes out clean. Remove from pan; cool on wire rack. Yield: 1 loaf.

Mrs. Gary L. Jones,
Austin, Texas.

CHERRY NUT BREAD

2½ cups all-purpose flour
1 cup buttermilk
1 cup chopped pecans or walnuts
½ cup sugar
½ cup firmly packed brown sugar
2 eggs, beaten
¼ cup shortening
¼ cup maraschino cherry juice
1 tablespoon baking powder
½ teaspoon salt
½ teaspoon soda
½ cup chopped maraschino cherries

Combine all ingredients except cherries in a mixing bowl. Blend on low speed of electric mixer 15 seconds; increase to medium speed, and blend 30 additional seconds. Stir in cherries.

Pour batter into a greased and floured 9- x 5- x 3-inch loafpan. Bake at 350° for 1 hour and 10 to 15 minutes or until wooden pick inserted in center comes out clean. Cool 10 minutes in pan; remove to wire rack, and cool completely. Yield: 1 loaf. *Judy Irwin, Mabank, Texas.*

QUICK MONKEY BREAD

½ cup chopped pecans
½ cup sugar
1 teaspoon ground cinnamon
3 (10-ounce) cans refrigerated buttermilk
   biscuits
1 cup firmly packed brown sugar
½ cup butter or margarine, melted

Sprinkle pecans evenly in the bottom of a well-greased 10-inch Bundt pan. Set aside.

Combine sugar and cinnamon. Cut biscuits into quarters; roll each piece in sugar mixture and layer in pan.

Combine brown sugar and butter; pour over dough. Bake at 350° for 30 to 40 minutes. Cool bread 10 minutes in pan; invert onto serving platter. Yield: one 10-inch coffee cake.
Judy Richardson, Pearland, Texas.

Tip: Compare costs of fresh, frozen, canned, and dried foods. To compute the best buy, divide the price by the number of servings. The lower price per serving will be the thriftiest buy.

Appetizers With A Texas Accent

Let your holiday guests enjoy the flavors of Texas cooking when you set out the appetizers at your next open house. Serve a large platter of hot Nachos Supreme and our spicy Avocado Dip with taco chips. To offset the jalapeño peppers and chili powder, serve our cool and creamy Shrimp Spread with slices of party rye bread.

NACHOS SUPREME

½ cup vegetable oil
12 corn tortillas, cut into quarters
1 large tomato, finely chopped
1 small onion, finely chopped
1 tablespoon vegetable oil
1½ cups tomato juice
¼ teaspoon salt
¼ teaspoon pepper
6 canned jalapeño peppers, seeded and
   sliced into rings
3 cups (12 ounces) shredded Cheddar
   cheese

Heat ½ cup oil to 375° in a medium skillet; add tortillas and fry until crisp and golden brown, turning frequently. Drain well on paper towels; set aside.

Sauté tomato and onion in 1 tablespoon oil in a medium saucepan until tender. Add tomato juice, salt, and pepper; simmer 10 to 12 minutes. Cover, and set aside.

Place tortilla chips on a cookie sheet or ovenproof platter. Place a slice of jalapeño pepper and a tablespoon of cheese on each chip. Top with a heaping teaspoon of tomato mixture. Broil 8 inches from broiler just until cheese melts. Serve immediately. Yield: 4 dozen.
Martha Walker, Beeville, Texas.

SHRIMP SPREAD

1 (4¼-ounce) can small shrimp, drained
   and divided
1 (3-ounce) package cream cheese,
   softened
½ cup mayonnaise
1 tablespoon chopped celery
Dash of onion salt

Place half of shrimp and remaining ingredients in container of electric blender; blend until smooth. Stir in remaining shrimp; chill well. Serve on party rye bread or crackers. Yield: about 1 cup.
Annette Crane, Dallas, Texas.

AVOCADO DIP

3 large ripe avocados, peeled and mashed
1 tablespoon chili powder
2 tablespoons finely chopped onion
3 tablespoons lemon juice
2 tablespoons mayonnaise
½ teaspoon salt
1 teaspoon taco sauce

Combine all ingredients, mixing well. Serve with taco chips. Yield: 2 cups.
Mrs. Bill Murphy, Big Spring, Texas.

Spark Appetites With Soup

Hot and brimming with flavor, appetizer soups begin meals on a warm note. Just a few sips of Easy Broccoli Soup or Cheesy Anytime Soup will spark any appetite.

Instead of serving the soup at the table, let the living room be the setting. Set up a minibuffet on your coffee table and ladle soup into your best china cups or fill mugs from a tureen in front of a roaring fire.

If you're looking for a light meal, an appetizer soup can be filling enough to serve as the main course. A crisp salad, some fruit, and wine make Toasty French Onion Soup a complete meal for a chilly day.

TOASTY FRENCH ONION SOUP

4 large onions, thinly sliced
¼ cup butter or margarine, melted
3 (10¾-ounce) cans beef broth, undiluted
1 teaspoon Worcestershire sauce
⅛ teaspoon pepper
4 or 5 slices French bread, toasted
Grated Parmesan cheese

Sauté onion in butter in a Dutch oven over medium heat until tender, stirring frequently. Add broth, Worcestershire, and pepper; bring to a boil. Reduce heat; cover and simmer 5 minutes.

Ladle soup into individual baking dishes; top each with a slice of toasted bread. Sprinkle with cheese. Place under broiler 2 or 3 minutes to brown top. Serve immediately. Yield: 4¼ cups.
Ann Elsie Schmetzer, Madisonville, Kentucky.

CHEESY ANYTIME SOUP

¼ cup butter or margarine
¼ cup plus 2 tablespoons all-purpose
   flour
2 (10¾-ounce) cans chicken broth,
   undiluted
2 cups milk
¼ teaspoon white pepper
2 tablespoons chopped pimiento
¼ cup plus 2 tablespoons dry white wine
½ teaspoon Worcestershire sauce
¼ teaspoon hot pepper sauce
2 cups (8 ounces) shredded sharp
   Cheddar cheese

Melt butter in a heavy saucepan over low heat; add flour, stirring until smooth. Cook 1 minute, stirring constantly. Gradually add broth and milk; cook over medium heat, stirring constantly, until thickened and bubbly. Stir in pepper. Add next 4 ingredients. Heat to boiling, stirring frequently. Remove from heat; add cheese, and stir until melted. Serve immediately. Yield: about 5 cups.
Jodie McCoy,
Tulsa, Oklahoma.

EASY BROCCOLI SOUP

¼ cup chopped onion
3 tablespoons butter or margarine, melted
3 tablespoons all-purpose flour
3 cups chicken broth
1 cup finely chopped fresh or frozen
   broccoli
1 small bay leaf
½ cup milk
½ teaspoon pepper

Sauté onion in butter until tender. Add flour, stirring well. Gradually stir in broth, broccoli, and bay leaf. Cook over medium heat until broccoli is tender, stirring frequently. Reduce heat and remove bay leaf; stir in milk and pepper. Serve immediately. Yield: 4 cups.
Kathy Helwick,
Dallas, Texas.

EGG FLOWER SOUP

⅓ cup water
1½ tablespoons cornstarch
6 cups chicken broth
1 cup (8 ounces) cubed tofu (soy bean
   curd)
1 (2- x 1- x ⅛-inch) slice gingerroot
½ teaspoon sugar
⅛ teaspoon pepper
3 eggs, beaten
1 teaspoon sesame seed oil
1 green onion, minced

Combine ⅓ cup water and cornstarch; stir well, and set aside.
Bring broth to a boil. Add tofu, gingerroot, sugar, and pepper; boil 1 minute. Stir in cornstarch mixture; boil 1 minute. Remove from heat. Slowly pour beaten egg into soup, stirring constantly. (The egg forms lacy strands as it cooks.) Remove gingerroot.
Stir in sesame seed oil, and sprinkle with onion. Serve immediately. Yield: about 7 cups.
Sue-Sue Hartstern,
Louisville, Kentucky.

CREAMY MUSHROOM SOUP

1 medium onion, minced
2 tablespoons butter or margarine, melted
¾ pound fresh mushrooms, sliced
3 tablespoons all-purpose flour
4½ cups beef consommé
1 cup whipping cream
Pinch of ground nutmeg
Pinch of pepper

Sauté onion in butter in a Dutch oven over medium heat until tender. Add mushrooms; cook over low heat 10 minutes. Stir in flour; cook 4 minutes, stirring mixture constantly. Gradually add consommé; bring to a boil, stirring often. Remove from heat, and stir in whipping cream, nutmeg and pepper. Serve immediately. Yield: 6 servings.
Ginger Barker,
Mesquite, Texas.

CREAM OF CARROT SOUP

2 cups peeled and thinly sliced carrots
¼ cup butter or margarine, divided
1 teaspoon sugar
½ teaspoon salt
½ cup water
2 tablespoons all-purpose flour
2¼ cups milk
½ teaspoon salt
⅛ teaspoon pepper
½ cup whipping cream

Combine carrots, 2 tablespoons butter, sugar, ½ teaspoon salt, and water in a medium saucepan. Cover and cook over low heat 15 to 20 minutes or until carrots are tender; set aside.
Melt remaining 2 tablespoons butter in a heavy saucepan over low heat; add flour, stirring until smooth. Cook 1 minute, stirring constantly. Gradually stir in milk; cook over medium heat, stirring constantly, until thickened and bubbly. Stir in ½ teaspoon salt and pepper.
Combine carrots and white sauce in container of electric blender and blend until smooth. Add whipping cream; blend well. Cook soup over low heat, stirring frequently, until thoroughly heated. Serve immediately. Yield: 3½ cups.
Darlene George,
Bon Aqua, Tennessee.

Doubly Good Yeast Rolls

Looking for rolls that melt in your mouth? Try Refrigerator Yeast Rolls. In addition to a delicious flavor, these rolls have another bonus. They can be stored in the refrigerator up to four days, letting you can enjoy the flavor of freshly baked rolls for several meals without repeating the mixing procedure.

REFRIGERATOR YEAST ROLLS

1 teaspoon sugar
1 teaspoon salt
1 package dry yeast
½ cup water
2 eggs
7 cups all-purpose flour
½ cup sugar
1 cup shortening
2 cups water

Combine first 5 ingredients in a mixing bowl; beat 2 minutes on low speed of electric mixer, and set aside.
Combine remaining ingredients in a large mixing bowl; beat 3 minutes with a heavy-duty electric mixer at medium speed. Add yeast mixture, and beat 3 minutes at medium speed. Cover and let rise in a warm place (85°), free from drafts, 3 hours or until doubled in bulk.
Punch dough down. Cover and refrigerate overnight. With lightly floured hands, shape dough into 1½-inch balls; place in 3 greased 9-inch cakepans. Let rise in a warm place (85°), free from drafts, about 2 hours or until doubled in bulk. Bake at 400° for 10 to 12 minutes. Yield: about 2½ dozen.
Note: Dough may be stored in the refrigerator up to 4 days.
Emma Lee Hester,
Creedmoor, North Carolina.

Don't Pass Up Brussels Sprouts

If brussels sprouts are one of those vegetables you tend to pass up on the winter produce counter, consider giving them a try in some dishes shared by our readers.

When purchasing fresh brussels sprouts, select small to medium heads that are bright green, firm, and compact; discolored leaves indicate poor quality. When out of season, you can substitute two 10-ounce packages of frozen brussels sprouts for 1 pound of the fresh vegetable.

BRUSSELS SPROUTS IN ONION SAUCE

¾ pound fresh brussels sprouts
2 tablespoons plus 2 teaspoons butter or margarine
1 cup minced onion
2 tablespoons plus 2 teaspoons all-purpose flour
1 cup milk
1 cup half-and-half
1½ teaspoons lemon juice
½ teaspoon salt
¼ teaspoon dried whole marjoram

Wash brussels sprouts thoroughly; drop into a small amount of boiling salted water. Return to a boil; cover and cook 8 to 10 minutes or until tender. Drain; transfer to serving dish, and keep warm.

Melt butter in a heavy saucepan over low heat; add onion, and cook until tender. Add flour and cook 1 minute, stirring constantly. Gradually stir in milk and half-and-half. Add lemon juice, salt, and marjoram; cook over medium heat, stirring constantly, until thickened and bubbly. Pour sauce over brussels sprouts, and serve immediately. Yield: 4 to 6 servings.

Jane Petrelli Greer,
Richardson, Texas.

FRIED BRUSSELS SPROUTS

1 pound fresh brussels sprouts
1 egg
1 tablespoon milk
¾ cup fine dry breadcrumbs
Olive or vegetable oil

Wash brussels sprouts thoroughly; drop into a small amount of boiling salted water. Return to a boil, cover, and cook 7 minutes. Drain.

Combine egg and milk; mix well. Dip brussels sprouts in egg mixture and dredge in breadcrumbs. Fry in hot oil (360°) until golden brown. Drain on paper towels. Yield: 6 to 8 servings.

Beth Waldorf,
Bardstown, Kentucky.

BRUSSELS SPROUTS STIR-FRY

1½ pounds fresh brussels sprouts
½ cup butter or margarine
⅓ cup chopped onion
1 small cucumber, peeled and sliced
1 tablespoon vinegar or lemon juice
1 teaspoon sugar
¼ teaspoon dried dillweed
½ teaspoon salt
⅛ teaspoon pepper
¼ cup chopped pimiento

Wash brussels sprouts, and pat dry; cut in half, and set aside.

Melt butter in a large skillet or wok. Add onion; cook over medium-high heat until tender. Add brussels sprouts and remaining ingredients; stir-fry 5 to 10 minutes or until brussels sprouts are crisp-tender. Yield: 8 to 10 servings.

Ruth E. Horomanski,
Satellite Beach, Florida.

Put Broccoli In A Pickle

You've tried dill pickles and sweet pickles, but what about broccoli pickles? Select tender broccoli flowerets, pack them into jars with tarragon vinegar and mixed pickling spices, and process. Serve these tangy pickles on appetizer trays and tossed into salads.

PICKLED BROCCOLI

3 pounds broccoli
2 quarts water
¾ cup pickling salt
3 cups tarragon vinegar (5% acidity)
1 cup water
2 tablespoons mixed pickling spices
1½ teaspoons whole peppercorns

Wash broccoli, and remove flowerets; reserve stems for use in another recipe.

Combine 2 quarts water and salt in a large bowl; stir until salt dissolves. Add broccoli; cover and let stand at room temperature 24 hours. Rinse broccoli several times in cold water; drain well.

Combine remaining ingredients in a heavy saucepan, mixing well. Bring to a boil; boil for 10 minutes.

Pack broccoli into hot sterilized jars, leaving ½-inch headspace. Pour vinegar mixture over broccoli, leaving ½-inch headspace. Cover at once with metal lids, and screw bands tight. Process in boiling-water bath 15 minutes. Refrigerate before serving. Yield: 3 pints.

Margaret Hunter,
Princeton, Kentucky.

Enjoy The Versatile Orange

One of the most versatile fruits in the kitchen, the sweet, juicy orange lends its refreshing citrus flavor and bright color to every part of the menu—from salads and sauces to numerous desserts.

ORANGE BASKETS

6 medium-size oranges
½ cup finely chopped dates
½ cup flaked coconut
½ cup coarsely chopped pecans
1 egg white
¼ cup sifted powdered sugar
Additional flaked coconut

Cut a thin slice from bottom of each orange so it will sit flat. Cut a ¾-inch slice from top of each orange. Gently remove pulp, leaving shells intact. Remove membrane from pulp; drain off juice (reserve juice for use in another recipe).

Combine orange pulp, dates, coconut, and pecans. Mix well, and spoon into orange shells.

Beat egg white (at room temperature) until foamy. Gradually add sugar, 1 tablespoon at a time, beating until stiff peaks form. Spread meringue over top opening of each orange shell, making sure edges are sealed, and sprinkle with coconut.

Broil orange shells 6 inches from heat about 1 minute or until coconut is lightly browned. Yield: 6 servings.

Mrs. Thomas F. Everett,
Blackville, South Carolina.

SUNSHINY CHICKEN

2 whole chicken breasts, halved and
   skinned
2 tablespoons shortening
1 (10¾-ounce) can chicken broth,
   undiluted
¾ cup orange juice
2 teaspoons brown sugar
⅛ teaspoon ground mace
Hot cooked rice (optional)
2 tablespoons water
2 tablespoons cornstarch
⅛ teaspoon grated orange rind
1 medium orange, peeled and sliced
   crosswise

Brown chicken in shortening in a large skillet over medium heat; drain off pan drippings. Combine broth, orange juice, brown sugar, and mace; stir well, and pour over chicken. Reduce heat to low; cover and simmer 30 minutes or until chicken is tender. Remove chicken to serving dish or platter of hot cooked rice, if desired.

Combine water, cornstarch, and orange rind; stir until smooth, and add to orange sauce in skillet. Cook over low heat, stirring constantly, until thickened. Arrange orange slices around chicken; pour orange sauce over top before serving. Yield: 4 servings.

Jodie McCoy,
Tulsa, Oklahoma.

ORANGE MERINGUE PIE

1¼ cups sugar
⅓ cup cornstarch
½ teaspoon salt
1½ cups water
3 eggs, separated
1 tablespoon grated orange rind
½ cup fresh orange juice, strained
2 tablespoons butter or margarine
1 baked 9-inch pastry shell
¼ teaspoon salt
¼ cup plus 2 tablespoons sugar

Combine 1¼ cups sugar, cornstarch, salt, and water in a saucepan, stirring

until smooth. Cook over medium heat, stirring constantly, until mixture comes to a boil. Reduce heat to low, and cook 1 to 2 minutes. Beat egg yolks until thick and lemon colored. Gradually stir about one-fourth of hot mixture into yolks; add to remaining hot mixture, stirring constantly. Stir in orange rind and orange juice. Remove from heat; stir in butter. Pour into pastry shell.

Combine egg whites (at room temperature) and salt; beat until foamy. Gradually add remaining sugar, 1 tablespoon at a time, beating until stiff peaks form. Spread meringue over filling, sealing to edge of pastry. Bake at 425° for 3 minutes or until golden brown. Cool to room temperature. Yield: one 9-inch pie.

Evelyn Howell,
Orange, Texas.

OVERNIGHT WALDORF SALAD

2 oranges, peeled, sectioned, and seeded
½ to 1 cup raisins
¾ cup chopped walnuts
2 cups seedless green grapes
2 cups miniature marshmallows
1 cup mayonnaise
2 bananas
1½ tablespoons lemon juice

Combine first 6 ingredients in a large bowl; mix well. Cover and refrigerate overnight.

Peel and slice bananas; sprinkle with lemon juice. Add bananas to fruit mixture, tossing gently; serve immediately. Yield: 10 to 12 servings.

Margaret O. Kaminsky,
Manassas, Virginia.

CHAMPAGNE FRUIT COMPOTE

4 oranges, peeled, seeded, and sectioned
1½ cups seedless green grapes, halved
1 (20-ounce) can pineapple chunks,
   drained
¼ cup sifted powdered sugar
1 teaspoon grated orange or lemon rind
1 (25.4-ounce) bottle champagne, chilled

Combine fruit in a large bowl; stir in sugar and orange rind. Chill several hours. Stir in the champagne. Serve in stemmed glasses. Yield: 10 to 12 servings.

Cindi Rawlins,
Dunwoody, Georgia.

Apple Flan From The Processor

No one knows better the advantages of using a food processor for everyday meal preparation than Nancy Eisele of Birmingham. With five children, Nancy does a lot of cooking, and the processor helps keep her from spending all her time in the kitchen.

Here Nancy shares with us her processor Apple Flan recipe. The processor is used to mix the pastry as well as to shred the apples for this delicious and attractive dessert.

APPLE FLAN

½ cup butter or margarine
1 cup all-purpose flour
2 tablespoons sugar
¼ teaspoon salt
1 tablespoon vinegar
5 to 6 medium cooking apples, peeled and
   cored
¾ cup sugar
2 tablespoons all-purpose flour
1 teaspoon ground cinnamon
Powdered sugar (optional)
Whipped cream (optional)

Cut butter into ½-inch pieces. Position knife blade in processor bowl. Add butter, 1 cup flour, 2 tablespoons sugar, and salt; top with cover. Process 10 to 15 seconds or until mixture resembles coarse meal.

With processor running, pour vinegar through food chute; process 15 to 20 seconds or until dough forms a ball. Press pastry into bottom and 1 inch up sides of a 9½-inch springform pan; set aside.

Cut apples into quarters. Position shredding blade in processor bowl. Position apples in food chute; shred, applying firm pressure with food pusher. Combine 3 cups shredded apples, ¾ cup sugar, 2 tablespoons flour, and cinnamon; mix well.

Spoon apple mixture evenly into prepared pastry. Bake at 400° for 45 minutes or until done. Cool; remove sides of pan. Sprinkle flan with powdered sugar, and top with whipped cream, if desired. Yield: 8 to 10 servings.

Nancy Eisele,
Birmingham, Alabama.

Appendices

EQUIVALENT WEIGHTS AND MEASURES

Food	Weight or Count	Measure or Yield
Apples	1 pound (3 medium)	3 cups sliced
Bacon	8 slices cooked	½ cup crumbled
Bananas	1 pound (3 medium)	2½ cups sliced, or about 2 cups mashed
Bread	1 pound	12 to 16 slices
	About 1½ slices	1 cup soft crumbs
Butter or margarine	1 pound	2 cups
	¼ - pound stick	½ cup
Cabbage	1 pound head	4½ cups shredded
Candied fruit or peels	½ pound	1¼ cups cut
Carrots	1 pound	3 cups shredded
Cheese, American or Cheddar	1 pound	About 4 cups shredded
cottage	1 pound	2 cups
cream	3 - ounce package	6 tablespoons
Chocolate morsels	6 - ounce package	1 cup
Cocoa	1 pound	4 cups
Coconut, flaked or shredded	1 pound	5 cups
Coffee	1 pound	80 tablespoons (40 cups perked)
Corn	2 medium ears	1 cup kernels
Cornmeal	1 pound	3 cups
Crab, in shell	1 pound	¾ to 1 cup flaked
Crackers, chocolate wafers	19 wafers	1 cup crumbs
graham crackers	14 squares	1 cup fine crumbs
saltine crackers	28 crackers	1 cup finely crushed
vanilla wafers	22 wafers	1 cup finely crushed
Cream, whipping	1 cup (½ pint)	2 cups whipped
Dates, pitted	1 pound	3 cups chopped
	8 - ounce package	1½ cups chopped
Eggs	5 large	1 cup
whites	8 to 11	1 cup
yolks	12 to 14	1 cup
Flour, all-purpose	1 pound	3½ cups
cake	1 pound	4¾ to 5 cups sifted
whole wheat	1 pound	3½ cups unsifted
Green pepper	1 large	1 cup diced
Lemon	1 medium	2 to 3 tablespoons juice; 2 teaspoons grated rind
Lettuce	1 pound head	6¼ cups torn
Lime	1 medium	1½ to 2 tablespoons juice
Macaroni	4 ounces (1 cup)	2¼ cups cooked
Marshmallows	11 large	1 cup
	10 miniature	1 large marshmallow
Marshmallows, miniature	½ pound	4½ cups
Milk		
evaporated	5.33 - ounce can	⅔ cup
evaporated	13 - ounce can	1⅝ cups
sweetened condensed	14 - ounce can	1¼ cups
Mushrooms	3 cups raw (8 ounces)	1 cup sliced cooked
Nuts		
almonds	1 pound	1 to 1¾ cups nutmeats
	1 pound shelled	3½ cups nutmeats
peanuts	1 pound	2¼ cups nutmeats
	1 pound shelled	3 cups
pecans	1 pound	2¼ cups nutmeats
	1 pound shelled	4 cups
walnuts	1 pound	1⅔ cups nutmeats
	1 pound shelled	4 cups

Food	Weight or Count	Measure or Yield
Oats, quick-cooking	1 cup	1¾ cups cooked
Onion	1 medium	½ cup chopped
Orange	1 medium	⅓ cup juice and 2 tablespoons grated rind
Peaches	4 medium	2 cups sliced
Pears	4 medium	2 cups sliced
Potatoes, white	3 medium	2 cups cubed cooked or 1¾ cups mashed
sweet	3 medium	3 cups sliced
Raisins, seedless	1 pound	3 cups
Rice, long-grain	1 cup	3 to 4 cups cooked
pre-cooked	1 cup	2 cups cooked
Shrimp, raw in shell	1½ pounds	2 cups (¾ pound) cleaned, cooked
Spaghetti	7 ounces	About 4 cups cooked
Strawberries	1 quart	4 cups sliced
Sugar, brown	1 pound	2¼ cups firmly packed
powdered	1 pound	3½ cups unsifted
granulated	1 pound	2 cups

EQUIVALENT MEASUREMENTS

3 teaspoons	1 tablespoon		2 cups .... .,............	1 pint (16 fluid ounces)
4 tablespoons...............	¼ cup		4 cups	1 quart
5⅓ tablespoons..............	⅓ cup		4 quarts	1 gallon
8 tablespoons..............	½ cup		⅛ cup....................	2 tablespoons
16 tablespoons..............	1 cup		⅓ cup....................	5 tablespoons plus 1 teaspoon
2 tablespoons (liquid) ...	1 ounce		⅔ cup....................	10 tablespoons plus 2 teaspoons
1 cup........................	8 fluid ounces		¾ cup....................	12 tablespoons

HANDY SUBSTITUTIONS

Ingredient Called For	Substitution
1 cup self-rising flour	1 cup all-purpose flour plus 1 teaspoon baking powder and ½ teaspoon salt
1 cup cake flour	1 cup sifted all-purpose flour minus 2 tablespoons
1 cup all-purpose flour	1 cup cake flour plus 2 tablespoons
1 teaspoon baking powder	½ teaspoon cream of tartar plus ¼ teaspoon soda
1 tablespoon cornstarch or arrowroot	2 tablespoons all-purpose flour
1 tablespoon tapioca	1½ tablespoons all-purpose flour
2 large eggs	3 small eggs
1 egg	2 egg yolks (for custard)
1 egg	2 egg yolks plus 1 tablespoon water (for cookies)
1 cup commercial sour cream	1 tablespoon lemon juice plus evaporated milk to equal 1 cup; or 3 tablespoons butter plus ⅞ cup sour milk
1 cup yogurt	1 cup buttermilk or sour milk
1 cup sour milk or buttermilk	1 tablespoon vinegar or lemon juice plus sweet milk to equal 1 cup
1 cup fresh milk	½ cup evaporated milk plus ½ cup water
1 cup fresh milk	3 to 5 tablespoons nonfat dry milk solids in 1 cup water
1 cup honey	1¼ cups sugar plus ¼ cup liquid
1 (1-ounce) square unsweetened chocolate	3 tablespoons cocoa plus 1 tablespoon butter or margarine
1 tablespoon fresh herbs	1 teaspoon dried herbs or ¼ teaspoon powdered herbs
¼ cup chopped fresh parsley	1 tablespoon dehydrated parsley
1 teaspoon dry mustard	1 tablespoon prepared mustard
1 pound fresh mushrooms	6 ounces canned mushrooms

Recipe Title Index

An alphabetical listing of every recipe by exact title

Month-by-Month Index

An alphabetical listing within the month of every food article and accompanying recipes

Month-by-Month Index   321

General Recipe Index

A listing of every recipe by food category and/or major ingredient

Chocolate *(continued)*
Pots de Crème, 15
Pudding, Hot Fudge, 208
Soufflé, Chocolate Mint, 16
Velvet, Chocolate Almond, 148

Chop Suey
Cabbage Chop Suey, 101
Chicken Chop Suey, 227
Salad, Chop Suey, 37

Clams
Backyard Clambake, 92
Casino, Clams, 125
Chowder, Clam, 32
Linguine in Clam Sauce, 83

Coconut
Cake, Coconut Cream, 179
Cake, Lemon-Coconut Cream, 179
Cake, Stately Coconut Layer, 70
Charlotte, Macaroon, 296
Filling, Coconut, 265
Frosting, Coconut-Pecan, 296
Pie, Coconut Cream, 136
Pie, Coconut Pecan, 161
Pie, Coconut-Pecan Chess, 248

Coffee
After-Dinner Coffee, 262
Brandied Coffee, 244
Creamy Coffee, 244
Dessert, Mocha-Almond, 62
Frosted Coffee, 244
Gingerbread, Mocha, 207
Pie, Chocolate-Mocha Crunch, 136
Punch, Creamy Coffee, 50
Squares, Frozen Mocha, 187
Tortoni, Coffee-Almond, 30

Cookies
Apricot Cookies, Frosted, 192
Bars and Squares
Apricot Bars, 247
Brownie Bars, Cinnamon, 230
Brownies, Chocolate Chip, 162
Brownies, Chocolate-Nut, 129
Brownies, Chocolate-Pecan, 64
Brownies, Nutty Blonde, 64
Brownies, Nutty Cocoa, 64
Butter Pecan Pie Squares, 262
Chocolate-Butterscotch Bars, 197
Chocolate Chip Bars, 130
Jam Squares, 289
Lemon Squares, 197
Pecan Squares, Easy, 230
Strawberry Bars, 301
Bourbon Balls, 254
Butter Cookies, Melt-Away, 20
Candy Bit Cookies, 192
Carrot Cookies, Frosted, 7
Cherry-Almond Drops, 20
Cherry Nut Nuggets, 286
Chocolate-Nut Chews, 92
Chocolate Sandwich Cookies, 192
Chocolate Snappers, Jumbo, 218
Cinnamon Wafers, 192
Double Chip Cookies, 301
Lemon Crinkle Cookies, 287
Lemon Yummies, 301
Lemon Zephers, 172
Mexican Tea Cakes, 196
Oatmeal Cookies, Nutty, 130
Oatmeal Cookies, Special, 236
Oatmeal Cookies, Spicy, 197
Peanut Butter-Oatmeal Cookies, 218

Peanut-Date Balls, 92
Refrigerator
Ambrosia Cookies, 301
Butter Cookies, Valentine, 20
Chocolate Meltaways, 302
Fruitcake Cookies, Holiday, 301
Peanut Butter Snaps, 237
Springerle, 251
Sugar Cookies, Red-, 21
Sugar 'n Spice Cookies, 21
Walnut Cookies, 301
Shortbread, Easy Roll-Out, 21
Swedish Heirloom Cookies, 129

Corn
Baked Corn on the Cob, Foil-, 128
Barbecued Corn on the Cob, 128
Casserole, Corn and Cheese, 128
Casserole, Corn and Tomato, 127
Chowder, Corn, 128
Chowder, Turkey-Corn, 98
Cold-Pack Corn, 216
Cornbread, Mexican, 137
Creamed Corn, Southern-Style, 165
Creole Corn, 128
Fritters, Golden Corn, 128
Medley, Okra-Corn-Tomato, 159
Medley, Zucchini-and-Corn, 25
Pudding, Corn, 128
Pudding, Creamy Corn, 267
Quick Corn Fix-Up, 4
Relish, Corn, 129, 175
Salad, Corn, 139
Salad, Shoepeg Corn, 23
Scalloped Corn, 128
Spoonbread, Corn and Bacon, 129
Stuffed Peppers, Ham-and-Corn, 87

Cornbreads
Carrot Cornbread, 163
Casserole, Cornbread, 91
Cheesy Beef Cornbread, 242
Corncakes, Lacy, 242
Corn Lightbread, 137
Cornsticks, Quick, 192
Corn Sticks, Southern, 242
Cowboy Cornbread, 188
Hoecake, Hot Water, 56
Hush Puppies, Easy, 191
Light Cornbread, Old Southern, 242
Mexican Cornbread, 137
Mexican Cornbread, Quick, 242
Old-Fashioned Cornbread, 242
Pastry, Cornmeal, 140
Skillet Cornbread, 31
Sour Cream Cornbread, 137
Southern Cornbread, 56
Spoonbread, 138
Tomato Corn Muffins, 137
Wampus Bread, 305

Cornish Hens
Brandied Cornish Hens, 259
Elegant Cornish Hens, 52
Flambé, Cornish Hens, 52

Crab
Cakes, Crab, 125
Dip, Hot Cheese and Crab, 261
Gumbo, Crab and Shrimp, 200
Salad, Crab-Avocado, 114
Salad, Macaroni-Crabmeat, 153
Salad, Super Shrimp, 37
Sandwiches, Deluxe Crabmeat, 74
Sandwiches, Open-Face Crab Tomato, 29
Soup, Steamboat's Cream of Crab, 127
Spread, Superb Crab, 235

Stuffed Mushrooms, Crab-, 190
Stuffed Shrimp Bundles, Crab-, 176
Stuffed Soft-Shell Crabs,
Steamboat's, 127

Cranberries
Bread, Raisin-Cranberry, 305
Cobbler, Cranberry, 275
Cobbler Roll, Cranberry, 248
Coffee Cake, Cranberry, 14
Coffee Cake, Cranberry-Nut, 250
Compote, Berry, 275
Daiquiris, Cranberry, 245
Glazed Ham, Cranberry, 274
Glazed Ham, Cranberry-Orange, 295
Jam, Christmas Brunch, 286
Jelly, Cranberry-Wine, 290
Muffins, Cranberry, 249
Pie, Cranberry-Apple Holiday, 269
Punch, Pink Lady, 100
Relish, Cranberry, 275
Relish, Cranberry-Orange, 289
Salad, Festive Cranberry, 264, 296
Salad, Holiday Jewel, 252
Squash, Cranberry-Filled Acorn, 231

Crêpes
Brunch Crêpes, Royal, 44
Cheese and Mushroom Crêpes, 88
Chicken Crêpes, Creamy, 200
Divan, Elegant Crêpes, 91
Fruit Filling, Crêpes with, 96
Spinach-Ricotta Crêpes, 52

Cucumbers
Pickles, Cucumber Sandwich, 174
Pickles, Dill, 174
Pickles, Mixed, 174
Salad, Dilled Cucumber and Tomato, 153
Salad, Tomato-Cucumber-Onion, 239
Sandwiches, Dainty Cucumber, 119
Soup, Cold Cucumber, 130
Soup, Cream of Cucumber, 98
Sour Cream, Cucumber and Onion in, 69
Stuffed Cucumbers, 237
Tomato, Onion, and Cucumber in Italian
Dressing, 83

Curry
Dip, Curried, 262
Dip, Curry, 9
Fruit, Hot Curried, 264
Lamb Curry with Rice, 10
Soup, Curried, 130
Sour Cream and Shrimp Curry, 10

Custards
Boiled Custard, Favorite, 181
Boiled Custard, Perfect, 34
Filling, Creamy Custard, 180
Lemon Custard in Meringue Cups, 172

Dates
Balls, Peanut-Date, 92
Bread, Chocolate Date-Nut, 284
Cake, Queen Bee, 237
Filling, Date Cream, 303

Desserts. *See also* specific types.
Apple Flan, 309
Apples, Brandied, 248
Banana-Berry Supreme, 205
Banana Cream Dessert, 180
Bananas Foster, Elegant, 59
Berry Compote, 275
Blueberry, Crumble, 84
Bourbon Praline Sauce, 170
Cantaloupe Compote, 147

Grits *(continued)*

Cheese Grits, Garlic, 197
Cheese Grits, Gruyère, 47
Nassau Grits, 47
Orange Grits, 47

Gumbos

Chicken and Oyster Gumbo, 198
Chicken Gumbo with Smoked
    Sausage, 199
Chicken-Ham-Seafood Gumbo, 6
Combo Gumbo, 198
Crab and Shrimp Gumbo, 200
Dove and Sausage Gumbo, 199
Fish Gumbo, Easy, 6
Ham and Seafood Gumbo, 199
Seafood Gumbo, 5
Shrimp Gumbo, 199

Ham

Balls with Spiced Cherry Sauce,
    Ham, 112
Barbecued Ham Slices, 110
Casserole, Ham and Broccoli, 133
Casserole, Macaroni-Ham, 177
Cordon Bleu, Chicken, 304
Country Ham in Wine, 260
Creamed Ham and Chicken, 74
Fritters with Creamy Sauce, Ham, 105
Glazed Ham, Cranberry, 274
Glazed Ham, Cranberry-Orange, 295
Glazed Ham Slice, Honey-, 104
Gumbo, Chicken-Ham-Seafood, 6
Gumbo, Combo, 198
Gumbo, Ham and Seafood, 199
Hideaways, Ham, 29
Hopping John with Ham, 7
Kabobs, Swiss-Ham, 124
Nuggets, Cheesy Ham, 290
Patties, Ham, 99
Quiche, Ham-and-Mushroom, 11
Ring, Chili-Sauced Ham, 122
Roll-Ups, Ham and Spinach, 143
Salad, Congealed Ham, 36
Salad, Fruited Ham, 36, 146
Salad, Ham 'n Egg, 36
Sandwiches, Baked Ham, 29
Sandwiches, Yummy, 229
Spread, Ham and Pimiento, 56
Stuffed Acorn Squash, Ham-, 239
Stuffed Peppers, Ham-and-Corn, 87
Stuffed Potatoes, Jalapeño-Ham, 61
Toast with Cheese Sauce, Ham and
    Eggs on, 43

Hominy

Bake, Chili Hominy, 282
Casserole, Chile-Hominy, 29
Sausage Skillet, Hominy-, 29

Ice Creams and Sherbets

Apricot Sherbet, 177
Apricot Yogurt Ice, 177
Bananas Foster, Elegant, 59
Caramel-Vanilla Helado (Caramel-
    Vanilla Ice Cream), 67
Chocolate-Mint Ice Cream Pie, 144
Coffee Punch, Creamy, 50
Fruit Ice, Mixed, 178
Hawaiian Frappé, 178
Lime Fizz, 172
Orange Sherbet Salad, 154
Peach Frosty, 156
Peach Ice, 178

Peach Ice Cream, 184
Peach Sundaes Flambé, 88
Peachy Orange Shake, 156
Peanut Butter Ice Cream, 103
Pineapple Sherbet, 177
Pumpkin Ice Cream Pie, 272
Strawberry Ice Cream, Very, 155
Strawberry Sundaes, Hot, 5
Vanilla Sherry Dessert, Glorified, 85
Watermelon Sherbet, Light, 147

Jams and Jellies

Apple Butter, 217
Apple Butter, Half-Hour, 203
Carrot-Citrus Marmalade, 148
Christmas Brunch Jam, 286
Citrus Marmalade, Mixed, 43
Crabapple Jelly, 217
Cranberry-Wine Jelly, 290
Fruit Marmalade, Delicious, 285
Orange Marmalade, 42
Peach Preserves, 147
Pineapple Jam, 147
Squares, Jam, 289
Strawberry Jelly, 147
Strawberry Preserves, 96
Teasers, Jam, 8

Jicama

Fried Jicama, French-, 88
Parsleyed Jicama, 88

Kabobs

Chicken Kabobs Supreme, 124
Ham Kabobs, Swiss-, 124
Salmon Kabobs, 182
Scallop-Bacon Kabobs, 111
Shish Kabobs, Overnight, 124
Steak with Vegetables, Skewered, 124
Vegetable Kabobs, Fresh, 158

Kiwi

in Meringue Cups, Kiwi and Cream, 279

Lamb

Curry with Rice, Lamb, 10
Hawaii, Lamb, 58
Rack of Lamb with Herb Mustard
    Glaze, 260
Roast of Lamb, Crown, 58
Shish Kabobs, Overnight, 124

Lasagna

for Two, Lasagna, 91
Simple Lasagna, 188
Spinach Lasagna, 243

Lemon

Chicken, Grilled Yogurt-Lemon, 111
Chicken, Lemon, 138
Desserts
    Cake, Lemon-Coconut Cream, 179
    Cake, Lightly Lemon Coffee, 14
    Cheesecake with Orange-Pineapple
      Glaze, Lemon, 270
    Cookies, Lemon Crinkle, 287
    Custard in Meringue Cups,
      Lemon, 172
    Pie, Buttermilk-Lemon, 120
    Pie, Deluxe Lemon Meringue, 172
    Pie, Lemon Cheese, 136
    Pie, Lemon Cottage Cheese, 143
    Pudding, Lemon, 99
    Squares, Lemon, 197
    Tarts, Lemon-Sour Cream, 304
    Yummies, Lemon, 301
    Zephers, Lemon, 172

Filling, Lemon, 172
Filling, Lemon-Orange, 71
Frosting, Lemon-Cream Cheese, 157
Lemonade, Fresh Squeezed, 172
Ribs, Lemon Baked, 166
Ribs, Lemon Grilled, 154
Salad, Cauliflower-Lemon, 23
Sauce, Lemon Parsley, 106
Spirals, French Lemon, 94

Lime

Fizz, Lime, 172
Mousse Freeze, Luscious Lime, 173

Linguine

Clam Sauce, Linguine in, 83

Liver

Chicken Livers. *See* under Chicken.
Patties, Beef Liver, 277
Saucy Liver, 277
Sauté, Liver, 277
Sweet-and-Sour Liver, 277
with Herbs, Liver, 277

Lobster

Clambake, Backyard, 92
How To Cook Lobster, 169

Macaroni

Bake, Cheesy Macaroni-Mushroom, 243
Casserole, Macaroni-Ham, 177
Salad for Two, Macaroni, 31
Salad, Gourmet Macaroni, 253
Salad, Macaroni-Crabmeat, 153
Salad, Salmon-and-Macaroni, 114

Melon. *See also* Fruit.

Cantaloupe Compote, 147
Cantaloupe Punch, 147
Cantaloupe Soup, Chilled, 156
Cocktail, Minted Melon, 146
Cooler, Melon, 146
Fruit Deluxe, Marinated, 146
Fruited Ham Salad, 146
Honeydew Fruit Boats, 147
Watermelon Rind Pickles, 174
Watermelon Sherbet, Light, 147

Microwave

Acorn Rings, Easy Glazed, 231
Black-Eyed Peas, Fresh, 165
Broccoli, Marinated Fresh, 139
Carrots, Orange-Glazed, 165
Cheese Sticks, Peppery, 289
Chicken, Lemon, 138
Chili-Cheese Dogs, 176
Corn Fix-Up, Quick, 4
Corn, Southern-Style Creamed, 165
Cupcakes, Cinnamon-Chocolate, 139
Egg Medley, Cheddary, 176
Frosting, Buttery Cinnamon, 139
Frosting, Caramel, 289
Haddock Italiano, 4
Ham and Chicken, Creamed, 74
Ham Ring, Chili-Sauced, 122
Macaroni-Ham Casserole, 177
Meat Loaf, Cheesy Pizza, 121
Meat Loaf, Oriental, 122
Meat Loaf, Swedish, 121
Okra and Tomatoes, Fresh, 165
Party Mix, Spicy, 138
Pastry, Basic, 268
Pastry, Microwaved Quiche, 74
Pecans, Spicy, 289
Pie, Cranberry-Apple Holiday, 269
Pie, Festive Pumpkin, 269
Pie, Fluffy Eggnog, 269
Pie, Old-Fashioned Pecan, 269

SOUTHERN LIVING 1981 ANNUAL RECIPES

Southern Living®:
  Foods Editor: Jean Wickstrom Liles
  Assistant Foods Editors: Margaret Chason, Susan Payne,
    Linda Welch
  Test Kitchens Director: Lynn Lloyd
  Test Kitchens Staff: Martha Hinrichs, Diane Hogan,
    Laura Nestelroad, Karen Parker, Peggy Smith
  Photo Stylist: Beverly Morrow
  Production Manager: Clay Nordan
  Photographers: Jerome Drown: cover, pages iii (above),
    iv, 27, 28, 79, 80 and 81, 82, 115, 116 and 117, 118,
    152, 292 (above), 293, 294; Charles Walton: pages i, ii,
    iii (below), 45, 46 (above right and below), 151, 185,
    186, 219, 220 and 221, 222, 255, 256 and 257, 258, 291,
    292 (below); Van Chaplin: page 46 (above left)

Oxmoor House, Inc.:
  Editor: Ann H. Harvey
  Assistant Editor: Annette Thompson
  Production: Jerry Higdon
          Joan Denman

  Designer: Carol Middleton
  Illustrator: Diana B. Smith

A WELCOME AID FOR BUSY HOMEMAKERS

Protect your favorite recipes from spills and splatters.

Get a clear view of your entire recipe behind a protective shield with this durable, acrylic cookbook stand. Your book sits firmly at an easy-to-read angle, open to your working recipe, safe from sticky fingers, mixing splatters and accidental spills. After cooking, the stand can be wiped clean with a damp sponge. A generous 16¾" wide by 12" high, this stand can accommodate most cookbooks.

Price and availability are subject to change without notice.

Send your order with a check or money order for $12.95 to:

Akra Data Cookbook Stand
P.O. Box 2463
Birmingham, AL 35201